The Pilot's Manual

3

Instrument Flying

The Pilot's Manual

3

Instrument Flying

Fourth Edition

A Step-by-Step Course Covering All Knowledge Necessary to Pass the FAA Instrument Knowledge and Oral Exams, and the IFR Flight Check

Foreword by Barry Schiff

Aviation Supplies & Academics, Inc.
Newcastle, Washington

The Pilot's Manual 3: Instrument Flying
Fourth Edition

Aviation Supplies & Academics, Inc.
7005 132nd Place SE
Newcastle, Washington 98059-3153

Originally published by Center for Aviation Theory
© 1990–1997

© 1997–2000 Aviation Theory Centre
All rights reserved. Published 1997 by Aviation Supplies & Academics, Inc.
Fourth Edition. Third Printing 2000.
No part of this manual may be reproduced in any manner whatsoever including electronic, photographic, photocopying, facsimile, or stored in a retrieval system, without the prior written permission of the publisher.

Nothing in this manual supersedes any operational documents or procedures issued by the Federal Aviation Administration, the National Ocean Service, Jeppesen Sanderson, Inc., aircraft and avionics manufacturers, flight schools, or the operators of aircraft.

Printed in the United States of America

02 01 00   9 8 7 6 5 4 3

ISBN 1-56027-415-8

ASA-PM-3

Acknowledgements

The Federal Aviation Administration (FAA), The National Ocean Service (NOS), The National Weather Service (NWS), Jeppesen Sanderson, Inc. *(Jeppesen charts have been reproduced with permission, and are copyrighted by Jeppesen Sanderson, Inc.)* Bendix/King (a division of Allied Signal Aerospace), II Morrow, Inc., Narco Avionics, Garmin Communication and Navigation. Dora Muir (ASA—design), Bookworks Ltd (origination), Bruce Landsberg (Executive Director, AOPA Air Safety Foundation).
Also, to the many students, instructors and FAA personnel whose comments have helped in developing and refining the material in this manual.

Contents

Foreword vii

Introduction 1

Section One *Attitude Flying*

1   **Instrument Scanning Technique** 19

2   **The Instruments** 31

3   **Straight-and-Level Flight** 73

4   **The Straight Climb and Descent** 95

5   **Turning** 111

6   **Unusual Attitudes** 133

7   **Normal Instrument Flight on a Partial Panel** 143

8   **Suggested Training Maneuvers** 163

Section Two *Radio Navigation Aids*

9   **Introduction to Radio Navigation Aids** 181

10 **Radar** 183

11 **DME** 207

12a **The NDB and the ADF** 213

12b **The Relative Bearing Indicator (RBI)** 231

12c **The RMI and Rotatable-Card ADF** 259

13 **The VOR** 273

14 **The Instrument Landing System (ILS)** 309

15 **Area Navigation (RNAV)** 357

16 **VHF Direction Finding (DF)** 367

Section Three *IFR Meteorology*

17 **Icing** 371

18 **Visibility** 379

19 **Clouds** 387

20 **Thunderstorms** 401

21 **High-Level Meteorology** 415

22 **Wind, Air Masses and Fronts** 419

23 **Weather Reports and Forecasts** 431

Section Four *The IFR System*

24 **Regulations Important to the Instrument Pilot** 477

25 **Preparation for Flight** 505

26 **Instrument Departures** 531

27 **En Route** 543

28 **Holding Patterns, Procedure Turns & DME Arcs** 553

29 **Instrument Approaches** 575

30 **Visual Maneuvering** 603

Glossary and Abbreviations 615

Index 619

Foreword

When it was time to take my private pilot written examination in 1955, my flight instructor handed me a pocket-size booklet. It was published by the Civil Aeronautics Administration (FAA's predecessor) and contained 200 true/false questions (including answers).

"Study these well," he cautioned with a wink, "because the test consists of 50 of these."

As I flipped through the dozen or so pages, my anxiety about the pending examination dissolved into relief. Nothing could be easier, I thought. One question, for example, stated "True or False: It is dangerous to fly through a thunderstorm." Really. (I passed the test with flying colors—but so did everyone else in those days.)

The modern pilot, however, must know a great deal more to hurdle today's more-challenging examinations. This has resulted in a crop of books developed specifically to help pilots pass tests. Unfortunately, some do little else, and the student's education remains incomplete.

An exciting exception is "The Pilot's Manual"—a series of outstanding books published by ASA and Aviation Theory Centre. These voluminous manuals provide far in excess of that needed to pass examinations. They are also chock-full of practical advice and techniques that are as useful to experienced pilots as they are to students.

"The Pilot's Manual" is a refreshingly creative and clever approach that simplifies and adds spice to what often are regarded as academically dry subjects. Reading these books is like sitting with an experienced flight instructor who senses when you might be having difficulty with a subject and patiently continues teaching until confident that you understand.

Barry Schiff
Los Angeles

Barry Schiff has over 26,000 hours in more than 260 types of aircraft. A thirty-four year veteran with Trans World Airlines, he flew the Lockheed L-1011 and Boeing 747, and has received numerous honors for his contributions to aviation. He is well known to flying audiences for his many articles published in some 90 aviation periodicals, notably *AOPA Pilot*.

About the Editorial Team

Amy Laboda. Freelance writer, editor, active flight instructor, executive board member, Women in Aviation, International; columnist for *Flight Training* magazine; contributor to numerous other aviation magazines; former editor at *Flying* magazine; has rotorcraft category, gyroplane rating, glider rating and multiengine ATP rating; holds a B.A. in Liberal Arts from Sarah Lawrence College.

Martin E. Weaver. An experienced flight and ground instructor in airplanes, helicopters and gliders; a former chief flight instructor and designated pilot examiner; has been closely involved with standardization procedures for the past 14 years; holds a B.S. from the University of Southern Mississippi; also currently a pilot in the Oklahoma Army National Guard.

Richard James. Experienced flight instructor, charter pilot and air ambulance pilot; currently flying Boeing 767s on international operations; recently Boeing 747, DC-10 and Fokker F-50 pilot; has represented pilots on new-aircraft evaluation committees, IFALPA Aircraft Design and Operation Study Group, and ICAO En Route Obstacle Clearance Criteria Study Group.

Ian Suren. Former chief, Personnel Licensing and Training with ICAO in Montreal for 10 years; senior examiner in charge of Flight Crew License Examinations with the Australian Department of Civil Aviation; certificated pilot.

Dr. Jacqueline A. Waide. Professor of Aviation, Ohlone College, CA, FAA-approved pilot examiner (flight & written); flight instructor; twice Oakland District Flight Instructor of the Year; holds a B.S. from Embry-Riddle. Started flying in 1956, was first woman to fly Lockheed L-1011; spent six years as Presidentially appointed consultant to FAA Administrator; former President of Northern California Pilot Examiner Assoc.

Dr. Gerald R. Fairbairn. An aviation educator for over 22 years; AOPA Air Safety Foundation lecturer in flight instructor revalidation clinics; National Accident Prevention Counselor; flight instructor with airplane, instrument, and glider ratings, over 6000 hours flight instruction given; formerly a Professor of Aeronautics at San Jose State University; currently Vice President for Academic Affairs at Daniel Webster College, New Hampshire.

Jeffery W. Hanson. An FAA inspector in the San Francisco Bay area; named National Flight Instructor of the Year 1988, and received FAA Certificate of Recognition for *Outstanding Support* in Accident Prevention Program the same year; former pilot examiner (flight and written), flight instructor, chief instructor of the Aeronautics Dept, College of the Redwoods, Eureka, CA; holds B.S. from Humboldt State College, CA.

Introduction

Air travel becomes much more reliable when airplane operations are not restricted by poor weather or by darkness. Greater reliability can be achieved with a suitably equipped airplane and a pilot skilled in instrument flying.

The instrument-qualified pilot and the instrument-equipped airplane must be able to cope with flying in restricted visibility, such as in cloud, mist, smog, rain, snow, or at night, all of which may make the natural horizon and ground features difficult, or even impossible, to see.

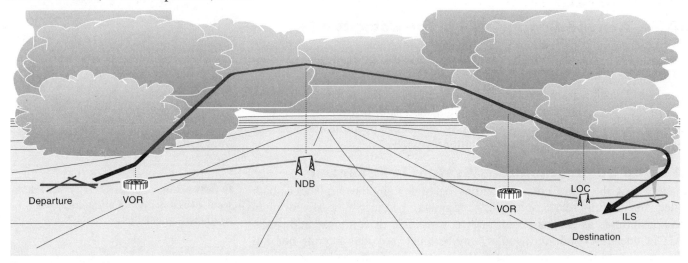

Figure 1. A typical flight on instruments

As an instrument pilot, you must learn to trust what you see on the instruments. We generally use vision to orient ourselves with our surroundings, supported by other bodily senses which can sense gravity, such as feel and balance. Even with the eyes closed, however, we can usually manage to sit, stand and walk on steady ground without losing control. This becomes much more difficult standing on the bed of an accelerating or turning truck, or even in an accelerating elevator.

In an airplane, which can accelerate in three dimensions, the task becomes almost impossible unless you have the use of your eyes.

The eyes must gather information from the external ground features, including the horizon, or, in poor visibility, gather substitute information from the instruments.

A pilot's eyes are very important, and the starting point in your instrument training will be learning to use your eyes to derive information from the instruments.

Figure 2. The eyes, and the instruments

The Three Fundamental Skills in Instrument Flying

The three fundamental skills in instrument flying are:

- **instrument cross-check** (also known as scanning the instruments);
- **instrument interpretation** (understanding their message); and
- **airplane control** (directing the airplane along the desired flightpath).

Make Yourself Comfortable In the Cockpit

Instrument flying is much easier if you are comfortable in the cockpit and know your airplane well. Adjust the seat position prior to flight to ensure that you can reach all of the controls easily, and so that you have the correct eye position. The view from the cockpit window must be familiar when you break out of the clouds at a low level, following a successful instrument approach, and see the rapidly approaching runway. A correct eye position will make the ensuing landing, possibly in poor visibility, so much easier.

A Good Communications System Is Essential

Ensure that the radio communications equipment in the airplane is both adequate and fully serviceable. This is of great importance. One of your main responsibilities as an instrument pilot is to remain in communication with ATC. Under IFR conditions, you will not be able to see other aircraft, nor will they be able to see you, hence the visual safety rule of "see and be seen" will not apply.

The separation of aircraft in IFR conditions is achieved by each pilot flying along a known route at a known altitude at known times, with ATC, in cooperation with the pilots, ensuring that there are no conflicting flightpaths. Good communications are therefore essential. On the rare occasions when a radio or electrical system fails, special procedures laid down for pilots to follow will minimize risk.

In instrument conditions (IMC) "see and be seen" does not apply. Communications equipment is essential.

During your instrument training, there will be a fair amount of talking in the cockpit. Your instructor will be explaining things to you, and offering words of encouragement as you perform the various maneuvers.

If this cockpit communication has to be done by shouting over the engine and air noise, as it was in the days when I learned to fly, then a lot of totally unnecessary stress will be introduced into the cockpit. A good intercom system will make life a lot easier for you and for your instructor, and will save you both time and money. Speak with your instructor about this.

Attitude Flying, and Applied Instrument Flying

The first step in becoming an instrument pilot is to become competent at **attitude flying** on the full panel containing the six basic flight instruments. The term *attitude flying* means using a combination of engine power and airplane attitude to achieve the required performance in terms of flightpath and airspeed.

Attitude flying on instruments is an extension of visual flying.

Attitude flying on instruments is an extension of visual flying, with your attention gradually shifting from external visual cues to the instrument indications in the cockpit, until you are able to fly accurately on instruments alone.

Partial panel attitude instrument flying, also known as limited panel, will be introduced fairly early in your training. For this exercise, the main control instrument, the attitude indicator, is assumed to have malfunctioned and is not available for use. The heading indicator, often powered from the same source as the AI, may also be unavailable.

Partial panel training will probably be practiced concurrently with full panel training, so that the exercise does not assume an importance out of proportion to its difficulty. You will perform the same basic flight maneuvers, but on a reduced number of instruments. The partial panel exercise will increase your instrument flying competence, as well as your confidence.

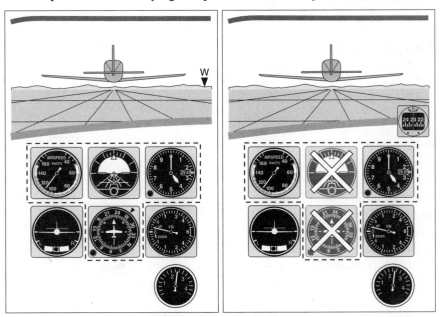

Figure 3. The full panel (left) and the partial panel (right)

An excessively high or low nose attitude, or an extreme bank angle, is known as an **unusual attitude**. Unusual attitudes should never occur inadvertently! Practice in recovering from them, however, will increase both your confidence and your overall proficiency. This exercise will be practiced on both a full panel and a partial panel.

After you have achieved a satisfactory standard in attitude flying, on both a full panel and a partial panel, your instrument flying skills will be applied to en route flights using radio navigation aids and radar.

Procedural instrument flying (which means getting from one place to another) is based mainly on knowing where the airplane is in relation to a particular radio ground transmitter (known as orientation), and then accurately tracking *to* or *from* the ground station. Tracking is simply attitude flying, plus a wind correction angle to allow for drift.

Typical radio aids used are the ADF, VOR, DME and ILS, as well as ground-based radar. In many ways, en route navigation is easier using the radio navigation instruments than it is by visual means. It is also more precise.

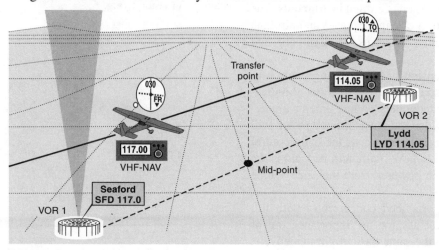

Figure 4. En route tracking on instruments

Having navigated the airplane on instruments to a destination, you must consider your approach. If instrument conditions exist, an **instrument approach** must be made.

If you encounter visual conditions, you may continue with the instrument approach or, with ATC authorization, shorten the flightpath by flying a visual approach or a contact approach.

Only published instrument approach procedures may be followed, with charts commonly used in the United States available from NOS (National Ocean Service) or Jeppesen. An instrument approach usually involves positioning the airplane over (or near) a ground station, and then using precise attitude flying to descend along the published flightpath at a suitable airspeed.

If visual conditions are encountered on the instrument approach at or before a predetermined minimum altitude is reached, then the airplane may be maneuvered for a landing. If visual conditions are not met at or before this minimum altitude, a **missed approach** should be carried out. The options are to climb away and position yourself for another approach, or to divert elsewhere.

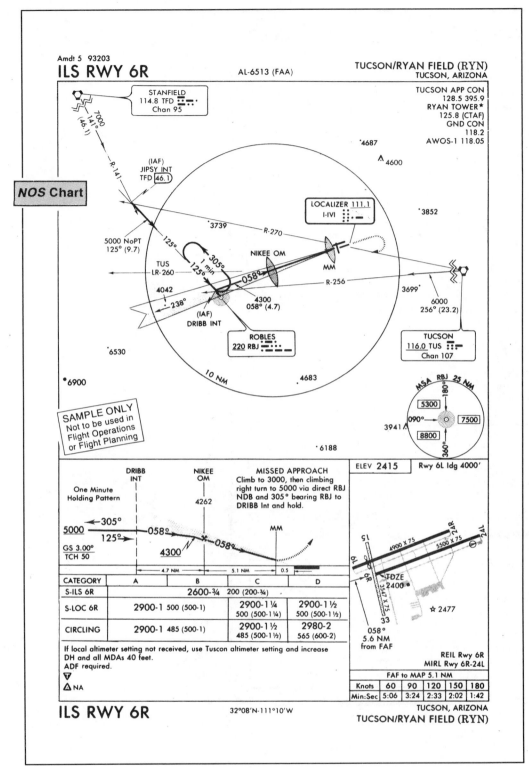

Figure 5. Plan and profile of a precision instrument approach

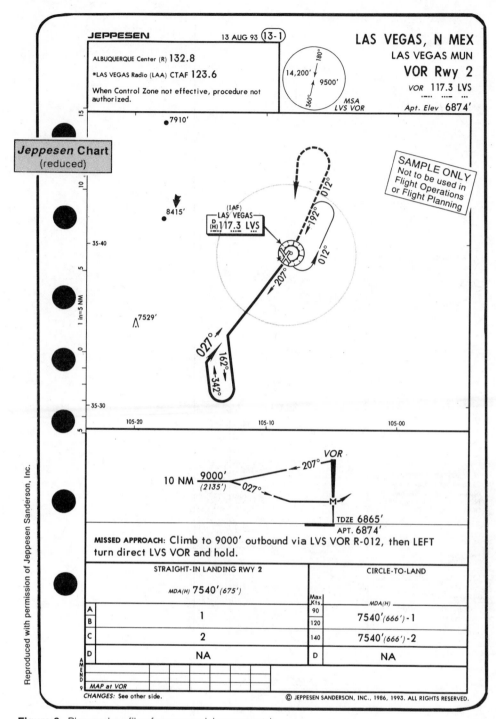

JEPPESEN   13 AUG 93 (13-1)   LAS VEGAS, N MEX
LAS VEGAS MUN
VOR Rwy 2

ALBUQUERQUE Center (R) 132.8

*LAS VEGAS Radio (LAA) CTAF 123.6

When Control Zone not effective, procedure not authorized.

VOR 117.3 LVS

14,200'   180°   9500'   360°

MSA
LVS VOR

Apt. Elev 6874'

7910'

8415'

(IAF)
LAS VEGAS
(H) 117.3 LVS

012°   192°   012°

207°

027°   162°   342°

7529'

VOR

10 NM   9000'
(2135')   207°   027°

M

TDZE 6865'
APT. 6874'

MISSED APPROACH: Climb to 9000' outbound via LVS VOR R-012, then LEFT turn direct LVS VOR and hold.

STRAIGHT-IN LANDING RWY 2		CIRCLE-TO-LAND	
MDA(H) 7540' (675')	Max Kts.	MDA(H)	
A		90	7540'(666')-1
B	1	120	
C	2	140	7540'(666')-2
D	NA	D	NA

MAP at VOR

CHANGES: See other side.

© JEPPESEN SANDERSON, INC., 1986, 1993. ALL RIGHTS RESERVED.

Figure 6. Plan and profile of a nonprecision approach

The Airplane, and the Ground Trainer

The simulator or ground trainer is an extremely valuable training aid for practicing both attitude flying and instrument procedures. It is a great time-saver. It allows certain maneuvers (for instance, climbing turns at 5000 feet) to be practiced without having to preflight check an actual airplane, then taxi out, wait in the queue, takeoff and climb for ten minutes, and so on. It is not dependent on weather—strong crosswinds on the runway making takeoff for airplanes impossible will not stop your practice. It allows easy conversation between student and instructor without the distraction of engine noise or radio calls. Time can be frozen, while the instructor discusses points of detail before the exercise continues.

Maneuvers can be repeated without delay and without interruption. Instrument procedures, such as an ILS approach to busy JFK International Airport in New York can be practiced repeatedly in the simulator—a situation probably not possible in a real airplane because of the heavy traffic in the New York area. Also, procedures at any airport that you are about to visit for the first time, or that you might have to divert to, can be practiced beforehand—very useful, and a great confidence builder when you are about to proceed into unfamiliar territory.

The fact that most ground trainers do not move, and experience only the normal earth-bound 1g gravity force, is not really a disadvantage for instrument training, since one of the aims of this training is to develop the ability to interpret the instruments using your eyes, and to disregard the other senses.

The ground trainer is also less expensive to operate than an airplane. This, and the many other advantages, make it an extremely valuable aid. But, it is still not an airplane!

Practice attitude instrument flying and procedures in a simulator or ground trainer first.

Figure 7. The ground trainer (left), and the airplane (right)

Instrument flying in the airplane is the real thing! It is important psychologically to feel confident about your instrument flying ability in an actual airplane, so in-flight training is important. There will be more noise, more distractions, more duties and different bodily feelings in the airplane. G-forces resulting from maneuvering will be experienced, as will turbulence, and these may serve to upset the senses. Despite the differences, however, the ground trainer can be used very successfully to prepare you for the real thing. Practice in it often to improve your instrument skills. Time in the real airplane can then be used more efficiently.

Attitude Instrument Flying

The performance of an airplane in terms of flightpath and airspeed is determined by a combination of the power set and the attitude selected. Airplane attitude has two aspects—pitch and bank, that is, nose position against the horizon, and bank angle. **Pitch attitude** is the angle between the longitudinal axis of the aircraft and the horizontal. **Bank attitude** is the angle between the lateral axis of the airplane and the horizontal.

Power plus attitude equals performance.

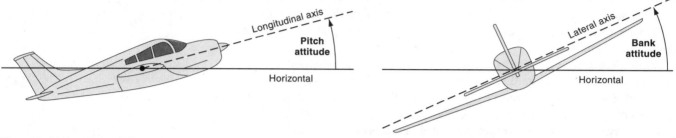

Figure 8. Pitch attitude (left) and bank attitude (right)

For a given airplane weight and configuration, a particular attitude combined with a particular power setting will always result in a similar flightpath through the air, be it a straight-and-level flightpath, a climb, a descent or a turn. Any change of power and/or of attitude will result in a change of flightpath and/or airspeed.

The pilot selects pitch attitude using the elevator. In visual conditions, you refer to the external natural horizon. At any time (in cloud, at night, or in visual conditions) you can select a specific pitch attitude with reference to the **attitude indicator (AI)** on the instrument panel. In visual flight, the pitch attitude can be estimated from the position of the natural horizon in the windshield. In instrument flight, pitch attitude is selected with reference to the AI, using the position of the center dot of the wing bars relative to the horizon bar. The center dot represents the nose of the airplane.

The pilot selects bank attitude (bank angle) using the ailerons. In visual conditions, you refer to the angle made by the external natural horizon in the windshield. On instruments, you select bank angle on the attitude indicator, either by estimating the angle between the wingbars of the miniature airplane and the horizon bar, or from the sky pointer (or bank pointer) position on a graduated scale at the top of the AI.

Figure 9.
Low pitch attitude, and wings level

Figure 10.
High pitch attitude, and right bank

Most of your attention during flight, both visual and on instruments, is concerned with achieving and holding a suitable attitude. A very important skill to develop when flying on instruments, therefore, is to check the attitude indicator every few seconds. There are other tasks to be performed, and there are other instruments to look at as well, but the eyes should always return fairly quickly to the AI.

Check the attitude indicator every few seconds.

To achieve the desired performance (in terms of flightpath and airspeed), you must not only place the airplane in a suitable attitude with the flight controls, you must also apply suitable power with the throttle. Just because the airplane has a high pitch attitude does not mean that it will climb—it requires climb power as well as climb attitude to do this. With less power, it may not climb at all. **Attitude flying** is the name given to this skill of controlling the airplane's flightpath and airspeed with changes in attitude and power. The techniques used in attitude flying are the same whether flying visually or on instruments.

Pitch Attitude

The **pitch attitude** is the geometric relationship between the longitudinal axis of the airplane and horizontal. Pitch attitude refers to the airplane's inclination to the horizontal, and not to where the airplane is actually going. The **angle of attack**, however, is the angle between the wing chord and the relative airflow. The angle of attack, therefore, is closely related to flightpath.

Pitch attitude is not angle of attack.

Pitch attitude and angle of attack are different, but they are related in the sense that if the pitch attitude is raised, then the angle of attack is increased. Conversely, if the pitch attitude is lowered, then the angle of attack is decreased.

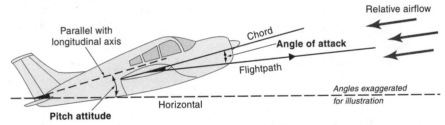

Figure 11. Pitch attitude and angle of attack are not the same

An Airplane Flies Identically, In or Out of Clouds

The principles of flight do not change when an airplane enters clouds. The airplane will fly identically, and be controlled in the same way, both in clouds and in clear skies. The only difference in clouds is that the pilot loses reference to external visual cues, and must derive substitute information from the instrument panel.

When flying visually, you are already deriving a lot of information from the instruments. The exact altitude, for instance, cannot be determined from external features—you must look at the altimeter to positively know the altitude. Similarly, the precise heading is found on the heading indicator or the magnetic compass, and not by reference to external features. The precise airspeed can only be determined from the airspeed indicator. Also, to set a precise power, you must look (briefly) at the power indicator.

Coordination, in turns as well as in straight-and-level flight, is maintained precisely with reference to the coordination ball, in both visual and instrument flight, although the "seat of your pants" can also be a good guide.

The main change, it seems, when switching to instrument flying from visual flying, is to transfer attention from the natural horizon outside the cockpit to the horizon bar of the AI in the cockpit.

Instrument-rated pilots are no different from other pilots, except that they have acquired more knowledge, and can derive more information from the instrument panel. An altimeter can tell you more than just the current altitude—it also says something about the rate of change of altitude, and if the selected pitch attitude is correct for altitude to be maintained. Similarly, the heading indicator can provide heading information, but it also can tell you if the wings are banked. If the heading is changing and the ball is centered, then the wings must be banked.

The skill of instrument interpretation (deriving all sorts of information from various instruments) will develop quickly during your instrument training. It is not difficult—it just takes practice. The airplane will fly exactly the same on instruments as when you are flying visually, and you will control it in the same way. The information required to do this is available on the instrument panel.

During instrument training, most maneuvers will be performed first in visual conditions, where the AI indications can be related to the appearance of the natural horizon in the windshield. After a satisfactory standard of visual flying is demonstrated, practice will occur in simulated instrument conditions—probably achieved by your instructor restricting your view of the outside world with a screen or hood.

His view, however, will remain unobstructed so that he can act as safety pilot, keeping a lookout for other aircraft, and monitoring the position of your airplane. You will concentrate on attitude flying using the instruments, interpreting their indications, and then responding with the controls. You should then be able to cope with actual instrument conditions.

A good understanding of each maneuver, and the ability to put it into practice in visual conditions, will speed up your instrument training. If you happen to be a little rusty, the first volume of this series—*Flight Training*—contains detailed briefings for each visual maneuver.

The skill of instrument interpretation is not difficult, but it does take practice to acquire and to maintain.

Scanning the Instruments

Scanning the instruments with your eyes, interpreting their indications and applying this information is a vital skill to develop if you are to become a good instrument pilot.

Power is selected with the throttle, and can be checked (if required) on the power indicator. Pitch attitude and bank angle are selected using the control column, with frequent reference to the attitude indicator. With both correct power and attitude set, the airplane will perform as expected. The attitude indicator and the power indicator, because they are used when controlling the airplane, are known as the **control instruments**.

The actual performance of the airplane, once its power and attitude have been set, can be cross-checked on what are known as the **performance instruments**—the altimeter for altitude, the airspeed indicator for airspeed, the heading indicator for direction, and so on.

A valuable instrument, important in its own right, is the clock or stopwatch. Time is extremely important in instrument flying. The stopwatch is used:

- in holding patterns (which, for example, may be racetrack patterns with legs of 1 or 2 minutes duration);

- in timed turns (a 180° change of heading at standard rate of 3° per second taking 60 seconds); and
- to measure time after passing certain ground beacons during certain instrument approaches (at 90 knots groundspeed, for instance, it would take 2 minutes to travel the 3 nm from a particular radio marker beacon to the published missed approach point).

Another area on the instrument panel contains the radio navigation instruments, which indicate the position of the airplane relative to selected radio navigation facilities. These radio navaids will be considered in detail later in your training, but the main ones are:

- **the VHF omni range (VOR) cockpit indicator**, which indicates the airplane's position relative to a selected course *to* or *from* the VOR ground station;
- **the automatic direction finder (ADF)**, which has a needle that points at an NDB or a compass locator ground station; and
- **the distance measuring equipment (DME)**, which indicates the slant distance in nautical miles to the selected DME ground station.

Instrument scanning is an art that will develop naturally during your training, especially when you know what to look for. The main scan to develop initially is that of the six basic flight instruments, concentrating on the AI and radiating out to the others as required. This is covered in detail in Chapter 1. Then as you move on to en route instrument flying, the radio navigation instruments will be introduced. Having scanned the instruments, interpreted the message that they contain, built up a picture of where the airplane is and where it is going, you can now control it in a meaningful way.

Your main scan is across six basic instruments:
•ASI •AI •ALT
•TC •HI •VSI

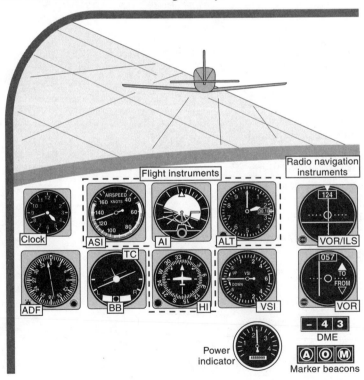

Figure 12. Layout of a typical instrument panel

Controlling the Airplane

During instrument flight, the airplane is flown using the normal controls according to the "picture" displayed on the instrument panel. From this picture, you will, with practice, know what control movements (elevator, aileron, rudder and throttle) are required to either maintain the picture as it is, or to change it.

When maneuvering the airplane, a suitable control sequence to follow (the same as in visual flight) is:

1. **Visualize** the desired new flightpath and airspeed.
2. **Select the attitude and the power required** to achieve the desired performance by moving the controls, and then checking when the airplane has achieved the estimated attitude on the AI.
3. **Hold the attitude** on the AI, allowing the airplane to settle down into its new performance, and allowing the pressure instruments that experience some lag to catch up.
4. **Make small adjustments** to attitude and power until the actual performance equals the desired performance.
5. **Trim** (which is vital, if you are to achieve accurate and comfortable instrument flight). Heavy loads can be trimmed off earlier in the sequence to assist in control, if desired, but remember that the function of trim is to relieve control loads on the pilot, and not to change aircraft attitude.

  Change  Check  Hold/adjust Trim

Figure 13. Control sequence

Some helpful hints follow.

- Derive the required information from the relevant instrument—direction from the heading indicator, altitude from the altimeter.
- **Respond to deviations** from the desired flightpath and/or airspeed. Use the AI as a control instrument, with power as required. For example, if you are 50 feet low on altitude, then raise the pitch attitude on the AI slightly and climb back up to altitude. Do not just accept steady deviations—it is just as easy to fly at 3000 feet as it is to fly at 2950 feet. A lot of instrument flying is in the mind and, in a sense, instrument flying is a test of character as well as of flying ability. Be as accurate as you can!
- **Do not over-control.** Avoid large, fast or jerky control movements, which will probably result in continuous corrections, over-corrections and then re-corrections. This can occur if attitude is changed without reference to the AI, or it might be caused by the airplane being out-of-trim, or possibly by a pilot who is fatigued or tense.
- **Do not be distracted** from a scan of the flight instruments for more than a few seconds at a time, even though other duties must be attended to, such as checklists, radio calls and navigational tasks.
- **Relax.** Easier said than done at the start, but it will come with experience.

Sensory Illusions

Most people live in a 1g situation most of the time, with their feet on the ground. 1g means the force of gravity. Some variations to 1g, however, do occur in everyday life—for instance, when driving an automobile. Accelerating an automobile, hard braking, or turning on a flat bend will all produce g-forces on the body different to the 1g of gravity alone. Passengers with their eyes closed could perhaps detect this by bodily feel or with their sense of balance.

A right turn on a flat road, for instance, could be detected by the feeling of being thrown to the left—but it might be more difficult to detect if the curve was perfectly banked for the particular speed. A straight road sloping to the left (and causing the passenger to lean to the left) might give the passenger the false impression that the automobile is turning right, even though it is in fact not turning at all.

The position sensing systems of the body, using nerves all over the body to transmit messages of feel and pressure to the brain, can be fooled in this and other ways.

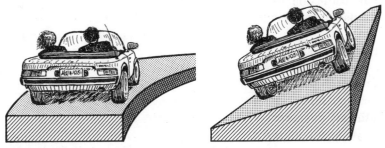

Figure 14. Turning right—or simply leaning?

The organs within the inner ear, used for balance and to detect accelerations, can also be deceived. For instance, if you are sitting in an automobile traveling around a suitably banked curve, the sensing system in your ears falsely interprets the g-force holding you firmly and comfortably in the seat as a vertical force, as if you were moving straight ahead rather than in a banked turn.

The inner ear organs also have other limitations, one being that a constant velocity is not detected, nor is a gradual change in velocity. For instance, you are sitting in a train and notice another train on the next track moving past your window. Is it moving forward? Are you moving backward? Are you both moving forward but at different speeds? It is sometimes difficult to tell.

False impressions of motion can also be caused by unusual g-forces—for instance, by rapid head motion, or by lowering the head. If you happen to drop your pencil while instrument flying, don't just lower your eyes and lean down to look for it in one motion—take it carefully step by step to avoid any feeling of vertigo.

Because an airplane moves in three dimensions, there is the possibility to accelerate and decelerate in three dimensions, and this can lead to more complicated illusions. Pulling up into a steep climb, for example, will hold you tightly in your seat, which is exactly the same feeling as in a steep turn. Banking the airplane and pulling it into a turn will increase the pressure on "the seat of your pants", which is a similar bodily feeling to suddenly entering a climb. As well as your muscles, the balance organs of your inner ear may be sending false signals to your brain. Rolling into and out of a turn may be interpreted as a climb or descent (or vice versa) by your bodily feel. With your eyes closed, it is sometimes difficult to say which maneuver it is.

A sudden change from a climb to straight-and-level flight or a descent may cause an illusion of tumbling backward. A sudden acceleration in straight-and-level flight, or during the takeoff roll, may cause an illusion of being in a nose-up attitude.

Decelerating while in a turn to the left may give a false impression of a turn to the right. Be aware that your sense of balance and bodily feel can lead you astray in an airplane, especially with rapidly changing g-forces in maneuvers such as this. The one sense that can resolve most of these illusions is sight. If the automobile passenger could see out, or if the pilot had reference to the natural horizon and landmarks, then the confusion, and the risk of not knowing your attitude in space (i.e. the risk of **spatial disorientation**), would be easily dispelled. A false horizon seen by the eyes, however, can be misleading—such as what a pilot might see flying above a sloping cloud formation, or on a dark night with ground lights and stars spread in certain patterns, or when the natural horizon is obscured. Believe the flight instruments!

Unfortunately, in instrument flight you do not have reference to ground features, but you can still use your sense of sight to scan the instruments and obtain substitute information. Therefore, an important instruction to the budding instrument pilot is: "believe your eyes and what the instruments tell you."

Believe only what your eyes tell you when flying on instruments.

It is good airmanship to avoid any situation in flight, or prior to flight, that will affect your vision. While in clouds at night, for instance, turn off the strobe light if it is bothering you. It could induce vertigo, a sense of dizziness or of whirling around, if sufficient of its flashing light is reflected into the cockpit. It is good practice to avoid strong white light, such as a flashlight, in the cockpit when night flying, so that the night adaptation of your eyes is not impaired. However, if flying in dark conditions with thunderstorms in the vicinity, turn the cockpit lights up bright to minimize the effects of nearby lightning flashes. If expecting to fly out of cloud tops and into bright sunlight, have your sunglasses handy. Protect your sight!

While sight is the most important sense, and must be protected at all costs, also make sure that you avoid anything that will affect your balance or position sensing systems.

Avoid alcohol, drugs (including smoking in the cockpit) and medication. Do not fly when ill or suffering with an upper respiratory infection (a cold). Do not fly when tired or fatigued. Do not fly with a cabin altitude higher than 10,000 feet MSL without using oxygen. Avoid sudden head movements, and avoid lowering your head or turning around in the cockpit.

Despite all these don'ts, there is one very important do—do trust what your eyes tell you from the instruments.

The Instrument Rating Test

Detailed information of the standards required for you to obtain an Instrument Rating is included in 14 CFR (Part 61) and in a small publication entitled *Practical Test Standards (PTS)*, published by the FAA and reprinted by ASA in both book form and digitized on CD-ROM. These standards change from time to time, so be sure that you are working from a current set of regulations and a current issue of the PTS book.

Terminology and Units

Terminology has always been a problem in international aviation, with some areas of the world using different terms to describe the same thing. For instance, the scale used to set the pressure level from which the altimeter will measure height may be called the *Kollsman window* (after the inventor of the sensitive altimeter), or the *pressure window,* or the *altimeter subscale.*

Pressure window is a good way to describe it, since it is indeed a "window" in the face of the altimeter in which the pilot sets the pressure datum from which the instrument will measure its height. You should be familiar with each of these terms.

Standard pressure is expressed in various units—in the US it is 29.92 *inches of mercury* (abbreviated in. Hg or "Hg), but in other parts of the world it is 1013.2 *hectopascals (hPa)* or 1013.2 *millibars (mb)*—all describing the same pressure value. Millibars are used in the United Kingdom, and hectopascals in Europe and Australia.

A variety of units are used for **distance** in aviation. For instance, runway lengths are specified in feet in the USA, but in *meters* in most other parts of the world; course distances are measured in *nautical miles,* and in the USA and some other countries visibility is quoted in *statute miles.* If you are flying internationally, you should be careful to acquaint yourself with these variations.

Elevations on most aeronautical charts are specified in *feet* MSL (or AMSL—above mean sea level), although in France, for example, they may be in *meters.* So, again, if flying internationally, be very careful of units.

The **heading** of an airplane is the direction in which its longitudinal axis is pointing. In radio navigation the reference direction is magnetic north and the heading is therefore known as *magnetic heading* (MH). Wind effect may cause the airplane's path over the ground to differ from its heading, and the result is known as the *ground track.* The aim of the instrument pilot is to ensure that the aircraft's ground track matches the required course as closely as possible.

Course is usually specified as *magnetic course* (MC) when, as is usual, it is based on magnetic north. (Some countries refer to course as required track.) Instruments in the cockpit, such as the VHF-NAV receiver display (VOR and ILS) with its CDI (course deviation indicator), inform the pilot if the aircraft's actual ground track is deviating from the MC.

Refer to the *Glossary and Abbreviations* at the end of the manual for information on the many abbreviations involved with instrument flying. The *Aeronautical Information Manual* is also a valuable reference source.

The Pilot's Manual **Instrument Flying**

Attitude Flying Section One

1   **Instrument Scanning Technique** 19
2   **The Instruments** 31
3   **Straight-and-Level Flight** 73
4   **The Straight Climb and Descent** 95
5   **Turning** 111
6   **Unusual Attitudes** 133
7   **Normal Instrument Flight on a Partial Panel** ... 143
8   **Suggested Training Maneuvers** 163

Instrument Scanning Technique 1

The three fundamental skills in instrument flying are:

- instrument cross-check (or scan);
- instrument interpretation; and
- airplane control.

In this chapter, we look at suitable flight instrument scanning techniques that allow you to cross-check the instruments efficiently, and to extract and interpret information relevant to the flight path and performance of your airplane.

The performance of an airplane is, as always, determined by the power set and the attitude selected. In *visual* flying conditions, the external natural horizon is used as a reference when selecting pitch attitude and bank angle. The power indicator in the cockpit is only referred to occasionally, for instance when setting a particular power for cruise or for climb.

In *instrument* conditions, when the natural horizon cannot be seen, pitch attitude and bank angle information is still available to the pilot in the cockpit from the **attitude indicator**. Relatively large pitch attitude changes against the natural horizon are reproduced in miniature on the attitude indicator.

In straight-and-level flight, for instance, the wings of the miniature airplane should appear against the horizon line, while in a climb they should appear one or two *bar widths* above it.

In a turn, the wing bars of the miniature airplane will bank along with the real airplane, while the horizon line remains horizontal. The center dot of the miniature airplane represents the airplane's nose position relative to the horizon.

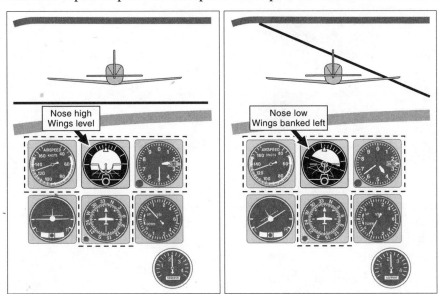

Figure 1-1. The AI is the master instrument for pitch attitude and bank angle

Simple Scans

Coordination. The AI, while it shows pitch attitude and bank angle directly, does not indicate coordination or yaw. Coordination (or balance) information can be obtained simply by moving the eyes from the attitude indicator diagonally down to the left to the **inclinometer**, to check that the ball is indeed being centered with rudder pressure. The eyes should then return to the AI.

Heading. Directional information can be obtained from the **heading indicator (HI)** or from the magnetic compass. From the AI, the eyes can be moved straight down to the HI to absorb heading information, before returning to the AI. Each eye movement to obtain particular information is very simple, starting at the attitude indicator and radiating out to the relevant instrument, before returning to the AI.

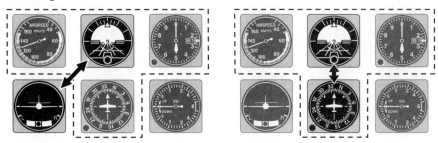

Figure 1-2.
A simple scan for coordination

Figure 1-3.
A simple scan for heading

Airspeed. Airspeed information is also very important, and this is easily checked by moving the eyes left from the AI to the **airspeed indicator (ASI)**, before returning them to the AI.

Altitude. The **altimeter** is the only means of determining the precise altitude of the airplane, in visual as well as in instrument conditions.

To obtain altitude information, the eyes can move from the AI toward the right where the altimeter is located, before moving back to the AI.

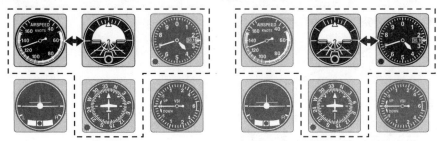

Figure 1-4.
A simple scan for airspeed

Figure 1-5.
A simple scan for altitude

Vertical Speed. The rate of change of altitude, either as a rate of climb or a rate of descent in feet per minute, can be monitored on the **vertical speed indicator (VSI)** by moving the eyes from the AI diagonally down to the right to the VSI, before returning to the AI. The VSI, since it is often used in conjunction with the altimeter, is located directly beneath it on most instrument panels.

Turning. A turn is entered using the AI to establish bank angle and the inclinometer ball to confirm coordination. Additional information on the turning rate is available from the **turn coordinator** once the bank angle is established. The normal rate of turn in instrument flying is 3° per second, known as *standard-rate* or *rate 1*, and this is clearly marked on the turn coordinator (or turn-and-slip indicator).

Figure 1-6.
Simple scan for vertical speed information

Figure 1-7.
Simple scan for turn rate

With these six basic flight instruments, plus the power indicator, it is possible to fly the airplane very accurately and comfortably without any external visual reference, provided the instruments are scanned efficiently, and you control the airplane adequately in response to the information derived from them.

Control and Performance

The attitude selected on the AI and the power set on the power indicator determines the performance of the airplane, hence these two instruments are known as the **control instruments**.

> **Control the airplane to achieve the desired performance.**

The attitude indicator is located centrally on the instrument panel directly in front of the pilot, so that any changes in attitude can be readily seen. Because continual reference to the power indicator is not required, it is situated slightly away from the main group of flight instruments, easy to scan occasionally, but not in the main field of view.

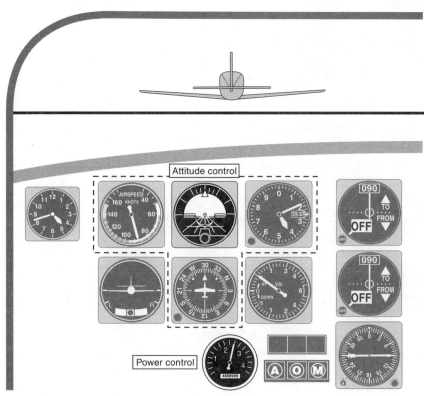

Figure 1-8. The control instruments are used to select attitude and power

The other flight instruments are **performance instruments** that display how the airplane is performing (as a result of the power and attitude selected) in terms of:

• altitude, on the altimeter and VSI;
• direction, on the HI and turn coordinator; and
• airspeed, on the ASI.

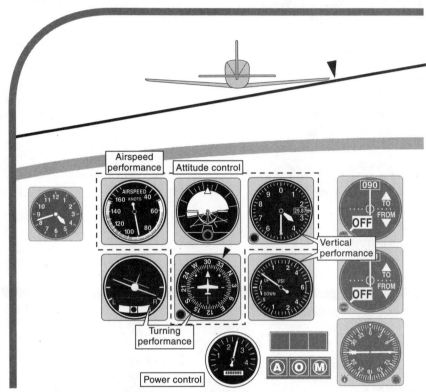

Figure 1-9. Performance is displayed on the performance instruments

Changes in **pitch attitude** are shown directly on the AI, and are reflected on the altimeter, VSI and ASI. Changes in **bank angle** are shown directly on the AI, and are reflected on the turn coordinator and the heading indicator. The "quality" of flight is shown by the coordination ball.

Figure 1-10.
The pitch instruments

Figure 1-11.
The bank instruments

The Selective Radial Scan

Of the six main flight instruments, the **attitude indicator** is the master instrument. It gives you a direct and immediate picture of pitch attitude and bank angle. It will be the one most frequently referred to (at least once every few seconds in most stages of flight). The eyes can be directed selectively toward the other instruments to derive relevant information from them as required, before being returned to the AI. This eye movement radiating out and back to selected instruments is commonly known as the **selective radial scan**.

The attitude indicator is the master flight instrument.

For instance, when climbing with full power selected, the estimated climb pitch attitude is held on the attitude indicator, with subsequent reference to the airspeed indicator to confirm that the selected pitch attitude is indeed correct. If the ASI indicates an airspeed that is too low, then lower the pitch attitude on the AI (say by a half bar width or by one bar width), allow a few seconds for the airspeed to settle, and then check the ASI again.

The key instrument in confirming that the correct attitude has been selected on the AI during the climb is the airspeed indicator. Because it determines what pitch attitude changes should be made on the AI during the climb, the airspeed indicator is the primary performance guide for pitch attitude in the climb. It is supported by the AI and the VSI.

Correct pitch attitude in the climb is checked on the airspeed indicator.

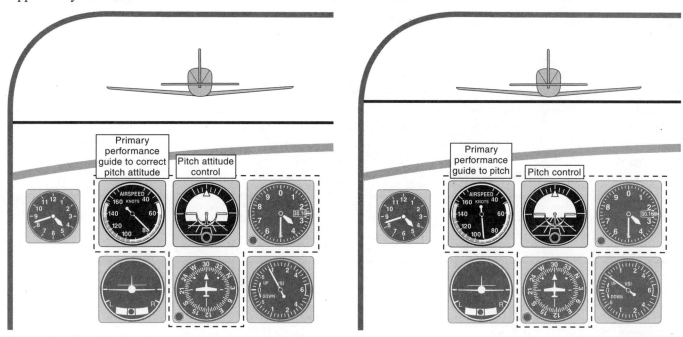

Figure 1-12. The ASI is the primary instrument in the climb to confirm correct pitch attitude

Approaching the desired cruise altitude, however, more attention should be paid to the altimeter to ensure that, as pitch attitude is lowered on the AI, the airplane levels off right on the desired altitude. When cruising, any minor deviations from altitude detected on the altimeter can be corrected with small changes in pitch attitude. Because the altimeter is now the instrument that determines if pitch attitude changes on the AI are required to maintain level flight, the altimeter is the primary performance guide for pitch attitude in the cruise. It is supported by the AI and the VSI.

Correct pitch attitude when cruising is checked on the altimeter.

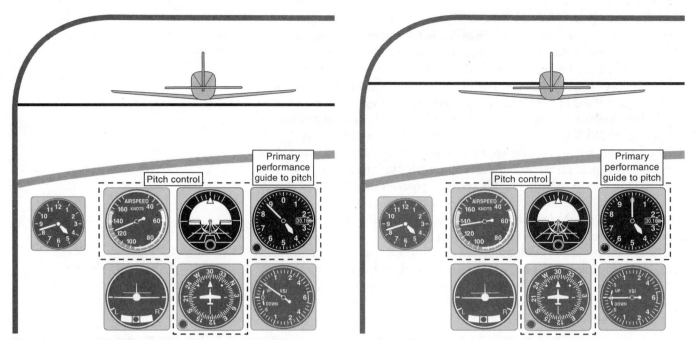

Figure 1-13. The altimeter is the primary instrument in the cruise to confirm correct pitch attitude

If climb power is still set after the airplane has been leveled off at cruise altitude, then the airplane will accelerate, shown by an increasing airspeed on the ASI. At the desired speed, the power should be reduced to a suitable value.

While it is usual simply to set cruise power and then accept the resulting airspeed, it is possible to achieve a precise airspeed by adjusting the power. Because the ASI indications will then determine what power changes should be made during level flight, the airspeed indicator is the primary performance guide to power requirements in the cruise.

Correct power when cruising is checked on the airspeed indicator.

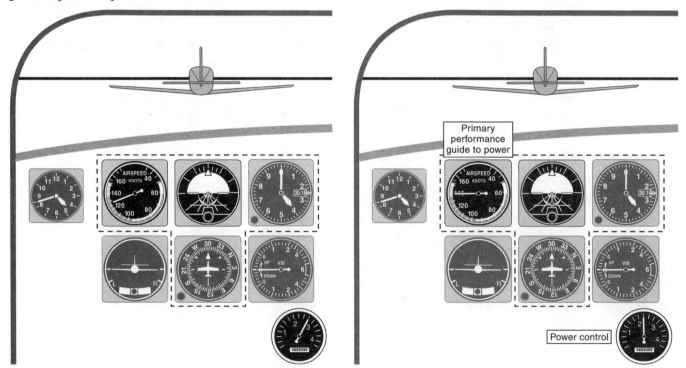

Figure 1-14. The ASI is the primary instrument in the cruise to confirm correct power

Heading is maintained with reference to the heading indicator (HI), and any deviations corrected with gentle coordinated turns. Because the indications on the HI will determine what minor corrections to bank angle should be made on the attitude indicator during straight flight, the heading indicator is the primary performance guide to zero bank angle in maintaining a constant heading for straight flight. It is supported by the turn coordinator and the AI. The ball should be centered to keep the airplane from slipping or skidding, to provide coordinated straight flight.

Check wings level on the heading indicator.

Keep the ball centered.

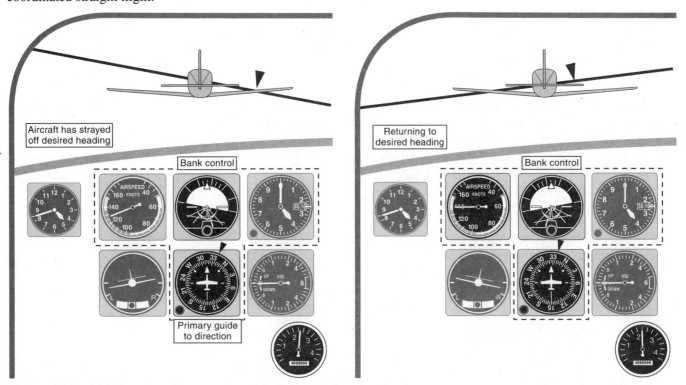

Figure 1-15. The HI is the primary instrument in straight flight to confirm wings level

The Basic-T Scan

A basic scan suitable for straight-and-level flight (where altitude, direction and airspeed need to be monitored) is centered on the AI, and radiates out and back, following the basic-T pattern on the panel, to the relevant performance instrument:

- the HI to confirm heading (and correct with shallow turns on the AI);
- the altimeter to confirm altitude (and correct with pitch changes on the AI);
- the ASI to confirm airspeed (and, if desired, correct with power changes).

Figure 1-16. The "basic-T" scan in level flight

If cruise power is set and left alone, and the resulting airspeed accepted (normally the case), then scanning the ASI need not be as frequent, and the scan can concentrate on the AI, HI and altimeter.

Also, once established and well trimmed on the cruise, the airplane will tend to hold altitude because of its longitudinal stability, making it less essential to scan the altimeter continually compared to when the airplane is out of trim. The airplane may not be as stable laterally as it is longitudinally, however, and so the HI should be scanned quite frequently to ensure that heading is maintained.

Visual pilots are already well practiced at scanning the altimeter regularly, since it is the only means of accurately holding altitude, but they may not be used to scanning the HI quite so frequently as is necessary in instrument conditions. This skill will have to be developed.

What About the other Flight Instruments?

In smooth air, the VSI will show a trend away from cruising altitude often before it is apparent on the altimeter, and can be used to indicate that a minor pitch attitude correction is required if altitude is to be maintained. The VSI provides supporting pitch information to that provided by the altimeter, although it is of less value in turbulence which causes the VSI needle to fluctuate.

If the wings are held level on the AI, and heading is being maintained on the HI, then it is almost certain that the airplane is coordinated (in balance), with the inclinometer ball centered. Normally, the inclinometer does not have to be scanned as frequently as some of the other instruments, but it should be referred to occasionally, especially if heading is changing while the wings are level, or if the "seat of your pants" tells you that the airplane is skidding or slipping.

The turn coordinator will show a wings-level indication during straight flight, and provides supporting information regarding bank to that provided by the heading indicator. In a standard-rate turn, it is the primary performance guide to confirm that the bank angle is correct.

Choice of Scan Pattern

Starting with your eyes focused on the AI, scan the performance instruments that provide the information required. Relevant information can be obtained from different instruments depending on the maneuver.

Use a logical scan for each maneuver.

Primary pitch information (to confirm whether or not the pitch attitude selected on the AI is correct) is obtained from the altimeter during cruise flight, but from the ASI during climbs and descents. There is no need to memorize particular scan patterns, since they will develop naturally as your training progresses.

Do not allow the radial scan to break down. Avoid fixation on any one instrument, since this will certainly cause a breakdown in the radial scan, and result in delayed recognition of deviations from the desired flight path and/or airspeed. Fixation on the HI, for instance, can lead to heading being maintained perfectly, but in the meantime altitude and airspeed may change—tendencies which would have been detected (and corrected for) if the altimeter, VSI and ASI had been correctly scanned. Keep the eyes moving, and continually return to the AI.

Keep your eyes moving, and continually return to the attitude indicator.

Occasionally, the eyes will have to be directed away from the main flight instruments for a short period, for instance when checking the power indicator during or following a power change, or when periodically checking the oil temperature and pressure instruments, the ammeter, or the suction (vacuum) gauge, or when re-aligning the heading indicator with the magnetic compass, or when referring to instrument approach charts, filling in the flight log, or tuning radios.

Do not neglect the radial scan for more than a few seconds at a time, even though other necessary tasks have to be performed. Avoid omission of any relevant instrument. For instance, after rolling out of a turn, check the HI to ensure that the desired heading is being achieved and maintained. The wings might be level and the airplane flying straight, but on the wrong heading.

Use all available resources. For instance, with correct power set and the correct attitude selected on the AI, it is possible to hold altitude at least approximately using only the AI and the power indicator but, if precision is required, then the altimeter must be included in the scan as the primary reference for altitude.

Furthermore, do not forget that supporting instruments can provide additional information to back-up primary instruments. For example, altitude is indicated directly on the altimeter, but any tendency to depart from that altitude may first be indicated on the VSI (especially in smooth air), which makes it a very valuable supporting instrument to the altimeter.

Supporting instruments can provide additional information to back-up primary instruments.

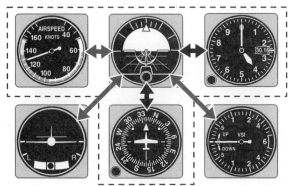

Figure 1-17. A suitable scan during straight-and-level flight

Other Scans

It is necessary on some occasions to have a fast scan, such as on final for an instrument approach. On other occasions, however, the scan can be more relaxed, for instance when cruising with the autopilot engaged. It may then be suitable just to have a fairly relaxed **circular scan**.

Figure 1-18. A circular scan

If you are performing other tasks while flying a constant heading, such as map reading, then a very simple scan to make sure things do not get out of hand is a **vertical scan** from the AI down to the heading indicator and back again.

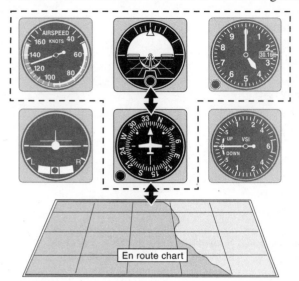

Figure 1-19. The vertical scan

If at any time, you suspect an instrument failure, then a very efficient means of establishing what instrument or system has failed is to commence with an **inverted-V scan**, centered on the AI and radiating to the turn coordinator and the VSI.

Figure 1-20. Use and inverted-V scan if you suspect instrument failure

Each of these instruments normally has a different power source—the vacuum system for the AI, the electrical system for the turn coordinator, and the static system for the VSI—so a false indication on one should not be reflected on the others. Confirmation of attitude and flight path can then be achieved using the other instruments.

With practice, you will develop scans suitable to every situation.

Review Questions and Answers

To assist you in reviewing this topic and consolidating your knowledge, you should now complete the questions that follow. Cover the answers by sliding a sheet of paper down to the appropriate arrowhead ➤, only uncovering the answer *after* you have decided firmly on your response to the question.

✍ Review 1

Introduction

1. To avoid spatial disorientation when flying in IFR conditions, you should believe (the flight instruments/your bodily feelings).

➤ the flight instruments

2. Flying visually in a clear, blue sky above a sloping cloud layer may not be as easy as it sounds, because a sloping cloud layer may cause a _____ horizon.

➤ false

3. A well-lit town situated on sloping ground (may/will not) cause a false horizon at night.

➤ may

4. An abrupt change from climb to straight-and-level flight can cause an illusion of (tumbling backward/a nose-up attitude) if you do not refer to your flight instruments.

➤ tumbling backward

5. The force that pulls an airplane into a turn can cause an illusion of (climb or descent/motion reversal) if you do not refer to your flight instruments.

➤ climb or descent

6. Abrupt head movement (can/cannot) cause spatial disorientation if you do not refer to your flight instruments.

➤ can

7. Rapid acceleration during straight-and-level flight or during takeoff can create the illusion of (being in a nose-up attitude/being in a nose-down attitude/turning) if you do not refer to your flight instruments.

➤ being in a nose-up attitude

8. To assist the adaptation of your eyes to darkness, you should (use/avoid) bright white light in the cockpit at night.

➤ avoid

Instrument Scanning Technique

1. The three fundamental skills in instrument flying are _____.

➤ instrument cross-check (scan), instrument interpretation, aircraft control

2. Sketch a simple diagram showing the relative positions of the six main flight instruments.

➤ ASI   AI   ALT
   TC   HI   VSI

3. The master instrument for pitch attitude and bank attitude is the _____.

➤ attitude indicator

4. Directional information is obtained from the _____.

➤ heading indicator

5. Information as to whether flight is coordinated or not is obtained from the _____.

➤ coordination ball

6. Airspeed information is obtained from the _____.

➤ ASI

7. Altitude information is obtained from the _____.

➤ altimeter

8. Vertical speed in terms of rate of climb, or rate of descent, is obtained from the _____.

➤ VSI

9. Changes in pitch attitude are shown directly on the _____.

➤ AI

10. Changes in pitch attitude are shown directly on the _____, and are reflected on the _____.

➤ AI, and reflected on the altimeter, VSI and ASI

11. Changes in bank attitude are shown directly on the _____.

➤ AI

12. Changes in bank attitude are shown directly on the _____, and are reflected on the _____.

➤ AI, and reflected on the turn coordinator and heading indicator

13. Eye movement radiating out and back to selected instruments is known as the _____ scan.

➤ selective radial scan

14. All changes of pitch attitude and bank angle should be made with reference to the _____.

➤ AI

15. In level flight, the primary performance guide to confirm that the pitch attitude selected on the AI is correct is the _____.

➤ altimeter

16. In level flight, the primary performance guide to confirm that the pitch attitude is correct is the _____. It is supported by the _____.

➤ altimeter, supported by the AI and VSI.

17. In climbing flight, the primary performance guide to confirm that the pitch attitude selected on the AI is correct is the _____.

➤ ASI

18. In climbing flight, the primary performance guide to confirm that the pitch attitude selected is correct is the _____. It is supported by the _____.

➤ ASI, supported by the AI and VSI.

19. For cruise at a specific airspeed, any need for a power change will be indicated by the _____.

➤ ASI

20. The primary performance guide to confirm that the bank angle selected on the AI is correct for a standard-rate turn is the _____.

➤ turn coordinator

21. The primary performance guide to confirm that the bank angle is correct for straight flight is the _____.

➤ heading indicator

22. Sketch a simple diagram showing the relative positions of the instruments that provide information in pitch.

➤ ASI   AI   Alt
  ___   ___   VSI

23. Sketch a simple diagram showing the relative positions of the instruments that provide information in bank.

➤ ___   AI   ___
TC   HI   ___

The Instruments

The first impression most people have of an airplane cockpit is just how many instruments there are. Yet, when you analyze the instrument panels of even the largest jet transport airplanes, the instrumentation is not all that complicated. In fact, the basic instruments in large passenger aircraft are very similar to those in the smallest training airplane.

The **flight instruments**, which provide vital flight information such as attitude, airspeed, altitude and direction, fall into two basic categories:

- those that use variations in **static and/or ram air pressure**, such as the airspeed indicator, the altimeter and the vertical speed indicator; and

- those that use the properties of **gyroscopic inertia**, such as the attitude indicator, the heading indicator and the turn coordinator.

Figure 2-1. The pressure flight instruments (left) and gyroscopic flight instruments (right)

We will consider each flight instrument individually, as well as the systems which might affect them, such as the pitot-static system for the pressure instruments and the vacuum system for the gyroscopic instruments.

We look first at the attitude indicator and the power indicator, since they are used as **control instruments** by the pilot to set flight attitude and power. It is power and attitude that determines the performance of the airplane, and this can be measured on the other flight instruments.

The Attitude Indicator

The attitude indicator is the only instrument that gives a direct and immediate picture of pitch attitude and bank attitude (or bank angle). Any changes to pitch attitude or bank angle by the pilot will normally be made with reference to the attitude indicator. The attitude indicator is commonly referred to as the AI.

The main features of an attitude indicator are an **artificial horizon line** (also known as the horizon bar) that remains horizontal as the airplane banks and pitches about it, and a **miniature airplane** that is fixed to the case of the instrument. This small symbolic airplane moves with the instrument case and the real airplane, while the horizon line remains level with the real horizon outside.

For the instrument pilot, the attitude indicator is the master instrument in the cockpit, providing a clear visual representation of the airplane's movement about two axes (pitch and roll). However, since the AI does not have any "landmarks" on its horizon line, it does not provide any information on yaw.

The attitude indicator is the master instrument in the cockpit.

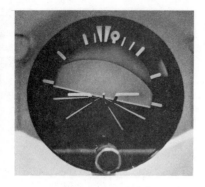

Figure 2-2. Typical attitude indicators

Pitch attitude is indicated on the AI by the relative positions of the miniature airplane and the horizon line. Ideally, they will be perfectly aligned when the airplane is in the level attitude, with the central dot in the wing bars directly over the horizon line.

When the airplane is pitched up into the climbing attitude, the miniature airplane moves with it, and appears above the horizon line. This is achieved within the instrument, not by the miniature airplane moving up, but by the horizon line moving down.

Conversely, when the airplane is pitched down into the descent attitude, the horizon line will move to a position above the miniature airplane. The pilot sees the airplane below the horizon and knows it is in a descent attitude.

Small horizontal lines marked above and below the horizon line indicate the number of degrees of pitch up or pitch down but, generally, there is no need to use these lines. Most pilots alter pitch in terms of bar width—one bar width being the thickness of the wing bar and the central dot on the miniature airplane (or the thickness of the horizon line if it is thicker than the wing bars). The central dot is easier to use than the wing bars when setting pitch attitude against the horizon line during a banked turn, since the wing bars will, of course, be at an angle to the horizon.

Bank attitude (angle) is displayed both by the bank pointer against a scale graduated in degrees at the top of the AI, and by the angle between the wing bar of the miniature airplane and the horizon line. Some instruments have converging lines marked on the "earth" part of the background to enhance the picture and assist in estimating the bank angle. Bank pointer displays vary in design, but are easy to interpret.

How the AI Works

The basis of the attitude indicator is a self-erecting gyroscope with a vertical spin axis. It may be driven either electrically or by an airflow induced over vanes on the edge of the gyroscope by suction. The gyroscope is connected to the horizon line. Once it is spinning fast enough, and the spin axis has stabilized vertically, the gyroscope acts to hold the horizon line of the AI horizontal. Because the spin axis is vertical, and the gyroscope spins in the horizontal plane, the AI cannot provide a reference in the yawing plane, but only in pitch and roll.

If the spin axis of the gyroscope moves off the vertical for some reason, the AI's internal self-erecting mechanism, which senses gravity, will realign it at a rate of approximately 3° per minute. The AI should work perfectly in steady 1g conditions, and the horizon line should remain exactly horizontal.

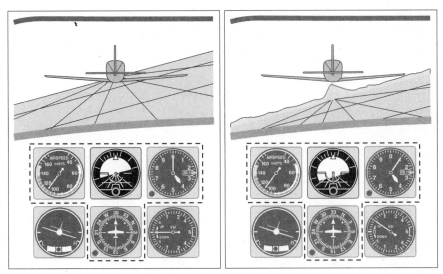

Figure 2-3. The AI provides pitch and bank information only

The miniature airplane attached to the case of the AI usually consists of a wing-bar on either side of a central dot that represents the nose of the airplane. In normal cruise flight, the miniature airplane will be on the horizon bar. In the normal climb it will appear above the horizon bar, and in the normal descent it will appear slightly below the horizon bar.

Occasionally the miniature airplane may require repositioning in flight. If so, it should be aligned with the horizon line when the airplane is flying straight-and-level at a steady speed.

Errors of the Attitude Indicator

The attitude indicator is an exceptionally useful and important instrument, but it is not perfect and is subject to power failures and precession errors.

Power source failure. If the AI experiences a failure of the power source, it will become unusable. An electrically driven AI will usually incorporate a red warning flag to alert the pilot to a power failure, but a vacuum-driven AI may not include this feature—the gyroscope may just wind down gradually, and the AI will provide false indications without any specific warning to the unwary pilot. So, if your airplane is fitted with a vacuum-driven AI, you should conscientiously check the suction gauge at regular intervals to ensure that an adequate vacuum of approximately 3–5 in. Hg is being provided. If not, treat the attitude indicator with caution (as well as the heading indicator which, most likely, will also be vacuum-driven).

Precession errors. The AI suffers from gyroscopic precession errors during rapid speed changes and turns, which can cause false indications of pitch attitude and bank angle. These errors are usually small, and are easily identified and corrected for. For instance, any attempt to follow a slightly incorrect horizon bar will be detected by scanning the other flight instruments, enabling you to take appropriate corrective action to maintain the desired pitch attitude and direction until the AI indications normalize.

Any acceleration (such as a rapid speed change or a turn) will exert additional g-forces on the airplane. Everything within it, including the pilot and the AI's self-erecting mechanism, will sense a false "gravity" force. This may cause the gyroscope's spin axis to move off the vertical briefly, thereby moving the horizon line to a slightly incorrect position.

The attitude indicator is subject to power failures and precession errors.

During a rapid acceleration, the horizon line will move down, and so the AI will indicate a false climb. If you follow the AI without reference to the other instruments and lowers the nose, the airplane will have a lower pitch attitude than desired. Conversely, during a deceleration, the horizon line will move up, causing a false pitch-down indication, i.e. the AI will display a greater pitch-down attitude than the airplane actually has. If you follow the slightly higher horizon line, the airplane will enter a climb. You will detect these small pitch errors in your scan of the vertical performance instruments, and either maintain altitude in level flight using the altimeter and VSI, or maintain airspeed in a climb or descent using the ASI.

Skids, slips and turns exert additional forces that may cause the horizon line to move off the horizontal briefly, resulting in a small error in bank angle display. You will detect this in your scan of the other instruments, and can maintain heading and wings level with reference to the heading indicator in straight flight, or maintain a particular turn rate during a heading change with reference to the turn coordinator. The small bank error in the AI from precession is greatest following a turn of 180° (possibly up to 5° of bank error in the direction opposite the turn), and there is also a slight climb falsely indicated. The errors cancel out at the completion of 360°.

These precession errors correct themselves fairly quickly and can, in general, be disregarded in light aircraft, which do not have high rates of acceleration and deceleration. A good scan ensures that errors in the AI will not affect the accuracy of instrument flying, with the pilot able to hold altitude, heading or airspeed quite accurately with reference to the other flight instruments.

Some attitude indicators have a gyroscope which may "tumble" when the airplane is in extreme attitudes well beyond normal flight attitudes (typically in excess of 60° of pitch and 100° of roll). This will temporarily render the AI useless.

Some older gyroscopes can be caged for aerobatic maneuvers to prevent tumbling, and then uncaged once the airplane is back in straight-and-level flight. Newer attitude indicators, however, can tolerate any aircraft attitude (360° of pitch and/or roll) without the gyroscope tumbling. If, however, the self-erecting mechanism of any attitude indicator is unable to cope with large errors, no matter what their cause, they will make the AI unusable.

If the attitude indicator becomes unusable in flight for any reason, accurate instrument flight is still attainable (although more difficult) using the other flight instruments. Chapter 7, *Normal Instrument Flight on a Partial Panel*, discusses this in detail.

Preflight Checks of the Attitude Indicator

The gyroscope of the attitude indicator must stabilize within 5 minutes of initial power-up (FAA requirement). This means within 5 minutes of engine start for AIs powered by an engine-driven vacuum pump, or within 5 minutes of supplying electrical power to an electrically driven AI. While 5 minutes is the requirement, most AIs will erect within one or two minutes.

After allowing the gyroscope time to stabilize, the attitude indicator should be checked for serviceability. The electrical-failure warning flag should be biased out of view for an electrically driven gyroscope, and there should be no unusual or irregular mechanical noise as the gyroscope winds up. Adequate

The gyroscope of the attitude indicator must stabilize within 5 minutes of initial power-up.

suction (3–5 in. Hg) should be indicated for a vacuum-driven gyroscope. The horizon line should appear horizontal, and the miniature airplane should be checked to ensure that it is aligned with the horizon line when the airplane is on level ground.

During the taxi to the takeoff position, if the brakes are eased on until the nose dips a little, the miniature airplane should appear slightly below the horizon line. As the brakes are released, the nose of the airplane will rise again and this should be reflected on the AI. (Do not apply the brakes too abruptly, however, as this could put excessive stress on the nosewheel strut or cause the propeller to strike the runway or long grass, both of which can result in severe damage.) During turns, the horizon line may tilt a little. For the AI to be considered serviceable, the maximum permissible tilt of the horizon bar in taxi turns is 5° false bank angle. Normally, there should be little or no tilt of the horizon bar, otherwise control of bank angle in flight will be more difficult.

Significant bank or pitch errors in the attitude indicator could indicate a malfunction within the gyroscopic system. If you suspect a problem in the attitude indicator, then you should not commence an instrument flight.

Be aware that some attitude indicators will precess slightly during an acceleration, causing the horizon bar to move down slightly. The miniature airplane will appear above the horizon line, thereby causing a false indication of a climb. This may occur during the takeoff acceleration.

For the AI to be considered serviceable, the maximum permissible tilt of the horizon bar in taxi turns is 5° false bank angle.

The Power Indicator(s)

Different types of engines and propellers require different types of power instruments. For this reason, the power indicator in the cockpit will be referred to throughout this manual as just that, the power indicator, whereas in a specific airplane it may actually be the tachometer, in another the tachometer and manifold pressure gauge, and in a jet, the EPR gauge.

In an airplane fitted with a fixed-pitch propeller (most basic trainers), the power instrument is a **tachometer**, which measures engine rpm. Moving the throttle forward increases power by increasing engine rpm, displayed by the tachometer needle moving clockwise.

More advanced airplanes have a constant-speed propeller whose rpm can be set to a constant value with a propeller control placed beside the throttle. With rpm set on the **tachometer**, a power increase is made by advancing the throttle, and is shown in the cockpit as an increase in manifold pressure (MP) on the **manifold pressure gauge**, which is now the main power indicator. Manifold pressure is usually abbreviated to MP or to MAP (manifold absolute pressure).

A power increase on a jet engine made by advancing the throttle may be shown on an **engine pressure ratio (EPR) gauge**, which may be the main power indicator to the jet pilot.

From the point of view of instrument flying, it does not matter what sort of airplane is being flown and what sort of power instruments it has—the important point is that there is always a power indicator in the cockpit to which you can refer when power changes are made. We use a nonspecific type of indicator in the illustrations, mainly to show power increases or decreases. Training for a Type Rating on a specific airplane with an instructor will include training in the use of its particular power indicators and engine/propeller controls.

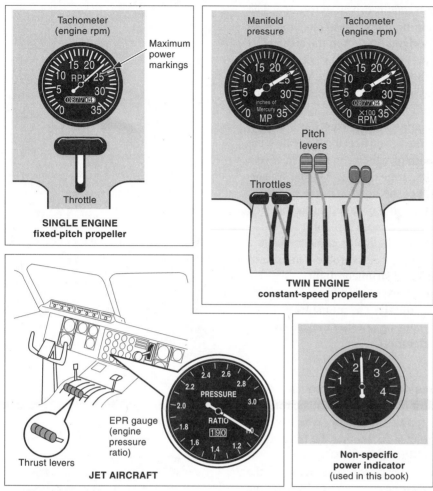

Figure 2-4. Typical power indicators

The Airspeed Indicator

The airspeed indicator (ASI) displays an airspeed referred to as the **indicated airspeed (IAS)**. It is related to the dynamic pressure, which is the difference between the total (or ram air) pressure and the static pressure. This is determined within the airspeed indicator by having a diaphragm with total pressure (from the pitot tube) being fed to one side of it, and static pressure (from the static port) being fed to the other side of it.

The diaphragm will position itself, and the pointer connected to it, according to the difference between the total pressure and the static pressure, that is, according to the dynamic pressure ($\frac{1}{2}$ *rho* V^2). *Rho* is the Greek letter used to symbolize air density, and is written ρ.

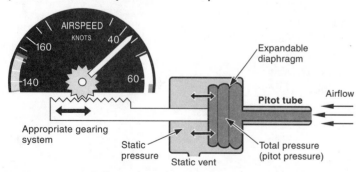

Figure 2-5. The airspeed indicator measures dynamic pressure

By assuming that the density of air (ρ) remains constant at its standard mean sea level value (which of course it does not), the airspeed indicator scale can be graduated in speed units. The most common airspeed unit is the **knot**, which is 1 nautical mile per hour, but you may see some older instruments graduated in mph. The airspeed indicator will only show the actual true airspeed at this one air density, that of standard MSL; at other densities, the indicated airspeed will differ from the true airspeed.

As airspeed increases, the dynamic pressure increases, but the static pressure remains the same. The difference between the total pressure or ram air pressure (measured by the pitot tube) and the static pressure (measured by the static vent or static line) gives us a measure of the dynamic pressure, which is related to indicated airspeed. This difference between the total and static pressures causes the diaphragm to reposition itself, and the pointer to indicate a higher airspeed.

Color Coding on the Airspeed Indicator

To assist the pilot, ASIs in modern aircraft have certain speed ranges and certain specific speeds marked according to a conventional color code.

Green arc. Denotes the **normal operating speed range**, from V_{S1} (stall speed at maximum gross weight, flaps up, wings level), up to V_{NO} (normal operating limit speed or maximum structural cruising speed), which should not be exceeded except in smooth air. Operations at an IAS in the green arc should be safe in all conditions, including turbulence.

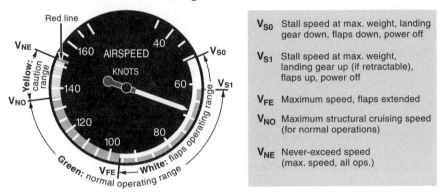

Figure 2-6. Indicated airspeed is what we read on the ASI

Yellow arc. Denotes the **caution range**, which extends from V_{NO} (normal operating limit speed) up to V_{NE} (the never-exceed speed). The aircraft should be operated at indicated airspeeds in the caution range only in smooth air.

White arc. Denotes the **flaps operating range**, from V_{S0} (stall speed at maximum gross weight in the landing configuration—full flaps, landing gear down, wings level, power off), up to V_{FE} (maximum flaps-extended speed).

Red radial line. Denotes V_{NE}, the never-exceed speed.

Note:

1. Some ASIs have a blue radial line to denote best single-engine rate of climb speed for a light twin-engined airplane V_{YSE}.

2. All ASI markings refer to indicated airspeed (IAS) and not true airspeed (TAS). Where weight is a factor in determining the limit speed (such as stall speeds) the value marked is for the maximum gross weight situation in all cases.

3. Some limiting speeds that you should know are not marked on the ASI. They appear in the Flight Manual and Pilot's Operating Handbook.

- V_{LO} is the maximum landing gear operating speed, for raising or lowering the landing gear. V_{LE} is the maximum landing gear extended speed, which for some airplanes exceeds V_{LO} once the gear is down and locked in place, making it structurally stronger.
- Maneuvering speed V_A should not be exceeded in turbulence, to avoid excessive g-loading on the airplane structure.
- V_X is best-angle climb speed.
- V_Y is best-rate climb speed.

Indicated Airspeed and True Airspeed

The fact that indicated airspeed (IAS) and true airspeed (TAS or V) are usually different seems to worry many inexperienced pilots, but it need not. IAS is an aerodynamic airspeed which is closely related to dynamic pressure ($\frac{1}{2}\, rho\, V^2$).

This is a vital aerodynamic quantity, because the amount of lift produced is a function of dynamic pressure ($\frac{1}{2} rho\, V^2$), the wing area (S) and the coefficient of lift (C_{Lift}, the lifting ability of the wing):

$$\text{Lift} = C_{Lift} \times \tfrac{1}{2}\rho V^2 \times S$$

—and the amount of drag created is also a function of dynamic pressure:

$$\text{Drag} = C_{Drag} \times \tfrac{1}{2}\rho V^2 \times S$$

Indicated airspeed (IAS) is important aerodynamically. The indicated airspeed is vital performance information for the pilot, because the aerodynamic qualities of the airplane depend on it. It affects the flight performance of the airplane (lift, drag, stalling speed, takeoff speed, maximum speeds, climbing speed, etc.).

True airspeed (TAS) is important for navigation. The true airspeed (TAS) is the actual speed of the airplane relative to the air. TAS (or V) is important for navigational purposes, such as describing speed through the air (TAS), from which can be found speed over the ground (GS).

True airspeed (TAS) usually exceeds indicated airspeed (IAS). If the IAS (which depends on $\frac{1}{2}\rho V^2$) is to remain the same, the value of V (the true airspeed) must increase as air density (ρ) decreases.

Air density decreases with altitude. Therefore, as an airplane climbs with a constant IAS, the TAS will gradually increase.

Air density also decreases with temperature rise. This will significantly affect performance items, such as the takeoff distance and rate of climb, which depend on IAS. For instance, to achieve the takeoff IAS at a hot, high and humid airport where air density (ρ) is low, V must be greater, so the airplane must be accelerated to a higher TAS to reach the takeoff IAS. This, coupled with possibly poorer performance from the engine/propeller, will mean a longer takeoff distance at hot and high airports.

Note:
At 5000 feet under standard conditions your TAS exceeds the IAS by about 8%. At 10,000 feet your TAS exceeds the IAS by about 17%. (You can perform this calculation on your flight computer.)

These are handy figures to remember for rough mental calculations, and also for understanding what experienced pilots are talking about when they are discussing the speeds that their airplanes "true-out at". If you are cruising at 5000 feet in standard atmosphere conditions with IAS 180 kt showing on the airspeed indicator, then your true airspeed will be approximately 8% greater (8% of 180 = 14), 194 kt TAS. If at any time the air density decreases, by climbing or by flying into warmer air, the TAS will be greater for the same IAS.

An easy method of mentally estimating the approximate TAS is simply to increase the IAS shown on the airspeed indicator by a percentage equal to double the number of thousands of feet. For instance:

- at 5000 feet MSL, increase IAS by 10% to obtain TAS;
- at 10,000 feet MSL, increase IAS by 20% to obtain TAS.

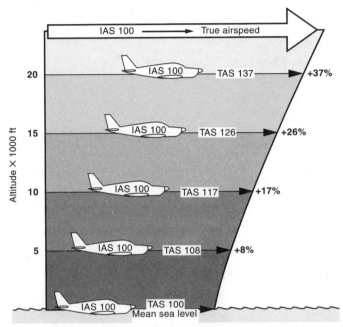

Figure 2-7. With IAS constant, TAS increases with increase in altitude

IAS/TAS indicators. Some airspeed indicators, as well as showing IAS, can also be made to show TAS. These airspeed indicators have a manually rotatable scale attached to them (known as the *temperature/altitude correction scale*), which allows the pilot to read TAS as well as IAS and which is valid up to speeds of approximately 200 knots TAS. (Above this speed the compressibility of the atmosphere needs to be allowed for—this is considered in the theory subjects for advanced pilot certificates.)

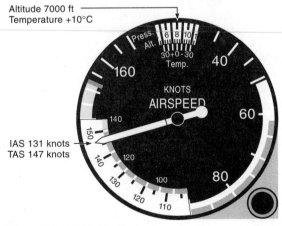

Figure 2-8. IAS/TAS indicator

Setting the temperature/altitude scale on the airspeed indicator performs exactly the same function as setting the same scale on the flight computer. It allows the indicated airspeed read on the ASI to be matched up with the true airspeed, which is of navigational value when on the cruise.

For performance purposes (takeoff, landing and stall speeds), it is IAS that is important, and not TAS. For this reason, some TAS scales do not extend into the low speed range. Knots IAS may be written KIAS; knots TAS may be written KTAS.

Errors in the Airspeed Indicator

Small errors will occur in each airspeed indicator. Errors caused by imperfections in manufacture and maintenance are known as **instrument error**. Errors caused by placement of the pitot tube and static vent on the airplane are known as **position error**. The result, after the indicated airspeed is corrected for these small errors, is called the **calibrated airspeed (CAS)**. It is a calculation not normally required by a pilot, because the correction is usually so small. A correction table to convert IAS to CAS is in the Pilot's Operating Handbook.

At high speeds, above about 200 KIAS, the air tends to compress in front of the pitot tube, thereby causing the airspeed indicator to read higher than it should. If the calibrated airspeed is corrected for this **compressibility error** at high speeds, which it rarely is in practice (since the pilot is probably more interested in Mach number), the result is **equivalent airspeed (EAS)**. EAS will be less than CAS.

High-Speed Flight

For high-speed flight at high levels, the most appropriate speed instrument is the **Mach indicator**, which displays the *Mach number*, the true airspeed of the airplane expressed as a ratio of the local speed of sound. Mach 0.78 means that the airplane is flying at 78% of the speed of sound.

$$Mach\ number\ =\ \frac{true\ airspeed}{local\ speed\ of\ sound}$$

Figure 2-9. The Mach indicator or Mach meter

The speed of sound, or Mach 1, is significant to high-speed flight because this is the speed at which pressure waves travel. As the airplane itself approaches the speed of sound, the pressure waves bank up and form shock waves (like bow waves of a ship). This causes a significant increase in drag and possible aerodynamic buffeting of the airplane. Most jet transport airplanes have a maximum operating Mach number (MMO), beyond which they must not be flown.

The Heading Indicator (HI)

Although it does not automatically sense magnetic direction, the heading indicator can indicate magnetic heading once it has been aligned with the magnetic compass. The heading indicator is a gyroscopic instrument, and the power source for its gyroscope will be either the vacuum system (along with the attitude indicator) or the electrical system.

The modern heading indicator comprises a circular compass card marked with a complete compass rose of 360°. This vertical compass card can rotate around a model airplane fixed in the center of the dial, with its nose pointing up. Typically, the rose is labeled every 30° with a number or letter, with large graduation marks every 10° and smaller markings for every intermediate 5°.

The compass card can be rotated using a manual alignment knob until the current magnetic heading, determined from the magnetic compass, appears at the top of the dial.

As heading changes, the compass rose rotates until the new heading is at the top of the dial, either under a fixed marker or at the nose of the model airplane. Note that for the indicated heading to increase, the compass card will rotate counterclockwise.

Figure 2-10. Typical modern heading indicators

Note: To be absolutely precise, you should also refer to the compass correction card as well as the magnetic compass to correct for any significant deviation error before aligning the heading indicator.

There may also be fixed markings relative to the nose of the model airplane at each 45° position around the instrument case. The reciprocal direction to the magnetic heading, if desired, can be read off the bottom of the dial. The abeam bearings can be read off the 90° markings. Mental arithmetic calculations are not necessary.

To turn left 45°, for instance, simply note the direction at the 45° left marking on the instrument casing or glass, and perform a banked turn to the left until the noted direction appears at the top of the dial.

The modern heading indicator is an easy instrument to interpret because, in a left turn, for instance, the model airplane appears to turn left relative to the compass rose. (In actual fact, it is the compass rose that rotates to the right.)

The heading indicator is a nonmagnetic instrument. It contains a gyroscope with a horizontal spin axis, which provides the heading indicator card with short-term directional stability.

The gyro-stabilized heading indicator is not subject to the problems that the magnetic compass experiences as a result of magnetic dip (turning and acceleration errors), nor does it oscillate in rough air. It is a much easier instrument to use than the compass, especially in turns and in turbulence, although the magnetic compass still remains the fundamental reference for magnetic direction.

Directional gyros. Older directional gyros (DGs) do not display a complete compass rose, but only a small part of a circular strip card that can rotate, with heading shown under a lubber line. In fact, it is not the card that rotates; it is the airplane as it changes heading that moves around the card, similar to the magnetic compass.

The DG is a more difficult presentation to interpret than the modern heading indicator, since only 30° either side of the current heading is shown and, if the airplane turns left, the lubber line moves to the right relative to the card.

Figure 2-11. An older directional gyro

For example, in the situation in Figure 2-11, to take up a magnetic heading of MH 275 from the current heading of MH 295, the airplane should turn left. To increase heading, turn right; to decrease heading, turn left.

Heading Indicator Errors

After initially being aligned with the magnetic compass, the heading indicator will gradually drift off the correct magnetic direction because of internal mechanical reasons (such as friction and gimbal effect), and also because of **apparent drift**.

Apparent drift results from the earth's rotation. As the earth rotates about its axis at 15° per hour, the direction in space from a point on the earth's surface to north continually changes. This effect increases toward the poles, and is zero on the equator. Even though the HI has preset precession for the expected latitude of operation to overcome this problem, most HIs will still drift off heading.

The airplane can compound apparent drift as it flies across the face of the earth. Realigning the heading indicator periodically with the magnetic compass solves the problem.

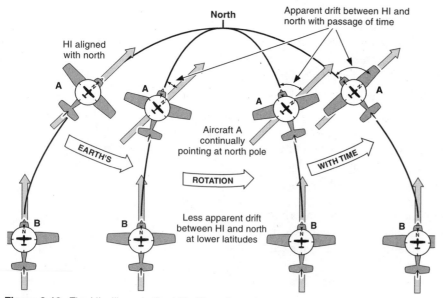

Figure 2-12. The HI will gradually drift off heading

Older heading indicators have internal limits that may cause them to lose their direction-holding ability if bank angle or pitch attitude exceed 55°. Newer types, however, have gyroscopes that will not tumble even in extreme attitudes.

For several reasons, therefore, the heading indicator must be periodically realigned with the magnetic compass, which is unaffected by the rotation of the earth and always points, at least within a few degrees, toward magnetic north during steady straight-and-level flight. Remember that a small correction may have to be made to the magnetic compass indication to allow for deviation arising from extraneous magnetic fields present in the airplane. The correction required is found on the compass correction card displayed in the airplane. If not allowed for, the deviation error of the compass will be carried through to the heading indicator.

Check HI alignment with the magnetic compass at least every 15 minutes.

The heading indicator should be checked at least every 15 minutes, and reset to the correct magnetic heading by reference to the magnetic compass (and compass correction card) during steady straight-and-level flight. For the heading indicator to be acceptable in normal operations, this correction should not exceed 3° in 15 minutes.

Complete failure of the heading indicator makes life a little more difficult for the instrument pilot since, to obtain heading information, you must scan right across the instrument panel to the magnetic compass, and must also allow for its turning and acceleration errors.

Because the attitude indicator and heading indicator often share the same power source, loss of one may mean the loss of the other, a situation considered in Chapter 7, *Normal Instrument Flight on a Partial Panel*.

Preflight Checks of the Heading Indicator

After start-up, the electrical or vacuum power source should be checked to ensure that the gyroscope will get up to speed. Once up to speed, which may take up to 5 minutes for a vacuum-driven gyroscope, the heading indicator should be aligned with the magnetic compass using the manual adjustment knob. The heading indicator can then help in orientation on the ground—for instance, in determining which direction the takeoff will be.

While taxiing, the heading indicator should be checked for correct functioning: "turning right, heading increases—turning left, heading decreases".

At the holding point, just prior to takeoff, the heading indicator should again be checked against the magnetic compass (but not while turning or accelerating), and it can be used to verify that the correct runway is about to be used.

The Remote Indicating Compass

The remote indicating compass (RIC) is a logical extension of the heading indicator. It combines the functions of the magnetic compass and the heading indicator.

The remote indicating compass employs a magnetic sensor, called the **magnetic flux detector** (or flux valve), which is positioned well away from other magnetic influences in the airframe, usually in a wingtip. This sensor detects magnetic direction and sends electrical signals to the heading indicator to automatically align it with the current magnetic heading of the airplane. This process is known as *slaving* of the compass card and it eliminates the need for the pilot to manually align the heading indicator, which now becomes known as a remote indicating compass.

Associated with the remote indicating compass is a slaving control and compensator unit. It contains a **slaving meter** that indicates any difference between the heading displayed on the compass card and the actual magnetic heading.

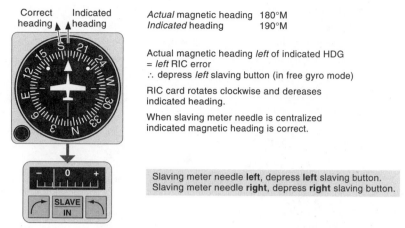

Correct heading Indicated heading

Actual magnetic heading 180°M
Indicated heading 190°M

Actual magnetic heading *left* of indicated HDG
= *left* RIC error
∴ depress *left* slaving button (in free gyro mode)

RIC card rotates clockwise and dereases indicated heading.

When slaving meter needle is centralized indicated magnetic heading is correct.

Slaving meter needle **left**, depress **left** slaving button.
Slaving meter needle **right**, depress **right** slaving button.

Figure 2-13. Manual slaving correction for the remote indicating compass

In the **slaved mode**, the normal mode of operation, the compass card is automatically aligned on start-up and, ideally, the meter will indicate no difference or error and the needle will be centered (zero deflection).

- **A left deflection** (–) of the slaving meter needle indicates a left (counterclockwise) error in the compass card. The compass card has rotated too far to the left and so the correct magnetic heading is to the left of the heading currently being indicated. The slaving meter needle is displaced into the "–" sector, indicating that it is necessary to decrease the reading on the RIC compass card to return it to the correct indication.

- **A right deflection** (+) in the slaving meter indicates a right (clockwise) error in the compass card. The compass card has rotated too far to the right, and so the correct magnetic heading is to the right of the heading currently being indicated. The slaving meter needle is displaced into the "+" sector, indicating that it is necessary to increase the reading on the RIC compass card to return it to the correct indication.

Note: During a turn, it is normal to see the slaving meter needle fully deflected to one side as the slaving process attempts to catch up with the change in the airplane's magnetic heading.

Example 1. In the case illustrated in Figure 2-13, the actual magnetic heading is 180° magnetic, but the indication on the RIC is 190.

The correct magnetic heading is left of the indicated heading
= left RIC error
= counterclockwise error
= clockwise correction.

That is, the compass card must be rotated right (clockwise) to correct the error.

Left RIC error = slaving meter needle deflected left into the "–" sector, which means that the compass reading must be decreased to obtain the correct magnetic heading indication on the RIC.

- rotate the RIC compass card clockwise and decrease the indicated heading toward the correct value (180); and

- center the slaving meter needle.

Example 2. The compass card of the RIC indicates 090 compared with 080 on the magnetic compass. What action is required to correct this?

The RIC has rotated 10° too far left. If this left RIC error is to be corrected, the compass card must be rotated 10° to the right (clockwise). Turn the heading knob to manually align the compass card to the correct heading.

Left error—left deflection of the needle—correct with the left button.

Example 3. The correct magnetic heading is MH 070. The compass card of the RIC indicates 065, 5° to the left of that desired. Would you expect the slaving meter needle to be deflected left or right? What action is required to correct this error?

The RIC has rotated 5° too far right, to an RIC error of 5° right. For this right RIC error to be corrected, the RIC compass card needs to be rotated 5° to the left (counterclockwise).

Right error—right deflection of the needle—use the right button.

Example 4. The magnetic compass indicates 270. The compass card of the RIC indicates 265, 5° to the left of that desired. What deflection would you expect to see on the slaving meter (left or right), and what corrective action would you take?

The RIC has rotated 5° too far right (clockwise) and so there will be a right deflection on the slaving meter. To correct this right RIC error, the RIC compass card needs to be rotated 5° to the left (counterclockwise). Right error—right deflection of the needle—use the right knob to slew to the correct heading.

To correct any lasting error, place the system in the **free gyro mode** using the push-button provided on the slaving control unit. The compass card is no longer slaved to the magnetic flux valve. You can then use the appropriate heading drive button to manually align the RIC for reference purposes only. The heading will reflect normal precession.

The Horizontal Situation Indicator (HSI)

The horizontal situation indicator is a slaved heading indicator (a remote indicating compass) with superimposed VOR/ILS navigation indications. The HSI, if fitted, will occupy the same position on the instrument panel as the standard heading indicator, directly below the attitude indicator. The HSI is considered in more detail in Chapter 13 and Chapter 14.

Figure 2-14. A typical horizontal situation indicator (HSI)

The Altimeter

Unlike an automobile, an airplane must be navigated in three dimensions, not only left and right, but also up and down. It must be navigated vertically as well as horizontally. The altimeter is the most important instrument for *vertical navigation*. You must use it correctly and understand exactly what it is telling you.

The altimeter relates the **static pressure** at the level of the airplane to a height in the **standard atmosphere**, a theoretical "average" atmosphere which acts as a convenient hypothetical yardstick. The main purpose of the standard atmosphere is to calibrate altimeters. Standard pressure at mean sea level (MSL) is 29.92 inches of mercury. (Its equivalent in SI units is 1013.2 hectopascals, usually written as 1013 hPa. The term *hectopascals* (hPa) has replaced the older term *millibar* (mb) in many countries.)

Standard pressure at MSL is 29.92 in. Hg.

Atmospheric pressure reduces by approximately 1 in. Hg (one inch of mercury) for each 1000 feet gain in altitude in the lower levels of the atmosphere, and the altimeter converts this reduction in atmospheric pressure to a gain in altitude. For instance, if the pressure falls by 0.45 in. Hg, the altimeter will indicate a 450 feet gain in altitude.

Atmospheric pressure reduces by approximately 1 in. Hg for each 1000 feet gain in altitude.

How the Altimeter Works

The altimeter contains a sealed, but expandable, aneroid capsule that is exposed within the instrument case to the current static pressure as measured by the static port. As the airplane climbs and static pressure decreases, the sealed capsule expands. Through a linkage, it drives a pointer around the altimeter scale to indicate the increased height above the selected pressure level. There may be a short time lag before changes in altitude are indicated on the altimeter.

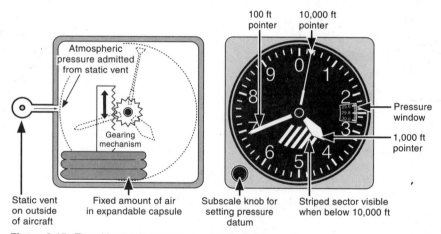

Figure 2-15. The altimeter is a pressure sensitive instrument

Unfortunately for altimeters, the real atmosphere existing at a particular place and time can differ significantly from the standard atmosphere. Atmospheric pressure at MSL will vary from place to place and from time to time as weather pressure patterns move across the country. If an altimeter is to measure height from any particular level, such as mean sea level (MSL), then it must be designed so that the appropriate pressure setting can be selected.

The Pressure Window

The altimeter incorporates a small adjustable subscale that allows a pilot to select the pressure level from which altitude will be measured. This subscale is known as the pressure window, or as the Kollsman window after Paul Kollsman, the inventor of the sensitive altimeter. If you want to measure the altitude of the airplane above the 29.92 in. Hg standard pressure level, then you set 29.92 in the pressure window.

If you want to measure the altitude of the airplane above the 30.10 in. Hg pressure level, then you set 30.10 in the pressure window. If 30.10 in. Hg happens to be the current MSL barometric pressure, then the altimeter will indicate the altitude of the airplane above MSL.

For flight operations in the United States below 18,000 feet MSL, the level from which altitude is measured is mean sea level (MSL). Although 29.92 inches of mercury is standard MSL pressure, the existing MSL pressure may differ significantly from this value. The pressure window allows the pilot to set the current MSL pressure, so that the altimeter will indicate the airplane's altitude above MSL.

The MSL pressure at a particular place and time is called the local **altimeter setting.** When this is set in the pressure window, the altimeter will display what is known as the **indicated altitude**. If the local altimeter setting is 30.10 in. Hg (higher than the standard pressure 29.92), then 30.10 should be set in the pressure window for the altimeter to display indicated altitude. When the setting in the pressure window is changed by winding the subscale, the altimeter needle will also move around the dial, since it measures altitude above the selected pressure level and the selected level is being changed.

If the pressure setting is wound up from 30.00 in. Hg to 30.50 in. Hg (which is a lower level in the atmosphere with a pressure increase of 0.50 in. Hg), the altimeter reading will increase by 500 feet. Conversely, if the pressure setting is wound down from 29.92 to 29.31, a pressure decrease of 0.61 in. Hg, the altimeter reading will decrease by 610 feet.

A one inch decrease in pressure in the lower levels of the atmosphere indicates approximately 1000 feet gain in altitude. Therefore, increasing the setting in the pressure window will increase the altimeter reading. This can be remembered as "Wind on inches, wind on altitude."

Check Altimeter Accuracy on the Ground

The only place you can really check the accuracy of an altimeter is while the airplane is on the ground at an airport. With the local altimeter setting in the pressure window, the altimeter should indicate airport elevation. This indication should be within ±75 feet of the known airport elevation for the altimeter to be acceptable for IFR flight.

In this check, allow for the fact that the published **airport elevation** is the altitude above MSL of the highest point on any of the usable runways. It may be that the parking area where you happen to check the altimeter is significantly lower than this, so use common sense when doing this check. If you have any doubts about the accuracy of the altimeter, refer it to an appropriately rated repair station for evaluation and possible correction.

Different airplanes have different cockpit heights, but their altimeters are calibrated so that they read similarly. This means that the altimeter in a small training airplane on the ground at an airport should read approximately the same as that in a nearby *Boeing 747*.

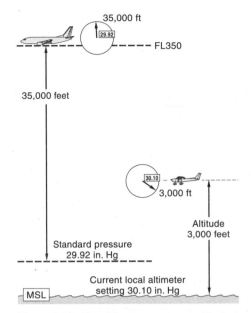

Figure 2-16. The altimeter measures altitude above the pressure level set in the pressure window

Wind on inches, wind on altitude.

An altimeter should read within ±75 feet of the known airport elevation for the altimeter to be acceptable for IFR flight.

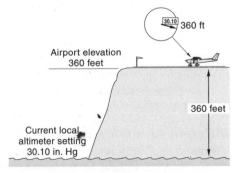

Figure 2-17. On the ground, all altimeters should read airport elevation

The current altimeter setting as passed to a pilot by ATC is measured or calculated so that the indicated altitude on the ground will be the same as the airport elevation (which is of course a true altitude), regardless of whether standard atmospheric conditions exist or not.

If, for some reason, ATC does not provide you with a local altimeter setting prior to flight, then you can set the subscale knob while the airplane is parked or taxiing until the altimeter indicates the published airport elevation. This will ensure that the current altimeter setting, at least approximately, will be in the pressure setting (or Kollsman) window. Once airborne and in radio contact with ATC, you can request the "official" altimeter setting. ATC will periodically provide the current altimeter setting for the area to aircraft operating in controlled airspace.

Whenever the current local altimeter setting is set in the pressure window, the altimeter will indicate the altitude of the airplane above MSL. This enables the pilot to fly at an altitude that is well separated vertically both from terrain and from other aircraft. Aeronautical charts display the height of terrain in feet above MSL.

When flying in the United States at or above 18,000 feet MSL, standard pressure 29.92 in. Hg should be set in the pressure window. Above 18,000 feet MSL there is adequate terrain clearance, and so vertical separation from other aircraft is the main concern. Having a common setting of 29.92 in. Hg gives all of these high-flying airplanes a common pressure level from which their flight level is measured, avoiding any conflict caused by altimeter settings from different geographic locations.

Above 18,000 feet MSL, set 29.92 in the pressure window

With standard pressure 29.92 set, the altimeter indicates pressure altitude. It is usual to remove the last two zeros of a pressure altitude and refer to it as a flight level. If the altimeter reads 21,000 feet with 29.92 in. Hg set, then this may be referred to as a pressure altitude of 21,000 feet or, more commonly, as FL210 (flight level two one zero).

It is correct procedure to use the current reported altimeter setting for all operations below 18,000 feet MSL, and to set 29.92 when climbing through 18,000 feet. Conversely, on descent, the setting in the pressure window should be changed from 29.92 to the latest reported local altimeter setting when descending through 18,000 feet.

Below 18,000 feet MSL, set the current local altimeter setting in the pressure window.

If you neglect to do this, then the altimeter will provide incorrect information (unless standard pressure exists). For flight operations in these lower levels, vertical separation from terrain, as well as from other aircraft, is of concern, hence the need to relate the altitude to MSL.

Example 5. An airplane previously cruising at FL230 (flight level two three zero) is on descent to land at an airport, elevation 600 feet. Local altimeter setting is 29.50 in. Hg. If the pilot forgets to reset the pressure window on descent through 18,000 feet, what will the altimeter read on landing?

With the correct altimeter setting of 29.50, the altimeter will read the elevation of 600 feet after the airplane has landed. With 29.92 set, which is 0.42 in. Hg too great, the altimeter will read 420 feet too high (since 1 in. Hg = 1000 feet altitude, and "wind on inches, wind on altitude"), i.e. 1020 feet.

Different Altimeter Presentations

You must be able to interpret the altimeter reading correctly since it provides absolutely vital information. Lives have been lost in the past because pilots (even professional pilots) have misread the altimeter by 10,000 feet. Learn how to read it accurately right at the start!

The most easily understood altimeter presentation is a simple digital readout of altitude, supported by a single pointer indicating 100s of feet. It will make one complete revolution of the dial for every 1000 feet gain or loss of altitude. The digital readout displays the actual altitude. The pointer does not indicate the complete altitude, but only the last three digits of it (at 15,200 feet it would indicate 200).

The pointer is very useful to an instrument pilot, however, because it gives a better indication of any tendency to depart from an altitude than does a set of changing digits. Trends of 20 or 50 feet either side of the precise altitude are more easily discerned on the pointer and then corrected with an attitude change on the attitude indicator.

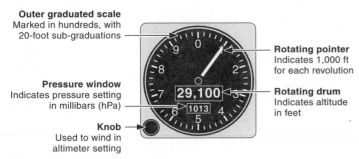

Outer graduated scale
Marked in hundreds, with
20-foot sub-graduations

Rotating pointer
Indicates 1,000 ft
for each revolution

Pressure window
Indicates pressure setting
in millibars (hPa)

Rotating drum
Indicates altitude
in feet

Knob
Used to wind in
altimeter setting

Figure 2-18. The digital altimeter, plus pointer

The most common altimeter presentation consists of three pointers of varying shapes and sizes.

- The long, medium-thickness pointer indicates 100s of feet. It will move once around the dial for each 1000 feet change in altitude. If it is on 7, then that means 7 × 100 = 700 feet.

- The short, thick pointer indicates 1000s of feet. It will move once around the dial for a change of 10,000 feet. If it is on 4 (or just past it), then that means 4000 feet. To reinforce to a pilot that the airplane is below 10,000 feet, a striped sector (see Figure 2-19) is visible in the display; it gradually becomes smaller as 10,000 feet is approached.

- The pointer with a thin needle and splayed tip indicates 10,000s of feet. If it is on 1 (or just past it), then that means 10,000 feet. This pointer is particularly easy to misread.

Figure 2-19.
Conventional altimeter display

All taken together, the altimeter reads 4700 feet.

100-foot pointer   1,000-foot pointer   10,000-foot pointer

Figure 2-20. The three pointers on a conventional altimeter—displaying 4700 feet

Note: An **encoding altimeter** may be an ordinary altimeter, except that it supplies altitude information electronically to the **transponder**. If the pilot selects "Mode C" (the altitude reporting mode of the transponder) the ground radar controller is presented with altitude information as well as the horizontal position of the airplane.

Preflight Checks of the Altimeter

During the external preflight inspection, check that the static port is clear, because a blocked static vent will seriously affect the altimeter, the VSI and the ASI. The current altimeter setting should be wound into the pressure window, causing the altimeter to read airport elevation to within ±75 feet. If the current altimeter setting is not known, then the knob can be turned until the altimeter indicates airport elevation. It is a requirement for IFR flight that the altimeter and static system be thoroughly inspected every 24 calendar months.

Altimeter Indication Error Caused By Nonstandard Temperatures

Density error is caused by changes in atmospheric conditions for which the altimeter does not automatically compensate, such as nonstandard temperatures.

The altimeter is calibrated to read the altitude above the pressure level selected in the pressure window as if the characteristics of the existing atmosphere (temperature, pressure, density and humidity) are identical to the standard atmosphere. This is rarely the case, however, which means that the altimeter indication will differ to some extent from the true altitude.

Normally, the difference between indicated altitude and true altitude is of no practical significance, since all airplanes in the one area will have their altimeters affected identically, and so vertical separation between aircraft will not be degraded. Airplanes are always flown by reference to the indicated altitude (what appears on the altimeter), and not to true altitude which is more difficult to determine.

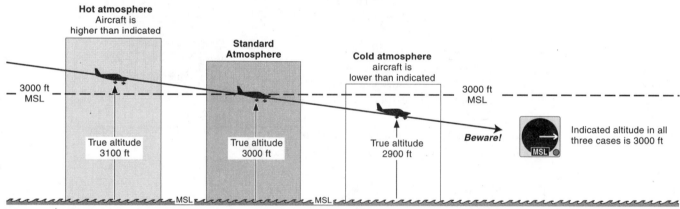

Figure 2-21. Indicated altitude may differ from true altitude

While the density error affecting the altimeter is of little significance for most flight operations, it may occasionally require some consideration during precision instrument approaches.

In very warm air, the density will be less than standard and the pressure levels will be expanded, so a given pressure level will be higher in a warm atmosphere compared with a standard atmosphere. After climbing a true 1000 feet, the altimeter will sense less than 1000 feet difference in pressure in the thinner air and will indicate a climb of less than 1000 feet, so the altimeter in warmer air will under-read. The altimeter may read 3000 feet but, in this air that is warmer than standard, the airplane may actually be at 3100 feet. This tendency is easily remembered as HI–LO (higher temperature than standard— lower altimeter reading). If you fly into a parcel of warmer air and maintain the same indicated altitude, the true altitude (and the true airspeed) will increase.

The altimeter will under-read in warm air.

Conversely, in air colder than ISA, the reverse is the case: the altimeter will indicate higher than the airplane actually is, LO–HI (lower temperature than standard—higher altimeter reading). The altimeter may read 3000 feet, but the airplane may actually be at 2900 feet.

The altimeter will over-read in cold air.

Example 6. A pilot carrying out an instrument approach to a runway by flying down an ILS glideslope will check altitude as he passes the outer marker. He might notice a small difference between the indicated altitude on the altimeter compared with the altitude published on the instrument approach charts.

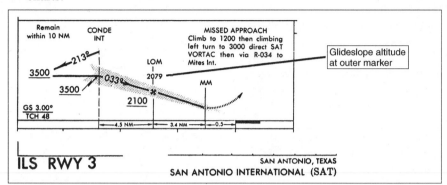

Figure 2-22. A typical ILS approach profile

The actual altitude at this crossing point is fixed in space (it is a true altitude that never changes) but, even if the airplane is exactly on slope, the altimeter reading may be a little different to the published value. This is because, in warm air, the altimeter will read a little too low (HI–LO); in cold air, it will read a little too high (LO–HI).

The difference is not great, because the altimeter setting is such that airport elevation is indicated on the altimeter when the airplane is on the runway, and the outer marker crossing point is usually only about 2000 feet higher. Indicated altitude in flight only equals true altitude if standard atmospheric conditions exist.

Density Altitude Determines Performance

The prevailing air density has a significant effect on the performance of the airplane and its engines—the lower the air density, the poorer the performance. Air density decreases with higher altitudes and higher temperatures.

Performance at a pressure altitude of 5000 feet will be poorer than at sea level; performance at 5000 feet and 20°C will be poorer than at 5000 feet and 5°C. This can be predicted from performance tables or charts published in the Flight Manual relating performance to particular density levels in the standard atmosphere. Density depends on pressure and temperature, and you can enter these tables or charts using pressure altitude and temperature to determine performance.

The term **density altitude** refers to the altitude in the standard atmosphere that has the same density as the existing air. Even though an airplane might be cruising with 5000 feet indicated on the altimeter, if the air is 10°C warmer than standard, then it will perform as if it were at 6200 feet in the standard atmosphere.

Density altitude is pressure altitude corrected for nonstandard temperature. The only time that density altitude will equal pressure altitude is when standard temperatures exist. Standard temperature at MSL is 15°C (59°F) and decreases by approximately 2°C for each 1000 feet gain in altitude.

Density altitude is pressure altitude corrected for nonstandard temperature.

Position Error Correction (PEC)

There are many variations in airflow around an airplane, thus it is difficult to position a static vent so that it senses the exact static pressure in all stages of flight. Altitude indications are often slightly in error, especially when the airplane is flown in certain flight attitudes such as nose high or in a sideslip. Because the magnitude of this sensing error depends to a large extent on where the static vent is located on the airplane, it is usually referred to as **position error**.

While it is not necessary to consider this small error when in flight well away from the ground, it may be necessary to make an appropriate allowance for it during instrument flight close to the ground—in particular, when calculating the altimeter reading to be used to indicate descent to the minimum altitude during an instrument approach. Discuss this with your flight instructor, to determine if the PEC for the altimeter in your particular airplane is significant. It is published in the Flight Manual.

The Vertical Speed Indicator

The vertical speed indicator is commonly referred to as the VSI. It provides a readout of the rate of change of altitude as an airplane climbs or descends. If the airplane climbs steadily through 250 feet in 30 seconds, then the VSI should read 500 feet per minute (fpm).

The VSI measures rate of change of altitude.

If the airplane descends steadily through 120 feet in 15 seconds, then the VSI should read 480 fpm DOWN. Its dial is usually marked in 100s of feet either side of a zero marking, with 500 fpm UP and 500 fpm DOWN clearly labeled.

The VSI, as well as being useful in climbs and descents, is a very useful instrument when trying to achieve precise level flight, when it should indicate zero. In smooth air, it will show any *trend* to move away from an altitude very quickly. It will respond faster to an altitude change than the altimeter, and allow a pitch attitude correction to be made on the AI before the altimeter has hardly registered any change in altitude. In rough air, however, the VSI pointer fluctuates, making it a less valuable instrument.

With large and sudden attitude changes, the VSI may briefly show a reversed reading because of disturbed airflow near the static vent, with some lag before a steady rate of climb or descent is indicated. Sometimes this lag is as long as 5 seconds. In such a case, allow the indication to stabilize before using its information.

The main value of the VSI is the support it gives to the altimeter when you are maintaining altitude, and the rate of climb or descent it displays during climbs and descents. It is, however, not a required instrument for IFR flight. If the VSI is not working, you are still permitted to commence an IFR flight, but it should be placarded.

How the VSI Works

The VSI has an expandable capsule to which is fed the current static pressure from the static vent. The VSI instrument case containing the capsule is also connected to the static line, but through a **metered leak**. As the airplane changes altitude, the static pressure within the capsule changes immediately, but the metered leak causes the pressure change surrounding the capsule to be more gradual.

On a climb, the pressure in the capsule changes instantaneously to the now lower static pressure. The case that surrounds the capsule, however, contains the original higher pressure which takes some time to change. The effect is to compress the capsule, driving a pointer around the dial to indicate a rate of climb.

The changed pressure gradually leaks into the instrument case. If the airplane continues to climb, the pressure within the instrument case never quite catches up with the external static pressure within the capsule, and so the VSI continues to indicate a rate of climb. Once the airplane levels off, however, the two pressures do gradually equalize, and the VSI reads zero.

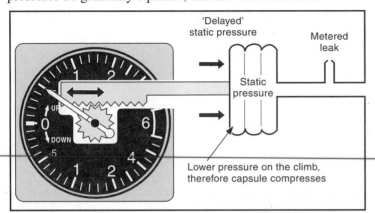

Figure 2-23. The VSI compares static pressure in the capsule with delayed static pressure in the case

The VSI is good as a trend instrument ("Am I going up?" or "Am I going down?"), as well as a rate instrument ("How fast am I going up or down?"). Whereas the trend is obvious almost immediately in smooth air, the precise rate will take a few seconds to settle down. In rough air, it may take longer.

Some advanced VSIs have accelerometers to reduce the lag and to give instantaneous indications of climb and descent rates. Such an instrument is known as an **instantaneous vertical speed indicator** and is labeled **IVSI**.

Preflight Checks of the VSI

Like all static pressure instruments, the VSI requires a static vent and line that is not blocked. The VSI should also indicate approximately zero while the airplane is on the ground. Indication errors may exist in some VSIs, for which allowance will have to be made in flight. For instance, if the VSI indicates 100 fpm UP while on the ground, then this 100 fpm UP must be the "zero" position in flight, verified, of course, against the altimeter when cruising.

The Turn Coordinator and Turn Indicator

The turn coordinator is a significant development of an earlier instrument, the turn indicator. They are both **rate gyroscopes**, where the rotating mass has freedom to move about two of its three axes and is designed to show movement of the aircraft about the third axis. The gyroscope in the turn indicator or turn coordinator will not tumble in extreme attitudes, making for a very reliable instrument. The gyroscope of the turn coordinator or turn indicator may be driven electrically or by suction.

Figure 2-24. The turn coordinator (left) and turn indicator

The **inclinometer**, a small ball which is displaced from its central position in coordinated flight (slips or skids), is usually incorporated into the instrument case of the turn indicator or turn coordinator, even though it is not part of the gyroscopic system. The turn indicator is sometimes called the turn-and-slip indicator.

Turn indicator. The turn indicator is the older of the two instruments and has a lateral horizontal spin axis (with a vertical spinning gyro) attached to a gimbal. The gimbal axis is fixed and aligned with the airplane's longitudinal axis. The turn indicator is designed to show motion about a vertical axis, and therefore show the rate of turn.

The turn indicator displays rate of turn.

Any turning motion of the aircraft is mechanically transmitted to the spin axis, and exerts a force on the spinning mass of the gyroscope. In Figure 2-25, the force exerted on the gyro in a left turn is translated 90° by the gyroscopic precession effect, causing the gyro and its spin axis to tilt. This tilting is opposed by a spring—the greater the turning force, the greater the tilt.

The tilt is transmitted to a pointer which moves on the turn indicator dial, usually calibrated to show **standard-rate turns** left or right. A standard-rate turn causes heading to change at 3° per second, hence a complete turn of 360° will take 2 minutes.

Note: Some instruments have their dials calibrated to turns other than standard-rate, a point which must be established before relying on the instrument.

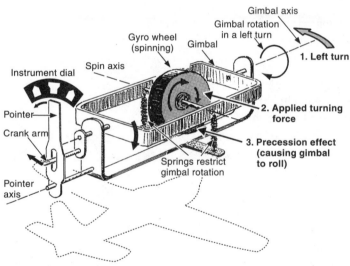

Figure 2-25. The turn indicator

Turn coordinator. The turn coordinator is a very clever development of the same gyroscopic principle. The gimbal axis is angled up at about 30° to the airplane's longitudinal axis, which makes the gyroscope sensitive not only to turning but also to rolling. Since a turn is commenced by banking the airplane, the turn coordinator will react to roll, even before the airplane actually starts turning.

The turn coordinator displays rate of turn and rate or roll.

The turn coordinator presentation is usually a set of wings pivoted in the center of the instrument, the wings moving to indicate the direction of bank. Calibrations around the edge of the instrument show standard-rate turns. Note that the wings are pivoted in the center and so will not move up or down to indicate pitch attitude.

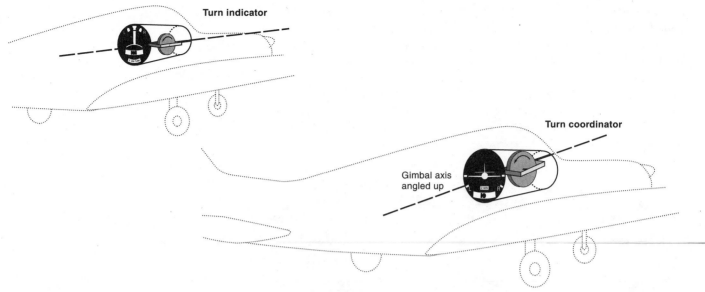

Figure 2-26. The turn coordinator gyro is angled to make it sensitive to banking as well as turning

Many turn coordinators are labeled "NO PITCH INFORMATION". The "2 MIN" label on many turn coordinators refers to a standard-rate turn taking 2 minutes to achieve a heading change of 360°.

A significant advantage of the turn coordinator is that it can be used quite comfortably to keep the wings level in straight flight if the attitude indicator has failed. The wings of the turn coordinator will react first to roll, and then to yaw. The turn coordinator shows rate of roll as well as rate of turn, whereas the older turn indicator shows only rate of turn.

Preflight Checks of the Turn Coordinator (and Ball)

During the taxi, a simple check is to turn the aircraft and observe the indications: "turning left (on the turn coordinator)—skidding right" (on the inclinometer), followed by "turning right—skidding left".

Any doubts about the standard-rate calibration can be checked with a timed standard-rate turn in flight, a full 360° at standard-rate requiring exactly 120 seconds (2 minutes).

The Coordination Ball, or Inclinometer

The coordination ball is a simple and useful mechanical device that indicates the direction of the g-forces, which are the combined effect of the earth's gravity force and any turning force. The coordination ball has no power source. It is known in various places as the inclinometer, the slip-skid indicator, the balance ball or the coordination ball.

The coordination ball is usually incorporated into the presentation of the turn coordinator (or turn indicator). It is simply a small ball, free to move like a pendulum bob, except that it moves in a curved cylinder filled with damping fluid. In straight flight it should appear at the lowest point in the curved cylinder (like a pendulum bob hanging straight down), and the airplane is then said to be *coordinated*, or *in balance*.

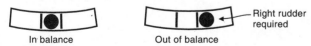

In balance   Out of balance   Right rudder required

Figure 2-27. The coordination ball

If there is any slip or skid, the ball will move to one side in the same way as a pendulum bob would swing out. Similarly, you feel a force pushing you out, usually through the seat of your pants. If the ball is out to the right, apply right rudder pressure to center it.

In a properly coordinated turn, you feel no sideways forces; and neither does the ball, which remains centered. Any sideways force (either a slip in toward the turn or a skid out away from the turn) will be shown by the coordination ball (and felt in the seat-of-your-pants). Use same-side rudder pressure to center the ball.

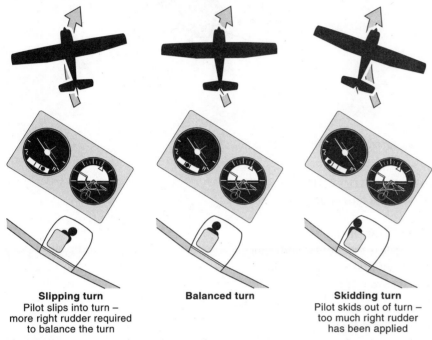

Slipping turn
Pilot slips into turn –
more right rudder required
to balance the turn

Balanced turn

Skidding turn
Pilot skids out of turn –
too much right rudder
has been applied

Figure 2-28. For coordinated flight, "step on the ball"

The Magnetic Compass

The magnetic compass is the fundamental source of directional information in the cockpit. In steady flight, it aligns itself with magnetic north so that the airplane's magnetic heading appears under the **lubber line**. Small errors in this reading caused by other known magnetic fields in the airplane are allowed for by the pilot by using information on the deviation card, which is also known as the **compass correction card**.

The magnetic compass experiences significant errors caused by magnetic dip when the airplane is turning (especially through north or south), and when accelerating (especially on easterly and westerly headings).

The easiest way to achieve accurate heading control is to periodically align the gyroscopic heading indicator (which is not subject to these errors) with the magnetic compass during steady, straight flight, and then use the heading indicator as a short term guide to direction, rather than the magnetic compass.

If, however, the heading indicator fails and the magnetic compass has to be used, certain allowances for these dip errors need to be made. These allowances apply to dip errors in the northern hemisphere. They increase toward the north pole, decrease toward the equator, and are reversed in the southern hemisphere.

Figure 2-29. The magnetic compass

Compass Turning Errors

- **Undershoot** the heading when turning through north.
- **Overshoot** the heading when turning through south.

Note:

1. When turning away from a northerly heading the compass will *lag* behind the actual turn and may initially show a turn in the opposite direction.

2. When turning away from a southerly heading, the compass will *lead* the turn.

3. When turning away from an easterly heading or westerly heading, the compass will read accurately if the roll into the turn is smooth. At high rates of turn the compass card may "hang up" or move erratically.

Compass Acceleration Errors

- Expect an *apparent* turn north on the magnetic compass when accelerating on east or west.
- Expect an *apparent* turn south on the magnetic compass when decelerating on east or west.

> Remember acceleration and deceleration errors in the northern hemisphere with "ANDS":
> Acceleration gives an apparent turn North;
> Deceleration gives an apparent turn South.

Preflight Checks of the Magnetic Compass

The magnetic compass should be checked that it is secure, and that the bowl is full of fluid, not discolored and without bubbles. Its reading can be checked against a known heading, at least approximately. Ensure that no magnetic materials are stored near it, as these could introduce large errors. During the taxi, the card can be checked for free movement during a turn.

The Vertical Compass

The conventional magnetic compass is a *wet* compass in the sense that the magnet is immersed in a damping fluid to reduce oscillations. Its compass card is horizontal. Some modern magnetic compasses, however, contain no fluid and have a vertical card presentation like a heading indicator. They do not "hang up" at high bank angles, but are still subject to the usual turning and acceleration errors.

The Clock

Accurate time-keeping is important to an instrument pilot, and it is a requirement that a serviceable timepiece with a sweep second pointer or a digital presentation be on board the airplane. It is usual to have the clock set to coordinated universal time (UTC) to simplify calculation of ETAs and the preparation of position reports, the calculation of latest divert time to an alternate airport, the validity periods of meteorological forecasts, end of daylight, operating hours of control towers, pilots' flight time limitations and rest periods, etc. The term "Zulu" is used when ATC procedures require a reference to UTC.

The second timer can be used for many purposes, such as timing the outbound leg of a holding pattern, for timing to a *missed approach point* (MAP), or for calculating accurate groundspeeds (GS) in conjunction with a DME (36 seconds is 1/100 of an hour, so 2.3 nm in 36 seconds = 230 kt GS).

Other Instruments

So far we have covered the main instruments that a pilot needs to continually refer to during instrument flight, in particular the six flight instruments. In flight, the pilot occasionally refers to a number of other instruments, such as the power indicator, the clock and the **navigation instruments**. The navigation instruments will be discussed in detail in Section 2.

There are other **engine instruments** associated with the main power indicator(s). For instance, each engine of a typical light twin has a manifold pressure gauge and a tachometer (rpm) as the main power indicators, with additional engine operating information available from a cylinder head temperature (CHT) gauge, an oil pressure gauge and an oil temperature gauge.

Never forget that it takes fuel for an engine to run and provide power, so fuel awareness is essential. The **fuel gauges** are in the cockpit, usually electrically powered, and not always accurate. A visual check of fuel quantity prior to flight is recommended, with fuel consumption in flight being progressively deducted, using the fuel gauges as a cross-check of your calculations.

Instrument flight often occurs in moist conditions, in clouds or rain, where there is an increased risk of icing. An **outside air temperature (OAT) gauge** helps you to determine if icing is a possibility and when to use anti-icing or de-icing equipment. Airframe icing (on the wings and tail) will only occur at temperatures near to or below freezing, but carburetor icing can occur at temperatures of +25°C (+77°F).

Advanced airplanes may have a **radar altimeter** (also known as a radio altimeter), which provides a reading of the height above ground level (AGL). These usually read from zero up to 2000 feet AGL, and provide a backup to the pressure altimeter during instrument approaches to the minimum descent altitude (MDA) or decision height (DH).

Radar altimeter readings are different than that of a co-located pressure altimeter, however, since the pressure altimeter reads altitude MSL and the radar altimeter reads height AGL.

Attitude indicators on some advanced airplanes incorporate a **flight director**, which has **command bars** indicating where the pilot (or autopilot) should place the miniature airplane to achieve the desired attitude or flightpath.

Figure 2-30. The radar altimeter

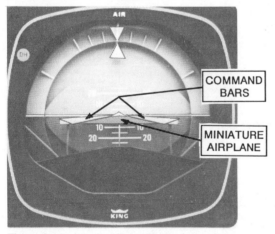

Figure 2-31. A typical flight director

The Pitot-Static System

Three vital flight instruments are connected to the pitot-static system:

- the altimeter (static pressure only);
- the VSI (static pressure only);
- the airspeed indicator (static pressure and pitot pressure).

The **pitot tube** measures total pressure, which is also known as the pitot pressure or the ram air pressure. The **static port**, or static vent, measures only the static pressure.

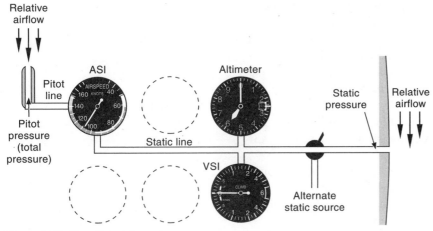

Figure 2-32. The pitot-static system

Many airplanes have two static ports, one on either side of the fuselage, rather than just having one port. This reduces errors when the airplane is yawing, and it also reduces the possibility of faulty indications from a blocked static vent.

An **alternate static source** may also be available in the event of a blockage. It usually measures the pressure in the cockpit, which is less than the external static pressure, and so causes slight errors in the instruments—the altimeter and the airspeed indicator will read slightly high, and the VSI will momentarily show a climb before settling down. If both normal and alternate sources of static pressure were blocked (a very remote possibility), breaking the glass of the VSI will introduce the cockpit pressure into the system.

Some airplanes have a combined **pitot-static tube**, where the pitot and the static vent are positioned in the one tube.

Problems in the static system may affect all three pressure instruments. Problems in the pitot system alone will only affect the airspeed indicator. There may occasionally be a problem with one individual instrument that does not affect the others.

Static system problems may affect all three pressure instruments. Problems in the pitot system alone will only affect the airspeed indicator.

Blockage of a Static Line

Blockage of a static port by ice, insects or maintenance tape, could affect all three instruments, since they would be fed a fixed static pressure even though, in fact, it would be changing in a climb or descent.

In a climb with a blocked static vent, the altimeter would indicate a constant altitude, the VSI would indicate zero, and the ASI would under-read (read lower than it should), because of the trapped static pressure being greater than the actual outside static pressure, which decreases in a climb.

In a descent with a blocked static vent, the altimeter reading would not change, the VSI would indicate zero, and the ASI would indicate a higher airspeed than it should. This could be dangerous for a pilot. He could be descending into high terrain even though no descent is indicated by the altimeter or the VSI, and might react to the over-reading ASI by raising the nose to reduce speed, inadvertently stalling the airplane.

Blockage of the Pitot Tube

If the pitot tube ices over, only the airspeed indicator is affected. The pitot tube is particularly vulnerable to icing because of the position of the ram air input in the airflow, hence most IFR aircraft have a **pitot heater** to prevent it from icing up. Drain holes prevent moisture accumulating in the probe.

If the pitot tube and the drain holes become clogged with ice while flying in icing conditions, then the total pressure in the pitot tube will stay constant. In a climb, the static pressure reduces, and so the airspeed indicator will read higher than it should. Conversely, in a descent, the ASI will read less than it should. Note that, with blocked pitot tube and drain holes, the ASI behaves like an altimeter—it reads high as the airplane climbs, and reads low as the airplane descends.

If only the pitot tube ram air inlet is blocked, and the drain holes are still free, then the total pressure will dissipate through the drain holes, and the ASI will indicate zero.

Don't forget that wasps and other insects, as well as ice, can block a pitot tube, so inspect it closely in your preflight check, and always make sure that the pitot cover is removed prior to flight. Use the electric pitot heater in icy conditions.

The Gyroscopes

Three of the main flight instruments are gyroscopic:

- the attitude indicator;
- the heading indicator; and
- the turn coordinator.

Gyroscopic instruments depend on the principle that a rapidly spinning wheel or disc is very resistant to any deflecting force, a property known as *rigidity in space*. If an external force is applied to a gyroscope, it will react as if this force had been applied at a position 90° further in the direction of rotation. This property is known as **gyroscopic precession**.

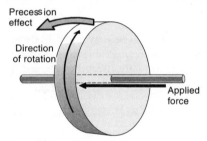

Figure 2-33. Gyroscopic precession

A good example of precession is leaning a spinning bicycle wheel over to the left. The leaning force applied effectively to the top of the wheel is translated 90° in the direction of rotation, and causes the front of the wheel to precess left.

The gyroscopes may be spun electrically or by a stream of high speed air directed at buckets cut into the perimeter of the rotor. This high-speed air is drawn (or induced) into the instrument cases and onto the gyro rotors by the vacuum system, usually powered by engine-driven suction pumps. Some instrument systems are operated by air pressure rather than by suction.

A common arrangement has the attitude indicator and the heading indicator driven by suction, but the turn coordinator driven electrically. This guards against all three failing simultaneously. With a loss of electrical power, the turn coordinator may be lost, but the attitude indicator and heading indicator remain.

With a loss of suction, the attitude indicator and heading indicator may gradually become erratic as they spin down and then become unusable, but the turn coordinator will remain. It is possible also that an individual instrument will fail from an internal fault.

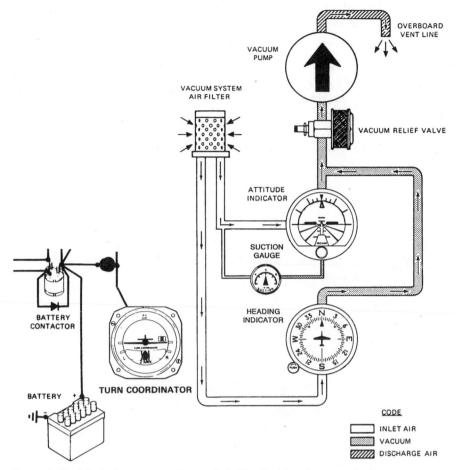

Figure 2-34. A typical vacuum system and electrically driven turn coordinator

The suction (vacuum) gauge should be checked periodically to ensure that sufficient high-speed air is available to drive the gyroscopes. Power failure to an electrically driven gyroscope is usually indicated by a red warning flag on the affected instrument.

When first switching electrical power on to the electric gyro instruments, you should listen for any unusual or irregular mechanical noise as the gyro spins up, which could indicate a faulty instrument.

Preflight Checks of the Flight Instruments

External inspection. During the preflight external inspection, check that the pitot cover is removed, and that the pitot tube and the static ports are not obstructed in any way.

In the cockpit, check that the instrument glass is intact, the turn coordinator's wings are level, the inclinometer contains fluid and the ball is at the lowest point, the magnetic compass contains clear fluid free of bubbles and the compass correction card is in place. After switching on the power, listen for any unusual mechanical noises as the electric gyros spin up.

The airspeed indicator should indicate zero, the VSI should indicate zero (if not, allow for this in flight), and the altimeter, once you have set the current reported altimeter setting, should read airport elevation to within ±75 feet after allowing for an uneven airport. Confirm that the static system and altimeter are not due for their 24 calendar month inspection. Check the stopwatch.

After start, and when the gyros are spun up, set the AI's miniature airplane against the horizon line, and align the heading indicator with the magnetic compass. Check suction.

During taxiing, check the turn coordinator and the inclinometer with gentle turns: "Turning left, heading decreasing, skidding right; turning right, heading increasing, skidding left". The horizon bar of the AI should remain steady. If desired, the AI can be checked by gently applying the brakes until the nose drops slightly. There should be no red warning flags on the electrical gyroscopic instruments, and there should be sufficient suction (3–5 in. Hg) for the suction-driven instruments.

In the holding position, and when stationary, the heading indicator can be realigned with the magnetic compass if necessary. Check that the reading on the heading indicator is logical, considering the runway to be used.

During the takeoff, confirm runway heading on the HI before starting to roll, and then, after applying power, an occasional glance at the instruments should be made to ensure that the airspeed is increasing and that the gyroscopic instruments look normal.

✍ Review 2

The Instruments

The Instruments

1. Name three gyroscopic flight instruments.

➤ the attitude indicator, the heading indicator, the turn coordinator (or turn-and-slip indicator)

2. Name three pressure flight instruments.

➤ the airspeed indicator, the altimeter, the vertical speed indicator

3. Name the two control instruments.

➤ the attitude indicator and the power indicator

4. The master instrument is considered to be the _____.

➤ attitude indicator

Attitude Indicator

1. The attitude indicator is a (gyroscopic/pressure) instrument.

➤ gyro

2. The pretakeoff check of the attitude indicator includes checking that the (horizon bar/miniature airplane) erects and becomes stable within 5 minutes.

➤ horizon bar

The Instruments

3. If the position of the miniature airplane requires adjustment prior to flight, it should be positioned against the horizon line when the airplane is on (level/sloping) ground.

➤ level

4. If the horizon bar in an attitude indicator tilts more than _____° while making taxi turns, then the attitude indicator should be considered unreliable.

➤ 5°

5. Acceleration and deceleration forces induce small (pitch/roll) errors in the attitude indicator.

➤ pitch

6. The attitude indicator provides a (direct/indirect) picture of pitch attitude and bank angle.

➤ direct

7. A properly functioning attitude indicator responds to any change in pitch attitude or bank angle (immediately/after a short lag time).

➤ immediately

8. When an airplane decelerates quickly, some attitude indicators will precess and incorrectly indicate a (climb/descent/turn).

➤ descent

9. When an airplane accelerates quickly, some attitude indicators will precess and incorrectly indicate a (climb/descent/turn).

➤ climb

10. While accelerating during the takeoff roll, the attitude indicator may indicate a false (climb/descent).

➤ climb

11. If the position of the miniature airplane requires adjustment during flight, it can be positioned against the horizon line when the airplane is

_____.

➤ flying straight-and-level at a steady speed

12. During turns, the centripetal turning force induces small (pitch/roll/pitch and roll) errors in the attitude indicator.

➤ pitch and roll

13. The greatest errors in an attitude indicator occur following a (90°/180°/360°) turn. When the airplane rolls out straight-and-level after such a turn, the attitude indicator will show a slight (climb/descent) and a turn in the (same/opposite) direction.

➤ 180°, climb, opposite

14. A pilot usually makes pitch attitude changes on the attitude indicator in terms of (bar widths/degrees).

➤ bar widths

15. A failure of the power supply to an electrically driven attitude indicator would probably be indicated immediately by a _____.

➤ red warning flag

16. If the indications of a vacuum-driven AI seem erratic and not consistent with the indications of other flight instruments, you should check the

_____.

➤ suction (vacuum) gauge

Power Indicators

1. The power indicators for an airplane fitted with constant speed propellers will be _____.

➤ a tachometer and a manifold pressure gauge for each engine

The Airspeed Indicator

1. The airspeed indicator is a (gyro/pressure) instrument.

➤ pressure

2. The ASI (will/will not) be affected if the pitot tube ices over.

➤ will

3. The ASI (will/will not) be affected if the static line becomes blocked.

➤ will

4. The indicated airspeed on the ASI will be numerically equal to the true airspeed (always/under standard MSL conditions).

➤ under standard MSL conditions

5. As an airplane climbs, the air density (increases/decreases/remains the same).

➤ decreases

6. As an airplane climbs at a constant IAS, the TAS (increases/decreases/remains the same).

➤ increases

7. Warm air is (less/more) dense than cold air.

➤ less

8. If an airplane flies into a parcel of warmer air and maintains the same IAS, the TAS will (increase/decrease/remain the same).

➤ increase

9. If the outside air temperature increases during a flight at constant power and at a constant indicated altitude, the true airspeed will (increase/decrease).

➤ increase

10. The yellow arc on the ASI is known as the _____ range, and airspeeds in this range (are/are not) suitable for turbulent conditions.

➤ caution, are not

11. The red radial line on an ASI indicates the _____ speed.

➤ never exceed

12. Normally, pilots do not correct the indicated airspeed for the position error correction found in the Flight Manual but, if you do, the result is called the _____ airspeed.

➤ calibrated

13. The ratio of the true airspeed to the speed of sound is called the _____.

➤ Mach number

14. An airplane traveling at Mach 0.80 is traveling at _____/tenths the speed of sound.

➤ eight/tenths

15. High speed airplanes have not only the indicated airspeed shown on the airspeed indicator, but also the Mach number shown on the _____.

➤ Mach meter

Heading Indicator

1. The heading indicator is a (gyro/pressure) instrument.

➤ gyro

2. The heading indicator, to read accurately, (should/need not) be regularly aligned with the magnetic compass.

➤ should

3. If an airplane turns to the right, its heading will (increase/decrease).

➤ increase

4. For the indicated heading to increase, the compass card will rotate (clockwise/counter-clockwise).

➤ counterclockwise

5. If an airplane turns to the left, its heading will (increase/decrease).

➤ decrease

6. For the indicated heading to decrease, the compass card will rotate (clockwise/counter-clockwise).

➤ clockwise

7. What pretakeoff check should be made of a vacuum-driven heading indicator in preparation for an IFR flight?

➤ Approximately 5 minutes after engine start (allowing the gyroscope sufficient time to spin up), set the indicator to the magnetic heading of the aircraft and check for proper alignment after taxi turns.

8. The magnetic sensor for a remote indicating compass is known as a magnetic (flux valve/compass).

➤ flux valve

9. In the slaved mode, the compass card of a remote indicating compass (is/is not) automatically slaved to the magnetic flux detector.

➤ is

10. In the free gyro mode, the compass card of a remote indicating compass (is/is not) automatically slaved to the magnetic flux detector.

➤ is not

11. A remote indicating compass should normally operate in the (slaved/free gyro) mode.

➤ slaved

12. A right deflection in the slaving meter of an RIC indicates that the compass card has rotated too far to the (right/left), and therefore a (clockwise/counterclockwise) correction is required.

➤ right, counterclockwise

13. A left deflection in the slaving meter of an RIC indicates that the compass card has rotated too far to the (right/left), and therefore a (clockwise/counterclockwise) correction is required.

➤ left, clockwise

14. If there is a left deflection in the slaving meter of an RIC, this can be corrected by selecting the correction knob on the (left/right).

➤ left

15. The heading on a remote indicating compass is 120° and the magnetic compass indicates 110°. To correctly align the heading indicator with the magnetic compass you should select the (free gyro/slave) mode and depress the (clockwise/counterclockwise) heading drive button.

➤ free gyro, clockwise

16. If an RIC is in the slaved gyro mode, choose the clockwise heading drive knob to rotate the compass card to the (left/right) to eliminate a (left/right) compass card error.

➤ right, left

17. The heading on a remote indicating compass is 5° to the left of that desired. To move the desired heading under the heading reference, you should slew the (clockwise/counterclockwise) heading drive button.

➤ free gyro, counterclockwise

18. The horizontal situation indicator (HSI) is a slaved heading indicator with superimposed (VOR and ILS/ADF) navigation indications.

➤ VOR and ILS

Altimeter

1. The altimeter is a (gyro/pressure) instrument.

➤ pressure

2. The altimeter (will/will not) be affected if the pitot tube ices over.

➤ will not

3. The altimeter (will/will not) be affected if the static line becomes blocked.

➤ will

4. Standard MSL pressure is _____ in. Hg.

➤ 29.92 in. Hg

5. In the metric system, standard MSL pressure is _____ hectopascals (millibars).

➤ 1013.2 hPa (or mb)

6. Actual MSL pressure (varies/never changes).

➤ varies

7. As an airplane climbs, the pressure (increases/decreases/remains the same).

➤ decreases

8. In the lower levels of the atmosphere, air pressure will decrease by approximately 1 in. Hg for every _____ feet gain in altitude.

➤ 1000 feet

9. To check the altimeter prior to an IFR flight, set the pressure window (known also as the Kollsman window or altimeter subscale) to _____ and check that it is within _____ feet of the actual elevation for acceptable accuracy.

➤ current local altimeter setting, ±75 feet

10. If 30.10 is set in the pressure window, then the altimeter will indicate the altitude of the airplane above _____.

➤ the 30.10 in. Hg pressure level

11. If the current altimeter setting is set in the pressure window, then the altimeter will indicate the altitude of the airplane above (ground/sea level).

➤ sea level

12. If the current airport altimeter setting is set in the Kollsman window, then the altimeter, when the airplane is on the runway, will indicate _____.

➤ field elevation

13. Field elevation is the (true/pressure) altitude of the airport above sea level.

➤ true

14. The local altimeter setting should be used by all pilots below 18,000 feet MSL in a particular area to provide for (vertical/horizontal) separation between aircraft.

➤ vertical

15. The local altimeter setting should be used by a pilot to help ensure (vertical/horizontal) separation from terrain.

➤ vertical

16. Which altimeter depicts 8000 feet?

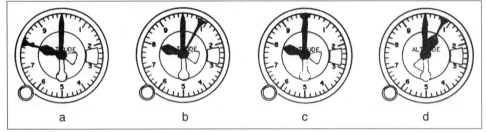

Figure 1.

➤ b

17. Which altimeter depicts 12,000 feet?

Figure 2.

➤ d

18. If you are departing from an airport where you cannot obtain an altimeter setting, you should:

(a) set 29.92 in. Hg in the pressure window of the altimeter.

(b) set the altimeter to read field elevation.

(c) set the altimeter to read zero.

➤ (b)

19. With 29.92 in. Hg set in the pressure window the altimeter will read (density/pressure/true/calibrated) altitude.

➤ pressure altitude

20. For an altimeter to read pressure altitude a pilot should wind _____ into the pressure window.

➤ 29.92

21. For an altimeter to read altitude above sea level a pilot should wind _____ into the pressure window.

➤ the local altimeter setting

22. How can you determine the pressure altitude at an airport without a Tower or Flight Service Station?

➤ set 29.92 in the pressure window and read pressure altitude off the altimeter

23. How can you determine the local altimeter setting at an airport without a Tower or Flight Service Station?

➤ while on the ground, set field elevation in the altimeter and read local altimeter setting in the pressure window

24. When cruising below 18,000 feet in the United States it is usual to set _____ in the pressure window so that the altimeter reads _____.

➤ local altimeter setting, altitude above sea level

25. If, for some reason, (say to compute a precise TAS) you want to determine the pressure altitude when you are cruising below 18,000 feet, then you should set _____ in the pressure window and read the altimeter.

➤ 29.92

26. For every 1000 feet of altitude gained, atmospheric pressure decreases by approximately _____ in. Hg.

➤ 1 in. Hg

27. The current altimeter setting is 30.42 in. Hg. If an airplane is cruising at an altitude of 6500 feet MSL, what is its approximate pressure altitude?

➤ 6000 feet

28. How does a pilot normally obtain the current altimeter setting during an IFR flight in controlled airspace below 18,000 feet?

➤ ATC periodically advises the pilot of the current altimeter setting

29. A cruising level of FL210 is a (true/pressure/calibrated/density) altitude.

➤ pressure altitude

30. When cruising above 18,000 feet in the United States, the pilot should set _____ in the Kollsman window of the altimeter.

➤ 29.92

31. When cruising below 18,000 feet in the United States, the pilot should set _____ in the pressure window of the altimeter.

➤ the local altimeter setting

32. Describe the procedure when departing from an airport where the altimeter setting is 29.40 in. Hg and climbing to maintain FL210.

➤ set local altimeter setting of 29.40 in the pressure window of the altimeter prior to takeoff; leave it set for the climbout until passing through 18,000 feet, when 29.92 should be set in preparation for cruise level FL210 (pressure altitude 21,000 feet).

33. You are cruising at FL250. You hear ATC advise another airplane that the altimeter setting is 28.92 in. Hg in your area. At what pressure altitude are you flying?

➤ 25,000 feet

34. You are maintaining FL250. You hear ATC advise another airplane that the altimeter setting is 28.92 in. Hg in your area. At what altitude MSL are you flying?

➤ 24,000 feet MSL

35. On descent from FL290 prior to landing at an airport, elevation 650 feet, ATC advises that the local altimeter setting is 30.37 in. Hg. For the landing, _____ in. Hg should be set in the altimeter and on landing the altimeter should read _____ feet. If the pressure window of the altimeter was not reset from the FL290 cruise setting of _____ in. Hg, on landing the altimeter would read _____ feet.

➤ 30.37, 650 feet, 29.92, 200 feet

36. On descent from FL210 prior to landing at an airport, elevation 134 feet, ATC advises that the local altimeter setting is 30.26 in. Hg. For the landing, _____ in. Hg should be set in the altimeter and on landing the altimeter should read _____ feet. If the pressure window of the altimeter was not reset from the FL210 cruise setting of _____ in. Hg, on landing the altimeter would read _____ feet.

➤ 30.26, 134 feet, 29.92, 206 feet below sea level

37. What conditions are required for the pressure altitude to be equal to the true altitude?

➤ standard atmospheric conditions must exist

38. Under what condition are pressure altitude and density altitude the same value?

➤ at standard temperature

39. Under what condition will true altitude be lower than indicated altitude if the altimeter setting is 29.92?

➤ in colder than standard temperature

40. Under what condition will true altitude be higher than indicated altitude?

➤ in warmer than standard temperature

41. If you change the setting in the pressure window of an altimeter from 29.92 to 30.00, the indicated altitude will (increase/decrease) by _____ feet.

➤ increase by 80 feet

42. If you change the setting in the pressure window of an altimeter from 30.11 to 29.96, the indicated altitude will (increase/decrease) by _____ feet.

➤ decrease by 150 feet

43. The altimeter will indicate a lower altitude than actually flown (true altitude) when the air temperature is (higher/lower) than standard.

➤ higher

44. When temperatures are (low/high), beware below.

➤ low

45. If the outside air temperature increases during a flight at constant power and at a constant indicated altitude, the true altitude will (increase/decrease).

➤ increase

46. The altimeter and static system, to be suitable for IFR flight, are required by the FAA to be checked every _____ calendar months.

➤ 24

47. The last static pressure system and altimeter test was on Sept 3rd, 1992, and was found to comply with FAA standards. This test is valid until _____, 19_____.

➤ Sept 30th, 1994

48. An encoding altimeter sends electronic altitude information to the _____.

➤ transponder

The Vertical Speed Indicator

1. The VSI is a (gyro/pressure) instrument.

➤ pressure

2. The VSI (will/will not) be affected if the pitot tube ices over.

➤ will not

3. The VSI (will/will not) be affected if the static line becomes blocked.

➤ will

4. The VSI functions by using a metered leak of the (static/pitot) pressure.

➤ static

5. If the VSI indicates 100 fpm DOWN when the airplane is on the ground, then an IFR flight (should not/may) commence.

➤ may

Turn Coordinator

1. The turn coordinator is a (gyro/pressure) instrument.

➤ gyro

2. Prior to start-up, the wings of the turn coordinator (should/need not) be horizontal.

➤ should

3. The turn coordinator indicates:

    (a) rate of roll while altering bank angle, and rate of turn.

    (b) rate of turn only.

    (c) rate of roll only.

    (d) pitch attitude and bank angle.

➤ (a)

4. The model airplane of the turn coordinator gives (a direct/an indirect) indication of the bank angle.

➤ indirect, in that it indicates the direction of turn, but not the bank angle.

5. The displacement of a turn coordinator during a coordinated turn will (increase/decrease/remain constant) if the bank angle is increased.

➤ increase

6. While taxiing, the pilot makes a left turn. The turn coordinator should show a turn to the (left/right) and the ball should show a skid to the (left/right).

➤ turn left, skid right

7. While taxiing, the pilot makes a right turn. The turn coordinator should show a turn to the (left/right) and the ball should move out to the (left/right).

➤ right, left

8. A turn coordinator with a 2 MIN marking indicates standard-rate turns of _____° per second, and a full 360° turn using this indication should take _____ min.

➤ 3° per second, 2 min

9. A turn coordinator with a 4 MIN marking indicates turns of _____° per second, and a full 360° turn using this indication should take _____ min.

➤ 1.5° per second, 4 min

Turn-and-Slip Indicator

1. The turn-and-slip indicator is a (gyro/pressure) instrument.

➤ gyro

2. Prior to starting an engine, you should check the turn-and-slip indicator to determine if the turn needle is (centered/horizontal) and the inclinometer tube is full of fluid.

➤ centered

3. To check the turn-and-slip indicator during taxiing prior to flight, you should turn the airplane and note that the turn needle deflects in the direction (of the turn/opposite the turn) and the ball deflects in the direction (of the turn/opposite the turn).

➤ of the turn, opposite the turn

The Magnetic Compass

1. The magnetic compass is a (gyro/pressure) instrument—or neither.

   ➤ neither

2. On the taxi check prior to flight, the magnetic compass should (swing freely/remain rigid) and indicate (known headings/north).

   ➤ swing freely, known headings

3. Turning error in a magnetic compass is caused by _____.

   ➤ magnetic dip

4. As you roll into a standard-rate turn to the right from an easterly heading in the northern hemisphere, the magnetic compass will indicate:

   (a) a turn to the right, but at a slower rate than is actually occurring.

   (b) a turn to the left initially.

   (c) due east for a short time, then gradually catch up with the heading of the aircraft.

   (d) the approximate correct magnetic heading if the roll into the turn is smooth.

   ➤ (d)

5. As you roll into a standard-rate turn to the left from an easterly heading in the northern hemisphere, the magnetic compass will indicate:

   (a) a turn to the left, but at a slower rate than is actually occurring.

   (b) a turn to the right initially.

   (c) due east for a short time, then gradually catch up with the heading of the aircraft.

   (d) the approximate correct magnetic heading if the roll into the turn is smooth.

   ➤ (d)

6. As you roll into a standard-rate turn to the right from a southerly heading in the northern hemisphere, the magnetic compass will indicate:

   (a) a turn to the right, but at a faster rate than is actually occurring.

   (b) a turn to the left initially.

   (c) due south for a short time, then gradually catch up with the heading of the aircraft.

   (d) the approximate correct magnetic heading if the roll into the turn is smooth.

   ➤ (a)

7. As you roll into a standard-rate turn to the left from a southerly heading in the northern hemisphere, the magnetic compass will indicate:

   (a) a turn to the left, but at a faster rate than is actually occurring.

   (b) a turn to the right initially.

   (c) due south for a short time, then gradually catch up with the heading of the aircraft.

   (d) a turn to the right, but at a slower rate than actually occurring, lagging by about 30°.

   ➤ (a)

8. A magnetic compass, during a 360° level turn with a 15° bank angle, will read most accurately as the aircraft passes through (045°/090°/135°/180°/225°/270°/315°/360°).

   ➤ 090° and 270°

9. As you roll into a standard-rate turn to the right from a westerly heading in the northern hemisphere, the magnetic compass will indicate:

   (a) a turn to the right, but at a faster rate than is actually occurring.

   (b) a turn initially in the opposite direction, but then in the correct direction but lagging behind the actual heading of the aircraft.

   (c) due west for a short time, then gradually catch up with the heading of the aircraft.

   (d) the approximate correct magnetic heading if the roll into the turn is smooth.

   ➤ (d)

10. As you roll into a standard-rate turn to the right from a northerly heading in the northern hemisphere, the magnetic compass will indicate:

   (a) a turn to the right, but at a slower rate than is actually occurring.

   (b) a turn to the left initially, and then a turn to the right but lagging behind the actual heading of the aircraft.

   (c) due north for a short time, then gradually catch up with the heading of the aircraft.

   (d) the approximate correct magnetic heading if the roll into the turn is smooth.

   ➤ (b)

11. As you roll into a standard-rate turn to the left from a westerly heading in the northern hemisphere, the magnetic compass will indicate:

   (a) a turn to the left, but at a slower rate than is actually occurring.

   (b) a turn initially in the opposite direction, but then in the correct direction but lagging behind the actual heading of the aircraft.

   (c) due west for a short time, then gradually catch up with the heading of the aircraft.

   (d) the approximate correct magnetic heading if the roll into the turn is smooth.

   ➤ (d)

12. As you roll into a standard-rate turn to the left from a northerly heading in the northern hemisphere, the magnetic compass will indicate:

   (a) a turn to the left, but at a faster rate than is actually occurring.

   (b) a turn to the right initially, and then a turn to the left but lagging behind the actual heading of the aircraft.

   (c) due north for a short time, then gradually catch up with the heading of the aircraft.

   (d) approximately 30° lag behind the actual heading of the aircraft.

   ➤ (b)

Pitot-Static Instruments

1. During flight, if the pitot tube becomes clogged with ice, the instruments that could be affected are the (AI/ASI/VSI/altimeter/HI/turn coordinator/inclinometer).

   ➤ ASI

2. Both the ram air input and the drain hole of the pitot system are blocked by ice while flying in severe icing conditions. The pilot applies climb power and raises the nose to the correct pitch attitude to climb out of the icing conditions. As the airplane climbs, with correct power and attitude, the indicated airspeed will:

   (a) continuously decrease.

   (b) continuously increase.

   (c) be zero.

   (d) be correct.

   ➤ (b)

3. Both the ram air input and the drain hole of the pitot system are blocked by ice while flying in severe icing conditions. The airspeed indicator will respond to altitude changes like an a_____. With the correct power and pitch attitude set for a climb, the indicated airspeed will (gradually increase and read too high/gradually decrease and read too low/read correctly). With the correct power and pitch attitude set for a descent, the indicated airspeed will (gradually increase and read too high/gradually decrease and read too low/read correctly).

   ➤ altimeter, gradually increase and read too high, gradually decrease and read too low

4. Both the ram air input and the drain hole of the pitot system are blocked by ice while flying in severe icing conditions. The airspeed indicator will respond to altitude changes like an a_____. If the pilot adds power to accelerate the airplane in level flight, the indicated airspeed will (increase/decrease/remain unchanged).

   ➤ altimeter, remain unchanged

5. If both the ram air input and the drain hole of the pitot system are blocked, there will be no variation in indicated airspeed in level flight even if large power changes are made. (true/false)?

➤ true

6. In level flight, it becomes necessary to use an alternate source of static pressure that is vented inside the airplane; this alternate static pressure will be (the same as/lower than/greater than) the normal static pressure measured outside the airplane.

➤ lower than

7. In level flight, it becomes necessary to use an alternate source of static pressure that is vented inside the airplane, the airspeed indicator will read (slightly lower than normal/slightly higher than normal/correctly).

➤ slightly higher than normal

8. In level flight, it becomes necessary to use an alternate source of static pressure that is vented inside the airplane, the altimeter will read (slightly lower than normal/slightly higher than normal/correctly).

➤ slightly higher than normal

9. In level flight, it becomes necessary to use an alternate source of static pressure that is vented inside the airplane; when the change is made, the vertical speed indicator will momentarily show a (climb/descent).

➤ climb

10. If the static ports ice over, then the vertical speed indicator will read _____ even if the airplane climbs or descends.

➤ zero

11. You check the flight instruments while taxiing and find that the VSI indicates a descent of 100 fpm. Must this be rectified prior to flight?

➤ No, treat the 100 fpm descent as the zero indication on the VSI.

12. If the outside air temperature suddenly increases as you fly at a constant indicated altitude into a warmer parcel of air, the true altitude will (increase/not change/decrease), and the true airspeed will (increase/not change/decrease).

➤ increase, increase

Gyroscopic Instruments

1. What test should be made on electrical gyro instruments prior to starting an engine?

➤ Turn on the electrical power and listen for any unusual or irregular mechanical noise.

2. The operation of a properly functioning gyroscope depends on the principle that a rapidly spinning wheel or disc (will/will not) resist deflection.

➤ will

Straight-and-Level Flight **3**

Flying *straight* means maintaining a constant heading, which can be achieved by holding the wings level with the ailerons and keeping the airplane coordinated (in balance) with the ball centered using rudder pressure.

Flying *level* means maintaining a constant altitude, which can be achieved by holding the correct pitch attitude for the power set.

Straight-and-level flying is important, since most flights contain a cruise segment which, on occasions, may be quite long. Accurate straight-and-level flying is important for aerodynamic efficiency, fuel efficiency and comfort, and is one sign of a good pilot.

The Control Instruments

The control instruments for straight-and-level flight, as for all flight, are:

- the attitude indicator; and
- the power indicator.

With reference to these control instruments, the pilot can use the controls (the control column for pitch and bank attitude, the throttle for power) to select straight-and-level flight at the desired altitude and airspeed. The AI gives a direct and instantaneous "picture" of the airplane's pitch attitude and bank angle, and the power indicator gives a direct reading of power.

The AI gives a direct and instantaneous picture of the airplane's pitch attitude and bank angle, and the power indicator gives a direct reading of power.

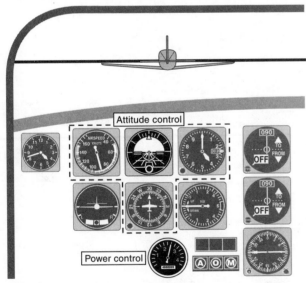

Figure 3-1. The control instruments

The Performance Instruments

Vertical performance of the airplane is indicated to the pilot primarily on:

- the altimeter;
- the vertical speed indicator (VSI); and, to a lesser extent;
- the airspeed indicator (ASI).

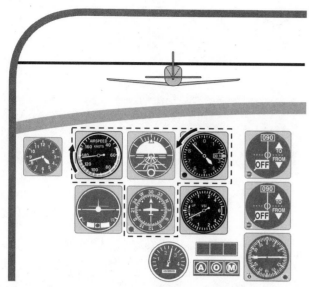

Figure 3-2. The vertical performance instruments showing a gradual loss of altitude

The altimeter indicates altitude directly. The VSI indicates any trend away from that altitude. The ASI indicates airspeed, but can also provide information indirectly regarding pitch attitude and altitude. For instance, an increasing airspeed at a constant power setting may mean that the pitch attitude is too low for straight-and-level flight, and that a loss of altitude is occurring.

For the altimeter reading to be meaningful, the pilot must have the appropriate pressure setting in the pressure window, since this will be the pressure level from which the altimeter measures height. The setting should be:

• the current local altimeter setting for operations below 18,000 feet; and
• Standard pressure 29.92 in.Hg for operations above 18,000 feet.

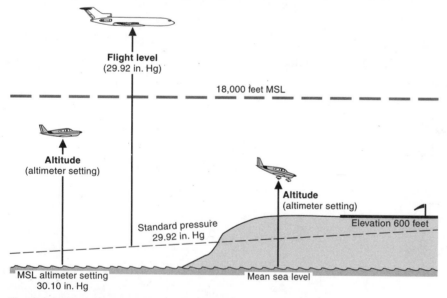

Figure 3-3. The correct pressure setting must be wound into the pressure window

Horizontal performance, in directional terms, is indicated to the pilot primarily on:

• the heading indicator (HI); and
• the turn coordinator (TC) and inclinometer.

The HI gives a direct reading of magnetic heading provided it has been correctly aligned with the magnetic compass during steady flight. It also gives an indirect indication of bank (because, if the heading is changing in coordinated flight, then the wings are banked), plus an indirect indication of rate of turn (by comparing the heading change with the time taken).

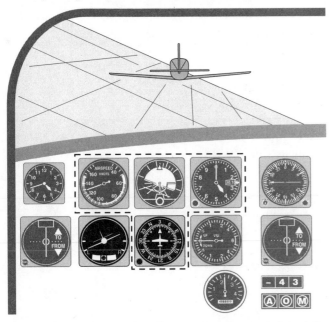

Figure 3-4. The directional performance instruments during a left turn toward north

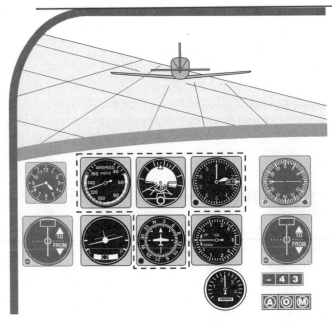

Figure 3-5. The full panel during a left turn to regain heading 360°M at altitude 2000 ft and 130 KIAS

The turn coordinator (or the older style turn-and-slip indicator) indicates the rate of turn. The coordination ball is important, since coordinated flight is almost always desirable to avoid any sideslip or skid through the air.

Horizontal performance in terms of airspeed is indicated on the airspeed indicator.

The Three Fundamentals of Instrument Flying

The three fundamentals of instrument flying are:
- instrument cross-check (scan);
- instrument interpretation; and
- aircraft control.

We have considered instrument cross-check and interpretation, and now we will look at aircraft control for straight-and-level flight.

Keep the Airplane In Trim

When properly trimmed, the airplane should maintain level flight with little or no assistance from the pilot. If not properly trimmed, level flight is much more difficult to maintain, and the pilot is likely to become fatigued and tense on the controls.

Remember that trim is used only to relieve steady control pressures exerted by the pilot, and not to change airplane attitude. Significant trim changes in straight-and-level flight will generally only be required when the pilot makes significant changes in airspeed, or changes in configuration, for instance by lowering the flaps.

Instrument flying requires a light touch, and this is only possible when the airplane is in trim and the pilot relaxed.

The natural stability designed into the airplane will help it to maintain pitch attitude in rough air as well as smooth air, even though there may be some significant deviations from altitude as a result of turbulence. The pilot can correct for altitude deviations with smooth elevator control, but should avoid constant retrimming in turbulence.

Stay Relaxed

A relaxed pilot with a good instrument scan and a light touch on the controls will be a good instrument pilot.

If at any time you feel tense on the controls, a good relaxation technique is to first ensure that the airplane is in trim and then (provided conditions are not turbulent) release all pressure on the elevator control for just a moment or two. Flex your fingers, before replacing them on the control column. The thumb and first two fingers will be more than sufficient for adequate control; a full hand grip may lead to lack of sensitive control and to further tenseness. Being in trim is vital!

Pitch Attitude and Cruise Speed

Different cruise speeds require different pitch attitudes. The pitch attitude established on the attitude indicator will vary for different cruise speeds. For instance, the pitch attitude required for low speed cruise will be higher than that for normal cruise, in order to generate sufficient lift at the lower speed to balance the weight. This is summarized in the lift formula— $(L = C_L \times \frac{1}{2}\rho V^2 \times S)$, which tells us that the lift produced (L) is a function of the angle of attack (related to C_L) and the airspeed (related to $\frac{1}{2}\rho V^2$).

A high angle of attack at a low airspeed is capable of producing the same lift as a low angle of attack at a high airspeed.

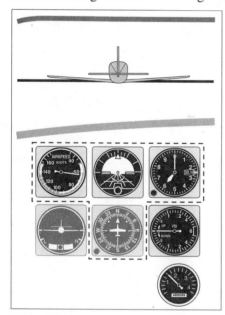

Figure 3-6. Low speed cruise   **Figure 3-7.** High speed cruise

The VSI and the altimeter will confirm if the pitch attitude selected on the AI is correct to maintain altitude with that power set. If not, then you will have to adjust the pitch attitude and/or the power setting. The power required will differ with each airspeed, but more of this later.

Also, compared with when it is light, a heavily laden airplane will require a greater lift force to support the greater weight, and so will require a higher angle of attack at a given cruise speed, hence a higher pitch attitude in the cruise. The pilot may not notice this directly, but reference to the VSI and altimeter will ensure that the correct pitch attitude is selected no matter what the weight is. What may be noticeable to the pilot, however, is the higher power required to maintain airspeed because of the higher drag.

The precise pitch attitude required to maintain level flight will be determined by airspeed, air density, airplane weight and configuration (position of flaps and/or landing gear). When establishing straight-and-level flight, the pilot uses the control instruments, namely the power indicator (throttle) and the AI (control column), to set the power and expected pitch attitude. Fine tuning to accurately hold altitude, confirmed on the appropriate performance instruments (the altimeter and VSI), is achieved by making minor corrections about this pitch attitude with the elevator.

Maintaining Heading

Keeping the wings level and the ball centered will ensure that the desired heading is maintained. The heading can be monitored on the heading indicator, with any tendency to turn being indicated on the turn coordinator.

The HI is the primary performance instrument used to maintain a constant heading. Remember that it should be realigned periodically with the magnetic compass (every 10 or 15 minutes while in steady flight).

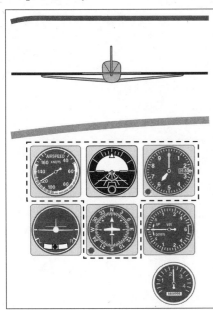

Figure 3-8. Keep wings level and ball centered to achieve straight flight

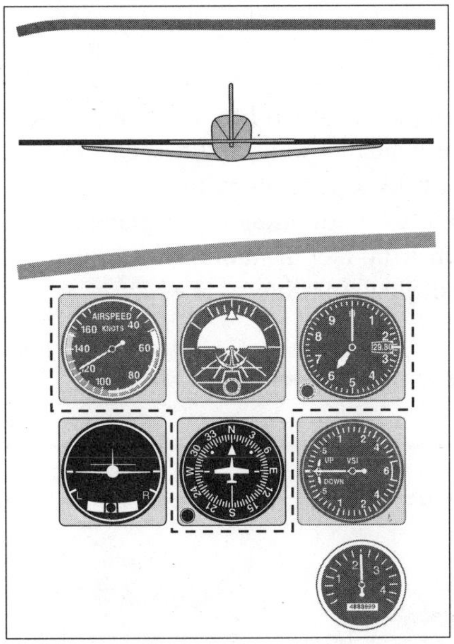

Figure 3-9. Monitor HI and TC for heading performance

If the airplane is allowed to drift off heading, then small coordinated turns (bank and rudder) should be made to regain it. With a reasonable scan, the pilot will always have the airplane within a few degrees of the desired heading. Aim for perfection as an instrument pilot, but at least remain within the acceptable heading limits of ±10°. As a guide, when correcting for small heading errors, limit the bank angle to the number of degrees to be turned, or even less. For instance, a heading change of 5° can be comfortably made with a bank angle of 5° or less.

If a significant heading change is required, however, do not exceed the bank required for a standard-rate turn. Approaching the desired heading, level the wings with aileron, and center the ball with rudder pressure to maintain coordinated flight.

To get an approximate bank angle required for a standard rate turn, divide the airspeed by 10, then add the answer to one-half itself again (at 120 kt this will be approximately 120/10 + 6 = 12 + 6 = 18° bank angle).

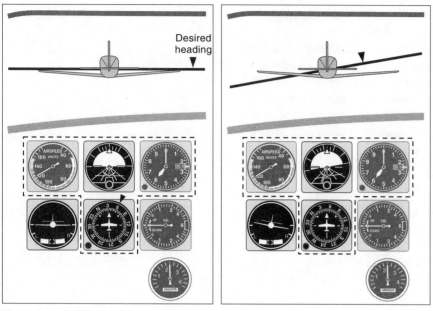

Figure 3-10. Making a slight turn right to regain heading

Maintaining Altitude

Perfectly level flight is almost impossible to achieve in real life. Level flight, in practice, actually consists of a series of very small climbs and descents as the airplane moves off altitude and is brought back to it again by the pilot.

Once again, aim for perfection, and certainly do not allow the airplane to deviate from the desired altitude by more than ±100 feet in smooth air; turbulence of course will make this accuracy more difficult to achieve, in which case do the best you can.

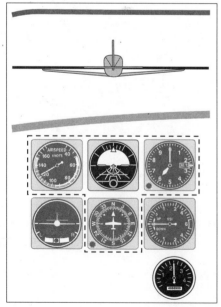

Figure 3-11. Set power and attitude

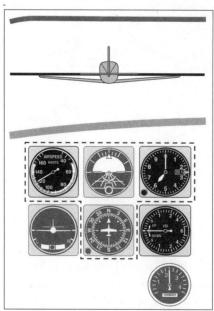

Figure 3-12. Monitor vertical performance

The pilot controls straight-and-level flight by setting the correct pitch attitude on the attitude indicator and the correct cruise power on the power indicator, and then monitors vertical performance on:

- the altimeter;
- the vertical speed indicator;
  and, to a lesser extent,
- the airspeed indicator.

The altimeter, with the correct setting in the pressure window, is used to ensure that the correct altitude is indeed being flown. The altimeter is the primary performance instrument in level flight to confirm that the pitch attitude is correct to maintain altitude. It will indicate deviations from this altitude but, in smooth air, the earliest sign of a tendency to deviate from altitude will be shown, not on the altimeter, but on the vertical speed indicator.

In smooth air, an altitude deviation will be indicated first on the VSI.

Often, a slight correction to pitch attitude can be made on the AI in response to a trend on the VSI before any significant deviation is registered on the altimeter. A large VSI indication may mean a large pitch attitude correction is required. A VSI reading of 600 fpm down might suggest an initial pitch correction of one bar width up, whereas a VSI reading of only 150 fpm might suggest that one-half bar width correction is adequate.

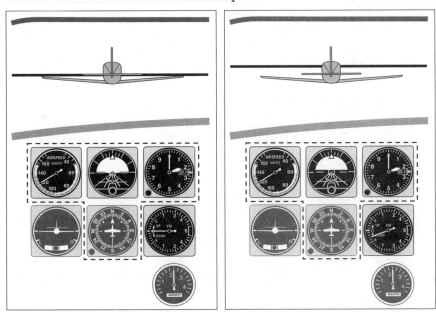

Figure 3-13. In smooth air, the VSI indicates the pitch error well in advance of the altimeter

In rough air, the VSI reading unfortunately will fluctuate considerably, making it of less value to the pilot. In this situation, the altimeter becomes the best guide to any tendency to deviate from altitude.

The airspeed indicator also provides valuable information regarding level flight. If cruise power is set, and the airspeed gradually increases, then the pitch attitude is too low and the airplane will be gradually descending. This will of course be evident on the VSI and altimeter, and corrective action taken by raising the pitch attitude.

Small Deviations from Altitude

In a stable cruise, a deviation of 100 feet or less above the desired altitude (a small inadvertent climb) will usually be accompanied by a small loss of airspeed. You need only make a minor adjustment to pitch attitude, say by lowering it a half bar width on the AI, to quickly regain altitude (and airspeed).

When the airplane is at or near altitude, the pitch attitude can be raised slightly to maintain level flight. No power alterations should be required during these small corrections to altitude. Minor adjustments to altitude using elevator alone can be thought of as gentle zooms and dives.

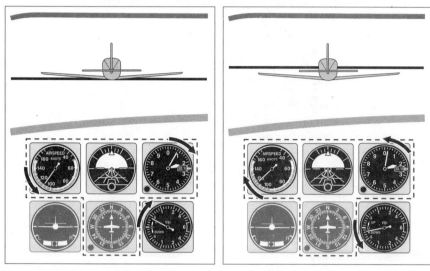

Figure 3-14. Make a small pitch correction for an altitude deviation of less than 100 ft high

Conversely, a small inadvertent descent in a stable cruise will usually be accompanied by a slight gain in airspeed. A deviation of 100 feet or less beneath the desired altitude can be corrected by a slight adjustment to pitch attitude, say by raising it one-half bar width on the attitude indicator to regain altitude (and airspeed).

When at or near altitude, the pitch attitude can then be lowered slightly to maintain level flight. No power alterations should be required.

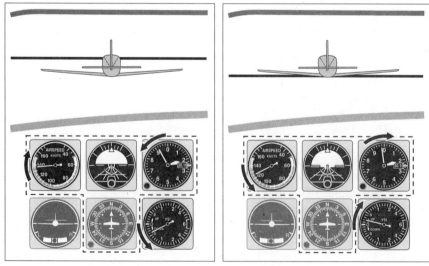

Figure 3-15. Pitch correction for an altitude deviation of less than 100 ft low

Larger Deviations from Altitude

Correction of a large deviation from altitude (in excess of 100 feet) requires an attitude change and possibly a power change as well.

Even if the altitude is changing rapidly, the correction made to pitch attitude by the pilot should still be smooth, with light control pressures, and can be thought of in two stages: one to stop the movement of the altimeter needle and reduce the VSI indication to zero, and a further pitch correction to return the airplane toward the desired altitude. The total pitch correction required still may be only one or two bar widths.

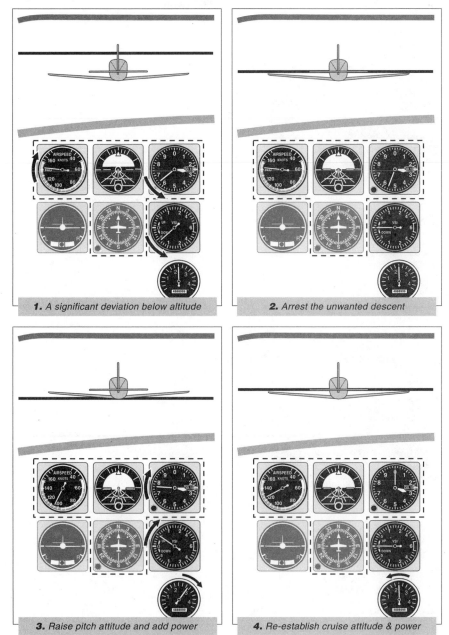

1. A significant deviation below altitude

2. Arrest the unwanted descent

3. Raise pitch attitude and add power

4. Re-establish cruise attitude & power

Figure 3-16. Attitude and power corrections for a significant deviation below altitude

Following a large deviation below altitude, a significant climb back to the desired altitude of 100 feet or more will probably require increased power for the period of the climb if airspeed is to be maintained. Once back on altitude at the desired airspeed, cruise power can be reset to maintain that airspeed.

Conversely, a significant descent to regain the desired altitude requires a lower pitch attitude, and a temporary reduction in power to avoid an unwanted airspeed increase. Once back on altitude with the correct pitch attitude set and at the desired airspeed, cruise power can be reset to maintain that airspeed.

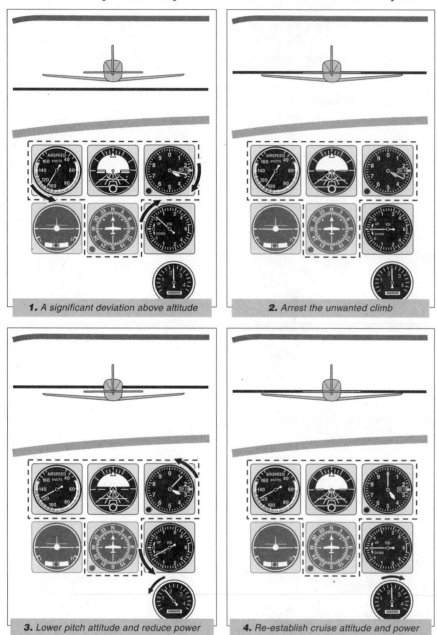

1. *A significant deviation above altitude*

2. *Arrest the unwanted climb*

3. *Lower pitch attitude and reduce power*

4. *Re-establish cruise attitude and power*

Figure 3-17. Attitude and power corrections for a significant deviation above altitude

Energy Transfer in Straight-and-Level Flight

Maintaining both a steady altitude and a steady airspeed can be thought of in terms of energy management. An airplane in flight has kinetic energy in the form of airspeed and potential energy in the form of altitude.

It is possible to convert between these two forms of energy either by zooming to a greater altitude and converting airspeed to altitude, or by diving and converting altitude to airspeed. Additional energy, if required, can be supplied to the airplane by adding power with the throttle.

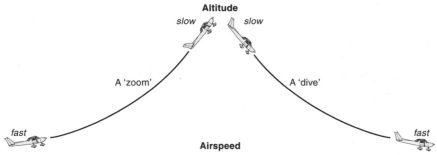

Figure 3-18. Converting airspeed to altitude, and vice versa

If, for instance, the airplane is below the desired altitude with the airspeed well in excess of that desired, then the pilot can convert the excess airspeed to altitude without the use of additional power. If there is no excess airspeed, however, then additional engine power is required to maintain airspeed. Conversely, excess height can be lost by lowering the pitch attitude with elevator and either accepting an airspeed increase or reducing power with the throttle to maintain airspeed.

Scanning the vertical performance instruments will tell the pilot what he should do. As in all flight, the performance of the airplane depends on a combination of both attitude and power but, in straight-and-level flight, it is easiest for the pilot to think in terms of controlling:

• altitude with elevator (pitch attitude); and

• airspeed with throttle (power).

Typical deviations and remedies include the examples shown in Figure 3-19. Desired airspeed is 125 KIAS; desired altitude is 2000 feet MSL.

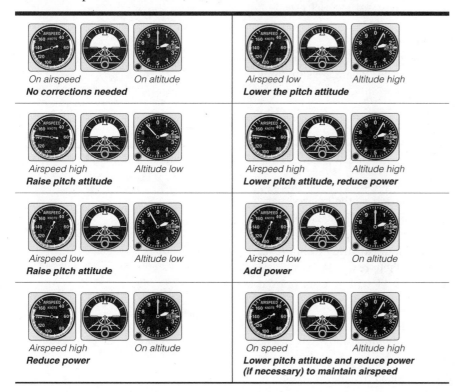

Figure 3-19. Typical deviations and remedies

Recovering From Slightly Unusual Attitudes

It is possible, indeed even probable, that during the early stages of your instrument training you will find the airplane in some slightly unusual attitudes. The remedies are quite straightforward:

- If the airplane is banked, level the wings on the AI with the ailerons.
- If the nose is too high or too low, ease it into the correct attitude on the AI with elevator.
- If the airspeed is excessively high or low, or if large alterations to altitude are required, some adjustment of power may be necessary.

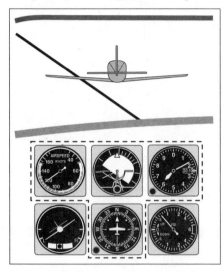

Figure 3-20. Nose high and tuning left: lower the pitch attitude and level the wings

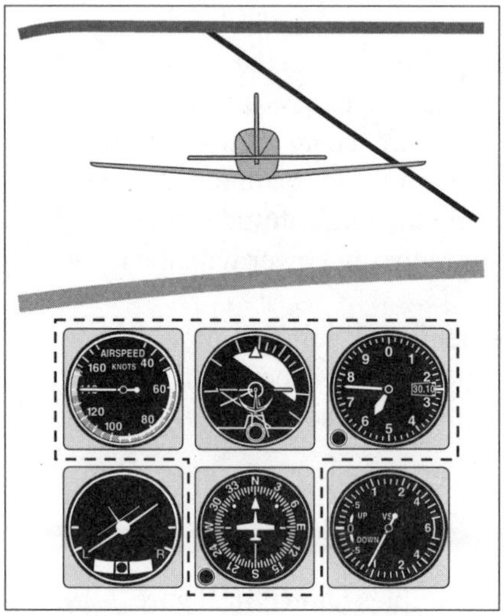

Figure 3-21. Nose low and turning left: level the wings and raise the pitch attitude

Coping with a Faulty Attitude Indicator

The attitude indicator is the master instrument for the pilot and, if it is not functioning correctly, the pilot's task is made that much harder. There are situations where it may fail totally, and others where its indications are not perfectly correct, but are still usable.

Resetting the Miniature Airplane

A symbol of the real airplane appears as a miniature airplane in the center of the attitude indicator. Its up and down position can be adjusted, when required, with a small adjustment knob. The miniature airplane should be positioned so that, during normal cruise flight, it appears superimposed on the horizon bar.

If the preflight check of the AI shows that the miniature airplane is not properly aligned, then it should be adjusted when the airplane is on level ground. If, for some reason, it requires resetting in flight, establish straight-and-level flight (monitored on the other instruments), and then reset the miniature airplane against the horizon bar. After resetting, the AI will give its normal indications in all attitudes.

Coping with a Faulty Wings-Level Indication

Occasionally you will come across an AI that gives a faulty wings-level indication, caused by either a miniature airplane that is slightly askew, or a horizon bar that is not perfectly horizontal. It may also be caused by small gyroscopic precession errors following strenuous maneuvers, causing the horizon bar to temporarily go off the horizontal. These precession errors correct themselves fairly quickly.

On level ground (tricycle landing gear)   *In straight and level flight*

Figure 3-22. Set the index airplane in the attitude indicator with the airplane in the straight-and-level attitude

The clue that the AI is not indicating bank correctly is that, with the wings held level according to the AI and with the ball centered, the heading indicator shows a gradually changing heading, and the turn coordinator shows a turn.

To cope with a suspected faulty wings-level indication on the AI:

- keep the ball centered with rudder pressure;
- hold the desired heading with reference to the heading indicator; and
- accept the slightly erroneous lopsided AI indication.

The AI may not be functioning correctly if, with the wings of the miniature airplane held level and the coordination ball centered, the heading indicator shows a gradually changing heading and the turn coordinator shows a turn.

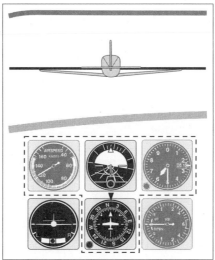

Figure 3-23. A faulty wings-level indication on the AI   **Figure 3-24.** Maintaining heading with a faulty AI

A complete failure of the attitude indicator is possible, although unlikely since it is generally a reliable instrument. However, a vacuum pump failure to a vacuum-driven AI, or an electrical failure to an electrically driven AI, or even an internal gyroscopic failure, will make the AI unusable as the gyroscope runs down.

Any failure of the AI prior to flight should be detected during the preflight checks of the instruments while the airplane is still on the ground.

The rare event of the AI failing in flight, causing the pilot to fly on instruments without reference to the most important one of all, is considered in Chapter 7, *Normal Instrument Flight on a Partial Panel.*

Changing Airspeed In Straight-and-Level Flight

Normal cruise involves setting cruise power, holding cruise altitude, and accepting the airspeed that is achieved, which should be close to the figure published in the Pilot's Operating Handbook.

On occasions, however, there is a need to fly at other than normal cruise airspeed. This requires a different pitch attitude and a different power setting. To slow the airplane down, the pilot throttles back and gradually raises the pitch attitude to maintain altitude; to increase airspeed, the pilot advances the throttle, and gradually lowers the pitch attitude to maintain altitude.

Once the desired airspeed is achieved, the pilot adjusts the power to maintain it. The precise power required for steady flight will depend upon the amount of total drag, which, in cruise, varies with angle of attack and airspeed. High power will be required for:

- high speed cruise (when total drag is high mainly due to parasite drag); and
- low speed cruise (when total drag is high mainly due to induced drag).

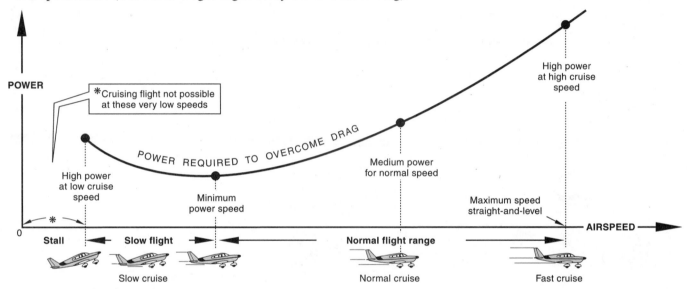

Figure 3-25. The power curve

Medium power is required for normal cruise. The ASI confirms whether or not correct power is set. If not, do something about it. The ASI is the primary performance guide to power requirements during level flight.

Practicing airspeed changes in cruise is excellent instrument flying practice since pitch, bank, balance and power changes must all be coordinated to maintain constant altitude and heading.

When the pilot changes power, a single-engined propeller-driven airplane will tend to move around all three axes of movement. If the propeller rotates clockwise as seen from the cockpit, which is the usual case, adding power will cause the nose to pitch up and yaw left, with a tendency for the airplane to bank left.

The pilot can counteract this by applying forward elevator pressure to prevent the nose pitching up, with right rudder and aileron pressure to overcome the tendency to yaw and roll left. The converse applies when reducing power, hold the nose up and apply left rudder pressure. Refer to the AI to keep the wings level and hold the pitch attitude, and refer to the Inclinometer to ensure the ball is kept centered.

The ASI is the primary performance guide to power requirements during level flight.

Some hints on changing cruising speed follow.

- The attitude indicator gives a direct picture of pitch and bank attitudes.
- The ball gives a direct indication of coordination.
- Useful performance instruments are the altimeter and VSI to ensure that altitude is being maintained, and the heading indicator to ensure that heading is being maintained.
- The airspeed indicator indicates the power requirements. If too slow, add more power; if too fast, reduce power.

The pilot's scan rate of the flight instruments during any power change needs to be reasonably fast to counteract the pitch/yaw effects smoothly and accurately. For this reason, it is good to develop the skill of judging power changes by throttle movement and engine sound, rather than only by observation of the power indicator. This allows the pilot to concentrate on the flight instruments until after the power change has been made, at which time a quick glance at the power indicator for fine adjustment suffices.

When you memorize the approximate power settings necessary to maintain the various cruise speeds, then power handling and airspeed changes become simpler to manage.

Small airspeed changes (say a few knots either way) can generally be handled by a single small power change, and then allowing the airplane to gradually slow down or accelerate to the desired speed.

Large airspeed changes, however, are most efficiently achieved within a few seconds by underpowering on the initial power change for a speed decrease, or overpowering on the initial power change for a speed increase. This allows more rapid deceleration or acceleration to the desired speed, at which time the necessary power to maintain that airspeed is set.

The degree of over- or under-powering will depend upon how fast the pilot wishes to achieve the desired speed (typically 200–300 rpm, or 3–4 in. MP), and also on engine limitations (which must not be exceeded).

Once the desired airspeed is achieved and suitable power is set, the ASI will indicate if further fine adjustment of power to maintain airspeed is required. In level flight, the ASI is the primary guide to power requirements.

To Increase Speed in Level Flight

A small airspeed increase, 5 kt for instance, may be achieved by a small power increase that allows the airspeed to gradually increase by the desired amount.

To achieve a large airspeed increase without delay, however, excess power should be applied to accelerate the airplane quickly, and then adjusted when the desired airspeed is reached. This can be thought of as overpowering on the initial power change, a typical amount being 200–300 rpm (or 3–4 in. MP for constant-speed propellers).

- Increase power with the throttle (overpower for large speed increases). Hold forward pressure to maintain altitude, referring to the VSI and altimeter; keep the ball centered with rudder pressure; keep wings level with aileron and check the HI for heading.
- Lower the pitch attitude slightly on the AI to maintain altitude (VSI and altimeter), and allow airspeed to increase to the desired value (ASI).
- At or approaching the desired airspeed, adjust the power to maintain it (ASI).
- Hold the pitch attitude (AI) using elevator, and trim off the elevator pressure.

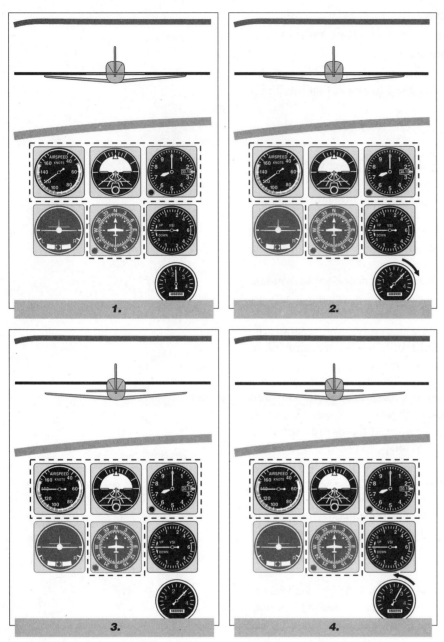

Figure 3-26. Increasing speed in level flight

To Decrease Speed in Level Flight

A small speed decrease can be achieved with a single small power change, but a large speed decrease without delay is best achieved with underpowering. Once the airplane has decelerated to the desired airspeed, power can be increased to maintain it.

- Decrease power with the throttle (underpower for large speed decreases). Hold backward pressure to maintain altitude referring to the VSI and altimeter; keep the ball centered with rudder pressure; keep wings level with aileron and check the HI for heading.

- Raise the pitch attitude slightly on the AI to maintain altitude (VSI and altimeter), and allow airspeed to decrease to the desired value (ASI).

- At or approaching the desired airspeed, adjust the power to maintain it (ASI).

- Hold the pitch attitude (AI), and trim.

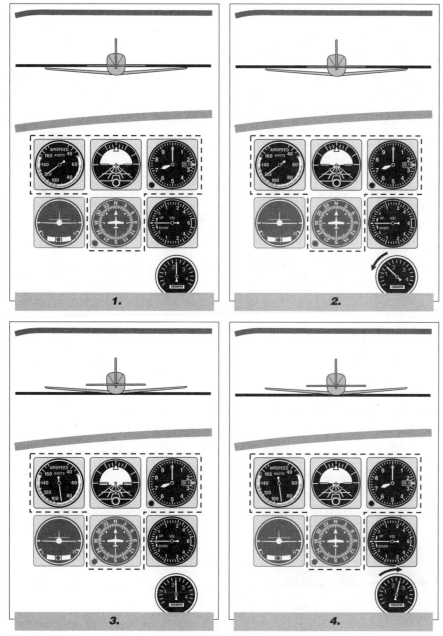

Figure 3-27. Decreasing speed in level flight

Once approximate level flight is achieved:

- the precise altitude can be accurately maintained with elevator; and
- the airspeed can be accurately maintained with power.

The FAA flight test requirement is to hold heading within ±10°, altitude within ±100 ft and any chosen airspeed within ±10 kt. You should aim for better accuracy than this. In smooth air, your airspeed can be held to ±2 knots, altitude to ±20 ft, and heading to ±5°. With a good scan, you can detect any trend away from the desired flightpath and airspeed, and make immediate corrections.

The FAA flight test requirement is to hold heading within ±10°, altitude within ±100 ft and any chosen airspeed within ±10 kt.

Changing Configuration In Level Flight

On occasions it is necessary to change the configuration of the airplane while maintaining level flight, for instance when lowering some flaps or lowering the wheels while maneuvering prior to landing. Before making any configuration changes, however, you must ensure that airframe limitations are satisfied. For instance, the airspeed must be less than V_{FE} before flaps are lowered, or below V_{LO} in a retractable landing gear airplane before the landing gear is extended.

Lowering the flaps or landing gear in most airplanes will cause an increase in total drag and therefore a tendency to lose airspeed, as well as a pitch change. With more familiarity, the pilot will be prepared to counteract these tendencies smoothly and comfortably.

Unwanted pitch changes can be counteracted using elevator pressure, with reference to the attitude indicator, altimeter and VSI.

Airspeed control is achieved using the throttle, with reference to the airspeed indicator—additional power being required to counteract the increased drag if airspeed is to be maintained. If, however, a further airspeed reduction is required, application of additional power can be delayed.

Unwanted pitch changes can be counteracted using elevator pressure, with reference to the attitude indicator, altimeter and VSI.

Lowering Flaps

To maintain altitude and airspeed as flaps are lowered:

- Ensure IAS is at or below V_{FE} with reference to the ASI;
- Lower the flaps, maintaining altitude with elevator pressure (monitoring the VSI and altimeter), and maintaining airspeed with power (monitoring the ASI). A lower pitch attitude and higher power can be expected.

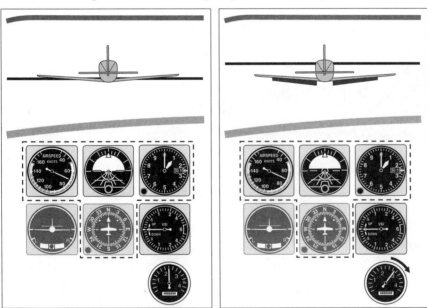

Figure 3-28. Maintaining altitude and airspeed as flaps are lowered

Raising Flaps

To maintain altitude and airspeed as flaps are raised:

- Ensure IAS is at or above V_{S1};
- Raise the flaps, maintaining altitude with elevator back pressure, and airspeed with reduced power. If an airspeed increase is desired, then the power can be adjusted, if necessary, to achieve this.

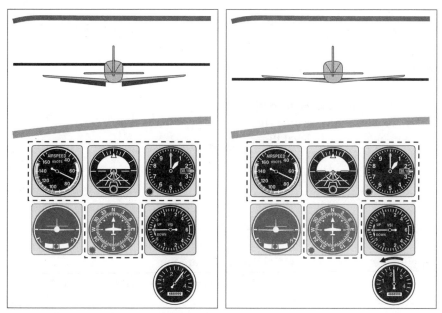

Figure 3-29. Maintaining altitude and airspeed as flaps are raised

Lowering Landing Gear

To maintain altitude and airspeed as landing gear is lowered:

- Ensure IAS is at or below V_{LO};
- Lower the landing gear, maintaining altitude with elevator pressure, and airspeed with additional power.

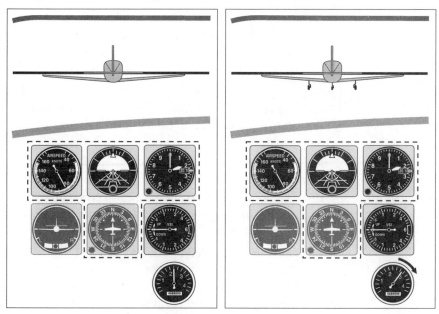

Figure 3-30. Maintaining altitude and airspeed as landing gear is lowered

Maintaining altitude and airspeed as the landing gear is lowered is a typical maneuver as the airplane is flown level to intercept the glideslope for an ILS approach.

Raising Landing Gear

To maintain altitude and airspeed as landing gear is raised:

- Ensure IAS is at or below V_{LO};
- Raise the landing gear, maintaining altitude with elevator pressure, and airspeed with power.

Usually the landing gear is raised during the initial climb-out after takeoff, although there are occasions when it may be required to raise the gear from the extended position at other times, for instance when maneuvering in level flight and deciding to discontinue an approach to land.

✍ Review 3

1. The three fundamentals of instrument flying are _____.

➤ instrument cross-check (scan); instrument interpretation; and aircraft control

2. The AI gives (a direct/an indirect) indication of pitch attitude.

➤ a direct

3. The AI gives (a direct/an indirect) indication of bank angle.

➤ a direct

4. The control instruments are the _____.

➤ AI and power indicator

5. The vertical performance instruments are the _____.

➤ altimeter, VSI and ASI

6. The horizontal performance instruments in terms of bank are the _____.

➤ heading indicator, turn coordinator and inclinometer

7. The horizontal performance instrument in terms of speed is the _____.

➤ ASI

8. Pitch instruments are the _____.

➤ AI, altimeter, VSI and ASI

Straight-and-Level Flight

9. Bank instruments are the _____.

➤ AI, turn coordinator and heading indicator

10. The instrument that displays the quality of flight, or the coordination, is the _____.

➤ coordination ball

11. The primary instrument to confirm correct pitch attitude in straight-and-level flight is the _____.

➤ altimeter

12. The primary instrument to confirm correct bank in straight-and-level flight is the _____.

➤ HI

13. The primary performance instrument to confirm correct power in straight-and-level flight is the _____.

➤ ASI

14. The primary instrument to confirm correct pitch attitude in straight-and-level flight is the _____, supported by the _____.

➤ altimeter, supported by AI, VSI and ASI

15. The primary instrument to confirm correct bank in straight-and-level flight is the _____, supported by the _____.

➤ HI, supported by AI and turn coordinator

16. If you experience a small deviation from altitude in straight-and-level flight, then you should make a pitch correction on the _____, and then confirm the effect of this pitch change on the _____ and _____.

➤ AI, altimeter and VSI

17. As a rule of thumb, altitude corrections of less than 100 feet can be accomplished by using a pitch correction of one (half/full) bar width on the AI.

➤ half

18. As power is reduced to change airspeed from high to low cruise in level flight, which instrument is primary for pitch?

➤ altimeter

19. As power is reduced to change airspeed from high to low cruise in level flight, which instrument is primary for bank?

➤ HI

20. As power is reduced to change airspeed from high to low cruise in level flight, which instrument is primary for power? Once the desired speed has been reached and the estimated power set, the primary performance instrument to confirm correct power is the _____.

➤ power indicator, ASI

21. Three conditions which determine the precise pitch attitude required to maintain level flight are (altitude/airspeed/air density/weight/wind velocity).

➤ airspeed, air density, weight

22. Desired heading should be maintained to an accuracy of within ±_____°.

➤ ±10°

23. Desired altitude should be maintained to an accuracy of within ±_____ feet.

➤ ±100 feet

24. Desired airspeed should be maintained to an accuracy of within ±_____ knots.

➤ ±10 knots

25. Cruising level below 18,000 feet MSL should be achieved with (29.92/local altimeter setting) in the pressure window of the altimeter.

➤ local altimeter setting

26. Cruising level above 18,000 feet MSL should be achieved with (29.92/local altimeter setting) in the pressure window of the altimeter.

➤ 29.92

27. The primary information for heading and bank in straight flight is the heading indicator, but its information is only valid if _____.

➤ it is aligned with the magnetic compass

28. To maintain a constant airspeed as the landing gear is lowered, _____.

➤ increase power

The Straight Climb and Descent 4

With the correct power and attitude set, the airplane should achieve the desired performance, which in this case is a straight climb or descent. The control instruments for the climb and descent are the same as for all maneuvers:

- the power indicator, used by the pilot to set power with the throttle; and
- the attitude indicator, used to set pitch attitude with the elevator (typically one or two bar widths above or below the cruise position).

These are the primary instruments used when making the transition from level flight to a climb or descent.

Remember that the three fundamental skills in instrument flying are:

- instrument cross-check (or scan);
- instrument interpretation; and
- aircraft control.

The Straight Climb

To Enter A Climb

As in visual flight, the procedure for entering the climb on instruments is A-P-T: attitude–power–trim.

- Select the climb **attitude** with reference to the AI using elevator.
- Set climb **power** using the throttle as desired climb speed is attained (with the mixture RICH if necessary).
- **Trim**.

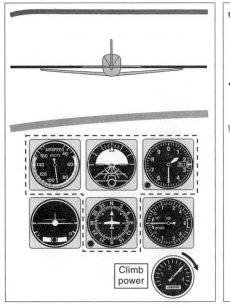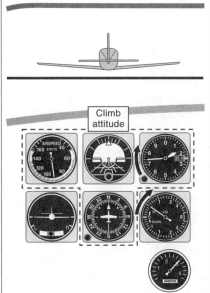

Figure 4-1. Enter the climb with attitude, power and trim

In the typical single-engined propeller-driven airplane there is a tendency for the nose to pitch up and yaw left as power is applied. To ensure that heading is maintained, the wings on the AI are kept level with aileron, and the ball kept centered with rudder pressure.

Hold the attitude and allow the airspeed to settle on the ASI, then make fine adjustments to the attitude with elevator to achieve the desired climbing speed precisely, and finally trim off any steady control pressure. It is a good idea to make a coarse trim adjustment initially, followed by a finer trim adjustment as the precise climb speed is achieved and maintained.

Once established in the climb, the climb performance of the airplane is monitored on:

- the altimeter;
- the vertical speed indicator; and
- the airspeed indicator.

With a smooth transition from level flight to a climb, the VSI will show an upward trend, and then the altimeter reading will start to increase. The VSI will eventually indicate a rate appropriate to the stabilized climb airspeed and pitch attitude for the power set.

Maintaining the Climb

Keeping the wings level with aileron and the ball centered with rudder pressure ensures that heading is maintained, which can be verified on the heading indicator. With climb power set (and this is often full power in light aircraft), the pilot achieves the desired climbing airspeed precisely with slight adjustments to pitch attitude on the AI using elevator. The airspeed indicator is the primary performance instrument in the climb to ensure that pitch attitude is correct.

The airspeed indicator is the primary performance instrument in the climb to ensure that pitch attitude is correct.

Airspeed low
Lower the pitch attitude

Airspeed high
Raise the pitch attitude

Figure 4-2. Make minor pitch attitude adjustments to maintain climbing airspeed

Once established in the climb, any fine adjustments to pitch attitude should be confined to just one-quarter or one-half bar width on the AI. If the climbing airspeed is correct, then the pitch attitude is correct. If the airspeed is low, then the pitch attitude is too high and should be lowered slightly.

If the climb airspeed is correct, then the pitch attitude is correct.

Conversely, if the airspeed is too high, then the pitch attitude should be raised slightly. Once the airspeed has settled to its new value, any steady control pressure can be trimmed off.

Heading is maintained by keeping the wings level on the AI and the ball centered, and direction can be monitored on the heading indicator. Small heading corrections can be made with gentle coordinated turns.

Once established in the climb, check that correct climb power is set. With a fixed-pitch propeller, the rpm will decrease as the climb attitude is assumed and airspeed decreases. With a constant-speed propeller, the manifold pressure will decrease as altitude is gained (for nonturbocharged engines).

The required accuracy in a climb is airspeed within ±10 kt, and heading within ±10°, but you should aim for perfection.

Clearing turns (that are made in a visual climb to look for other aircraft) are meaningless in clouds and in nil visibility but, if you happen to be in visual conditions (which is often the case during an instrument flight), clearing turns may be made. During training, your instructor will probably restrict your outside vision to simulate instrument conditions, but he will require clearing turns to be made periodically for him to adequately perform his function as safety pilot.

Engine temperatures and pressures should be checked periodically on the climb, since the engine is working hard and the cooling airflow is less, but do not be distracted from your scan of the flight instruments for more than a few seconds at a time. Periodically check that correct climb power remains set.

As the desired cruise altitude or level is approached, the altimeter should be scanned more frequently. You should also check that the correct barometric setting has been wound into the pressure window: current local altimeter setting for operations below 18,000 feet MSL, or standard pressure 29.92 in.Hg (or 1013 mb or hPa) for operations above 18,000 feet.

Leveling Off from the Climb

As for visual flight, the procedure for leveling off from a climb on instruments is A-P-T: attitude–power–trim. As the desired altitude is approached, the focus for changes in pitch attitude shifts from the airspeed indicator to the altimeter – the aim being to lower the pitch attitude to capture the desired altitude. Leveling off should be commenced before actually reaching the altitude, a suitable lead-in altitude being "10% of the rate of climb", which, at a rate of climb of 500 fpm would be 50 feet before reaching the desired altitude.

Raise the pitch attitude and reduce the rate of climb to capture the desired altitude.

Commencing at the lead-in altitude, gradually lower the pitch attitude toward the level flight position on the AI. The VSI will show a gradually reducing climb rate, and movement of the altimeter needle will slow down. The aim is to reduce the rate of climb to zero just as the desired altitude is captured. The required accuracy is to level off within ±100 feet of the desired altitude, but your aim, of course, should be to level off right on altitude and, if you are a little out, to correct this immediately.

Normally, climb power is retained after leveling off to allow the airplane to accelerate to the cruise speed. Once at the desired airspeed, reduce to cruise power, holding the desired pitch attitude with elevator, and then trim.

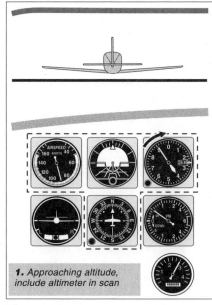

1. Approaching altitude, include altimeter in scan

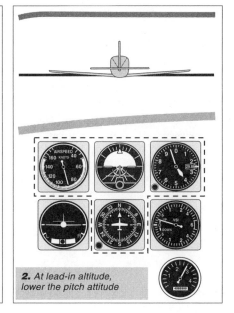

2. At lead-in altitude, lower the pitch attitude

Figure 4-3 (continued on page 98)

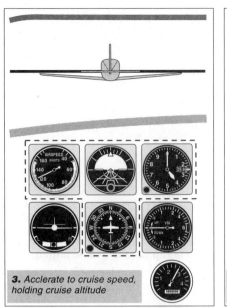
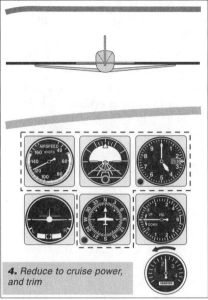

3. *Acclerate to cruise speed, holding cruise altitude*

4. *Reduce to cruise power, and trim*

Figure 4-3. Leveling off from a climb

Heading is monitored on the heading indicator, and will remain constant if the wings are kept level and the ball centered. Heading corrections can be made using shallow coordinated turns. Minor adjustments to pitch attitude using the elevator will be required to maintain the exact altitude. If a particular cruise airspeed is desired, then power adjustments may also be required.

Climbing at Different Airspeeds

With climb power set, climbing airspeed is selected with pitch attitude on the AI, a higher pitch attitude resulting in a lower airspeed. Different climb airspeeds are used to achieve different objectives, for instance:

- **the best angle of climb** airspeed (V_X) to clear obstacles;
- **the best rate of climb** airspeed (V_Y) to gain altitude as quickly as possible;
- **the cruise-climb airspeed**, sacrificing rate of climb for a higher airspeed, is often used to provide faster flights, better airplane control because of the increased airflow over the control surfaces, better engine cooling, and a more comfortable (lower) airplane attitude.

The precise values of V_X and V_Y appear in the Pilot's Operating Handbook. To achieve the desired airspeed, simply adjust the pitch attitude on the AI; the airspeed indicator is the primary performance instrument to verify that pitch attitude is correct in the climb.

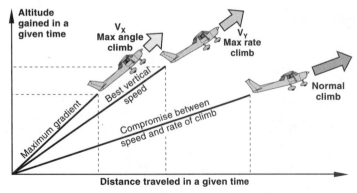

Figure 4-4. Different climbing airspeeds to achieve different objectives

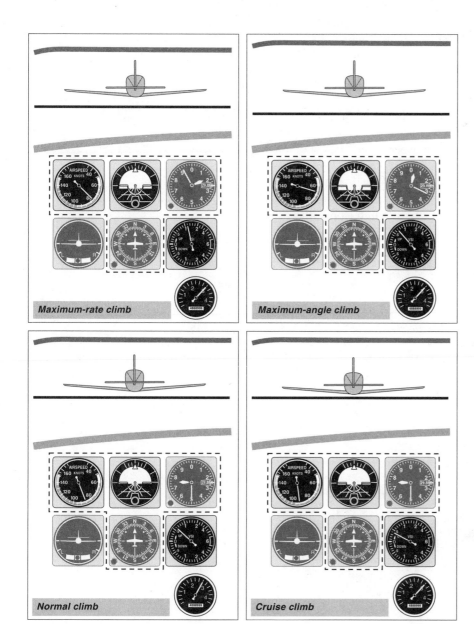

Figure 4-5. Different climb pitch attitudes

Variations On Entering the Climb

The technique used to enter the climb from level flight depends on the level airspeed and the desired climb speed. If the same airspeed is to be used both cruising and climbing, simultaneously apply power and gently raise the pitch attitude to maintain the airspeed and then, once settled into the climb, trim off any steady pressure.

If, however, the climb airspeed is to be less than the cruising airspeed (which is generally the case), then the pilot can either:

• raise the pitch attitude and allow the speed to bleed off before applying power to maintain the desired climb speed (A-P-T); or

• apply power and raise the pitch attitude, allow the airspeed to bleed off to climb speed, and then make minor pitch adjustments to maintain the desired climb speed (the usual P-A-T).

In general, the order A-P-T is acceptable, but some instructors prefer the P-A-T. The initial pitch attitude selected on the AI should be that appropriate to the desired climb speed.

Climbing at a Particular Rate

Limiting the rate of climb to a specific value is not generally required in most light aircraft because of their relatively modest performance capabilities, even at full power. High-powered airplanes, however, may occasionally be required to climb at a particular rate.

The airspeed in a climb is controlled by small alterations in pitch attitude using elevator, with the airspeed indicator as the primary performance instrument for climb speed. The pilot has a measure of rate of climb from either:

- the vertical speed indicator (VSI); or
- the clock and the altimeter combined.

500 ft/min rate of climb indicated on the VSI

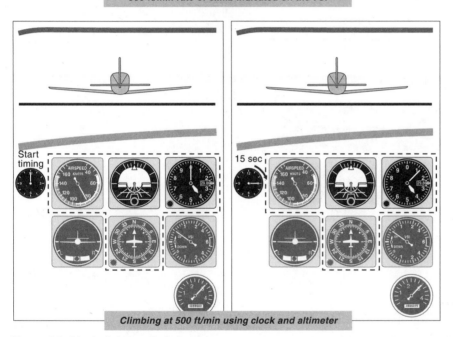

Climbing at 500 ft/min using clock and altimeter

Figure 4-6. Monitoring rate of climb

The VSI, after it has stabilized, is normally the primary performance instrument for rate of climb but, if turbulence causes the VSI to fluctuate, then the pilot can either estimate the average reading of the VSI or use the clock and altimeter to time the climb. In Figure 4-6 the airplane has climbed 125 feet in 15 seconds ($\frac{1}{4}$ minute), a rate of 500 fpm.

Power can be adjusted until the desired rate of climb is achieved precisely, accompanied by minor adjustments of pitch attitude on the AI to hold airspeed. For instance, as illustrated in Figure 4-7, a decrease in power to reduce the rate of climb from 900 fpm to 500 fpm will require a slight lowering of the pitch attitude to maintain a constant airspeed of 80 knots.

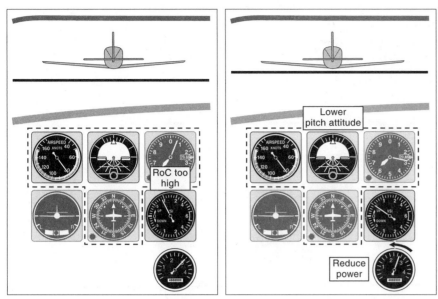

Figure 4-7. Establishing a precise rate of climb

Conversely, the rate of climb can be increased at a constant airspeed by adding power and raising the pitch attitude. If, however, maximum power is already being used (as is often the case in light aircraft), the only way of improving rate of climb is to fly closer to V_Y, the best rate of climb airspeed.

Be warned that raising the pitch attitude too high, and reducing the airspeed to below V_Y, will lead to a poorer rate of climb. In an extreme case, the airplane may simply stagger along in a nose-high attitude with a poor rate of climb (if any), facing the possibility of a stall, and with the risk of poor engine cooling because of the high power and reduced cooling airflow.

Climbing Into Clouds After Takeoff

The actual takeoff ground run and lift-off is made with external visual reference to the runway and its surroundings.

When airborne and climbing away from the ground, however, it is possible that visual reference to ground objects and to the natural horizon will be lost. This will occur if the airplane enters clouds, but it may also occur in conditions of poor visibility (mist, haze, smog, rain, snow or dust), or at night. The pilot must transfer his attention to the instruments before losing external visual reference.

The importance of the instrument checks made prior to takeoff is obvious, since these instruments may now suddenly become your only source of attitude and performance information.

When instrument conditions are expected to be entered shortly after becoming airborne, carry out a visual takeoff and stabilize the airplane in the climb-out, with climb power and climb attitude set, and with the airplane in trim for the climb speed. In other words, make a normal visual takeoff. Then, prior to entering clouds or otherwise losing visual reference, transfer your attention from external references to the instrument panel.

The scan is the same as for a normal climb:

• Maintain pitch attitude and wings level on the AI, with the ball centered.
• Hold airspeed on the ASI with small pitch changes on the AI.

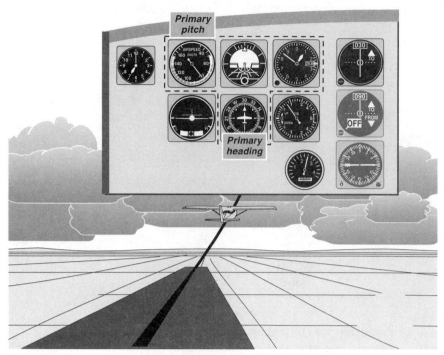

Figure 4-8. Transfer attention to the instrument panel shortly after takeoff

- Keep in trim.
- Maintain heading on the heading indicator with small coordinated turns.
- Monitor climbing performance on the altimeter and VSI.

Transferring attention to the flight instruments shortly after liftoff and when established in the climb-out is especially important at night, when there is little ground lighting, or when low clouds might be encountered unexpectedly.

The Straight Descent

With the correct power and attitude, the airplane should achieve the desired performance, which in this case is a straight descent. The control instruments for the descent are the same as for all maneuvers:

- the power indicator, used by the pilot to set or remove power with the throttle;
- the attitude indicator, used to set pitch attitude with the elevator (slightly below the horizon bar for a powered descent, and typically one or two bar widths below the horizon bar for the glide).

To Enter a Descent

As in visual flight, the procedure for entering a descent on instruments is P-A-T: power–attitude–trim.

Reduce the power by placing the mixture control to RICH (fully in), the carburetor heat control to HOT (fully out) if the power reduction is significant, and smoothly move the throttle out until the desired descent power is set. Back pressure on the control column and left rudder pressure is required to counteract the pitch down/yaw right tendency as power is reduced. Keep the wings level with aileron, and the ball centered with rudder pressure, to ensure that heading is maintained.

Hold altitude until airspeed reduces to that desired, and then lower the pitch attitude one or two bar widths beneath the horizon bar to maintain airspeed. (If the descent speed is to be the same as the level speed, then the power reduction and the lowering of pitch attitude on the AI should be simultaneous.)

Hold the pitch attitude and allow the airspeed to settle, then make any minor pitch adjustments required, and trim. It is a good idea to make an initial coarse trim adjustment after the power and attitude have been selected, followed by a finer trim adjustment once the precise airspeed is achieved and maintained.

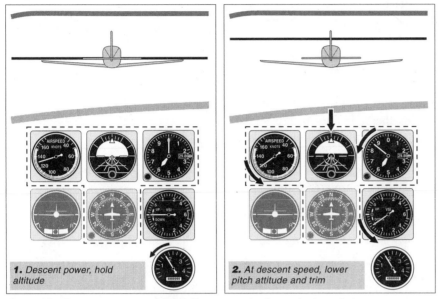

1. Descent power, hold altitude

2. At descent speed, lower pitch attitude and trim

Figure 4-9. Enter the descent with P-A-T, power reduction, attitude and trim

The descent performance is monitored on:
- the altimeter;
- the vertical speed indicator; and
- the airspeed indicator.

With a smooth transition from level flight to a descent, the VSI will show a downward trend, and then the altimeter reading will start to decrease. The VSI will eventually indicate a rate appropriate to the stabilized descent airspeed and pitch attitude for the power set.

Maintaining the Descent

Keeping the wings level with aileron and the ball centered with rudder pressure ensures that heading is maintained, which can be verified on the heading indicator. With descent power set (often throttle fully closed), the pilot achieves the precise descent airspeed desired with slight adjustments to pitch attitude on the AI using elevator. The airspeed indicator is the primary performance instrument in the descent (as in the climb) to verify that pitch attitude is correct.

Figure 4-10. Monitoring descent performance

The airspeed indicator is the primary performance instrument in the descent to verify that pitch attitude is correct.

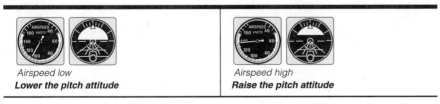

Airspeed low
Lower the pitch attitude

Airspeed high
Raise the pitch attitude

Figure 4-11. Make minor pitch attitude adjustments to maintain descent airspeed

When established in the descent, any fine adjustments to pitch attitude should be confined to just one quarter or one half bar widths. If the descent airspeed is correct, then the pitch attitude is correct. If the airspeed is low, then the pitch attitude is too high and should be lowered slightly. Conversely, if the airspeed is too high, then the pitch attitude should be raised slightly. Once the airspeed has settled to its new value, any steady control pressure can be trimmed off. The required accuracy is airspeed within ±10 knots, and heading within ±10° but, of course, you should aim for better accuracy than this.

If the descent airspeed is correct, then the pitch attitude is correct.

If the power is kept constant, then a pitch attitude change is the only way of achieving a change in airspeed, and this will be accompanied by a change in the rate of descent. If a precise rate of descent is required, as well as a precise airspeed, then a combination of power and attitude is used (see page 106).

In a prolonged descent with low power, thought should be given to clearing the engine every 1000 feet or so by applying 50% power, or power into the green arc, for a few seconds. This will keep the engine and oil warm, avoid carbon fouling on the spark plugs, and ensure that the carburetor heat is still supplying warm air. Be prepared to counteract the pitch/yaw tendencies as power is changed.

As the desired altitude or flight level is approached, the altimeter should be increasingly brought into the scan. Ensure that the correct altimeter setting has been set in the pressure window:

- local altimeter setting for operations below 18,000 feet; or
- Standard pressure 29.92 in.Hg (1013 hPa) for operations above 18,000 feet.

Leveling Off from a Descent

The procedure for leveling off from a descent is P-A-T: power–attitude–trim. As the desired altitude is approached, the focus for changes in pitch attitude shifts from the airspeed indicator to the altimeter, the aim being to raise the pitch attitude to capture the desired altitude, and to use power to achieve the desired cruise speed. A suitable lead-in altitude is 10% of the rate of descent, which at rate of descent 500 fpm would be 50 feet before reaching the desired altitude.

Raise the pitch attitude to capture the desired altitude.

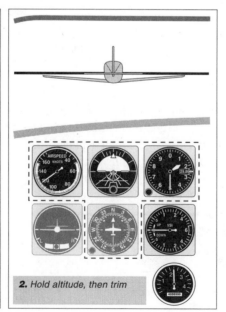

1. Apply power, and raise the pitch attitude

2. Hold altitude, then trim

Figure 4-12. Leveling off from a descent

Commencing at the lead-in altitude, smoothly apply cruise power (carburetor heat COLD), and gradually raise the pitch attitude toward the level flight position on the AI, keeping the ball centered with rudder pressure. The VSI will show a gradually reducing descent rate, and movement of the altimeter needle will slow down. The aim is to reduce the rate of descent to zero just as the desired altitude is captured. A fairly quick scan rate helps to make this a smooth and comfortable maneuver. Once established in level flight at the desired airspeed, trim off any steady pressures.

The required accuracy is to level off at the desired altitude ±100 feet but, with a little care, you can be much more accurate than this. If not quite accurate enough to begin with, make small corrections and place the airplane right on altitude.

Heading is monitored on the heading indicator, and will remain constant if the wings are kept level and the ball centered. Heading corrections can be made using shallow coordinated turns. Minor adjustments to pitch attitude using the elevator will be required to maintain altitude. If a particular cruise airspeed is desired, then power adjustments may also be required.

If the cruise airspeed is significantly greater than the descent airspeed, then power can be added a little earlier than usual, say 100 feet before reaching the desired altitude, and the airplane can commence accelerating to be at or near the higher cruise speed just as leveling-out is completed. If the cruise speed is the same as descent speed, however, then applying power simultaneously with raising the pitch attitude (at about 50 feet to go if the rate of descent is 500 fpm) is sufficient.

Climbing Away from a Descent

This is a very important instrument maneuver, since it is used when you elect to go-around from a *missed approach* to land, as well as at any other time you want to go directly from a descent into a climb. The procedure is still P-A-T: power–attitude–trim, except that it is climb power and climb attitude that are selected, and the change in control pressures and trim are much greater than in previous maneuvers.

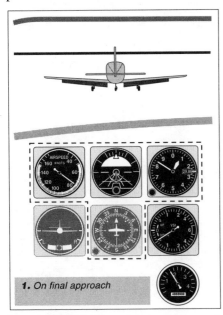
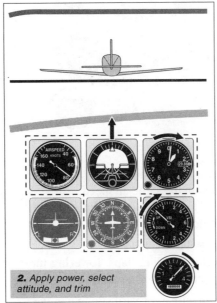

1. On final approach

2. Apply power, select attitude, and trim

Figure 4-13. Climbing away from a descent

A greater pitch/yaw tendency can be expected with the large power increase in the go-around, and this must be counteracted. In a genuine go-around, full power will probably be used (with carburetor heat COLD and mixture RICH). Once established in the climb, it is acceptable to make an initial trim adjustment, and then fine tune the trim as the airplane stabilizes in the climb.

For a go-around from final approach you may also have to think about retracting the landing gear and raising the flaps, as shown in Figure 4-13. As a general rule, the retraction of gear and flaps should only be initiated on a go-around after a positive rate of climb has been established.

A greater pitch/yaw tendency can be expected with the large power increase in the go-around.

Descending at a Particular Rate

Airspeed in the descent at constant power is controlled with small pitch attitude changes, using the ASI as the primary performance instrument. Rate of descent is shown directly on the VSI, or can be determined from the clock and altimeter.

Descent at a constant airspeed and a specific rate of descent can be achieved by adjusting the power and the pitch attitude suitably. Again, it is the interplay of power and attitude that determines the performance of the airplane. If the rate of descent is too great, it can be reduced by raising the pitch attitude and increasing power to maintain the same airspeed. Retrimming to relieve steady control pressures is necessary once the airplane has stabilized in the new descent.

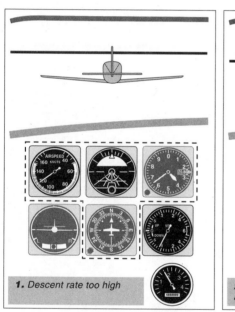
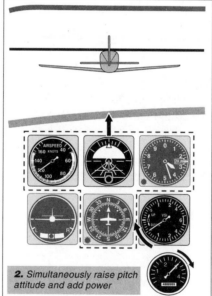

Figure 4-14. Reducing the rate of descent

Conversely, the rate of descent can be increased by simultaneously lowering the pitch attitude, and reducing power to maintain the same airspeed.

If the pilot cannot reduce power because the throttle is already fully closed, then the rate of descent can be increased by other means:

- by lowering the pitch attitude and accepting a higher airspeed; or
- by increasing drag, which can be achieved by lowering flaps, lowering the landing gear, or by deploying spoilers or speed brakes if fitted.

Note: The rate of descent can also be increased with a forward slip maneuver, but this is definitely not a recommended procedure for IFR.

The Precision Approach

While the precision instrument approach will be fully covered in the latter stages of your instrument training, it is appropriate to introduce it here in our consideration of the straight descent maneuver.

The precision approach is a very accurate instrument descent toward the touchdown zone on a runway. If the runway is not sighted by a certain minimum altitude, then a go-around is made; if the runway is sighted and the airplane is in a position to land, then a landing may be made.

The most common precision approach in instrument flying is achieved using the electronic **instrument landing system (ILS)** that provides:

- course guidance (left or right of a **localizer** path aligned along the extended runway centerline); and
- approach slope guidance (referred to as the **glideslope** even though the airplane will not in fact be gliding, but in a powered descent).

The ILS glideslope is an inclined surface, typically 3° or 1:20 to the horizontal, that intersects the runway in the touchdown zone, usually about 1000 feet in from the threshold. It is generally intercepted 1500 feet to 3000 feet above the touchdown zone elevation, some 5 to 10 nm from the airport and in line with the runway.

The position of the glideslope relative to the airplane is displayed to the pilot in the cockpit on an instrument associated with the VHF-NAV radio, the VOR/ILS cockpit display.

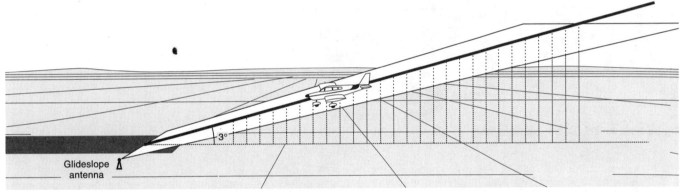

Figure 4-15. The glideslope onto the touchdown zone of a runway

Maintaining the glideslope at the desired airspeed during an instrument approach is one of an instrument pilot's major tasks, but it is quite similar to maintaining straight-and-level cruise flight.

Hold the glideslope with elevator.
Hold airspeed with power.

In both cases, the pilot is trying to direct the airplane along a particular surface (horizontal for level flight, sloping for the approach) while maintaining a particular airspeed. The easiest control technique in both cases is:

- hold the glideslope (or altitude) with elevator, making small pitch changes; and
- hold the airspeed with throttle.

As always, power and attitude (controlled by throttle and elevator respectively) determine the performance of the airplane. Often a change in one will necessitate a change in the other, but it is still easier to separate the functions in your own mind as stated above – maintain glideslope with attitude and airspeed with power.

In a powered descent down an ILS glidepath, it may be necessary to readjust the power setting as altitude decreases if a constant power is desired. For instance, at a constant throttle setting, the manifold pressure will tend to increase as the airplane descends into denser air during final approach. To maintain the desired power and avoid an unwanted speed increase, it may be necessary to close the throttle a little. The need for this will be detected in your scan of the flight instruments, however, it is always an advantage to be fore-warned.

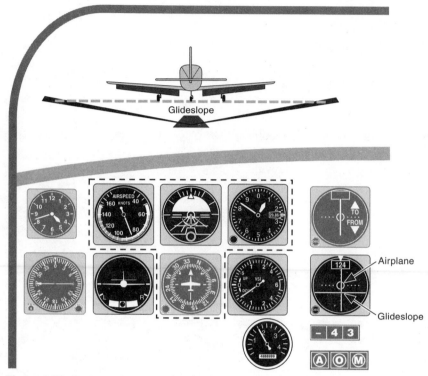

Figure 4-16. An accurate approach to land

1. Any changes in pitch attitude should be made with reference to the _____.
➤ AI

2. Any changes in pitch attitude made on the AI will be reflected on the _____.
➤ altimeter, VSI and ASI

3. What instrument is primary for pitch attitude when transitioning from level flight into a climb?
➤ AI

4. What instrument is primary for power when transitioning from level flight into a climb?
➤ power indicator

5. The ball is kept centered using _____.
➤ rudder pressure

6. If the ball is out to the right, (left/right) rudder pressure is required.
➤ right

7. The primary performance guide that the pitch attitude selected on the AI is correct during a climb or descent is the _____.
➤ ASI

8. If the airspeed in the climb is too low, then you should _____.
➤ lower the nose slightly

9. If the airspeed in the climb is too high, then you should _____.
➤ raise the nose slightly

10. If the airspeed in the descent is too low, then you should _____.
➤ lower the nose slightly

11. If the airspeed in the descent is too high, then you should _____.
➤ raise the nose slightly

12. Any changes in bank attitude should be made on the _____.
➤ AI

13. The requirement for a bank attitude change to achieve straight flight is indicated on the _____.
➤ heading indicator

14. In a straight climb or descent, the primary performance guide that the bank attitude selected on the AI is correct is the _____.
➤ heading indicator

15. What are the supporting bank instruments in a straight climb or descent?
➤ AI and turn coordinator

16. To enter a climb at the same speed the airplane is flying level at:
    (a) add power and raise the nose simultaneously.
    (b) add power first, and then raise the nose.
    (c) raise the nose first, and then add power.
➤ (a)

17. While cruising at 160 knots you wish to establish a climb at 130 knots. When entering the climb, it is proper to make the initial pitch change by increasing back elevator pressure until the:
    (a) ASI reaches 130 knots.
    (b) AI, ASI and VSI indicate a climb.
    (c) VSI reaches the predetermined rate of climb.
    (d) AI shows the approximate pitch attitude appropriate for the 130 knot climb.
➤ (d)

18. To enter a descent at the same speed the airplane is flying level at:

    (a) reduce power first, and then lower the nose.

    (b) reduce power and lower the nose simultaneously.

    (c) lower the nose first, and then reduce power.

➤ (b)

19. When making significant pitch attitude changes, you should refer to the _____.

➤ AI

20. As power is increased to enter a 500 fpm rate of climb in straight flight, the primary instruments for pitch, bank and power are respectively _____.

➤ AI, HI and power indicator

21. The best rate of climb speed found in the Pilot's Operating Handbook is written as _____.

➤ V_Y

22. Rate of climb or descent can be seen on the _____, or it can be calculated using the _____ and the _____.

➤ VSI, clock and altimeter

23. Approximately what percentage of the indicated vertical speed should be used to determine the number of feet to lead the level-off from a climb or descent to a specific altitude?

➤ 10%

24. If you are descending at 500 fpm to a new cruising level of 6000 feet, you should start raising the pitch attitude at approximately _____ feet.

➤ 6050 feet

25. When climbing above 18,000 feet MSL, the pressure window of the altimeter should be set to _____.

➤ 29.92 in.Hg

26. When operating below 18,000 feet MSL, the Kollsman window of the altimeter should be set to _____.

➤ local altimeter setting

Turning 5

The aim of a turn is to change heading. This is achieved by banking the airplane and tilting the lift force produced by the wings. The horizontal component of the tilted lift force (known as the *centripetal force*) pulls the airplane into the turn.

If altitude is to be maintained, the magnitude of the tilted lift force must be increased so that its vertical component will equal the weight. This is achieved with back pressure on the control column to increase the angle of attack (raising the pitch attitude), thereby increasing the lift generated by the wings.

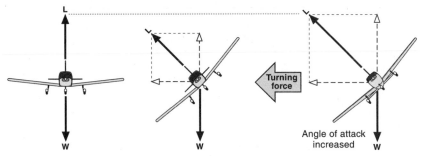

Figure 5-1. Lift must be increased to maintain altitude in a level turn

A consequence of the increased lift is increased induced drag. The airplane will therefore slow down unless power is applied. In a medium turn, the loss of a few knots is usually acceptable, and so additional power is not normally applied. The airspeed loss is regained fairly quickly once the airplane is returned to straight-and-level flight.

Bank Angle and Rate of Turn

The **standard rate** of turn in instrument flying is 3° change of heading per second (known as *rate 1* in some countries). At standard rate, it will therefore take 30 seconds to turn through a heading change of 90°, 1 minute to turn through 180°, and 2 minutes to turn through 360°. The standard rate of turn is marked on most turn coordinators, which may also be labeled 2 MIN. A half-standard-rate turn would, of course, be at 1.5° per second, and a complete 360° turn would take 4 minutes at this rate.

The rate of turn is a function of airspeed and bank angle—a higher airspeed requiring a greater bank angle to achieve the same rate of turn. A quick method of estimating the bank angle required for a standard-rate turn is:

Divide airspeed by 10, then add one-half the answer.

At an airspeed of 100 KIAS, the bank angle for a standard-rate turn is:

$$\frac{100}{10} + \left(\frac{1}{2} \times \frac{100}{10}\right) = 15° \, bank \, angle$$

At 140 KIAS airspeed, the required bank angle is:

$$\frac{140}{10} + \left(\frac{1}{2} \times \frac{140}{10}\right) = 21° \, bank \, angle$$

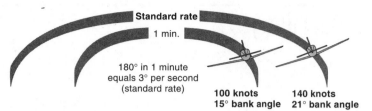

Figure 5-2. A standard-rate turn requires a steeper bank at a higher airspeed

It is permissible to use a turn in excess of standard rate, but it is strongly recommended not to exceed a bank angle of 30° in instrument conditions (although your instructor may use steep turns during your training to give you practice in coordination of eyes, hands and feet).

Do not exceed a bank angle of 30° in normal instrument flight.

A Constant-Speed Turn. At a constant airspeed, the greater the bank angle, the tighter the turn (the smaller the radius of turn) and the greater the rate of turn (in degrees per second).

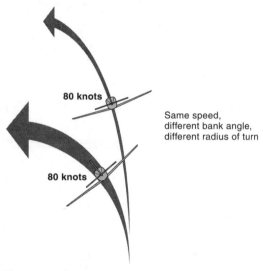

Figure 5-3. Same speed, steeper bank angle → tighter turn and higher rate of turn

A Constant-Radius Turn. To fly a turn of the same radius at a higher speed requires a greater bank angle. This is one reason why you should slow down for any tight maneuvering in a terminal area, so that tight turns are possible without excessive bank angles.

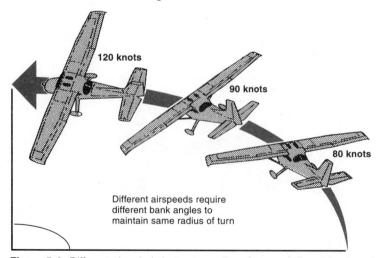

Figure 5-4. Different airspeeds but same radius of turn → different bank angles

A Constant-Bank Turn. An airplane in a 30° banked turn will travel around different circular paths depending on the airspeed.

At low speed, the turn is tighter (the radius of turn is less) than at high speed, and the rate of turn is greater.

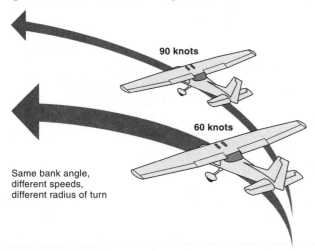

90 knots

60 knots

Same bank angle,
different speeds,
different radius of turn

Figure 5-5. Different speeds, same bank angle → different radius of turn

Be In Trim Before Commencing The Turn

A turn is usually commenced from straight flight. It can be flown more accurately if the airplane, prior to being banked, is exactly on altitude, on speed, and in trim.

There is no requirement to retrim during the turn, since it is only a transient maneuver and the airplane will most likely be returned to straight flight quickly. If the airplane is trimmed in the turn, then it will require retrimming when returned to straight flight.

In Visual Conditions, Keep a Good Lookout

A good lookout is essential in visual flight but, in clouds with zero visibility, there is little point. A surprising amount of a typical instrument flight occurs in visual conditions, however, and a good lookout then shows good airmanship.

During training, your instructor will act as *safety pilot* and maintain a good lookout for you.

Roll-In and Roll-Out Rate

All instrument flying should be smooth and unhurried. Turns should be entered at a comfortable rate with coordinated aileron and rudder pressure, with time allowed to check the attitude indicator for bank angle and to keep the ball centered.

As training progresses, and the rate of scanning and interpreting the instruments increases, roll-in and roll-out of turns can occur at a faster rate.

Strive to achieve a fairly constant rate of roll-in and roll-out for all turns, which will make it easier to judge when to commence the roll-out to a precise heading.

Remember that the three fundamentals of instrument flying are:
- instrument cross-check (scan);
- instrument interpretation; and
- aircraft control.

Part (a)
The Medium Level Turn

Rolling Into a Medium Level Turn

Note the position of the miniature airplane on the attitude indicator in steady straight-and-level flight before entering the turn, and then roll into the turn at a comfortable roll rate with coordinated aileron and rudder pressure. At the desired bank angle on the AI, the roll-in can be stopped by neutralizing the ailerons and keeping the ball centered with rudder pressure, and then holding a steady bank angle. The primary bank instrument when rolling into (and out of) a turn is the AI.

Early in the roll-in, the pitch attitude can remain the same as before entry but, as the bank angle increases, an altitude loss will be seen on the VSI and altimeter unless the pitch attitude is raised slightly with back pressure.

The VSI is the best guide in smooth air for correct pitch attitude in the level turn, since it will show a tendency to depart from altitude before the altimeter registers any change. In rough air, however, the VSI fluctuates and is of less value, the altimeter then becoming the primary guide to correct pitch attitude.

The primary bank instrument when rolling into (and out of) a turn is the AI.

The VSI is the best guide in smooth air for correct pitch attitude in the level turn. In rough air the altimeter should guide you.

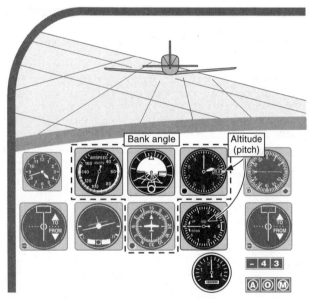

Figure 5-6. Rolling into a level turn

Maintaining a Medium Level Turn

Bank angle and pitch attitude are maintained on the AI, which is a control instrument, and the ball is kept centered. The **bank pointer** on the AI will give an accurate indication of the degrees of bank angle.

Turning performance can be confirmed on the turn coordinator, which is graduated to indicate a standard-rate turn of 3° per second. While the AI was the primary bank instrument when rolling into the turn, once in the turn the turn coordinator becomes the primary performance instrument to confirm that the bank angle is correct. Small bank angle corrections, when required, can be made on the AI using aileron.

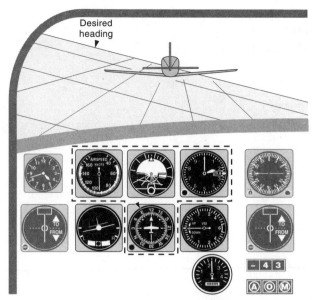

Figure 5-7. Maintaining a level turn on instruments

There is generally no need to check the heading indicator until well established in the turn and approaching the desired heading (which, for a 90° change of heading at standard rate, will be 30 seconds away).

Confirm **vertical performance** on the VSI and altimeter, making any small pitch corrections on the AI using elevator. In general, a slight back pressure will be required, increasing as the bank angle becomes steeper. The altimeter is the primary performance instrument in the level turn to ensure that pitch attitude is correct.

Confirm that the turn is **coordinated** with the ball, and keep it centered with rudder pressure. The position of the ball in the inclinometer indicates the quality of the turn—a high quality turn has the ball right in the center throughout the maneuver. Confirm **airspeed** with the airspeed indicator and be prepared for a loss of several knots. If a constant airspeed is required, then increase power slightly.

It is difficult to hold bank angle, altitude and balance perfectly, but a good instrument pilot will notice trends quickly and act to correct them. Aim for perfection, and at least stay well within the limits of ±5° bank angle and ±100 feet of altitude during the turn.

Remember that the **performance instruments** (VSI, altimeter, turn coordinator) may indicate a need for change, but that these changes should be made with reference to the **control instruments**. In particular, use the attitude indicator for any pitch attitude or bank angle changes. The throttle can be used for airspeed control in the level turn, if required.

Rolling Out of a Level Turn

Commence the roll-out a few degrees before the desired heading. A suitable lead is by one half of the bank angle. For example, if the bank angle in the turn is 20°, commence roll-out 10° before reaching the desired heading. Aim to level the wings just as the desired heading is reached.

Roll out of the turn at a comfortable roll rate with coordinated aileron and rudder pressure. The **attitude indicator** is monitored for control of the bank angle during the early part of the roll-out, with the **heading indicator** being monitored to check that the desired heading is being achieved. The primary bank instrument when rolling out of (or into) a turn is the AI.

If airspeed is decreased in a turn, the lift generated will be less. Altitude may be maintained by either decreasing the angle of bank (to restore the vertical component of lift) and/or increasing the angle of attack (to increase the lift generated).
Conversely, if airspeed is increased in a turn, altitude may be maintained by increasing the angle of bank and/or decreasing the angle of attack.

Vertical performance is confirmed on the VSI and altimeter, with small pitch adjustments on the AI to maintain altitude. The back pressure applied on entering the turn can now be released, and the pitch attitude lowered slightly. The primary pitch instrument to confirm that the pitch attitude is correct for level flight, straight or turning, is the altimeter.

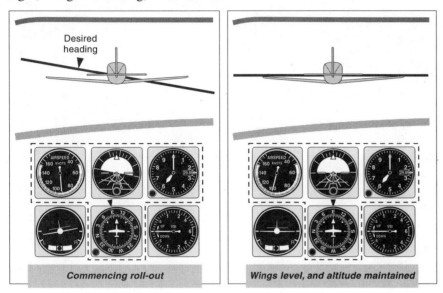

Figure 5-8. Rolling out of a turn

After the roll-out, the scan should revert to the normal straight-and-level scan:

- use the AI to set the pitch attitude and hold the wings level;
- keep the ball centered;

Confirm:

- vertical performance on the VSI and altimeter (hold altitude with elevator);
- directional performance on the heading indicator and turn coordinator (adjust heading with gentle coordinated turns if necessary); and
- monitor airspeed on the ASI (controlling with power if necessary).

The few knots of airspeed that were lost in the turn will gradually return. If additional power was applied in the turn to maintain airspeed, however, it should be removed in the roll-out to avoid an unwanted airspeed increase.

Instrument Turns to a Specific Heading

Turns to a particular heading can be achieved using:

- the heading indicator; or
- timed turns, with the clock and turn coordinator, knowing that standard rate is 3° per second; or
- the magnetic compass.

The primary source of direction information in the airplane is the magnetic compass, but this is an awkard instrument to use, especially when the airplane is turning. Since directional information is very important in a turn, pilots are provided with a more stable instrument, the heading indicator, driven by a gyroscope and not subject to turning errors.

The HI occupies a central position on the instrument panel where it can easily be scanned by the pilot, whereas the magnetic compass is quite remotely located, generally somewhere above the cockpit glare shield near the windshield, not out of sight, but certainly outside the primary scanning area.

Using the Heading Indicator

Unlike the magnetic compass, the most common HI does not automatically align itself with magnetic north (although some, such as the HSI or the remote indicating compass are slaved to north). For its reading to be meaningful, ensure that the heading indicator is realigned with the magnetic compass during steady straight-and-level flight every 10 or 15 minutes.

Before commencing a turn, the HI can be used to decide whether to turn left or right to the new heading. Usually, the turn is made in the shorter direction, but not always. For instance, in a *teardrop turn* carried out in certain instrument maneuvers, the turn is made in the longer direction and exceeds 180°.

Check that the heading indicator is correctly aligned with the magnetic compass at least every 15 minutes.

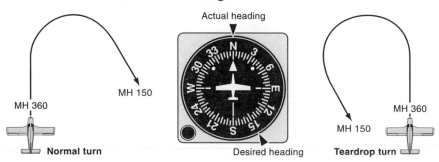

Figure 5-9. Orient yourself, and decide which way to turn

Having decided which way to turn, the HI need not be scanned until the airplane is approaching the desired heading. The roll out should be commenced a few degrees before the desired heading is reached. Anticipate the heading by half the bank angle.

For instance, if the bank angle is 20°, commence rolling out 10° before the required heading is reached—the roll-out for a right turn to MH 150 commencing as the HI passes through MH 140. Aim to level the wings just as the desired heading is reached.

Settle into normal straight flight, checking direction on the HI, and altitude on the VSI and altimeter. Hold the desired heading accurately by making small coordinated turns as needed. Aim for perfection, and certainly stay within the limits of 5° of heading. If aiming to maintain airspeed, stay within 10 knots.

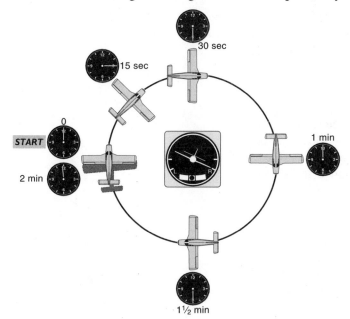

Figure 5-10. Timed turns with the clock and turn coordinator can be very accurate

Timed Turns Using Turn Coordinator and Clock

Timed turns are useful in instrument flying, and it is a good habit to develop the skill of estimating time to turn. Standard rate is 3° per second, so a 45° turn at standard rate will take 15 seconds. A **standard-rate turn** is achieved at a particular bank angle dependent on airspeed (airspeed/10 + $\frac{1}{2}$ the answer—so that 15° bank angle will be required at 100 knots), and can be monitored on the turn coordinator (or turn indicator).

A 15° change of heading at standard rate will therefore require $\frac{15}{3} = 5$ seconds (not allowing for roll-in and roll-out), 30° will take 10 seconds, 45° will take 15 seconds, 90° will take 30 seconds, 180° will take 1 minute, and 360° will take 2 minutes. By establishing a standard-rate turn on the turn coordinator and measuring the time on a clock, accurate turns can be made without reference to the HI or magnetic compass.

It is usual to use standard-rate turns in instrument flying but, especially if the heading change required is only small, half standard rate on the turn coordinator could be used, in which case the heading would change at only 1.5° per second, a 12° heading change requiring 8 seconds.

To carry out a standard-rate timed turn:

1. Calculate heading change and divide by 3 (a right turn from MH340 to MH100 is 120° change at 3° per second = $\frac{120}{3}$ seconds = 40 seconds); and

2. Start the stopwatch or note the reading of the secondhand (say against 12, 3, 6 or 9 to make it easier), and roll into the turn with the coordinated use of aileron and rudder, achieving the estimated bank angle for a standard-rate turn.

3. Confirm turning performance is standard rate on the turn coordinator, and make slight adjustments to bank angle on the AI if required. Confirm vertical performance on the VSI and altimeter. Keep the ball centered with rudder.

4. Commence the roll-out when the second hand reaches the calculated number of seconds. If the roll-in and roll-out rates are approximately the same, then they will compensate each other, and will not require consideration.

5. At the end of the timed turn, with the wings level and the ball centered, check heading on the heading indicator, or on the magnetic compass once it settles down. Make minor adjustments to heading with gentle coordinated turns.

Calibration of the Turn Coordinator

The accuracy of the turn coordinator can be checked by banking the airplane until the turn coordinator indicates standard rate precisely, and then timing the rate of actual heading change using the heading indicator and clock. In 10 seconds, if the turn is exactly at standard rate, the heading should change by 30°.

If the airplane only turns through 27° in this time, you know that the turn coordinator is over-reading in that direction, and need to increase bank until the turn coordinator is indicating slightly more than standard rate for a standard-rate turn in fact to occur.

Conversely, if the heading changes say 34° in the 10 seconds, you must decrease bank until the turn coordinator indicates slightly less than standard rate for a standard-rate turn to occur. You can then make allowances for any known peculiarities of your particular turn coordinator.

Using the Magnetic Compass

Since the magnetic compass suffers considerable indication errors in a turn it is the least preferred method of making accurate turns. It can, however, be used to achieve at least an approximate heading, which can then be checked and modified once the compass has settled down in steady, straight flight and the oscillations of the compass card have ceased.

The construction of the magnetic compass is such that, when an airplane is turning (especially through north or south), it will give false indications of magnetic heading. To allow for magnetic compass errors in the northern hemisphere, observe the following:

In the northern hemisphere, undershoot north and overshoot south. In the southern hemisphere, overshoot north and undershoot south.

- When turning to northerly headings, roll out when the magnetic compass indicates approximately 30° before the desired heading (undershoot on north).

- When turning to southerly headings, roll out when the magnetic compass indicates approximately 30° past the desired heading (overshoot on south).

These allowances should be reduced when turning to headings well removed from north and south (in fact when turning to east or west, no allowance at all need be made).

Note: In the southern hemisphere, these allowances must be reversed (overshoot on north, and undershoot on south).

Part (b)
Climbing Turns

The technique for flying a climbing turn is the same as for a level turn, except that airspeed (rather than altitude) is maintained. This makes the ASI an important performance guide to the correct pitch attitude in the climbing turn.

Rolling Into a Climbing Turn

Note the position of the miniature airplane relative to the horizon on the AI, and then roll into the turn with coordinated aileron and rudder until the estimated bank angle is reached.

Monitor the ASI, and be prepared to lower the pitch attitude slightly to maintain a constant climbing airspeed. There will be a natural tendency for the airplane to drop its nose when it is banked, so (even though the pitch attitude in the climbing turn is slightly lower than when the wings are level) slight back pressure may have to be applied to prevent the nose dropping too far.

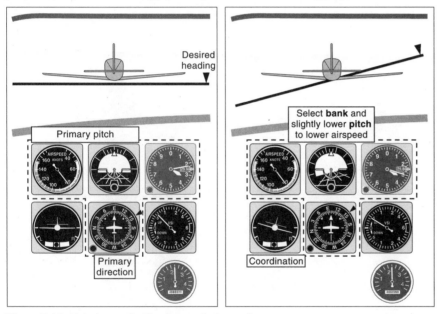

Figure 5-11. Entering a climbing turn on instruments

Maintaining a Climbing Turn

The AI is used to maintain bank angle and pitch attitude, with the ball kept centered with rudder pressure. Airspeed is monitored on the ASI and, if the airspeed is slightly lower than desired, the pitch attitude should be lowered slightly on the AI. The ASI is the primary performance indicator in the climb that correct pitch attitude is being held. Aim for perfect accuracy in maintaining the airspeed, and stay well within the normal flight tolerance of 10 knots, and desired bank angle 5°.

The **vertical performance** in a climbing turn will be less than in the straight climb, indicated by a reduced rate of climb on the VSI, and slower movement of the altimeter needle.

The **turning performance** can be monitored on the turn coordinator, and the bank angle adjusted with reference to the AI to achieve the desired rate of turn.

Keep the ball centered with rudder—this may require a reduced or an increased rudder pressure on a particular pedal compared with that in the straight climb. The heading indicator should be brought increasingly into the scan as the desired heading is approached.

Rolling Out of a Climbing Turn

As the desired heading on the HI is approached, roll out of the bank with coordinated aileron and rudder, aiming to level the wings on the AI just as heading is reached. Monitor airspeed on the ASI, and select a slightly higher pitch attitude on the AI to maintain climbing airspeed. The heading should be within 10° and the airspeed within 10 knots, but you should aim for much better accuracy than this.

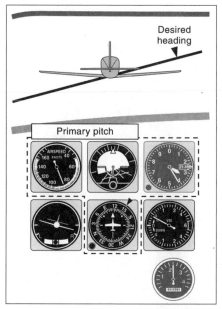

Figure 5-12. Maintaining a climbing turn   **Figure 5-13.** Rolling out of a climbing turn

Part (c)
Descending Turns

The technique for flying a descending turn is the same as for a level turn, except that airspeed (rather than altitude) is maintained. This makes the ASI an important performance guide to the correct pitch attitude.

Rolling Into a Descending Turn

Note the position of the miniature airplane relative to the horizon on the AI, and then roll into the turn with coordinated aileron and rudder until the desired bank angle is reached.

Monitor the ASI and be prepared to lower the pitch attitude slightly to maintain a constant descent airspeed.

There will be a natural tendency for the airplane to drop its nose when it is banked, so (even though the pitch attitude in the descending turn is slightly lower than in the straight descent) slight back pressure may have to be applied to stop the nose dropping too far.

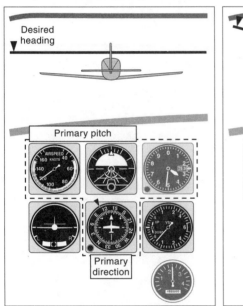 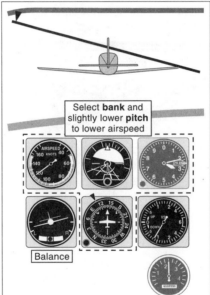

Figure 5-14. Entering a descending turn

Maintaining a Descending Turn

The AI is used to maintain bank angle and pitch attitude, with the ball kept centered with rudder pressure. Airspeed is monitored on the ASI and, if the airspeed is slightly lower than desired, the pitch attitude should be lowered on the AI. If the airspeed is slightly high, then the pitch attitude should be raised.

The ASI is the primary performance indicator that correct pitch attitude is being maintained in the descent.

The **vertical performance** of the airplane can be monitored on the VSI, and altimeter. An increased rate of descent in a descending turn is to be expected but, if desired, this can be reduced by the addition of power and the selection of a slightly higher pitch attitude.

The **turning performance** can be monitored on the turn coordinator, with the bank angle being altered with reference to the AI to achieve the desired rate of turn. The ball is kept centered with rudder pressure. The heading indicator should be brought increasingly into the scan as the desired heading is approached.

Rolling Out of a Descending Turn

As the desired heading on the HI is approached, roll out of the bank with coordinated aileron and rudder, aiming to level the wings on the AI just as heading is reached. Monitor airspeed on the ASI, and select a slightly higher pitch attitude on the AI to maintain descent airspeed. The roll out should be within 10° of the desired heading, but aim for perfection and roll out right on the heading.

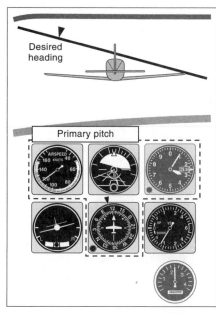

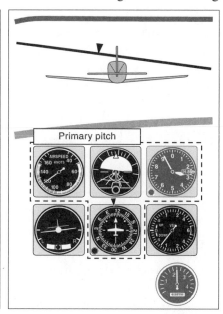

Figure 5-15. Maintaining a descending turn

Figure 5-16. Rolling out of a descending turn

Part (d)
Steep Turns

A typical turn in instrument flight is made at standard rate. At 120 knots, this can be achieved with a bank angle of 18°. When required, turns at greater than standard rate may be used in instrument conditions, but do not exceed a bank angle of 30°. Any turn made on instruments at a bank angle greater than 30° is considered a steep turn.

It is poor airmanship to exceed a 30° bank angle in normal IFR operations, since the required coordination of hands, eyes and feet makes accurate instrument flying more difficult. The end result, if it gets out of hand, could be a spiral dive. Steep turns under instrument conditions with an instructor on board, however, can be good practice in:

- improving basic flying skills;
- speeding up the scan rate; and
- recovering from flight attitudes neither usual, nor desirable, in normal instrument flight (see Chapter 6, *Unusual Attitudes*).

The Steep Level Turn

Tilting the lift force as the airplane banks will reduce its vertical component. Back pressure on the control column is therefore required to increase the angle of attack of the wings and increase the magnitude of the lift force so that its vertical component will still balance the weight and avoid a loss of altitude (monitored on the VSI and altimeter).

The load factor (lift/weight) increases significantly in a steep turn—two consequences being a greater g-loading on the airplane and pilot, and a higher stalling speed.

The increased angle of attack in a steep turn means not only increased lift, but also greatly increased drag. Airspeed will decrease significantly unless additional power is applied (with airspeed monitored on the ASI).

A positive application of power in the early stages of a steep turn is particularly important, since the higher load factor means an increased stall speed (a 40% increase at 60° bank angle).

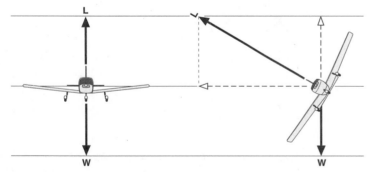

Stall speed increases by 40% in a 60° banked turn.

Maintain airspeed with added power.

Figure 5-17. A steep turn requires increased lift to maintain altitude, and increased power to maintain airspeed

Prior to Entering a Steep Level Turn. Achieve straight-and-level flight at the desired altitude and airspeed, and be in trim. Note the heading on the heading indicator, and decide which way you will turn and to what heading. Ask the safety pilot to check outside for other aircraft.

Rolling Into a Steep Level Turn

Roll into the steep turn with coordinated aileron and rudder the same as you would for a medium turn except that, as the bank angle increases through 30°:

- progressively increase back pressure to raise the pitch attitude on the AI to maintain altitude; and
- progressively add power to maintain airspeed.

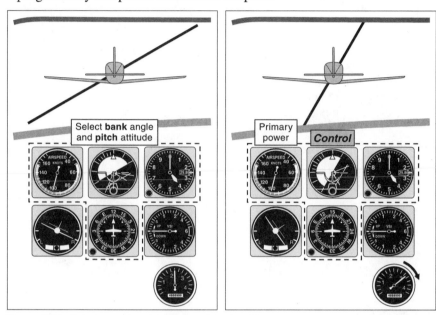

Figure 5-18. Entering and maintaining a steep level turn

Maintaining a Steep Level Turn

Increase your scan rate of the instruments as the turn steepens, to cope with all of the variables. The secret of an accurate steep level turn on instruments is to:

- have a good scan;
- hold the correct bank angle and pitch attitude on the attitude indicator; and
- maintain airspeed with power.

The secret of an accurate steep level turn on instruments is to have a good scan, hold the correct bank angle and pitch attitude on the attitude indicator and maintain airspeed with power.

Bank Angle and Coordination

The required accuracy is to hold bank angle (for instance 45°) ±5°, altitude ±100 feet, airspeed ±10 knots, and to roll out of a 180° or 360° turn within 10° of the specified heading. The steep turn in Figure 5-18 is 60° bank angle.

Control of the bank angle and balance is achieved with coordinated use of aileron and rudder, with reference to the attitude indicator and the ball. The turn coordinator is of little use in a steep turn, since the turn rate will be well in excess of standard rate. However it is still useful as an indication of the direction of the turn, left or right. The desired bank angle is held on the AI.

Pitch Control

Pitch control is more difficult to achieve than bank control, because of the considerably increased back pressure required (and for some people, the slightly unpleasant g-forces that increase as back pressure is applied). The pitch attitude is higher in the steep turn than in level flight. Vertical performance can be monitored on the VSI and altimeter to ensure that altitude is

The altimeter is the primary performance indicator for pitch attitude.

being maintained. The primary performance indicator that the pitch attitude held on the AI is correct is the altimeter, supported by the VSI.

Airspeed

Airspeed control is achieved with the throttle. If insufficient additional power is applied, then airspeed can diminish quite rapidly. The power should be increased progressively as the bank angle steepens during the roll-in, and the pilot should imagine that there is a direct link from the airspeed indicator to his hand on the throttle—any hint of an airspeed loss requiring an immediate increase in power. The primary performance indicator for power in level flight (including turns) is the ASI. There is no need to monitor the power indicator directly, however, unless there is a possibility of exceeding engine limitations.

The ASI is the primary performance indicator for power in level flight.

Altitude

Loss of altitude will result if insufficient back pressure is applied as the steep turn is entered, the nose will drop, the VSI and altimeter will indicate a rapid loss of altitude, and the ASI will indicate an increasing airspeed. Simply increasing back pressure at a steep bank angle when the nose has already dropped will only tighten the turn without raising the nose.

The recommended technique if altitude is lost is:
* reduce bank angle with aileron;
* raise pitch attitude with elevator (back pressure); and
* re-apply bank.

If altitude is being gained:
* relax some of the back pressure, and lower the pitch attitude slightly; and/or
* steepen the bank angle slightly.

Extreme cases of nose-high or nose-low attitudes are considered in Chapter 6, *Unusual Attitudes*. They can result from a poorly flown steep turn, especially under instrument conditions, and especially when you have a slow scan rate or are not prepared to exert your authority over the airplane and make it do exactly what you want.

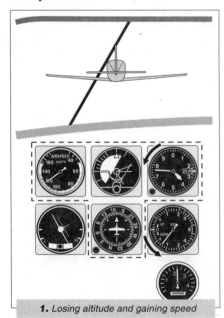

1. *Losing altitude and gaining speed*

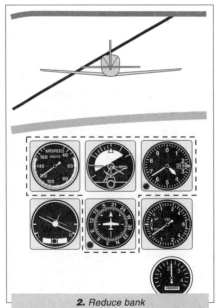

2. *Reduce bank*

Figure 5-19 (continued on page 127)

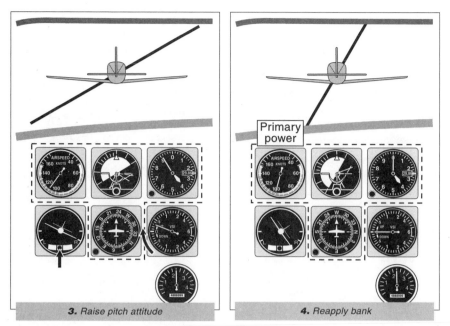

3. *Raise pitch attitude*   **4.** *Reapply bank*

Figure 5-19. Regaining an altitude loss in a steep level turn

Rolling Out of a Steep Level Turn

If the aim is to roll out from a steep turn to a particular heading, then approximately 30° lead should be allowed because of the high rate of turn. Roll out of the steep turn using coordinated aileron and rudder.

Gradually release the back pressure on the control column and lower the pitch attitude on the AI to maintain altitude (as monitored on VSI and altimeter). Gradually reduce power to maintain the desired airspeed (as monitored on ASI).

You should roll out to within 10° of the specified heading and, if not exactly on it, make small corrections to be as accurate as possible. Airspeed should be within 10 knots and altitude within 100 feet.

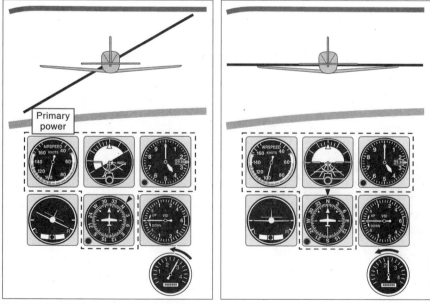

Figure 5-20. Rolling out of a steep level turn

Steep Descending Turns

The steep descending turn is never flown in normal instrument flight operations, but it may be used during your training (with your flight instructor on board as safety pilot) as a practice maneuver to improve coordination. Note that there is no steep climbing turn, since this is beyond the performance capability of most training aircraft, and a useful rate of climb could not be maintained.

It is usual to allow airspeed to increase in a steep descending turn in order to maintain an adequate safety margin over the stalling speed (which increases during a turn). Suitable speed increases for an aircraft that stalls at 50 knots straight-and-level are:

- 10 knots for a 45° bank in a steepdescending turn; and
- 20 knots for a 60° bank in a steep descending turn.

Rolling Into a Steep Descending Turn

From a steady descent, roll on bank with coordinated aileron and rudder. Keep the ball centered with whatever rudder pressure is required; in a gliding turn, there will be more rudder pressure required one way compared to the other because of the lack of a significant slipstream over the tail fin.

Lower the pitch attitude slightly on the AI, using elevator to maintain the desired nose position to achieve the higher airspeed. The nose will tend to drop in a descending turn and so, even though the pitch attitude on the attitude indicator will be lower to achieve a higher airspeed, some back pressure on the control column will be needed to stop the nose dropping too far.

Maintaining a Steep Descending Turn

Increase your scan rate as the turn steepens to cope with all of the variables. Hold the desired pitch attitude and bank angle with reference to the AI, and monitor the ASI closely.

Control bank angle with coordinated use of aileron and rudder. Apply whatever rudder pressure is required to keep the ball centered. Control pitch attitude on the AI with elevator to achieve the desired airspeed. The ASI is the primary performance indicator that pitch attitude is correct in any descent.

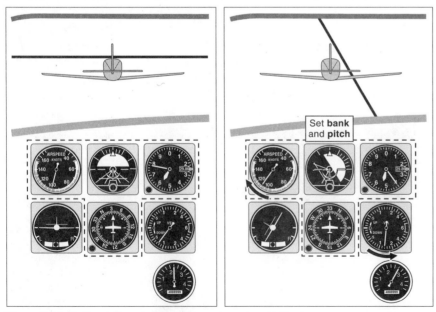

Figure 5-21. Rolling into and maintaining a steep descending turn

If the pitch attitude is too low and the airspeed becomes excessive:

- reduce the bank angle on the AI using ailerons;
- raise the pitch attitude on the AI with elevator to reduce airspeed; and
- re-apply the bank.

If the bank angle is not reduced, then simply applying back pressure may only serve to tighten the turn without decreasing airspeed, and the g-loading may increase beyond acceptable limits. A spiral dive can result if pitch attitude, bank angle and airspeed are not kept within acceptable limits.

The rate of descent in a steep descending turn will increase significantly, not only because of the lower pitch attitude for the higher airspeed, but also because the tilting of the lift force reduces its vertical component.

If desired, the rate of descent can be controlled with power, and monitored on the VSI and altimeter. Increasing power, and raising the pitch attitude to maintain airspeed, results in a reduced rate of descent.

Rolling Out of a Steep Descending Turn

With reference to the attitude indicator, roll-off bank with coordinated aileron and rudder, and select the slightly higher pitch attitude with elevator required for the straight descent.

Monitor the ASI and adjust pitch attitude on the AI to achieve the desired airspeed. The ASI is the primary guide to a correct pitch attitude in the descent. If the aim is to roll out to a specific heading, then approximately 30° lead should be allowed because of the rapid rate of turn. The required accuracy is ±10° of the specified heading.

A steep descending turn that is not monitored carefully can result in a spiral dive, an unusual attitude best avoided. How to recover from a spiral dive is discussed in Chapter 6, *Unusual Attitudes*.

✍ Review 5

1. The three fundamental skills of instrument flying are _____.
   ➤ instrument crosscheck (scan), instrument interpretation and aircraft control

2. Bank angle is directly indicated on the _____.
   ➤ attitude indicator

3. Pitch attitude is directly indicated on the _____.
   ➤ attitude indicator

4. Altitude is indicated on the _____.
   ➤ altimeter

5. Heading is indicated on the _____.
   ➤ heading indicator

6. Rate of turn is indicated on the _____.
   ➤ turn coordinator

7. The quality of a turn is indicated by the _____.
   ➤ coordination ball (inclinometer)

8. The normal method of turning an airplane is to (tilt the lift force by banking the airplane/use the rudder).
   ➤ tilt the lift force by banking the airplane

9. The force that causes an airplane to turn is called the (centripetal/centrifugal/horizontal) force.
   ➤ centripetal

10. The (horizontal/vertical) component of the tilted lift force causes an airplane to turn.
    ➤ horizontal

11. The rate of turn at any airspeed depends on the magnitude of the (horizontal/vertical) component of the lift force.
    ➤ horizontal

Turning

12. If altitude is to be maintained in a turn, the magnitude of the lift force must be (increased/decreased).
    ➤ increased

13. If altitude is to be maintained in a turn, the magnitude of the lift force must be increased by (increasing/decreasing) the angle of attack with (forward/neutral/backward) pressure on the control column.
    ➤ increasing, backward

14. If altitude is to be maintained in a turn, the magnitude of the vertical component of the lift force, compared to straight-and-level flight, must be (increased/decreased/the same).
    ➤ the same

15. If the airplane is banked left and turning left, but the ball is out to the right, the airplane is in a (skidding/coordinated/slipping) turn.
    ➤ skidding

16. If the ball is out to the right, (right/left) rudder pressure is required for flight to be coordinated.
    ➤ right

17. If airspeed is decreased in a turn, altitude may be maintained by either decreasing the angle of (bank/attack) and/or increasing the angle of (bank/attack).
    ➤ decreasing the angle of bank and/or increasing the angle of attack.

18. If airspeed is increased in a turn, altitude may be maintained by either increasing the angle of (bank/attack) and/or decreasing the angle of (bank/attack).
    ➤ increasing the angle of bank and/or decreasing the angle of attack.

19. In instrument flying, the standard rate of turn is _____° per second.
    ➤ 3° per second

20. If a standard rate of turn is maintained, it would take _____ seconds, or _____ minutes, to turn a full 360°.

➤ 120 seconds, 2 minutes

21. If a half standard rate of turn is maintained, it would take _____ minutes to turn a full 360°.

➤ 4 minutes

22. If a standard rate of turn is maintained, it would take _____ seconds to turn 60°.

➤ 20 seconds

23. If a standard rate of turn is maintained, it would take _____ seconds to turn 270°.

➤ 90 seconds

24. If a standard rate of turn is maintained, it would take _____ seconds to turn 45°.

➤ 15 seconds

25. If a standard rate of turn is maintained, it would take _____ seconds to turn right from MH 050 to MH 120.

➤ 23 seconds

26. If a standard rate of turn is maintained, it would take _____ seconds to turn left from MH 050 to MH 120.

➤ 97 seconds

27. If a standard rate of turn is maintained, it would take _____ seconds to turn left from MH 050 to MH 320.

➤ 30 seconds

28. If a half standard rate of turn is maintained, it would take _____ seconds to turn left from MH 050 to MH 320.

➤ 60 seconds

29. Radius of turn can be decreased by (increasing/decreasing) bank angle.

➤ increasing

30. Radius of turn can be decreased by (increasing/decreasing) airspeed.

➤ decreasing

31. Rate of turn can be increased by (increasing/decreasing) bank angle.

➤ increasing

32. Rate of turn can be increased by (increasing/decreasing) airspeed.

➤ decreasing

33. In a constant bank level turn, a decrease in airspeed would (increase/decrease/not alter) the rate of turn, and (increase/decrease/not alter) the radius of turn.

➤ increase, decrease

34. In a constant bank level turn, an increase in airspeed would (increase/decrease/not alter) the rate of turn, and (increase/decrease/not alter) the radius of turn.

➤ decrease, increase

35. What is the initial primary bank instrument when establishing a turn?

➤ the attitude indicator

36. What is the primary bank instrument once a standard-rate turn is established?

➤ the turn coordinator

37. The primary performance instrument for pitch attitude when establishing a level turn is the _____.

➤ altimeter

38. The primary performance instrument for pitch attitude when established in a standard-rate level turn is the _____.

➤ altimeter

39. The primary performance instrument for pitch attitude when rolling out of a level turn is the _____.

➤ altimeter

40. The primary performance instrument for pitch attitude when establishing a climbing turn is the _____.

➤ ASI

41. The primary performance instrument for pitch attitude when established in a standard-rate climbing turn is the _____.

➤ ASI

42. The primary performance instrument for pitch attitude when rolling out of a climbing turn is the _____.

➤ ASI

43. When establishing a level standard-rate turn, the primary instrument for bank is the _____, supported by the _____.

➤ attitude indicator, turn coordinator

44. Once established in a level standard-rate turn, the primary instrument for bank is the _____, supported by the _____.

➤ turn coordinator, attitude indicator

45. The primary performance instrument for pitch attitude when establishing a descending turn is the _____.

➤ ASI

46. The primary performance instrument for pitch attitude when established in a standard-rate descending turn is the _____.

➤ ASI

47. The primary performance instrument for pitch attitude when rolling out of a descending turn is the _____.

➤ ASI

48. The quality of any turn is indicated by the position of the _____.

➤ coordination ball

49. The primary instrument used in a level turn to confirm that the correct power is being used is the _____.

➤ ASI

50. The primary indicator for pitch when changing airspeed in a level turn is the _____, supported by the _____ and the _____.

➤ altimeter, attitude indicator and VSI

51. If an airplane is banked right and turning right, with the coordination ball out to the left, the airplane is in a (skidding/coordinated/slipping) turn, and the remedy is to apply (right/left/the same) rudder pressure.

➤ skidding, left

52. If the airplane is banked right and turning right, with the coordination ball out to the right, the airplane is in a (skidding/coordinated/slipping) turn, and the remedy is to apply (right/left/the same) rudder pressure.

➤ slipping, right

53. If the airplane is banked right and turning right, with the coordination ball centered, the airplane is in a (skidding/coordinated/slipping) turn.

➤ coordinated

Unusual Attitudes

An **unusual attitude** in instrument flying is any attitude not normally used during flight solely on instruments, including:

- bank angles in excess of 30°;
- nose-high attitudes with a decreasing airspeed; and
- nose-low attitudes with an increasing airspeed.

Unusual attitudes are potentially hazardous, so you should learn to recognize and recover from them before they develop into hazardous situations.

An unusual attitude may result from some external influence such as turbulence, or it can be induced by pilot error. For instance, if you become disoriented or confused (Where am I? Which way is up?), or become preoccupied with other cockpit duties (such as radio calls, or the study of charts) at the expense of an adequate scan, or if you overreact or under-react on the controls, interpret the instruments incorrectly, or follow an instrument that has failed (unknown to you), then the airplane may enter an unusual attitude.

Whatever the cause of the unusual attitude, the immediate problem is to recognize exactly what the airplane is actually doing, and to return it safely to normal acceptable flight (generally straight-and-level flight). After the recovery, you should try to determine the cause of the event, to prevent any recurrence.

In unusual attitudes, the physiological sensations may be disconcerting, but do not allow these to influence either the recognition of the attitude, or the subsequent recovery action.

To recover from an unusual attitude you must recognize exactly what the airplane is doing and return it safely to normal acceptable flight.

Recognizing an Unusual Attitude

If you notice any unusual instrument indication or rate of change not expected in the normal gentle instrument flight maneuvers, or if you experience unexpected g-forces or air noise, assume that the airplane could be in (or is about to enter) an unusual attitude.

Increase your scan rate to determine the actual attitude and/or if any instrument has malfunctioned.

If all instruments are functioning normally, then an **excessive bank angle** will be indicated directly on the AI, supported by an excessive rate of turn on the turn coordinator, and a rapidly turning heading indicator. Which way the wings are banked can be determined from the attitude indicator, supported by the turn coordinator. (Be aware that some attitude indicator gyroscopes can tumble and become unusable when the airplane is in an extreme attitude. This is discussed shortly.)

Increase your scan rate to determine the actual attitude and/or if any instrument has malfunctioned.

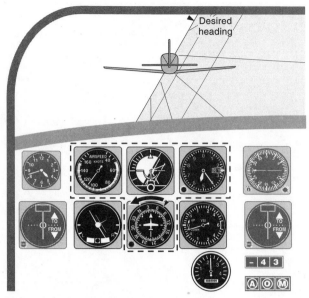

Figure 6-1. An excessive bank angle

A **nose-low attitude** will be indicated by a low pitch attitude on the AI, supported by descent indications on the altimeter and VSI, and an increasing airspeed on the ASI. An excessive bank angle will often lead to a nose-low attitude as well, since the nose tends to drop naturally when the wings are banked. The result could be a spiral dive—an undesirable attitude that, uncorrected, can result in tragedy.

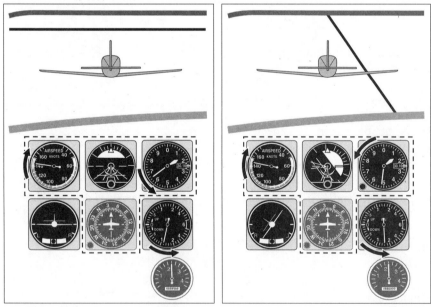

Figure 6-2. Nose-low unusual attitudes

If all instruments are functioning correctly, a **nose-high attitude** will be indicated by a high pitch attitude on the AI, supported by climb indications on the altimeter and VSI, and a decreasing airspeed on the ASI. In an extreme nose-up attitude, however, a stall could result, with the VSI and altimeter indicating a descent, and the ASI a low airspeed.

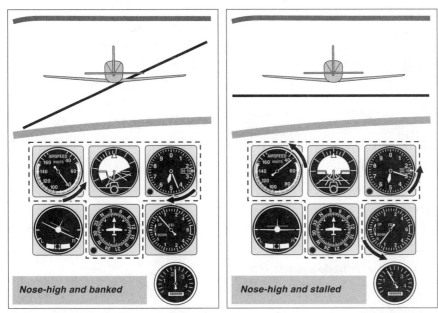

Figure 6-3. Nose-high unusual attitudes

If any instrument has failed, then a cross-check of the others should enable the pilot to isolate it and disregard its indications. For instance, if limits are exceeded the AI gyroscope could tumble and become unusable, which can happen in some aircraft as a result of the unusual attitude.

Similarly, a suction failure in some aircraft can lead to both the AI and HI becoming unusable. (This situation is considered in Chapter 7, *Normal Instrument Flight on a Partial Panel*.) In such a case:

• nose-high or nose-low information can be derived from the ASI, altimeter and VSI; and

• bank information can be derived from the turn coordinator.

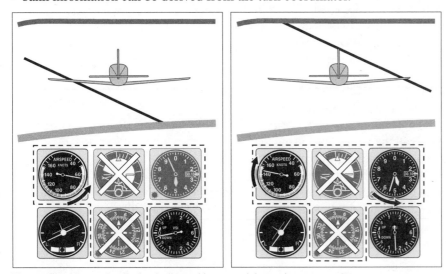

Figure 6-4. Unusual attitudes indicated by a partial panel

In recognizing an unusual attitude, the key points to establish are:

1. Is the airplane nose-high or nose-low?

2. Is it banked?

Recovery from Unusual Attitudes

It is easy for an inexperienced pilot to over-react to an unusual attitude with rapid and excessive control movements, since he does not expect to find himself in an unusual attitude during normal instrument flight. Over-reaction can lead to a worsened situation and, possibly, an overstressed aircraft or an over-revved engine.

Having recognized the unusual attitude for what it is, do not overreact.

One important aspect of instrument training, therefore, is to place the airplane into unusual attitudes on purpose and to develop recovery techniques that allow the pilot, having recognized the nature of the unusual attitude, to return the airplane to normal flight calmly, quickly and safely.

Each unusual attitude, and the recovery, should be practiced:
- in fully visual conditions with external references; then
- on a full panel of instruments; and then
- on a partial panel of instruments.

It is possible that some AIs may tumble during an unusual attitude and become unusable. As a result, the pilot may suddenly have to revert to partial panel techniques quite unexpectedly. For this reason, we have included partial panel recovery techniques in this chapter for ease of reference after your training has been completed.

During your training, however, your instructor may prefer to consider the full panel techniques alone at this stage, and return to the partial panel later.

Nose-Low Attitudes With Increasing Airspeed

If the pitch attitude is too low, then the airspeed will start to increase. In an extreme situation, the airplane may end up in a steep dive, either straight or spiral. If not corrected, the airplane may exceed V_{NE} (the never-exceed speed shown on the ASI as a red line), possibly suffering excessive airframe stress in the dive and in the recovery, if not handled correctly.

To reduce the rate at which the airspeed is increasing, and to avoid unnecessary loss of altitude, reduce the power with the throttle, even closing it completely if necessary. Engine overspeed is possible if this is not done soon enough. As well as reducing the thrust as an accelerating force, the windmilling propeller will increase drag, further reducing the tendency for airspeed to increase.

Reduce power.

A steep bank angle and a nose-low attitude may develop into a spiral dive. If the control column is simply pulled back to raise the nose while the airplane is still steeply banked, then the spiral dive will be tightened without the descent being stopped. Therefore, it is most important to roll the wings level using the AI and the turn coordinator, changing a banked or spiral dive into a straight dive, before raising the pitch attitude to ease the airplane out of the dive.

Level the wings.

Throttling back and rolling the wings toward the level attitude can be done simultaneously, with the ball being kept centered with rudder pressure. Once the wings are level, the airplane will be in a straight dive. Then, to ease the airplane out of the straight dive, smoothly raise the pitch attitude through the level flight position on the AI.

Smoothly raise the pitch attitude to ease the airplane out of the dive.

There is a danger of overstressing the airframe at high airspeeds with large and sudden elevator control movements, hence the instruction to "ease" the airplane out of the dive with firm elevator pressure rather than with sudden and large movements of the elevator control.

On reaching the level flight attitude, the airspeed will "check" (stop increasing), and the altimeter will move from a descent indication to a level (or even climbing) indication.

The VSI initially may be erratic and unusable because of the large change in attitude (possibly showing a reversed reading), although it will settle down fairly quickly to a steady and usable reading once the recovery is completed.

After the initial recovery actions have been taken, the rate of scanning the flight instruments should be increased to ensure that there is no over-controlling, which is a possibility since the control pressures at the start of the recovery (when the airspeed is high) may be quite heavy.

To regain lost altitude after recovering from a spiral dive or a straight dive, apply power, raise the pitch attitude to the climbing attitude and commence a normal climb.

Once in steady straight-and-level flight, the heading indicator should be checked to ensure that it is aligned with the magnetic compass.

The ASI and altimeter needles will stop and reverse direction as the aircraft's pitch attitude passes through level.

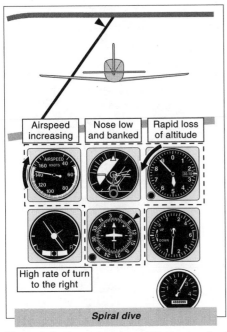
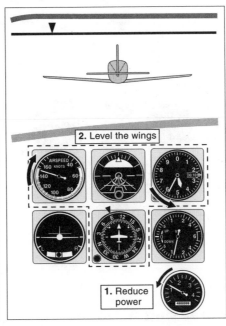
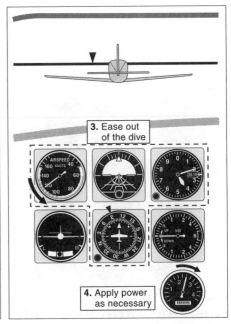

Figure 6-5. Regaining normal flight using the full panel

Note:

1. The airspeed will continue to increase until the aircraft passes through the level flight attitude, when it will check (reverse direction).

2. Unless the wings are fairly level when the pilot raises the pitch attitude with back pressure, the turn coordinator will show an exaggerated turn rate, and the spiral will tighten. This is undesirable. Always roll the wings toward level before easing out of the dive.

3. With the fairly large initial pitch up control movement to achieve the level flight attitude, the VSI may initially show a reverse indication of an initial increase in the rate of descent, even though the reverse is in fact occurring. Excessive attitude corrections can cause VSI indication reversal due to disturbed airflow near the static ports, and so this instrument should be disregarded in the first few seconds following a large pitch change.

Always level the wings before easing out of the dive.

Partial panel. On a partial panel, with no usable information available from the AI, the indication of a nose-low attitude will be an increasing airspeed on the ASI, with secondary information from the altimeter and VSI showing a high and possibly increasing rate of descent, and with bank angle (if any) indicated on the turn coordinator.

The recovery maneuver is the same for visual and instrument flight—both full and limited panel. The only difference is the instruments available to provide information.

On a partial panel:

- reduce power;
- level the wings (using the turn coordinator on a partial panel);
- ease out of the dive (a level pitch attitude is indicated on the partial panel when the airspeed checks, and the altimeter stabilizes).

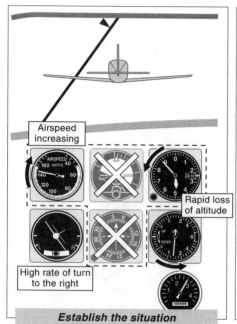
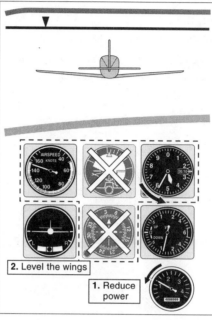
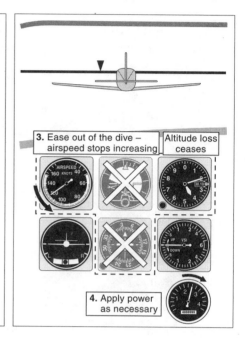

Figure 6-6. Recovery from "nose low and high airspeed" on a partial panel

Nose-High Attitudes With Decreasing Airspeed

If the pitch attitude is too high, then the airspeed will start to decrease.

A high pitch attitude will be shown on the AI, with the ASI indicating a decreasing airspeed, and the altimeter and VSI showing a climb (depending on the power used). Whether the wings are level or not will be shown on the AI and the turn coordinator.

In an extreme situation the airplane may stall, either wings level or with a wing drop, and the altimeter and VSI will show a descent. The nose attitude may be high to begin with, but may drop, depending on the airplane. A vigilant instrument pilot, however, will never allow the airplane to inadvertently approach a stall. Recovery action will have been initiated well ahead of the stall occurring.

The recovery maneuver when the airplane is in a nose-high/airspeed-reducing attitude, but not in or near a stalled condition, is to simultaneously increase power, lower the pitch attitude and roll the wings level on the AI with coordinated use of aileron and rudder. Which wing (if any) is low, is indicated by the AI and the turn coordinator.

Simultaneously: increase power, level the wings, and lower the pitch attitude.

The level flight attitude, when this has been achieved, will be shown directly on the AI. It will also be indicated by the fact that the airspeed stops decreasing. The altimeter reading will also stabilize. Following a large pitch attitude change, however, the VSI may be erratic, and even show a reversed reading, so it should initially be disregarded.

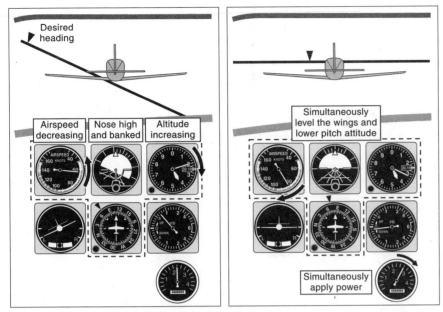

Figure 6-7. Regaining normal flight using the full panel

Having regained normal steady straight flight following recovery from an unusual attitude, check the heading indicator against the magnetic compass, to ensure that it is aligned.

Partial panel. Using a partial panel, with no usable information available from the AI, the indication of a nose-high attitude will be:

• a decreasing airspeed on the ASI, with supporting information from the altimeter and VSI; and with

• direction of bank (if any) indicated on the turn coordinator.

Recovery is the same, with the level pitch attitude being indicated on the ASI when the airspeed is checked and stops decreasing, and the altimeter stabilizes. The wings-level bank attitude is achieved when the wings are level on the turn coordinator.

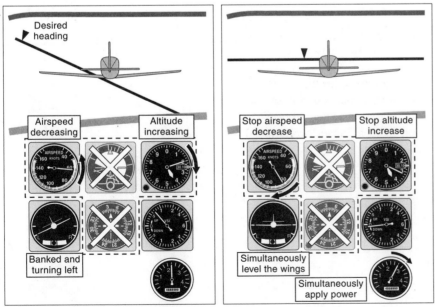

Figure 6-8. "Nose high and decreasing airspeed" on the partial panel

The recovery from an unusual attitude using only a partial panel is a very important technique for an instrument pilot, since it is possible that an instrument such as the AI may gradually fail, rather than suddenly fail, possibly leading a pilot with a faulty scan into an unusual attitude. His first maneuver on a partial panel will then be recovery from an unusual attitude, rather than just maintaining a steady flight condition.

Nose-High, and Approaching the Stall

A "nose-high/airspeed decreasing" situation can ultimately result in a stall. In this situation, it should be possible to regain normal flight, with the maximum loss of altitude being 50 feet or less.

Note: An **accelerated stall** will occur in any phase of flight if the critical angle of attack is exceeded. The 50 feet loss of altitude refers only to a stall recovery in "level" flight.

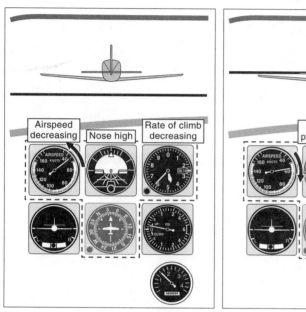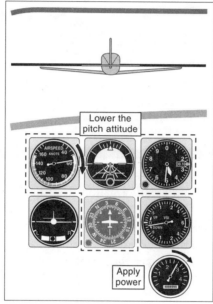

Figure 6-9. Recovering from the incipient stall

There is little danger of overstressing the airframe at low airspeeds with large elevator control movements, because the airplane will stall before any load limits are reached, as shown in the V-n diagram in Figure 6-10.

If the recovery from a nose-high attitude is not followed through correctly and the airplane placed into a normal acceptable flight condition, a nose-low attitude could develop, resulting in either a straight or spiral dive with rapidly increasing airspeed, from which recovery action from a "nose-low/airspeed increasing" situation (as previously discussed) will be required.

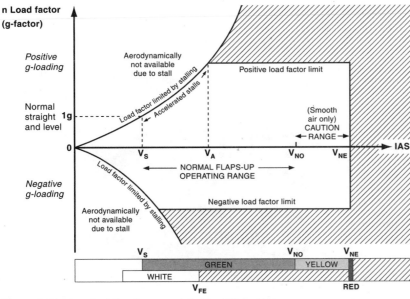

Figure 6-10. A typical V-n diagram related to ASI markings

Partial panel. Using a partial panel, with no usable information available from the AI, the indication of a nose-high attitude approaching the stall will be a decreasing airspeed on the ASI, with secondary information from the altimeter and VSI (which may show a decreasing rate of climb, or even a descent). Any departure from wings level will be indicated by deflections on the turn coordinator.

The recovery procedure is the same. Simultaneously:

- lower the nose to the level pitch attitude (or lower if necessary, with the level pitch attitude on a partial panel being indicated when the airspeed checks and stops decreasing, and the altimeter stabilizes); and
- apply full power.
- Prevent further yaw with rudder and, once a safe flying speed is achieved on the ASI, level the wings on the turn coordinator with coordinated aileron and rudder.

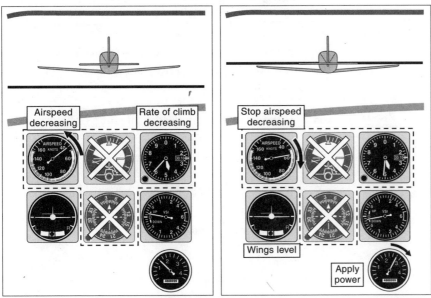

Figure 6-11. Stall recovery on a partial panel

1. What instruments indicate a nose-high or nose-low attitude?

➤ AI, altimeter, VSI and ASI

2. What instruments indicate bank, directly or indirectly?

➤ AI, HI, turn coordinator (and magnetic compass)

3. What is the correct sequence for recovery from a spiraling, nose-low, increasing airspeed, unusual flight attitude?

➤ reduce power, correct the bank attitude, and raise the nose to a level attitude

4. What is the correct sequence for recovery from a nose-high, banked turn, reducing airspeed, unusual flight attitude?

➤ apply power, lower the nose to a level attitude, and correct the bank attitude

5. During recovery from unusual attitudes on a partial panel, level flight is attained the instant:

(a) the horizon bar on the AI is exactly overlapped with the miniature airplane.

(b) a zero rate of climb is indicated on the VSI.

(c) the altimeter and ASI needles stop prior to reversing their direction of movement.

(d) the turn coordinator shows no turn.

➤ (c)

Unusual Attitudes

6. What is the correct sequence for recovery in the following situation?

Figure 1.

➤ a climbing turn to the right—apply power, lower the nose to a level attitude, and correct the bank attitude

7. What is the correct sequence for recovery in the following situation?

Figure 2.

➤ a nose-low spiral to the right—reduce power, level the wings, and raise the nose to a level pitch attitude

8. If the AI malfunctions, the direction of bank can be determined using the _____.

➤ turn coordinator

9. If the AI malfunctions, the pitch attitude can be determined using the _____.

➤ ASI, altimeter and VSI

Normal Instrument Flight on a Partial Panel 7

The three fundamental skills of instrument flying are:
- instrument cross-check (scan);
- instrument interpretation; and
- aircraft control.

For the exercises on the partial panel, one or more of the flight instruments is assumed to have failed. A good scan to begin with if you suspect a failure is the inverted-V scan, which helps you to quickly establish which instrument or system has failed.

Figure 7-1. Use the inverted-V scan to establish a failure

It is possible to cope quite comfortably once you know what instruments are available to you on a partial panel. Even though there is less information available, the airplane flies exactly the same and responds in exactly the same way to any pilot control inputs, regardless of which instruments are or are not working.

Cross-Check Available Instruments

If any instrument has failed, then a cross-check of the other instruments should enable the pilot to isolate it and disregard its indications. The AI is the master instrument, and its loss is perhaps the most difficult to cope with. The AI could be lost as a result of its power source failing (electrical or vacuum), or its gyroscope could tumble and become unusable during an extreme unusual attitude. It may re-erect itself after some time.

Vacuum Failure

In many aircraft, both the AI and HI are powered by suction. Their gyroscopes are driven by an airflow induced through them by the vacuum system. A suction failure could lead to the loss of both of these instruments. This is the common partial panel situation (unusable attitude indicator and heading indicator). In such a case, the aircraft is controlled by reference to the **performance instruments**:

1. Nose-high or nose-low information can be derived from the ASI, altimeter and VSI.

2. Bank information can be derived from the turn coordinator, with the magnetic compass available to supply heading information.

3. Coordination, is shown by the simple ball that never suffers a power failure.

The ASI, altimeter, VSI and magnetic compass may experience some lag or delay before the precise performance is indicated after some attitude or power change, so any new attitude should be held for a few seconds to allow the readings to settle down, before additional control adjustments are made.

Electrical Failure

An electrical failure may make electrically driven instruments unusable. This could include the attitude indicator, the heading indicator and the turn coordinator. An electrical failure could also make the pitot heater unavailable, leading to icing problems with the pitot-static system unless the pilot avoids icing conditions.

Electrical failure will make the radios unusable, unless there is an emergency source of power available (such as the battery). Instrument navigation without VHF-NAV or the ADF is difficult. Radar assistance may be requested, but this requires VHF-COM to be working.

Following an electrical failure, check that the master switch is ON, and check any circuit breakers or fuses for the particular item. Do not interrupt your scan of the operating flight instruments for more than a few seconds at a time. If an electrically powered instrument has indeed failed and cannot be restored, then cross-checking the other instruments will help to compensate for its loss.

Note: The master switch in some aircraft also acts as a circuit breaker, particularly those master switches that are split rocker switches, and so they can be turned off and on to recycle. This may restore full or partial electrical power.

Pitot Tube Blockage

A damaged pitot tube affects the airspeed indicator, as will an iced-up pitot tube, but the use of electric pitot heat in icing conditions generally prevents the occurrence of icing problems in the pitot-static system.

A more serious situation is a pitot cover that has not been removed prior to flight. As well as probably being impossible to remedy in flight, it indicates that the pilot has been derelict in his duties at the preflight stage. Preflight checks of the pitot tube are important. Remove the pitot cover, and check the pitot tube for damage and blockages, possibly by insects.

If the ASI becomes unusable in flight, then all is not lost. Selecting a suitable attitude on the AI and suitable power on the power indicator should result in the desired performance, even though airspeed information is not available.

Static Vent Blockage

A damaged or blocked static system affects the airspeed indicator, the altimeter, and the VSI. If totally blocked, a constant static pressure may be trapped in the system. The altimeter indication will not alter, and the VSI will remain on zero, even when the airplane changes altitude. In clouds or at night, this could be dangerous.

The ASI will indicate an incorrect airspeed. The indicated airspeed is a measure of *dynamic pressure = pitot (total) pressure – static pressure*. Therefore, as the airplane climbs, the too-high static pressure trapped will cause the ASI to read too low. The danger on the climb is to follow the false ASI reading and speed up, possibly exceeding V_{NE}.

Conversely, on descent the trapped static pressure will be too low, causing the ASI to read too fast. The danger on descent is to follow the false ASI indication and slow up, possibly to the point of stalling.

As a safeguard against the undesirable effects of a blocked static system on pressure instrument indications, most aircraft are fitted with an alternate static source in the cockpit. If this is selected by the pilot when a static blockage occurs, or is suspected, then the affected instruments should become usable again.

As a last resort, if both normal and alternate static sources are blocked and unusable (a most unlikely event), the instrument glass of the VSI can be broken to admit cabin static pressure into the whole static system. If you do not damage the inner mechanism of the VSI, it will read in reverse, showing a descent when the aircraft is climbing, and vice versa. This is because the direction of the airflow through the "metered leak" is reversed.

If you do damage the inner workings of the VSI when you break the glass, then the VSI could indicate anything.

Cabin pressure in a nonpressurized aircraft is slightly lower than the external static pressure, because of the venturi effect caused by the airplane's motion through the air. This slightly lower static pressure will cause the altimeter to read 50–100 feet too high, and the ASI to read 5 knots or so too high. The VSI will show a brief climb as the lower static pressure is introduced, but will then settle down and read accurately.

Adapt to Suit the Situation

Whatever instrument fails, the resourceful pilot should be able to cope, using whatever resources remain, and adapting his control of the aircraft to suit the situation. For instance, without the aid of the attitude indicator, which responds directly and immediately to any attitude changes, the effects of inertia appear to be more marked than usual. Therefore, when using only a partial panel, the pilot must develop the ability to make smooth and gentle changes using the "Change—Check—Hold—Adjust—Trim" technique, using the instruments that are available, and avoiding chasing the needles.

When using only a partial panel make smooth and gentle changes using the "Change—Check—Hold—Adjust—Trim" technique. This allows time for performance instruments to stabilize.

Because the immediate and direct presentation of attitude changes on the attitude indicator is missing on a partial panel, and because performance instruments like the ASI, altimeter and VSI suffer some lag, it is even more important that the pilot holds any new attitude to allow time for the performance instruments to stabilize, before further adjustments are made.

Therefore, in a partial panel situation, reduce the rate and extent of control movements compared with when operating on a full panel. The lag in readings will be less severe, and there will be less tendency to over-react by chasing the needles. Small control movements should be made, then checked and held while the performance instruments catch up with the change and settle into their correct readings. Then, fine-tune with further adjustments if necessary, before trimming off any steady control pressures.

The scan for each maneuver when using a partial panel will need to be modified to increase reference to the serviceable instruments, and to bypass the unusable instruments. This is simpler than it sounds—just look at the instrument that will give you the information that you want. If it is bank angle you want, and the AI is not usable, then refer to the turn coordinator. It will not tell you bank angle directly, but it will tell you if the airplane is turning and, if it is, which way and at what rate. From this information, you can gain some idea of bank angle.

On partial panel, just look at the instruments that give you the information that you want.

During your early learning stages, actually covering the instruments not to be used will ensure that you do not respond to incorrect information obtained subconsciously from them.

Interpreting Pitch Attitude on a Partial Panel

The attitude indicator is a control instrument. It is the best guide to pitch attitude, since it gives a direct and immediate picture of the attitude of the airplane relative to the horizon. However, for practice in flying on a partial panel, it may not be available. If the attitude indicator is indeed unusable, then the pilot can determine the pitch attitude of the airplane using the three pressure instruments which derive their information from the pitot-static system. They are the airspeed indicator, the altimeter and the vertical speed indicator.

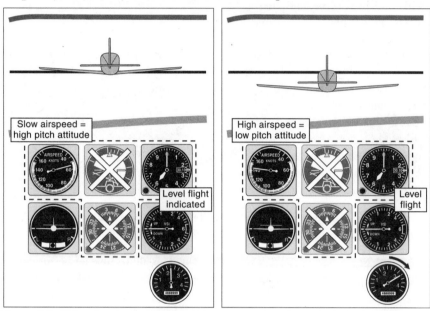

Figure 7-2. Using the pitot-static instruments to determine pitch attitude (without the attitude indicator)

The **altimeter** not only indicates altitude, but can also provide information regarding pitch attitude. If altitude is remaining constant, then the pitch attitude is correct for level flight at that power setting, whereas increasing or decreasing altitude would indicate a pitch attitude that is too high or too low.

The **airspeed indicator**, as well as indicating airspeed, can also provide information regarding pitch attitude. If the ASI shows that the desired airspeed is being maintained, then the pitch attitude for the power set is correct. If it indicates an increasing airspeed, or an airspeed that is too high, then the pitch attitude is too low for the power set. Conversely, if the ASI indicates a decreasing airspeed, or an airspeed that is too low, then the pitch attitude is too high for the power being used.

Used in conjunction with the altimeter, the ASI is an extremely valuable guide to pitch attitude, but it should be remembered that, because of its inertia, an airplane will take some time to change speed and, therefore, the ASI indication must have settled before it can confidently be regarded as an accurate indication of pitch attitude. In other words, hold any new attitude for a few seconds to allow the airspeed and the ASI to settle.

The **vertical speed indicator** not only indicates the rate of climb or descent, but also can provide information regarding pitch attitude. If the VSI indication remains approximately zero, then the pitch attitude is correct for level flight at that power, whereas a significant and sustained departure from zero on the VSI would indicate a pitch attitude that is either too high or too low for level flight.

In a climb or descent, a steady and fairly constant VSI reading can be used to support information on pitch attitude from the other performance instruments. Remember that large or sudden changes in pitch attitude may cause the VSI to initially give reverse indications—another reason for avoiding dramatic attitude changes when flying on a partial panel. Similarly, the VSI may read erratically in turbulence, so only use sustained VSI readings as a source of information regarding pitch attitude.

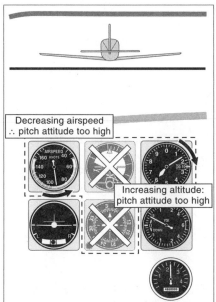

Figure 7-3. Pitch attitude too high

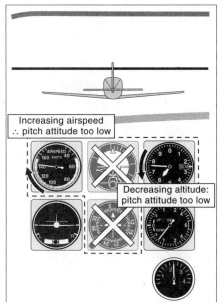

Figure 7-4. Pitch attitude too low

Interpreting Bank Attitude on a Partial Panel

The attitude indicator is the best guide to bank attitude, since it gives a direct picture of the attitude of the airplane relative to the horizon. However, for practice in flying on a partial panel, it may not be available. If the attitude indicator is indeed unusable, then the pilot can determine the bank attitude from the turn coordinator and ball, and the heading indicator (if it is working, which it may not be) or the magnetic compass.

For the purpose of this exercise, the heading indicator is assumed to be unusable (say because the suction has failed both to it and to the attitude indicator). If, in a real situation, the HI is working, then use it.

A steady zero reading on the turn coordinator, with the ball centered, means that the wings are level. If the turn coordinator reading is not zero and the ball is centered, then the direction and rate of turn will be indicated. In most instrument flying, the normal rate of turn is standard rate, which is a change of heading at 3° per second.

If the airplane is in coordinated flight (ball centered), any indication of turning will mean that the airplane is banked.

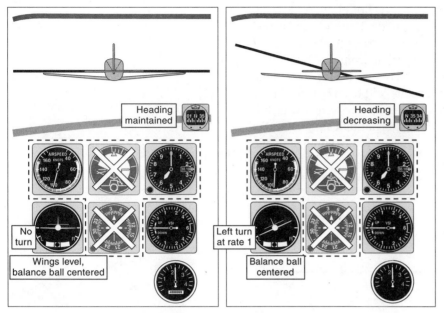

Figure 7-5. Determining bank attitude on a partial panel

While most modern aircraft are fitted with a turn coordinator, there are some still fitted with a turn-and-slip indicator. The modern turn coordinator is a superior instrument. As well as indicating *rate-of-turn* (as does the turn-and-slip indicator), the turn coordinator also shows *rate-of-bank* because of the slightly angled internal mounting of its gyroscope.

The turn coordinator responds immediately when an airplane banks, even before the airplane actually starts turning. It is therefore an easier instrument to use when trying to keep the wings level. The turn coordinator shows both roll and yaw; the turn-and-slip indicator shows yaw only.

The turn coordinator is especially valuable for lateral control if the attitude indicator is unusable. But remember that, even though it has symbolic wings to indicate banking and turning, the turn coordinator does not give pitch information.

The modern turn coordinator indicates both rate-of-turn and rate-of-bank. The turn coordinator does not give pitch information.

Remember that the turn coordinator does not give pitch information.

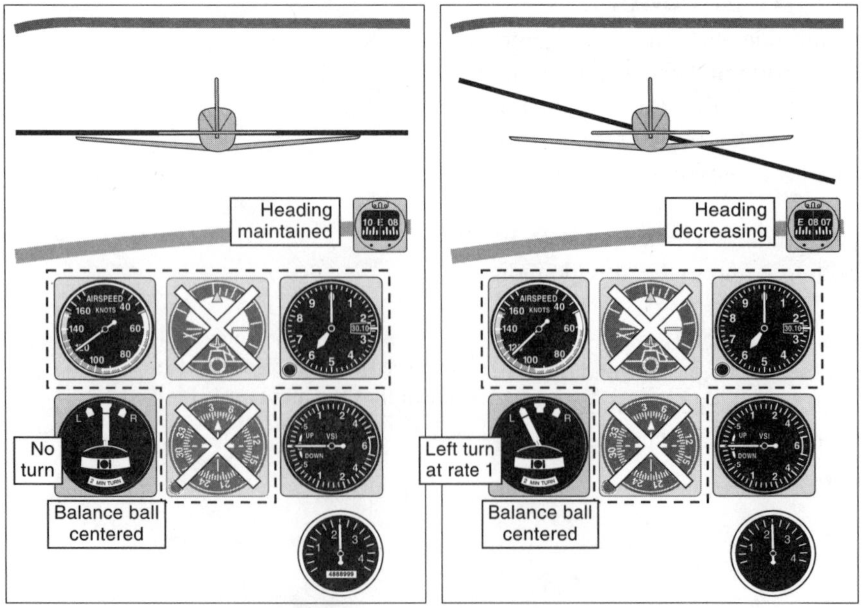

Figure 7-6. Determining bank attitude on a partial panel with a turn indicator

If, for some reason, the turn coordinator or turn-and-slip indicator is not working, then bank information can be derived from the heading indicator or magnetic compass.

If the heading is constant on the HI and the ball centered, then the wings are level. If the heading is changing at 3° per second (15° heading change in 5 seconds) and the ball is centered, then the wings are banked sufficiently to give a standard-rate turn (bank angle = airspeed/10 + $\frac{1}{2}$ the answer).

If the heading is constant and the ball is centered, the wings are level.

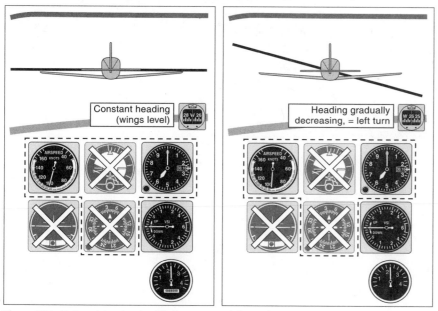

Figure 7-7. Determining bank attitude on a partial panel

If All Gyros Fail

If all gyroscopes fail (extremely improbable, but see Figure 7-6), then the best technique is to fly toward an area where you can become visual, keeping the wings level by maintaining a constant heading on the magnetic compass. This is easiest on a heading of south when you are in the northern hemisphere, because the magnetic compass is most sensitive on this heading (vice versa in southern hemisphere).

Straight Flight on a Partial Panel

Straight-and-Level Flight on a Partial Panel

Setting cruise power and placing the airplane in the cruise attitude will provide cruise performance, with the airplane in straight-and-level flight.

To achieve straight-and-level flight at a particular altitude on a partial panel without the use of the AI:

- set cruise power on the power indicator;
- hold the wings level with reference to the turn coordinator, with the ball centered; and
- adjust the pitch attitude with reference to the altimeter and VSI; and then
- trim.

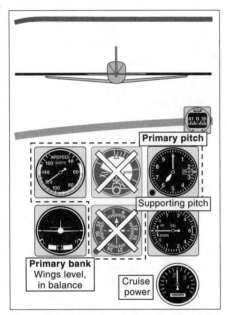

Figure 7-8. Achieving straight-and-level flight on a partial panel

To maintain straight-and-level flight at the chosen altitude, once it has been achieved:

Heading

Maintain heading by keeping the wings level using the turn coordinator, and the ball centered. Heading can be checked on the heading indicator if it is working, otherwise on the magnetic compass.

Any corrections to heading should be made with gentle coordinated turns (half standard rate on the turn coordinator, which is 1.5° per second, should be more than adequate). The heading indicator, if usable, will indicate heading directly but, if the magnetic compass is used, then some allowance will be needed to undershoot on northerly headings and overshoot on southerly headings.

Altitude

Any tendency to drift off altitude caused by a slightly incorrect pitch attitude will first be shown on the VSI, and minor adjustments with the elevator can be made almost before any change is registered on the altimeter. In turbulent conditions, however, the VSI tends to fluctuate, in which case the altimeter will be the more useful instrument. Aim to stay right on altitude. Minor deviations of less than 100 feet can generally be corrected with very small pitch alterations; any deviation in excess of 100 feet may also require a small power change as well as an attitude change. Keep in trim to make the task easier.

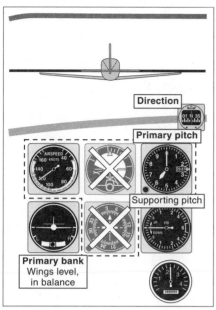

Figure 7-9. Maintaining heading and altitude

Airspeed

Airspeed is normally just accepted once cruise power has been set. If, however, precise airspeed control is desired, then this can be achieved with power. Once cruise speed is achieved, ensure that the airplane is in trim, otherwise altitude and/or airspeed will be difficult to maintain.

To change airspeed in straight-and-level flight, a coordinated change of both power and pitch attitude will be required. Greater precision using only a partial panel of instruments can be achieved if these changes are gradual and smooth.

Higher airspeed. A higher speed requires more power and a lower pitch attitude. Remember that a power increase causes a *pitch up/yaw left* tendency in most aircraft, and this should be resisted with gentle control pressures. Therefore, as power is slowly increased with the throttle to achieve a speed increase, monitor the VSI (backed up by the altimeter) to determine the small increases in forward pressure required on the control column to maintain altitude, and keep the ball centered with a slight increase in (right) rudder pressure.

Refer to the turn coordinator to ensure that wings are kept level, so that heading is maintained. Power adjustment may be required to maintain the desired airspeed. Once stabilized at the desired speed, retrim the aircraft. The heading indicator (if available) or the magnetic compass (once it has settled down) can be checked to verify heading.

Lower airspeed. Reducing the airspeed requires less power and a higher pitch attitude. The power reduction will cause a *pitch down/yaw right* tendency, which the pilot should be ready to counteract.

The VSI can be used to avoid any tendency to lose altitude, prevented by use of the elevator, and the turn coordinator and ball can be used to prevent any tendency to drift off heading.

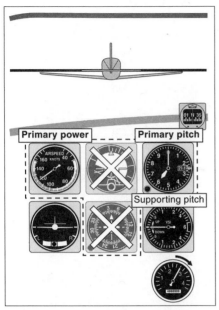

Figure 7-10. Changing airspeed on a partial panel

Once the desired lower airspeed is achieved, minor power adjustments with the throttle may be required. The airplane should then be retrimmed.

Climbing on a Partial Panel

Entering a Climb

The procedure to enter a climb using only a partial instrument panel is the same as with a full panel: A-P-T, attitude–power–trim. Raise the pitch attitude slightly with back pressure on the control column; smoothly apply climb power (mixture RICH if necessary) as the desired climb speed is attained—remember there will be a pitch-up tendency as power is applied. Keep the wings level on the turn coordinator, and the ball centered to maintain coordination.

Use A-P-T, attitude–power–trim to climb on partial panel.

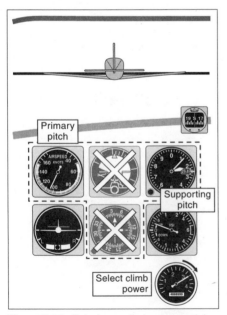

Figure 7-11. Entering a climb on a partial panel

Hold the new pitch attitude until the airspeed indicator stabilizes. The VSI will show a climb and, once you are familiar with the particular airplane, this will provide useful backup information to the ASI regarding correct pitch attitude. An initial trim adjustment will assist in maintaining the new attitude. Once the airspeed has settled, minor adjustments can be made with the elevator to fine tune the airspeed, and then the airplane can be trimmed precisely to maintain the desired climbing speed. Adjustment of power may be required to ensure correct power is set.

Maintaining a Climb

To maintain a straight climb on a partial panel, hold the pitch attitude with reference to the ASI, which is the primary indicator of correct pitch attitude during the climb. Use the VSI for rate climbs. Maintain heading by keeping the wings level on the turn coordinator and the ball centered. Heading can be checked on the heading indicator or magnetic compass. Being in trim will make life easier.

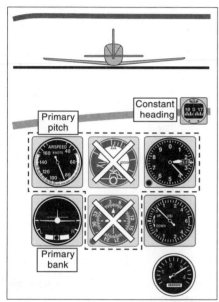

Figure 7-12. Maintaining the climb on a partial panel

It is good airmanship to periodically check engine temperatures and pressures on the climb. The engine is working hard and the cooling airflow is less, but this check should not take more than one or two seconds and should not distract you from your main scan of the flight instruments.

Leveling Off from a Climb

To level off at a particular altitude, it is important that the altimeter has the correct setting in its pressure window (the current local altimeter setting for operations below 18,000 feet MSL, and standard pressure 29.92 in.Hg above).

The altimeter should be scanned more frequently as the desired altitude is approached, and the focus for pitch control shifted to it from the ASI. Leveling off should be commenced smoothly before the desired altitude is actually reached, a suitable lead-in being 10% of the rate of climb (say 40 feet before the altitude for a rate of climb of 400 fpm).

The procedure to level off is A-P-T, attitude–power–trim. Gradually lower the pitch attitude toward the level flight position, noting a decreasing climb rate on the VSI, and capture the desired altitude with reference to the altimeter. Keep the wings level and the ball centered to maintain heading. Once the airspeed has increased to the desired cruising value on the ASI, smoothly reduce power, and then trim the airplane.

Use A-P-T, attitude–power–trim when leveling off from a partial panel climb.

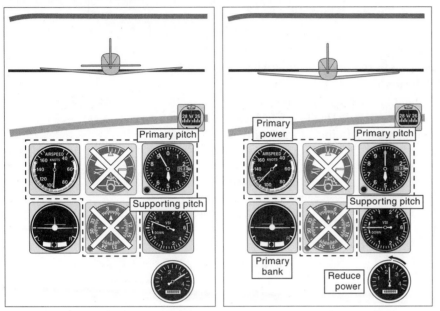

Figure 7-13. Leveling off from a climb on a partial panel

Once the airplane is stabilized, the scan becomes that for normal straight-and-level flight, although particular attention should be paid to the ASI in the early stages to ensure that adequate power is set to maintain the desired airspeed.

Descending on a Partial Panel

Entering a Descent

A descent will require less power and a lower pitch attitude than for level flight. To enter a descent, the procedure is P-A-T, power–attitude–trim. Smoothly reduce the power (mixture control RICH as required, carburetor heat HOT if necessary) with the throttle.

Use P-A-T, power–attitude–trim to descend on partial panel.

Hold the wings level and the ball centered to maintain heading, and hold the pitch attitude with slight back pressure until the desired descent airspeed on the ASI is almost reached in level flight, at which time the nose can be gently lowered slightly to maintain airspeed.

If the descent airspeed is to be the same as the level airspeed, then the pitch attitude should be lowered simultaneously with the power reduction. Remember that there will be a natural tendency for the nose to drop and yaw as power is reduced.

The VSI can be used to monitor trends in vertical performance. An initial trim adjustment as soon as the descent attitude is adopted is acceptable to remove most steady control pressure, followed by fine adjustments to the pitch attitude to maintain the desired airspeed and a final fine trim adjustment.

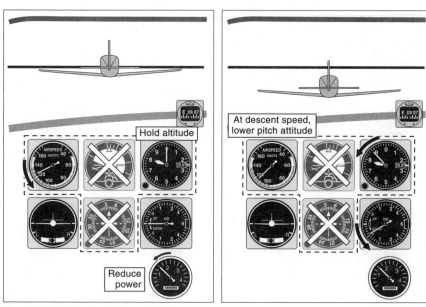

Figure 7-14. Entering a descent

Maintaining a Descent

To maintain the descent on a partial panel:

- Maintain heading with wings level on the turn coordinator and the ball centered, checking heading against the heading indicator or the magnetic compass; and
- Maintain airspeed with gentle changes in pitch attitude, using the ASI and VSI. If a particular rate of descent is required, then coordinated use of power and attitude can be used to achieve it, with the airspeed being monitored on the ASI, and the rate of descent being monitored on the VSI.

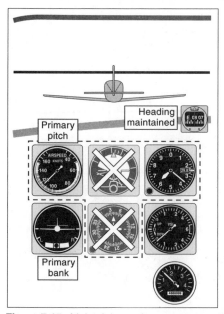

Figure 7-15. Maintaining a descent on a partial panel

In a powered descent, minor adjustments to power may be required to ensure that the correct descent power is set.

In a prolonged descent with low power, thought should be given to clearing the engine every 1000 feet or so by applying power into the green arc for a few seconds to keep the engine and oil warm, to avoid carbon fouling of the spark plugs and to keep warm air available to the carburetor heat.

Applying the extra power, and then removing it, should not distract you from scanning the flight instruments for more than a few seconds. Be prepared to counteract pitch/yaw tendencies as the power is changed.

Leveling Off from a Descent

To level off from a descent at a particular altitude, it is important that the altimeter has the correct setting in its pressure window. As the desired altitude is approached, the focus for pitch attitude control should shift from the ASI to the altimeter, and the leveling off maneuver commenced before the altitude is actually reached (a suitable lead-in being 10% of the rate of descent).

The procedure to level off from a descent is P-A-T, power–attitude–trim. Smoothly increase power to the cruise setting and raise the pitch attitude, noting that the VSI shows a reducing rate of descent, and aim to capture the desired altitude precisely on the altimeter.

Trim the airplane.

Revert to the normal straight-and-level scan, checking the altimeter for altitude, and initially checking the ASI to ensure that the desired airspeed is indeed being maintained. If not, adjust the power, hold altitude with elevator, and retrim.

Level off from a descent with P-A-T, power–attitude–trim.

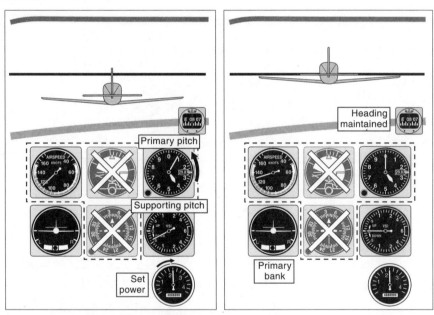

Figure 7-16. Leveling off from a descent on a partial panel

Entering a Climb from a Descent

Entering a climb from a descent, such as in a go-around, is a more demanding maneuver on a partial panel than on a full panel, since a large and fairly rapid power increase, accompanied by a higher pitch attitude, is required. The large pitch attitude change may cause the VSI to give a reversed reading initially, so it must be disregarded until its reading has stabilized. Practicing a go-around on a partial panel is an essential maneuver for the prudent pilot to master.

Turning on a Partial Panel

To turn to a specific heading, the best instruments to use for directional guidance are (in order of preference):

- the heading indicator; or
- the stopwatch (for timed turns—standard rate being 3° per second); or
- the magnetic compass (with its associated turning and acceleration errors).

Heading indicator. If the heading indicator is used, then it must first have been aligned with the magnetic compass while in steady straight-and-level unaccelerated flight. The HI is the simplest direction instrument to use.

Clock and turn coordinator. If the HI is not usable, then a timed turn with clock and turn coordinator is the preferred method. This method can be quite accurate. Once established in straight flight on the new heading, the magnetic compass will soon settle down and allow the heading to be cross-checked.

Magnetic compass. If, however, the magnetic compass has to be used during the turn, then the roll-out should occur before any desired northerly heading is indicated on the compass (by about 30° in a standard-rate turn), and after any desired southerly heading is indicated. These corrections are for the northern hemisphere, and are reversed in the southern hemisphere.

No allowances need be made when using the magnetic compass to turn to easterly or westerly headings, and lesser corrections will be required for intermediate headings.

Before Entering a Turn

Prior to commencing a turn, ensure that you are stabilized in steady straight-and-level flight, exactly on altitude, on speed, and in trim. Check the heading indicator (if available) or the magnetic compass for the present heading, establish the required direction for the turn (left or right) to take up the new heading, and decide on the rate of turn that will be used.

Standard rate is suitable for significant heading changes, but just a few degrees of heading change can be achieved satisfactorily at half standard rate. Calculating the time required for the turn, whether using the HI or the compass, always provides a convenient backup. The ASI, altimeter and VSI should all be stable before rolling into a level turn using a partial panel.

Entering a Level Turn

To enter a level turn, note the time in seconds on the clock (or set the stopwatch going), bank in the desired direction using coordinated aileron and rudder until the turn coordinator shows standard rate, (at which point the ailerons should be neutralized to stop further banking) and keep the ball centered with rudder pressure.

Altitude can be maintained by counteracting any trend on the VSI with elevator, which will probably require a slight back pressure. In turbulent conditions, the altimeter may be more useful than the VSI which could be fluctuating. Neutralizing the ailerons will hold the bank angle fairly constant, but minor corrections will have to be made continually to maintain standard rate on the turn coordinator.

Maintaining a Level Turn

To maintain a level turn, hold standard rate on the turn coordinator using the ailerons, and keep the ball centered with rudder pressure. Hold altitude on the altimeter by picking up any trend on the VSI and counteracting it with elevator. The altimeter will confirm that the precise altitude is being maintained.

The ASI will show the expected loss of several knots, which is acceptable, unless a constant airspeed is desired, in which case you must add some power while turning. It is not necessary to trim in the turn, since it is a transient maneuver and straight flight will shortly be resumed. As the desired heading is approached, bring the heading indicator (HI, clock or compass) increasingly into the scan.

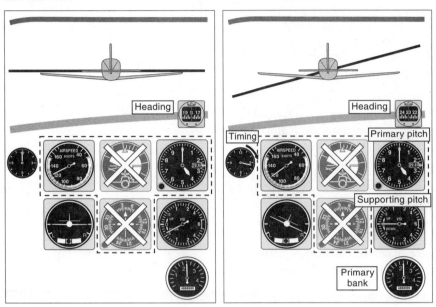

Figure 7-17. Entering and maintaining a level turn using a partial panel

Rolling Out of a Level Turn

To roll out of a level turn, anticipate the desired heading by some degrees and decrease bank with coordinated aileron and rudder until the turn coordinator shows wings level. Hold altitude using the VSI and altimeter, smoothly relaxing any back pressure held during the turn. Allow the magnetic compass to settle down in steady straight flight, then check it for heading and make any necessary adjustments with small coordinated turns.

Climbing Turn on a Partial Panel

The climbing turn is normally entered from a straight climb, and is more easily achieved if the airplane is first well-established and trimmed in the straight climb. Climbing airspeed should be maintained in the climbing turn, therefore the primary performance guide to pitch attitude is the ASI.

To enter a climbing turn, bank the airplane with coordinated aileron and rudder until the desired rate of turn is indicated on the turn coordinator. Adjust the pitch attitude with reference to the ASI. It will be slightly lower than in the straight climb, if airspeed is to be maintained.

Maintain the climbing turn with reference to the turn coordinator and the ASI, and bring the heading indicator (HI, clock or magnetic compass) into the scan as the desired heading is approached.

Roll out of the climbing turn into a straight climb with coordinated aileron and rudder, achieving wings level with the turn coordinator, ball centered, and maintain climbing airspeed with reference to the ASI.

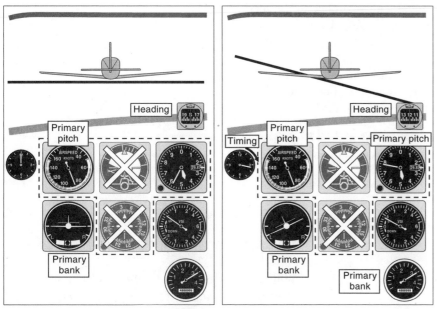

Figure 7-18. Entering and maintaining a climbing turn on a partial panel

Descending Turn on a Partial Panel

The descending turn is normally entered from a straight descent, and is more easily achieved if the airplane is well-established and trimmed in the straight descent. Descent airspeed should be maintained in the descending turn, therefore the primary performance guide to pitch attitude is the ASI.

To enter a descending turn, bank the airplane with coordinated aileron and rudder until the desired rate of turn is indicated on the turn coordinator. Adjust the pitch attitude with reference to the ASI. Pitch attitude in a descending turn will be slightly lower than in the straight descent for airspeed to be maintained.

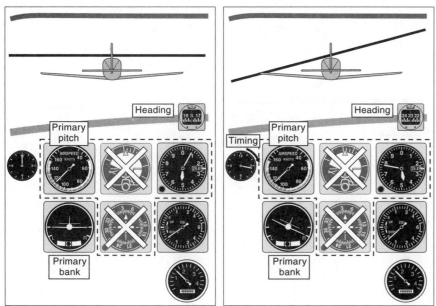

Figure 7-19. Entering and maintaining a descending turn on a partial panel

To maintain the descending turn, hold bank angle with reference to the turn coordinator, and hold pitch attitude with reference to the ASI. Bring the heading indicator (HI, clock or magnetic compass) into the scan as the desired heading is approached.

Roll out of the descending turn into a straight descent with coordinated aileron and rudder, achieving wings level with the turn coordinator, ball centered, and maintain descent airspeed with reference to the ASI.

Recovery From Unusual Attitudes on a Partial Panel

This topic was discussed in Chapter 6. It is recommended that you now read it again.

✍ Review 7

Normal Instrument Flight on a Partial Panel

1. Which instruments, in addition to the AI, are pitch instruments?
➤ altimeter, ASI and VSI

2. Which instrument provides the most pertinent information (primary) for pitch correction requirements in straight-and-level flight?
➤ altimeter

3. Which instrument provides the most pertinent information (primary) for pitch correction requirements in level turning flight?
➤ altimeter

4. Which instrument provides the most pertinent information (primary) for pitch correction requirements in climbing flight?
➤ ASI

5. Which instrument provides the most pertinent information (primary) for pitch correction requirements in descending flight?
➤ ASI

6. Which instruments, in addition to the AI, are bank instruments?
➤ HI, magnetic compass and turn coordinator

7. Which instrument provides the most pertinent information (primary) for bank correction requirements in straight flight?
➤ HI

8. Which instrument provides the most pertinent information (primary) for bank correction requirements in a standard-rate turn?
➤ turn coordinator

9. If the heading indicator is malfunctioning, direction indication is available on the _____.
➤ magnetic compass

10. Name the pressure instruments.
➤ ASI, altimeter, VSI

11. Which instruments use static pressure?
➤ ASI, altimeter, VSI

12. Which instruments use pitot (ram air) pressure?
➤ ASI

13. Name the gyroscopic instruments.
➤ AI, HI, turn coordinator

14. Name the gyroscopic instruments typically powered from the vacuum system.
➤ AI, HI

15. What is the flight situation?

Figure 1.

➤ climbing turn to the right; AI has failed—right turn (turn coordinator and HI, not supported by AI); climb (altimeter VSI and ASI, not supported by AI); coordinated (ball)

16. What is the situation if maximum power has been applied?

Figure 2.

➤ straight-and-level flight; failure of ASI (perhaps iced-up pitot tube)—wings level (AI, turn coordinator and HI); level flight (AI, altimeter and VSI); coordinated (ball); pitot system has failed (ASI indication not supported by other instruments)

17. What is the flight attitude?

Figure 3.

➤ descending right turn—right turn (AI, turn coordinator and HI); nose down (AI); pitot-static system failed since there is no movement on the ASI, altimeter and VSI

18. What is the flight situation? Cruise power is applied.

Figure 4.

➤ level turn to the right, ASI has malfunctioned— right turn (AI, turn coordinator and HI); level (AI, altimeter and VSI); ASI reading not supported by other instruments

19. While recovering from an unusual flight attitude without the aid of the attitude indicator, reaching approximate level attitude is indicated by the ASI and altimeter (stopping/increasing) their movement.

➤ stopping

20. If the airplane is in an unusual flight attitude and the AI has exceeded its limits, which two instruments should be relied on to determine the pitch attitude before starting recovery?

➤ ASI and altimeter

21. Interpret the flight attitude.

Figure 5.

➤ straight-and-level flight, with a malfunctioning vacuum system (AI and HI unreliable)—wings level (turn coordinator, not supported by AI that shows a bank to the right, and not supported by the HI that shows a turn to the left); level flight (AI, altimeter and VSI)

22. Interpret the flight attitude.

Figure 6.

➤ climbing right turn, with a malfunctioning turn coordinator—bank to the right (AI and HI, not supported by turn coordinator); climb (AI, altimeter and VSI)

23. Interpret the flight attitude, and determine the action to take (if any) to return the airplane to normal straight-and-level flight.

Figure 7.

➤ climbing right turn with a faulty static system—right bank (AI, turn coordinator and HI); nose high (AI with no support, but fixed indications on the altimeter and the VSI along with a decreasing airspeed are consistent with a climb with a blocked static system)—therefore lower the nose and level the wings with reference to the AI

24. What is the primary bank instrument in unaccelerated level flight on a specific heading?

➤ the heading indicator

25. The heading indicator is inoperative. What is the primary bank instrument in unaccelerated level flight for holding a specific heading?

➤ the magnetic compass

Suggested Training Maneuvers **8**

All instrument instructors have their own preferred methods of teaching, including training patterns that can be flown in the simulator or in the airplane. We have included a few suggested patterns in this chapter.

To begin with, start on cardinal headings such as MH 360 or MH 090 and fly at straightforward altitudes such as 3000 feet MSL or 5500 feet MSL. Later, start the patterns on headings such as MH 030, MH 155, MH 235 and altitudes like 4200 feet MSL. Initially fly the patterns at a steady speed; later you can try speed changes and configuration changes.

As your training progresses, you will advance from flying these patterns on a *full panel* of instruments to flying them on a *partial panel*. When you can fly the later patterns comfortably on a partial panel, you have reached a high standard of attitude instrument flying, and you are ready to proceed on to instrument flying using radio navigation aids. Do not be in a hurry to move on—it is the attitude flying that is the real instrument flying—get it right and the rest follows.

Ground Trainers

Simulators and ground trainers are very effective, especially in the early days of your instrument training. The patterns suggested above are suitable for both simulators and real airplanes.

Take advantage of ground trainers.

At airline level the quality of simulator training is so high that pilots can practically fly the real airplane safely the first time they get into it—so do not be disappointed that you spend quite a few hours practicing in a ground trainer before you actually step into the airplane.

Ground trainers save you a lot of time and money—but treat a session in them exactly as you would a session in real flight. This is serious training.

The Seven-Ts

Each time an instrument pilot reaches an en route turning point or a reporting point, there are certain things to do. An easy method of remembering what they are is to think of the 7-Ts.

The 7-Ts are: time, turn, twist, track, throttle, transmit, think.

- **Time**—note the time.
- **Turn**—turn to the new heading.
- **Twist**—"twist" the OBS knob of the VOR indicator to display the new course.
- **Tracking**—make minor heading adjustments to fly the course.
- **Throttle**—adjust the throttle if altitude or speed changes are required.
- **Transmit**—transmit any radio reports that are required.
- **Think**—Is that all I have to do? What is the next thing for me to think about?

Section 1 of this manual, which you are now completing, covers *Attitude Instrument Flying*. Tracking with the assistance of radio aids such as the VOR is yet to come, so the third T above does not, at the present time, have any real meaning for you. But it will be relevant shortly, so learn it now.

If you get into the habit of using the 7-Ts right from your very first training patterns in the ground trainer, then they will soon become second nature, and this will help you greatly in the future. The order of the 7-Ts is consistent with a comfortable scan across the panel, and this is a good way of remembering them. Simply follow the scan illustrated in Figure 8-1.

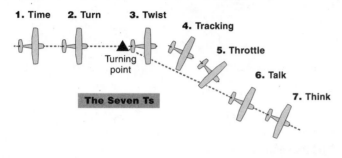

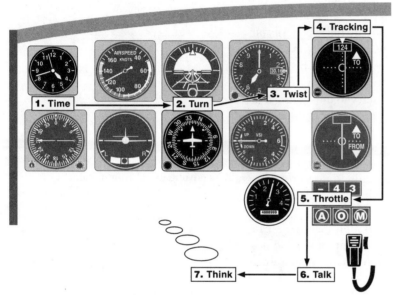

Figure 8-1. The 7-Ts at each turning point

Performance Sheets

To help you adjust to a new airplane type, we have included a **Type Performance Table**. You can fill this table in as you become familiar with the power settings and attitudes required to achieve the desired performance in the various phases of flight. Attitude can be shown on the AI by inserting a horizon line. Knowing the numbers simplifies the game!

Warm-Ups

At the start of each advanced instrument training session, it is not a bad idea to fly a few simple warm-up procedures. The *vertical-Ss* are a good example. You can fly them as shown in this chapter, and you can fly them with variations, such as constant speed, maximum rate climb and 500 fpm descent, then repeat the maneuver with flaps extended, then with landing gear extended, and so on.

PERFORMANCE TABLE

	Configuration		Power	Attitude	Performance	V-speeds
	Flaps	Gear	MP rpm		Airspeed VSI	
TAKE-OFF	............°	down				
	............°	up				
CLIMB	............°	up				V_{S1} = ... (stall speed, clean) V_X = ... (best angle) V_Y = ... (best rate)
CRUISE						V_A = ... (maneuvering speed) V_{NO} = ... (normal maximum) V_{NE} = ... (never exceed)
CRUISE DESCENT (500 fpm)						
HOLDING						
APPROACH Level	............°	up				V_{FE} = ... (flaps extended) V_{LO} = ... (landing gear operation)
PRECISION APPROACH Descent (approx. 500 fpm)	............°	down				
NONPRECISION APPROACH Descent (800–1000 fpm)	............°	down				
LANDING	............°	down		Visual		V_{S0} = ... (Stall speed, landing configuration)

A	**Level flight:** straight-and-level; timed turns (standard-rate)	*page 166*
B	**Level flight:** straight-and-level;	*page 167*
C	**Level flight:** straight-and-level;	*page 168*
D	**Level flight:** straight-and-level;	*page 169*
E	**Level flight:** straight-and-level;	*page 170*
F	**Climbs/descents** at normal airspeeds	*page 171*
G	**Climbs/descents** at a specific airspeed	*page 171*
H	**Vertical Ss** at a specific airspeed	*page 171*
I	**Climbs/descents/turns** with airspeed changes	*page 172*
J	**Climbs/descents/turns** with airspeed changes and configuration changes	*page 173*
K	**S-turns** across a cardinal heading with configuration changes and heading changes	*page 174*
L	**Climbs/descents/turns** with airspeed changes and configuration changes	*page 175*

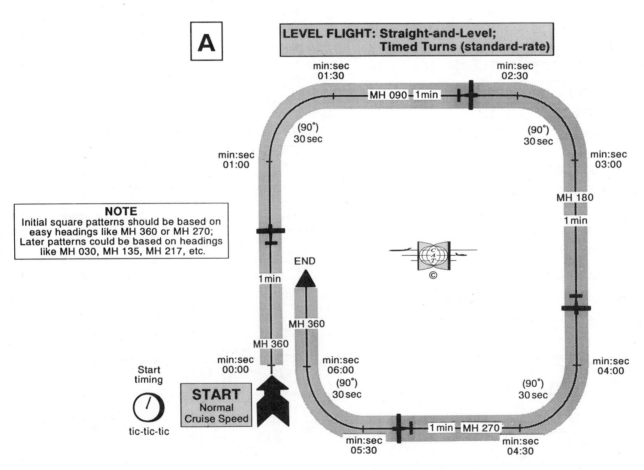

Figure 8-2. Pattern A

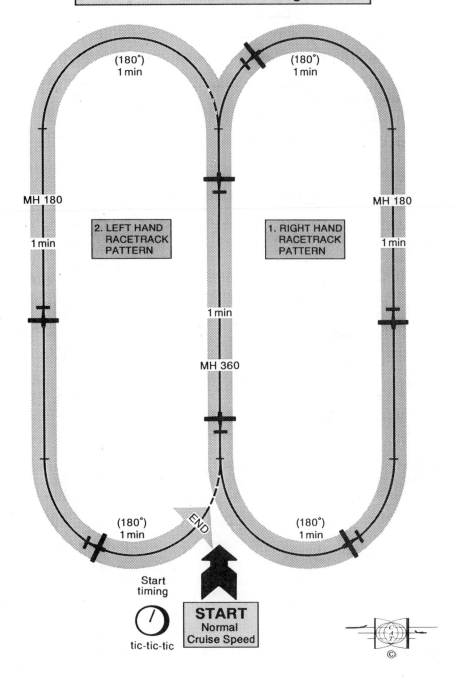

LEVEL FLIGHT: Straight-and-Level;
Timed Turns (standard-rate);
Racetrack Holding Pattern

(180°)
1 min

(180°)
1 min

MH 180

MH 180

2. LEFT HAND
RACETRACK
PATTERN

1. RIGHT HAND
RACETRACK
PATTERN

1 min

1 min

1 min

MH 360

(180°)
1 min

(180°)
1 min

END

Start
timing

tic-tic-tic

START
Normal
Cruise Speed

NOTE: We have included the *cumulative time intervals* for Pattern A only — we suggest
that you mark in the cumulative times for the remainder of the patterns yourself.

Figure 8-3. Pattern B

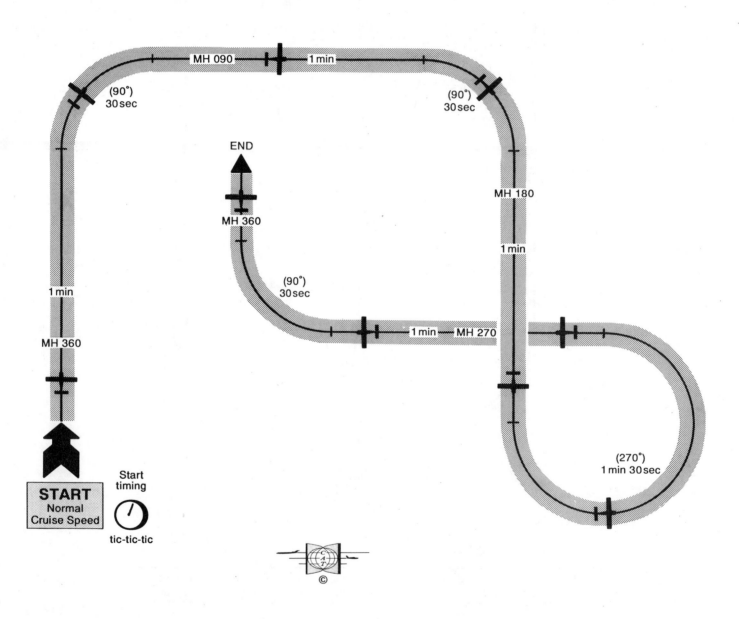

C

LEVEL FLIGHT: Straight-and-Level;
Timed Turns (standard-rate)

MH 090 — 1 min

(90°)
30 sec

(90°)
30 sec

END

MH 360

MH 180

1 min

(90°)
30 sec

1 min — MH 270

1 min

MH 360

START
Normal
Cruise Speed

Start
timing

tic-tic-tic

(270°)
1 min 30 sec

Figure 8-4. Pattern C

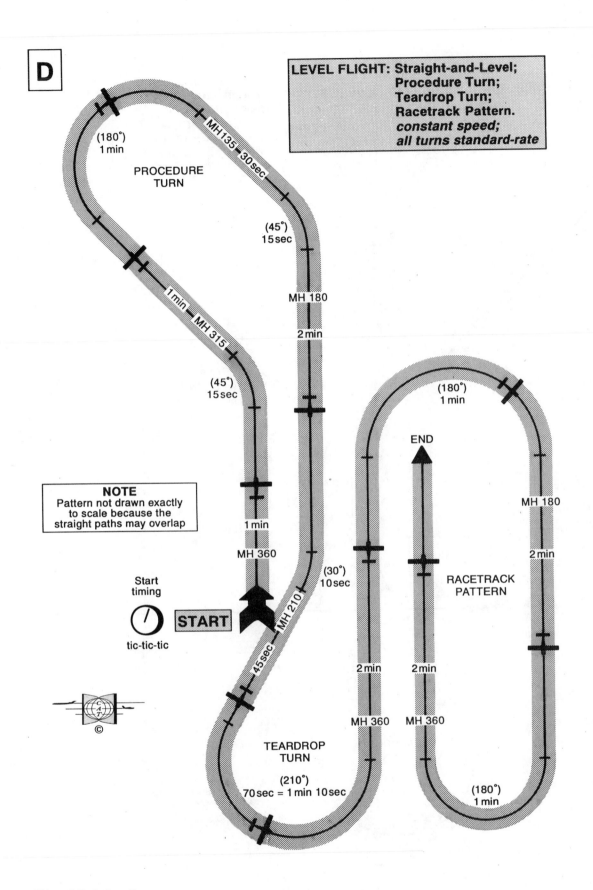

D

LEVEL FLIGHT: Straight-and-Level;
Procedure Turn;
Teardrop Turn;
Racetrack Pattern.
*constant speed;
all turns standard-rate*

(180°)
1 min

PROCEDURE
TURN

MH135 30 sec

(45°)
15 sec

MH 180

2 min

1 min MH 315

(45°)
15 sec

NOTE
Pattern not drawn exactly
to scale because the
straight paths may overlap

(180°)
1 min

END

MH 180

1 min

2 min

MH 360

Start
timing

START

tic-tic-tic

(30°)
10 sec

MH 210

RACETRACK
PATTERN

45 sec

2 min

2 min

MH 360

MH 360

TEARDROP
TURN

(210°)
70 sec = 1 min 10 sec

(180°)
1 min

Figure 8-5. Pattern D

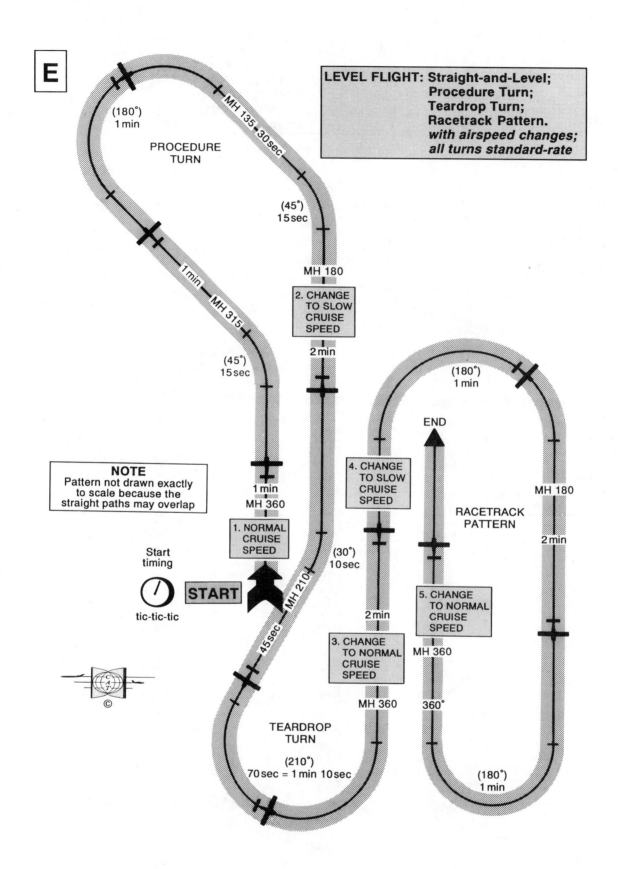

E

PROCEDURE TURN

(180°) 1 min

MH 135 ━ 30 sec

LEVEL FLIGHT: Straight-and-Level;
Procedure Turn;
Teardrop Turn;
Racetrack Pattern.
*with airspeed changes;
all turns standard-rate*

(45°) 15 sec

MH 180

2. CHANGE TO SLOW CRUISE SPEED

2 min

1 min ━ MH 315

(45°) 15 sec

NOTE
Pattern not drawn exactly to scale because the straight paths may overlap

(180°) 1 min

MH 180

2 min

RACETRACK PATTERN

END

4. CHANGE TO SLOW CRUISE SPEED

1 min

MH 360

1. NORMAL CRUISE SPEED

Start timing

tic-tic-tic

START

MH 210

45 sec

(30°) 10 sec

2 min

3. CHANGE TO NORMAL CRUISE SPEED

MH 360

5. CHANGE TO NORMAL CRUISE SPEED

MH 360

360°

TEARDROP TURN

(210°) 70 sec = 1 min 10 sec

(180°) 1 min

Figure 8-6. Pattern E

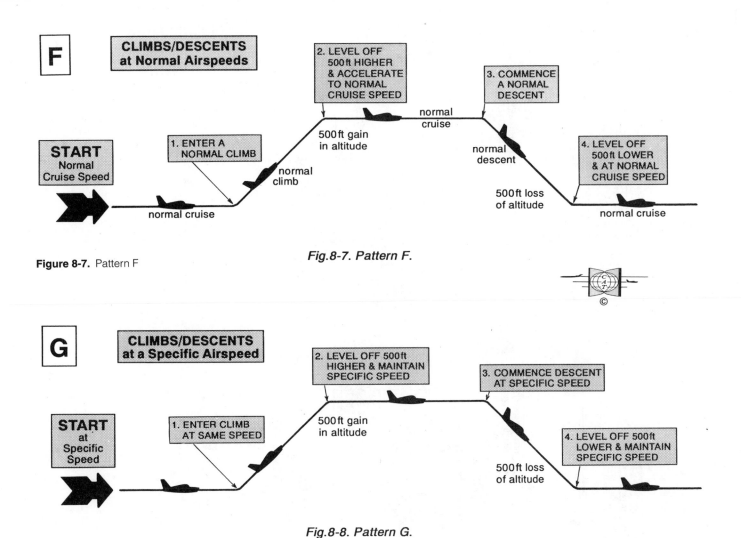

Figure 8-7. Pattern F

Fig.8-7. Pattern F.

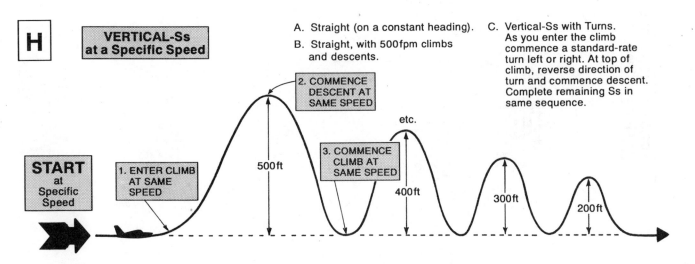

Figure 8-8. Pattern G

Fig.8-8. Pattern G.

VERTICAL-Ss at a Specific Speed

A. Straight (on a constant heading).

B. Straight, with 500fpm climbs and descents.

C. Vertical-Ss with Turns. As you enter the climb commence a standard-rate turn left or right. At top of climb, reverse direction of turn and commence descent. Complete remaining Ss in same sequence.

Figure 8-9. Pattern H

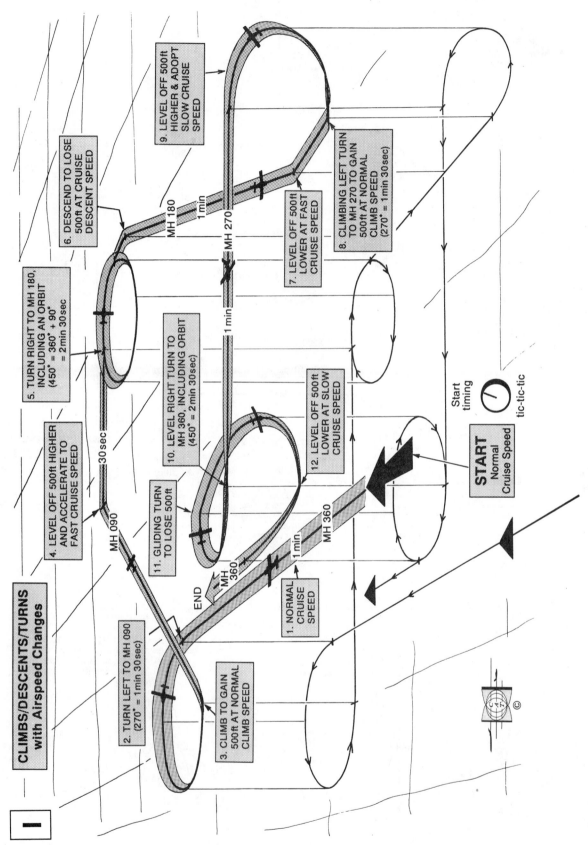

CLIMBS/DESCENTS/TURNS with Airspeed Changes

9. LEVEL OFF 500ft HIGHER & ADOPT CRUISE SLOW SPEED

6. DESCEND TO LOSE 500ft AT CRUISE DESCENT SPEED

8. CLIMBING LEFT TURN TO MH 270 TO GAIN 500ft AT NORMAL CLIMB SPEED (270° = 1min 30sec)

7. LEVEL OFF 500ft LOWER AT FAST CRUISE SPEED

5. TURN RIGHT TO MH 180, INCLUDING AN ORBIT (450° = 360° + 90° = 2min 30sec)

MH 180

MH 270

1 min

1 min

Start timing

tic-tic-tic

4. LEVEL OFF 500ft HIGHER AND ACCELERATE TO FAST CRUISE SPEED

10. LEVEL RIGHT TURN TO MH 360, INCLUDING ORBIT (450° = 2min 30sec)

12. LEVEL OFF 500ft LOWER AT SLOW CRUISE SPEED

30 sec

MH 090

11. GLIDING TURN TO LOSE 500ft

START Normal Cruise Speed

END

MH 360

MH 360

1 min

1. NORMAL CRUISE SPEED

2. TURN LEFT TO MH 090 (270° = 1min 30sec)

3. CLIMB TO GAIN 500ft AT NORMAL CLIMB SPEED

Figure 8-10. Pattern I

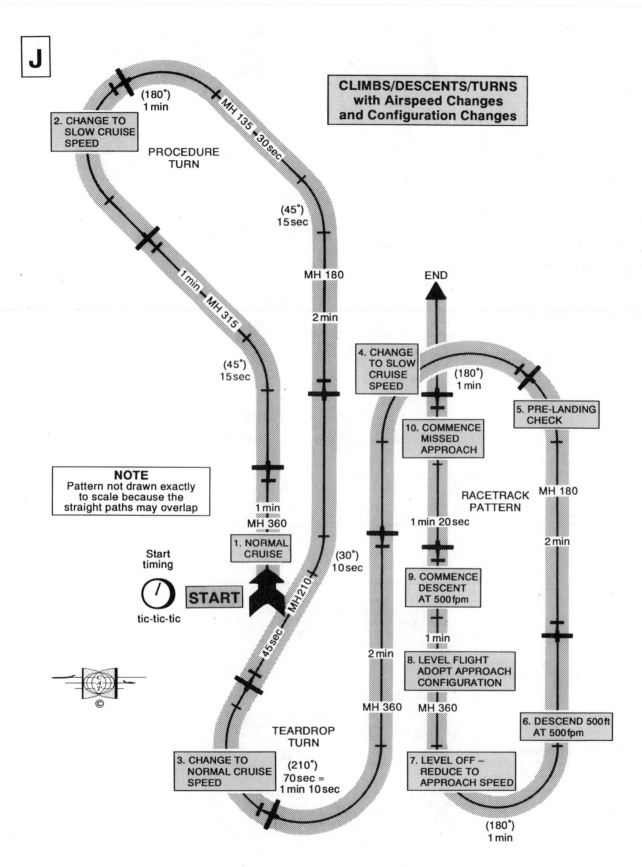

J

CLIMBS/DESCENTS/TURNS
with Airspeed Changes
and Configuration Changes

PROCEDURE TURN

(180°) 1 min

MH 135 – 30 sec

2. CHANGE TO SLOW CRUISE SPEED

(45°) 15 sec

MH 180

2 min

1 min – MH 315

(45°) 15 sec

END

4. CHANGE TO SLOW CRUISE SPEED

(180°) 1 min

5. PRE-LANDING CHECK

10. COMMENCE MISSED APPROACH

RACETRACK PATTERN

MH 180

1 min 20 sec

2 min

NOTE
Pattern not drawn exactly to scale because the straight paths may overlap

1 min
MH 360

1. NORMAL CRUISE

Start timing

tic-tic-tic

START

MH 210

(30°) 10 sec

9. COMMENCE DESCENT AT 500 fpm

1 min

8. LEVEL FLIGHT ADOPT APPROACH CONFIGURATION

2 min

6. DESCEND 500 ft AT 500 fpm

45 sec

2 min

MH 360

MH 360

TEARDROP TURN

3. CHANGE TO NORMAL CRUISE SPEED

(210°) 70 sec = 1 min 10 sec

7. LEVEL OFF – REDUCE TO APPROACH SPEED

(180°) 1 min

Figure 8-11. Pattern J

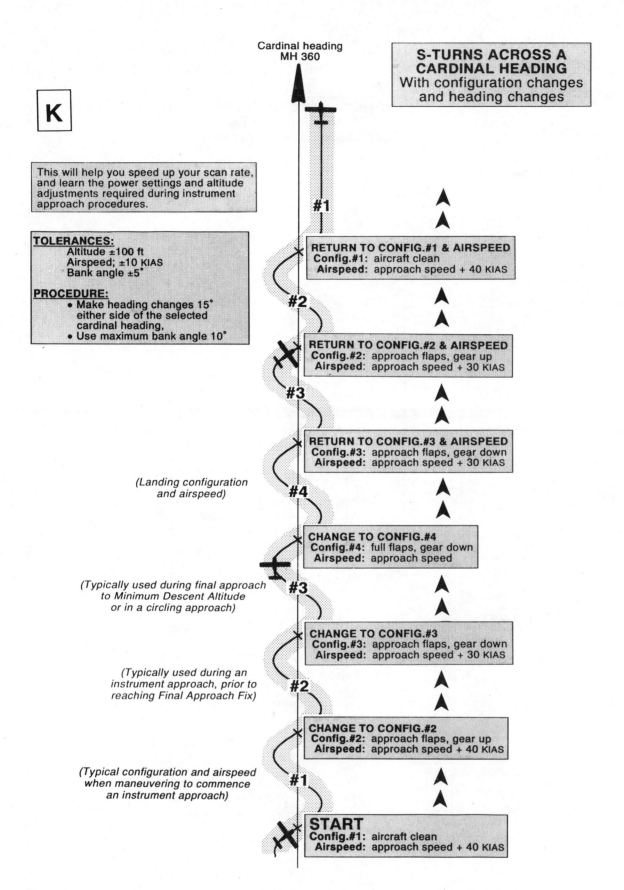

Cardinal heading
MH 360

S-TURNS ACROSS A CARDINAL HEADING
With configuration changes and heading changes

K

This will help you speed up your scan rate, and learn the power settings and altitude adjustments required during instrument approach procedures.

TOLERANCES:
 Altitude ±100 ft
 Airspeed; ±10 KIAS
 Bank angle ±5°

PROCEDURE:
 • Make heading changes 15° either side of the selected cardinal heading,
 • Use maximum bank angle 10°

#1

RETURN TO CONFIG.#1 & AIRSPEED
Config.#1: aircraft clean
Airspeed: approach speed + 40 KIAS

#2

RETURN TO CONFIG.#2 & AIRSPEED
Config.#2: approach flaps, gear up
Airspeed: approach speed + 30 KIAS

#3

RETURN TO CONFIG.#3 & AIRSPEED
Config.#3: approach flaps, gear down
Airspeed: approach speed + 30 KIAS

(Landing configuration and airspeed)

#4

CHANGE TO CONFIG.#4
Config.#4: full flaps, gear down
Airspeed: approach speed

(Typically used during final approach to Minimum Descent Altitude or in a circling approach)

#3

CHANGE TO CONFIG.#3
Config.#3: approach flaps, gear down
Airspeed: approach speed + 30 KIAS

(Typically used during an instrument approach, prior to reaching Final Approach Fix)

#2

CHANGE TO CONFIG.#2
Config.#2: approach flaps, gear up
Airspeed: approach speed + 40 KIAS

(Typical configuration and airspeed when maneuvering to commence an instrument approach)

#1

START
Config.#1: aircraft clean
Airspeed: approach speed + 40 KIAS

Figure 8-12. Pattern K

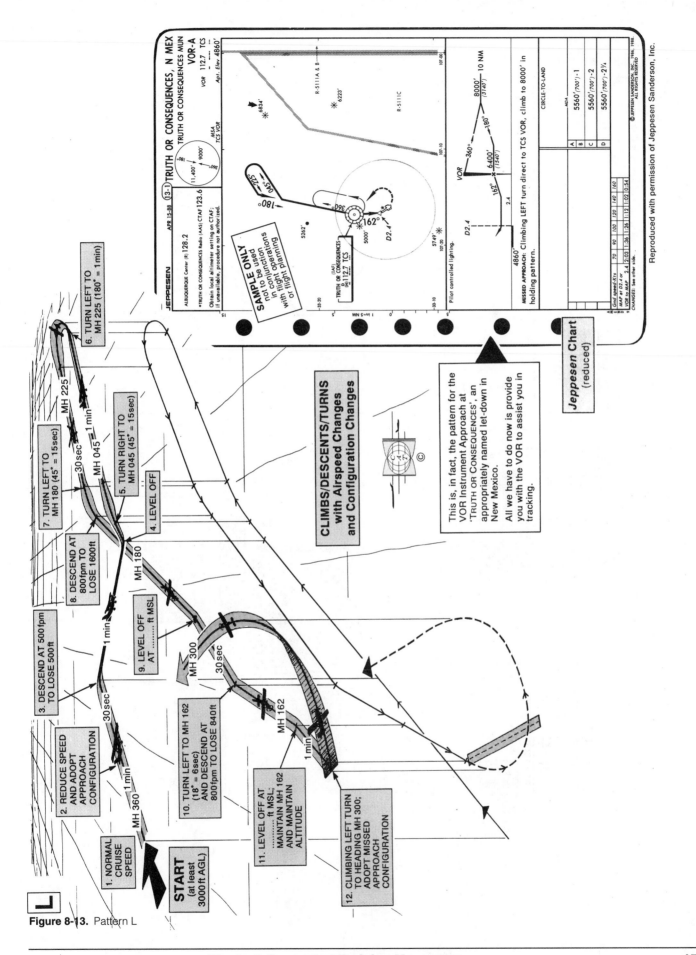

CLIMBS/DESCENTS/TURNS
with Airspeed Changes
and Configuration Changes

This is, in fact, the pattern for the VOR Instrument Approach at 'TRUTH OR CONSEQUENCES', an appropriately named let-down in New Mexico.

All we have to do now is provide you with the VOR to assist you in tracking.

Jeppesen Chart
(reduced)

Reproduced with permission of Jeppesen Sanderson, Inc.

1. NORMAL CRUISE SPEED

START
(at least 3000 ft AGL)

2. REDUCE SPEED AND ADOPT APPROACH CONFIGURATION

3. DESCEND AT 500 fpm TO LOSE 500 ft

4. LEVEL OFF

5. TURN RIGHT TO MH 045 (45° = 15 sec)

6. TURN LEFT TO MH 225 (180° = 1 min)

7. TURN LEFT TO MH 180 (45° = 15 sec)

8. DESCEND AT 800 fpm TO LOSE 1600 ft

9. LEVEL OFF AT .... ft MSL

10. TURN LEFT TO MH 162 (18° = 6 sec) AND DESCEND AT 800 fpm TO LOSE 840 ft

11. LEVEL OFF AT .... ft MSL; MAINTAIN MH 162 AND MAINTAIN ALTITUDE

12. CLIMBING LEFT TURN TO HEADING MH 300; ADOPT MISSED APPROACH CONFIGURATION

MH 360 1 min
MH 180
MH 225
MH 045 1 min
MH 300
MH 162
30 sec
1 min

Figure 8-13. Pattern L

Chapter 8 **Suggested Training Maneuvers**

JEPPESEN

(11-2)

MANCHESTER, U.K.
MANCHESTER
ILS Rwy 06
NDB Rwy 06
LOC *108.9 IMM

Apt. Elev. 256'

*ATIS 128.17
MANCHESTER Control Approach (R) 119.4 121.35
MANCHESTER Tower 118.7
Ground 121.7

Alt Set: hPa
Rwy Elev: 8 hPa

Trans level: By ATC
Trans alt: 4000'(3789')

MSA
MCR Lctr

LYLAK
D27.0 WAL VOR R-076
WAL 114.1
HOLDING
076°
D271'23
256°
MHA 5000
or FL 50

❶ IF POL VOR OUT OF
SERVICE, USE LYLAK
HOLDING WITH SAME
POSITION AS BOLIN.

❶BOLIN
D16.0 POL VOR
R-230
230°
181°
14.3
3000
050°
230°
D16/20
MHA 5000
or FL 50

NOT TO SCALE

MANCHESTER
396 ME

MANCHESTER
D 113.55 MCT

CONGLETON
360.5 CON
155°
5000 or FL 50
335°
323°
8.9
3000

057°
3000
057°
237°
309°
MM

(IAF)
MANCHESTER
388 MCR
237°
192°
012°
378'
057°

ILS
057° *108.9 IMM

SAMPLE ONLY
Not to be used in conjunction
with Flight Planning or
Flight Operations

1 in = 5 NM

Procedure restricted to max IAS 185 KT.

WARNING: RA fluctuations may occur due to Bollin Valley.

OCA (H) RWY 06
ILS A: 371'(160')
     B: 381'(170')
     C: 391'(180')
     D: 411'(200')

TCH Displ
thresh 57'

MM
NDB
LOC
GS 507'(296')
RWY 06 211'
0.8
APT. 256'

LOM 3000'
(2789')
237° 057°
GS 151'(1300')

1520'
(1309')

2520'
(2309')
Start
turn at
❶ 1 Min
150 KT TAS

NDB
❷ 2 Min above

3.9
3.1

TO DISPLACED THRESHOLD
MISSED APPROACH: Climb STRAIGHT AHEAD to ME NDB continue climb in holding
to 3000'(2789').

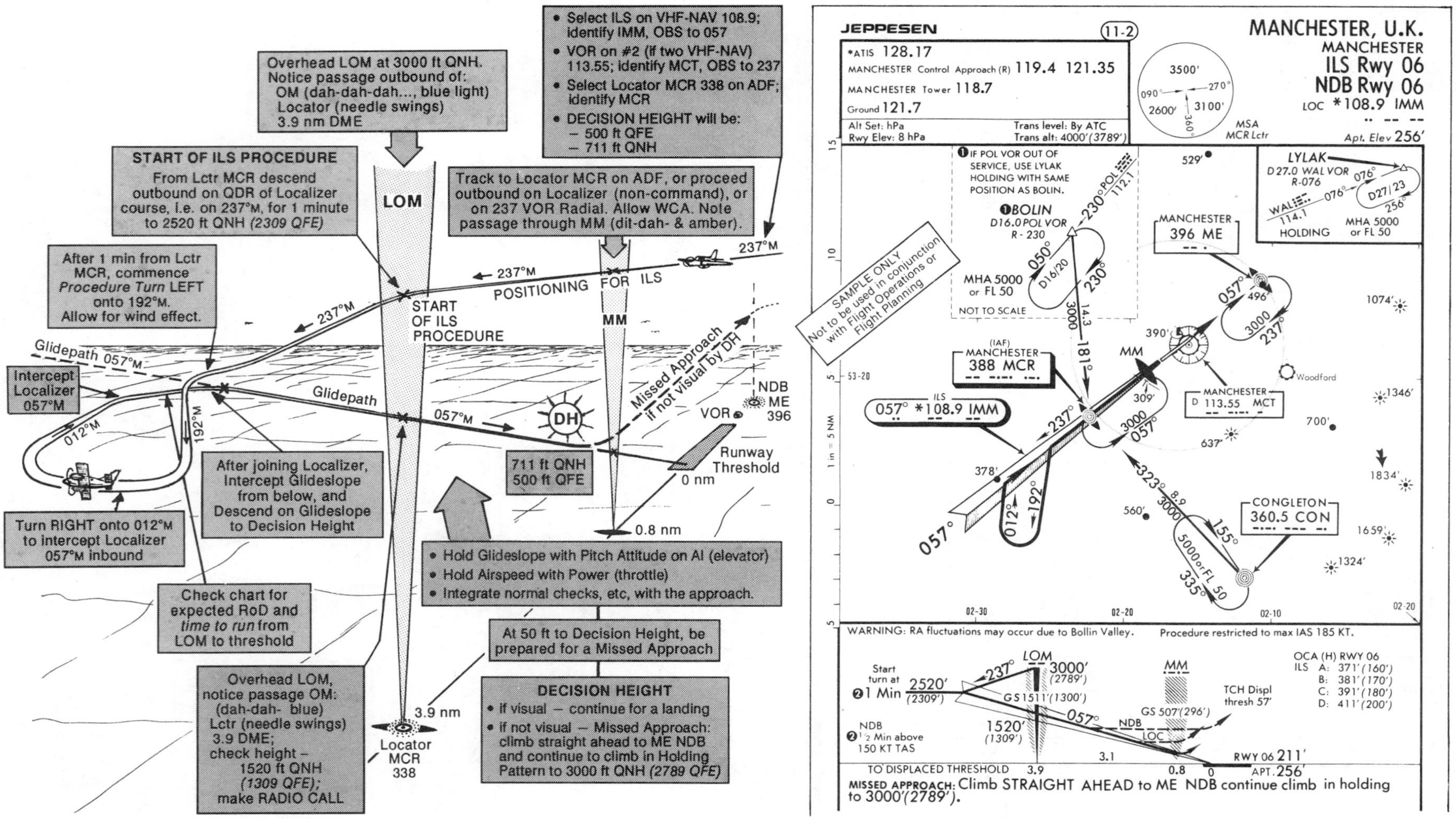

Figure 8-14. Maneuvering procedure to carry out a UK ILS approach—Manchester ILS Rwy 06. Note that UK terminology for altimeter settings and radio navaid reference is used in the drawing and should be disregarded.

Annotation boxes:

- Select ILS on VHF-NAV 108.9;
  identify IMM, OBS to 057
- VOR on #2 (if two VHF-NAV)
  113.55; identify MCT, OBS to 237
- Select Locator MCR 338 on ADF;
  identify MCR
- DECISION HEIGHT will be:
  — 500 ft QFE
  — 711 ft QNH

Track to Locator MCR on ADF, or proceed
outbound on Localizer (non-command), or
on 237 VOR Radial. Allow WCA. Note
passage through MM (dit-dah- & amber).

237°M

POSITIONING FOR ILS

237°M

NDB
ME 396

VOR

Runway
Threshold
0 nm

Missed Approach
if not visual by DH

MM

DH

711 ft QNH
500 ft QFE

0.8 nm

- Hold Glideslope with Pitch Attitude on AI (elevator)
- Hold Airspeed with Power (throttle)
- Integrate normal checks, etc, with the approach.

At 50 ft to Decision Height, be
prepared for a Missed Approach

DECISION HEIGHT

- If visual — continue for a landing
- If not visual — Missed Approach:
  climb straight ahead to ME NDB
  and continue to climb in Holding
  Pattern to 3000 ft QNH (2789 QFE)

Overhead LOM at 3000 ft QNH,
Notice passage outbound of:
OM (dah-dah-dah... blue light)
Locator (needle swings)
3.9 nm DME

START OF ILS PROCEDURE

From Lctr MCR descend
outbound on QDR of Localizer
course, i.e. on 237°M, for 1 minute
to 2520 ft QNH (2309 QFE)

START
OF ILS
PROCEDURE

LOM

237°M

Glidepath

057°M

3.9 nm

Locator
MCR
338

After joining Localizer,
intercept Glideslope
from below, and
Descend on Glideslope
to Decision Height

Check chart for
expected RoD and
time to run from
LOM to threshold

Overhead LOM,
notice passage OM:
(dah-dah- blue)
Lctr (needle swings)
3.9 DME;
check height —
1520 ft QNH
(1309 QFE);
make RADIO CALL

After 1 min from Lctr
MCR, commence
Procedure Turn LEFT
onto 192°M.
Allow for wind effect.

192°M

210°M

Glidepath 057°M

Intercept
Localizer
057°M

Turn RIGHT onto 012°M
to intercept Localizer
057°M inbound

Instrument Rating
FAA Practical Test Standards

Flight By Reference to Instruments

The examiner will require the performance of all Tasks. At least two of the Tasks, A through E as selected by the examiner, will be performed without the use of the attitude and heading indicators. Task F should be performed using all available instruments; Task G will be performed without the use of the attitude indicator.

A. Task: Straight-and-Level Flight

Objective. To determine that the applicant:

1. Exhibits adequate knowledge of the elements relating to attitude instrument flying during straight-and-level flight.
2. Maintains straight-and-level flight in the aircraft configuration specified by the examiner.
3. Maintains the heading within 10 degrees, altitude within 100 feet, and airspeed within 10 knots.
4. Uses proper instrument cross-check and interpretation, and applies the appropriate pitch, bank, power, and trim corrections.

B. Task: Change of Airspeed

Objective. To determine that the applicant:

1. Exhibits adequate knowledge of the elements relating to attitude instrument flying during change of airspeeds in straight-and-level flight and in turns.
2. Establishes a proper power setting when changing airspeed.
3. Maintains the heading within 10 degrees, angle of bank within 5 degrees when turning, altitude within 100 feet, and airspeed within 10 knots.
4. Uses proper instrument cross-check and interpretation, and applies the appropriate pitch, bank, power, and trim corrections.

C. Task: Constant Airspeed Climbs and Descents

Objective. To determine that the applicant:

1. Exhibits adequate knowledge of the elements relating to attitude instrument flying during constant airspeed climbs and descents.
2. Demonstrates climbs and descents at a constant airspeed, between specific altitudes in straight or turning flight as specified by the examiner.
3. Enters constant airspeed climbs and descents from a specified altitude, airspeed and heading.
4. Establishes the appropriate change of pitch and power to establish the specified climb and descent performance.
5. Maintains the airspeed within 10 knots, heading within 10 degrees or, if in a turning maneuver, within 5 degrees of the specified bank angle.
6. Performs the level-off within 100 feet of the specified altitude.
7. Uses proper instrument cross-check and interpretation, and applies the appropriate pitch, bank, power, and trim corrections.

D. Task: Rate Climbs and Descent

Objective. To determine that the applicant:

1. Exhibits adequate knowledge of the elements relating to attitude instrument flying during rate climbs and descents.
2. Demonstrates climbs and descents at a constant rate between specified altitudes in straight or turning flight as directed by the examiner.

3. Enters rate climbs and descents from a specified altitude, airspeed, and heading.

4. Establishes the appropriate change of pitch, bank, and power to establish the specified rate of climb or descent.

5. Maintains the specified rate of climb and descent within 100 feet per minute, airspeed within 10 knots, heading within 10 degrees, or if in a turning maneuver, within 5 degrees of the desired bank angle.

6. Performs the level-off within 100 feet of the desired altitude.

7. Uses proper instrument cross-check and interpretation, and applies the appropriate pitch, bank, power, and trim corrections.

E. Task: Timed Turns to Magnetic Compass Headings

Note: If the aircraft has a turn-and-slip indicator, the term "miniature aircraft of the turn coordinator" applies to the turn needle.

Objective. To determine that the applicant:

1. Exhibits adequate knowledge of procedures relating to calibrating the miniature aircraft of the turn coordinator, the operating characteristics and errors of the magnetic compass, and the performance of timed turns to specified compass headings.

2. Establishes indicated standard rate turns, both right and left.

3. Applies the clock correctly to the calibration procedure.

4. Changes the miniature aircraft position, as necessary, to produce a standard rate turn.

5. Makes timed turns to specified compass headings.

6. Maintains the altitude within 100 feet, airspeed within 10 knots, bank angle 5 degrees of a standard or half-standard rate turn, and rolls out on specified headings within 10 degrees.

F. Task: Steep Turns

Objective. To determine that the applicant:

1. Exhibits adequate knowledge of the factors relating to attitude instrument flying during steep turns.

2. Enters a turn using a bank of approximately 45 degrees for an airplane and 30 degrees for a helicopter.

3. Maintains the desired angle of bank for either 180 degrees or 360 degrees of turn, both left and right.

4. Maintains altitude within 100 feet, airspeed within 10 knots, 5 degrees of specified bank angle, and rolls out within 10 degrees of the specified heading.

5. Uses proper instrument cross-check and interpretation, and applies the appropriate pitch, bank, power, and trim corrections.

G. Task: Recovery From Unusual Flight Attitudes

Note: Any intervention by the examiner to prevent the aircraft from exceeding any operating limitations, or entering an unsafe flight condition, shall be disqualifying.

Objective. To determine that the applicant:

1. Exhibits adequate knowledge of the factors relating to attitude instrument flying during recovery from unusual flight attitudes (both nose-high and nose-low).

2. Uses proper instrument cross-check and interpretation, and applies the appropriate pitch, bank, and power corrections in the correct sequence to return the aircraft to a stabilized level flight attitude.

Radio Navigation Aids Section Two

9   **Introduction to Radio Navigation Aids** 181

10 **Radar** 183

11 **DME** 207

12a **The NDB and the ADF** 213

12b **The Relative Bearing Indicator (RBI)** 231

12c **The RMI and Rotatable-Card ADF** 259

13 **The VOR** 273

14 **The Instrument Landing System (ILS)** 309

15 **Area Navigation (RNAV)** 357

16 **VHF Direction Finding (DF)** 367

Introduction to
Radio Navigation Aids

Now that you have achieved a high standard in attitude flying using the flight instruments, it is time to apply this ability to cross-country navigation on instruments.

It is, in fact, possible to fly cross-country using attitude flying only, without referring to any radio navigation instrument in the cockpit, simply by following instructions passed to you by a radar controller. Instructions such as "Turn right heading three four zero", and "Descend to and maintain seven thousand", can be followed, even to the point of breaking out of the clouds for a straight-in landing on a particular runway.

Radar is the first of the radio navigation aids, or radio *navaids*, that we consider in this section, since it does not involve a great deal of understanding before you can benefit from it. As well as explaining the ways in which radar is used, we will also discuss some of the basic theory underlying its operation.

The **transponder**, used as part of a secondary radar system, is also discussed. It is required equipment in airplanes for flight in a large proportion of United States airspace, to enable better radar control and, consequently, safer flight.

Your instructor may wish to follow an order of study different to that presented here. If so, simply bypass the other chapters and proceed to the one desired. Each chapter stands well alone, and reading the earlier chapters is not necessary to understand the content of a later one.

VHF direction finding (VDF or DF), like primary radar, does not require additional instrumentation in the cockpit. You can request a FSS to provide you with a magnetic bearing to the station. The FSS determines your position by detecting the direction from which your VHF radio communications are received. The procedure used is not much more complicated than simply steering radar headings. VDF is more primitive than radar and rarely used in the United States. It is used in the United Kingdom, however, even to the point of making instrument approaches at some airports.

Radio navigation aids that do have instruments in the cockpit include:
- the automatic direction finder (ADF), which indicates the direction of the selected ground-based nondirectional beacon (NDB). The ADF has various presentations, such as the relative bearing indicator (RBI) or the radio magnetic indicator (RMI);
- the VHF omni range (VOR);
- distance measuring equipment (DME);
- the instrument landing system (ILS);
- area navigation (RNAV);
- the microwave landing system (MLS);
- LORAN; and
- global positioning systems (GPS).

Radar controllers can vector you from your departure through your arrival.

An FSS can determine your bearing from its station by doing a DF steer.

It may sound a little complicated at this stage, but careful consideration of each of the radio navigation aids one at a time will make it easy for you.

There is a certain amount of jargon associated with instrument flying, but it will not take long before you are familiar with all the terms.

This section of the manual will help you to understand how the aids work and how to use them, especially for tracking to or from a ground station.

In Section 4, we consider the more advanced instrument procedures, such as:

- instrument departure procedures (DPs);
- holding patterns;
- standard terminal arrivals (STARs);
- instrument approaches;
- straight-in landings after a successful instrument approach;
- circling maneuvers to land after a successful instrument approach; and
- missed approaches if you do not become visual on an instrument approach.

Your skills in these maneuvers will depend to a large extent on the lessons learned in Section 1 on attitude flying and in this Section 2 on radio navigation aids. A good instrument approach consists mainly of accurate attitude flying using the flight instruments, and accurate tracking using a radio navaid.

Radar 10

In the high-volume traffic environment of today's airspace, **radar** is the primary tool used by Air Traffic Control to provide many vital services to IFR (and VFR) aircraft, such as radar vectoring, radar separation and sequencing. The air traffic controller is presented with an electronic map of his area of responsibility, showing the position of aircraft within it. Amongst the advantages of this system are:

- reduced air-ground radio communication; for instance, there is no need for a pilot to transmit regular position reports;
- an ability to handle an increased number of aircraft in the same volume of airspace, with reduced, but still safe, separation distances;
- an ability to *radar vector* an aircraft along any desired course by passing headings to steer directly to the pilot; and
- an ability to sequence aircraft, that is, to feed them onto final approach to land, either to the commencement of a published instrument approach procedure, such as an ILS (instrument landing system), or until the pilot becomes visual, without the need for excessive pre-approach maneuvering, and with more than one airplane on the approach at any one time.

Radar used for these purposes is called **surveillance radar**. In the U.S. there are two basic types of surveillance radar in use:

- **Air Route Surveillance Radar (ARSR)** is a long-range radar system used by Air Route Traffic Control Centers (ARTCCs) to monitor aircraft during the en route phase of flight. ARSR sites are widely distributed to provide continuous coverage of airspace over most of the continental U.S.

- **Airport Surveillance Radar (ASR)** is a relatively short-range system that is used to monitor aircraft operating within the airspace immediately surrounding an airport.

FAA radar units operate continuously at the locations shown in the Airport/Facility Directory (A/FD). Their primary role is to provide positive direction and coordination for IFR flights, but they are also used to provide a varying level of service to VFR flights, depending on the facilities available, the type of airspace, and controller workload.

The radar controller can also provide a **radar traffic information service** to alert pilots to other nearby and possibly conflicting traffic. Even if in receipt of this service, you are still responsible, in suitable conditions, for continual vigilance to "see and avoid" other traffic. The radar controller will pass what he considers relevant information using the clock system to specify the position of the other traffic relative to your course. He sees your course on his screen rather than your heading, so you will have to allow for the drift angle when you look out the window for other traffic.

ATC radar that is approved for approach control is used for:
- **track guidance to final approach course;**
- **ASR radar instrument approaches; and**
- **monitoring of nonradar approaches.**

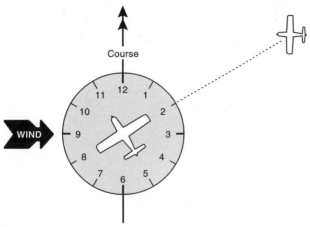

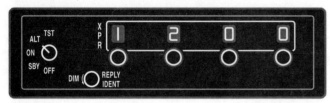

Figure 10-1. Radar traffic information service. "Traffic two o'clock, one mile, westbound."

An important component of the surveillance radar systems used in the U.S. is the **Air Traffic Control Radar Beacon System (ATCRBS)**, sometimes referred to as **secondary surveillance radar**, or **SSR**. The operating principles of this system, and its advantages over primary radar, will be explained later in this chapter.

Figure 10-2. A typical SSR transponder

An essential component of the SSR system is the **transponder**, a piece of equipment now common in most aircraft. A transponder transmits a unique reply signal in response to radar signals received from the ground, allowing a radar controller to identify and track individual aircraft with greater accuracy and safety. The term *transponder* is a contraction of *transmitter/responder.*

At some airports, ATC may use SSR information to provide course guidance down a final approach path for what is known as an **Airport Surveillance Radar (ASR)** approach, usually referred to simply as a **surveillance approach**. This procedure is normally only considered if equipment failure has ruled out all other types of instrument approach. It is a back-up procedure only.

A very small number of airports are equipped with a special type of approach radar equipment, known as **Precision Approach Radar (PAR)**, which enables ATC to provide extremely accurate guidance, along both a specific final approach course and a descent slope, to land on a particular runway. The PAR approach is rarely used by civilian pilots.

In this chapter, we first consider radar vectoring, and then look at radar approaches to land. There is no need for you to understand the theoretical aspects of radar operation to be able to fly according to instructions issued by ATC, and so we will reserve consideration of the principles of radar until the end of the chapter.

The availability of radar at a particular airport is indicated on NOS instrument approach charts by the letters ASR near the communications frequencies, and on *Jeppesen* instrument approach charts by the letter (R) in brackets following the particular communications frequency.

There are many airports and much airspace in the world that is in a nonradar environment. Without the protection of radar, you should comply with any published departure and approach procedures, and expect ATC to request additional reports to enable them to monitor the progress of your flight.

Radar Vectoring

Radar vectoring is a procedure in which a radar controller passes a *heading* to steer to a pilot, with an instruction like:

Seven zero seven four delta
Turn left heading two five zero

The aim of the controller when issuing these headings is to get the aircraft to follow a particular *course* over the ground. Because he will not know precisely the actual wind at your level, or the amount of drift it is causing, he will occasionally issue modified vectors to achieve the desired course.

No radio navigation instruments are required in the aircraft to follow radar vectoring, but radio communication is essential. The pilot concentrates on attitude flying (maintaining the desired heading, altitude and airspeed), while the radar controller concentrates on getting the aircraft to follow the desired course. This does not, however, relieve the pilot of his responsibility to be aware of the aircraft's approximate position at all times, especially in the vicinity of high terrain or obstructions—such an awareness is essential in the event of a communications failure.

Departures. Radar vectors may be assigned by ATC during a **radar departure** from a terminal area. On initial radio communication with the departures controller, you should ensure that he uses the phrase *"Radar contact"* during the reply, which indicates that your aircraft has been positively identified. This may occur while still below the minimum vectoring altitude, and you are still responsible for terrain and obstruction clearance. Once the controller starts giving radar vectors, ATC will assume responsibility for monitoring terrain and obstruction clearances, however you should still retain an awareness of where you are and height above terrain and obstructions. Termination of radar vectoring by ATC will be indicated to you by the phrase *"Resume own navigation"*, as in:

Intercept Victor 55, resume own navigation.

En route. En route radar vectoring off a previously assigned course or airway may be used by ATC for traffic separation, terrain clearance or weather avoidance purposes. Vectors will continue to be assigned until you are reestablished on the assigned route, with ATC indicating termination of vectoring by giving your present position, and then appending the phrase *"Resume own navigation"*.

Approach. Radar vectors during the approach phase are often used extensively for flights into suitably equipped airports, either for guidance to intercept an instrument approach procedure or establish the airplane in the traffic pattern for a visual approach.

When you are being radar vectored prior to commencing an instrument approach, ATC will aim to have the airplane established on the final approach course before the final approach fix (FAF). Clearance for the approach is normally issued with a suitable final intercept vector (usually about a 30° intercept of the final approach course) but, for traffic separation or sequencing purposes, ATC may sometimes vector you through the final approach course. In this case, they are required to inform you of this additional maneuvering, using such phraseology as:

Expect vectoring across final approach course ...

It is most important that you maintain the last assigned heading and/or altitude until you are in receipt of a positive approach clearance, signified by phraseology like:

Turn right heading 180
Maintain 3600 until established on the localizer
Cleared for ILS Runway 21 approach

Minimum vectoring altitudes (MVAs) are established for each part of a terminal area, and it is ATC's responsibility to ensure that aircraft being radar vectored remain at or above the appropriate MVA. MVAs are designed to provide at least 1000 feet clearance from terrain and obstructions (2000 feet in designated mountainous areas), and are not less than 300 feet above the lower limit (floor) of controlled airspace. Minimum Vectoring Altitudes are known to the radar controller, but not to the pilot. All the same, as a pilot you should always keep in mind what is a reasonable altitude by reference to your en route and approach charts.

Minimum vectoring altitudes will keep you inside controlled airspace and clear of obstacles.

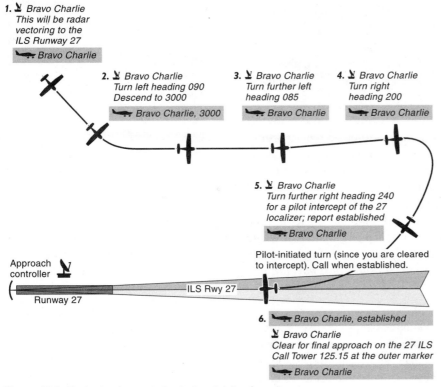

1. *Bravo Charlie*
This will be radar vectoring to the ILS Runway 27

Bravo Charlie

2. *Bravo Charlie*
Turn left heading 090
Descend to 3000

Bravo Charlie, 3000

3. *Bravo Charlie*
Turn further left heading 085

Bravo Charlie

4. *Bravo Charlie*
Turn right heading 200

Bravo Charlie

5. *Bravo Charlie*
Turn further right heading 240 for a pilot intercept of the 27 localizer; report established

Bravo Charlie

Pilot-initiated turn (since you are cleared to intercept). Call when established.

Approach controller

Runway 27

ILS Rwy 27

6. *Bravo Charlie, established*

Bravo Charlie
Clear for final approach on the 27 ILS
Call Tower 125.15 at the outer marker

Bravo Charlie

Figure 10-3. Typical radar vectoring in the vicinity of an airport

When being radar vectored for an approach, keep well ahead of the airplane by organizing your approach navigation aids in preparation for resuming your own navigation once you intercept the final approach course. Remember that each approach aid must be identified before you may use it for navigation. Stay aware of your height above terrain, and be prepared at all times to resume pilot-navigation in case of radio failure.

On **visual approaches** that are being monitored by the approach radar controller, radar service is terminated without advising the pilot when the landing is completed, or when instructed to change to the advisory frequency at uncontrolled airports, whichever occurs first.

If there is a **radar failure**, ATC will use *procedural separation*, which is separating aircraft vertically and horizontally using pilot position reports.

Radar Approaches

There are two types of radar approach that an instrument-rated pilot may make:

- **Airport Surveillance Radar (ASR) approach**—usually called a surveillance approach, this is a *nonprecision* radar approach, executed according to instructions issued by a radar controller whose equipment provides *range* and *azimuth* (course) information only (no accurate altitude information); these approaches may be made straight-in to a specific runway, or down to a circling altitude; and

- **Precision Approach Radar (PAR) approach**—usually referred to simply as a PAR, this is a *precision* radar approach conducted straight-in to a specific runway, down to a much lower altitude than is possible with a surveillance approach. PAR is a precision approach aid, because *slope guidance* is provided. It is an approach and landing aid, rather than an aid for sequencing and separating aircraft.

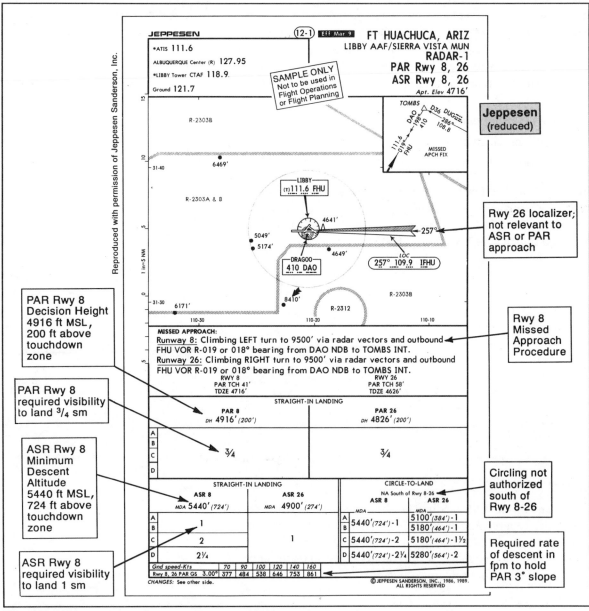

Figure 10-4. Approach plate for a surveillance radar approach (*Jeppesen*)

PARs are only possible at a small number of airports, where radar equipment that provides very accurate range, azimuth and height information is installed.

Radar approaches are only available at those airports with published Civil Radar Instrument Approach Minimums, which are listed in each NOS Instrument Approach Procedures booklet. Special radar approach plates are published by *Jeppesen* for these airports. Figure 10-4 shows information for the radar approaches at Fort Huachuca, AZ, an airport with both ASR and PAR approaches. Note that the ASR minimums are higher than for the more precise PAR.

Surveillance Approaches

A surveillance approach is carried out by the pilot under the guidance of a radar approach controller who uses a special VHF-COM frequency (callsign "... *Radar*") to issue:

- **horizontal navigation (course) instructions** in the form of a series of radar vectors, (headings to steer) to intercept and then maintain the final approach path, aligned with the extended centerline of the landing runway;
- **vertical navigation (descent) advice**, in the form of an instruction of when to commence descent to the previously advised Minimum Descent Altitude (MDA) and, if requested, a recommended altitude for each mile along the final approach path; and
- **arrival** at the Missed Approach Point (MAP).

The recommended altitudes provided by the controller will usually correspond to the normal instrument approach slope of 3° horizontal, which is a slope of 1-in-20 (derived from the 1-in-60 rule, which means that an angle of 3° is equivalent to 3 in 60, or 1 in 20). For every 1 nm (approximately 6000 feet) traveled horizontally, the airplane must descend $\frac{1}{20}$ of this distance to maintain a 3° slope (300 feet). Therefore, a 3° slope is approximately 300 ft/nm, which at 60 knots is 300 fpm, and at 120 knots is 600 fpm.

A 3° slope is approximately 300 feet per nautical mile.

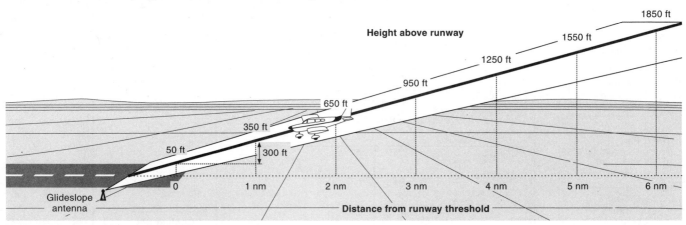

Figure 10-5. The normal instrument approach slope is 3°

Given that the airplane should cross the landing threshold at a height of 50 feet, it is relatively easy to derive a recommended *height/distance profile* for a 3° approach slope to any runway you like. Imagine the airplane moving backward up the 3° slope, from a point 50 feet above the threshold—it will pass through a series of points 300 feet higher for each 1 nm covered.

The figures shown in Figure 10-5 represent the recommended **height above touchdown (HAT)** for a 3° slope. When you are actually flying an instrument approach (including a surveillance approach), the current local altimeter setting is selected in the pressure window, and so you must calculate an altitude indication equivalent to each HAT to monitor descent down the approach slope, the recommended altitude at each mile = touchdown zone elevation + HAT. The recommended altitudes provided by the radar controller during a surveillance approach are determined using the same sort of procedure.

Maintaining a 3° Descent

There is no instrument in the cockpit that is able to indicate descent in terms of feet/nm, although such an instrument would certainly make it easy to follow a 3° approach slope. However, you do have a vertical speed indicator that measures rate of descent in fpm, and an airspeed indicator that measures indicated airspeed in knots (nm/hr). With these instruments, it is possible to estimate the required descent rate for a 300 ft/nm slope. Because the approach path is measured in ground nautical miles, you should use the approximate groundspeed achieved at the approach IAS to increase the accuracy of the descent rate estimate:

- at a GS of 60 knots, the airplane will travel 1 nm in 1 minute, and so to maintain a slope of 300 ft/nm, a descent rate of 300 fpm will be required;
- at a GS of 120 knots, the airplane will travel 2 nm in 1 minute, and so to maintain a slope of 300 ft/nm, a descent rate of 600 fpm will be required; and
- at a GS of 90 knots, the airplane will travel 1.5 nm in 1 minute, and so to maintain a slope of 300 ft/nm, a descent rate of 450 fpm will be required.

Example 1. An airplane has an approach speed of 75 KIAS (and assume IAS = TAS). To achieve a 3° slope of 300 ft/nm, the required rate of descent is:

1. in zero wind: TAS 75 knots, GS 75 knots, 375 fpm.
2. in 15 knots headwind: TAS 75 knots, GS 60 knots, 300 fpm.
3. in 30 knots headwind: TAS 75 knots, GS 45 knots, 225 fpm.
4. in 15 knots tailwind: TAS 75 knots, GS 90 knots, 450 fpm; in this case, you should be wary of continuing the approach to avoid exceeding the tailwind limitation for landing.

An easier method for rapid determination of an approximate descent rate to achieve a 3° slope is:

Rate of descent (fpm) for 3° slope = 5 × groundspeed

Example 5. At GS 80 knots, required descent rate = 5 × 80 = 400 fpm.

Rate of descent in fpm for a 3° slope = 5 × groundspeed.

Flying a Surveillance Approach

For a surveillance approach, the controller will radar vector your airplane to the final approach path, and then advise:

- the published Minimum Descent Altitude (MDA) for the approach;
- the Missed Approach Point (MAP), and the missed approach procedure; and
- when you are approaching the descent point.

Note: If the landing is not to be made straight-in, then the controller will request your airplane's performance category, and provide the appropriate circling MDA.

The controller will instruct you when to commence descent to the MDA, at which point you should establish the airplane in a stable straight descent at a rate appropriate for a 3° slope (as discussed above).

On final approach, the controller will provide:

- course guidance instructions (vectors) to keep the airplane tracking on the extended centerline; and
- distance from the runway or MAP at each mile on final and, if you have specifically requested this, the recommended altitude for each mile.

Guidance will be provided all the way to the MAP where, unless you have reported visual contact with the runway, the controller will instruct you to commence the missed approach procedure.

Landings from surveillance approaches are normally made straight-in. It is also possible to break off at a higher MDA to make a circling approach to the into-wind runway, should this be preferable for any reason. For instance, if use of the straight-in approach course for Runway 18 is not advisable because of weather to the north of the airport, then it may still be possible to make a surveillance approach from the south on Runway 36 instead, and then circle close-in to land on Runway 18.

PAR Approaches

A PAR approach is similar to an ASR approach, except that the radar information used is much more precise, allowing a highly accurate approach to be made to a lower Decision Height (DH) than the Minimum Descent Altitude (MDA) for an ASR approach. The PAR approach is a precision approach, based on both course and slope guidance. This means the pilot has a better chance of establishing visual contact with the runway in poor weather conditions.

Very sensitive radar equipment, separate from the standard ASR installation, is required for PAR approaches. A typical PAR installation consists of two antennas, scanning the vertical and horizontal planes within a narrow corridor covering the final approach path to a particular runway. The specialist PAR controller uses a radar screen that provides an accurate display of the airplane's position relative to both the final approach course (along the extended runway centerline), and the glidepath, right down to the runway touchdown zone.

There are only a handful of airports in the continental U.S. where published PAR approaches are available for civil users (plus several more in Alaska), but many military airports are equipped to provide precision radar approaches (called GCAs, for Ground Controlled Approaches). PAR or GCA approaches by civil aircraft are normally only used in an emergency, but they are quite easy to fly, and extremely accurate.

The PAR controller will vector you to the final approach course, and advise when you are approaching the descent point. As the airplane intercepts the glidepath, he will instruct you to *"Begin descent"*, and you should then commence a stabilized descent at the desired rate to maintain a 3° slope.

During more-or-less continuous transmissions while you are on final approach, the controller will advise you of the distance to go to the threshold, and any deviation from the required course and glidepath. You must use gentle and coordinated alterations of pitch and heading to make immediate corrections in response to controller instructions.

You will be advised when the airplane reaches the DH (although you should, of course, monitor this yourself, and commence to scan for the runway as you approach the DH). If visual contact with the runway is not established at the DH, or if a safe landing is not possible, then you should initiate a missed approach. If you continue for a landing, the controller will provide course and glidepath advice until you are over the threshold.

No-Gyro Approaches

If the heading indicator, and/or any other gyro-driven flight instrument, should fail or become unreliable during instrument flight (a partial panel situation), then you should declare an emergency and request a no-gyro approach. This may consist simply of radar vectors for a descent through the cloud base to establish in the landing pattern, but if available, ATC will direct you for a straight-in PAR or surveillance approach to a suitable runway.

Under these circumstances, you will usually not have reliable heading indications, and so the controller will tell you when to commence and stop all turns that are required to intercept and maintain the final approach course. The controller will command you to *"Turn left"* and *"Stop turn"*. You should conduct the descent according to usual radar approach procedures, but must make all turns at standard rate (3° per second) until established on final approach, after which half standard rate is required. All turn instructions must be complied with immediately.

Using the Transponder

Most aircraft are now equipped with a transponder that transmits a strong responding signal to a secondary ground radar, which can provide ATC with additional information such as aircraft identification and altitude. The theory of secondary surveillance radar (SSR or ATCRBS) is discussed in detail at the end of this chapter, however, the operating techniques are considered here.

The transponder is usually warmed-up in the STANDBY position while taxiing prior to takeoff. (It should also go to STANDBY at the end of a flight before the master avionics switch is moved to OFF). The four-figure discrete code to be used for the flight will probably be assigned by ATC when they issue an IFR clearance, and this should be selected immediately by the pilot.

The transponder should be selected to the ON position, or the ALT position if it is a Mode C system, as the airplane lines up on the runway for takeoff. If your airplane is equipped with a serviceable transponder, then it must be used in flight, even when you are operating in airspace where its carriage is not mandatory.

Even though transponders produced by various manufacturers vary slightly in design, they are all operated in basically the same manner. However, as a responsible pilot, you should become thoroughly familiar with your particular transponder.

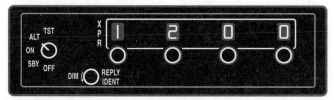

Figure 10-6. Typical transponder panel

The Function Selector Knob

This enables you to select the transponder on and off, and to operate it in one of its various modes. Typical transponder operating modes include:

OFF: transponder deactivated completely.

STANDBY: warmed up, and ready for immediate use. This is the normal position until you are ready for takeoff, when you would select ALT or ON.

ON: transmits the selected code in Mode 3/A (to assist with aircraft identification only) at the normal power level.

LO SENS: for those transponders provided with this function, the selected code is transmitted in Mode 3/A, but at a lower power level. This may be requested by the radar controller to prevent overly strong blips appearing on the screen from aircraft close to the interrogating antenna. After landing, you would normally switch to STANDBY or OFF for the same reason.

ALT: altitude-reporting mode (Mode C), which may be used if the aircraft is fitted with a suitable altitude encoding device, either an encoding altimeter or a blind encoder. These feed the current altitude to the transponder for transmission onto the ATC radar screen. (If not installed, the transponder still transmits in Mode A, aircraft identification without altitude reporting).

TST: tests the transponder by causing it to generate an internal self-interrogation signal—correct operation is indicated by illumination of the reply monitor light.

Code Selection

Suitable knobs are provided to allow selection of the required code on the transponder, the selected code being prominently displayed in digital form.

Whenever codes are selected or altered, it is important to avoid passing through such vital codes as 7700 (for emergencies), 7600 (for radio failure) and 7500 (for hijack) when the transponder is switched ON, as these codes will activate unnecessary alarms in nearby ATC radar facilities. This can be prevented by making it your standard procedure to select STANDBY while the transponder code is being changed. Your flight instructor will explain further.

The Reply-Monitor Light

The reply light flashes to indicate that the transponder is replying to an interrogation pulse from a ground station. The reply-monitor light will glow steadily when you:

- press the TEST button, or move the function switch to the TEST position (depending on the design of your particular transponder), to confirm correct functioning; or
- transmit an *ident* pulse.

The IDENT Switch or Button

The IDENT button is pressed whenever the radar controller requests the pilot to *"squawk ident"*. A special reply pulse is transmitted by the transponder to the interrogating ground station, which causes a special symbol to appear for a few seconds on the radar screen alongside the normal return from your aircraft, thus allowing positive identification by the radar controller.

Note: Your particular transponder may have minor variations to the functions described above, but will certainly be fundamentally the same. It may, for instance, have a separate mode selector to select Mode A (position reporting) or Mode C (position and altitude reporting).

Radio Terminology for Transponder Operation

The term **squawk** that is commonly used by ATC in connection with transponder operation is basically intended to mean "transmit". It is usually followed by an instruction describing the type of transmission required by the controller, for instance: squawk ident, squawk code 4000, squawk mayday (7700).

To squawk is to transmit via your transponder.

ATC: *"... (callsign) squawk code 4000."*

Pilot response is to read back: "... (callsign) code 4000", and to select the transponder to that code.

ATC: *"... (callsign) squawk code.... and ident."*

Pilot response is to change the code and then press the IDENT button, allowing the radar controller to identify you positively on his screen.

ATC: "… (callsign) squawk standby."

Pilot response is to move the function switch from ALT or ON to the STANDBY position, for a temporary suspension of transponder operation (maintaining present code).

ATC: "… (callsign) squawk normal."

Pilot response is to reactivate the transponder from STANDBY to ON, or to ALT if it is a Mode C system, retaining the existing code.

ATC: "… (callsign) stop squawk."

Pilot response is to select the transponder to OFF.

ATC: "… (callsign) stop altitude squawk."

Pilot response is to move the function selector from ALT to ON, so that the altitude information is removed from the transponder's reply signals.

Further information on transponder operating procedures may be found in the Airman's Information Manual (AIM).

How Radar Works

The remainder of this chapter discusses the basic theory of radio waves, and of radar in particular. It is not essential knowledge but it will help your understanding of radio, radar and radio navigation aids.

Radio utilizes the ability to transmit electromagnetic energy, in the form of radio waves, from one place to another. Radio has played a vital role in the development of aviation—**radar** is an important type of radio system.

Waves of electromagnetic energy emanating from a radio transmitter can carry information, such as speech, music, and Morse code out into the surrounding environment. Radio receivers tuned to the same frequency may detect and utilize these signals, often at quite long distances from the transmitter.

Important aeronautical uses of radio include:

• air/ground voice communication; and

• radio navigation (the ADF/NDB combination, VOR and ILS).

Figure 10-7. Radio involves the transmission and reception of electromagnetic energy between distant locations

The Reflection of Radio Waves

Radio waves and light waves are both forms of electromagnetic radiation, differing only in their frequency.

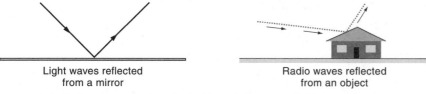

Light waves reflected from a mirror

Radio waves reflected from an object

Figure 10-8. Radio waves can be reflected in a similar way to light waves

Electromagnetic radiation can be reflected from certain surfaces. Light waves, for instance, will be reflected by the metallic coating on a mirror. Similarly, radio waves of certain frequencies will be reflected from metallic and other surfaces, some of the radio energy returning to the point from which it was transmitted as a return echo. Other surfaces and objects, such as wood, may not cause reflection of the radio waves, which will simply pass through like X-rays pass through a body.

Radar

The detection of reflected radio waves at the point from which they were originally transmitted is the fundamental basis of radar. The basic operating principles of radar were first developed during the late 1920s, and subsequent rapid improvements in the ability to detect objects, such as aircraft, and to measure their range, was often a decisive factor during World War II (1939–45). The term *radar* was derived from **ra**dio **d**etection **a**nd **r**anging.

A typical radar system consists of a combined transmitter-receiver unit, which is equipped with a parabolic dish antenna that is designed to be efficient both in the transmission of a focused beam of radio signals, and in the reception of any reflected signals from the same direction. The dish can be rotated slowly, so that the whole sky can be scanned systematically, if desired.

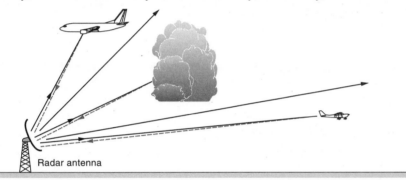

Radar antenna

Figure 10-9. Radar is the transmission of electromagnetic radio energy and the detection of some of the reflected energy back at the point of transmission

The properties and behavior of radio waves (their reflectivity and range) depends on their frequency. Radio signals from the upper range of the radio frequency spectrum, with very short wavelengths, are the most suitable for use in radar systems. Radars usually operate in the UHF (ultra-high frequency) and SHF (super-high frequency) bands.

Figure 10-10. A typical radar antenna

Radars usually operate in the UHF (ultra-high frequency) and SHF (super-high frequency) bands.

The Relationship of Time and Distance

All electromagnetic energy travels at the speed of light, 162,000 nautical miles per second (300,000 kilometers per second), the equivalent of almost eight journeys around the world in one second. Some common forms of electromagnetic energy are light, radio waves, X-rays, ultraviolet radiation and infrared radiation.

It is possible to measure the elapsed time between the transmission of a very short burst, or pulse, of radio energy, and the reception of any reflected echo back at the source. Given the known velocity of radio waves, a relatively simple mathematical calculation will allow determination of the distance or range of the reflecting object from the transmitter.

Radar converts an elapsed *time* to a *distance:*

$$\frac{\text{distance}}{\text{time}} = \text{speed}$$

Multiplying both sides of this equation by *time* gives an expression for *distance* in terms of the known speed of light and the measured elapsed time.

$$\text{distance} = \text{speed} \times \text{time}$$

During the elapsed time between transmission of the pulse and reception of its reflection (measured electronically at the radar site), the distance between the radar site and the object will have been traveled twice, once out and once back, so the elapsed time needs to be halved. This is done electronically.

The speed of light being so great, means that the time intervals involved are extremely short. A stream of rapidly repeating pulses can be transmitted, with reception of any echoes still being possible during the intervening short time periods between each pulse transmission.

As a matter of interest, the time taken for a radar pulse to travel to and from a reflector 20 nm away (a total of 40 nm) is 0.000250 seconds, or 250 millionths of a second.

$$40 \text{ nm } (2 \times 20) \textit{ at speed of light } 162{,}000 \text{ nm/sec} = \frac{40}{162{,}000} \text{ sec}$$
$$= 0.000250 \text{ sec}$$

- If the measured elapsed time interval is 250 millionths of a second, then the object is 20 nm distant.
- If the measured elapsed time interval is 750 millionths of a second, then the object is 60 nm distant.
- If the measured elapsed time interval is 125 millionths of a second, then the object is 10 nm distant.
- If the measured elapsed time interval is 12.5 millionths of a second, then the object is 1 nm distant. A time interval of 12.5 millionths of a second (or microseconds) can be thought of as a radar mile.

At What Range can Radar Detect Targets?

Radar uses ultra-high frequency (UHF) transmissions, which basically follow a straight line-of-sight path, so that signal coverage will be limited by significant obstructions (buildings and terrain), and by the curvature of the earth. They will cause radar shadows, and objects in these shadow areas will not be detected.

The curvature of the earth means that the higher an aircraft is flying, the greater the distance at which it can be detected by radar. The relationship between the maximum detection distance (in nautical miles) and aircraft altitude is given by the expression:

$$\text{Radar range in nm} = \sqrt{1.5 \times \text{altitude in feet}}$$

Note: $\sqrt{1.5 \times \text{altitude}}$ is the same as $1.22 \times \sqrt{\text{altitude}}$, which some people prefer. It is a similar expression, since the square root of 1.5 is 1.22.

Example 6. At 5000 feet AGL over flat terrain with no obstructions, an aircraft will be detected up to approximately 87 nm.

$$\text{Radar range in nm} = \sqrt{1.5 \text{ alt in ft}} \qquad or \qquad = 1.22\sqrt{\text{alt in ft}}$$
$$= \sqrt{1.5 \times 5000} \qquad\qquad = 1.22\sqrt{5000}$$
$$= \sqrt{7500} \qquad\qquad\quad = 1.22 \times 71$$
$$= 87 \text{ nm} \qquad\qquad\quad = 87 \text{ nm}$$

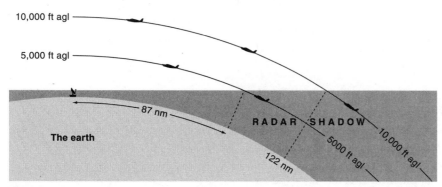

Figure 10-11.

Example 7. At 10,000 feet AGL over flat terrain with no obstructions, an aircraft will be detected out to approximately 122 nm.

$$\text{Radar range in nm} = \sqrt{1.5 \text{ alt in ft}} \qquad or \qquad = 1.22\sqrt{\text{alt in ft}}$$
$$= \sqrt{1.5 \times 10{,}000} \qquad\qquad = 1.22\sqrt{10{,}000}$$
$$= \sqrt{15{,}000} \qquad\qquad\quad = 1.22 \times 100$$
$$= 122 \text{ nm} \qquad\qquad\quad = 122 \text{ nm}$$

Note: These are expected ranges under ideal conditions; in reality, the range of a radar may be significantly less than this, and it may experience blind spots and radar shadows.

Radar range may be increased if the radar antenna is sited at a high elevation, both to raise it above nearby obstacles that would cause shadows, and to allow it to see further around the curvature of the earth. Hence radar dishes are often sited on the tops of hills and buildings. The approximate range at which an aircraft can now be detected by an elevated radar installation is given by a slight revision of the previous formula:

$$\text{Radar range} = \sqrt{1.5 \text{ altitude of radar dish}} + \sqrt{1.5 \text{ altitude of aircraft}}$$

or

$$\text{Radar range} = 1.22\sqrt{\text{altitude of radar dish}} + 1.22\sqrt{\text{altitude of aircraft}}$$

Example 8. At 5000 feet AGL over flat terrain with no obstructions, an aircraft will be detected up to approximately 99 nm if the radar dish is elevated 100 feet above a uniform surface.

$$\text{Radar range in nm} = \sqrt{1.5 \times 100} + \sqrt{1.5 \times 5000}$$
$$= (\sqrt{150} + \sqrt{7500})$$
$$= (12 + 87)$$
$$= 99 \text{ nm}$$

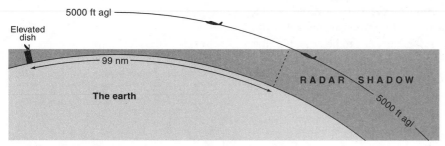

Figure 10-12. Radar range is increased if the radar dish is elevated

If the radar dish can be elevated 400 feet, then its range will increase by:

$$\sqrt{1.5 \times 400} = 24 \text{ nm}$$

Another technical design feature (apart from the positioning of the radar dish) that determines the range of a radar is the interval existing between pulse transmissions to allow the transmitter to act as a receiver. The greater the time interval, the greater the range from which echoes can be received, prior to the next transmission. The number of separate pulses transmitted in one second is known as the **pulse repetition rate (PRR)**. A radar with a low PRR has a greater detection range than a radar with a high PRR.

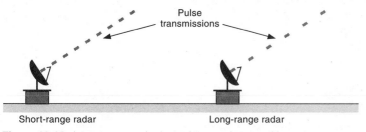

Figure 10-13. Long-range radar has a lower pulse repetition rate

Bearing Measurement by Radar

The bearing (direction) of reflecting objects from a radar site is determined by slowly rotating the dish antenna, a typical rate being between two and ten revolutions per minute.

As it rotates, a narrow beam of multiple radar pulses is directed around the horizon, with any reflected signals being received almost instantaneously along each bearing that is scanned. The angle of the antenna relative to north at the moment a return is received will provide the bearing (or azimuth) of the object.

Both the bearing and the range of an object can therefore be determined by radar, so that its position can be precisely pinpointed, and the *returns* displayed as *blips* on a suitable screen.

Primary Surveillance Radar

Radar that makes use of reflected radio energy is known as **primary radar**, and it is used for a number of purposes in aviation including:

- **Surveillance Radar,** to provide an overview of a wide area, and used in Air Route Surveillance Radar (ARSR) and Airport Surveillance Radar (ASR), and also used for ASR instrument approaches; and

- **Precision Approach Radar (PAR),** used for extremely accurate azimuth and slope guidance on final approach to land.

Surveillance radar is designed to give a radar controller an overview of his area of responsibility. It does not transmit pulses in all directions simultaneously, but rather as a beam, which is slowly rotated. For an aircraft to be detected, the beam must be directed roughly toward it. If the radar controller has his radar tilted up, then it may miss lower aircraft at a distance; conversely, nearby high aircraft may not be detected if the tilt is down.

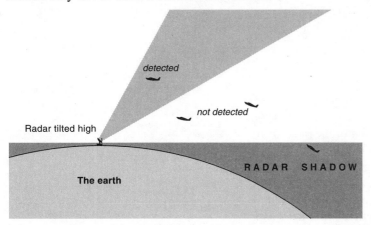

Figure 10-14. To be detected, aircraft must be within the radar transmitter's beam

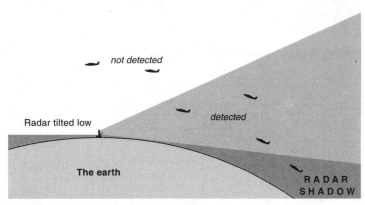

Figure 10-15. Radar tilted low cannot detect targets directly above

The Radar Screen

Most radar screens are simply cathode ray tubes (CRTs) that resemble circular television screens. Using the same principle as television, a beam of electrons is directed at the fluorescent coating of the CRT to provide a radar picture. Radar controllers generally have circular displays showing the position of the radar antenna in the center, with range marks to aid in estimating distance. The radar screen is also known as a **plan position indicator (PPI)**.

The actual radar dish may be located away from the position of the radar controller, possibly on a nearby hill or tower. As the radar antenna rotates slowly, the small electron beam in the controller's CRT also rotates, leaving a faint line or trace on the screen in a direction aligned with the direction of the antenna at that moment. Any radar return signal along that same bearing appears as a *blip* or *paint* at the appropriate spot on the screen.

The direction of north is indicated on the screen, allowing the controller to estimate the bearing, or azimuth, of each target. Concentric range marks assist in the estimation of target distance. The paint of the target remains visible for some seconds after the small trace line has moved on, and will still be visible, but fading, as its next paint occurs in the following revolution. This fading trail of blips allows the controller to determine the motion of the target in terms of direction and speed.

In areas of high traffic density, the radar responsibility may be divided between various controllers, each with his own screen and radio communications frequency, and will go under such names as *Approach Control, Center,* and *Departure Control.*

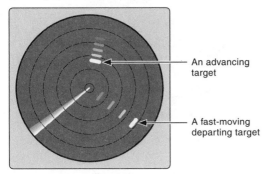

Figure 10-16. A radar screen

In addition to the range marks, various symbols and lines may be superimposed on an ATC radar screen, using a video overlay, so that it effectively becomes an electronic map of the scanned area.

The video image for a terminal area radar typically shows:

- the location of both primary and satellite airports, common flight paths to them, radio navaids (VORs, LOMs), and significant obstructions;
- airways, and extended runway centerlines; and
- the controlled airspace structure, and boundaries of any special use airspace (such as Prohibited and Restricted Areas).

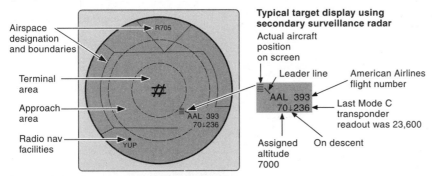

Figure 10-17. A typical ATC radar screen

Some Disadvantages of Primary Radar

While a big advantage of primary radar is that no special equipment is required in the aircraft, it does have some operational disadvantages including:

- **clutter**, caused by spurious returns reflected from precipitation, ground obstacles and buildings or mountains;
- **variation** in the size and intensity of radar returns, according to the reflectivity of different aircraft (for instance, a Cessna 172 is harder to plot than a Boeing 747); and
- **shadows** or blind spots, from screening by high terrain features or areas of heavy precipitation.

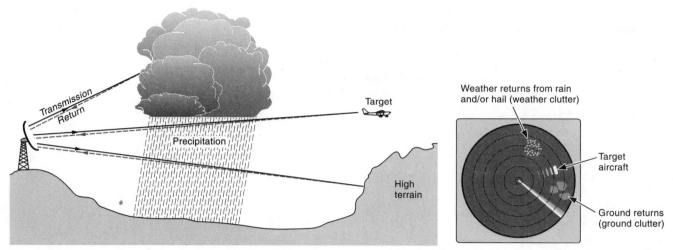

Figure 10-18. Primary Surveillance Radar is subject to clutter

The radio energy in the reflected signal received at the radar dish may be quite small, depending on the strength of the original transmission, how good a reflector the target is, its distance from the radar antenna, and so on. A radar that is sensitive enough to pick up weak returns from targets may also pick up returns from terrain and precipitation, leading to ground clutter and weather clutter on the screen. During periods of heavy rain, primary radar may be significantly degraded.

Some radars incorporate an electronic sifting device known as a **moving target indicator (MTI)** that only allows signals from moving targets to be shown on the screen, in an attempt to eliminate clutter from stationary objects.

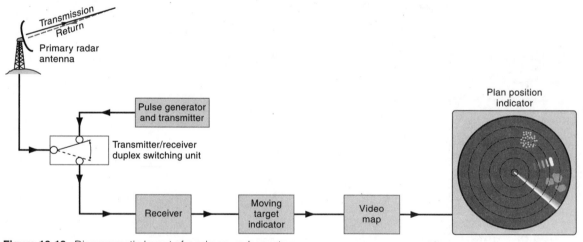

Figure 10-19. Diagrammatic layout of a primary radar system

On screens relying solely on primary radar returns, it will often be difficult for a controller to identify and track a particular aircraft, especially when there are other aircraft returns in close proximity, or in the presence of clutter caused by weather or terrain. The aircraft may have to execute a significant turn, for instance, in order for the controller to establish positive identification, a time-wasting and tedious process at best.

Secondary Surveillance Radar (SSR) or
Air Traffic Control Radar Beacon System (ATCRBS)

Secondary surveillance radar overcomes most of the limitations of primary radar simply by ensuring that a conspicuous, high-energy return pulse is produced by any aircraft that is equipped with a device known as a **transponder**.

Primary radar detects radar energy passively reflected from a target and displays it as a blip, or fading series of blips, on a screen; this is similar to seeing an aircraft reflected in the beam of a searchlight at night.

Secondary radar is much more than this, and involves an active response by the aircraft every time it is scanned by a ground-based radar. It is as if each time a searchlight strikes a target, the target is triggered to light itself up very brightly in response, rather than just passively reflect some of the light energy transmitted from the ground site. Secondary radar actually consists of two sets of radar "talking" to each other.

The strength of the reflected signals received by a primary radar system is usually only a tiny fraction of the energy of the original pulse transmissions. Consequently, primary radars need powerful transmitters and large antennas.

As only a small amount of radio energy transmitted from the ground is required to trigger a response from an airborne SSR transponder, the ground-based secondary radar transmitter and antenna systems tend to be quite compact in comparison. In fact, the typical long, narrow SSR antenna is small enough to be mounted above the larger primary radar dish at many radar ground sites.

The SSR ground equipment consists of:

- an interrogator that provides a coded signal asking a transponder to respond;
- a highly directional rotating radar antenna that transmits the coded interrogation signal, then receives any responding signals, and passes them back to the interrogator; and
- a decoder, which accepts the signals from the interrogator, decodes them and displays the information on a radar screen.

The SSR airborne equipment consists of a transponder carried in each individual aircraft.

The original interrogation pulses transmitted from the ground station trigger an automatic response from the aircraft's transponder. It transmits strong coded reply pulses, which are then received back at the ground station. These reply pulses are much, much stronger than the simple reflected signals used in primary radar. Even a very weak interrogation pulse received at the aircraft will trigger a strong response from the transponder.

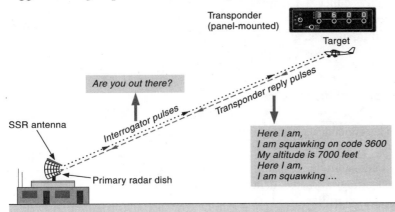

Figure 10-20. SSR is two radars talking to each other

The secondary responding pulse sent by a transponder not only enhances the basic positional information available to a controller, but can also carry coded information that will help distinguish that aircraft from all others on the same radar screen. Depending on the type, or *mode*, of the transponder, and the *code* selected on it by the pilot (as requested by ATC), it can convey additional information such as:

- the specific identity of an aircraft;
- its altitude (if Mode C has been selected by the pilot);
- any abnormal situation affecting the aircraft, such as radio failure, distress, emergency, etc.

Other significant advantages of SSR systems include:

- they are not degraded to the same extent as primary radar by weather or ground clutter;
- they present targets of the same size and intensity to the controller, regardless of the relative reflectivity of individual aircraft; and
- they minimize blind spots.

Radar Screens and SSR

In the United States, secondary surveillance radar is referred to as the **Air Traffic Control Radar Beacon System (ATCRBS)**. The role of the SSR transponder is becoming more and more crucial, not only within the busy terminal areas, but also in those areas of the ATC en route environment beyond the effective coverage of primary radar, where SSR is the only source of position information available.

On the radar screens used by most controllers, information from both primary and secondary radars is combined on the one display. In many cases, these "broadband" radar screens are actually synthetic radar displays, showing radar position symbols that are generated by automated computer processing of primary and secondary radar signals, sometimes from widely separated radar sites.

Different symbols are used to indicate whether the position information and track "history" for a particular aircraft have been derived from primary, secondary, or combined radar sources. Associated with each symbol will be other information regarding the aircraft concerned, which may include its identity, level, destination and groundspeed. This information may be obtained either directly from the coded SSR signals sent by the aircraft, from calculations by the radar's digital processor, or from manual entries made by the controller himself into the ATC computer.

We recommend that you visit an ATC radar facility, either a terminal approach/departure facility or an en route center, to see the system in action from the air traffic controller's point of view. Understanding his task, and how it interacts with yours as pilot-in-command, will lead to greater professionalism.

Transponder Modes

Two different types, or modes, of transponder equipment are fitted in civil aircraft:

- Mode 3/A: the basic transponder type, with 4096 different codes selectable by the pilot; and
- Mode C: the same as Mode 3/A sets, but with an automatic altitude-reporting capability (provided the aircraft is fitted with an encoding altimeter, or a "blind" encoder). This sends altitude information to the controller based on 29.92 in. Hg irrespective of what the pilot has set in the pressure window.

So that a radar controller can distinguish a particular aircraft from others operating in its vicinity, ATC will usually assign a unique discrete transponder code to each aircraft, using the phraseology *"Squawk code ..."*. When this code is selected by the pilot, the aircraft's alphanumeric identification (N number or flight number, whatever the controller desires) is displayed on the radar screen next to its position symbol.

If the aircraft is fitted with a Mode C transponder, then its current altitude will be automatically displayed (to the nearest 100 feet), no pilot or controller input being necessary. If the radar display is an automated type, then the current groundspeed, as calculated by the radar's digital processor, can also be called up and displayed by the controller. All this information assists the controller in the rapid interpretation of the situation presented on a radar screen, and eases his task in separating aircraft and maintaining a safe and efficient traffic flow.

You may be specifically requested by ATC to *"squawk ident"*, when they want positive identification of an aircraft. This is the only time that you should touch the IDENT button on your transponder. Pressing this button once will cause a special "ID" symbol to appear adjacent to the aircraft's position on the screen. The IDENT button should not be held in, just firmly pressed once and released.

Transponder Codes

A total of 4096 different codes can be selected on a transponder, but not all of them are available to be assigned as discrete codes to assist with identification.

There are certain standard codes allocated for military and civilian use. For instance, all transponder-equipped VFR aircraft should squawk Code 1200, unless they are assigned another discrete code. Other standard codes are allocated for use in emergencies only, and will trigger visual and aural alarms in ATC facilities:

- Emergency situations—7700;
- Hijack—7500;
- Radio communications failure—7600.

Mandatory Transponder Requirements

14 CFR requires carriage and use of a transponder with *altitude-reporting* capability in a considerable amount of US airspace. This is primarily to assist in reducing the risk of midair collisions in congested airspace where the old "see-and-avoid" system of traffic separation is considered inadequate.

A Mode C transponder must be carried by all aircraft operating:

- in Class A airspace, Class B airspace and Class C airspace, and, within the lateral boundaries of Class B and C airspace areas designated for an airport, up to 10,000 feet MSL;
- from the surface up to 10,000 feet MSL when operating within 30 nm of an airport listed in Appendix D, Section 1, of 14 CFR Part 91 (list contains most major US airports, including Atlanta, Denver, Los Angeles, Miami, Minneapolis, both New York airports, St. Louis, Seattle & both Washington airports);
- in all airspace of the 48 contiguous states and the District of Columbia at or above 10,000 feet MSL (except when flying at or below 2500 feet AGL); and
- from the surface to 10,000 feet MSL within a 10-nm radius of any airport in 14 CFR Part 91 Appendix D, section 2, except the airspace below 1200 feet outside the lateral boundaries of the surface area of the airspace designated for that airport; (currently only one airport is listed in section 2 of Appendix D—Billings, MT).

Mode S

A new type of transponder, known as Mode S, and also referred to as the **discrete address beacon system**, has been developed to reduce the workloads of both controllers and pilots, as well as reducing the congestion on normal radio communications frequencies.

In addition to the altitude information provided by Mode C systems, Mode S transponders can automatically transmit an aircraft's registration and type whenever it is interrogated by ground-based radar. This eliminates the need for the controller to enter the identification of each aircraft manually into the ATC computer, and means that a pilot does not have to select a discrete code. This improvement is significant enough on its own, but fully optioned Mode S installations will provide further benefits.

By a process known as *select addressing*, it is possible for ATC to transmit other information, such as weather reports, ATIS, and clearances to a specific aircraft, which can then be displayed on a suitable screen or printer in the cockpit. This promises to decrease the volume of radio transmissions considerably.

TCAS

TCAS stands for **traffic alert and collision avoidance system**. The regulations state that no person may operate a large aircraft that has a passenger seating configuration, excluding any pilot seat, of more than 30 seats unless it is equipped with an approved TCAS II traffic alert and collision avoidance system and the appropriate class of Mode S transponder.

The TCAS II system installed in large passenger jets allow the pilots to see the transponder returns of the surrounding aircraft. The TCAS II computer warns pilots of possible traffic conflicts, and will even command an avoidance procedure (resolution) if a collision seems imminent. Pilots operating TCAS II equipped aircraft should follow the commands of the TCAS first, and advise ATC of their change of flight path second. Once the collision threat has passed, pilots should maneuver their aircraft back onto the ATC cleared routing or altitude.

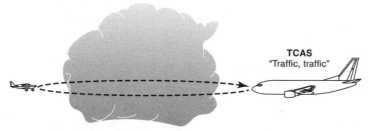

Figure 10-21. TCAS in action

✍ Review 10

1. The process of separating aircraft and positioning them by ATC passing headings to steer is known as radar _____.

➤ radar vectoring

2. If a radar service is not available, then ATC will separate aircraft using procedures based on their estimated positions and known altitudes. This is known as:

    (a) nonradar separation.

    (b) procedural separation.

    (c) standby separation.

➤ (b)

3. Primary surveillance radar can detect aircraft, even if they carry no airborne equipment. Secondary surveillance radar (SSR) on the ground detects strong responding signals transmitted from aircraft that carry a _____.

➤ transponder

4. In the United States, secondary surveillance radar is known as _____.

➤ Air Traffic Control Radar Beacon System (ATCRBS)

5. In providing a radar traffic information service, ATC report the position of a possibly conflicting aircraft as "two o'clock northbound". The "two o'clock" is related to the (heading/ground track) of your airplane.

➤ ground track

6. Is ATC radar that is approved for approach control service able to be used for course guidance to the final approach course?

➤ yes

7. Is ATC radar that is approved for approach control service able to be used for ASR approaches?

➤ yes

8. Is ATC radar that is approved for approach control service able to be used for the monitoring of nonradar approaches?

➤ yes

9. The radar ground equipment for a PAR approach (is/is not) the same as for an ASR approach.

➤ is not

10. Altitude-reporting capability of a transponder is called Mode _____.

➤ Mode C

11. When ATC request you to "squawk ident", you should press the IDENT button (once firmly/for 15 seconds).

➤ once firmly

12. The standard transponder code for an emergency is _____.

➤ 7700

13. The standard transponder code for radio failure is _____.

➤ 7600

14. The standard transponder code for a VFR airplane is _____.

➤ 1200

15. FAA radar locations are found in the _____ booklet.

➤ Airport/Facility Directory (A/FD)

16. Availability of radar at a particular airport is indicated on NOS approach charts by _____.

➤ the letters ASR in the communications area on the chart

17. The availability of radar at a particular airport is indicated on *Jeppesen* instrument approach charts by _____.

➤ the letter (R) following the particular frequency in the communications area on the chart

18. An approach to a runway under the guidance of a radar controller who passes tracking instructions and recommended altitudes is known as an _____ approach.

➤ Airport Surveillance Radar approach

19. What approximate rate of descent in fpm is required to achieve a 3° glideslope, which is 300 feet per nm, if the groundspeed of the airplane is 60 knots?

➤ 300 fpm

20. What approximate rate of descent in fpm is required to achieve a 3° glideslope, which is 300 feet per nm, if the groundspeed of the airplane is 90 knots?

➤ 450 fpm

21. The approximate range of any VHF signals for an aircraft at 6000 feet above the level of a ground station is _____ nm.

➤ 95 nm

22. The approximate range of any VHF signals for an aircraft at 2000 feet above the level of a ground station is _____ nm.

➤ 55 nm

23. The approximate range of any VHF signals for an aircraft at 2500 feet above the level of a ground station is _____ nm.

➤ 61 nm

24. During an ASR approach, the controller will provide headings to align the airplane with the extended centerline of the runway and also provide without request three additional items, which are _____.

➤ when to commence descent to the MDA, the airplane's position each mile on final from the runway, and arrival at the MAP

25. Must a particular surveillance approach have been previously authorized and established by the FAA for a particular runway for it to be available? Must it have an approach chart and/or published minimums?

➤ yes, yes

26. During a no-gyro approach, and prior to being handed off to the final approach controller, all turns should be made at (standard rate/half standard rate) unless otherwise advised.

➤ standard rate

27. During a no-gyro approach, and after being handed off to the final approach controller, all turns should be made at (standard rate/half standard rate) unless otherwise advised.

➤ half standard rate

Slant Distance

Distance measuring equipment (DME) can provide pilots with extremely useful information, their distance from a DME ground station. DME uses radar principles to measure this distance, which is the *slant* distance in nautical miles, rather than the *horizontal* distance (or range).

For most practical purposes, the DME distance can be considered as range, except when the airplane is within a few miles of the DME ground station. As a general rule of thumb, the DME distance may be considered as an accurate horizontal distance (with negligible slant range error) if the airplane is 1 nm or more from the DME ground facility for each 1000 feet above the facility. For instance, if the airplane is 12,000 feet higher than the elevation of the DME ground station, DME distances greater than 12 nm will provide an accurate range. The greatest errors occur at high altitudes close to the DME ground station.

DME measures slant distance.

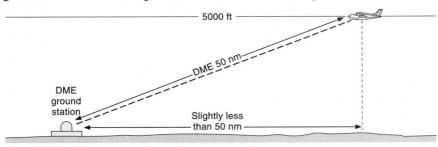

Figure 11-1. DME measures slant distance

Passing directly over the ground beacon, the DME indicator in the cockpit will either show the altitude of the airplane above the ground in nautical miles (1 nm = 6000 feet approximately), or the DME indication will drop out.

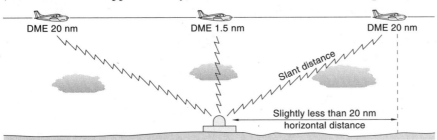

Figure 11-2. Passing over a DME ground station

DME Cockpit Displays

DME distance may be displayed in the cockpit as either a digital read-out, or by a pointer that moves around a calibrated scale. The pilot selects the DME by selecting the VOR or ILS frequency on the VHF-NAV radio (since most DMEs are paired with a VOR frequency or a localizer frequency). Once the DME is locked on, and a DME reading and ident obtained, the DME indications can be used for distance information regardless of whether the VOR (or localizer) is used for tracking or orientation purposes.

Most airborne DME equipment is capable of computing and displaying the rate of change of DME distance (the *rate of closure* of the airplane with the DME ground station). If it is assumed that slant distance equals horizontal distance, and that the airplane is tracking either directly toward or directly away from the DME ground station, then the rate of closure read-out will represent groundspeed, a useful piece of information.

DME measures rate of closure to the ground station and displays your groundspeed and time to the station.

Some DME indicators can also display **time to the station (TTS)** in minutes at the current rate of closure, by comparing the groundspeed with the DME distance. If the airplane is not tracking directly toward or away from the DME ground station, then these readings will not represent groundspeed and TTS.

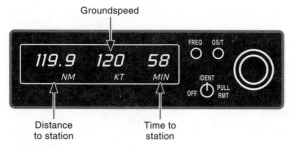

Figure 11-3. A digital DME panel

If the DME equipment in the airplane does not give a groundspeed read-out, then the pilot can simply note the DME distance at two particular times, and carry out a simple calculation of *groundspeed = distance/time* either mentally or on his navigation computer. Again, this is only accurate when the airplane is tracking directly to or from the DME ground beacon.

Example 1. A pilot notes DME distance and time as he tracks directly toward a DME ground station. Calculate groundspeed.

DME 35	Time 0215 UTC		
DME 25	Time 0220 UTC		
10 nm	5 min	=	**GS 120 kt**

Circular Position Lines

The DME provides a circular position line. If the DME reads 35 nm, for instance, then the pilot knows that the airplane is somewhere on the circumference of a 35 nm circle centered on the DME ground station.

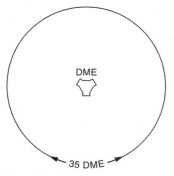

Figure 11-4. A circular position line from a DME

Information from another radio aid may provide a positive fix of the position of the airplane, provided the two position lines give a good *cut* (angle of intercept), ideally as close to perpendicular as possible.

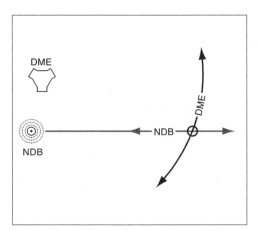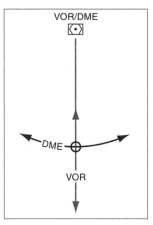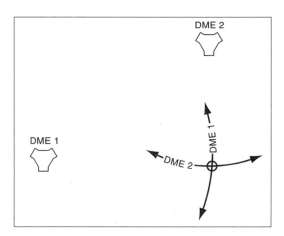

Figure 11-5. Using two radio navigation aids to fix position

How DME Works

DME uses the principle of secondary radar. Radar is covered thoroughly in Chapter 10, where both primary and secondary radar are discussed. Primary radar detects its own transmissions that are reflected from some object; secondary radar detects responding transmissions from a transponder activated by an interrogation signal.

Distance measuring equipment operates, using the secondary radar principle, by the airborne transmitter (the interrogator) sending out a stream of radio pulses in all directions on the receiving frequency of the DME ground beacon, which acts as a transponder.

At the target DME ground beacon, these pulses are passed through an electronic gate. If the pulses and the gate match up, the DME ground beacon is triggered, and responds by transmitting a strong answering signal. The airborne DME equipment detects this answering signal and measures the time between the transmission of the interrogating pulse from the airplane and the reception of the ranging reply pulse from the DME ground station. It converts this time to a distance in nautical miles and the DME indicator, when it displays this distance, is said to have *latched on* or *locked on.*

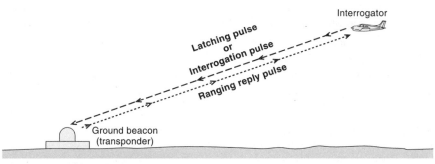

Figure 11-6. Operation of the DME

Each DME ground transponder can cope with about 100 different airplanes at any one time before becoming saturated, and the system is designed so that there is no possibility of interrogation pulses from one airplane causing an incorrect range indication in another airplane.

Because the frequencies are carefully chosen so that stations with like frequencies are situated well apart geographically, there is no likelihood of interference from the wrong DME ground station. The DME must still be identified, however, before you may use it for navigation. If your DME does not lock-on, try another ground station in case the first one is saturated.

You must positively identify a DME ground station before using it for navigation.

DME signals are line-of-sight transmissions (like VHF voice communications, radar and VOR), with an approximate usable range (in nautical miles) equal to the square root of (1.5 × altitude in feet).

Approximate DME range (nm) = $\sqrt{1.5 \times \text{altitude in feet}}$

DME Frequencies

DME operates in the UHF (ultra-high frequency) band from 962–1213 MHz which, with 1 MHz spacing, gives 252 possible frequencies. Each DME channel consists of two frequencies (an *interrogation* frequency from the airplane and a paired *response* frequency from the ground station).

There are 126 channels currently in use for the International DME system, numbered from 1 to 126, followed by the suffix "X", such as Channel 122X (there are an additional 126 channels allocated for the system, using the same numbers but suffixed with a "Y", which are not presently used). Each DME channel consists of two separate frequencies (an interrogation frequency used by the airborne transmitter, and a corresponding response frequency used by the transponder at the DME ground station).

There is no need for a pilot to know these details, since these channel numbers and frequencies are not used to select the DME—the correct DME channel is selected automatically when the frequency of an associated VOR or ILS station is selected on the VHF-NAV set.

VOR/DME Pairing

Each VOR frequency has a specific DME channel paired with it. For instance, VOR frequency 112.10 MHz has DME Channel 58 paired with it, so that the VOR's associated DME will automatically be interrogated when the pilot selects the VOR frequency 112.10 on his VHF-NAV. The purpose of this pairing is to reduce the pilot's workload in the cockpit, with only one selection instead of two required, and to reduce the risk of a pilot selecting the right VOR but the wrong DME station.

Co-located VORs and DMEs are frequency paired, and each will have the same Morse code *ident*, the VOR identifier modulated on 1020 Hz and broadcast about every 10 seconds, and the DME identifier modulated on 1350 Hz and broadcast about every 30 seconds, which is about one DME ident for every three VOR idents, with the DME ident being heard with a higher pitch tone.

A single coded identifier received only once every 30 seconds, and not mixed in with another identifier broadcast every 10 seconds, means that the DME component of the VORTAC station is operative, but the VOR component is not.

VOR ground stations are often combined with TACAN installations (Tactical Air Navigation system), which provide azimuth and distance information to military aircraft on UHF frequencies. The combined VOR/TACAN facility is known as a VORTAC. Civil aircraft obtain azimuth (course) information from the VOR, and distance information from the DME component of the TACAN.

A paired VOR and DME (or vortac) can provide a very good position fix, consisting of:

- the **radial** from the VOR; and
- the **distance** from the DME.

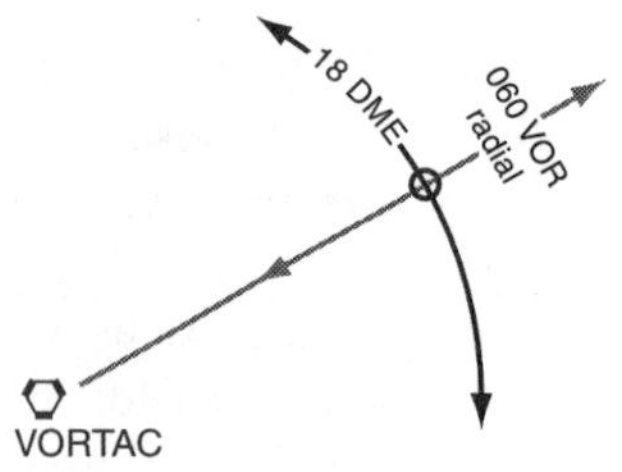

Figure 11-7. Fixing position with VOR and DME

ILS/DME Pairing

Some instrument landing systems (ILSs) have their localizer frequency paired with a DME located close to the runway threshold. This provides the pilot with indications of the *distance to go* to the runway threshold during an ILS or localizer approach to that runway, which can be useful.

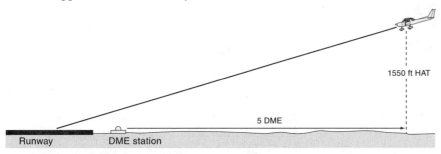

Figure 11-8. Using a paired localizer/DME

Some ILSs, however, are flown using the ILS for course and slope guidance, with a DME associated with some other nearby aid, such as a VOR, providing distance information. The need for this will be noted on the instrument approach chart.

DME Arcs

Many instrument approach procedures use a DME arc along which the airplane should track to intercept the final approach course. DME arcs are sometimes used in Departure Procedures (DPs) also.

The DME arc is a circular path centered on the DME ground facility. The airplane is flown to stay, at least approximately, at a fixed DME distance. Another aid, such as an RMI, is normally used to assist in tracking. Flying DME arcs is discussed in detail in Chapter 28.

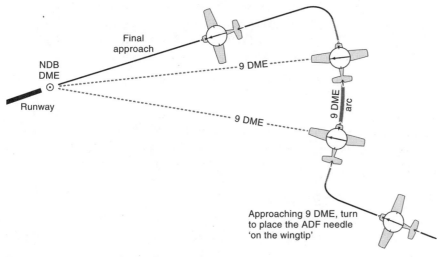

Figure 11-9. Example of a DME arc maneuver

✎ Review 11

1. The letters DME are an abbreviation for _____; a DME measures (horizontal/vertical/slant) distance.

➤ distance measuring equipment, slant

2. The DME is selected on the _____ radio, usually along with a co-located VOR.

➤ VHF-NAV

3. The coded identifier of the DME is transmitted about once every _____ seconds and is modulated to _____ Hz.

➤ 30 seconds, 1350 Hz

4. The coded identifier of the VOR is transmitted about once every _____ seconds and is modulated to _____ Hz.

➤ 10 seconds, 1020 Hz

5. For each time you hear the DME identifier, you should hear the VOR identifier about _____ times.

➤ 3 times

6. DME readings give an accurate range if the airplane is further than 1 nm per _____ feet above the elevation of the DME ground station.

➤ 1000 feet

7. For an airplane cruising at 12,000 feet MSL approaching an airport, elevation 2000 feet, the DME read-out from a VORTAC sited on the airport may be considered an accurate range down to _____ DME.

➤ 10 DME

8. For an airplane cruising at 15,000 feet MSL approaching an airport, elevation 210 feet, the DME read-out from a VORTAC sited on the airport may be considered an accurate range down to _____ DME.

➤ 15 DME

9. If an airplane flies 12,000 feet directly above a DME ground beacon, the DME indicator will either drop out temporarily or reduce to a DME distance of _____ nm.

➤ 2 nm

10. Flying at 12,000 feet MSL and passing over a DME ground beacon elevation 3000 feet, the DME indicator will either drop out temporarily or reduce to a DME distance of _____ nm.

➤ 1.5 nm

11. If an airplane tracking directly toward a DME is at 37 DME at time 0115, and at 27 DME at time 0120, what is its groundspeed?

➤ 10 nm in 5 min = GS 120

12. If an airplane tracking directly away from a DME is at 22 DME at time 1223, and at 32 DME at time 1230, what is its groundspeed?

➤ 10 nm in 7 min = GS 86

13. Passing abeam a DME ground station, the DME readings change in the following manner as you proceed: 25, 21, 17, 15, 14, 15, 17, 21. What was your abeam distance from the DME ground station?

➤ 14 nm

14. A DME can provide a (circular/straight) position line.

➤ circular

The NDB and the ADF

General Description

The **nondirectional beacon** (NDB) is the simplest form of radio navigation aid used by aircraft. It is a ground-based transmitter which transmits radio energy in all directions, hence its name—the *nondirectional* beacon.

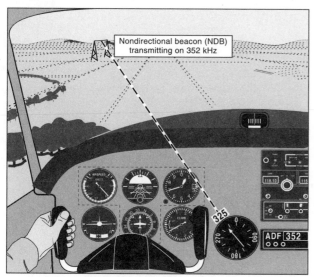

Figure 12a-1. A correctly tuned ADF indicates the direction of the selected NDB from the aircraft

The ADF, or **automatic direction finder**, installed in an airplane has a needle that indicates the direction from which the signals of the selected NDB ground station are being received. This is extremely useful information for pilots flying in instrument conditions and/or at night. In days past, the ADF was referred to as the *radio compass*.

Flying to an NDB in an airplane is similar to following a compass needle to the north pole—fly the airplane toward where the needle points, and eventually you will arrive overhead.

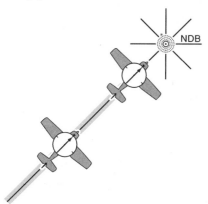

Figure 12a-2. Flying to a station is straightforward

Flying away from the north pole, however, with the magnetic compass needle pointing behind, could take the airplane in any one of 360 directions. Similarly, flying away from an NDB using only the ADF needle will not lead the airplane to a particular point (unlike flying to an NDB). The airplane could end up anywhere! Further information is required.

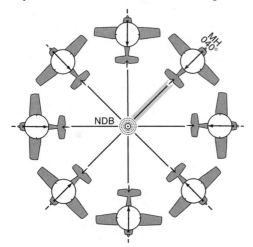

Figure 12a-3. Flying away from a station to somewhere else requires further information than just the needle on the tail

The ADF and the Heading Indicator

The extra information required by the pilot, in addition to that supplied by the ADF needle, comes from the magnetic compass or, more commonly, from the heading indicator (which is kept manually aligned with the compass by the pilot, and is easier to use). Accurate navigation can be carried out using these two references:

• **an ADF needle** that points at an NDB ground station; plus

• **a heading indicator** that indicates the airplane's magnetic heading (MH).

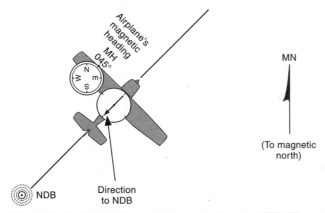

Figure 12a-4. To be really useful for navigation, the ADF/NDB combination needs support from a magnetic compass (or from a HI)

Note: Since a heading indicator will slowly drift out of alignment, it is vital that you periodically realign it with the magnetic compass in straight flight at a steady speed, say every 10 minutes or so.

A drift out of alignment of 3° in 15 minutes is the maximum acceptable for the HI to be considered serviceable.

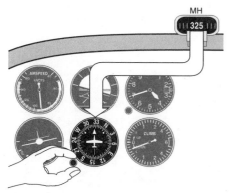

Figure 12a-5. Periodically realign the HI with the magnetic compass in steady flight

The NDB/ADF Combination

Before using an ADF's indications of the bearing to a particular NDB, the airplane must be within the operational range of the NDB and you must have:

- correctly selected the NDB frequency;
- identified its Morse code ident; and
- tested the ADF needle to ensure that it is indeed "ADFing".

Also, the HI should have been aligned with the magnetic compass (plus or minus the deviation correction, as given on the compass card).

If the NDB bears 40 degrees to the left of the airplane's magnetic heading, say MH 070, then the situation can be illustrated as in Figure 12a-6. Since the NDB is 40 degrees left of the nose or, if you prefer, on a *relative bearing* of 320 (RB 320), it will have a magnetic bearing of 030 (MB 030) from the airplane. This gives you some idea of where the airplane is, and in what direction to travel to reach the NDB.

The ADF/NDB combination, in conjunction with the heading indicator, can be used by the pilot:

- **to track** to the NDB on any desired course, pass over the NDB, and track outbound on whatever course is desired; or
- **to fix** the airplane's position.

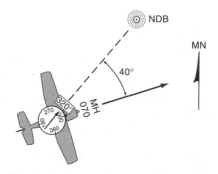

Figure 12a-6. A diagrammatic representation

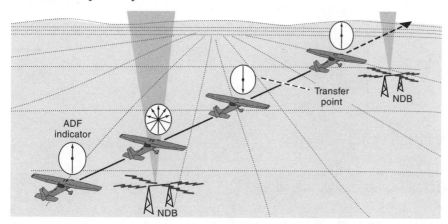

Figure 12a-7. Flying toward, over, and past an NDB, and then on to the next one

The ADF in the airplane should, whenever possible, be selected to an NDB relevant to the desired path of the airplane. If tracking en route between two NDBs, the changeover point from one NDB to the next would reasonably be the halfway point, depending of course on their relative ranges.

If the NDB is ahead, the ADF needle will point up the dial; if the NDB is behind, the ADF needle will point down the dial. As the airplane passes over the NDB, the ADF needle will become quite sensitive and will swing from ahead to behind.

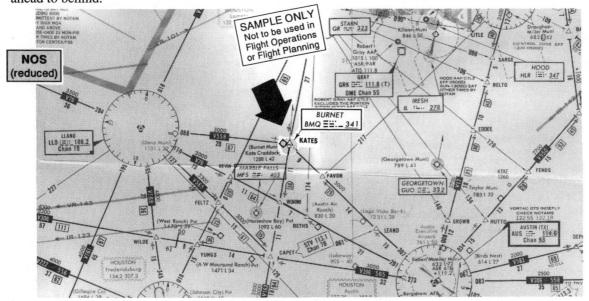

Figure 12a-8. Burnet NDB is available to confirm arrival at KATES intersection

The ADF can also be used for more advanced procedures such as:

- flying an accurate "racetrack" holding pattern based on the NDB; or
- using the NDB for guidance when maneuvering in the vicinity of an airport, either as a nonprecision approach aid in its own right, or as a lead-in to a precision approach aid such as an ILS (instrument landing system).

Low-powered NDBs, known as **compass locators**, are often co-located with one of the marker beacons associated with an ILS. A co-located compass locator and outer marker is designated on approach charts by LOM (for locator outer marker), as illustrated at Columbus Muni, Indiana (Figure 12a-9).

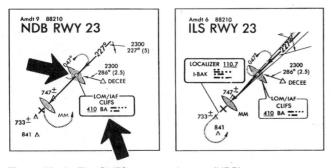

Figure 12a-9. The CLIFS compass locator (NDB)

The compass locator CLIFS (frequency 410 kHz and coded ident *dah-dit-dit-dit dit-dah*) may be used as:

- a point over which to hold in a racetrack pattern inbound MC 227;
- the sole tracking aid for the NDB approach for Runway 23; or
- an additional tracking guide when using the Runway 23 instrument landing system, and as an outer marker (LOM) or check point on this ILS approach.

Some NDBs are not available for holding or for instrument approaches, but only for en route navigation. This information is available in the green Airport/Facility Directory (A/FD).

The NDB/ADF combination is the simplest form of radio navigation in theory, yet it requires a competent instrument pilot to use it accurately in practice. Other advanced systems, such as the VOR, are more complicated in principle, but easier to use in practice.

The NDB

The nondirectional beacon (NDB) is the ground-based part of the combination. It is referred to as nondirectional because no particular direction is favored in its transmissions; the NDB radiates identical electromagnetic energy in all directions.

Each NDB transmits on a given frequency in the low-frequency or medium-frequency LF/MF band (somewhere between 200 and 1750 kHz), the transmission mast being either a single mast or a large T-antenna strung between two masts.

Figure 12a-10. NDB transmission antennas

To avoid confusion between various NDBs, and to ensure that the pilot is using the correct beacon, each NDB transmits its own particular identification signal (or *ident*) in the form of a two- or three-letter Morse code signal, which should be checked by the pilot before using the NDB for navigation.

If the NDB is the only aid being used for navigation, for instance during a typical NDB approach, the ident should be continuously monitored in the cockpit by the pilot, since the ADF has no failure flag to indicate a faulty signal or, indeed, no signal at all.

Monitor the ident continuously if an NDB is the only aid you are using.

Example 1. The Burnet NDB (Figure 12a-8) operates on frequency 341 kHz and may be identified by the coded ident for BMQ, *dah-dit-dit-dit dah-dah dah-dah-dit-dah*. A nearby NDB is Marble Falls, which operates on frequency 403 kHz, and may be identified by the coded ident for MFS, *dah-dah dit-dit-dah-dit dit-dit-dit*.

The normal sources of NDB frequency and identification information are the en route charts, or the approach charts, which you should be carrying in the cockpit. More detailed information on a particular NDB, or any other radio aid, is available in the Airport/Facility Directory (A/FD).

§ **BURNET MUNI KATE CRADDOCK FLD** (T27) 1 SW UTC–6(–5DT) 30°44′16″N 98°14′19″W **SAN ANTONIO**
1288 B S4 **FUEL** 100LL, JET A **L-15D**
RWY 01-19: H4201X75 (ASPH) S-30 MIRL **IAP**
RWY 01: SAVASI(NSTD)—GA 3.5°TCH 12′. Trees. Rgt tfc.
RWY 19: SAVASI(NSTD)—GA 3.5°TCH 12′. Trees.
AIRPORT REMARKS: Attended 1300–0100Z‡. For arpt attendant after ~~...~~ y 01–19 one
box SAVASI left side.
COMMUNICATIONS: CTAF/UNICOM 122.8
AUSTIN FSS (AUS) TF 1–800–WX–BRIEF. NOTAM FILE AUS.
HOUSTON CENTER APP/DEP CON 132.35
RADIO AIDS TO NAVIGATION: NOTAM FILE AUS.
LAMPASAS (H) VORTAC 112.5 LZZ Chan 72 31°11′07″N 98°08′30″W 183° 27.3 NM to fld.
1290/08E.
➡ **NDB (MHW)** 341 BMQ 30°44′20″N 98°14′13″W at fld

Figure 12a-11. An extract from the A/FD

NDB Range

For long-range en route navigation where no other aids are available, a reasonably powerful NDB with a range of 100 nm or more is usually required. Some NDBs used for long-distance overwater tracking, such as in the Pacific area, may have a range of 400 nm. In the U.S., however, where route segments are relatively short and there are many aids, especially VORs, most NDBs have only a short range.

A compass locator positioned at an outer marker of an ILS to assist in holding and local maneuvering may have a range of only 15 nm; an en route NDB might have a range of 75 nm.

The range of an NDB depends on:

- the power of transmission (10–2000 watts);
- the frequency of transmission;
- atmospheric conditions existing at the time—electrical storms, which can generate spurious signals, and periods of sunrise and sunset, which can distort or reflect the signals from an NDB; and
- the nature of the earth's surface over which the signals travel.

In the U.S., NDBs are classified according to their range, or **standard service volume** (SSV) radius, as follows:

Class	Range
Compass locator	15 nm
MH	25 nm
H	50 nm*
HH	75 nm

*The range of individual H-class NDB stations may be less than 50 nm—such restrictions will be published in NOTAMs, and in the A/FD.

The distances are the same at all altitudes. The classification (and range) for an individual NDB can be checked in the Airport/Facility Directory (A/FD).

NDB Signal Accuracy

An ideal NDB signal received at an airplane may be accurate to ±2°, however various factors may reduce this accuracy considerably. These factors include:

Thunderstorm effect: causing the ADF needle to be deflected toward a nearby electrical storm (cumulonimbus cloud) and away from the selected NDB.

Night effect: at night, NDB signals can be refracted by the ionosphere and then return to earth as strong *skywaves*, causing interference with the normal

NDB surface waves, and resulting in a fading signal and a wandering ADF needle (most pronounced at dawn and dusk).

Interference: from other NDBs transmitting on similar frequencies (this can be particularly significant at night).

Mountain effect: caused by reflections of the NDB signals from mountains.

Coastal effect: caused by the NDB signal bending slightly toward the coastline when crossing it at an angle.

NDB Identification

Each NDB is identifiable by a three-letter Morse code identification signal that is transmitted along with its normal signal. This is known as its **ident**.

Each compass locator is identified by a two-lettered coded ident. If it is associated with the outer marker (LOM), the compass locator ident will be the first two letters of the localizer identification group. If it is associated with the middle marker (LMM), the compass locator ident will be the last two letters of the localizer identification group.

You must identify an NDB or compass locator before using it for any navigational purposes within its operational range and, if using it for some length of time, then it should be periodically re-identified. During an NDB approach, the NDB or compass locator ident should be monitored continuously.

The lack of an ident may indicate that the NDB is out of service, even though it may still be transmitting (say for maintenance or test purposes), and it must not be used for navigation. When under test, the coded word *test* may sometimes be transmitted: *dah dit dit-dit-dit dah.* If an incorrect ident is heard, then those signals must not be used.

To identify most NDBs and compass locators, simply select AUDIO on the ADF, listen to the Morse code signal, and confirm that it is indeed the correct one. All NDBs in the U.S. can be identified with the ADF mode selector in the ADF position. In continental Europe and some of the Pacific Islands, however, there are still some NDBs that require the pilot to select BFO (beat frequency oscillator) to enable identification. The BFO imposes a tone onto the NDB carrier wave to make it audible.

Many NDBs carry voice transmissions, such as the Automatic Terminal Information Service (ATIS) at some airports, and the Transcribed Weather Broadcast (TWEB). It is also possible, in a situation where the communications radio (VHF COM) has failed, for ATC to transmit voice messages on the NDB frequency, and to receive them on the ADF if AUDIO is selected. Those that do not have a voice capability will have "W", which stands for *without voice,* included in their class designator in the A/FD, for instance as "HW".

Note: Broadcast stations may also be received by an ADF, since they transmit in the LF/MF bands. It is not good airmanship, however, to use broadcast stations as navigation aids, since they are difficult to identify precisely. Even if an announcer says *"This is the Memphis Country Hour"*, it is possible that the transmission is coming, not from the main transmitter, but from an alternative or emergency transmitter located elsewhere, or even a relay station many miles away from the main transmitter.

To use information from a broadcast station, you must be certain of its geographical position—something which is difficult to determine. Listening to broadcast stations in flight is also distracting from your main operational tasks. Broadcast stations are not used for IFR navigation in the United States—they are not required to have standby generators and do not have to advise the FAA if they are not transmitting for some reason.

You must positively identify an NDB before using it for navigation.

Monitor the ident continuously during an NDB approach.

If you hear an incorrect or test ident, the NDB must not be used for navigation.

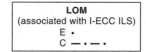

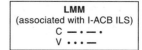

Figure 12a-12. Typical NDB and compass locator idents

The ADF

The airborne partner of the ground-based NDB is the automatic direction finder, usually referred to as the ADF. It operates on the radio compass principle whereby the ADF needle indicates the direction from which the signals are coming. Under ideal conditions, the ADF needle will point directly at the NDB antenna; under less-than-ideal conditions, the signals from the NDB antenna may not follow a straight path, and so the direction indicated by the ADF needle will be somewhat in error.

The automatic direction finder has three main components:

The ADF receiver, installed in the cockpit radio panel, which the pilot tunes to the frequency of the desired NDB and verifies with the ident.

The antenna system, comprising a loop antenna and a sense antenna (or their modern equivalent, a single combined unit) which together determine the signal direction.

The ADF cockpit display, either a fixed-card or a rotatable-compass-card, with a pointer or needle indicating the signal direction. The ADF cockpit instrument is usually installed to the right of the attitude flight instruments, with the top of the dial representing the nose of the airplane and the bottom of the dial representing its tail. Ideally, the ADF needle will point continually and automatically toward the NDB ground station.

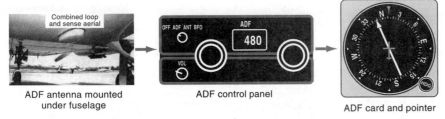

ADF antenna mounted under fuselage   ADF control panel

ADF card and pointer

Figure 12a-13. The airborne ADF equipment

ADF Antennas

Improved reception on a portable radio is sometimes possible by rotating it to a particular position, because of the directional properties of its receiving antenna. The automatic direction finder works on the same principle.

The Loop Antenna

The loop antenna, when it is aligned with the plane of a radio wave (in the position illustrated in Figure 12a-14), will have slightly different voltages induced either side of it because, at any instant, the two sides will be receiving different parts of the radio wave. This will cause a small electric current to flow from one side of the loop to the other, and this current is measurable. The strength of the electric current is greatest when the loop antenna is aligned with the radio wave, which occurs in two positions 180° apart.

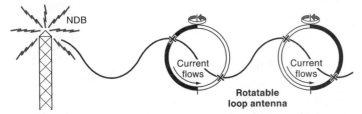

Figure 12a-14. The loop antenna having a maximum electric current induced in it by a radio wave

If the loop antenna is rotated until it is perpendicular to the radio wave, then each side of the loop will be receiving similar parts of the radio wave simultaneously, there will be no difference in potential, no voltage difference across the loop, and hence no current, so it is a *null* position.

The null positions can be thought of as the radio wave slipping through the loop. For one complete 360° rotation of the loop antenna, the null, or zero, signal will occur in two positions, 180° apart.

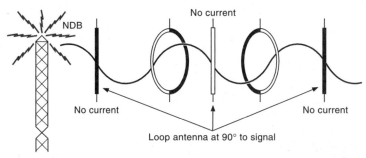

Figure 12a-15. The loop antenna in its null position, having zero electric current induced in it by a radio wave

For one 360° rotation of the loop antenna, the received signal will pass through two maximums and two nulls, with the nulls (zero current) being much more sharply defined than the maximums, as illustrated in Figure 12a-16.

Small angular deflections of the loop antenna near its null positions produce larger changes in current than similar angular changes near to the loops maximum positions. For this reason, a null position of the loop antenna, rather than a maximum position, is used for direction finding purposes.

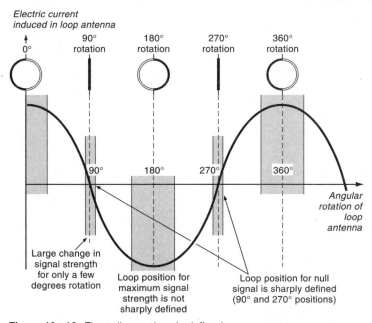

Figure 12a-16. The nulls are sharply defined

If a loop antenna is rotated into a null position where no current is generated, then the NDB transmitter is either directly ahead of the loop or 180° away and directly behind the loop. This is a very ambiguous situation, but it can be resolved using a *sense antenna*.

The Sense Antenna

The sense antenna is a single stationary antenna. It has the same sensitivity as the loop in its maximum position, and so it generates a continuous maximum current. Unlike the loop antenna, it has no directional properties.

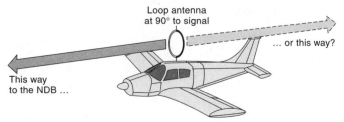

Figure 12a-17. Which way to the NDB? (using only a loop antenna)

By adding the steady signal from the sense antenna to the alternating signal from the loop as it rotates, there is now only one null position as the loop rotates 360°. This position acts as a phase reference point, allowing the correct null position to be correctly identified. In other words, the 180° ambiguity has been removed, and the pilot can be certain of the direction to the NDB.

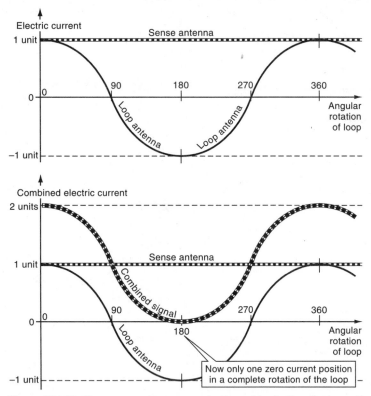

Figure 12a-18. The sense antenna removes the ambiguity from the loop signal

Modern ADF Antenna Systems

In days gone by, the loop had to be turned manually by the pilot, navigator or radio operator for the radio compass needle to point toward the ground station. Then came a loop antenna that was rotated electrically, so that the ADF needle pointed continuously and automatically at the NDB.

Modern equipment uses a loop antenna that does not have to be rotated at all, but is rather a fixed loop antenna (or *goniometer*) that is directionally sensitive to radio signals. This has allowed the ADF antenna system to become compact, especially if the sense antenna is internally mounted.

Figure 12a-19. A modern ADF antenna system

The ADF Control Panel

There are various types of ADF that may be fitted to an airplane and, prior to flight, you must be familiar with the set that you will use.

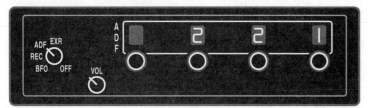

Figure 12a-20. Typical ADF control panel

You must be able to select and positively identify the NDB that you wish to use, and then verify that the ADF needle is indeed responding to the signals from that NDB. The correct procedure, any time a new NDB is to be used, is to confirm (verbally if so desired):

- **selected**;
- **identified**; and
- **ADFing** (and giving a sensible bearing to the NDB).

The Mode Selector or Function Switch

The mode selector switches between ADF modes of operation:

OFF: to switch the ADF off.

ADF: the normal position when the pilot wants bearing information to be displayed automatically by the needle. Most NDBs can be identified with the mode selector in this position (and the volume knob adjusted suitably).

ANT (or REC): abbreviations for antenna or receiver. In this position, only the signal from the sense antenna is used, with no satisfactory directional information being available to the ADF needle. The reason for this function position is that it gives the best audio reception to allow easier identification, and better understanding of any voice messages. Never leave the mode selector in this position if you are navigating using the ADF—the ADF needle will remain stationary with no obvious indication that it is not responding! It is possible, however, to identify most NDBs with the mode selector in the ADF position (which is a safer position), and for the ANT position to be avoided.

BFO (or CW): abbreviations for beat frequency oscillator or continuous wave. This position, rarely required in the United States, is selected when identifying the few NDBs that use A0/A1 or A1 transmissions, which are unmodulated carrier waves whose transmission is interrupted to provide the NDB's Morse code identification. Since no audio message is carried on an unmodulated carrier wave, the BFO (as part of the airborne equipment) imposes a tone onto the carrier wave signal to make it audible to the pilot so that the NDB signal can be identified. Again, do not leave the mode selector switch in this position when navigating using the ADF.

TEST: Placing the mode selector into the TEST position will deflect the ADF needle from its current position. Placing the mode selector back to ADF should cause the needle to swing back and indicate the direction of the NDB. This function should be tested every time as part of the selected, identified, ADFing tuning procedure. Some ADF sets have a separate TEST button which only needs to be pressed to deflect the needle, and then released to check the return of the needle. You only have to deflect the needle approximately 30°, and watch the return, for the test to be satisfactory.

Note: On some ADF equipment, the TEST function is achieved using the ANT/REC position, which drives the needle to the 090 position. Returning the mode selector to ADF should see the needle start ADFing again.

VOL: The volume knob will probably be separate to the mode selector. With audio selected to the pilot's headset or to the cockpit speakers, the volume should be adjusted so that the ident or any voice messages on the NDB or compass locator may be heard. If signal reception is poor in ADF, then try ANT/REC; if there is no signal reception, try BFO/CW. Remember to return the mode selector to ADF!

> **Whenever you select an ADF mode, remember to return the mode selector to ADF when you have completed the task!**

Frequency Knobs

NDBs transmit on frequencies in the range 200–1750 kilohertz, the most common band being 200–400 kHz. To allow easier and accurate selection of any particular frequency, most modern ADFs have knobs that allow digital selection, in 100, 10 and 1 kHz steps. Some ADFs may have a band selector (200–400; 400–800; 800–1600 kHz), with either a tuning knob or digital selection for precise tuning.

ADF Cockpit Displays

The basic purpose of an automatic direction finder (ADF) in an airplane is for its needle to point directly toward the selected NDB ground station. The ADF cockpit display is a card or dial placed vertically in the instrument panel so that:

> **The ADF needle always points directly toward the selected NDB ground station.**

- if the ADF needle points up, the NDB is ahead;
- if the ADF needle points down, then the NDB is behind;
- if the ADF needle points to one side, then the NDB is located somewhere to that side of the fore–aft axis of the airplane.

To convey this information to the pilot, various presentations are used, three of which we will consider:

- the fixed-card ADF, also known as the relative bearing indicator (RBI);
- the rotatable-card ADF (the "poor man's" RMI); and
- the radio magnetic indicator (RMI).

Fixed-card ADF or Relative Bearing Indicator (RBI)

A fixed-card display has an ADF needle that can rotate against the background of a fixed-azimuth card of 360°, with 000 (360) at the top, 180 at the bottom, etc. The fixed-card ADF is also known as the relative bearing indicator (RBI), and is common in many general aviation aircraft. On the fixed-card ADF, the needle indicates the relative bearing (RB) of the NDB from the airplane.

On the fixed-card ADF, the needle indicates the relative bearing (RB) of the NDB from the airplane.

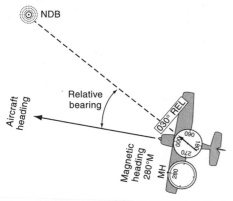

Figure 12a-21. A fixed-card ADF is a relative bearing indicator (RBI)

The **relative bearing** of the NDB from the aircraft is the angle between the aircraft's heading and the direction of the NDB. Relative bearings are usually described clockwise from 000 to 360, however it is sometimes convenient to describe the bearing of the NDB relative to the nose or tail of the airplane.

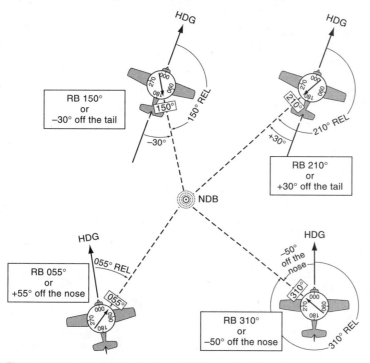

Figure 12a-22. The RBI or fixed-card ADF shows relative bearings

Each time the airplane changes its magnetic heading, it will carry the fixed card with it. Therefore, with each change of magnetic heading, the ADF needle will indicate a different relative bearing (RB).

With each change of magnetic heading, the ADF needle will indicate a different relative bearing.

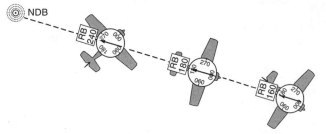

Figure 12a-23. Each time heading is changed, the relative bearing also changes

It is not the needle that moves, but rather the fixed-card—the needle continues to point at the station. The principle is easily understood if you stand, point at an object, and then turn and face another direction while continuing to point at the object. Your arm indicates the same direction to the object, but it makes a different angle with your body because you have changed your heading. The relative bearing of the object has changed because your heading has changed.

Orientation Using the RBI or Fixed-Card ADF

The airplane can be oriented with respect to the NDB knowing:

- the magnetic heading (MH) of the airplane (from the magnetic compass or heading indicator); plus
- the relative bearing (RB) of the NDB from the airplane.

In practice, magnetic heading is flown using the heading indicator, which should be realigned with the magnetic compass in steady flight every 10 minutes or so. Our illustrations will therefore display the heading indicator instead of the magnetic compass. In Figure 12a-24, the pilot is steering MH 280, and the ADF indicates RB 030 to the NDB.

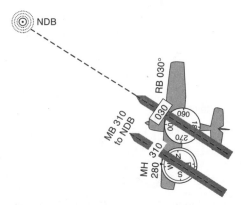

Figure 12a-24. Orientation (Where am I?) using an RBI

MH 280	+	RB 030	=	MB 310 to NDB
Aircraft Magnetic Heading	+	Relative Bearing of NDB from aircraft	=	Magnetic Bearing of NDB from aircraft

Visualizing Magnetic Bearing To the NDB (MB)

A quick pictorial means of determining MB to an NDB, using a relative bearing indicator and a heading indicator, is to translate the ADF needle onto the HI, by paralleling a pencil or by using your imagination. MH + RB = MB to ground station.

Visualizing Magnetic Bearing From the NDB

The magnetic bearing of the aircraft from the NDB is the reciprocal of the magnetic bearing to the NDB. In Figure 12a-25, this is MB 130 from the NDB. MB from can be visualized as the tail of the pencil (or needle) when it is transferred from the RBI onto the HI.

Note: An easier method of finding reciprocals than adding or subtracting 180°, is to either:

- add 200 and subtract 20; or
- subtract 200 and add 20.

Figure 12a-25. A pictorial (but clumsy) method of finding MB

Example 2.

MB 310 to NDB	MB 270 to NDB	MB 085 to NDB
−200	−200	+200
+ 20	+ 20	− 20
MB 130 from NDB	MB 090 from NDB	MB 265 from NDB

The Rotatable-Card ADF

The rotatable-card ADF is an advance on the fixed-card ADF, because it allows the pilot to rotate the card so that the ADF needle indicates, not relative bearing, but magnetic bearing to the NDB. The pilot does this by aligning the ADF card with the HI compass card each time the airplane's magnetic heading is changed.

To align a manually rotated ADF card:

- note magnetic heading on the heading indicator; then
- rotate the ADF card, setting magnetic heading under the index.

When the ADF card is aligned with the HI, the ADF needle will indicate the magnetic bearing to the NDB. This eliminates the need for mental arithmetic—an obvious advantage. Note also that the tail of the needle, 180° removed from its head, indicates the magnetic bearing of the airplane from the NDB.

Any time the aircraft changes magnetic heading, the pilot should manually align the ADF card with the HI (after ensuring, of course, that the HI is aligned with the magnetic compass).

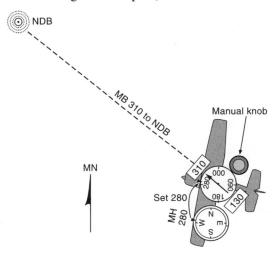

Figure 12a-26. Using a rotatable-card ADF

If desired, the rotatable-card can still be used as a fixed-card simply by aligning 000 with the nose of the airplane and not changing it.

The next step up from a rotatable-card ADF is an instrument whose card remains aligned automatically, known as the radio magnetic indicator, or RMI.

The Radio Magnetic Indicator (RMI)

The RMI display has the ADF needle superimposed on a card that is continuously and automatically being aligned with magnetic north. It is, if you like, an automatic version of the rotatable-card ADF—an automatic combination of the heading indicator and RBI.

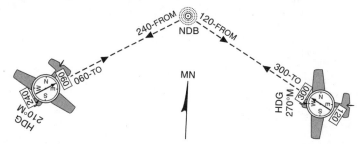

Figure 12a-27. The RMI compass card remains aligned with magnetic north

The RMI is the best ADF presentation, and the easiest to use, but unfortunately the most expensive and usually only encountered in more sophisticated aircraft. In such aircraft, the RMI usually occupies the position in the instrument panel previously occupied by the manually slaved HI.

• The RMI needle will always indicate the magnetic bearing *to* the NDB; and

• The tail of the RMI needle will indicate the magnetic bearing *from* the NDB.

As an airplane turns and its magnetic heading alters, the RMI card (which automatically remains aligned with magnetic north) will appear to turn along with the ADF needle. In reality, of course, it is the compass card and the RMI needle that remain stationary, while the airplane turns about them. Before, during and after the turn, the RMI's needle will continue to indicate the current MB to the NDB.

Gyro-Stabilized Compass Equipment

In most airplanes fitted with an RMI, the initial magnetic north reference for the RMI card is provided by a **fluxgate** or **fluxvalve**, a detector that is sensitive to magnetic north, and situated in a fairly nonmagnetic part of the airplane such as in a wingtip. A directional gyroscope is electrically slaved to this magnetic reference so that the gyroscope is continually being aligned with magnetic north, and it is this directional gyroscope that drives the RMI compass card in a process known as slaving.

FLUX VALVE
provides
Magnetic Reference to   DIRECTIONAL   which
                     GYRO   drives   RMI COMPASS CARD

Figure 12a-28. The RMI compass card is drived by a fluxvalve and directional gyro

Most gyro-stabilized compasses have an annunciator near the compass card. This contains a small needle, often triangular in shape, that oscillates when automatic slaving is in process (which should be all the time). When the annunciator needle is hard over to one side, it indicates that the compass card is a long way out of alignment; this can usually be remedied using a manual knob to quickly realign the compass card with the magnetic heading of the airplane, after which the slower, automatic slaving should be sufficient to maintain alignment.

If slaving is not occurring because of some fault in the system (indicated by the annunciator being stationary and not oscillating) then the pilot can revert to using the RMI as a rotatable-card ADF ("poor man's RMI") or as a fixed-card ADF (relative bearing indicator).

Indicators With Two Pointers

Some airplanes are fitted with two ADF receivers, and have two needles superimposed on the one indicator (which may be a fixed-card twin-ADF indicator, or a dual-pointer RMI).

Most RMIs have function switches that allow you to select either an NDB or a VOR ground station for the RMI needle to point at. This gives you more flexibility in using radio navigation aids, since you can select the RMI to any suitable NDB or VOR within range or, with two needles, select one to ADF and the other to VOR.

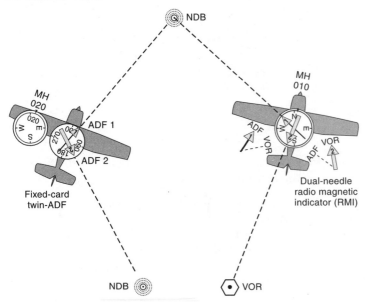

Figure 12a-29. An indicator with two needles

What Follows ...

The next two chapters consider the in-flight operation of:

• the relative bearing indicator (RBI) or fixed-card ADF; and

• the radio magnetic indicator (RMI), including the manually rotatable card.

Initially you need only read the chapter that applies to the ADF instrument in your training aircraft.

✍ Review 12a

1. The letters NDB are an abbreviation for _____.
> nondirectional beacon

2. The NDB is (a ground-based transmitter/an airborne receiver).
> ground-based transmitter

3. NDBs transmit on a frequency in either the _____ or _____ band.
> low frequency or medium frequency band (LF/MF)

4. The letters ADF are an abbreviation for _____.
> automatic direction finder

5. The ADF is (a ground-based transmitter/an airborne receiver).
> airborne receiver

6. A particular NDB may be identified by _____.
> its Morse code ident

7. The three basic steps that you should follow before using a particular NDB are _____.
> select the NDB frequency, identify the NDB, and check that the needle is indeed "ADFing"

8. The term RBI is an abbreviation for _____.
> relative bearing indicator

9. If an airplane steering MH 250 has a reading of 030 on its relative bearing indicator (RB030), what is:
    (a) the magnetic bearing to the NDB from the airplane?
    (b) the magnetic bearing of the airplane from the NDB?
> (a) MB 280 to the NDB; (b) MB 100 from the NDB

10. If an airplane steering MH 250 has a reading of RB 350 on its RBI, calculate:
    (a) the magnetic bearing to the NDB from the airplane.
    (b) the magnetic bearing of the airplane from the NDB.
> (a) MB 240 to the NDB; (b) MB 060 from the NDB

11. An NDB used to locate the airplane on an instrument approach may be called a _____.
> compass locator

12. An NDB positioned so that it provides a fix for an airplane during an instrument approach, and co-located with the outer marker, may be designated on the instrument approach chart with the letters _____.
> LOM (locator outer marker)

13. If a localizer has the coded ident I-UKI, you would expect the ident of the LOM to be _____.
> UK, the first two letters of the localizer identifier

14. If a localizer has the coded ident I-RDD, you would expect the ident of the LOM to be _____.
> RD

15. If a localizer has the coded ident I-DAN, you would expect the ident of the LMM, if there is one, to be _____.
> AN, the last two letters of the localizer identifier

16. Atmospheric conditions, such as electrical storms or the periods of sunrise and sunset, (may/will not) distort NDB signals, making ADF indications less reliable.
> may

17. Mountains (may/will not) reflect and distort NDB signals, making ADF indications less reliable.
> may

Operational Use of the RBI

Orientation

Using the RBI to Obtain a Position Line

A **position line** is a line along which the airplane is known to be at a particular moment. A position line (PL), or line of position line (PL), may be obtained by a pilot either visually, or by radio means.

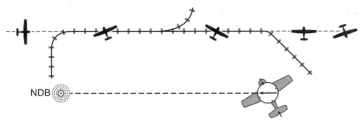

Figure 12b-1. A visual position line, and a radio position line

Two position lines that "cut" at a reasonable angle, ideally close to 90°, are needed for a fix. For the airplane to be on both position lines simultaneously, it must be at their point of intersection.

Figure 12b-2 shows a radio fix obtained using two NDBs in an airplane fitted with two ADFs. It is possible to fix position using a combination of radio aids including NDBs, VORs and DMEs.

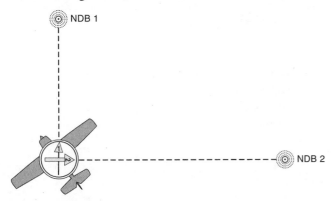

Figure 12b-2. Two lines of position with a good cut can provide a fix

A position line can be considered from two perspectives:

- **to the NDB** from the airplane, that is, the position line to the NDB that a pilot would see from the airplane, as either a relative bearing (RB 030 to NDB 1), or as a magnetic bearing to the NDB (MB 360 to NDB 1); or

- **from the NDB** to the airplane, as a magnetic bearing from the station (such as MB 180 from NDB 1). The magnetic bearing from the NDB may be converted to a true bearing by applying magnetic variation, if for instance you wanted to plot the airplane's position on a chart.

Example 1. An airplane is steering MH 015. Its ADF needle points toward a nondirectional beacon 75° to starboard (to the right of the nose) on a relative bearing indicator (also known as a fixed-card ADF). Magnetic variation is 5°W. Calculate:

(a) the relative bearing (RB) to the NDB from the airplane;

(b) the magnetic bearing to the NDB from the airplane;

(c) the magnetic bearing from the NDB to the airplane; and

(d) the true bearing from the NDB to the airplane.

While it is possible to calculate all of this mentally, at this early stage it is a good idea to sketch a clear diagram to help visualize the situation.

Step 1. Sketch the airplane on MH 015.

Step 2. Indicate RB 075.

Step 3. Draw in the position line to the NDB.

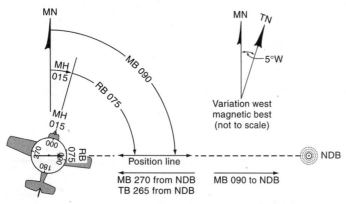

Figure 12b-3. Magnetic heading MH 015, relative bearing RB 075

MH 015	MB 090 to NDB	*Variation west,*	MB 270 from NDB
+ RB 075	+ 180	*magnetic best*	Variation −5
MB 090	**MB 270 from NDB**		**TB 265 from NDB**

Answers: RB 075; MB 090 to NDB; MB 270 from NDB; TB 265 from NDB.

True Bearings From an NDB

Normally, an instrument pilot would not bother to actually plot positions on a chart. However, if for some reason you decide to, then the easiest method on an en route chart is to plot the *true* bearings from the NDB, which are bearings from the NDB related to true north, using a protractor or plotter. True north is indicated on the chart by the meridians of longitude that run north-south.

Note: It is possible to plot *magnetic* bearings from a VOR, known as **radials**, since each VOR has a compass rose around it oriented to magnetic north—NDBs do not. True bearing = magnetic bearing plus east variation (minus west variation).

Example 2. MH is 280. RB is 050. What is the true bearing (TB) from the NDB? Magnetic variation in the area is 6°W.

MH 280 + RB 050 = MB 330 to NDB

−200
+20
MB 150 from NDB
−6° west variation
TB 144 from NDB

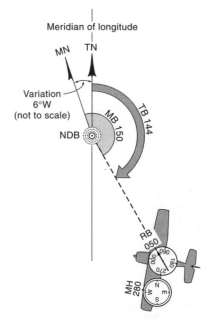

Figure 12b-4. Example 2. Finding true bearing from an NDB

Example 3. An airplane steering MH 120 has the needle on its fixed-card ADF indicating RB 290. The variation is 13°E. Calculate:

(a) the relative bearing (RB) to the NDB from the airplane;

(b) the magnetic bearing (MB) to the NDB from the airplane;

(c) the MB from the NDB to the airplane; and

(d) the true bearing (TB) from the NDB to the airplane.

(After doing this, see below for a quicker method of visualizing magnetic bearing.)

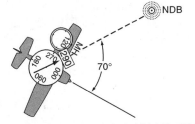

Figure 12b-5. Example 3. MH 120, RB 290

MH 120			
+ RB 290			
MB 410 to NDB	MB 050 to NDB	*Variation east*	MB 230 from NDB
−360	+180	*magnetic least*	Var'n +13
MB 050 to NDB	**MB 230 from NDB**		**TB 243 from NDB**

Answers: RB 290; MB 050 to NDB; MB 230 from NDB; TB 243 from NDB.

Easy Method of Visualizing MB

A relative bearing, as well as being specified using the 360° method clockwise from the nose of the airplane, can be specified as either *left* or *right* of the nose (or the tail). For instance, a relative bearing of 290 may be thought of as –70, since the corresponding MB will be 70° less than the current magnetic heading. Similarly, RB 030 may be thought of as +30, since the corresponding MB to the NDB will be 30° greater than the magnetic heading.

Relative bearings off the tail of the airplane may be treated in a similar shorthand fashion. For instance, RB 160 may be thought of as –20 off the tail; and RB 210 as +30 off the tail. This *quadrantal* approach to relative bearing and MB problems can simplify your in-flight visualization.

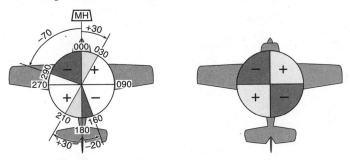

Figure 12b-6. "Quadrants" for converting relative bearings to magnetic bearings

Example 4. An airplane is steering MH 340. The ADF needle shows RB 010. Determine the MB to the NDB.

MH 340
  +10 off the nose (RB 010)
MB 350 to NDB

Figure 12b-7. MH 340 + 10 off the nose = MB 350

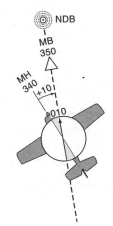

Chapter 12b **The Relative Bearing Indicator (RBI)**

Example 5. An airplane is steering MH 358. The ADF needle shows RB 352. Determine the MB to the NDB.

MH 358
   –8 off the nose (RB 352)
MB 350 to NDB

Notice that, by coincidence, this airplane has the same magnetic bearing to the NDB as the airplane in Example 4, MB 350 to the NDB. In fact, it may even be the same airplane, which has simply altered heading by turning right from MH 340 to MH 358.

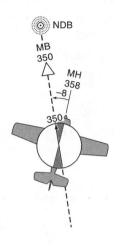

Figure 12b-8. MH 358 – 8 off the nose = MB 350

Example 6. An airplane is steering MH 340. The ADF needle shows RB 190. Determine the MB from the NDB to the airplane.

MH 340
   +10 off the tail (RB190)
MB 350 from the NDB

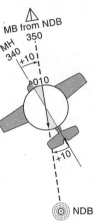

Figure 12b-9. MH 340 + 10 off the tail = MB 350 from the NDB

Example 7. An airplane is steering MH 010. The ADF needle shows RB 160. Determine the MB from the NDB.

MH 010
   –20 off the tail (RB 160)
MB 350 from NDB

Notice that, by coincidence, this airplane has the same magnetic bearing from the NDB as the previous one, MB 350 from the NDB. In fact, it may even be the same airplane, which has simply altered heading by turning right from MH 340 to MH 010.

Figure 12b-10. MH 010 – 20 off the tail = MB 350 from the NDB

Visualizing Position on the Heading Indicator

Mentally transferring the RBI needle onto the HI allows quick visualization of MB to NDB on the head of the needle, and MB from NDB on its tail.

If you now imagine a model airplane attached to the tail of the needle, with the model airplane oriented with the actual heading, you have a very good picture of the whole situation.

Example 8. Visualize the situation of MH 070 and RB 260 (Figure 12b-11).

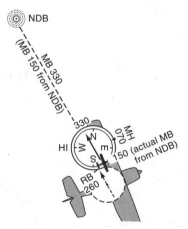

Figure 12b-11. Example 8. Visualizing position on the HI; MB 330 and MH 070

Intercepting a Course

Having oriented yourself with respect to an NDB, you know the answer to the question "Where am I?" Now ask "Where do I want to go?" and "How do I get there?"

Step 1. Orient the airplane relative to the NDB, and to the desired course.

Step 2. Turn to take up a suitable intercept heading, after considering where you want to join the desired course.

Step 3. Maintain the intercept heading and wait:
– for the head of the needle to fall if inbound;
– for the tail of the needle to rise if outbound:
    to ±030 for a 30° intercept; to ±045 for a 45° intercept;
    to ±060 for a 60° intercept; to ±090 for a 90° intercept, etc.

Step 4. Turn to the desired course, and apply a suitable wind correction angle to maintain it.

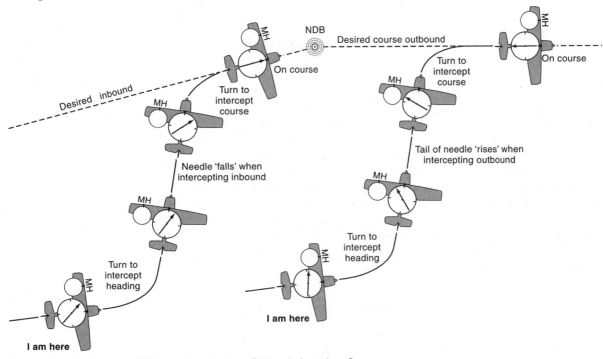

Figure 12b-12. Where am I? Where do I want to go? How do I get there?

Visualizing Where You Are, and Where You Want To Go

The heading indicator (HI) can assist greatly in visualizing the situation. In the previous example, the situation MH 070 and RB 260 was visualized, with MB 330 to the NDB. What now if the pilot wishes to intercept a magnetic course (MC) 270 to the NDB?

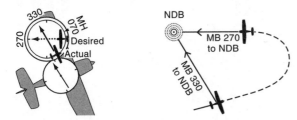

Figure 12b-13. Visualizing an intercept on the HI

All that the pilot needs to do is visualize the desired course on the heading indicator. With a model airplane on the tail of the needle tracking as desired, it becomes quite clear what turns are necessary to intercept the desired course. First turn left to a suitable intercept heading, say MH 360 for a 90° intercept of MC 270 to the NDB.

Note: If you become disoriented, a simple procedure is to take up the heading of the desired course. Even though not on course, the airplane will at least be parallel to it, and the ADF needle will indicate which way to turn to intercept it.

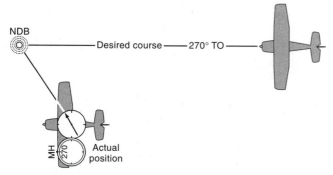

Figure 12b-14. Paralleling course to help in visualization

Suppose the situation is MH 340, RB 080, and you wish to intercept a course MC 090 to the NDB. The current magnetic bearing to the NDB is easily found to be MB 060 (MH 340 + RB 080). By continuing to steer MH 340, the airplane will eventually intercept MC 090 to the NDB, but it would be a rather untidy intercept, with the airplane tracking somewhat away from the NDB, and with an intercept turn of 110° being required.

A tidier and more efficient intercept may be achieved by turning to an initial heading of MH 360 for a 90° intercept; or MH 030 for a 60° intercept. (Turning further right to MH 060 would of course point the airplane at the NDB, and MC 090 to the NDB would not be intercepted.)

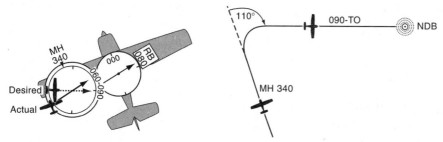

Figure 12b-15. Visualizing the intercept

Figure 12b-16. An inefficient intercept of course

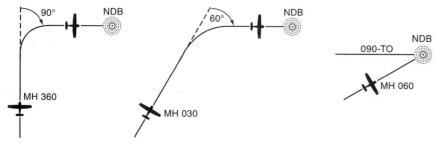

Figure 12b-17. Different intercepts of course

Using the ADF to Intercept an Inbound Course

Example 9. An airplane is steering MH 355, and the RBI indicates RB 005 when tuned to a particular NDB. The pilot is requested to track inbound on course MC 340 to the station, intercepting the course at 60°.

Step 1. Orient the airplane. MH 355 + RB 005 = MB 360 to NDB, or MB 180 from NDB. The airplane is south of the NDB and heading MH 355. The desired course is MC 340 to the NDB (which is on the position line MB 160 from the NDB), to the right of the airplane.

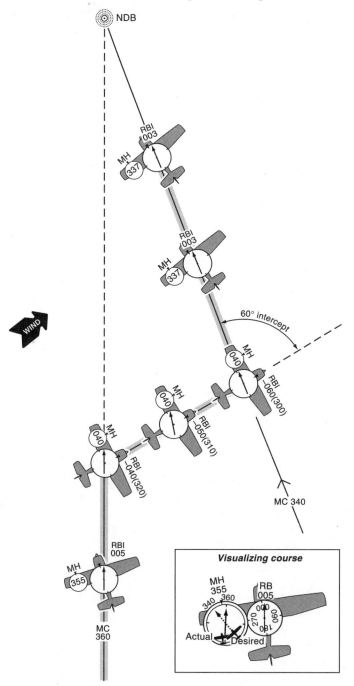

Figure 12b-18. Intercepting MC 340 inbound, from south of the station

Step 2. To intercept the course MC 340 from the left at 60°, the airplane should steer (340 + 60 = 400 =) MH 040. As the airplane's heading alters,

---

the ADF needle will continue to point at the NDB and so the relative bearing will change (in this case, even though it is not an important calculation, from RB 005 to RB 320, or –40 off the nose, with the 45° right turn).

Step 3. Maintain MH 040 and periodically observe the RBI as the head of the needle falls. Since it is a plus 60 intercept, wait until the head of the needle falls to minus 60 (or RB 300). You are steering course plus 60, waiting for minus 60.

Step 4. At MB 340, and as the needle is falling to RB –60, turn left to take up the desired course to the NDB, allowing for the estimated crosswind effect on tracking. In this case, a wind correction angle (WCA) of 3° left is used. Maintain the desired course of MC 340 to the station by continually checking that MH + RB = MB 340, for example: MH 337 + RB 003 = MB 340.

Note: An airplane takes some distance to turn, and so you should anticipate the desired course by commencing the turn onto course just before MB 340 is reached. You can do this by observing the rate at which the ADF needle falls toward –060, and commence the turn accordingly.

Example 10. ATC gives you radar vector 010 to steer, and instructs you to intercept 055 inbound to an NDB off that heading.

Step 1. Orient the airplane. With radar vector 010 to intercept MC 055 inbound, the airplane must be south of the required course.

Step 2. The intercept has been organized by the radar controller so that the airplane will intercept course at 45° (055 – 010 = 45).

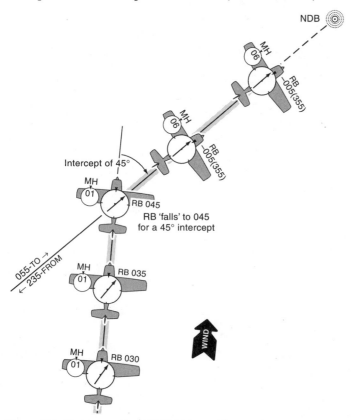

Figure 12b-19. Intercepting MC 055 inbound from radar vector 010

Step 3. Maintain MH 010 and periodically observe the RBI as the head of the needle falls. Since it is a –45 intercept, wait until the head of the needle falls to +045 (RB 045). You are steering course minus 45, waiting for plus 45.

Step 4. Shortly before MB 055 to the NDB is reached, and as the needle falls to +45, turn right to take up the desired course to the NDB, allowing for the estimated wind drift. In this case, a WCA of 5° right is used, by steering MH 060 with the RBI on –5 off the nose (RB 355). Maintain the desired course MC 055 to the station by continually checking that MH + RB = MB 055, e.g. MH 060 + RB –005 = MB 055.

Another means of achieving a smooth intercept is to reduce the closing angle as the desired course is approached, say from 45° to 30° to 15° and, finally, to zero as the course is intercepted.

Using the ADF to Intercept an Outbound Course

Example 11. The radar controller gives you a radar vector of 340 to intercept an outbound course of 280.

Step 1. Orient the airplane. It must be south of the outbound course.

Step 2. Consider the intercept. A radar vector of 340 to intercept MC 280 outbound means a +60° intercept.

Step 3. Monitor the intercept by steering a steady MH 340 and periodically checking the RBI to see the tail of the needle rising to –60 (RB 300). You are steering course plus 60, waiting for minus 60.

Step 4. As MC 280 outbound is approached, indicated by the tail of the needle rising to –60, turn left to pick it up, in this case allowing a WCA of 10° for a wind from the right, to MH 290.

Periodically check that MH ± ADF tail = MB from NDB. In this case, the tail of the ADF needle should be –10 off the nose (on RB 350), so that MH 290 – 10 = MC 280 from NDB.

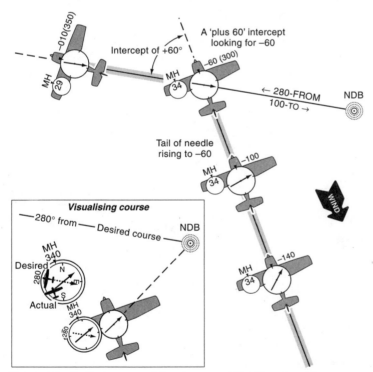

Figure 12b-20. Radar vector 340 to intercept MC 280 outbound

Example 12. You are steering MH 120, with RB 080. You wish to track outbound from the NDB on MC 090, intercepting as soon as possible.

Step 1. Orient the airplane. MH 120 + RB 080 = MB 200 to NDB, or MB 020 from NDB The airplane is north-northeast of the NDB, steering MH 120. The desired course is MC 090 from the NDB, which is to the right of the airplane.

Step 2. Continuing on MH 120 would give a 30° intercept of MC 090-outbound. To intercept MC 090-outbound as soon as possible, with a 90° intercept, the airplane should be turned to steer (090 + 90 =) MH 180.

Step 3. Maintain MH 180 and periodically observe the RBI as the tail of the needle rises. Since it is a plus 90 intercept, wait until the tail of the needle rises to minus 90 (270). You are steering course plus 90, waiting for minus 90.

Step 4. At MB 090 from the NDB, or shortly before MB 090 from the NDB is reached, and as the tail of the needle approaches –90, turn left from your current MH 180 to take up the desired course 090 from the NDB, allowing for the estimated crosswind effect on tracking. In this case, with no wind, steer MH 090. The tail of the ADF needle should be on 000. Periodically check that MH ± ADF tail = MB 090 from NDB. For instance, with a northerly wind, you might require WCA 10° left, so that MH 080 + 10 off the tail = MB 090 from NDB.

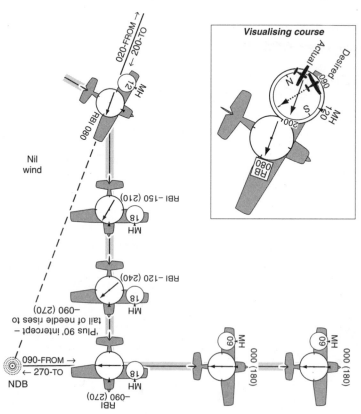

Figure 12b-21. A 90– intercept of 090-outbound

Note: With such a large intercept angle, 90° in the above case, you will have to watch the rate at which the tail of the ADF needle rises, and anticipate the turn to intercept the desired course. If you do not anticipate the intercept, the airplane will fly through the course, which will then have to be re-intercepted from the other side—not a tidy maneuver.

Tracking

Using the RBI to Track Inbound to an NDB

The ADF/NDB combination is often used to provide guidance for an airplane from a distant position to a position overhead the NDB ground station. This is known as tracking. Just how the pilot achieves this depends to a certain extent on the prevailing wind direction and speed, since an airplane initially pointed directly at the NDB will be blown off course by a crosswind.

Tracking Toward an NDB, with no Crosswind Effect

With no crosswind, a direct inbound course can be achieved by simply pointing the airplane directly at the NDB and steering a heading that keeps the ADF needle on the nose (RB 000).

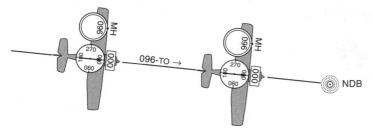

Figure 12b-22. Tracking inbound, with no crosswind

If there is no crosswind to blow the airplane off course, then everything will remain constant as in Figure 12b-22—the MH 096, the RB 000, and the MB 096 to the NDB will all remain constant. This can only occur in:

- no-wind conditions;
- a direct headwind; or
- a direct tailwind.

Tracking Inbound with a Crosswind

If no wind correction angle is applied, and the airplane is pointed directly at the NDB, so that the ADF needle indicates RB 000, then any crosswind will cause the airplane to be blown off course.

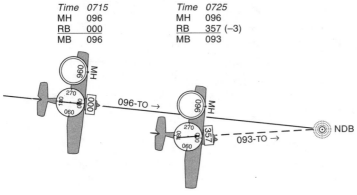

Figure 12b-23. Crosswind causes drift

In the case illustrated in Figure 12b-23, a wind with a northerly component has blown the airplane to the right of course. This is indicated by the ADF needle starting to move down the left of the dial. To return to the desired course, the airplane must be turned to the left, toward the direction in which the head of the needle is moving.

If you turn left to put the NDB on the nose again, so that the relative bearing is RB 000, then after a short while the airplane will again be blown to the right of course, and the ADF needle will again move to the left of the nose. A further turn to the left will be required—and the process will need to be repeated again and again. In this way, the airplane's ground track to the NDB will be curved and it will finally arrive overhead the NDB heading roughly into the wind. This rather inefficient means of tracking to the NDB is known as homing (keeping the NDB on the nose). It is not a tidy procedure and will involve traveling a greater distance than that required to fly a direct course to the NDB from the original position. Professional pilots never use it!

With the correct wind correction angle applied, the airplane will track directly toward the ground station in a straight line—a far better procedure than homing. If 5° left is indeed the correct wind correction angle, you can achieve a course of MC 096 direct to the NDB by steering MH 091.

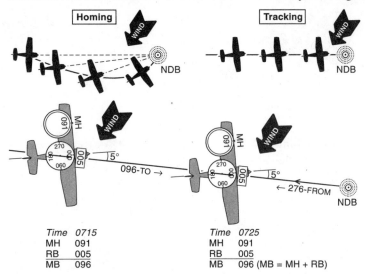

	Time 0715		Time 0725
	MH 091		MH 091
	RB 005		RB 005
	MB 096		MB 096 (MB = MH + RB)

Figure 12b-24. Tracking direct to the NDB

Wind Correction Angles

Different winds require different wind correction angles. An airplane is on course when the relative bearing is equal-and-opposite to the difference between the actual magnetic heading (MH) and the desired magnetic course (MC). This is illustrated in Figure 12b-25. In each situation, the airplane is on the desired course of MC 010, but using a different wind correction angle (WCA) to counteract the drift under different wind conditions.

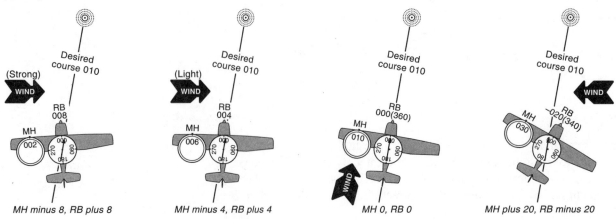

Figure 12b-25. Laying off drift to achieve the desired course

If the precise wind effect is not known, then initially use a best guess WCA estimated from the available information. For the same crosswind, slower airplanes will need to allow a greater WCA than faster airplanes. See how the estimated WCA works, then make an adjustment to heading if required.

It is possible that the wind effect will change as you track toward an NDB, and so regular adjustments to the heading may be required. This is often the case as an airplane descends while using the NDB as the tracking aid, due to variations of wind speed and/or direction, and of airplane TAS, that occur with changes in level.

If an incorrect drift correction is made by the pilot, then the airplane will move off the desired course, so the RB indication and the MB to the NDB will change. If a steady heading is being flown, then any divergence from course will become obvious through a gradually changing relative bearing, with the ADF needle moving left or right down the dial.

Suppose you fly a heading with a 5° wind correction angle to the left to counteract the effects of a wind from the left. If the wind effect turns out to be less than expected, then the airplane will gradually move to the left of the desired course to the NDB, and the RB will gradually increase (naturally, the MB to the NDB will also increase). Typical cockpit indications could be:

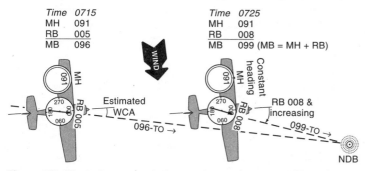

Figure 12b-26. An incorrect wind correction angle causes MB to change

The head of the ADF needle falling away to the right indicates that a turn right must be made to track to the NDB. Conversely, the head of the ADF needle falling away to the left indicates that a left turn must be made to track to the NDB. Just how great each correcting turn should be depends on the deviation from course.

Note: Be careful of terminology. Drift is the angle between heading and the achieved ground track, which may not be the desired course. The perfect wind correction angle will counteract any drift exactly, and the actual ground track will follow the desired course; this is the aim of tracking.

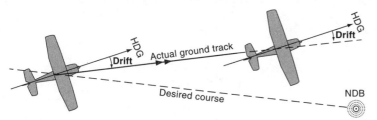

Figure 12b-27. Drift is the angle between heading and achieved ground track

Maintaining Course

In reality, flying level is a series of small and gentle climbs and descents made by the pilot in an attempt to maintain the desired altitude precisely. Similarly, tracking is a series of small turns made in an attempt to maintain the desired course perfectly.

Re-intercepting a course, having deviated from it, involves the same procedure as the initial intercept of a new course, except that the intercept angles will be smaller (provided that the pilot is vigilant and does not allow large deviations to occur). Realizing that the airplane is diverging from the direct course to the NDB, the pilot has several options—either:

- fly direct from the present position (along a new course); or
- regain the original course.

To fly direct to the NDB from your present position (even though the present position is not on the originally desired course), turn slightly right (say 3° in this case), and fly direct to the NDB from the present position. Normally, this technique is used only when within one or two miles from the NDB, when there is insufficient distance remaining to regain the original course.

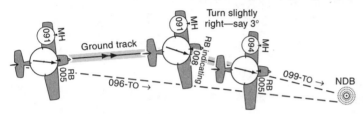

Figure 12b-28. Flying a new course to the NDB—needle head falling right; turn right

To regain the original course, turn further right initially (say 5° to MH 096), and reintercept the original course by allowing the wind to blow the airplane back onto it. Once the desired course is regained, turn left and steer a heading with a different wind correction angle (say WCA 3° left instead of 5° left), say MH 093 instead of MH 091. This is a relatively minor correction, something you would expect to see from an experienced instrument pilot who would have noticed any deviation from course fairly quickly.

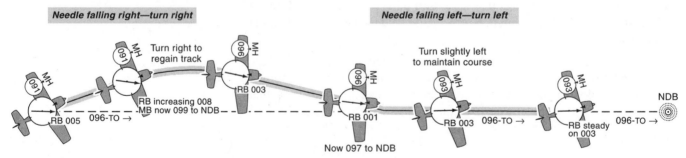

Figure 12b-29. Regain the desired course

Attempting to maintain the desired course (remaining on a constant MB to the NDB) is the normal navigational technique when at some distance from the NDB. If, when steering a steady magnetic heading, the ADF needle indicates a constant relative bearing near the top of the dial, then the airplane is tracking directly to the NDB, and no correction to heading is necessary.

Tracking is a series of small turns made in an attempt to maintain the desired course perfectly.

If MH + RB = desired MB constantly, then ADF tracking is good.

Just how great each correcting turn should be depends on the deviation from course. A simple method is to **double the error**. If the airplane has deviated 10° left indicated by the RBI moving 10° right, then alter heading by 20° to the right. (If you alter heading by only 10° to the right, the result will probably be a further deviation to the left, a further correction to the right, with this being repeated again and again, resulting in a curved homing to the NDB.)

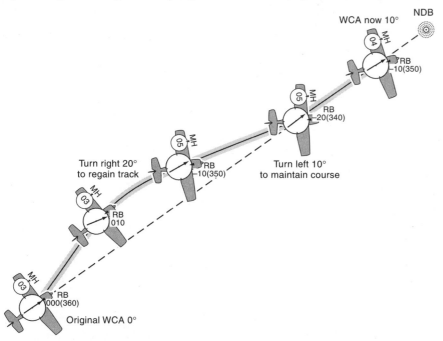

Figure 12b-30. Regain course by "doubling the error" and maintain course thereafter

Having regained course, turn left by only half the correcting turn of 20°, that is, turn left 10° to intercept and maintain course. This leaves you with a WCA different to the original one (remembering that the original WCA caused you to deviate from course).

The new WCA should provide reasonable tracking. If not, make further minor corrections to heading.

"Bracketing" Course

In practice, an absolutely perfect direct course is difficult to achieve. The actual ground track by the pilot will probably consist of a series of short segments either side of the desired course, which corresponds to minor corrections similar to those described above. This technique is known as bracketing the course, and involves making suitable heading corrections, left or right as required, to regain and maintain the desired course.

The aim of bracketing is to find the precise WCA needed to maintain course. If, for instance, a WCA of 10° right is found to be too great and the airplane diverges to the right of course, and a WCA of only 5° right is too little and the wind blows the airplane to the left of course, then try something in between, say WCA 8° right.

Monitor the tracking of the airplane on a regular basis, and make corrections earlier rather than later, the result being a number of small corrections rather than just one big correction. However, if a big correction is required, as may be the case in strong winds, make it.

Bracketing involves making suitable heading corrections, left or right as required, to regain and maintain the desired course.

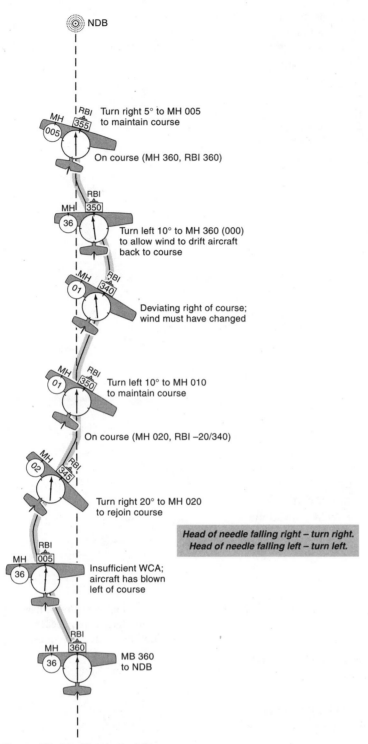

NDB

Turn right 5° to MH 005
to maintain course

On course (MH 360, RBI 360)

Turn left 10° to MH 360 (000)
to allow wind to drift aircraft
back to course

Deviating right of course;
wind must have changed

Turn left 10° to MH 010
to maintain course

On course (MH 020, RBI –20/340)

Turn right 20° to MH 020
to rejoin course

*Head of needle falling right – turn right.
Head of needle falling left – turn left.*

Insufficient WCA;
aircraft has blown
left of course

MB 360
to NDB

Figure 12b-31. "Bracketing" the course

Wind Effect

If the wind direction and strength is not obvious, then the best technique is to initially **steer course as heading** (make no allowance for drift). The effect of the wind will become obvious as the ADF needle moves to the left or right. Observe the results, and then make appropriate heading adjustments to bracket course.

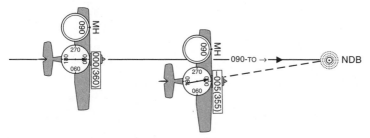

Figure 12b-32. If uncertain of wind, initially steer course as heading

Tracking Over an NDB

The ADF needle will become more and more sensitive as the NDB station is approached. Minor displacements left or right of course will cause larger and larger changes in RB and MB. For a very precise course to be achieved, you must be prepared to increase your scan rate as the NDB is approached, and to make smaller corrections more frequently.

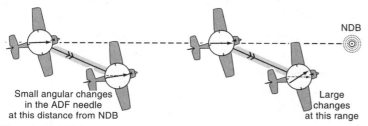

Figure 12b-33. Approaching the NDB, the ADF needle becomes more sensitive

Close to the station and just prior to passing over the NDB, however, the ADF needle can become very sensitive and agitated. Relax a little and steer a steady heading until the airplane passes over the NDB, indicated by the ADF needle moving toward the bottom of the dial.

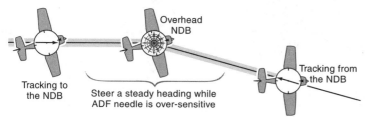

Figure 12b-34. Do not overcorrect when close to the station

Having passed over the NDB, tracking *from* the NDB should be checked and suitable adjustments made to heading. If the course outbound is different from that inbound, then a suitable heading change estimated to make good the new desired course could be made as soon as the ADF needle falls past the 090 or 270 position on its way to the bottom of the dial.

The ADF needle becoming extremely active, and then falling rapidly to the bottom of the dial, indicates that the airplane has passed directly over the NDB.

The ADF needle moving gradually to one side, and slowly falling to the bottom of the dial indicates that the airplane is passing to one side of the beacon, the rate at which the needle falls being an indication of the airplane's proximity to the NDB. If it falls slowly, then the tracking by the pilot could have been better.

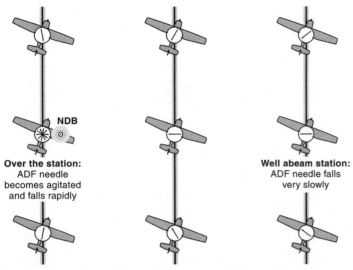

Figure 12b-35. Good ADF tracking (left), reasonable tracking and poor tracking

Time over (or abeam) the NDB with no WCA can be taken as the needle falls through the approximate 090 or 270 position.

Time over (or abeam) the NDB with a WCA 10° right can be taken as the needle falls through the approximate 080 (090 – WCA 10) or 260 (270 – WCA 10) position.

Tracking Away From an NDB

When tracking away from an NDB, the head of the ADF needle will lie toward the bottom of the dial.

Tracking Away From an NDB with no Crosswind Effect

If the pilot tracks over the NDB and then steers course as heading, the airplane will track directly away from the NDB with the head of the ADF needle steady on 180, and the tail of the ADF needle steady at the top of the dial on 000. The airplane in Figure 12b-36 has MB 040 from the NDB, and MB 220 to the NDB.

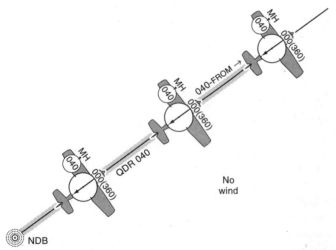

Figure 12b-36. Tracking away from an NDB with no crosswind effect

Tracking Away From an NDB with a Crosswind

Suppose that the desired course outbound from an NDB is MC 040, and the pilot estimates that a WCA of 5° to the right is necessary to counteract a wind from the right. To achieve this, he steers MH 045, and hopes to see the tail of the ADF needle stay on –5 off the nose (RB 355). The magnetic course away from the station is found from:

MB from NDB = MH ± deflection of the tail of the needle.

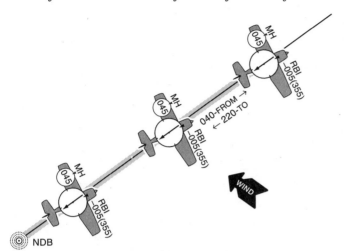

Figure 12b-37. Tracking away from an NDB, with a WCA of 5° into wind

In this case, MH 045 – 005 tail = MB 040 from NDB, and the chosen WCA and magnetic heading to steer are correct.

If the estimated WCA is incorrect, then the actual ground track achieved by the airplane will differ from the desired course. If, in the previous case, the wind is stronger than expected, the airplane's ground track may be 033, to the left of the desired course MC 040.

Whereas inaccurate tracking to an NDB is indicated by the ADF needle falling, incorrect tracking away from an NDB can occur with the ADF needle indicating a steady reading. Having passed overhead the NDB, an airplane can track away from it in any of 360 directions. You must always ensure that you are flying away from the NDB along the correct course, and the easiest way to do this is to calculate MB from the NDB using the HI and the RBI.

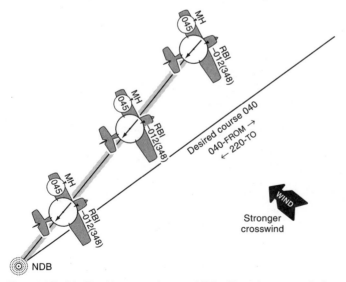

Figure 12b-38. Tracking away from an NDB with an incorrect wind correction angle

Regaining Course Away From an NDB in a Crosswind

If an incorrect wind correction angle is flown, then the airplane will be blown off the desired course. The vigilant pilot will observe the incorrect ground track, probably by visualizing MB from the NDB (or MB to the NDB), while steering a constant magnetic heading.

Example 13. The pilot is flying course as heading, initially making no allowance for wind effect. If the head of the ADF needle moves right from RB 180 into the negative quadrant, then the airplane must be turned right to regain course.

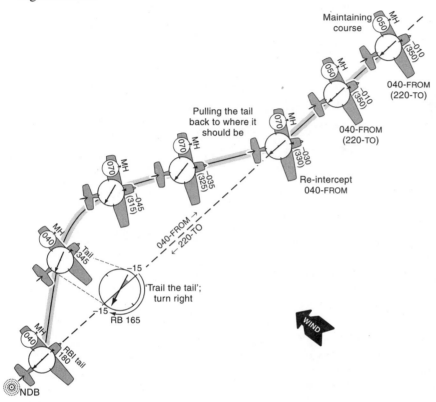

Figure 12b-39. Turning right to "trail the tail" or "pull the tail around"

Note: It is generally easier to work off the top of the dial, since that is where the airplane is going, rather than off the bottom of the dial. The right turn necessary to regain course, turning right toward the head of the needle and therefore away from the tail of the needle, can be thought of as pulling the tail of the ADF needle around or *trailing the tail*. Some instructors, however, prefer to say that if the head of the needle is moving right, then turn right (and vice versa), even though the head of the needle is at the bottom of the dial. Your instructor will recommend a method.

In Example 13, the airplane has been blown to the left of course. The off-course MB from the NDB is given by:

MH 040 – 015 tail = MB 025 from NDB;
which is left of the desired MB 040 from the NDB.

To regain course, the pilot has turned right by 30° (double the error) from MH 040 to MH 070, which causes a simultaneous change in the relative bearing of the NDB, the ADF needle tail moving from –015 (345) to –045 (315). (The head of the needle, indicating relative bearing, will move from

RB 165 to RB 135, but this is not a calculation for the pilot to make, only an observation.)

The relative bearing will naturally change as the airplane is turned but, once the airplane is flown on its steady intercept heading of MH 070, the tail of the needle will be gradually pulled around.

The pilot will continue to steer the intercept heading until the airplane approaches the desired course, MC 040 from the NDB. This is indicated by the tail of the needle moving up toward –30 (since MB 040 from NDB = MH 070 –30 tail). For a 30° intercept of MC 040 outbound, the pilot will steer a MC + 30 heading (MC 040 + 30° intercept = MH 070), waiting for the tail of the needle to rise to –30 off the nose. *Steering course plus 30, waiting for minus 30 on the tail of the needle.*

As the desired outbound course MC 040 is intercepted from MH 070, the pilot turns left to maintain MC 040 from the NDB. Estimating a WCA of 10° into the wind to be sufficient, the pilot steers MH 050 and checks regularly that the needle tail stays on –010.

Example 14. Conversely, if the head of the ADF needle moves left from RB 180 into the positive quadrant, then the airplane must be turned left to regain course.

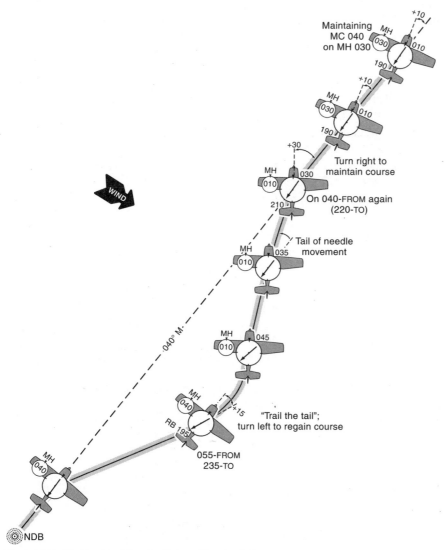

Figure 12b-40. Turning left to "trail the tail" or "pull the tail around"

Looking at the top of the ADF dial and the tail of the needle, turn left and *trail the tail*. In Figure 12b-40, the airplane has been blown to the right of course. The off-course MB from the NDB is given by: MH 040 + 015 tail = MB 055 from NDB; right of desired MC 040-FROM.

To regain course, the pilot has turned left by 30° from MH 040 to MH 010, which causes a simultaneous change in the relative bearing of the NDB, the tail of the ADF needle moving from 015 to 045.

The relative bearing will naturally change as the airplane is turned but, once the airplane is flown on its steady intercept heading of MH 010, the tail of the needle will be gradually pulled around.

For a 30° intercept of MC 040 outbound, the pilot is steering a heading equal to MC–30 (MC 040 – 30° intercept = MH 010), waiting for the tail of the needle to rise to +30 off the nose. *Steering course minus 30, waiting for +30 on the tail of the needle.*

The pilot will continue with the intercept heading until the airplane approaches the desired MC 040 outbound from the NDB. This is indicated by the tail of the needle moving up toward RB 030 (since MB 040 from NDB = MH 010 + 30 tail).

As the desired course outbound is approached, the pilot turns right to maintain MC 040 from the NDB. Estimating a WCA of 10° into the wind to be sufficient, the pilot steers MH 030 and checks regularly that the tail of the needle stays on +10 (RB 010).

The NDB Approach

The NDB/ADF combination can be used for an instrument approach procedure called the **NDB approach**—typical examples follow. The top section of each instrument approach chart shows a plan view for tracking purposes, and the bottom section shows a profile view for vertical navigation (descent).

The Monte Vista NDB Rwy 20 approach uses an NDB sited on the airport for tracking; the Valparaiso NDB Rwy 27 approach uses an NDB sited well away from the airport. As you will see later, the same situation can apply with VOR approaches—some use a VOR on, or very near to, the airport, others use a VOR sited some distance away. NDB and VOR approaches are similar in design, the only significant difference being the type of tracking aid employed.

The Monte Vista NDB Rwy 20 Approach

Ensure that the chart is current, and then review it thoroughly. Chart review will be considered in Chapter 25—here we will consider only the general outline of the approach.

It is clear that Monte Vista is a high altitude airport (airport elevation 7608 feet MSL) surrounded by mountains. The Minimum Safe Altitude (MSA) is up to 15,400 feet MSL in the northeast sector. The MSA provides 1000 feet obstruction clearance within 25 nm of the MVI NDB in the specified sectors. However, it may not provide good navigational signal reception at this altitude, so you should transition from the en route phase of flight to overhead the NDB at an altitude higher than the MSA. If you are arriving from the Alamosa VOR on MC 301, however, an altitude of 9800 feet MSL or higher is satisfactory on this specific course, as noted on the chart.

Before using the NDB for any navigational purposes, you should verify it is:

- selected;
- identified (MVI: *dah-dah dit-dit-dit-dah dit-dit*); and
- ADFing.

Since the ADF does not have a warning flag, you should monitor the ident continuously throughout the approach, although the volume may be turned down so that it is not too distracting.

From overhead the NDB, maneuver to take up a course of MC 011 from the NDB, descent to 9100 feet MSL now being permitted. This is provided you have the current Alamosa altimeter setting; if not, the NDB approach is not authorized, since your vertical navigation must be based on a guaranteed altimeter setting in the pressure window. The lowest altitude permitted outbound, 9100 feet MSL, is 1494 feet above the touchdown zone elevation (TDZE).

The ADF needle will be sensitive initially, when you are close to the NDB, but will settle down as you track outbound away from it.

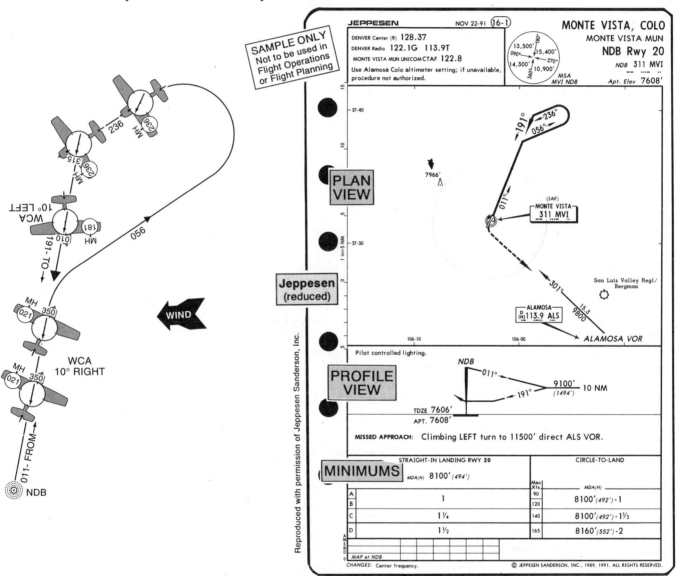

Figure 12b-41. Plan and profile of the Monte Vista, Co, NDB Rwy 20 approach chart (*Jeppesen*)

To reverse course, you may begin a procedure turn to the right to MH 056, plus or minus a wind correction angle, for 1 minute, followed by a left turn to MH 236 to intercept the inbound MC 191. Stay within 10 nm of the MVI NDB.

When established inbound on MC 191 (±5°), you are permitted to commence descent to the **minimum descent altitude (MDA)**, which is

8100 feet MSL (494 feet HAT) for a straight-in landing on Runway 20. This is 494 feet above the touchdown zone elevation (TDZE). If you plan on using another runway, the **circling MDA**, in this case, is the same at 8100 feet MSL (or 492 feet above the airport—HAA).

If you become visual at or above the MDA 8100 feet, you may descend further for a landing. A landing is permitted if the minimum visibility of 1 statute mile is satisfied. This is a matter for pilot judgment.

If you do not become visual at or above the MDA 8100 feet, then you may continue tracking inbound at this altitude in the hope of breaking clear of clouds and becoming visual, and then maneuvering as necessary for a landing. Tracking to the NDB at the MDA in clouds, you need to concentrate on maintaining altitude and tracking accurately. The ADF needle will become more and more sensitive as you fly closer to the NDB, so frequent small corrections may be required.

If you do become visual, and are right on course, then the runway should lie directly ahead. If you do not become visual, and reach the NDB, which is the designated missed approach point (MAP), at MDA 8100 feet, then you must commence a missed approach by initiating a climb and turning left and tracking to the Alamosa VOR, climbing to 11,500 feet MSL. From there you will have to decide whether to make another approach, or to hold for a while in the hope that conditions will improve, or to divert at a safe altitude to another airport.

The Valparaiso Rwy 27 NDB Approach

This approach is based on the compass locator VP situated at the outer marker (LOM) 5.3 nm from the Runway 27 threshold. From overhead the LOM, track outbound on MC 092 and descend to not below 2600 feet MSL. You must remain within 10 nm of the LOM.

Course reversal is achieved with a procedure turn to the right, to MH 137 for 1 minute, followed by a left turn to MH 317 to intercept the inbound course of MC 272.

Track into LOM not below 2600 feet MSL, continuously monitoring the VP ident. The ADF needle will become increasingly sensitive as you approach the compass locator, and then fall toward the bottom of the dial as you pass over it. The LOM is the final approach fix (FAF), and you should start timing as you pass it. This allows you to determine arrival at the MAP, which will be in 3 minutes 32 seconds if your groundspeed is 90 knots (as per the timing table at bottom right of approach plate).

From the FAF, you will be back-tracking on the compass locator, remaining on course by trailing the tail of the needle. Descent is now approved to the MDA 1240 feet MSL (470 feet above the airport) if you intend landing straight-in on Rwy 27, and also to 1240 feet MSL if you intend circling to another runway. This is provided you have the current Valparaiso altimeter setting; if not, and you are forced to use the South Bend altimeter setting, the MDA and the circling minimums are raised 140 feet to 1380 feet MSL, 610 feet above the airport (assuming that the South Bend altimeter setting is the same as at Valparaiso—if not, your altitude above the airport will be different, hence the caution).

To land straight-in, you require a visibility of $^3/_4$ sm; to circle to another runway, you require a visibility of 1 sm.

If you do not become visual at or above the minimum, then you must commence a **missed approach**, climbing away and turning right at the MAP (determined by stopwatch) direct to the VP LOM at 2600 feet MSL, where you should enter the holding pattern and consider your options.

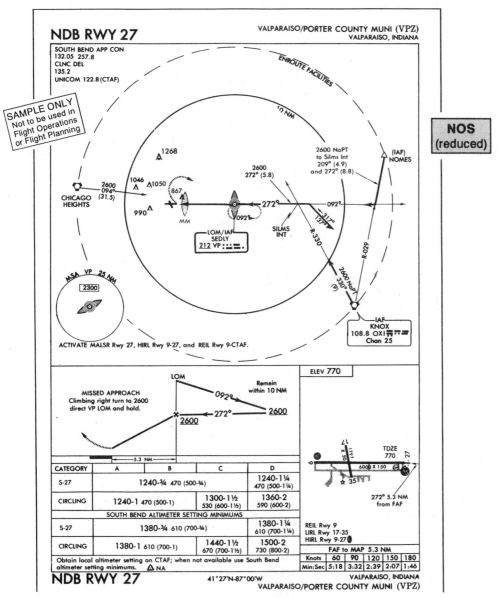

Figure 12b-42. Plan and profile of the Valparaiso/Porter County Municipal NDB Rwy 27 Approach (NOS)

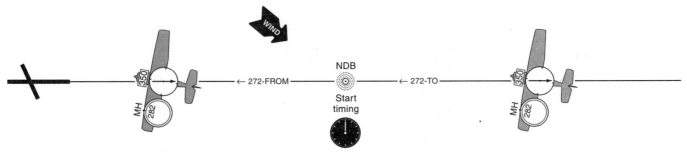

Figure 12b-43. Tracking on the Valparaiso NDB Rwy 27 approach

✍ Review 12b

The Relative Bearing Indicator (RBI)

1. On MH 020 with RB 010, the MB to the NDB is _____.

➤ MB 030 to NDB

2. On MH 020 with RB 005, the MB to the NDB is _____.

➤ MB 025 to NDB

3. On MH 020 with RB 000, the MB to the NDB is _____.

➤ MB 020 to NDB

4. On MH 020 with RB 355, the MB to the NDB is _____.

➤ MB 015 to NDB

5. When steering MH 180, MB 240 to the NDB is indicated by RB _____.

➤ RB 060

6. When steering MH 315, MB 060 to the NDB is indicated by RB _____.

➤ RB 105

7. When steering MH 340 with RB 010, the MB to the NDB is _____, and the MB from the NDB is _____.

➤ MB 350 to NDB, MB 170 from NDB

8. On MH 150 with RB 350, the MB to the NDB is _____, and the MB from the NDB is _____.

➤ MB 140 to NDB, MB 320 from NDB

9. On MH 340 with RB 180, the MB to the NDB is _____, and the MB from the NDB is _____.

➤ MB 160 to NDB, MB 340 from NDB

10. On MH 340 with RB 190, the MB to the NDB is _____, and the MB from the NDB is _____.

➤ MB 170 to NDB, MB 350 from NDB

11. When steering MH 270, MB 120 from the NDB is indicated by RB _____.

➤ RB 030

12. When steering MH 225, MB 255 from the NDB is indicated by RB _____.

➤ RB 210

13. When steering MH 315, MB 090 from the NDB is indicated by RB _____.

➤ RB 315

14. An airplane is steering MH 035. Its RBI indicates 040. Magnetic variation in the area is 4°W. Calculate:
(1) MB to the NDB; (2) MB from the NDB; (3) True bearing from the NDB.

➤ MB 075 to the NDB, MB 255 from the NDB, TB 251 from the NDB

15. An airplane is steering MH 335. Its RBI indicates 355. Magnetic variation in the area is 4°W. Calculate:
(1) MB to the NDB; (2) MB from the NDB; (3) True bearing from the NDB.

➤ MB 330 to the NDB, MB 150 from the NDB, TB 146 from the NDB

16. MH 080; RBI 000. What heading would you steer to make a 90° intercept of a course of MC 040 to the NDB? What would the RBI indicate at the point of intercept?

➤ right turn to MH 130, RBI 270

17. MH 080; RBI 000. What heading would you steer to make a 60° intercept of a course of MC 040 to the NDB? What would the RBI indicate at the point of intercept?

➤ right turn to MH 100, RBI 300

18. MH 070, RBI 010. Which way would you turn to intercept MC 075 to the NDB?

➤ right

19. MH 155, RBI 180. Which way would you turn to intercept a course of MC 140 away from the NDB?

➤ left.

20. MH 155, RBI 180. Which way would you turn to intercept a course of MC 180 away from the NDB?

➤ right

21. When tracking toward an NDB, the ADF readings are:
Time 1: MH 055, RBI 005; Time 2: MH 055, RBI 005.
What course is the airplane maintaining to the NDB?

➤ MC 060

22. When tracking toward an NDB, the ADF readings are:
Time 1: MH 055, RBI 005 and on course; Time 2: MH 055, RBI 002.
Is the airplane (left/right) of the desired MC, which is ..... .?

➤ right of MC 060 inbound to the NDB

23. To track toward an NDB on MC 340, with an expected crosswind from the right causing 5° of drift, what magnetic heading would you steer, and what would you expect the RBI to indicate?

➤ MH 345, RB 355

24. To track away from an NDB on MC 120, with an expected crosswind from the right causing 8° of drift, what magnetic heading would you steer, and what would you expect the RBI to indicate?

➤ MH 128, RB 172

25. You wish to track MC 360 in no-wind conditions. What magnetic heading would you steer? What would the RBI indicate as you pass abeam an NDB 10 nm to the right of course (when the NDB is on magnetic bearing MB 090 to the course)?

➤ MH 360, RB 090

26. You wish to track MC 360 and expect 10° of drift caused by a wind from the east. What magnetic heading would you steer? What would the RBI indicate as you pass abeam an NDB 10 nm to the right of course?

➤ MH 010, RB 080

27. You wish to track MC 030 in no-wind conditions. What magnetic heading would you steer? What would the RBI indicate as you pass abeam an NDB 10 nm to the right of course?

➤ MH 030, RB 090

28. You wish to track MC 030 in no-wind conditions. What magnetic heading would you steer? What would the RBI indicate as you pass abeam an NDB 10 nm to the left of course?

➤ MH 030, RB 270

29. You wish to track MC 030 and expect 7° left drift. What magnetic heading would you steer? What would the RBI indicate as you pass abeam an NDB 10 nm to the left of course?

➤ MH 037, RB 263

30. You are tracking MC 278 with 6° of left drift. You can determine your position abeam an NDB to the right of track by waiting until the RBI indicates _____.

➤ RB 084

31. You are tracking MC 278 with 6° of left drift. You can determine your position abeam an NDB to the left of course by waiting until the RBI indicates _____.

➤ RB 264

32. You are tracking MC 278 with 5° of right drift. You can determine your position abeam an NDB to the left of course by waiting until the RBI indicates _____.

➤ RB 275

The **radio magnetic indicator** combines the **relative bearing indicator** and the heading indicator into the one instrument, where the ADF card is aligned automatically with magnetic north. This considerably reduces your workload by reducing the amount of visualization and mental arithmetic required.

Even the manually rotatable-card (the "poor man's RMI" which allows you to align the ADF card manually with magnetic north) lightens the workload, since it also reduces the amount of visualization and mental arithmetic required.

The following discussion applies to both the RMI and the manually rotatable-card ADF, except that:

- the RMI is continuously and automatically aligned with magnetic north; while

- the manually rotatable-card must be realigned with the heading indicator by hand following every heading change (and of course the HI must be realigned with the magnetic compass by hand every 10 minutes or so).

The RMI, compared with the RBI, significantly reduces pilot workload.

Figure 12c-1.
The manually rotatable ADF card

Figure 12c-2. Examples of radio magnetic indicators (single and double ADF pointers)

Orientation

An RMI gives a graphic picture of where the airplane is:

- the *head* of the RMI needle displays magnetic bearing *to* the ground station; and

- the *tail* of the RMI needle displays magnetic bearing *from* the ground station.

One significant advantage of the RMI over the RBI is that you can select it to either an NDB or a VOR ground station. The method of use is the same in each case. If the head of the RMI needle indicates 030, then we write this as RMI 030. It tells us that the magnetic bearing to the ground station from the airplane is 030 degrees magnetic. The bearing from the ground station to the airplane is, of course, the reciprocal 210 degrees magnetic.

Example 1. The RMI is selected to an NDB. Orient the airplane with MH 320 and RMI 050. Determine the magnetic bearing to the ground station, and the magnetic bearing from the ground station.

Note: RMI 050 means MB 050 to the NDB (whereas RB 030 means a *relative bearing* of 030 to the NDB, relative to the airplane's nose and its heading).

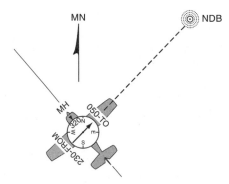

Figure 12c-3. Example 1. RMI orientation is quite straightforward—MB 050 to NDB, MB 230 from NDB.

The Initial Interception of Course

Intercepting an Inbound Course

A common use for the RMI, after you have used it to orient yourself with respect to the NDB, is to track to the NDB. The RMI makes it easy to visualize:

- where you are;
- where you want to go; and
- how to get there.

Example 2. An airplane has MH 340 and RMI 030. You are requested to intercept a course of 090 to the NDB.

Step 1. Orienting the airplane is made easy by the RMI. The magnetic bearing to the NDB from your present position is 030. If you now imagine a model airplane attached to the tail of the needle, with the airplane on the actual heading (which in this case is MH 340), then you have a clear picture of the situation.

The desired course of 090 to the NDB is ahead of the present position of the airplane. If you visualize the desired course on the RMI, with the model airplane on the tail of the needle tracking as desired, it becomes quite clear what turns are required to intercept the desired course.

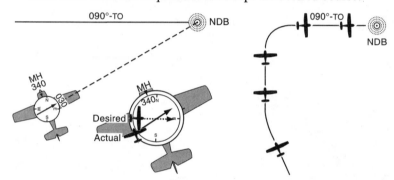

Figure 12c-4. Visualizing course on an RMI

Step 2. To intercept MC 090 to the NDB, the airplane should be turned to a suitable intercept heading, as in Figure 12c-5.

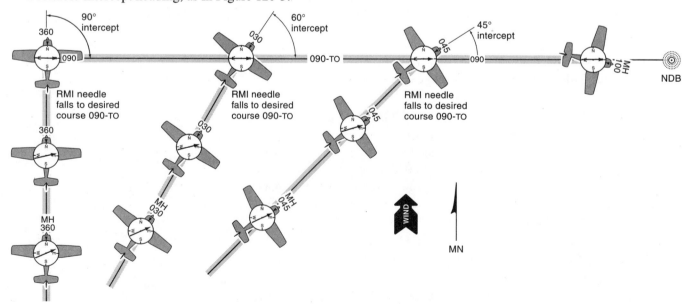

Figure 12c-5. Intercepting course at 90°, 60° or 45°

Step 3. Maintain the chosen intercept heading and periodically observe the RMI needle as it falls toward the desired inbound course of 090.

Step 4. As MC 090 to the NDB is approached (indicated by the RMI needle approaching 090) turn right to take up the desired course to the NDB, allowing for any estimated wind drift. In this case, a WCA of 10° right has been used. With MH 100, and the RMI steady on 090, the airplane now tracks MC 090 to the NDB.

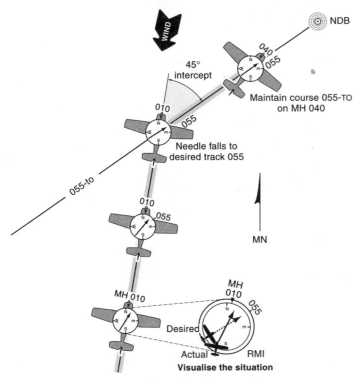

Figure 12c-6. Intercepting MC 055 inbound from radar vector 010

Example 3. An airplane is given a radar vector by ATC to steer MH 010, and then to intercept MC 055 inbound to an NDB.

Visualizing the situation confirms that radar vector 010 will intercept the inbound MC 055, and it will in fact be a 45° intercept (055 − 010 = 45). The RMI needle falls toward 055 approaching the desired course inbound, and you should commence a turn shortly before reaching it to avoid over-shooting the course. This is known as *leading in* (which is really anticipating), and the amount of lead-in can be judged by the rate at which the needle is falling, and the distance required for the airplane to turn to a suitable heading to fly inbound.

Another means of achieving a smooth intercept is to progressively reduce the closing angle as the course is approached, say from 45° to 30° to 15° and, finally, to zero, as the course is intercepted.

In this case, the pilot has chosen to fly inbound with a WCA of 15° left to counteract drift caused by a strong northerly wind. Correct tracking to the NDB will be confirmed by the RMI needle staying on 055.

Intercepting an Outbound Course

Example 4. You are given a radar vector of 340 to intercept 280 outbound from an NDB.

Step 1. Orient the airplane.

Step 2. Consider the intercept, 60° in this case (340 – 280 = 60). Visualize the situation. Again, the model airplane imagined on the tail of the needle helps.

Step 3. Monitor the intercept by steering a steady MH 340 and periodically checking the tail of the RMI needle rising to 280.

Step 4. As the desired course 280 outbound is approached, and as the tail of the needle approaches 280, turn left to pick up the MC 280, in this case allowing no wind correction angle, since you expect no crosswind effect.

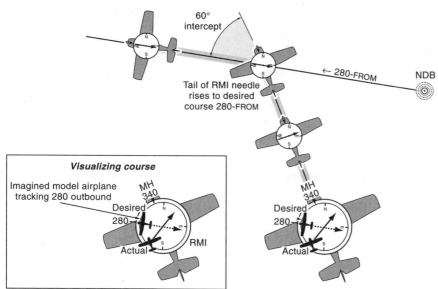

60°
intercept

← 280-FROM   NDB

Tail of RMI needle
rises to desired
course 280-FROM

Visualizing course

Imagined model airplane
tracking 280 outbound

MH 340
Desired 280
Actual
RMI

MH 340
Desired 280
Actual

Figure 12c-7. Intercepting 280 outbound off radar vector 340

Maintaining Course

Tracking Toward an NDB, with no Crosswind Effect

With no crosswind, a direct course inbound can be achieved by pointing the airplane directly at the NDB.

The magnetic heading will, in this case, be the same as the desired course, and the RMI needle will be on the nose indicating the course.

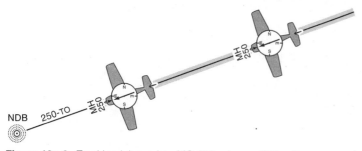

NDB   250-TO   MH 250   MH 250

Figure 12c-8. Tracking inbound on MC 250 using an RMI, with no crosswind

If there is no crosswind to blow the airplane off course, then everything will remain constant as in Figure 12c-8—MH 250 and RMI 250 will remain constant. This can only occur in:

- no-wind conditions;
- a direct headwind; or
- a direct tailwind.

Tracking Inbound with a Crosswind

If no correction for drift is made by the pilot, and the airplane is pointed straight at the NDB with the RMI needle initially on the nose, any crosswind will cause the airplane to be blown off course.

Time 0715	Time 0725
MH 250	MH 250
RMI 250	RMI 255

In Figure 12c-9, the wind, with a northerly component, has blown the airplane to the left of course. This is indicated by the head of the RMI needle starting to move down the right of the dial. To return to course, the airplane must be turned toward the right, toward the direction in which the head of the needle is moving.

If you turn right to put the NDB on the nose again, MH = RMI 255, then after a short period the airplane will again be blown to the left of course, and the RMI needle will move to the right of the nose. Another turn to the right will be required.

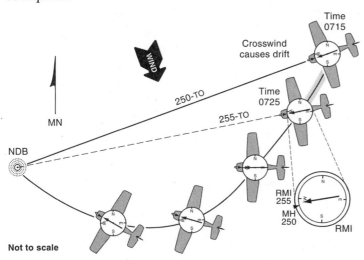

Figure 12c-9. Homing to the NDB

In this way the path to the NDB will be curved, with the airplane finally approaching the NDB heading roughly into the wind, and a longer distance will be traveled compared with the direct course from the original position. This is known as homing (keeping the NDB on the nose). It is not a tidy procedure. Professional pilots rarely use it.

If a correct drift correction is made by the pilot—a far better procedure than homing—then the airplane tracks direct to an NDB by heading into the wind and laying off a wind correction angle (WCA) to counteract drift. If 15° right is indeed the correct WCA, then the airplane will fly MC 250 direct to the NDB by steering MH 265.

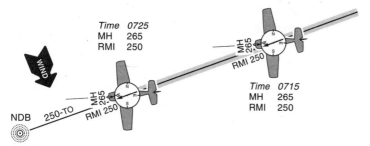

Figure 12c-10. Tracking direct to the NDB

Wind Correction Angles

Different winds require different wind correction angles. An airplane is on the desired course when the RMI indicates that same course. This is illustrated in Figure 12c-11. In each situation, the airplane is on the desired MC 355, but using a different wind correction angle to counteract the drift under different wind conditions.

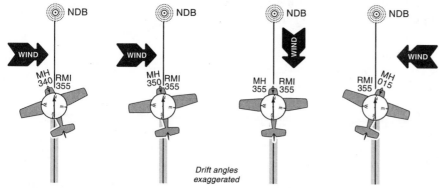

Drift angles exaggerated

Figure 12c-11. Laying off drift to achieve the desired course

If the precise wind effect is not known, then initially use a best-guess WCA, estimated from the available information. For the same crosswind, slower airplanes will need to allow a greater WCA than faster airplanes.

It is possible that the wind effect will change as you fly toward an NDB, and so regular alterations of heading may be required. This is often the case as an airplane descends using the NDB as the approach tracking aid.

If an incorrect drift correction is made by the pilot, then the airplane will move off the desired course and the magnetic bearing to the NDB will change. This will become obvious through a gradually changing RMI reading (since the RMI indicates MB to the ground station).

Suppose, for instance, the pilot steers a heading with a 5° wind correction angle to the right to counteract the effects of a wind from the right.

If the wind effect turns out to be greater than expected, the airplane will gradually deviate to the left of the desired course to the NDB, and the RMI reading will gradually increase. Typical cockpit indications could be:

Time 0715	Time 0725
MH 020	MH 020
RMI 015	RMI 018

The head of the RMI needle falling away to the right indicates that a turn right must be made to track to the NDB. Conversely, the head of the RMI needle falling away to the left indicates that a left turn must be made to track to the NDB. Just how great each correcting turn should be depends on the deviation from course.

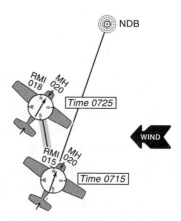

Figure 12c-12. An incorrect wind correction angle causes the RMI reading to change

Maintaining Course

Re-intercepting a course, once having deviated from it, requires basically the same procedure as the initial intercept of a new course, except that the angles will be smaller, provided the pilot is vigilant and does not allow large deviations to occur.

Realizing that the airplane is diverging from the direct course to the NDB, you have several options. You may either:

- track direct to the NDB from the present position even though it is slightly off the original course; or
- regain the original course.

To track direct to the NDB: Turn slightly right (say 5° in this case), and track direct to the NDB from the present position, even though it is not on the originally desired course. Normally, this technique is used only when very close to the station (say 1 or 2 nm).

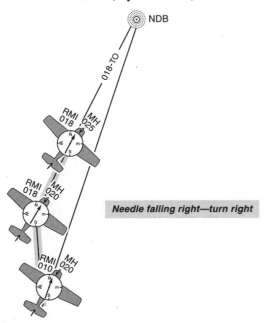

Figure 12c-13. Flying a new course to the NDB

To regain the original course: Turn further right initially (say 10° to MH 030), and reintercept the original course, indicated by the RMI needle moving down to read 015 again.

Once course is regained, turn left (say by half the correcting turn of 10°) to MH 025. This is a moderate correction, something you would expect to see from an experienced instrument pilot.

Attempting to maintain the desired course (maintaining a constant MB to the ground station) is the normal navigational technique when at some distance from the NDB. If the RMI remains on a steady reading, then the airplane is tracking directly to the NDB.

Just how great each correcting turn should be depends on the displacement from course and the distance from the station. A simple method is to initially alter heading by **double the error**.

If the airplane has deviated 10° left (indicated by the RMI moving 10° right), then alter heading by 20° to the right. (If you alter heading by only 10° to the right, the result will probably be a further deviation to the left, a further correction to the right, ultimately resulting in a curved homing to the NDB.)

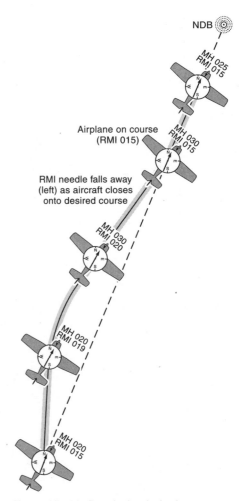

Figure 12c-14. Regain the desired course

Having regained course, turn left by only half the correcting turn of 20°, i.e. turn left 10° to intercept and maintain course. This leaves you with a WCA different to the original one (that caused you to deviate from course), and one that should provide reasonable tracking. If not, make further corrections to heading!

Bracketing Course

In practice, absolutely perfect tracking along the desired course is difficult to achieve. The actual ground track achieved will probably consist of a series of minor corrections to heading, a technique known as *bracketing* the course, making regular corrections, left or right as required, to maintain or regain the desired course.

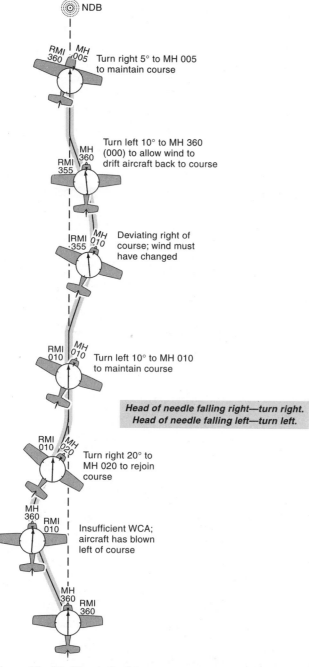

Figure 12c-15. "Bracketing" the course

The aim of bracketing is to find the precise WCA needed to maintain course. If, for instance, a WCA of 10° right is found to be too great and the airplane diverges to the right of course, and a WCA of only 5° right is too little and the wind blows the airplane to the left of course, then try something in between, say WCA 8° right.

A precise instrument pilot will monitor the tracking of the airplane on a regular basis and make corrections earlier rather than later, the result being a number of small corrections rather than just one big correction.

Wind Effect

If the wind direction and strength is not obvious, then a useful technique is to initially steer the course to the station as heading (make no allowance for drift), observe the results, and then make heading adjustments to bracket course. This is illustrated in Figure 12c-15.

Tracking Over an NDB

The RMI needle will become more and more sensitive as the NDB station is approached, minor movements left or right of course causing larger and larger changes in the RMI reading.

For a precise course to be achieved, you must be prepared to increase your scan rate and respond more frequently.

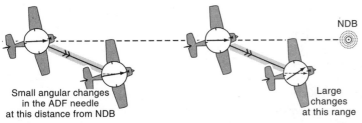

Figure 12c-16. Approaching the NDB, the RMI needle becomes more sensitive

Close to the station and just prior to passing over the NDB, however, the RMI needle can become agitated, and the pilot should relax a little and steer a steady heading until the RMI needle moves toward the bottom of the dial and settles down, at which time tracking from the NDB should be checked and suitable adjustments made to heading.

If the course outbound is different to that inbound, then a suitable heading change estimated to make good the new desired course could be made as soon as the RMI needle falls past the mid-position on its way to the bottom of the dial.

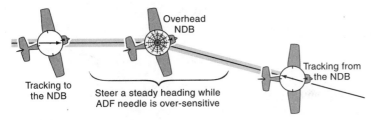

Figure 12c-17. Do not overcorrect when close to the station

The RMI needle becoming extremely active and then falling rapidly past the abeam position to the bottom of the dial indicates that the airplane has passed directly over the NDB.

The RMI needle moving gradually to one side and slowly falling to the bottom of the dial indicates that the airplane is passing to one side of the beacon—the rate at which the needle falls being an indication of the airplane's proximity to the NDB. If it falls very slowly, then possibly the tracking by the pilot could have been better. Time over (or abeam) the NDB can be taken as the needle falls through the approximate mid-position.

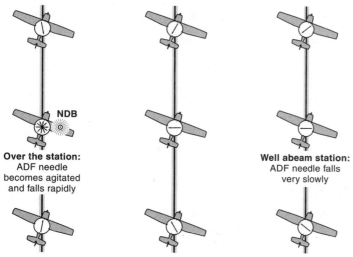

Over the station:
ADF needle becomes agitated and falls rapidly

Well abeam station:
ADF needle falls very slowly

Figure 12c-18. Good ADF tracking; reasonable tracking; poor tracking

Tracking Away From an NDB

When tracking away from an NDB, the head of the RMI needle will lie toward the bottom of the dial, and the tail of the RMI needle will be toward the top of the dial.

Tracking Away From an NDB with no Crosswind Effect

If the pilot tracks over the NDB and steers course as heading, the airplane will track directly away from the NDB with the head of the RMI needle steady at the bottom of the dial, and the tail of the RMI needle steady at the top of the dial under the MH lubber line.

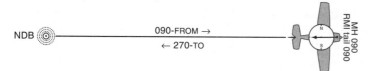

Figure 12c-19. Tracking away from an NDB with no crosswind effect

The airplane in Figure 12c-19 has a magnetic bearing from the station to the airplane indicated by the tail of the RMI needle, and a magnetic bearing to the station from the airplane indicated by the head of the RMI needle. Since it is course outbound that is being considered here, the position of the tail of the needle is of more use to the pilot.

Tracking Away From an NDB with a Crosswind

Suppose that the desired course outbound from an NDB is MC 340, and the pilot estimates that a WCA of 12° to the right is necessary to counteract a wind from the right. To achieve this, he steers MH 352, and hopes to see the tail of the RMI needle stay on 340, the desired outbound course. In Figure 12c-20, the chosen WCA and MH are correct, and the desired MC 340 outbound is maintained.

If the estimated WCA is incorrect, then the actual ground track achieved by the airplane will differ from that desired. If, in Figure 12c-20, the wind is stronger than expected, the airplane's ground track may be 335°M, and to the left of the desired course of MC 340.

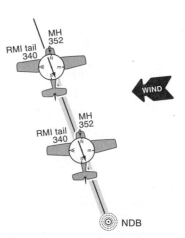

Figure 12c-20. Tracking away from an NDB with a WCA of 12° into the wind

Whereas inaccurate tracking to an NDB is indicated by the RMI needle falling, incorrect tracking away from an NDB can occur with the RMI needle indicating a steady reading—but the airplane may be on the wrong MC. Having passed over the NDB, an airplane can track away from it in any of 360 directions.

You must always ensure that you are flying away from the NDB along the correct course, and the easiest way to do this is to observe the MB from the ground station on the tail of the RMI needle. A magnetic course outbound from a VOR is known as a radial so, if you have the RMI selected to a VOR or VORTAC, the tail of the RMI needle will tell you what radial you are on.

Regaining Course Away From an NDB in a Crosswind

If an incorrect wind correction angle is flown, then the airplane will be blown off course. The vigilant pilot will observe the incorrect ground track, probably by noting that the tail of the RMI needle is indicating something other than the desired outbound course.

Example 5. The pilot is flying course as heading, initially making no allowance for drift. If the tail of the RMI needle moves right, then the airplane must be turned left to regain course.

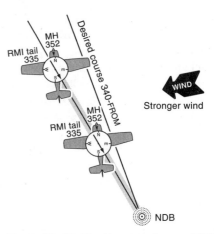

Figure 12c-21. Tracking away from an NDB with an incorrect wind correction angle

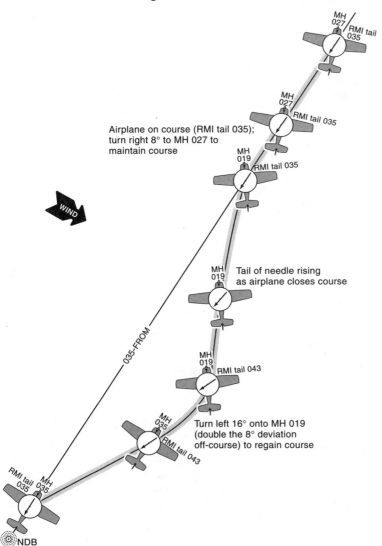

Figure 12c-22. Turning left to "trail the tail" or "pull the tail around"

In Figure 12c-22, the airplane has been blown to the right of the desired MC 035, to MB 043 from the NDB, as indicated by the tail of the RMI needle.

To regain course, the pilot has turned left by 16° (double the error) from MH 035 to MH 019. As the airplane is flown on its steady intercept heading of MH 019, the tail of the needle will be gradually pulled around.

The pilot will continue with the intercept heading until the airplane approaches the desired course, MC 035. This is indicated to the pilot by the tail of the RMI needle moving up the dial toward 035.

As the desired course outbound is approached, the pilot turns right to maintain the RMI tail on 035, which is MB 035 from the NDB. Estimating a WCA of 8° into the wind to be sufficient, the pilot steers MH 027 and checks regularly that the tail of the RMI needle stays on 035.

Similarly, if the tail of the RMI needle is left of where it should be, then the desired course is out to the right, and a right turn should be made to trail the tail.

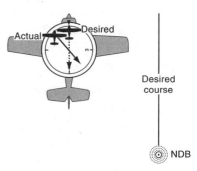

Figure 12c-23. Turn right to "trail the tail"

Note: If using the head of the needle is the preferred technique, then the need for a left turn is indicated by the head of the needle moving to the left of the datum MB 215 to the NDB.

It is generally easier to work off the top of the dial, since that is where the airplane is going, rather than off the bottom of the dial. The left turn necessary to regain course (turning left toward the head of the needle and therefore away from the tail of the needle) can be thought of as pulling the tail of the RMI needle around or "trailing the tail". Some instructors, however, prefer to use the head of the needle—in this case, the head of the needle (now at the bottom of the dial) moves left, indicating that a correcting turn to the left is required. Your instructor will recommend a method.

The NDB Approach

The NDB approach discussed at the end of the previous chapter is made simpler for pilots with an RMI to use for NDB tracking, rather than an RBI.

The actual NDB approach procedure for the pilot to follow in terms of flight path is identical for all ADF presentations—the fixed-card ADF (or RBI), the manually rotatable-card ADF, and the RMI.

Using the RMI to Fly a DME Arc

The RMI simplifies flying a DME arc, and this is considered in the Chapter 28, *Holding Patterns, Procedure Turns & DME Arcs.*

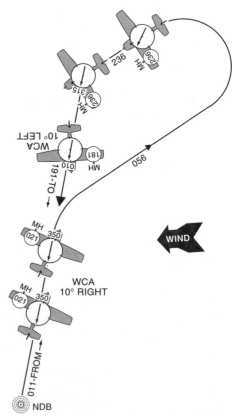

Figure 12c-24. Tracking using an RMI during an NDB approach; (Monte Vista, Co, NDB RWY 20 Approach—see *Jeppesen* chart, plan and profile on page 253)

1. If the head of the RMI needle reads RMI 070, the magnetic bearing to the ground station from the airplane is MB _____ to ground station.

➤ MB 070 to ground station

2. If the head of the RMI needle reads RMI 070, the magnetic bearing from the ground station to the airplane is MB _____ from ground station.

➤ MB 250 from ground station (the reciprocal of 070)

3. An airplane is flying MH 035. Its RMI indicates RMI 075. Calculate:
   (1) MB to the NDB;
   (2) MB from the NDB.

➤ MB 075 to the NDB, MB 255 from the NDB

4. An airplane steers MH 335. Its RMI indicates RMI 330. Calculate:
   (1) MB to the NDB;
   (2) MB from the NDB.

➤ MB 330 to the NDB, MB 150 from the NDB

5. The desired course is MC 040 inbound to an NDB or VOR. The WCA is 10° left. The airplane is achieving this course when the head of the RMI needle indicates RMI _____.

➤ RMI 040

6. The desired course is MC 230 inbound to an NDB or VOR. The WCA is 7° right. The airplane is achieving this course when the head of the RMI needle indicates RMI _____.

➤ RMI 230

7. The desired course is MC 120 outbound from an NDB or VOR. The WCA is 3° left. The airplane is achieving this course when the head of the RMI needle indicates RMI _____.

➤ RMI 300

8. MH 080; RMI 080. What heading would you steer to make a 90° intercept of a course of MC 040 to the NDB? What would the RMI indicate at the point of intercept?

➤ right turn to MH 130, RMI 040

9. MH 080; RMI 080. What heading would you steer to make a 60° intercept of MC 040 to the NDB? What would the RMI indicate at the point of intercept?

➤ right turn to MH 100, RMI 040

10. MH 070, RMI 080. Which way would you turn to intercept MC 075 to the NDB? What would the RMI indicate at the point of intercept?

➤ right, RMI 075

11. MH 155, RMI 330. Which way would you turn to intercept MC 140 away from the NDB? What would the RMI indicate at the point of intercept? What would the tail of the RMI pointer indicate?

➤ left, RMI 320, RMI tail on 140

12. MH 155, RMI 130. Which way would you turn to intercept MC 090 away from the NDB? What would the RMI indicate at the point of intercept? What would the RMI tail indicate?

➤ left, RMI 270, RMI tail on 090

13. When tracking toward an NDB, the RMI readings are:
    Time 1: MH 055, RMI 060; Time 2: MH 055, RMI 060.
    What course is the airplane maintaining to the NDB?

➤ MC 060

14. When flying toward an NDB, the RMI readings are:
    Time 1: MH 055, RMI 060 and on course; Time 2: MH 055, RMI 057.
    Is the airplane off course to the left or right?

➤ right

15. To track toward an NDB on MC 340, with an expected crosswind from the right causing 5° of drift, what magnetic heading would you steer, and what would you expect the RMI to indicate?

➤ MH 345, RMI 340

16. To fly away from an NDB on MC 120, with an expected crosswind from the right causing 8° of drift, what magnetic heading would you steer, and what would you expect the RMI to indicate?

➤ MH 128, RMI 300, RMI tail 120

17. You wish to fly MC 360 in no-wind conditions. What magnetic heading would you steer? What would the RMI indicate as you passed abeam an NDB 10 nm to the right of course?

➤ MH 360, RMI 090

18. You wish to fly MC 360 and expect 10° of drift caused by a wind from the east. What magnetic heading would you steer? What would the RMI indicate as you passed abeam an NDB 10 nm to the right of course?

➤ MH 010, RMI 090

19. You wish to track MC 030 in no-wind conditions. What magnetic heading would you steer? What would the RMI indicate as you passed abeam an NDB 10 nm to the right of course?

➤ MH 030, RMI 120

20. You wish to fly MC 030 in no-wind conditions. What magnetic heading would you steer? What would the RMI indicate as you passed abeam an NDB 10 nm to the left of course?

➤ MH 030, RMI 300

21. You wish to fly MC 030 and expect 7° left drift. What magnetic heading would you steer? What would the RMI indicate as you passed abeam an NDB 10 nm to the left of course?

➤ MH 037, RMI 300

22. You are flying on MC 239 with 7° of left drift. At a position directly abeam an NDB to the left of course, the RMI will read _____?

➤ RMI 149

23. The (head/tail) of an RMI selected to a VOR tells you what radial you are on.

➤ tail

24. If the head of the RMI needle selected to a VOR reads RMI 010, you are on the _____ radial.

➤ 190

25. If the tail of the RMI needle selected to a VOR reads 089, you are on the _____ radial.

➤ 089

The VOR 13

The VOR is a very high frequency (VHF) radio navigation aid that is extensively used in instrument flying. Its full name is the **very high frequency omni-directional radio range**, commonly abbreviated to the VOR, VHF omni range, or omni. VOR is pronounced *"vee-oh-are"*.

Each VOR ground station transmits on a specific VHF frequency between 108.00 and 117.95 megahertz (MHz), which is immediately below the frequency range used for VHF communications. A separate VHF-NAV radio is required for navigation purposes, but is usually combined with the VHF-COM in a NAV/COM set.

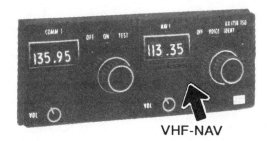

VHF-NAV

VOR INDICATOR

Figure 13-1. VOR equipment in the cockpit

The VOR was developed in the United States during the late 1940s, and was adopted by the International Civil Aviation Organization (ICAO) as the standard short-range radio navigation aid in 1960. When introduced, it offered an immediate improvement over previously existing aids such as the ADF/NDB combination, most of which operated in lower frequency bands than the VOR and suffered significant limitations such as night effect, mountain reflections and interference from electrical storms.

Principal advantages of the VOR over the NDB include:

- a reduced susceptibility to electrical and atmospheric interference (including thunderstorms);
- the elimination of night effect, since VHF signals are line-of-sight and not reflected by the ionosphere (as are NDB signals in the low and medium frequency band).

The reliability and accuracy of VOR signals allow the VOR to be used with confidence in any weather conditions, by day or by night, for purposes such as:

- orientation and position fixing (where am I?);
- tracking to or from a VOR ground station;
- holding (for delaying action or maneuvering); and
- instrument approaches to land.

The Main Use of the VOR is for Tracking

The VOR can be used by a pilot to indicate the desired course and the angular deviation from that course.

For a desired course of MC 015, the pilot would expect to steer a heading of MH 015, plus or minus a wind correction angle (WCA). By selecting an omni bearing of 015 under the course index of the VOR cockpit display, the pilot can obtain tracking information as shown in Figure 13-2.

Many VORs are paired with DME (distance measuring equipment). Selection of the VOR on the VHF-NAV set in the cockpit also selects the paired DME, thereby providing both tracking and distance information.

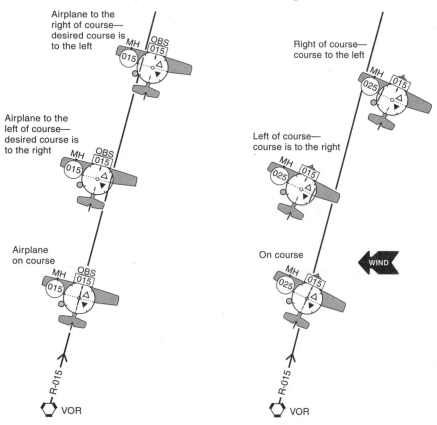

Figure 13-2. The VOR is used to indicate course

Figure 13-3. The VOR cockpit display is not heading sensitive

The VOR cockpit display is not heading sensitive, which means that the display will not change as a result of the airplane changing heading. The case illustrated in Figure 13-3 shows the same situation as Figure 13-2, except that a wind correction angle (WCA) of 10° right is being used by the pilot to counteract a wind from the right, and so the airplane's magnetic heading is now MH 025 (rather than the previous MH 015).

Note that:

- the VOR indication depends on the angular deviation of the airplane relative to the selected course;
- the VOR indication will not change with any heading change of the airplane.

VOR Radials

As its name *omni* suggests, a VOR ground transmitter radiates signals in all directions. Its most important feature, however, is that the signal in any particular direction differs slightly from its neighbors. These individual directional signals can be thought of as courses or position lines radiating out from the VOR ground station, in much the same way as spokes from the hub of a wheel.

By convention, 360 different tracks away from the VOR are used, each separated from the next by 1°, and each with its direction related to magnetic north. Each of these 360 VOR courses or position lines is called a **radial**. The 075 radial may be written R-075. A radial is the magnetic bearing outbound *from* a VOR.

An airplane tracking outbound on the 060 radial will diverge from an airplane tracking outbound on the 090 radial.

Conversely, if they both reverse direction and track inbound on the 060 radial (240-TO the VOR) and the 090 radial (270-TO), their tracks will converge.

When a VOR is operating normally, the radials are transmitted to an accuracy of ±2° or better.

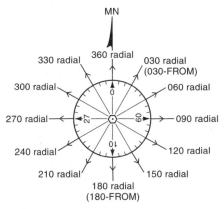

Figure 13-4. A radial is a magnetic bearing outbound *from* a VOR ground station

How the VOR Works

The VOR ground station transmits two VHF radio signals:

1. the **reference phase** signal, which is omni-directional (the same in all directions); and

2. the **variable phase** signal, which rotates uniformly at a rate of 1800 rpm, with its phase varying at a constant rate throughout the 360°.

The antenna of the VOR airborne receiver picks up the signals, whose *phase difference* (the difference between the wave peaks) is measured, this difference depending on the bearing of the airplane from the ground station. In this manner, the VOR can determine the magnetic bearing of the airplane from the VOR ground station.

Figure 13-5. A VOR antenna (left) and a VOR ground station (right)

The two signals transmitted by the VOR ground station are:

• in-phase on magnetic north, which is the reference for VOR signals;

• 90° out of phase at magnetic east 090°M;

• 180° out of phase at magnetic south 180°M;

• 270° out of phase at magnetic west 270°M; and

• 360° out of phase (back in-phase) at magnetic north 360°M, or 000°M.

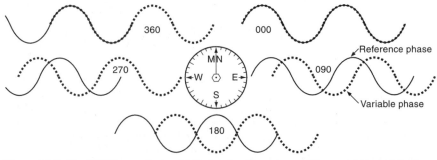

Figure 13-6. The VOR transmits two VHF signals with a phase difference between them

Every 10 seconds or so a Morse code identifier signal (or **ident**) is transmitted, modulated at 1020 Hz, allowing the pilot to positively identify the VOR. The coded identifier for the Redmond VOR is RDM (*dit-dah-dit dah-dit-dit dah-dah*). Any associated DME will have a coded identifier broadcast about every 30 seconds, modulated at 1350 Hz, about one DME ident at a higher pitch tone for every three or four VOR idents.

Some VORs may also carry voice transmissions either identifying them (for example, "Linden VOR", alternating with the coded identifier), or carrying a message such as a relevant Automatic Terminal Information Service (ATIS) or Transcribed Weather Broadcast (TWEB). The voice identifier of the VOR must have the word VOR or VORTAC stated after its name for the VOR to be considered identified.

If the VOR ground station is undergoing maintenance, the coded identifier is not transmitted, but it is possible that navigation signals will still be received. Sometimes a coded *test* signal (*dah dit dit-dit-dit dah*) is transmitted. Do not use these aids for navigation. No radio navigation signal should be used until positive identification is made.

VOR Range

The VOR is a very high frequency aid operating in the frequency band 108.0 to 117.95 MHz. It allows high quality "line-of-sight" reception because there is relatively little interference from atmospheric noise in this band. Reception may be affected by the terrain surrounding the ground station, the height of the VOR beacon, the altitude of the airplane and its distance from the station.

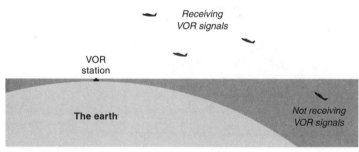

Figure 13-7. VHF line-of-sight signals

The approximate maximum range of a VHF signal is given by the formula (which is printed here for your convenience):

$$VHF\ range\ in\ nm\ =\ \sqrt{1.5 \times altitude\ in\ feet}$$

Example 1. At 7000 feet, approximate VHF range:

$$= \sqrt{1.5 \times 7000}$$
$$= \sqrt{10,000}$$
$$= 100\ nm$$

Different VORs may operate on the same frequency, but they will be well separated geographically so that there is no interference between their VHF line-of-sight signals. The higher the airplane's altitude, however, the greater the possibility of interference.

Standard Service Volumes

There are prescribed standard service volumes for three classes of VORs (High Altitude—H, Low Altitude—L, and Terminal—T) which define the reception limits usable at various altitudes. The transmitting power of each VOR is designed to achieve its specified volume.

Use standard service volumes when planning routes that are not on Federal Airways.

Use standard service volumes when planning an off-airway route. Standard service volume limitations do not apply to published IFR routes or procedures. For example, if planning an off-airway flight 17,000 feet above the level of a high altitude VOR ground station, the signal is officially usable out to 100 nm. For complete VOR coverage along the route, the H-class VOR ground stations should be within 200 nm of each other, so that their signals overlap and the airplane will always be within range (100 nm at that altitude) of a VOR.

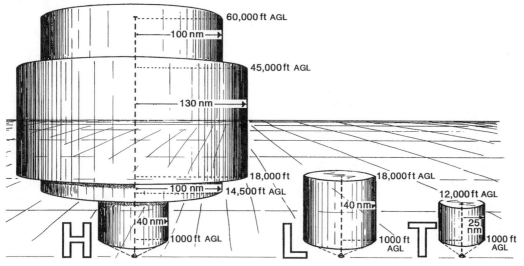

Figure 13-8. Standard service volumes

The class of a VOR is specified in the Airport/Facility Directory (A/FD), and also any restrictions on its use, such as unreliability between certain radials. The A/FD also contains, in its Directory Legend, a table of altitudes versus distances related to the standard service volumes, and this will help you when planning off-airway routes. The class of a VOR, other than H, is also specified in the navaid box on NOS En route Charts.

Minimum En Route IFR Altitude (MEA)

The MEA is the lowest published altitude between radio fixes that:

- assures acceptable navigational signal coverage between those fixes; and
- meets obstacle clearance requirements between those fixes.

Minimum Obstruction Clearance Altitude (MOCA)

The MOCA is the lowest published altitude between radio fixes that:

- meets obstacle clearance requirements between those fixes; but
- assures acceptable navigational signal coverage only within 22 nm (25 sm) of a VOR.

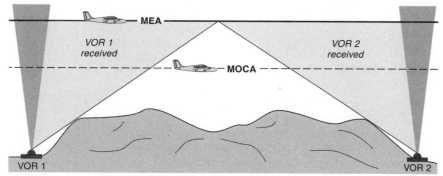

Figure 13-9. MEA and MOCA

The MOCA may be lower than the MEA, but of course can never be higher. For example, the route between two radio fixes may be labeled with an MEA of 6000, and a MOCA of 5000 (written as "*5000" on NOS charts and "5000T" on Jeppesen charts).

VOR Change-Over Point (COP)

It is usual, when tracking en route from one VOR to another, to select the next VOR when the airplane is approximately halfway between them, unless a **designated change-over point** is specified on the low altitude chart. Selecting the next VOR at the change-over point will mean that the stronger signal is being used.

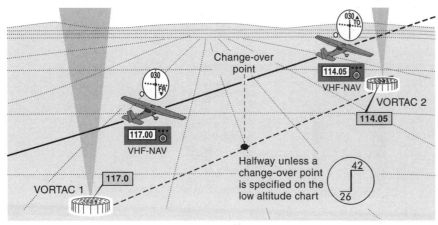

Figure 13-10. Tracking between two VORs

Change VORs at the specified change-over point, otherwise at the approximate mid-point between them, or at the point where the airway changes direction. This occurs at some intersections, so watch for this. Certain intersections have a specified **minimum reception altitude (MRA)** published on charts, this being the minimum altitude at which this intersection can be identified; at altitudes lower than the MRA, navigational coverage is not assured.

VORs on Aeronautical Charts

Most aeronautical charts show the position, frequency and Morse code *ident* of each VOR ground station. Information on a particular VOR may be found in the Airport/Facility Directory (A/FD), and any changes in this information will be referred to in NOTAMs (to which a pilot should refer prior to flight). You should take time to read the Directory Legend at the front of the A/FD regarding Radio Aids to Navigation.

A VOR ground station may be represented in various ways on a chart, the common forms are shown in Figure 13-11. Since magnetic north is the reference direction for VOR radials, a magnetic north arrowhead usually emanates from the VOR symbol, with a compass rose heavily marked each 30° and the radials shown in 10° intervals. This is generally adequate for in-flight estimation of an off-airway course to an accuracy of ±2°, however, when flight planning prior to flight, it is advisable to be more accurate than ±2°.

Most routes are published on the en route charts as airways, with the courses marked in degrees *magnetic*, thereby making it easy for the pilot to plan without having to use a protractor or plotter. If, for some reason, the pilot measures the course in true using a protractor, then variation needs to be applied to convert to magnetic ("Variation west, magnetic best" or "East is least, west is best").

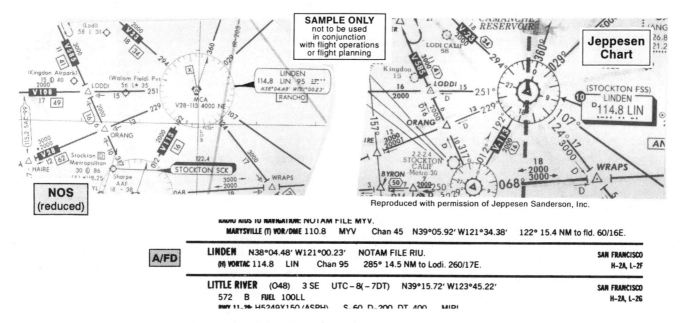

Figure 13-11. A VOR and its radials represented on various charts, and in the A/FD

The **Victor airways** between VORs shown on the low-altitude en route charts are marked at either end with the radial out of that VOR. These radials are not always exact reciprocals of each other, especially on east–west tracks, because:

- great circles (which the airways are) cross the north–south meridians of longitude at different angles; and

- magnetic variation changes slightly across the country (and this affects the calculation of the magnetic course, which a radial is, from the true course).

There are two sets of en route charts available—those published by *Jeppesen*, and those published by NOS (National Ocean Service).

VOR/DME, TACAN and VORTAC

Most civil VORs have an associated DME, providing both azimuth and distance information, and are known as **VOR/DMEs**. The VOR operates in the VHF range, but the DME, even though automatically selected along with the VOR selection, operates in the UHF range.

The military has developed a different navigation system, called TACAN (Tactical Air Navigation system), which operates in the UHF band, and also provides both azimuth and distance information. It requires special airborne equipment (installed only in military aircraft) for the azimuth information to be received, however civil aircraft can receive the TACAN distance information using the DME.

When a TACAN ground station has been integrated with a VOR/DME ground station, the combined facility is known as a **VORTAC**. The end result for a civil pilot using a VORTAC is the same as using a VOR/DME—both VOR and DME information are available.

On Jeppesen en route charts, a small letter D in the VOR box indicates that DME is also available when the VOR frequency is selected. On NOS en route charts, a (channel) number after the navaid three-letter ident (SEA 115 at Seattle), indicates DME is automatically available when the VOR frequency is selected. Underlined navaid frequencies on NOS charts means no voice is transmitted.

The VOR Cockpit Instrument

There are various types of VOR cockpit displays, however they are all reasonably similar in terms of operation. The VOR cockpit display, or VOR indicator, or omni bearing indicator (OBI), displays the omni bearing selected by the pilot on the course card using the **omni bearing selector (OBS)**, a small knob that is geared to the card. The omni bearing selector is also known as the course selector.

If the airplane is on the selected radial, then the VOR needle, known as the **course deviation indicator (CDI)**, is centered. If the airplane is not on the selected course, then the CDI will not be centered.

Whether the selected course would take the airplane *to* or *from* the VOR ground station is indicated by the TO/FROM flag, removing any ambiguity.

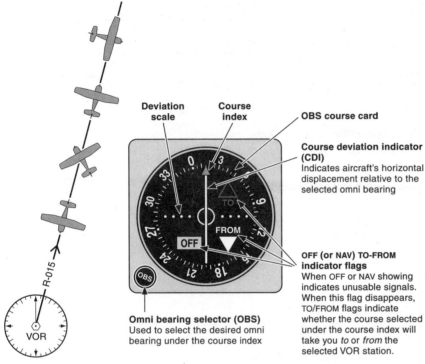

Figure 13-12. The VOR cockpit display (OBI) for airplanes on the 015 radial

The VOR is only to be used for navigation if:

- the red OFF warning flag is hidden from view;
- the correct Morse code or voice *ident* is heard; and
- the CDI is not moving erratically.

The red OFF flag showing indicates that the signal strength received is not adequate to operate the airborne VOR equipment, which may be the case if the airplane is too far from the VOR ground facility, too low for line-of-sight reception, or directly overhead where there is no signal. Also, it will show OFF if the equipment is switched off.

Course Deviation

The course deviation indicator (or CDI) in the VOR cockpit instrument indicates off-course deviation in terms of angular deviation from the selected course. At all times, the reference when using the VOR is the selected course under the course index. (This is a totally different principle to that of the ADF needle which simply points at an NDB ground station and indicates its relative bearing.)

The CDI indicates angular deviation from the selected course.

The amount of angular deviation from the selected course is referred to in terms of dots, there being 5 dots either side of the central position. The inner dot on both sides is often represented by a circle passing through them. Each dot is equivalent to 2 degrees course deviation.

Each "dot" on the CDI equals 2 degrees course deviation.

- If the airplane is on the selected course, the CDI is centered.
- If the airplane is 2° off the selected course, the CDI is displaced 1 dot from the center (on the circumference of the inner circle).
- If the airplane is 4° off the selected course, the CDI is displaced 2 dots.
- If the airplane is 10° or more off the selected course, the CDI is fully deflected at 5 dots.

A full-scale deflection of the VOR at 5 dots indicates a course deviation of 10 degrees or more.

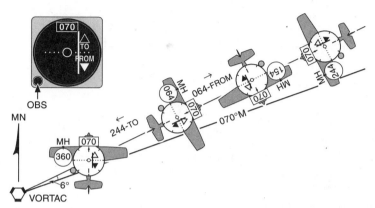

Figure 13-13. Each of these airplanes is displaced 6° from the 070 radial

Since the CDI indicates angular deviation, the actual distance off-course for a given CDI indication will be smaller the closer the airplane is to the ground station. In a manner of speaking, airplanes tracking inbound are funneled in toward the VOR ground station. At 1 nm distance from the VOR ground facility, a 1 dot deviation from the selected course is a lateral deviation of approximately 200 feet, so:

- at 1 nm, 1 dot on the VOR indicator = 200 feet laterally;
- at 2 nm, 1 dot on the VOR indicator = 2 × 200 = 400 feet;
- at 30 nm, 1 dot on the VOR indicator = 30 × 200 = 6000 feet = 1 nm;
- at 60 nm, 1 dot on the VOR indicator = 60 × 200 = 12,000 feet = 2 nm

Deviation "dots" on the CDI match up with the 1-in-60 rule: 1 nm off-course in 60 nm = 1° course error, therefore 2 nm off-course in 60 nm = 2° course error, or 1 dot on the VOR.

To or From

The 090 radial, which is a magnetic bearing of 090 away *from* the station, is the same position line as 270-TO the station. If an airplane is on this position line, then the CDI will be centered when either 090 or 270 is selected with the OBS. Any ambiguity in the pilot's mind regarding the position of the airplane relative to the VOR ground station is resolved with the TO/FROM indicator.

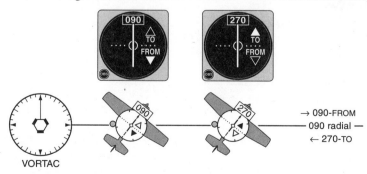

Figure 13-14. Using the TO/FROM flag

The TO or FROM flags or arrows indicate to the pilot whether the selected omni bearing will take the airplane *to* the VOR ground station, or away *from* it. In the case shown in Figure 13-14, the pilot can center the CDI by selecting either 090 or 270 (which are reciprocals) with the OBS. A course of 090 would take the airplane *from* the VOR, whereas a course of 270 would lead it *to* the VOR.

Example 2. Illustrate two indications on the VOR cockpit display informing the pilot that the airplane is on the 235 radial.

The 235 radial is either:

– 235-FROM the VOR; or

– 055-TO the VOR;

so, with the CDI centered, the VOR cockpit display could indicate either 235-FROM or 055-TO. See Figure 13-15.

At all times, the reference when using the VOR indicator is the course selected under the course index. The selected course determines CDI deflection and whether the TO or the FROM flag shows.

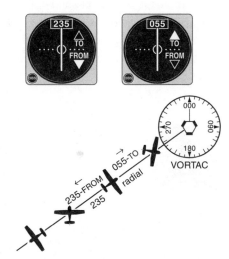

Figure 13-15. Indications that the airplane is on the 235 radial

Different Presentations of the Omni Bearing Indicator

There are various presentations of VOR cockpit information. In all cases, full-scale deflection is 10° either side of the selected omni bearing (a total arc of 20°), with five dots either side of center. In many VOR cockpit displays the two inner dots are joined by the circumference of a circle. The dots may be actual dots on some indicators, or they may be tick marks or hash marks.

The course deviation indicator (CDI) may also differ between instruments. On some displays, the whole CDI moves laterally (rectilinear movement); on others, the CDI hinges at the top and swings. Similarly, the means of displaying the selected omni bearing may differ between instruments. It may be shown under a course index, or it may be shown in a window. In some equipment, the TO and the FROM flags may be displayed in the one window, in others they may have separate windows.

In instruments where the VOR cockpit display also doubles as the ILS (instrument landing system) display, which is the usual case, vertical dots may be marked to indicate glideslope deviation (using a second needle which lies horizontal, or is hinged horizontally, so that it can move up or down). When being used for the VOR (and not the ILS), the glideslope needle may be biased out of view, and there may be a red GS warning flag showing.

Preparing the OBI for Use

A radio navigation aid is of little value if the pilot does not use it correctly. Prior to using the VOR, a pilot must:

• ensure that the VOR has been checked as suitable for IFR flight (see *The VOR Receiver Check* on page 283);

• ensure electrical power is available, and switch the VHF-NAV on;

• select the desired frequency (as found on the en route charts or in the A/FD);

• identify the VOR (*dit dit-dit-dah dah-dah-dit,* which is EUG in Morse code, the coded identifier specified on the charts for Eugene);

• check that the OFF flag is not showing (the signal is usable, otherwise the OFF flag would be visible).

The VOR Receiver Check

It is required that, for a pilot to use the VOR for IFR flight, the VOR equipment of that aircraft either:

- is maintained, checked and inspected under an approved procedure; or
- has been operationally checked within the preceding 30 days as specified below, and is within the limits of the permissible indicated bearing error.

There are five ways in which the VOR receiver may be checked for accuracy prior to IFR flight.

1. VOT (FAA VOR test facility), or a radiated test signal from an appropriately rated radio repair station (usually on 108.0 MHz). These are test signals which allow the VOR to be tested for accuracy on the ground. To use the VOT service:

(a) Tune the VOT frequency (found in the Airport/Facility Directory or on the A/G Communications panel of the Enroute Low Altitude Chart). The VOT radiates the 360 radial (360-FROM) in all directions.

(b) Center the CDI by turning the OBS; the omni bearing indicator (OBI) should read 360-FROM or 180-TO, with an acceptable accuracy of ±4° (356-FROM to 004-FROM, or 176-TO to 184-TO is acceptable). Should the VOR operate an RMI, its needle should point to 180°±4° with any OBI setting, between 176° and 184° is acceptable.

2. FAA Certified Ground Checkpoint (specified in the A/FD). This is a certified radial that should be received at specific points on the airport surface.

(a) Position the airplane on the ground checkpoint at the airport.

(b) Tune the VOR and select the designated radial with the OBS. The CDI must be within ±4° of the radial, with the FROM flag showing (since it is a radial), for the accuracy of the VOR receiver to be acceptable.

3. FAA Certified Airborne Checkpoint (specified in the A/FD). This is a certified radial that should be received over specific landmarks while airborne in the immediate vicinity of the airport.

(a) Tune the VOR and select the designated radial with the OBS.

(b) Visually position the airplane over the landmark, and center the CDI with the OBS. The course reading on the OBI must be within ±6° of the designated radial for the accuracy of the VOR receiver to be acceptable.

4. Dual System VOR Check. If a dual system VOR (units independent of each other except for the antenna) is installed in the aircraft, one system may be checked against the other.

(a) Tune both systems to the same VOR ground facility and center the CDI on each indicator using the OBS.

(b) The maximum permissible variation between the two indicated bearings is 4°, and this applies to tests carried out both on the ground and in the air.

5. Course Sensitivity Check. This is not a required check.

(a) Center the CDI and note the indicated bearing.

(b) Turn the OBS until the CDI lies over the last (5th) dot which, ideally, indicates a bearing difference of 10°. Between 10° and 12° is acceptable sensitivity.

Orientation using the VOR

Orientation

Using the VOR to Obtain a Position Line

Orientation means "to determine an airplane's approximate position". The first step in orientation is to establish a position line along which the airplane is known to be at a particular moment.

To obtain a position line using the VOR:

- rotate the OBS (omni bearing selector) until the CDI (course deviation indicator) is centered; and

- note whether the TO or FROM flag is showing.

Example 3. A pilot rotates the OBS until the CDI is centered, which occurs with 334 under the course index and the TO flag showing. Illustrate the situation. Could another reading be obtained with the CDI centered?

In this location, the CDI will be centered with either 334-TO or 154-FROM.

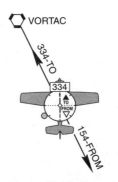

Figure 13-16. Example 3. On the 154 radial

Using Two Position Lines to Fix Position

One position line alone does not allow a pilot to positively fix the position of the airplane; it only provides a line somewhere along which the airplane lies. It requires two or more position lines to positively fix the position of an airplane.

To be of any real value for position fixing, the two position lines need to cut, or intersect, at an angle of at least 45°; any cut less than this decreases the accuracy of the fix. Radio position lines can be provided by any convenient radio navigation aids, including VORs, NDBs and DMEs. Positions defined on charts by this means are known as **intersections**.

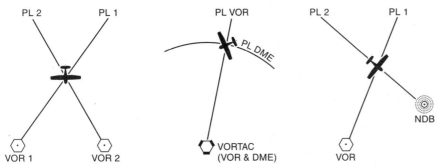

Figure 13-17. Fixing position requires two position lines with a good intersection

Fixing Position using Two VORs

Most IFR airplanes are fitted with two independent VHF-NAV systems, enabling two different VORs to be tuned at the same time. Two position lines from two different VOR ground stations can then be obtained simultaneously. In an airplane with only one VHF-NAV set, a pilot can, if he so desires, obtain two position lines using the one VHF-NAV by retuning it from one VOR to another—a bit tedious, and an increased workload, but still satisfactory.

Example 4. An airplane fitted with two VHF-NAVs is tracking MC 134-TO to VOR-A. The pilot obtains the following indications:

- **VOR 1:** VOR-A 115.2 is selected, the *tracking* VOR, and the CDI centers with 134-TO.

- **VOR 2:** VOR-B 113.8 is selected, the *crossing* VOR, and the CDI centers with 220-FROM.

The two VOR position lines intersect at a good angle, and the pilot has a fairly positive indication of where the airplane is. He has a VOR/VOR *fix*. Often an intersection of two radials from two VORs is used to define a position on the route, and such a position is known as an intersection. These intersections are clearly marked on the en route charts by triangles, with a five-letter name such as CISSI, GLADD, MUSKS, RADEX and ADOBE.

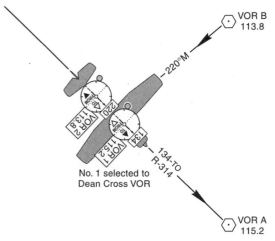

Figure 13-18. Fixing position using two VORs

Fixing Position Using a VOR and a DME

A common form of en route position fixing between aids is the VOR/DME fix, based on a ground station where the DME (distance measuring equipment) is co-located with the VOR ground station. This is also the case with a VORTAC.

The VOR can provide a straight position line showing the radial that the airplane is on, and the DME can provide a circular position line showing the distance that the airplane is from the ground station. The intersection of the lines is the position of the airplane.

Example 5. An airplane tracking north from Squaw Valley (SWR 113.2) has the cockpit indications of SWR VOR 002-FROM, and SWR DME 16 nm. Where is the airplane?

As the en route chart extract in Figure 13-19 shows, the airplane is at the TRUCK position, an in-flight position determined purely by radio navaids.

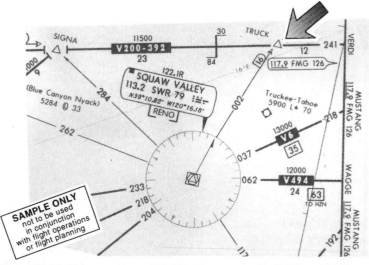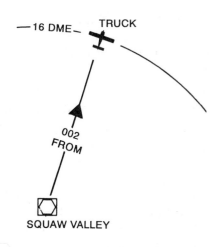

Figure 13-19. Fixing position at TRUCK using a co-located VOR and DME

Fixing Position Over a VOR

As an airplane approaches a VOR, the CDI will become more and more sensitive as the ±10° funnel either side of course becomes narrower and narrower.

As the airplane passes through the *zone of confusion* over the VOR ground station, the CDI may flick from side to side, before settling down again as the airplane moves away from the VOR. The flag will also change from TO to FROM (or vice versa), and the red OFF flag may flicker in and out of view because of the unusable signal. The zone of confusion can extend in an arc of 70° over the station, so it may take a minute or so for the airplane to pass through it before the CDI and the FROM flag settle down, and the OFF flag totally disappears.

VOR *station passage* is indicated by the first positive complete reversal of the TO/FROM flag.

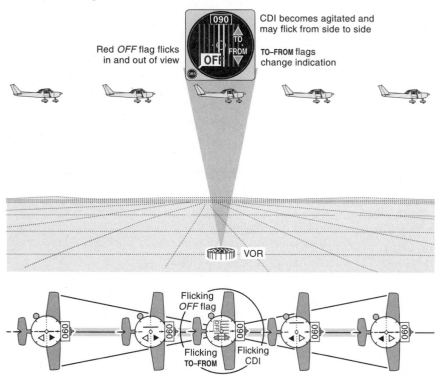

Figure 13-20. Fixing position over a VOR

Fixing Position Passing Abeam a VOR

A common means of checking flight progress is to note the time passing *abeam* (to one side of) a nearby VOR ground station. The most straightforward procedure is to:

- select and identify the VOR; and
- under the course index, set the radial perpendicular (at 90°) to your course.

Example 6. An airplane is tracking MC 350, and will pass approximately 20 nautical miles abeam a VOR ground station out to its right.

The VOR radial perpendicular to course is the 260 radial, and so 260 should be set with the OBS.

The CDI will be fully deflected to one side if the airplane is well away from the abeam position, and will gradually move from full deflection one side to full deflection on the other side as the airplane passes through the ±10° arc either side of the selected radial. The airplane is at the abeam position when the CDI is centered.

It is suggested that you set the radial (the bearing *from*) the off-course VOR on the OBI, in which case the CDI will be on the same side as the VOR until you have passed the radial. In Figure 13-21, the VOR is off-course to the right, and before passing abeam the ground station, the CDI will be out to the right. It will center to indicate the abeam position, and then move to the other side.

The abeam position can also be identified by setting the bearing *to* the VOR under the course index (rather than radial *from* the VOR), in which case the movement of the CDI will be from the opposite side. It is better practice to standardize on one method, and we suggest setting the radial *from*.

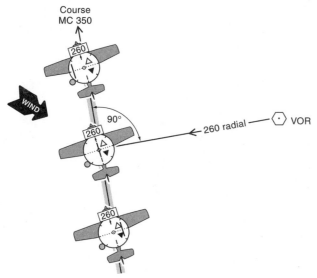

Figure 13-21. Passing abeam a VOR

The 1-in-60 rule, frequently used in navigation, states that 1 nm off-course in 60 nm subtends an angle of 1°. In rough terms, this means that the airplane, as it flies at right angles through the 10° from when the CDI first starts to move to when it is centered, will travel approximately 10 nm abeam the VOR when it is located 60 DME from the VOR ground station (or 5 nm at 30 DME). At say GS 120 knots (2 nm/min), passing through a 10° arc abeam the VOR will take 5 minutes at 60 DME, or 2.5 minutes at 30 DME.

In a no-wind situation, you can estimate the time it would take to fly directly to the station, by measuring the time for a bearing change as you fly abeam the station, and using the simple expression:

$$\textit{Minutes to the station} \ = \ \frac{\textit{seconds between hearings}}{\textit{degrees of bearing change}}$$

Example 7. A 10° bearing change abeam a VOR takes 5 minutes. By turning and flying direct to the VOR, the time required to reach the station is:

$$\textit{Minutes to VOR} \ = \ \frac{300 \ \textit{seconds}}{10°} \ = \ 30 \ \textit{minutes}$$

At a groundspeed of 120 knots (2 nm/min), this would mean that you are: $2 \times 30 = 60$ nm from the station.

Crossing a Known Radial From an Off-Course VOR

It is a simple procedure to identify passing a known radial from an off-course VOR and, indeed, many intersections are based on this.

Example 8. (Figure 13-22) LODDI intersection en route on Victor airway V-108 west of Linden VORTAC on the Linden 251 radial, intersecting with the 317 radial of the Manteca VORTAC.

In an airplane fitted with two VHF-NAVs, it would be normal procedure to track using NAV-1 on Linden, and check LODDI intersection with NAV-2 on Manteca. Selecting the radial on NAV-2 (rather than the bearing *to* the VOR), the CDI will be deflected to the same side of the NAV indicator as the VOR ground station until the airplane passes the radial.

With only one VHF-NAV, normal procedure would be to leave it on the main tracking aid (Linden) until almost at LODDI intersection (say 3 minutes before ETA), and then select Manteca VORTAC and the 317 radial. Having identified the LODDI intersection (on crossing this radial), the VHF-NAV can then be re-selected to the tracking aid (Linden and later the aid ahead).

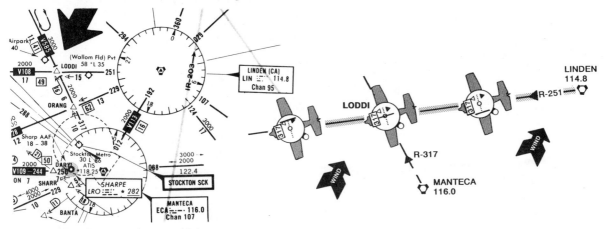

Figure 13-22. Crossing a known radial

If a 1:500,000 Sectional chart is being used (rather than an IFR en route chart), you can construct your own checkpoints along the planned course using nearby off-course VORs.

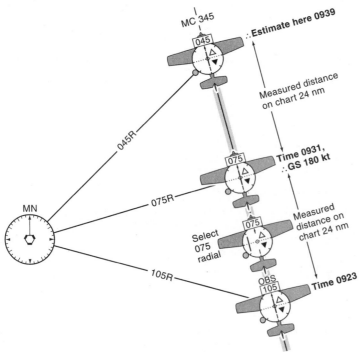

Figure 13-23. Using an off-course VOR to monitor progress

In Figure 13-23, the pilot has chosen to check his position crossing the 105, 075 and 045 radials from an *off-course* VOR. By measuring the distance between these planned fixes en route and noting the time of reaching them, the pilot can calculate the groundspeed and revise estimates for positions further along the planned course.

The VOR Display is not Heading Sensitive

The VOR indicates the position of the airplane with respect to the selected VOR course, and the actual VOR display in the cockpit will be the same regardless of the airplane's heading. If the airplane could turn in a circle on-the-spot, the VOR indications would remain the same, and the CDI would not move. Each of the airplanes in Figure 13-24 will have the same VOR display, provided the same course is set under the course index with the OBS.

The CDI position will not change as the airplane changes heading.

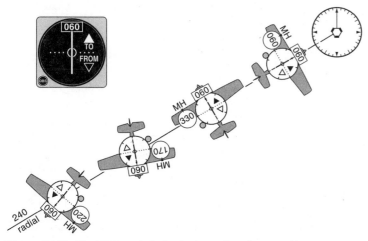

Figure 13-24. The VOR cockpit display is not heading sensitive

Orientation Without Altering the OBI

It is possible, without altering the omni bearing selector, to determine which quadrant the airplane is in with respect to the selected course.

In Figure 13-25, the selected omni bearing is 340.

- The CDI is deflected left, which indicates that, when looking in direction 340, the airplane is out to the right (of the line 340–160); and

- The FROM flag indicates that tracking 340 would take the airplane from the VOR ground station. The airplane is ahead of the line 250–070 when looking in the direction 340.

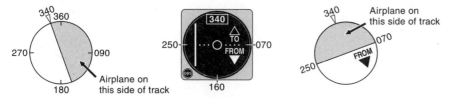

Figure 13-25. Using the CDI and the TO/FROM flag for orientation without moving the omni bearing selector

This puts the airplane in the quadrant:

- away from the CDI; and
- away from the TO/FROM flag.

So it is between the 340 and 070 radials (omni bearings from the VOR ground station). See Figure 13-26.

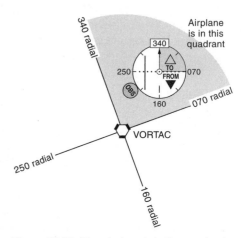

Figure 13-26. The airplane is in the quadrant away from the CDI and TO/FROM flag

Note: Remember, no information is available from the VOR cockpit display regarding airplane heading. Heading information in degrees magnetic must be obtained from the heading indicator.

Example 9. With 085 under the course index, the VOR indicator shows CDI deflected right with the TO flag showing. Position the airplane with respect to the VOR. This method is just a quick means of determining the approximate position of the airplane with respect to the VOR ground station.

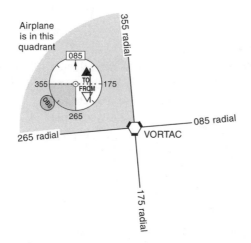

Figure 13-27. The airplane is between the 355 and 265 radials

Tracking using the VOR

Tracking To a VOR

To track to a VOR:

- **select** the VOR frequency;
- **identify** the station (Morse code ident as shown on the chart, or voice ident with VOR stated after the name);
- **check** that the red OFF warning flag is not displayed; and
- **select** the omni bearing of the desired course with the OBS.

Orient the airplane with respect to the desired course, and then take up a suitable *intercept heading* using the heading indicator (aligned with the magnetic compass). If the airplane is heading approximately in the direction of the desired course, the center circle will represent the airplane, and the CDI the desired course; to intercept course in this case, the pilot would turn toward the CDI.

This is using the VOR indicator as a **command instrument**, commanding the pilot to turn toward the CDI to regain course. Be aware, however, that this only applies when the airplane's heading is in roughly the same direction as the selected omni bearing.

On intercepting the course, the pilot should steer a reasonable heading to maintain the course, allowing a suitable wind correction angle to counter any wind effect. Remaining on course is indicated by the CDI remaining centered.

Example 10. In Figure 13-28, with the desired course 030 set under the course index, the CDI is out to the right.

Since the airplane's initial heading agrees approximately with the course of 030, the pilot concludes that the course is out to the right of the airplane. The CDI out to the right commands him to turn right to regain track and center the CDI.

The pilot has taken up a heading of MH 050 to intercept a course of 030-TO the VOR, which will give him a 20° intercept. This shallow intercept is satisfactory if the airplane is close to the course.

If the airplane is well away from the course, then a 60° or 90° intercept might be more appropriate. This would be MH 090 or MH 120.

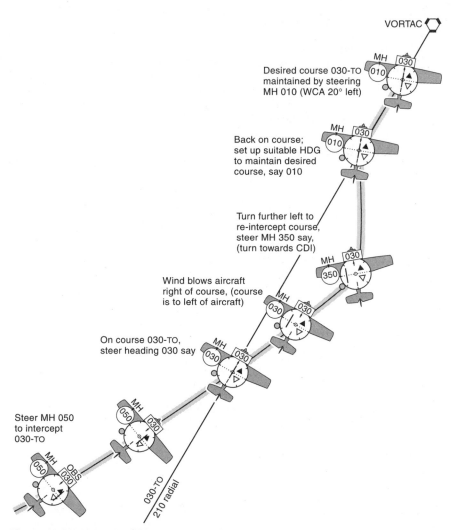

Figure 13-28. Using the CDI as a command instrument

Determining Wind Correction Angle
When Tracking on the VOR

When tracking inbound on 360-TO a VOR with 360 set under the course index, MH 360 will allow the airplane to maintain course provided there is no cross-wind component. If, however, there is a westerly wind blowing, then the airplane will be blown to the right of course unless a wind correction angle (WCA) is applied and the airplane steered on a heading slightly into wind. This is MH 352 in Figure 13-29.

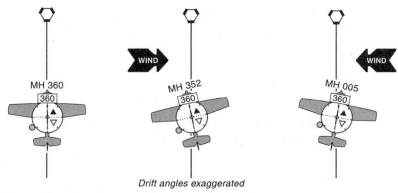

Drift angles exaggerated

Figure 13-29. Tracking inbound and allowing for drift

If, on the other hand, there is an easterly wind blowing, the airplane will be blown left of course, unless a wind correction angle is applied and the airplane steered on a heading slightly into wind, such as MH 005 in Figure 13-29.

Just how great the WCA need be is determined in flight by trial and error (preflight calculations using the navigation computer may suggest a starting figure for WCA). If the chosen WCA is not correct, and the airplane gradually departs from course causing the CDI to move from its central position, then the heading should be altered to regain the course (CDI centered), and then a new magnetic heading flown with an improved estimate of WCA. This process of achieving a suitable WCA by trial and error is known as **bracketing**.

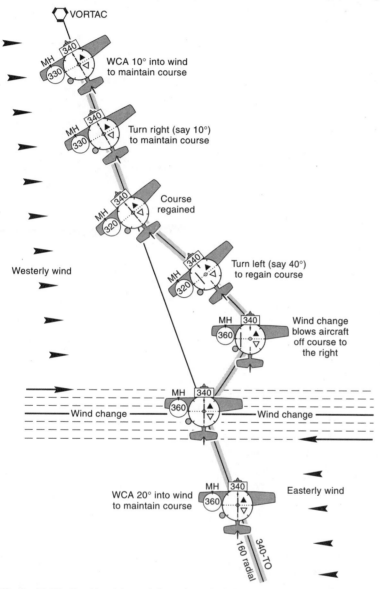

Figure 13-30. Tracking inbound through a wind change

In the real world the wind frequently changes in both strength and direction, and so the magnetic heading required to maintain course will also change from time to time. This becomes obvious by gradual movements of the CDI away from its central position, which the pilot will notice in his regular scan of the radio navigation instruments, and which he will correct by changes in magnetic heading using the heading indicator.

Tracking From a VOR

To track *from* a VOR (assuming the VOR has not already been selected and identified):

- **select** the VOR frequency;
- **identify** the station (Morse code ident or voice ident);
- **check** that the red OFF warning flag is not displayed; and
- select the **omni bearing** of the desired course with the OBS.

Orient the airplane with respect to the course, and then take up a suitable intercept heading using the heading indicator (aligned with the magnetic compass). If the airplane is heading approximately in the direction of the course, the center circle will represent the airplane, and the CDI will represent the course.

To intercept course in this case, the pilot would turn toward the CDI. This is using the CDI as a command instrument, commanding the pilot to turn toward the CDI to regain course. Be aware, however, that this only applies when the heading is roughly in the same direction as the selected omni bearing.

On intercepting course, the pilot steers a suitable heading to maintain it, keeping in mind the wind direction and strength. If the course is maintained, the CDI will remain centered.

Example 11. In Figure 13-31, with the course 140 set with the omni bearing selector (OBS), the CDI is out to the right. Since the airplane's initial heading agrees approximately with the course of 140, the pilot concludes that the course is out to the right of the airplane (or, in this case, straight ahead and to the right).

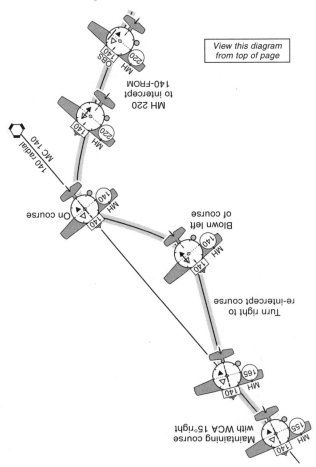

Figure 13-31. Using the CDI as a command instrument (Example 11)

The pilot steers MH 220 to intercept a course of 140-FROM the VOR, which will give an 80° intercept. This is satisfactory if the airplane is well away from the course. If the airplane is close to course, then a 60° or 30° intercept might be more suitable which, in this case, would be MH 200 or MH 170.

Using the CDI as a Command Instrument

With the course set on the OBI, and the airplane headed at least roughly in the same direction as the selected course, the CDI will act as a command instrument. By flying toward the deflected CDI, the pilot can center it, and thereby regain course. For example:

- tracking 060-TO the VOR, set 060 under the course index;
- tracking 030-FROM the VOR, set 030 under the course index.

A minor complication arises when the airplane is steered on a heading approximating the reciprocal of the course selected on the OBI. Under these circumstances, the CDI is *not* a command instrument. This situation is called **reverse sensing**.

Example 12. Suppose a pilot has been tracking 140-FROM a VOR, with 140 selected on the OBI and by steering MH 140. The airplane has drifted left of course, and so the CDI will be deflected to the right of center. Examine Figure 13-33—to regain the 140-FROM course, the pilot must turn toward the needle, in this case to the right. Heading and OBI selection are similar, so it is used as a command instrument.

Suppose now that he wants to return to the VOR ground station on the reciprocal course, which is 320-TO the VOR, and so turns through approximately 180° to MH 320 without altering the 140 set under the course index. The VOR indicator, because it is not heading sensitive, indicates exactly as it did before the turn, with the CDI out to the right of center.

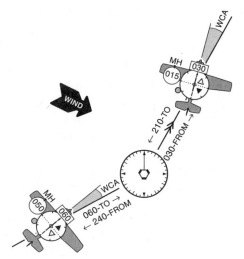

Figure 13-32. Use the CDI as a command instrument

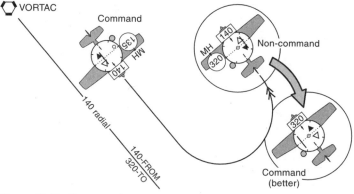

Figure 13-33. For ease of operation, use the CDI as a command instrument

To regain course on this reciprocal heading, the pilot would turn, not toward the CDI, but away from it. Turning toward the CDI on this reciprocal heading to the selected course would take the pilot further away from the selected course and the VOR is no longer a command instrument. This inconvenience can be easily removed, and the OBI returned to being a command instrument, by setting the new course under the course index of MC 320, which approximates the heading being flown. The immediate effect will be for the TO flag to appear, replacing the FROM flag, and the CDI to swing across to the other side. The CDI will now be out to the left, and a turn toward it will bring the airplane back toward the selected course. The VOR indicator is once again a command instrument, easier to understand, and easier to fly.

To keep the VOR indicator as a command instrument when flying on a VOR (so that the pilot can regain course by flying toward the CDI), set the OBI to the course to be flown. A good example of this is a base turn that is used in some instrument approaches to reverse direction:

- outbound on 160-FROM, where the pilot should set 160 with the OBS; and
- inbound on 325-TO, where the pilot should set 325 with the OBS.

The 15° between the 2 minute outbound leg in still air and the inbound leg of the descent allows sufficient arc for a standard-rate turn or less to align the airplane nicely for the final descent inbound to the VOR.

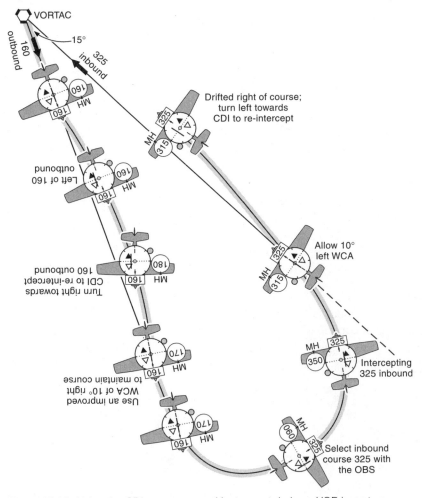

Figure 13-34. Using the CDI as a command instrument during a VOR base turn

Slow aircraft doing a standard-rate turn have a smaller turning radius than fast aircraft (for which the approach plates are designed), and so may tend to undershoot the inbound track (unless there is a strong tailwind in the turn). To avoid undershooting the inbound leg, the airplane should be rolled out of the standard-rate base turn to a suitable heading to allow for a reasonable intercept of the inbound leg (say a 60°, 45° or 30° intercept).

A lot depends on the actual wind strength and direction at the time. For instance, a strong tailwind during the base turn will cause the airplane to intercept the inbound leg more quickly than in no-wind or headwind conditions.

Note: The instrument landing system (ILS) uses the same cockpit instrument as the VOR. Whereas the pilot can select any VOR course, there is only one

ILS course. This is discussed in detail in Chapter 14, but the main points to consider are:

- when flying inbound on the ILS course (known as the localizer), the cockpit display is a command instrument (fly toward the CDI to center it and regain course); but

- when back-tracking from overhead the airport toward the ILS commencement point (flying outbound on the inbound localizer), sensing is reversed and the cockpit indicator is no longer a command instrument.

Intercepting a VOR Course

Visualizing Where You Are, and Where You Want To Go
You need to know:

- Where am I?;
- Where do I want to go?; and
- How do I get there?

The easiest method of orienting the airplane using the VOR is to rotate the omni bearing selector (OBS) until the CDI centers. This can occur on one of two headings (reciprocals of each other); choose the one with the omni bearing that most resembles the airplane's magnetic heading. If the airplane is heading toward the VOR ground station, then the TO flag will show; if it is heading away from the VOR, then the FROM flag will show.

Select the desired course in degrees magnetic with the OBS. Determine which way to turn to intercept the course, then steer a suitable intercept heading.

Intercepting an Outbound Course
The VOR is just as useful tracking away from a VOR ground station as tracking toward it, and it is much easier to use than the NDB/ADF combination.

Example 13. An airplane is tracking inbound on the 170 radial to a VOR (350-TO). ATC instructs the pilot to take up a heading to intercept the 090 radial outbound (090-FROM).

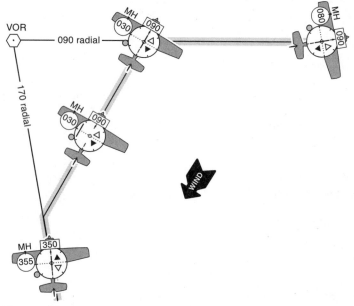

Figure 13-35. Intercepting a course outbound from a VOR

Orientation is not a problem in this example since the pilot already knows where he is (the usual situation). The better method tracking inbound on the 170 radial is to have 350 set under the course index, since the airplane is tracking 350-TO the VOR. This ensures that the VOR indicator is a command instrument (fly toward the CDI needle to regain course). See Figure 13-35.

The pilot visualizes the situation:

- tracking northward toward the VOR;
- the course, 090-FROM, lying ahead to the right.

To intercept the 090-FROM course, the pilot:

- sets 090 under the course index;
- takes up a suitable intercept heading (MH 030 for a 60° intercept); and
- maintains MH 030 until the CDI moves from full-scale deflection toward the center. To avoid overshooting the course, the pilot would anticipate the interception, and lead-in by commencing a turn just prior to intercepting course with the CDI centered. A 60° intercept will require a 60° turn which, at standard rate of 3° per second, will take 20 seconds.

Intercepting an Inbound Course

Example 14. ATC instructs a pilot to track inbound on the 010 radial to a particular VOR.

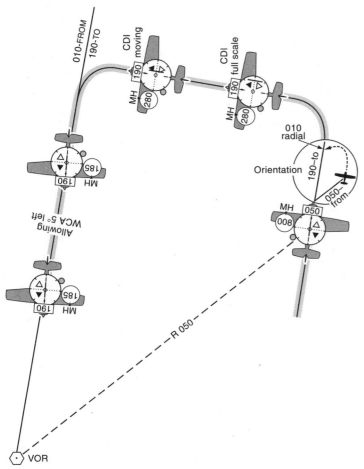

Figure 13-36. Intercepting an inbound course to a VOR

The pilot:
- selects and identifies the VOR; then
- orients himself with respect to the VOR (perhaps by centering the CDI suitably);
- sets the desired course under the course index; inbound on the 010 radial, 190-TO; and determines the relative position of this course;
- takes up a suitable intercept heading, and waits for the CDI to center.

In Figure 13-36:
- the CDI centers on 050-FROM (it would also center on 230-TO);
- the pilot has chosen a 90° intercept, steering MH 280 to intercept 190-TO; and as the CDI starts to move (within 10° of the selected course), the pilot leads in to smoothly join course, and allows a wind correction angle of 5° to counter a wind from the east.

Other VOR Presentations

There are various presentations of the VOR cockpit indicator with which a pilot should be familiar. In some aircraft, it is also possible to use an RMI needle to point to the VOR ground station as if it were an NDB. (The tail of the RMI needle shows the radial the airplane is on.) This can, on occasions, be quite useful.

The Radio Magnetic Indicator (RMI)

The radio magnetic indicator (RMI) combines a remote indicating compass and a relative bearing indicator into the one instrument. The RMI is a remote indicating compass with one or two ADF/VOR needles.

The RMI compass card is continually being aligned so that it indicates magnetic heading, and the RMI needles point at the ground stations to which they are tuned. These ground stations, on many RMIs, may be either an NDB or a VOR, the selection of either ADF or VOR being made with small switches at the base of the RMI.

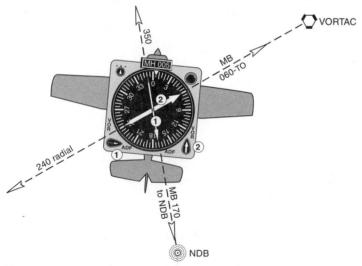

Figure 13-37. RMI needle 1 indicating NDB; RMI needle 2 indicating VOR

In Figure 13-37, the pilot has selected RMI needle 1 to the ADF, hence:
- the head of needle 1 indicates magnetic bearing *to* the NDB; and
- the tail of needle 1 indicates magnetic bearing *from* the NDB.

RMI needle 2 has been selected to the VOR, hence:
- the head of needle 2 indicates magnetic bearing *to* the VOR; and
- the tail of needle 2 indicates magnetic bearing *from* the VOR (radial).

Using the RMI with one needle selected to a VOR allows the VOR to be used as if it were an NDB for orientation and tracking purposes. Refer to Chapter 12c for more about the RMI and NDBs.

Orientation with VOR Selected to one Needle on the RMI

This makes orientation with the VOR easy, and it does not involve altering the OBI (omni bearing indicator). In Figure 13-38, RMI needle 2 indicates that the magnetic bearing *to* the VOR is MB 043 (so the airplane is on the 223 radial).

Note that there is no need to alter the OBI to determine this, as would be necessary if an RMI were not installed. Without an RMI, the pilot would have had to alter the OBI until the CDI centered at either 043-TO or 223-FROM.

Intercepting a Course with the RMI Selected to a VOR

If the pilot wishes to intercept the 090 inbound course to the VOR, then he would (since he has already oriented the airplane using the RMI):
- set 090 under the course index with the OBS (already done); and
- take up a suitable intercept heading.

If the pilot is uncertain of his orientation, he can use the ADF technique of imagining (Figure 13-39):
- the airplane on the tail of the needle in its current situation; and
- the airplane on the tail of the needle where he wants to go (090-TO).

On MH 010, it would be an 80° intercept. If the pilot wanted a 60° intercept, he would turn to MH 030. Tracking on MH 030, the RMI needle will gradually fall toward 090. Once the airplane is within 10° of the selected course on the VOR cockpit display, the CDI will start to move.

At this stage, the pilot could shift his attention to the VOR indicator, and turn in to track on 090-TO. In this case, he is tracking in on 090-TO, allowing a wind correction angle of 5° left to counteract the wind from the north by steering MH 085.

The Horizontal Situation Indicator (HSI)

The HSI is a remote indicating compass with a VOR indicator superimposed on it. It provides an easily understood pictorial display and is one of the most popular navigation instruments ever devised. It shows the magnetic heading and the position of the airplane relative to the selected course. Figure 13-40 shows the airplane on MH 175, about to intercept 205-TO the VOR.

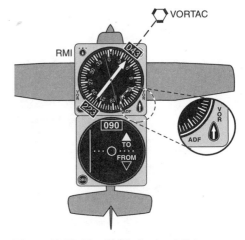

Figure 13-38. The RMI indicates 043 to the VOR

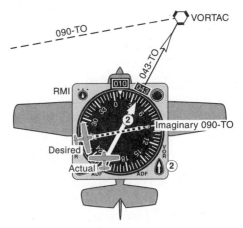

Figure 13-39. Determining "where to go?" using the RMI

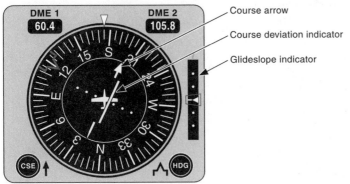

Course arrow
Course deviation indicator
Glideslope indicator

Figure 13-40. The horizontal situation indicator is always a command instrument

An outstanding benefit of the HSI over the traditional VOR indicator is that the HSI is always a command instrument. If the airplane turns, the remote indicating compass card turns, carrying the VOR display with it, and so the HSI will always show the pilot a CDI deflection toward the selected course. In Figure 13-40, the selected course is out to the left. If the airplane turns 180°, to MH 355, the HSI will show the selected course 205 out to the right of the airplane, which it actually is. There is no reverse sensing with an HSI.

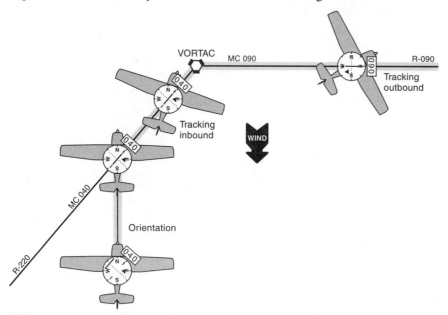

Figure 13-41. Tracking using an HSI

The VOR Instrument Approach

When carrying out a VOR approach, such as that published for Casa Grande (Figure 13-42), the VOR is used as the tracking aid. Of course the VOR must be identified before you may use it for navigation. The coded ident for the Stanfield VORTAC near Casa Grande, on which the instrument approach is based, is TFD (*dah dit-dit-dah-dit dah-dit-dit*).

The top part of the instrument approach chart is a plan view for tracking, and the bottom part of the chart is a profile view for vertical navigation.

You may track to the VORTAC at a safe altitude well above the minimum safe altitude (MSA), which is 4200 feet MSL to the north and 5600 feet MSL to the south and west. Note the high terrain (4373 feet MSL) southwest of the airfield at approximately 12 DME TFD. The airport elevation is 1462 feet MSL, and the runway 5 touchdown zone elevation (TDZE) is 1456 feet MSL. The airport elevation is always higher than the TDZEs, since it is the highest point on any of the runways.

When overhead the VORTAC, you must enter the holding pattern based on the TFD VORTAC as the holding fix, holding southwest on the 228 radial, one minute inbound legs. The inbound holding course is 048-TO the VORTAC. Have 048 selected on the OBI and keep the CDI centered when tracking inbound. You may descend to not below 3500 feet MSL in the holding pattern.

When ready to start the approach, commence the prelanding checks, and adopt an appropriate approach configuration (flaps/gear). You may fly inbound 048-TO the VORTAC not below 3500 feet MSL and, once past the VORTAC (indicated by the first complete reversal of the flag from TO to FROM), you should start the stopwatch and commence descent. Overhead the VORTAC is the final approach fix (FAF) for this approach. With 048 still set on the OBI, and FROM showing, you should fly a heading that keeps the CDI centered.

DME is available at Casa Grande, however it is not mandatory for this VOR approach. If it were, the approach would be published as a VOR/DME approach. Starting the stopwatch as you pass the VORTAC allows you to determine the position of the missed approach point (MAP) if the DME is not available to begin with, or if it fails while you are completing the approach. The table at the bottom right indicates that, if your groundspeed is 90 knots, then you will reach the MAP 5 minutes 12 seconds after passing over the VORTAC, which is the FAF. At GS 120 knots, it will take only 3 minutes 54 seconds.

You must not descend below the minimum descent altitude (MDA) 1940 feet MSL until you are visual. The MDA 1940 for a straight-in approach is 484 feet above the runway 5 touchdown zone elevation (TDZE) of 1456 feet MSL (HAT 484 feet).

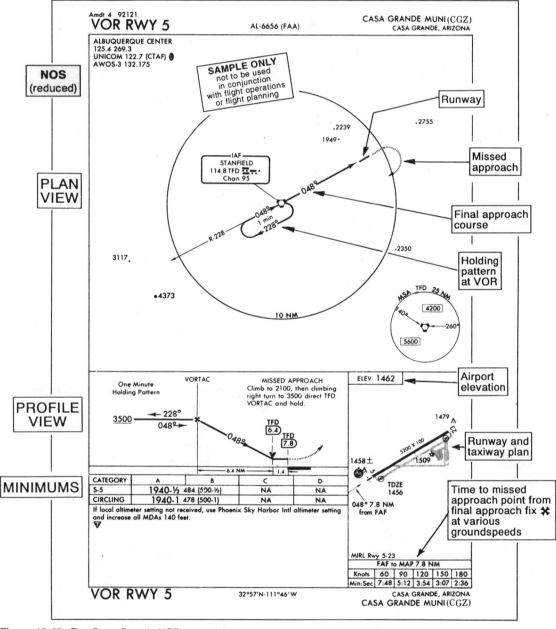

Figure 13-42. The Casa Grande VOR approach

Note that if the current Casa Grande altimeter setting is not available, you have to use the altimeter setting for Phoenix Sky Harbor International airport, which is some distance away; the minimum descent altitudes (MDAs) must be raised 140 feet to 2080 feet MSL.

If you fly out of the clouds during the approach and are visual at the MDA, then at 6.4 DME (noted on the chart as a visual descent point, VDP) a normal descent to the runway 5 touchdown point may be commenced, provided you can see the approach end of the runway and wish to make a straight-in landing.

You should plan your descent from the final approach fix overhead the VORTAC to be at the MDA at or before the visual descent point if you want to make an unhurried and stable normal descent to land straight-in on runway 5. This means descending 1560 feet (3500 – 1940) in 6.4 nm, which means a profile of (1560 feet ÷ 6.4 nm = 244 feet per nm) approximately 250 feet per nm. At a groundspeed of 60 knots this would require a rate of descent of 250 fpm; at a GS of 120 knots it would be 500 fpm; and at GS 90 knots, rate of descent would be 375 fpm. Descending to the MDA at or above these descent rates should position you well.

If you wish to circle to land, then the minimum altitude for this maneuver is also 1940 feet MSL, the 1/2 sm visibility required for a straight-in landing is increased to 1 sm for a circling approach to land on runway 23. This is logical because you will have to maneuver away from the runway a little to position for the landing on Rwy 23. The circling MDA 1940 feet MSL is 478 feet above the airport elevation, 1462 feet MSL (the highest point on any of the runways), and is 478 feet HAA. (Height above touchdown zone (HAT), is not shown for circling minimums because you might circle-to-land on either runway.)

If you are not visual at the MDA, then you may track in at the MDA in IFR conditions to the missed approach point (MAP) at 7.8 DME, or until the appropriate time has expired. If you become visual at the MDA, you may maneuver to land straight-in or to circle, depending on how you see the situation; otherwise commence a missed approach at the MAP. The missed approach is shown by a dotted line, and detailed on the profile diagram.

✍ Review 13

The VOR

1. The VOR is a (VHF/LF/MF) radio navigation aid.

    ➤ VHF

2. Many VORs are coupled with an (ILS/DME/NDB).

    ➤ DME

3. An airplane at 3000 feet MSL should be able to receive a VOR situated at sea level out to a range of approximately _____ nm.

    ➤ 67 nm

4. A radial is the (magnetic/true) bearing (to/from) a VOR ground station.

    ➤ magnetic bearing, from

5. You are instructed by ATC to track outbound on the 070 radial from a VOR. The more suitable heading is (070/250).

    ➤ MH 070

6. You are instructed to track inbound on the 050 radial. The more suitable heading is (050/230).

    ➤ MH 230

---

7. A particular VOR may be identified by its _____.
➤ Morse code ident or voice ident

8. A VOR ground station should transmit to an accuracy of at least ±_____° accuracy.
➤ ±2° accuracy

9. VOR stands for _____.
➤ VHF omni-directional radio range

10. The radio set in the cockpit used to select a VOR is the (VHF-COM/VHF-NAV/ADF).
➤ VHF-NAV

11. The needle in the VOR cockpit display is known as the CDI, which stands for _____.
➤ course deviation indicator

12. Any one of 360 tracks may be selected on the VOR cockpit display using the OBS, which stands for _____.
➤ omni bearing selector

13. The position of the VOR receiver checkpoint(s) can be found in the _____.
➤ Airport/Facility Directory

14. A 1 dot deviation of the CDI on the VOR cockpit display indicates a displacement of _____° from the selected course.
➤ 2°

15. A 2 dot deviation of the CDI on the VOR cockpit display indicates a displacement of _____° from the selected course.
➤ 4°

16. A 3 dot deviation of the CDI on the VOR cockpit display indicates a displacement of _____° from the selected course.
➤ 6°

17. A 4 dot deviation of the CDI on the VOR cockpit display indicates a displacement of _____° from the selected course.
➤ 8°

18. A 5 dot deviation of the CDI on the VOR cockpit display indicates a displacement of _____° from the selected course.
➤ 10° or more

19. If the CDI is centered with 090 set on the OBI, and the FROM flag is showing, what radial is the airplane on?
➤ 090 radial

20. If the CDI is centred with 090 set on the OBI, and the TO flag is showing, what radial is the airplane on?
➤ 270 radial

21. If the CDI is 2 dots right with 090 set on the OBI, and the TO flag is showing, what radial is the airplane on?
➤ 274 radial (094-TO)

22. If the CDI is 1 dot left with 090 set on the OBI, and the FROM flag is showing, what radial is the airplane on?
➤ 092 radial

23. You are flying MH 080, with the OBI selected to 080, CDI needle showing 2 dots right, and the FROM flag showing. Desired course is the 080 radial outbound. Is the desired course out to your left or right?
➤ desired course is out to the right

24. You are flying MH 300, with the OBI selected to 300, the CDI needle showing 3 dots left, and the TO flag showing. Desired course is 300°M to the VOR. Is the desired course out to your left or right?
➤ desired course is out to the left

25. You are flying MH 300, with the OBI selected to 300, the CDI needle showing 3 dots left, and the TO flag showing. If the airplane is now turned to the reciprocal heading of MH 120, would the indications in the VOR cockpit display change in any way (assuming the OBI is left unaltered).
➤ no, the VOR cockpit display is not heading sensitive.

26. Specify which of the airplanes in Figure 1 could have the following VOR indications.

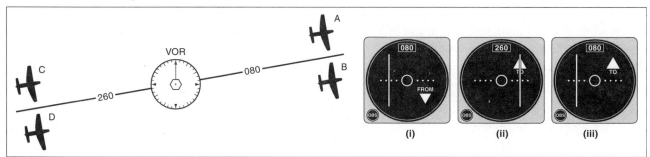

Figure 1.

➤ (i) airplane B; (ii) airplane B; (iii) airplane D

---

27. When checking a dual VOR system by use of a VOT, which illustration indicates that the VORs are satisfactory?

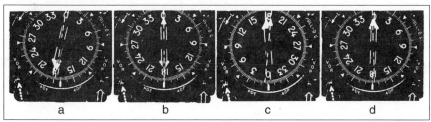

Figure 2.

➤ (a)

---

28. Which is an acceptable operational check of dual VORs using one system against the other?

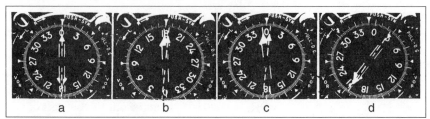

Figure 3.

➤ (d)

---

29. When making an airborne VOR check, what is the maximum allowable tolerance between the two indicators of a dual VOR system (units independent of each other except the antenna)?

➤ 4° between the two indicated bearings to a VOR

30. For a VOR receiver check with the airplane located on the designated checkpoint on the airport, set the designated (radial/bearing) on the OBI. The CDI must be within _____° of the radial, and the flag should show (TO/OFF/FROM).

➤ radial, 4°, FROM

31. The A/FD specifies an airborne checkpoint as overhead Lafayette (Louisiana) Regional Airport rotating beacon at altitude 1000 feet, azimuth and distance from LFT VORTAC 340°/25 nm. To meet the requirements for an airborne receiver check of ±(0°/2°/4°/6°/8°), acceptable VOR indications are between _____-FROM and _____-FROM or between_____-TO and _____-TO.

➤ ±6°, 334-FROM and 346-FROM, 154-TO and 166-TO

32. The VOT frequency for a particular airport can be found in the _____ Directory and on the _____ panel of the En route Low Altitude Chart.

➤ Airport/Facility Directory, A/G Voice Communication panel of the En route Low Altitude Chart

33. When testing your two VOR receivers using a VOT, which transmits the _____ radial in (one/all) direction(s), are readings of 176-TO and 003-FROM acceptable?

➤ 360, all, yes since they are within ±4° of 360-FROM and 180-TO

34. A VOR may be positively identified by either a _____ code identification or, in some cases, by a recorded _____ identification.

➤ Morse code, voice

35. A pilot (should/should not) use a VOR for navigation if he cannot identify it.

➤ should not

36. If a VOR is undergoing maintenance, then its identification (is/is not) removed. It (may/will not) transmit navigation signals.

➤ is, may

37. A VOR identification signal is transmitted about once every _____ seconds.

➤ 10

38. If a single coded identification from a VORTAC is received only once approximately every 30 seconds, then the VOR (may/must not) be used for navigation, and the DME (may/must not) be used for navigation.

➤ must not, may

39. For an airplane flying at the MOCA, acceptable navigational signal coverage is assured for a distance of _____ from the VOR.

➤ 22 nm (25 sm)

40. A particular intersection is defined by intersecting radials from two different VORs and is labeled with MRA 6000. How many VHF-NAV sets do you require to identify when you are at the intersection, and what is the significance of "MRA 6000"?

➤ one VHF-NAV set, adequate VOR coverage not assured below 6000 feet MSL

41. A 10° bearing change abeam a VOR takes 4 mins 30 secs. If you turned and flew to the VOR, how long would it take, and what is the approximate distance (assume groundspeed 180 knots)?

➤ 27 mins, 81 nm

42. A full-scale deflection of the CDI represents an angular deviation of _____° or greater.

➤ 10°

43. At 17,000 feet above the level of a H-class VORTAC in the contiguous United States, its range will be at least _____ nm.

➤ 100 nm

44. To use two H-class VORTACs to define a direct route off an established airway at 17,000 feet, they should be situated no farther apart than _____ nm.

➤ 200 nm

45. VOR station passage is indicated by:

    (a) the first full-scale deflection of the CDI.

    (b) the first movement of the CDI as the airplane enters the zone of confusion.

    (c) the moment the TO/FROM indicator becomes blank.

    (d) the first positive, complete reversal of the TO/FROM indicator.

➤ (d)

46. To check the sensitivity of a VOR receiver, changing the OBI to move the CDI from the center to the last dot on either side should cause a bearing change of between _____° and _____°.

➤ 10° and 12°

47. What angular deviation from a VOR course is represented by a half-scale deviation of the CDI?

➤ 5°

48. At 60 nm, a half-scale deflection of the CDI with a VOR tuned represents a distance of _____ nm from the course centerline.

➤ 5 nm (5° = 5 nm at 60 DME)

49. At 30 nm, a half-scale deflection of the CDI with a VOR tuned represents a distance of _____ nm from the course centerline.

➤ 2.5 nm (5° = 5 nm at 60 DME = 2.5 nm at 30 DME)

50. If the VOR shows a three dot deflection at 30 nm from the station, the airplane is displaced approximately _____ nm from the radial.

➤ 3 nm (3 dots = 6° = 6 nm at 60 DME = 3 nm at 30 DME)

51. After overflying a VOR ground station, you select the desired radial and fly a heading estimated to keep you on that course. If, however, there is a steady half-scale deflection of the CDI as you fly some miles away from the station, you will be (flying parallel to/diverging from) the radial.

➤ diverging from

52. The RMI combines the functions of a _____ and ADF/VOR needles.

➤ remote indicating compass

53. The HSI combines the functions of a _____ and a VOR indicator.

➤ remote indicating compass

54. Refer to Figure 4. The aircraft is located (northwest/northeast/southeast/southwest) of the VORTAC.

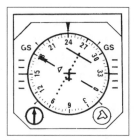

Figure 4.

➤ northeast

Refer to Figure 5 for Questions 55–62.

55. No. 1 NAV is a (VOR indicator/HSI).

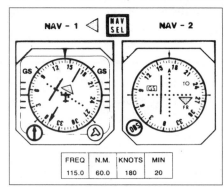

FREQ	N.M.	KNOTS	MIN
115.0	60.0	180	20

Figure 5.

➤ HSI

56. No. 2 NAV is a (VOR indicator/HSI).

➤ VOR indicator

57. The lateral displacement from the course selected on VHF-NAV 1 is _____ nm.

➤ 5 nm (2.5 dots = 5° which, at 60 nm, = 5 nm)

58. No. 1 NAV indicates the aircraft is on _____ radial.

➤ R-345
(2.5 dots = 5° before the selected R-350 FROM)

59. Which OBI selection on the No. 1 NAV would center the CDI and change the ambiguity indication to a TO?

➤ 165 (345-FROM to center the CDI = 165-TO)

60. The angular displacement from the desired radial on the No. 2 NAV is _____°.

➤ 4°

61. Which OBI selection on the No. 2 NAV would center the CDI?

➤ 174 (aircraft is 2 dots = 4° to the right of the selected R-170)

62. Which OBI selection on the No. 2 NAV would center the CDI and change the ambiguity indication to a TO?

➤ 354 (174-FROM to center the CDI = 354-TO)

Refer to Figures 6 and 7 for questions 63–68.

63. HSI presentation D corresponds to aircraft position (4/5/15/17).

➤ 17

64. HSI presentation E corresponds to aircraft position (5/6/15/17).

➤ 6

65. HSI presentation F corresponds to aircraft position (2/10/14/16).

➤ 16

66. HSI presentation A corresponds to aircraft position (1/8/11/18).

➤ 1

67. HSI presentation B corresponds to aircraft position (3/9/13/19).

➤ 19

68. HSI presentation C corresponds to aircraft position (6/7/12/20).

➤ 12

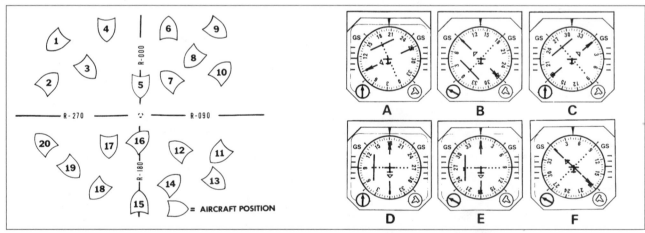

Figure 6. Aircraft position

Figure 7. HSI presentation

The Instrument Landing System (ILS) 14

The instrument landing system is known as the ILS (pronounced "*eye-ell-ess*"). It enables a suitably equipped airplane to make a **precision approach** to a particular runway. A precision approach is one in which electronic *slope* guidance, as well as *tracking* guidance, is given. Each ILS is known by the airport and runway it serves, for example, the *Lafayette ILS Rwy 10*, in Indiana.

The instrument landing system has four main elements:

1. the **localizer**, which provides course guidance along the extended centerline of the runway (guidance in *azimuth* left or right of the extended centerline);

2. the **glideslope**, which provides vertical guidance toward the runway touchdown point, usually at a slope of approximately 3° to the horizontal, or 1:20 (vertical guidance above or below the glideslope);

3. **marker beacons**, which provide accurate range fixes along the approach path (usually an *outer marker* and a *middle marker*) are provided; and

4. **approach lights, VASI** (visual approach slope indicator), and other lights (touchdown zone lighting, runway lights, etc.) to assist in transitioning from instrument to visual flight.

There may be supplementary radio aids available, including:

- a compass locator (NDB); and
- DME.

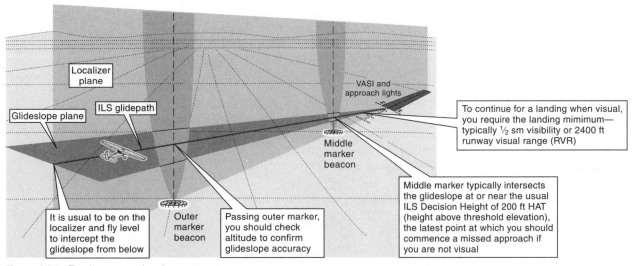

Figure 14-1. The instrument landing system

The **outer marker** may be replaced as a range marker on some ILSs by a compass locator, a DME distance, or an ASR or PAR radar position from ATC. The **middle marker**, where more accuracy is required, may be replaced as a range marker on some ILSs by a compass locator or PAR radar position from ATC (but not by a DME distance or ASR radar position). These range markers provide you with an accurate distance fix along the localizer.

A co-located compass locator and outer marker will appear on the approach chart as "LOM". A co-located compass locator and middle marker will appear on the approach chart as "LMM".

The ideal flightpath on an ILS approach, where the localizer plane and the glideslope plane intersect, is referred to as the **glidepath**. The word *glide* is really a misnomer carried over from earlier days, since modern airplanes make powered approaches down the glidepath, rather than glide approaches. However, the term glidepath is still used.

Since ILS approaches will often be made in conditions of poor visibility or at night, there is always associated visual information that can be used once the pilot becomes "visual". This may include approach lights leading toward the runway, runway lights, touchdown lights, and centerline lights. Lighting is indispensable for night operations, but it can also be invaluable during daylight hours in conditions of restricted visibility.

There may also be a visual approach slope indicator (VASI) situated near the touchdown zone to provide visual slope guidance during the latter stages of the approach. This, and other visual information, will assist you in maintaining a stable descent path toward the runway, where you can complete the flare and landing, and the ground run.

The ILS is selected in the cockpit on the VHF-NAV radio. Its cockpit display is usually the same instrument as for the VOR except that, as well as the vertical localizer needle (CDI) that moves left and right for course guidance, there is a second needle that comes into view. It is horizontal, and is able to move up and down to represent the position of the glideslope relative to the airplane. Some ILS indicators have needles that are hinged and move like wipers, others have needles that move rectilinearly. The airplane may be thought of as the center dot, and the intersection of the needles as the relative position of the glidepath.

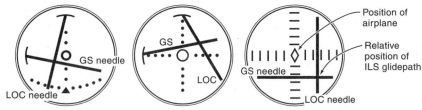

Figure 14-2. The ILS cockpit display

The Localizer

The localizer provides directional guidance along the extended centerline of the landing runway. Its transmitting antenna, which may be 60 feet wide and 10 feet high, is positioned at the far end of the runway and typically 1000 feet beyond the end so as not to be an obstacle to airplanes taking off.

Figure 14-3. The localizer transmitting antenna

The localizer transmits a highly directional beam on a frequency in the VHF band between 108.10 and 111.95 MHz, the specific frequency being published on charts and in the Airport/Facility Directory (A/FD). There are 40 localizer frequencies available, with all of them having an odd number as the first digit after the decimal point, such as 109.1, 108.3, and 110.5.

The Localizer Ground Equipment

The localizer antenna at the far end of the runway transmits two overlapping lobes of radio energy on the localizer's carrier frequency (such as 109.9 MHz for Los Angeles International Airport ILS Rwy 25 Right). The lobe on the left hand side of the approach course is modulated at 90 Hz (traditionally known as the *yellow* sector), and the lobe on the right hand side of the approach path is modulated at 150 Hz (the *blue* sector). The two lobes overlap to provide a path in line with the extended centerline of the runway.

The colors blue and yellow were once painted on the localizer cockpit display, but this is not the case on modern instruments. You will, however, sometimes hear blue and yellow sectors mentioned.

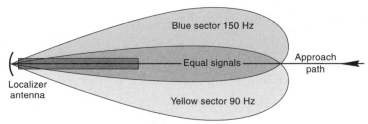

Figure 14-4. The localizer's radiation pattern

The transmission pattern is adjusted for each ILS so that the course width, from full-scale FLY LEFT to full-scale FLY RIGHT, is 700 feet at the approach runway threshold. Since runways are of varying lengths, and since the localizer antenna is positioned beyond the far end of the runway, the angular width of localizer beams will vary between 3 and 6 degrees to achieve the 700 feet course width at the approach threshold.

A typical angular width of the localizer course, from full-scale FLY LEFT to full-scale FLY RIGHT (peg to peg), is 5°, that is, 2.5° either side of the localizer course centerline, but for different localizers this may vary from 1.5° to 3°.

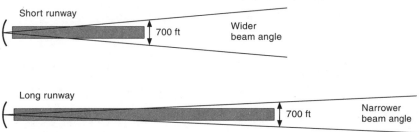

Figure 14-5. Peg-to-peg deflection is 700 feet at the landing threshold

The localizer course information is accurate within the sectors shown in Figure 14-6, from an altitude of 1000 feet above the highest terrain along the course line to 4500 feet above the elevation of the antenna site. Correct cockpit indications are assured if the airplane is in this airspace volume.

Outside this airspace, a correct localizer signal is not assured, and it is possible you may not even receive its coded *ident*.

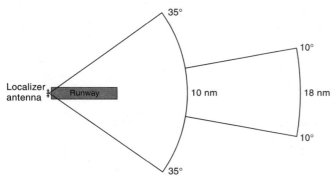

Figure 14-6. The protected airspace volume for the localizer signal

The main function of the localizer is to provide *azimuth* guidance to an airplane on final approach to a particular runway. The signal transmitted out along the approach path is sometimes called the localizer **front course**.

Many localizers also transmit a **back course** (BC). This can be used for tracking when continuing overhead the runway and straight ahead following a missed approach, or when taking off and departing. In some countries, like the United Kingdom and Australia, the localizer back course is suppressed.

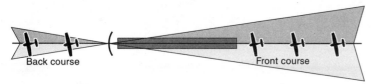

Figure 14-7. A localizer with both a front course and a back course

The back course of a localizer does not have an associated glideslope for a precision approach in the opposite direction, although *false glideslope* signals might exist. Some localizer back courses are available for a nonprecision approach in the opposite direction to the normal front course approach, in which case a LOC BC instrument approach chart is published.

Do not confuse the back course of a localizer with an ILS for the reciprocal runway, which will be a totally different installation with its own transmitting antennas. ATC will never have opposing ILSs in service simultaneously. For instance, you would not expect to find *ILS Rwy 8 Left* and *ILS Rwy 26 Right* operating simultaneously, since they would be directing airplanes to opposing ends of the one runway.

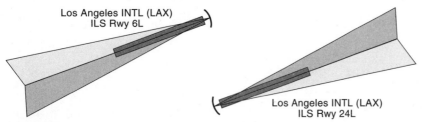

Figure 14-8. Two different ILSs serving opposite runways

The Localizer Airborne Equipment

The localizer transmits on one of 40 frequencies in the VHF band between 108.10 and 111.95 MHz. The specific frequency is published on the relevant instrument approach chart. You can select this frequency on the VHF-NAV radio, and must identify the localizer by its Morse code *ident* before using it. The localizer ident is always a four-letter coded identifier beginning with I, "*dit-dit*".

Always positively identify a localizer before using it for navigation.

Oakland ILS Rwy 11 is I-AAZ on frequency 111.9 MHz; Oakland ILS Rwy 27R is I-OAK on frequency 109.9 MHz; Cincinnati ILS Rwy 20L is I-LUK on frequency 110.9 MHz; and, as expected, the Cincinnati LOC BC 2R is the same localizer I-LUK on 110.9 MHz, since the 2L LOC BC is part of the 20R localizer. Have a look at your own Instrument Approach Procedures booklet for similar examples.

Identifying the localizer serves to identify the ILS (including the glide-slope). For instance, identifying the Cincinnati 20L localizer I-LUK, also identifies its glideslope. Correct identification is vital before an ILS (or any radio aid for that matter) is used.

For the localizer to be usable, it must be identified, and there should be no red OFF flag associated with the vertical needle. If the OFF flag is visible, then the signal being received at the airplane is not sufficiently strong, and so the CDI (course deviation indicator) indications will be unreliable and should not be used.

The airplane's VHF-NAV receiver, when tuned to a localizer frequency, compares the strengths of the two signals (150 Hz and 90 Hz) it receives, and produces a voltage that energizes the localizer needle in the cockpit instrument. If the 150 Hz signal is stronger (which will occur if the airplane on approach is out to the right), then a voltage is fed to the localizer needle that moves it to the left. This indicates that the localizer centerline is to the left of the airplane on approach. On some instruments, the needle will point to a blue marking, as a further indication that the airplane is to the right of centerline and in the blue sector.

If the signals are of equal strength, then the localizer needle is centered, providing an ON COURSE indication. If the 90 Hz signal predominates, then the voltage fed to the localizer needle moves it to the right, indicating that the airplane is in the yellow sector and, on approach, will need to move to the right to get back on centerline.

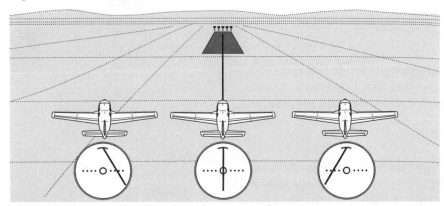

Figure 14-9. An airplane on approach—fly toward the CDI

Full-scale deflection will occur when the airplane is displaced approximately 2.5° or more from the localizer centerline. This means that the CDI (with the five dots either side of center) is four times more sensitive when it is tuned to a localizer (at 0.5° per dot), compared with when it is tuned to a VOR (at 2° per dot). Full-scale deflection of the CDI selected to a localizer is 2.5° or more off the localizer centerline; full-scale deflection of the CDI selected to a VOR is 10° or more off the selected radial. Usable localizer signals may be obtained up to ±35° from course centerline, giving full-scale deflection beyond ±2.5°. Outside the protected signal volume, the OFF flag will come into view, and no ident will be heard.

Note: The angular width of a localizer beam is adjusted to provide a beam width (peg-to-peg) of 700 feet at the approach-end runway threshold for all ILS approaches. Consequently, full-scale deflection of the localizer needle can actually represent angles between 1.5° and 3°, depending on the length of the runway and the distance of the localizer antenna from the upwind end. The angular deviation per dot varies for the localizer needle, with 0.5° per dot being average.

The localizer course is a single fixed course, unlike the VOR, which gives the pilot a choice of 360 radials using the omni bearing selector (OBS). With a localizer frequency selected on the VHF-NAV, the OBS has absolutely no significance, and changing it will have no effect on the indications of the CDI needle. It is good operating procedure, however, to dial in the inbound track of the localizer, using the OBS, simply as a reminder. It is also a habit that you will find useful if you happen to fly an airplane equipped with more advanced instruments like an HSI.

The localizer cockpit indicator does not provide any heading information, but only position information. It simply indicates how many degrees the airplane is displaced from the localizer course, and in which sector it is (blue or yellow). A one-dot deviation on the localizer is approximately 0.5°, which is roughly equivalent to 50 ft/nm left or right of centerline.

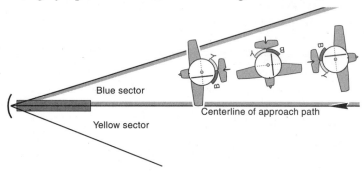

Figure 14-10. The CDI indicates angular displacement from the localizer, and does not give heading information

Localizer failure. If the localizer signal fails, then the whole ILS approach becomes unauthorized (including the glideslope), and an ILS approach in such a situation is not permitted. If only the glideslope signal fails, the localizer is still usable.

Flying the Localizer

The ILS cockpit instrument is a *performance* instrument. It should be included in the selective radial scan when information from it is desired. Having gained that information (which, in this case, is the position and/or movement of the localizer needle), your eyes should return to the attitude indicator.

Any corrections to heading to regain or maintain the localizer course can then be made with small coordinated turns on the attitude indicator. The heading indicator can be checked for heading, and the ILS cockpit indicator can be checked again for position and/or movement of the localizer needle. Concentrate on the HI and AI for your attitude flying, with an occasional glance at the CDI to see how the tracking is going. Do not chase the CDI.

The localizer beam is quite narrow, full-scale FLY LEFT to full-scale FLY RIGHT being only about 5°, and so any intercept of the localizer should be made at no more than 30°. Even when the CDI is pegged at full-scale deflection during the intercept, other radio aids, such as a compass locator, if available, should be used to monitor closure with the localizer.

Once the CDI starts moving, indicating that you are approaching the center-line, turn immediately onto course and steer the localizer course ± estimated WCA. Hold this heading for a few seconds, even if the CDI needle is not centered, and then observe its position and motion, if any. Then, with gentle turns using the flight instruments, position the airplane on the localizer center-line and steer a suitable reference heading to maintain it.

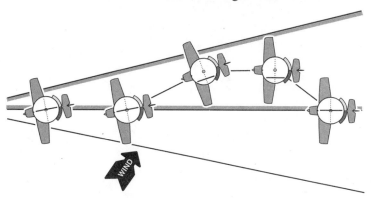

Figure 14-11. Typical heading corrections for a deviation right of centerline

The aim is to fly a heading that will maintain the airplane on centerline. If a crosswind exists, a wind correction angle will be required, and the airplane heading will differ slightly from the published inbound course of the localizer. The wind will probably back (swing counterclockwise) and weaken in strength as the airplane descends, and there will also be gusts and lulls, so periodic adjustments to heading can be expected.

Apply a wind correction angle that will keep the airplane on centerline.

For an airplane on approach, the localizer needle indicates which way the airplane should move to regain the centerline. If the localizer needle is to the left, then the airplane should be moved left. On approach, the CDI acts as a command instrument; to regain centerline, fly toward the needle.

On approach the CDI is a command instrument—fly toward the needle.

You should aim to capture the localizer as soon as possible on the approach, and ensure that small deviations are corrected before they can become large deviations. An ILS approach normally requires many such heading corrections to regain and maintain the localizer centerline. This is only to be expected, because wind effect will almost certainly vary along the glidepath.

The CDI needle displays angular displacement from the centerline and, because the localizer beam width narrows as the runway is approached (a bit like a funnel), it will become more and more sensitive during the descent. Heading corrections should become finer and finer, ±5° at the start of the approach, ±2° toward the end.

A typical *heading bug* on a heading indicator has an angular width of about 12°, or 6° either side of center. If such a heading bug is used as a heading datum on the HI, then most heading changes necessary to maintain the localizer can be contained within its angular width.

You should initially steer a heading that stops the needle moving, even if it is not perfectly centered, and hold that heading for a few seconds as a reference heading using the HI. Glance at the CDI to observe its position and any move-ment, then make gentle turns using the flight instruments to return the airplane to the localizer centerline and keep it there. Employ normal attitude instrument flying techniques using the flight instruments, with just an occasional glace at the CDI. You should aim to have the localizer tied down by the time you reach the outer marker, with the CDI centered and steady. Any tendency for the CDI to move after you have passed the outer marker can be remedied with small changes of heading, about ±2°.

Tracking over the runway and outbound on the back course, the CDI remains a command instrument, so fly toward the needle to regain course centerline. If you reverse heading, however, the CDI becomes a non-command instrument. When tracking outbound on a localizer front course, which is sometimes necessary when positioning the airplane for an ILS, the CDI needle will still indicate which sector the airplane is in (blue or yellow), and will display the angular displacement from centerline as if the airplane were on approach. To regain centerline the airplane must be turned away from the CDI needle because it is acting as a non-command instrument when the airplane is flying outbound. When "flying" a non-command instrument, you must fly away from the CDI to pull it back into the center.

When tracking outbound from a localizer, the CDI is a noncommand instrument.

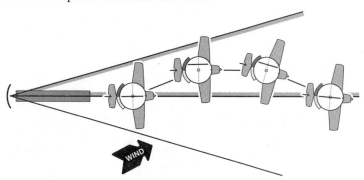

Figure 14-12. Tracking outbound on a localizer

The situation is the same tracking inbound on a localizer back course, when the basic CDI becomes a non-command instrument. Some runways have a LOC BC nonprecision approach, based on tracking inbound on the back course of the ILS serving the opposite runway.

Some ILS indicators have a BC switch that enables the pilot to electronically reverse the signals to the CDI and, when flying inbound on a localizer back course or outbound on a front course, convert the CDI back to a command instrument. The switch needs to be reversed with each reversal of heading.

Additional tracking guidance is always useful (especially when tracking outbound on a localizer, or inbound on a back course using a non-command instrument), and in many ILS and LOC BC approaches this additional guidance can be obtained from a compass locator.

Flying the Localizer with an HSI

The horizontal situation indicator (HSI) combines a slaved compass card and CDI, providing the pilot with an excellent plan view of the airplane's position relative to the localizer course. Even though the HSI course arrow setting does not affect the deviation of the localizer needle, the picture presented will be much more meaningful and useful if you set the inbound localizer course.

A significant advantage of the HSI over the basic ILS indicator is that, because the course arrow and CDI are carried around with the slaved compass card as the airplane changes heading, the HSI remains a command instrument at all times (provided you have the localizer blue-right course set), even when you are tracking outbound on an ILS or inbound on a LOC BC. Another advantage is that one instrument (the HSI) replaces two (the HI and CDI), thereby reducing the scanning workload for the pilot.

The HSI is always a command instrument.

The horizontal situation indicator simplifies the interception of a localizer because of the clear plan view it presents to you. For instance, Figure 14-13 shows the airplane steering MH 175 about to intercept the localizer MC 200, an approximate 25° intercept. If you maintain MH 175, the CDI will center and then pass to the left of the model airplane, indicating that you have flown through the localizer. To intercept the course without flying through the radial, lead out of the turn before the CDI actually centers. A good technique is to achieve a rate of turn that keeps the top of the CDI aligned with the heading index—the faster the CDI is moving, the faster the rate of turn will have to be. You should be able to roll out exactly on course.

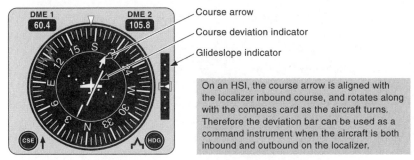

Course arrow
Course deviation indicator
Glideslope indicator

On an HSI, the course arrow is aligned with the localizer inbound course, and rotates along with the compass card as the aircraft turns. Therefore the deviation bar can be used as a command instrument when the aircraft is both inbound and outbound on the localizer.

Figure 14-13. A horizontal situation indicator display tuned to an ILS

Note: If you accidentally set the reciprocal of the inbound localizer course, you will get reverse sensing—not a good technique. Always set the inbound localizer course on the HSI (the course direction when the blue sector is on the right) then, even when flying a localizer back-course approach, you will always have a command instrument.

The Glideslope

The most suitable approach path to a runway for large modern airplane to follow is a slope of approximately 3° to the horizontal (a gradient of 1 in 20, or 5%) which intersects the runway approximately 1000 feet in from the approach threshold. The 3° slope provides a descent of approximately 300 feet for every 1 nm traveled horizontally, which gives a reasonable rate of descent for most airplanes at typical approach speeds—600 fpm at 120 knots ground-speed, for instance, and 450 fpm at 90 knots groundspeed.

Some instrument approach charts show a *rate-of-descent versus ground-speed* table, specifying what rate of descent is required, at that groundspeed, to remain on the glideslope. (This is especially valuable information if the electronic glideslope fails and you are forced to fly a localizer-only approach).

The glideslope is the component of an ILS that provides vertical guidance during the approach, and it is usually adjusted to allow airplanes to precisely follow this "ideal" 3° descent path (a slightly different angle may be used for some ILS installations). With a slope of 300 feet per nautical mile, you can expect a 3° glideslope to be:

• 3000 feet HAT (height above touchdown) at approximately 10 nm to touchdown;

• 2100 feet HAT at approximately 7 nm; and

• 1500 feet HAT at approximately 5 nm.

2,100 ft
HAT

1,500 ft
HAT

0   5 nm   7 nm

Figure 14-14. A 3° glideslope loses altitude by about 300 feet per nautical mile

The approximate altitude on-slope can be checked by multiplying the distance from the runway in miles by 300. For example, at 2 nm from touchdown the airplane should be about 600 feet above the touchdown zone elevation (TDZE). If the TDZE is 2350 feet MSL, 600 feet HAT is indicated on the altimeter by 2950 feet MSL.

The Glideslope Ground Equipment

The glideslope transmitting antenna is usually situated 750–1250 feet in from the runway threshold to ensure that any airplane flying the glideslope will have adequate wheel clearance over the threshold and any objects and/or terrain on approach. On some runways, the glideslope transmitting antenna may be positioned further in if there are high and restricting obstacles on the approach path. The **threshold crossing height (TCH)** of the glideslope is published on the ILS approach chart. The main wheels on some larger airplanes follow a much lower flightpath than the glideslope receiving antenna, which could be located near the nose of the airplane or somewhere else significantly higher than the wheels. A pilot of a large airplane should be aware of this.

The aim when flying a glideslope is not to touchdown on the numbers, but to touchdown in the designated **touchdown zone (TDZ)**, near where the glideslope intersects the runway.

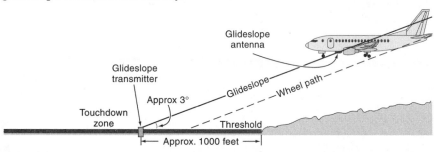

Figure 14-15. The typical glideslope transmitting antenna is approximately 1000 feet in from the runway threshold

As well as being located, on average, some 1000 feet in from the threshold, the glideslope transmitting antenna is usually offset by some 300 feet to the side of the runway, both to avoid being an obstacle to aircraft operating on the runway, and to prevent interference with the glideslope signal by nearby aircraft on the ground. The glideslope is transmitted on an ultra high frequency (UHF) carrier wave using a similar principle to the localizer transmission (that of two overlapping lobes), but the transmission pattern is slightly more complex.

A large 90 Hz lobe overlaps a 150 Hz lobe in the vertical plane. The actual glideslope, formed where the two signals are equal, is typically inclined at 3° to the horizontal, but some glideslopes may be shallower at 2.5°, and others may be steeper at 3.5°. It may not seem much of an increase in approach angle, but a 4° slope is extremely steep, very noticeable in the cockpit and possibly difficult to maintain in some jet transport airplanes.

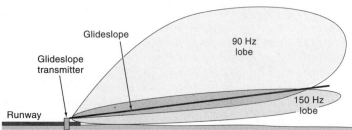

Figure 14-16. The glideslope

The overlap area of the two signals is about 1.4° thick, which means the useful signals extend 0.7° above and below the precise glideslope. The glidepath is calibrated out to 10 nm, although signals can be received at greater distances.

Unfortunately, because of ground reflection of some of the transmissions, there may be more than one overlapping of the lobes, giving rise to a **false glideslope**. The first false glideslope may be formed at approximately 12.5° to the horizontal—well above the true glideslope. One or more false glideslopes may exist, and do not be surprised when a false on-slope indication is given in the cockpit when the aircraft could not possibly be on slope, for instance at 12,000 feet HAA when only 10 nm from the airport, or when maneuvering around the airport to intercept the ILS.

There will also be *reverse sensing* with a false glideslope, and usually the glideslope needle will oscillate, making it fairly obvious that the signal is a false one. If the localizer transmits a back course, then there will probably be false glideslope signals in that area which can cause the glideslope OFF flag to flicker in and out of view. Be prepared to recognize a false glideslope signal for what it is when you see one, and to disregard it.

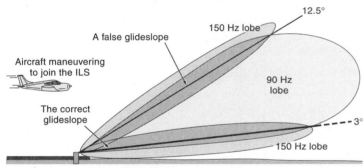

Figure 14-17. Beware of false glideslopes

The problem of false glideslopes is easily solved if the pilot has in his mind the altitude/distance relationship of the true glideslope, which is 300 ft/nm. Also, and most importantly, there is no false glideslope below the true glideslope— any false glideslopes will be above it, and will be inclined at least 10° (probably 12.5°) to the horizontal. For this reason it is recommended that you should always intercept the glideslope from below.

It is preferable, for example, to fly in from 10 nm at 2500 feet HAA to intercept the glideslope at about 8 nm to go, than to carry out a steep descent from above the glideslope in an attempt to intercept it. Transitions from the en route phase of flight on a published ILS approach are normally designed so that interception of the glideslope from below will occur.

False glideslopes will not occur below the true glideslope, so intercept the glideslope from below.

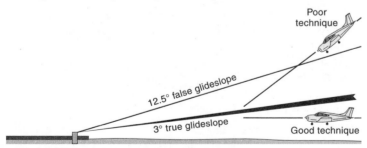

Figure 14-18. Ideally, intercept the glideslope from below

The glideslope signals are usually accurate out to about 10 nm, but descent based on the glideslope indication should not be commenced until the airplane has first intercepted the localizer.

The ILS Rwy 27 at South Bend, Indiana, is designed so that an airplane over any of the initial approach fixes (IAFs) may maneuver quite comfortably to join the localizer inbound not below 2200 feet MSL, and then intercept the glideslope from below. From LINGS IAF (initial approach fix) and GOSHEN IAF, the localizer intercept is a turn onto final course. From MISHA IAF, fly MC 092 outbound followed by course-reversal using a procedure turn to join MC 272 inbound.

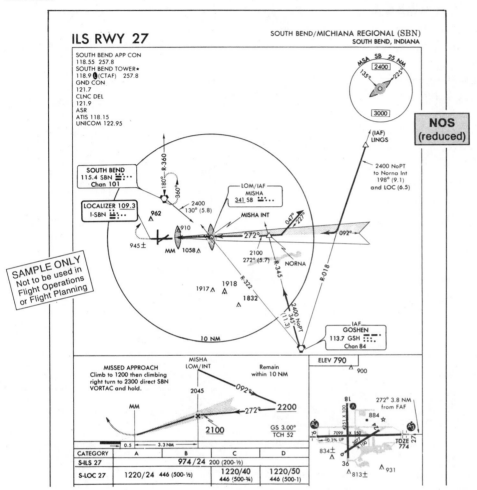

Figure 14-19. The South Bend, Indiana, ILS Rwy 27

The Airborne Glideslope Equipment

The position of the glideslope relative to the airplane is indicated by the horizontal needle of the VHF-NAV cockpit display. This needle may be hinged, and move like a wiper, or it may move rectilinearly. To be certain that the glideslope signal is usable, the red OFF flag must be out of view. The vertical glideslope scale on the typical ILS indicator consists of 5 dots above and below the central position, although the first dots UP and DOWN may be joined in a circle.

Figure 14-20. Different displays of glideslope

A unique glideslope transmission frequency is paired with each localizer frequency, so that the pilot automatically selects the associated glideslope when he selects the localizer on the VHF-NAV, without even knowing what the glideslope frequency is.

The glideslope receiver in the airplane compares the relative strength of the two signals, producing a voltage that positions the glideslope needle. If the 90 Hz signal is stronger because the airplane is above the glideslope, then the glideslope needle moves down. This indicates that the airplane must FLY DOWN to recapture the glideslope. It is the airplane which moves to the glideslope (and not vice versa).

Conversely, if the airplane is below the glideslope, the needle will move up—indicating FLY UP to rejoin the glideslope. This does not mean that the airplane must actually climb to recapture the glideslope. Flying level, or even just reducing the rate of descent, as the airplane flies toward the runway may be sufficient.

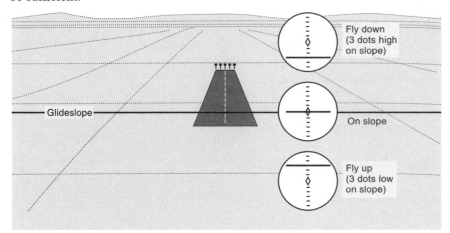

Figure 14-21. The glideslope needle indicates where the glideslope is with respect to the airplane

A full-scale FLY UP indication means that the airplane is 0.7° or more below the glideslope. Deviation from the glideslope is referred to in terms of dots rather than degrees, there being 5 dots up and 5 dots down on the instrument.

Keep the airplane right on glideslope, to the best of your ability, and do not exceed more than one-half full-scale FLY UP deviation below slope to retain adequate obstacle clearance toward the end of the approach. Half-scale FLY UP puts the airplane 0.3 or 0.4° below slope, which is significant, since the glideslope is inclined at only about 3° to the horizontal, and full-scale deviation is 0.7° below this.

As a general rule, make a strong effort to stay right on glideslope throughout the approach. A full-scale FLY DOWN indication means that the airplane is 0.7° or more above the slope.

Full-scale deflections once the ILS approach has been commenced are not acceptable, since the deviation from slope is at least 0.7°, and it could be even more! There is no indication of just how far the airplane is above or below slope when the glideslope needle is fully deflected.

The typical 0.7° full-scale deviation (above or below the ideal 3° glideslope) is equivalent to about 70 feet per nautical mile from touchdown, which is a vertical deviation in feet from the glideslope slope of:

- 700 feet at 10 nm;
- 350 feet at 5 nm;
- 210 feet at 3 nm;
- 140 feet at 2 nm;
- 70 feet at 1 nm; and
- a few feet at the runway threshold.

From peg-to-peg on the glideslope is 1.4°; peg-to-peg on the localizer is typically 5°; peg-to-peg on the VOR is 20°. Thus the glideslope needle is 3 times as sensitive as the localizer needle, and 12 times as sensitive as a VOR needle.

Do not go below the glideslope by more than half the full-scale FLY UP deflection.

The glideslope signal is only approved for navigation use down to the lowest authorized **decision height (DH)** for that particular ILS, and any reference to glideslope indications below that altitude must be supplemented by visual reference to the runway environment. A Category I ILS is approved for use down to DH 200 feet HAT, a Category II ILS is approved for use down to DH 100 feet HAT, and a Category III ILS is approved for use down to DH 0 feet HAT (requiring sophisticated equipment and highly trained pilots).

If the glideslope fails, but not the localizer, then you may still be permitted to carry out a nonprecision **localizer approach**, without electronic slope guidance, using the localizer for guidance in azimuth, and using range markers (such as the marker beacons, DME distances or a compass locator) for descent to suitable altitudes which will be marked on the profile part of the instrument approach chart.

Referring back to the South Bend ILS Rwy 27 profile, you may cross the SB LOM not below 2100 feet MSL and, for a straight-in approach to runway 27 in instrument conditions, descend further:

- for a *precision* ILS approach, using the electronic glideslope, down to a decision height (DH) of 974 feet MSL; or

- for a *nonprecision* localizer approach, without electronic slope guidance, down to a minimum descent altitude (MDA) of 1220 feet MSL.

If only the full ILS procedure is approved for a particular runway, and a localizer only approach without the use of a glideslope is not authorized, then the chart will carry the warning LOC ONLY N/A.

Flying the Glideslope

Flying the glideslope is similar to flying straight-and-level, except that the aim is to keep the airplane on a constant descent plane, rather than on a level plane at constant altitude. In level flight, the altimeter is checked regularly to ensure altitude is being maintained; during an ILS, the glideslope needle is checked regularly to ensure that the desired slope is being maintained.

The typical 3° glideslope requires a loss of altitude of 300 feet per nautical mile which:

- at a groundspeed of 60 kt (1 nm/min) requires a rate of descent of 300 fpm;

- at a groundspeed of 90 kt (1 nm/min) requires a rate of descent of 450 fpm;

- at a groundspeed of 120 kt (2 nm/min) requires a rate of descent of 600 fpm.

Notice that a quick method of estimating the required rate of descent for an ILS is simply 5 × groundspeed. By estimating your groundspeed, and then flying an appropriate rate of descent on the VSI, you will go close to holding the glideslope without even looking at the ILS indicator.

For instance, an approach speed of 90 KIAS into a 20-knot headwind will result in a groundspeed of 70 knots, so the correct rate of descent to hold glideslope will be (5 × 70) = 350 fpm. If the headwind decreases, your groundspeed will be greater for the same airspeed, and so you would require a higher rate of descent to hold slope. Periodically refer to the glideslope needle, and adjust the rate of descent as required to hold the glideslope.

The ILS indicator is a *performance* instrument. It should be included in the selective radial scan when information from it is desired. Having gained that information (which, in this case, is the position and/or movement of the glideslope needle), your eyes should return to the attitude indicator. Any corrections to regain or maintain the glideslope can then be made with a small pitch attitude change on the AI. The ILS indicator can then be checked again for position and/or movement of the glideslope needle.

Hold the glideslope with small pitch attitude changes. A process similar to bracketing track is used to regain and then maintain the glideslope, although in this case it is pitch attitude that is altered slightly, rather than heading.

If, for instance, the airplane goes below glideslope while a particular pitch attitude is held, then it should be raised slightly and held until the glideslope is regained. Once back on slope, the pitch attitude can be lowered slightly (but not quite as low as before), so that the glideslope is maintained.

Hold airspeed with power. There is also a target airspeed to be achieved on an ILS approach and, as in level flight, airspeed can be controlled with power. With pitch attitude changes to regain and maintain glideslope, small airspeed changes will occur. Fluctuations of ±5 knots are normally acceptable, but any trend beyond this should be corrected by a power alteration. Typically 1 inch MP or 100 rpm is sufficient, although greater power changes may be required in strong and gusty wind conditions or in windshear.

Maintaining glideslope and airspeed is one sign of a good instrument pilot. Flightpath and airspeed (in other words the performance of the airplane) are controlled by attitude and power on an ILS approach. If you have a good scan and quick response, then small deviations from the glideslope will be corrected with a small pitch change immediately, and will not develop into large deviations which might require a power adjustment as well.

Flying the glideslope involves energy management. If the airplane is slightly below glideslope slope and slightly fast, then the excess speed can be converted to height (or to a reduced rate of descent) by raising the pitch attitude on the AI, and flying up to regain slope.

Conversely, if the airplane is above glideslope and slightly slow, the pitch attitude on the AI can be lowered slightly, and the airplane flown down to regain glideslope, possibly with a small speed increase.

- Hold glideslope with pitch attitude on the AI.
- Hold airspeed with power.

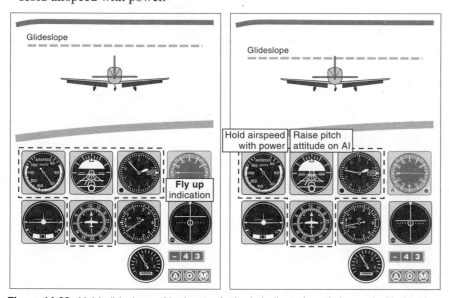

Figure 14-22. Hold glideslope with elevator (attitude indicator), and airspeed with throttle

Since it displays angular displacement, the glideslope needle will become more accurate and more sensitive as the airplane flies closer to the runway. Therefore, corrections on the attitude indicator to hold glideslope should become finer and finer as the runway is approached.

Hold the glideslope with small pitch attitude changes.

Hold airspeed with power.

Marker Beacons

ILS marker beacons transmit a highly focused vertical signal pattern, often described as elliptical or fan-shaped, which can only be received by an airplane as it passes directly overhead. Because the radio energy is transmitted upward, it is not possible to track to a marker beacon (unlike an NDB or compass locator whose energy is transmitted in all directions).

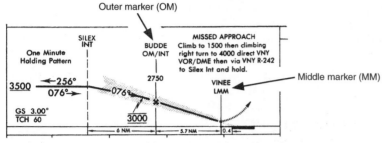

Figure 14-23. The outer marker and the middle marker

A typical ILS has two markers positioned along the localizer to provide range (or distance) check points. They are:

- **the outer marker (OM)** at between 4 and 7 nm from the runway threshold; and
- **the middle marker (MM)** at 3500 feet (0.6 nm) from the runway threshold.

Both markers operate on the same VHF frequency of 75 MHz, but each is amplitude-modulated to provide a different aural Morse code identification. There is no interference between the signals because their transmission volume is upward and very localized.

The airborne equipment consists of a marker receiver which indicates passage of the airplane over a marker by a light flashing in the cockpit and an aural Morse code ident. You can hear the ident through the headset or speaker, and see the light flashing (one of three color-coded lights on the instrument panel). You do not have to make any specific selection in the cockpit to receive the marker beacons, other than have the marker beacon switch ON.

The **outer marker** (OM) is located between 4 and 7 nm from the runway threshold. The airplane, if it is on glideslope, should therefore be at approximately 1400 feet HAT as it passes overhead the OM. The precise MSL altitude crossing the OM is specified on the profile diagram of the particular ILS, and you should check this on the altimeter as the airplane passes over the OM.

The cockpit indications of passage over the outer marker are:

- a continuous aural series of low-pitched (400 Hz) dashes transmitted at two per second (-*dah-dah-dah-dah-dah-dah-dah*-); and
- a flashing blue (or aviation purple) light synchronized with the aural "*dah-dahs*".

The middle marker (MM) is located approximately 3500 feet (0.6 nm) from the landing threshold, where the glideslope is approximately 200 feet HAT (height above touchdown). This is near the decision height DH and missed approach point (MAP) for the ILS approach. The middle marker crossing altitude may or may not be specified on the charts, since at this stage in the approach the pilot may be visual, depending on the particular approach minimums.

"*dah-dah-dah-dah-dah-dah-dah-*"

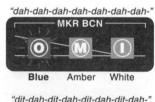

"*dit-dah-dit-dah-dit-dah-dit-dah-*"

Figure 14-24. Cockpit indications of the outer marker (top), and middle marker (below)

The cockpit indications of passage over the middle marker are:

- an aural series of alternating medium-pitched (1300 Hz) dots and dashes transmitted at six per second (*-dah-dit-dah-dit-dah-dit-dah-dit-*); and

- a flashing amber light synchronized with the aural *dah-dits*.

Some ILSs have an **inner marker (IM)** between the middle marker and the landing threshold that has an aural *"-dit-dit-dit-dit-"* signal at 3000 Hz (high-pitched) and six per second, and a synchronized flashing white light.

Some localizer back courses have a **back course marker (BCM)** that has an aural *"dit-dit dit-dit dit-dit"* signal, and a synchronized flashing white light. The BC marker is used to indicate the LOC BC final approach fix (FAF).

Marker beacons are sometimes used to provide en route fixes along airways. These are known as **fan markers (FM)**, and have an aural *"dit-dah-dit dit-dah-dit"* ident signal at 3000 Hz (high-pitched) that is synchronized with a flashing white light in the cockpit. The same white light is used for the IM, BC and FM markers, and is normally labeled "I", although on older airplanes it may be "A" or "FM/Z".

The marker beacon signals increase in strength fairly quickly as the airplane nears the marker beacon, remain very strong for a number of seconds, and then quickly fade away as the airplane moves further along the approach. Some airborne receivers have a HIGH/LOW sensitivity switch, LOW sensitivity giving a much narrower vertical pattern. For instrument approaches, the sensitivity switch is normally set to HIGH, because the airplane will be at a low level during the instrument approach, and the marker beacon signal will only be heard and seen for a few seconds.

Other Means of Checking Glideslope

Not all ILS installations have an outer marker and/or middle marker. For example, the Hayden, Colorado, ILS/DME Rwy 10 has neither. The glideslope, however, can be checked at the final approach fix (FAF) at 7.8 DME from the *I-HDN* DME (automatically selected along with the ILS on the VHF-NAV). If you are exactly on glideslope at 7.8 DME, the altimeter should read close to 8608 feet MSL.

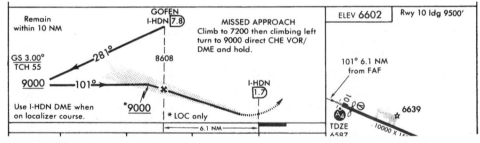

Figure 14-25. Hayden/Yampa Valley, CO, ILS/DME Rwy 10 profile diagram

The DME can be helpful in providing approximate slope guidance, or protection from underlying obstructions, if the electronic glideslope is not working or is not part of the approach. For example, the localizer back course approach at Tucson International, Arizona, LOC/DME BC Rwy 29R, has a number of DME/altitude restrictions. Descent from 8000 feet MSL may be commenced at 20 DME using the *I-TUS* localizer back course and DME, followed by an approach slope:

- not below 7200 feet until 13.5 DME;

- not below 6100 feet until 9.5 DME;

- not below 4800 feet until 5 DME, the final approach fix (FAF);

- not below 3600 feet until 2.3 DME; and
- not below MDA 3120 feet until visual, otherwise a missed approach at 0.3 DME.

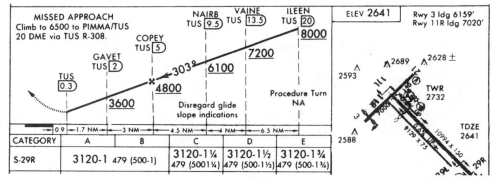

Figure 14-26. Tucson International, AZ, LOC/DME BC Rwy 29R profile diagram

Approach Lights, and other Lights

The aeronautical lighting facilities provided at an airport, which can assist a pilot to maneuver his airplane in conditions of poor visibility or at night, consist of:

- approach lighting;
- a visual approach slope indicator (VASI);
- touchdown zone lighting; and
- runway lighting.

Particulars of airport lighting are shown in the instrument approach procedures (IAP) publications.

Approach Light Systems (ALS)

At many airports, the approach lighting system (ALS) extends out from the approach end of the runway to well beyond the physical boundaries of the runway, possibly into forested or built-up areas.

Approach lights do not mark the boundaries of a suitable landing area—they simply act as a lead-in to a runway for a pilot on approach to land.

ALS lighting is a standardized arrangement of white and red lights, consisting basically of **extended centerline lighting**, with **crossbars** sited at specific intervals back along the approach path from the threshold, out to a distance of:

- 2400–3400 feet for precision instrument approach runways; or
- 1400–1500 feet for nonprecision instrument approach runways.

Approach light systems assist you to transition from instrument flight to visual flight for a landing. In minimum visibility conditions at the decision height, say visibility $\frac{1}{2}$ statute mile (2400 feet), the approach lights might be the only part of the runway environment that you can see, the runway and the VASI still being more than $\frac{1}{2}$ mile away, yet you may continue with the approach.

The approach lighting provides you with a visual indication of how well the airplane is aligned with the extended runway centerline (lateral guidance), as well as helping you to estimate the distance the airplane has to fly to touchdown during the latter stages of the instrument approach. This is especially useful in conditions of low visibility. In situations where no visible horizon exists, the approach lights can also assist you to visually judge the bank attitude of the airplane.

There are various types of approach light systems in use, the sophistication of the system depending on the importance of the airport and the frequency and type of operations. Some typical precision instrument runway ALSs are shown in Figure 14-27.

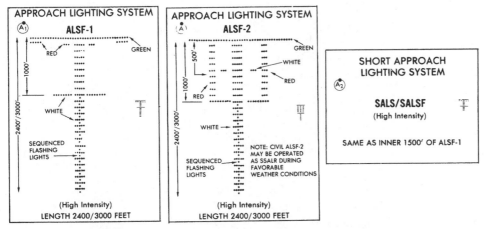

Figure 14-27. Approach lighting systems for precision instrument runways

Some approach lighting systems include **sequenced flashing lights (SFL)**, or **runway alignment indicator lights (RAIL)**, which appear to the pilot as a ball of white light traveling toward the runway at high speed (twice per second) along the extended centerline.

The runway threshold is marked with a row of green lights, and some runway thresholds have flashing strobes either side to act as **runway end identifier lights (REIL)**.

The view from the cockpit approaching a typical precision instrument runway in poor conditions is shown on the front cover of this book.

Visual Approach Slope Indicator (VASI)

In conditions of poor visibility and at night, when the runway environment and the natural horizon may not be clearly visible, it is often difficult for a pilot to judge the correct approach slope of the airplane toward the touchdown zone of the runway. A number of effective visual slope indicators have been invented to assist a pilot to stay on the slope in this situation; lateral guidance is provided by the runway, the runway lights or the approach light system.

2-Bar VASI

The typical 2-bar VASI has two pairs of wingbars extending outboard of the runway, usually at 500 feet and 1000 feet from the approach threshold. It is sometimes known as the *red/white system*, since the colors seen by the pilot tell him if he is right on slope, or too high or too low. He will see:

- all bars white if high on approach;
- the near bars white and the far bars red if right on slope; and
- all bars red if low on slope.

Remember: Red over white: you are all right. White over white: you are high as a kite. Red over red: you are dead.

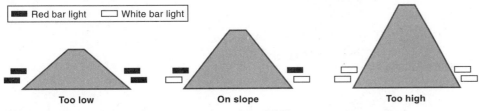

Figure 14-28. Perspectives on approach using a 2-bar VASI

During the approach, the airplane should be maintained on a slope within the white sector of the near bars and the red sector of the far bars. If the airplane flies above or below the correct slope, the lights will change color, there being a pink transition stage between red and white.

The plane of the VASI approach slope only provides guaranteed obstacle clearance in an arc 10° left or right of the extended centerline out to a distance of 4 nm from the runway threshold, even though the VASI may be visible in good conditions out to 5 nm by day and 20 nm by night. Before using VASI information, therefore, the airplane should be within this arc, and preferably aligned with the extended runway centerline.

In general, an approach descent using VASI should not be initiated until the airplane is visually aligned with the extended runway centerline. On instrument approaches, once the VASI comes into view you may use it to adjust your approach path.

There are other operational considerations when using the red/white VASI. At maximum range, the white bars may become visible before the red bars, because of the nature of red and white light. In haze or smog, or in certain other conditions, the white lights may have a yellowish tinge about them.

When extremely low on slope, the two wingbars (all lights red) may appear to merge into one red bar. At close range to the threshold this would be a critical situation with respect to obstacle clearance, and require urgent pilot action.

Some VASI systems use a reduced number of lights, in which case they may be known as an Abbreviated VASI or AVASI.

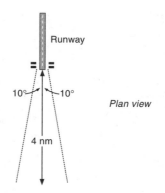

Figure 14-29. The extent of useful VASI information

Do not begin a VASI descent until the airplane is visually aligned with the extended centerline.

3-Bar VASI

The 3-bar VASI has an additional bar at the far end, intended to assist the pilots of long-bodied airplanes such as the *Boeing 747* or the *Airbus A300*. The approach slope guidance given by any VASI depends on the position of the pilot's eyes. Since the wheels of an airplane with a very long fuselage will be much further below the pilot's eyes, it is essential that his eyes follow a parallel but higher slope to ensure adequate mainwheel clearance over the runway threshold. The additional wingbar further into the runway makes this possible.

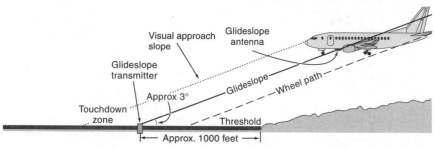

Figure 14-30. A 3-bar VASI ensures adequate wheel clearance over the threshold for long-bodied aircraft

Pilots of such airplanes should use the second and third wingbars, and ignore the first. When the pilot's eyes are positioned on the correct slope for a long-bodied airplane, he will see the top bar red, the middle bar white (and ignore the lower bar which is also white).

Pilots of smaller airplanes should refer to only the two nearer wingbars, and ignore the further "long-bodied" wingbar. On slope, the indications should be (top bar red and ignored), middle bar red and lower bar white.

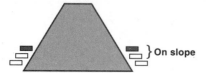

Figure 14-31. Correct view for the pilot of a long-bodied airplane using the 3-bar VASI

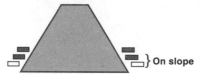

Figure 14-32. Correct view for the pilot of a smaller airplane using the 3-bar VASI

Precision Approach Path Indicator (PAPI)

PAPI is a development of the VASI, and also uses red/white signals for guidance in maintaining the correct approach angle, but the lights are arranged differently and their indications must be interpreted differently. PAPI has a single wingbar, which will consist of four light units on one or both sides of the runway adjacent to the touchdown point. There is no pink transition stage as the lights change from red to white.

If the airplane is on slope, the two outer lights of each unit are white and the two inner lights are red. Above slope, the number of white lights increase, and below slope the number of red lights increase.

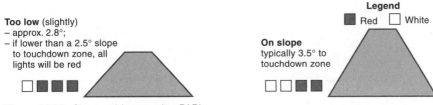

Figure 14-33. Slope guidance using PAPI

Pulsating Visual Approach Slope Indicator (PVASI)

PVASI consists of a single light unit, positioned on the left side of a runway adjacent to the touchdown point, which projects three or four different "bands" of light at different vertical angles, only one of which can be seen by a pilot on approach at any one slope position. The indications provided by a typical PVASI are:

- well above glideslope: fast-pulsing white;
- above glideslope: pulsing white;
- on glideslope: steady white (or alternating red/white for some systems);
- below glideslope: pulsing red;
- well below glideslope: fast-pulsing red.

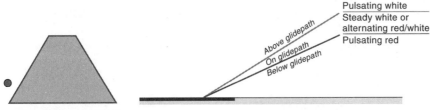

Figure 14-34. The PVASI

Tri-Color VASI

The tri-color VASI is a short-range visual slope aid (½ mile by day, 5 miles by night), and consists of a single-light unit that indicates:

- amber if above slope;
- green if on slope; and
- red if below slope.

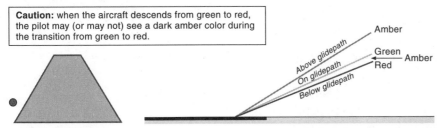

Figure 14-35. The tri-color VASI

T-VASI

The T-VASI is a system that has a horizontal bar of white lights either side of the runway aiming point. If the airplane is right on slope, you will only see these lights. If you are high on slope, single lights will appear above this bar, forming an inverted-T, and indicating FLY DOWN. If you are low on slope, single lights will appear below the bar, forming a T, and indicating FLY UP. The number of vertical lights give an indication of how far off slope you are. If you are extremely low, the lights turn red.

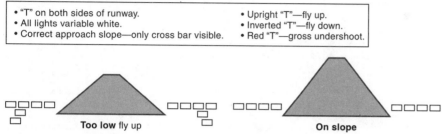

- "T" on both sides of runway.
- All lights variable white.
- Correct approach slope—only cross bar visible.

- Upright "T"—fly up.
- Inverted "T"—fly down.
- Red "T"—gross undershoot.

Too low fly up   **On slope**   **Too high** fly down

Figure 14-36. The T-VASI

Runway Lighting

Runway lighting defines the boundaries of the actual landing area, and some systems provide you with distance-down-the-runway information as well.

Runway Edge Lights

Runway edge lights outline the edges of runways during periods of darkness or restricted visibility. They are classified according to the intensity or brightness they are capable of producing:

- HIRL: High Intensity Runway Lights;
- MIRL: Medium Intensity Runway Lights;
- LIRL: Low Intensity Runway Lights.

Runway edge lights are white, except on instrument runways where amber replaces white for the last 2000 feet (or last-half on runways shorter than 4000 feet), to form a caution zone for landings in restricted visibility. When the pilot sees the white edge lights replaced by amber, he has some idea of how much runway is left for stopping.

Runway End Lights

The runway end lights show green to aircraft on approach, and red to airplanes stopping at the far end.

Runway End Identifier Lights (REIL)

Runway End Identifier Lights (REIL) consist of a pair of synchronized white flashing lights located each side of the runway threshold at the approach end. They serve to:

- identify a runway end surrounded by many other lights;
- identify a runway end which lacks contrast with the surrounding terrain; and
- identify a runway end in poor visibility.

In-Runway Lighting

Some precision approach runways have additional in-runway lighting embedded in the runway surface consisting of:

- **touchdown zone lighting (TDZL)**: bright white lights either side of the runway centerline in the touchdown zone (from 100 feet in from the landing threshold to 3000 feet or the half-way point, which ever is the lesser);

- **runway centerline lighting (RCLS)**: flush centerline lighting at 50 feet intervals, starting 75 feet in from the landing threshold to within 75 feet of the stopping end; RCLS also includes runway remaining lighting, where the centerline lighting seen by a stopping airplane is:
    - initially all white;
    - alternating red and white from 3000 feet-to-go point to 1000 feet-to-go;
    - all red for the last 1000 feet.
- **taxiway turn-off lights**: flush lights spaced at 50-foot intervals defining the curved path of aircraft travel from the runway centerline to a point on the taxiway.

Taxiway Lights

While not directly associated with a precision approach, it does help if you can exit the runway onto a taxiway with confidence. Taxiways are lighted in one of two ways for the guidance of pilots with either:

- one line of **centerline green** taxiway lights; or
- two lines of taxiway **blue edge** lights.

At some airports, there is a mixture of the two types, centerline green on some taxiways, and blue edge on others.

At certain points on the taxiway, there may be **red stop-bars** installed, to indicate the position where an airplane should hold position, for instance before entering an active runway.

Control of Lighting Systems

The approach lights and runway lights at an airport are controlled by:

- the control tower personnel (when the tower is active);
- the FSS, at some locations where no control tower is active (but this FSS function is gradually being eliminated); or
- the pilot (at selected airports).

The pilot may request ATC or FSS to turn the lights on (or off), or to vary their intensity if required. On a hazy day with restricted visibility, but with a lot of glare, maximum brightness might be necessary; on a clear dark night, a significantly lower brightness level will be required.

At selected airports, when ATC and/or FSS facilities are not manned, airborne control of the lights is possible using the VHF-COM. The A/FD specifies the type of lighting available, and the VHF-COM frequency used to activate the system.

To use an FAA-approved pilot-controlled lighting system, simply select the appropriate VHF frequency on the VHF-COM, and depress the microphone switch a number of times. A good technique involves keying the mike 7 times within 5 seconds, which will activate the lights at maximum intensity, and then subsequently keying it a further 5 or 3 times, for medium or low intensity respectively, if desired.

All pilot-controlled lighting operates for 15 minutes from the time of the most recent transmission. If pilot-controlled lights are already on as you commence an approach, it is good airmanship to reactivate them and thereby ensure availability for the duration of the approach and landing.

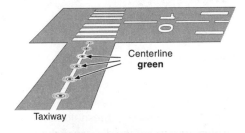
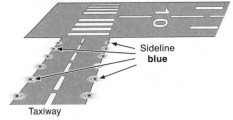

Figure 14-37. Taxiway lighting

All pilot-controlled lighting operates for 15 minutes from the most recent transmission.

Precision Instrument Runway Markings

To assist pilots landing and stopping at the conclusion of a precision instrument approach, some precision instrument runways have specific markings.

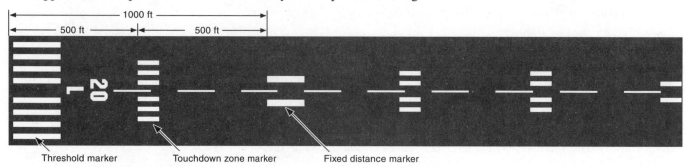

Figure 14-38. Markings on a precision instrument runway

A displaced threshold on an instrument runway is indicated by arrows in the middle of the runway leading to the displaced threshold mark. The runway edge lights to the displaced threshold appear red to an airplane on approach, and to an airplane taxiing to the displaced threshold from the absolute end of the runway. They appear white when taxiing back from the displaced threshold toward the absolute end of the runway. The green runway end lights seen on approach to a runway with a displaced threshold are found off the edge of the runway.

The runway surface with arrows to the displaced threshold is available for taxiing, takeoff and landing roll-out, but not for landing. The initial part of this runway is a non-touchdown area. If chevrons rather than arrows are used to mark the displaced threshold, then the surface is not available for any use.

Inoperative ILS Components

If some component of an ILS, or a visual aid, is inoperative (say, approach lighting), then higher minimums may be required. This is specified in the *Inoperative Components* or *Visual Aids Table* in each *NOS* Terminal Procedures book, and on each *Jeppesen* chart. If more than one ILS component is inoperative, use the highest minimum required by any single unusable component.

ILS glideslope inoperative (or "GS out") minimums are published on *NOS* and *Jeppesen* instrument approach charts as localizer (LOC) minimums.

(1) ILS, MLS, and PAR

Inoperative Component or Aid	Approach Category	Increase Visibility
ALSF 1 & 2, MALSR, & SSALR	ABCD	¼ mile

(2) ILS with visibility minimum of 1800 RVR

Inoperative Component or Aid	Approach Category	Increase Visibility
ALSF 1 & 2, MALSR, & SSALR	ABCD	To 4000 RVR
TDZI RCLS	ABCD	To 2400 RVR
RVR	ABCD	½ mile

(3) VOR, VOR/DME, VORTAC, VOR (TAC), VOR/DME (TAC, LOC, LOC/DME, LDA, LDA/DME, SDF, SDF/DME, RNAV, and ASR

Inoperative Component or Aid	Approach Category	Increase Visibility
ALSF 1 & 2, MALSR, & SSALR	ABCD	½ mile
SSALS, MALS, & ODALS	ABC	¼ mile

(4) NDB

Inoperative Component or Aid	Approach Category	Increase Visibility
ALSF 1 & 2, MALSR, & SSALR	C	½ mile
	ABD	¼ mile
MALS, SSALS, ODALS	ABC	¼ mile

Figure 14-39. *NOS* Inoperative Components and Visual Aids tables (Note: The tables may be amended by notes on the particular approach plate)

Flying a Typical ILS

The relevant instrument approach procedure (IAP) chart should be checked for currency, and thoroughly studied before commencing the approach. Even though the chart can be referred to during the actual approach, it is helpful to build up an overall view of where the airplane is and what path it will follow. As an example, the published *NOS* Burbank-Glendale-Pasadena ILS RWY 8 chart (plan and profile) follows, with a sketch (Figure 14-41) of how the approach will be flown.

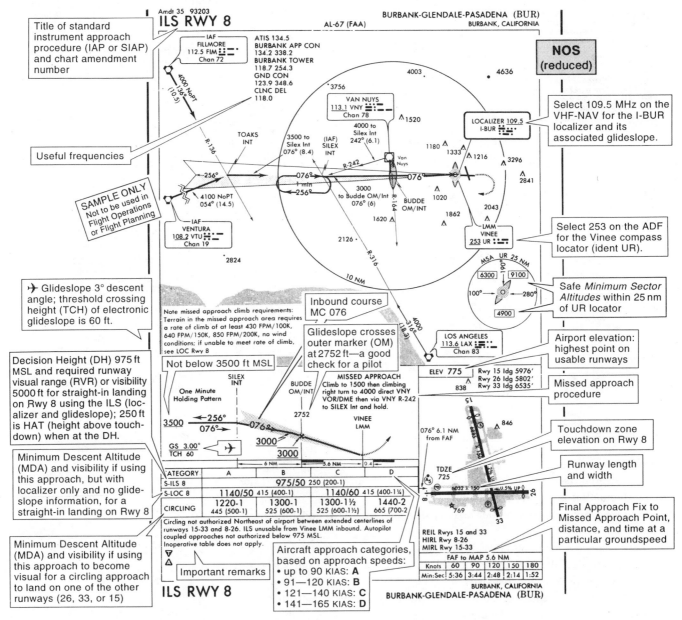

Figure 14-40. Burbank Rwy 8 ILS approach plate

The appropriate minimums should be determined. For a straight-in approach on Runway 8 using the full ILS (S-ILS 8), the **decision height** (DH) for a Category A airplane (a typical light aircraft) is DH 975 feet MSL, with a visibility or runway visual range (RVR) of 5000 feet (1 sm) being required to land. If the electronic glideslope is not available, and the approach is made using the localizer only without the glideslope (S-LOC 8), the minimums increase to a **minimum descent altitude** (MDA) of 1140 feet MSL, with 1 sm visibility required for landing. To circle and land on another runway, the minimums are further raised to 1220 feet and 1 sm.

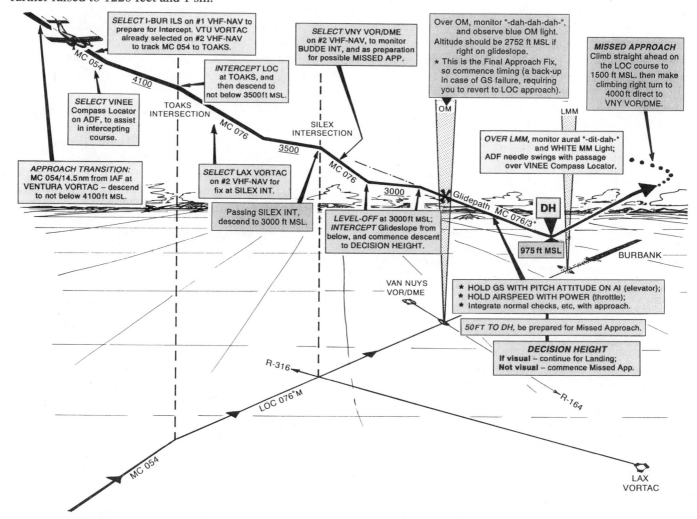

Figure 14-41. Flying the Burbank ILS Rwy 8 approach

The **missed approach** procedure should always be reviewed and alternative action planned if there is any doubt that a successful landing can be made. Low clouds fluctuating around the decision height, poor visibility, heavy rain, or anything that might prejudice your arrival, should lead you to consider alternate airports.

There is always a (remote) possibility that an essential ground aid required for the landing will become unserviceable (caused by a lightning strike or flooding during a storm, for instance).

The fuel situation must be considered, and the minimum fuel on board required for diversion should be calculated. Allow for reserves. Is there fuel enough for more than one approach before diverting, how much fuel is available for holding, is the weather at the alternate airport still suitable for an approach? Prepare for the approach well before reaching the airport, so that, once there, you can devote sufficient attention to flying the ILS approach.

Track to the airport following the normal route and using the normal en route tracking aids, maintaining the appropriate altitude. The minimum safe altitudes within 25 nm of Vinee compass locator (UR) are quite high, up to 9100 feet MSL in the northeast sector, but ATC may clear you to lower altitudes and provide radar vectors to expedite your arrival. All clearances, headings, altitudes and pressure settings passed by ATC should be repeated. All radio aids must be identified before being used.

If a **holding pattern** has to be entered, then plan to use the correct entry procedure based on the airplane's heading when it reaches the holding fix (see Figure 14-42).

"Stacking" airplanes in holding patterns until a slot on the ILS becomes available is common during busy periods at major airports. As each airplane departs the bottom of the stack and proceeds into the ILS, the other airplanes can be cleared down one at a time. This will be the procedure used if ATC informs you that "timed approaches are in progress."

In some instrument approach procedures, a **DME arc** may be flown to position an airplane on an ILS (Figure 14-43).

For the Burbank Rwy 8 ILS, the airplane will fly from the Ventura initial approach fix (IAF) to join the localizer at 4100 feet at Toaks intersection.

- Select VHF-NAV-1 to the Rwy 8 ILS I-BUR, 109.5 MHz, inbound 076, and identify.
- To assist in the intercept, select the ADF to Vinee compass locator, 253 kHz, identify UR, and test that it is "ADFing".
- Continue tracking MC 054 from Ventura with its VOR selected on VHF-NAV-2.

Use the ADF to assist the intercept, since the CDI will not start to move until you are within 2.5° of the localizer. The intercept, from MC 054 to localizer MC 076, is only 22°, which is satisfactory. If the intercept was greater, say 60°, it would be a good technique to break the intercept to about 30° just prior to the CDI starting to move. You can judge this using the position and rate of closure of the ADF needle.

If you are approaching the localizer centerline and have not yet been authorized for the approach, query ATC as to whether they want you to either maintain the last assigned heading (possibly for traffic reasons) or to intercept the localizer.

If you are authorized to make the approach, turn to MC 076 as soon as the CDI starts to move. Hold your reference heading, MC 076 plus or minus the estimated wind correction angle and check the CDI. There is no need for you to center it immediately, just so long as it does not move to the peg (full-scale deflection); it is more important to establish a reference heading that stops CDI movement, and then subsequently make gentle turns about the reference heading to center the CDI. Heading changes of ±5° may required early in the approach while you are becoming established, but after the final approach fix you should be able to manage with small adjustments of ±2°.

Integrate the normal operational requirements into the approach so that the whole thing flows smoothly, without undue haste or panic. Radio calls, prelanding checks, configuration and airspeed changes—the sorts of things that occur on all approaches—still must be attended to. Having prepared for the approach early in order to reduce the workload later on, you should now be able to sit back (more or less) and calmly follow the procedure, attending briefly to other duties as required.

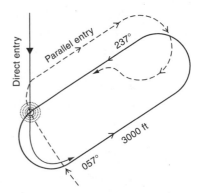

Figure 14-42. Holding pattern entry

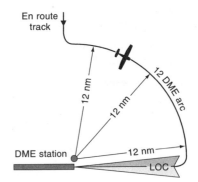

Figure 14-43. A DME arc

Thorough preparation will reduce your workload during the approach.

After intercepting the localizer at Toaks, track to the Silex Intercept, descending to not below 3500 feet MSL, indicated on the chart by 3500. While not essential, VHF-NAV-2 (if available) may be selected to the 316 radial of the LAX VOR, since its intersection with the localizer defines Silex. You are now in a good position if ATC request you to hold at Silex.

Passing Silex, descend to not below 3000 feet, indicated on the chart by 3000. The glideslope needle will move from the upper peg as you intercept the glideslope from below. Commence a descent at your estimated rate of descent. There are various techniques recommended for intercepting the glideslope, and your instructor will give you good advice, possibly to:

• lower the landing gear, thereby increasing drag, and pitch slightly down to maintain speed and achieve the desired rate of descent; or

• reduce power, and pitch slightly down to maintain speed and achieve the desired rate of descent.

Again, there is no need to immediately center the needle. It is more important to establish the correct rate of descent and hold the desired airspeed, provided the glideslope needle does not go to the upper or lower peg. The VSI can be of great assistance.

When settled down in the descent, make minor pitch adjustments to center the glideslope needle. Airspeed changes, if required, may be made with power (followed by a pitch change, if necessary, to hold the glideslope). Changes in wind speed and/or direction (*windshear*) will require a response. A brief section on windshear begins on page 343.

The ILS indicator is a navigation *performance* instrument—do not use it to make attitude changes, nor to "fly the needles". Periodically note the position of the localizer and glideslope needles, then return to the flight instruments and make appropriate minor attitude adjustments on the AI, and steer your selected heading on the HI. Several seconds later, check the ILS indicator, and then move your eyes back to the flight instruments.

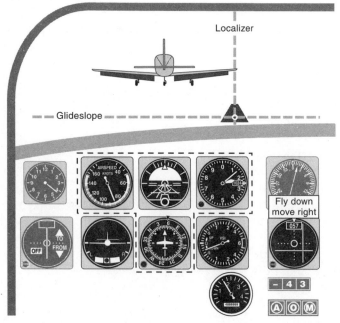
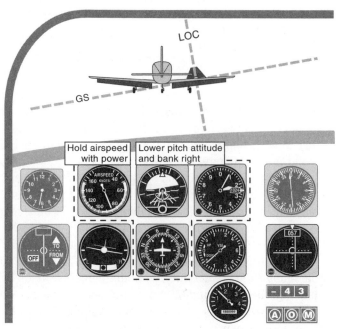

Figure 14-44. Flying the ILS on final approach

Remember that the flightpath in clouds or out of clouds is the same, the airplane does not know the difference; the main difference, if any, is in your psychological state—and if you treat the instrument indications merely as substitute visual indications, and keep visualizing your progress down the glidepath toward the runway, you can proceed comfortably as in a normal visual approach.

When past Silex, VHF-NAV 2 may be selected to Van Nuys VOR (VNY), in preparation for a potential missed approach. VHF-NAV 1, with the Burbank Rwy 8 ILS selected, is still your primary navigation instrument.

You should pass the **outer marker** (flashing blue light and "*dah-dah-dah-dah-*") at 2752 feet on the altimeter. Start the stopwatch. The outer marker is the final approach fix (FAF), and you should have the localizer and the glideslope tied down, with only small pitch and heading changes being required. You should be right on speed, with your hand on the throttle. Before landing checks should be complete, with only final flaps to go.

Note: If there is a glideslope failure prior to the outer marker, and you have to revert to a **localizer approach**, you should cross the outer marker at 3000 feet, indicated by $\overline{3000}$, and then descend to the minimum descent altitude (MDA) 1140 feet. You may hold the MDA in the hope of becoming visual before the missed approach point (MAP), whose position you can determine with the stopwatch (at groundspeed 90 knots, 3 minutes 44 sec-onds after the outer marker).

Assuming the full ILS is working (including the glideslope), proceed down to the decision height (DH) 975 feet MSL, occasionally looking up from the instruments for signs of the runway environment, such as approach lights or the runway itself. If you break out of the clouds at the DH or above, and the required visibility of 1 sm or more exists, you may proceed with the landing. Select final flaps, as required.

If you do not break out of the clouds at or above the DH, or if the required minimum visibility of 5000 feet (1 sm) does not exist, then you should imme-diately commence the **missed approach** at the DH, by initiating a climb, adopting the missed approach configuration, and commencing a climbing right turn, after passing through 1500 feet MSL, toward the Van Nuys VOR, climb-ing to 4000 feet. Van Nuys is already selected on your VHF-NAV 2. If you have only one VHF-NAV, turn to an estimated heading, say MH 290, and then select Van Nuys VOR when comfortable.

The missed approach is not an emergency procedure, but simply part of the normal instrument approach procedure that provides you with a safe flightpath if weather is below minimums, or if, for any reason, you decide not to proceed with the landing. The missed approach is, however, a maneuver that you must commence efficiently and without delay when you reach the DH.

International Terminology

Jeppesen charts for U.S. airports now use international (ICAO) terminology for presenting the minimum altitude on an approach; this differs slightly from the *NOS* instrument approach chart presentation of minimums.

• **Precision approaches** (ILS, MLS): *Jeppesen* charts use the term **decision altitude (height)**, abbreviated DA(H), in place of just **DH** (decision height), as on *NOS* charts. For example, DA(H) 492´(200´) means the decision alti-tude is at 492 feet MSL, which is 200 feet height above touchdown (HAT).

Refer to the example in Figure 14-45 on page 338: the *Jeppesen* Visalia, CA, ILS approach chart excerpt.

- **Nonprecision approaches** (VOR, NDB): *Jeppesen* uses the term **minimum descent altitude (height)**, abbreviated MDA(H). *NOS* charts use just **MDA**. For example, the *Jeppesen* Las Vegas, N Mex, VOR approach Rwy 2 chart shows the minimum as: MDA(H) 7540′(675′), where 7540 feet is the MDA (MSL altitude) and 675 feet is the height above airport (HAA).

Note: United Kingdom, European and Australian ILS approach plates use the international system.

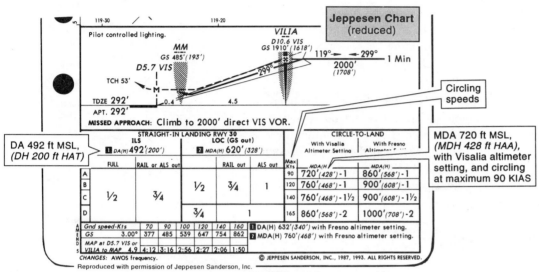

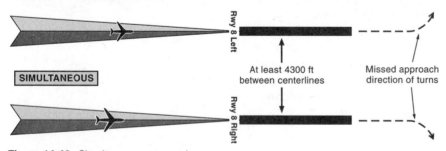

Figure 14-45. Excerpt from the Visalia, California ILS Rwy 30 *Jeppesen* approach chart

Simultaneous Approaches

At some airports with parallel instrument runways separated by at least 4300 feet, simultaneous ILS (or MLS) approaches may occur, with different aircraft flying down different parallel paths to different runways. When simultaneous approaches are in progress, you should monitor the tower frequency for radar advisories or instructions.

Figure 14-46. Simultaneous approaches

Note: At some airports with parallel runways with only 2500 feet MSL between centerlines, so-called **parallel ILS approaches** may be conducted, but aircraft on the adjacent localizers will be staggered by at least two miles. At some airports with converging runways, ATC may conduct simultaneous **converging ILS approaches**. The two approach courses will be well separated, the two missed approach points must be at least three miles apart, and the two missed approach courses must be well separated.

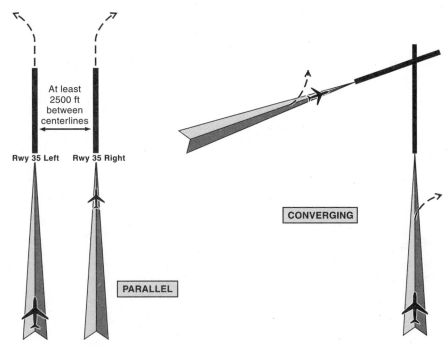

Figure 14-47. Parallel and converging approaches

The Sidestep Maneuver

The sidestep maneuver is a visual maneuver accomplished by the pilot after flying an instrument approach to one runway, becoming visual, and then side-stepping (with well-coordinated turns) to land straight-in on a parallel runway which is not more than 1200 feet to either side of the runway on which the instrument approach is based.

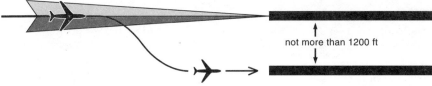

Figure 14-48. The sidestep maneuver

You should commence the sidestep maneuver as soon as you are visual and have the runway environment in sight.

The Localizer-type Directional Aid (LDA)

The localizer-type directional aid (LDA) is comparable to a localizer but is *not* aligned with the runway. In other words, using an LDA you will have to maneuver for a landing after becoming visual. The LDA does not have a glide-slope as part of the LDA procedure (unless specified in the approach title).

Straight-in LDA minimums may be published if the alignment does not exceed 30° between the LDA course and the runway. Circling minimums only are published where this alignment exceeds 30°.

A good example of efficient ATC use of radio navaids is the LDA approach at Van Nuys airport using the localizer part of the Burbank ILS. Since the Van Nuys runway is at almost 90° to the LDA course, only circling minimums are published. If you break out of the clouds at or above MDA 1480, and if the required minimum visibility of 1 sm exists, you may commence a circle-to-land maneuver at Van Nuys. If you have both the localizer and the VOR, the MDA is lower, at 1300 feet MSL.

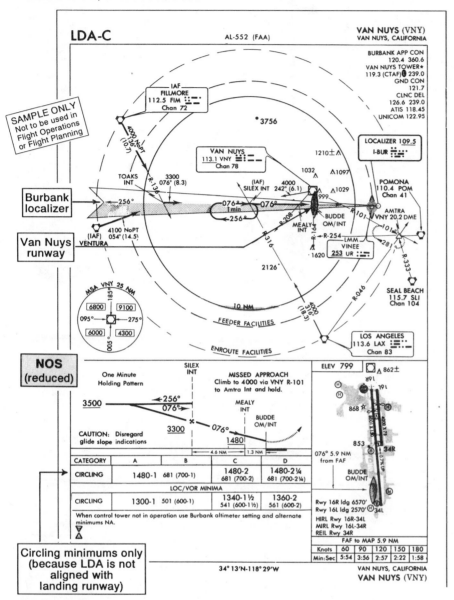

Figure 14-49. Van Nuys LDA-C

The Simplified Directional Facility (SDF)

The SDF is similar to a localizer except:

- its course width may be greater at 6° or 12°, resulting in less precise course guidance (but still good); and
- the SDF course may be offset slightly from the runway centerline, but this will be noted on the SDF approach chart.

The full-scale FLY LEFT or FLY RIGHT signals of the SDF are not usable outside 35° either side of course. Like the LDA, the SDF does not have a glideslope.

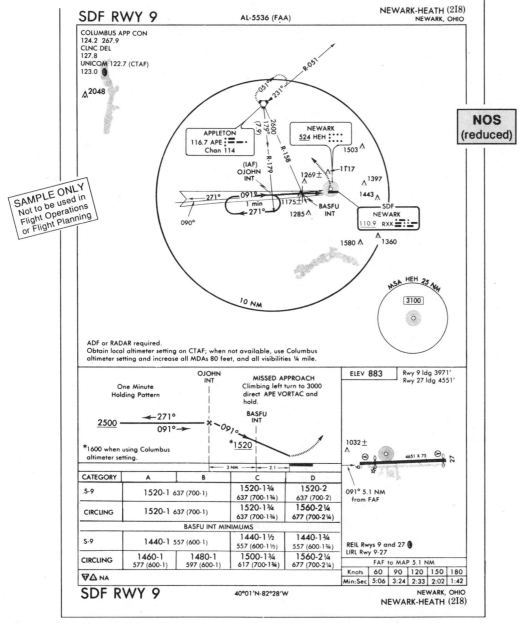

Figure 14-50. Newark, Ohio, SDF RWY 9

The Microwave Landing System (MLS)

A program has been underway for some years aimed at developing a replacement for the instrument landing system (ILS). The project, known as the microwave landing system (MLS), has not moved as rapidly or as smoothly as was expected, however there are a few MLSs in service, for instance at Richmond, Virginia. They have not replaced ILSs, and therefore are not a consideration for the average instrument pilot. Special MLS equipment is required in the airplane for MLS to be used.

MLS is a precision approach aid that operates in the microwave (SHF) band of 5031–5091 MHz. A coded 4-letter identifier is transmitted at least 6 times a minute, the first letter being M ("*dah-dah*"), instead of I ("*dit-dit*") for an ILS. For instance, M-DBE is an MLS; I-HRE is an ILS.

The MLS provides azimuth, elevation, distance information and other data in at least the service volume shown in Figure 14-51. The lateral and vertical guidance may be displayed on a conventional ILS indicator, and the MLS precision DME (known as DME/P) may be displayed on the conventional DME indicator; or they may all be displayed on one of the new multipurpose displays now available in sophisticated aircraft. The pilot using the conventional displays flies the MLS the same as he would the conventional ILS, simply guiding the airplane along the desired flightpath.

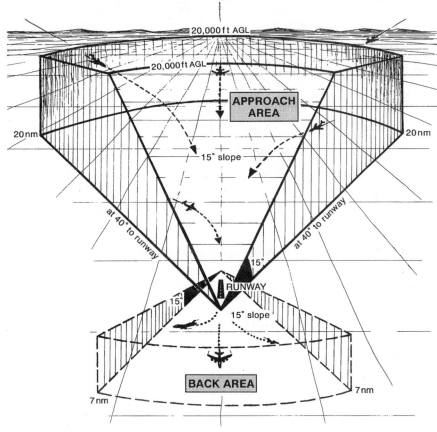

Figure 14-51. The MLS service volume

A significant advantage of MLS over the ILS is that it can provide precise electronic course and slope guidance on any flightpath in its approach area, including varying slopes and segmented approach paths. This means curved approach paths at any angle are possible, allowing ATC greater flexibility in handling traffic using simultaneous multi-path approaches.

The approach service volume is:
• laterally: at least 40° either side of the extended runway centerline;
• in elevation: at least 15° up from landing runway, to at least 20,000 feet AGL;
• range: at least 20 nm.

In the back service volume airspace, MLS provides guidance in azimuth, which is useful for missed approach navigation and departure navigation. The back service volume is:
• laterally: at least 40° either side of the extended runway centerline;
• in elevation: at least 15° up from landing runway;
• range: at least 7 nm.

Windshear on the Approach

An understanding of windshear helps explain why alterations of pitch attitude and/or power are continually required to maintain a desired flightpath, just as changes in heading are required to maintain a steady course.

The study of windshear and its effect on airplanes, and what protective measures can be taken to avoid potentially dangerous results, is still in its infancy and much remains to be learned.

What is certain is that every airplane and every pilot will be affected by windshear—usually the light windshears that occur in everyday flying, but occasionally a moderate windshear that requires positive recovery action from the pilot. On rare occasions, severe windshears can occur from which a recovery may even be impossible. A little knowledge can help you understand how to avoid significant windshear, and how best to recover from an inadvertent penetration.

Windshear Terminology

- A **windshear** is defined as a change in wind direction and/or wind speed in space. This includes updrafts and downdrafts. Any change in the wind velocity (be it a change in speed or in direction) as you move from one point to another is a windshear. The stronger the change and the shorter the distance within which it occurs, the stronger the windshear.
- **Updrafts** and **downdrafts** are the vertical components of wind. The most hazardous updrafts and downdrafts are those associated with thunderstorms.
- The term **low-level windshear** is used to specify any windshear occurring along the final approach path prior to landing, along the runway and along the takeoff/initial climb-out flightpath. Windshear near the ground (below about 3000 feet) is often the most critical in terms of safety for the airplane. Windshear is quite common when there is a low-level temperature inversion.
- **Turbulence** is eddy motions in the atmosphere which vary both with time and from place to place.

The Effects of Windshear on Aircraft

Most of our studies have considered an airplane flying in a reasonably stable air mass which has a steady motion relative to the ground, in a steady wind situation. We have seen how an airplane climbing out in a steady headwind will have a better climb gradient over the ground compared to the tailwind situation, and how an airplane will glide further over the ground downwind compared to into wind.

An actual air mass does not move in a totally steady manner—there will be gusts and updrafts and changes of wind speed and direction etc., which the airplane will encounter as it flies through the air mass. These windshears will have a transient effect on the flightpath of an airplane.

An Example of Windshear

Even when the wind is relatively calm on the ground, it is not unusual for the light and variable surface wind to suddenly change into a strong and steady wind at a level only a few hundred feet above the ground. If we consider an airplane making an approach to land in these conditions, we can see the effect the windshear has as the airplane passes through the shear.

An airplane flying through the air will have a certain inertia depending on its mass and its velocity relative to the ground. Its inertia makes it resistant to change. If the airplane has an airspeed of 80 knots and the headwind component is 30 knots, then the inertial speed of the airplane over the ground is (80 − 30) = 50 knots.

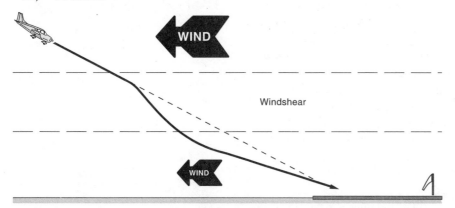

Figure 14-52. A typical windshear situation—calm on the ground with a wind at altitude

When the airplane flies down into the calm air, the headwind component reduces reasonably quickly to (let us say) 5 knots. The inertial speed of the airplane over the ground is still 50 knots, but the new headwind of only 5 knots will mean that its airspeed has suddenly dropped back to 55 KIAS.

The pilot will observe a sudden drop in indicated airspeed and a change in the performance of the airplane—at 55 KIAS the performance will be quite different to that available at 80 KIAS. The first indication of windshear to a pilot is usually a sudden change in indicated airspeed.

The normal reaction with a sudden loss of airspeed is to add power or to lower the nose to regain airspeed, and to avoid undershooting the desired flightpath. The stronger the windshear, the greater the changes in power and attitude that will be required. Any fluctuations in wind will require adjustments by the pilot, and this is why you have to work so hard sometimes, especially when approaching to land.

Windshear Effects on an Aircraft's Flightpath

The effects of windshear on an airplane's flightpath depend on the nature and location of the shear, as follows:

- **Overshoot effect** is caused by a windshear which results in the airplane flying above the desired flightpath and/or an increase in indicated airspeed. The nose of the airplane may also tend to rise. Overshoot effect may result from flying into an increasing headwind, a decreasing tailwind, from a tailwind into a headwind, or an updraft. Overshoot effect is sometimes referred to as a *performance-increasing* windshear, since it causes an increase in airspeed and/or altitude.

- **Undershoot effect** is caused by a windshear which results in an airplane flying below the desired flightpath and/or a decrease in indicated airspeed. The nose of the airplane may also tend to drop. Undershoot effect may result from flying into a decreasing headwind, an increasing tailwind, from a headwind into a tailwind, or into a downdraft. Undershoot effect is sometimes referred to as a *performance-decreasing* windshear, since it causes a loss of airspeed and/or altitude.

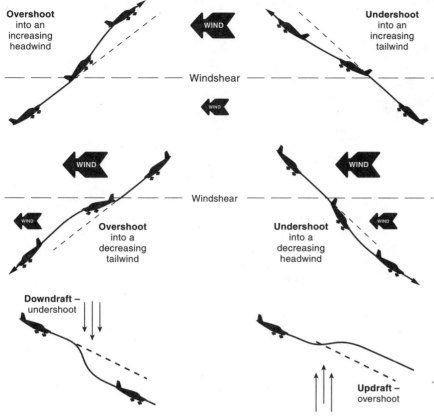

Figure 14-53. Six common windshear situations

Note that the actual effect of a windshear depends on:

1. the nature of the windshear;
2. whether the airplane is climbing or descending through that particular windshear; and
3. in which direction the airplane is proceeding.

- **Windshear reversal effect** is caused by a windshear which results in the initial effect on the airplane being reversed as the aircraft proceeds further along the flightpath. It would be described as overshoot effect followed by undershoot, or undershoot followed by overshoot effect, as appropriate.
  Windshear reversal effect is a common phenomenon that pilots often experience on approach to land, when things are usually happening too fast to analyze exactly what is taking place in terms of wind. The pilot can, of course, observe undershoot and overshoot effect and react accordingly with changes in attitude and/or power.

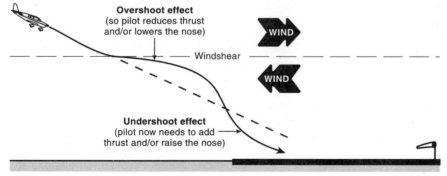

Figure 14-54. Windshear reversal effect

- **Crosswind effect** is caused by a windshear which requires a rapid change of aircraft heading to maintain a desired track (not uncommon in a crosswind approach and landing because the crosswind component changes as the ground is neared).

Figure 14-55. Crosswind effect

The Causes of Windshear

There are many causes of windshear. They include obstructions and terrain features which disrupt the normal smooth wind flow, localized vertical air movements associated with cumulonimbus (thunderstorms) and large cumulus clouds (gust fronts, downbursts and microbursts), low-level temperature inversions, sea breezes and jet streams.

The following phenomena are known to be strongly associated with the occurrence of windshear, and a pilot should exercise appropriate caution if any are observed, especially during takeoff and landing:

- roll clouds and/or dust raised ahead of an approaching squall line;
- strong, gusty surface winds at an airport with hills or large buildings located near the runway;
- windsocks on various parts of the airport indicating different winds (some airports are equipped with LLWAS—a Low Level Windshear Alert System—which is designed to detect such a situation, allowing ATC to provide advisory warnings to landing and departing aircraft);
- curling or ring-shaped dust clouds raised by downdrafts beneath a convective cloud (even if the ceiling is relatively high);
- virga associated with a convective cloud (rain falling from the base of the cloud and evaporating before reaching the ground causing a cold parcel of air which may descend rapidly); or
- thunderstorms.

In particular, we strongly recommend that all thunderstorms and cumulonimbus clouds be avoided. A strong downburst from the base of one of these clouds will spread out as it nears the ground. If an airplane encounters one of these on takeoff or landing, the initial effect may be an overshoot followed immediately by an extreme undershoot. You should delay the approach and hold in the vicinity until the storms move on, or divert. Takeoff should also be delayed.

Pilots are strongly encouraged to promptly report any windshear encounters. Windshear PIREPs will assist other pilots in avoiding windshear on takeoff and landing. Reports should always include a description of the effect of the shear on the airplane, such as "loss of 30 knots at 500 feet."

As well as considering the potential for windshear on final approach to land, you should also think about the possibility of wake turbulence caused by the wingtip vortices from preceding aircraft (especially heavy aircraft flying slowly at high angles of attack).

Avoid thunderstorms and cumulonimbus (Cb) clouds.

If possible, stay above the flightpath of a preceding heavy jet aircraft, and land beyond its touchdown point. Be especially cautious in light quartering tailwinds—the crosswind component can cause the upwind vortex to drift onto the runway and the tailwind component can drift the vortices into your touchdown zone.

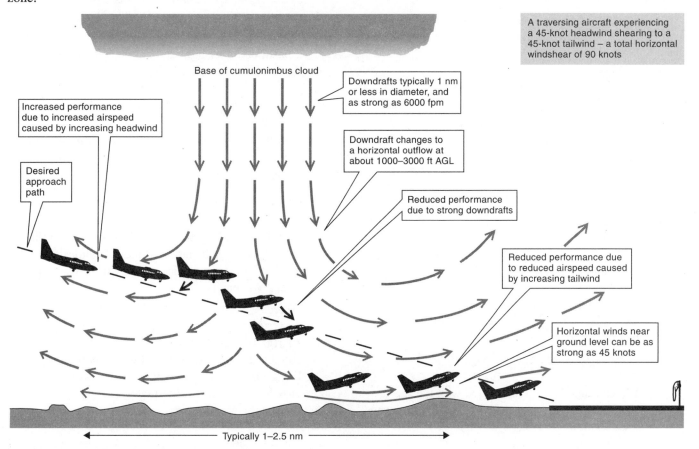

A traversing aircraft experiencing a 45-knot headwind shearing to a 45-knot tailwind – a total horizontal windshear of 90 knots

Base of cumulonimbus cloud

Downdrafts typically 1 nm or less in diameter, and as strong as 6000 fpm

Increased performance due to increased airspeed caused by increasing headwind

Downdraft changes to a horizontal outflow at about 1000–3000 ft AGL

Desired approach path

Reduced performance due to strong downdrafts

Reduced performance due to reduced airspeed caused by increasing tailwind

Horizontal winds near ground level can be as strong as 45 knots

Typically 1–2.5 nm

Figure 14-56. Avoid thunderstorms

ILS Specifications

1. Minimums for an ILS approach with all components operative normally establish a DH with a HAT of _____ feet.

➤ 200 feet

___

2. At the middle marker MM, the glideslope of a typical ILS will be approximately _____ feet above touchdown.

➤ 200 feet HAT

___

3. If all ILS components are operating and the required visual references are not established, the latest you should commence a missed approach is _____.

➤ immediately you reach the DH

___

4. Which range facility associated with the ILS is identified by the first two letters of the localizer identification group?

➤ outer compass locator

___

5. Which range facility associated with the ILS is identified by the last two letters of the localizer identification group?

➤ middle compass locator

___

6. The Pueblo, Colorado ILS RWY 26R has a coded identifier I-TFR, which in Morse code dits and dahs is _____. What coded identifier, in dits and dahs, would you expect to hear on the outer marker?

➤ *dit-dit dah dit-dit-dah-dit dit-dah-dit*, TF—*dah dit-dit-dah-dit*

___

7. What visual and aural indications will you receive on an ILS as you pass over the outer marker?

➤ a flashing blue marker light and continuous dashes (*dah-dah-dah-dah-dah*)

___

8. What visual and aural indications will you receive on an ILS as you pass over the middle marker?

➤ a flashing amber light and alternate dots and dashes (*dit-dah-dit-dah-dit-dah-dit-dah*)

___

9. What visual and aural indications will you receive on an ILS as you pass over the inner marker, if one is associated with the approach?

➤ a flashing white light and rapid dots (*dit-dit-dit-dit-dit-dit-dit-dit*)

___

For questions 10–14, refer to Figure 1.

10. At 500 feet HAT, approximately 1.9 nm from the runway, a 1 dot deviation of the ILS glideslope needle indicates a deviation above or below slope of approximately _____ feet.

➤ 70 feet

___

11. At 100 feet HAT, approximately 1300 feet horizontally from the runway, a 1 dot deviation of the ILS glideslope needle indicates a deviation above or below slope of approximately _____ feet.

➤ 14 feet

___

12. At 500 feet HAT, approximately 1.9 nm from the runway, a 1 dot deviation of the ILS localizer needle indicates a deviation left or right the localizer of approximately _____ feet.

➤ 355 feet

___

13. At 100 feet HAT, approximately 1300 feet horizontally from the runway, a 1 dot deviation of the ILS localizer needle indicates a deviation left or right of the localizer of approximately _____ feet.

➤ 215 feet

___

14. At 1.9 nm, the glideslope needle is 2 dots below its central position, and the localizer needle is 2 dots left of its central position. What is the lateral and vertical deviation from the desired flightpath?

➤ 140 feet high, and 710 feet right of the localizer

___

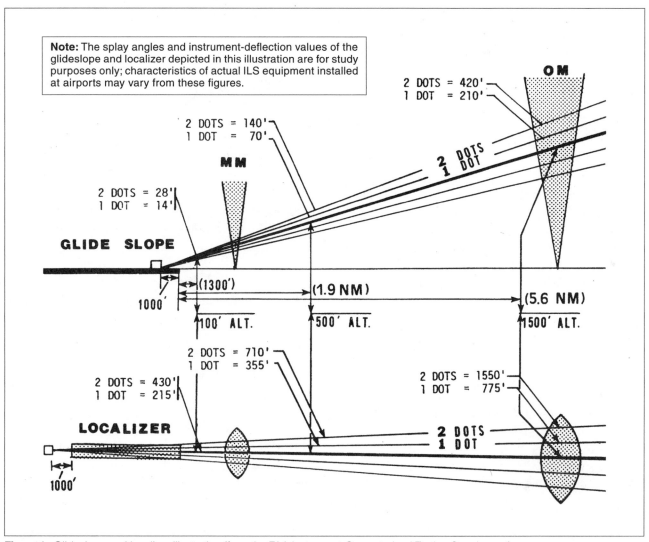

Note: The splay angles and instrument-deflection values of the glideslope and localizer depicted in this illustration are for study purposes only; characteristics of actual ILS equipment installed at airports may vary from these figures.

Figure 1. Glideslope and localizer illustration (from the FAA Instrument Computerized Testing Supplement)

15. Having become visual on an ILS approach, a typical landing minimum required is ½ sm or RVR _____ feet, where RVR stands for _____.

➤ 2400 feet, runway visual range

HSI and ILS

1. When using an HSI to fly a localizer, the better technique is to set the (inbound/outbound) localizer course, so that it is a (command/noncommand) instrument.

➤ inbound, command

2. If you accidentally set the reciprocal of the inbound localizer course on the HSI, you (will/will not) have reverse sensing; the HSI will act as a (command/noncommand) instrument. This is a (good/poor) technique.

➤ will, noncommand, poor

For questions 3–15, refer to Figures 2 and 3.

3. HSI presentation G will cause the HSI to act as a (command/noncommand) instrument; it indicates that the aircraft could be at position (1/2/3/4/7).

➤ command, 7

4. At position 4, with the HSI set correctly, the indication will be presentation (F/G/H/A).

➤ F

5. At position 6, with the HSI set correctly, the indication will be presentation (F/G/H/A).

➤ A

6. At position 11, with the HSI set correctly, the indication will be presentation (F/G/H/A).

➤ G

7. HSI presentation A corresponds to position(s) _____.

➤ 9, 6

8. HSI presentation B corresponds to position(s) _____.

➤ 5, 13

9. HSI presentation C corresponds to position(s) _____.

➤ 12

10. HSI presentation D corresponds to position(s) _____.

➤ 2

11. HSI presentation E corresponds to position(s) _____.

➤ 8, 3

12. HSI presentation F corresponds to position(s) _____.

➤ 4

13. HSI presentation G corresponds to position(s) _____.

➤ 7, 11

14. HSI presentation H corresponds to position(s) _____.

➤ 1

15. HSI presentation I corresponds to position(s) _____.

➤ 7, 11

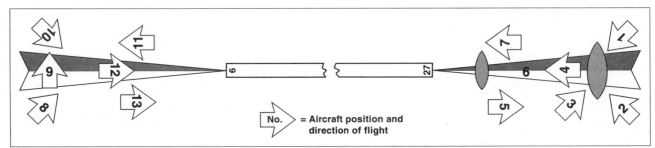

No. ⟩ = Aircraft position and direction of flight

Figure 2. 27 Localizer with back course

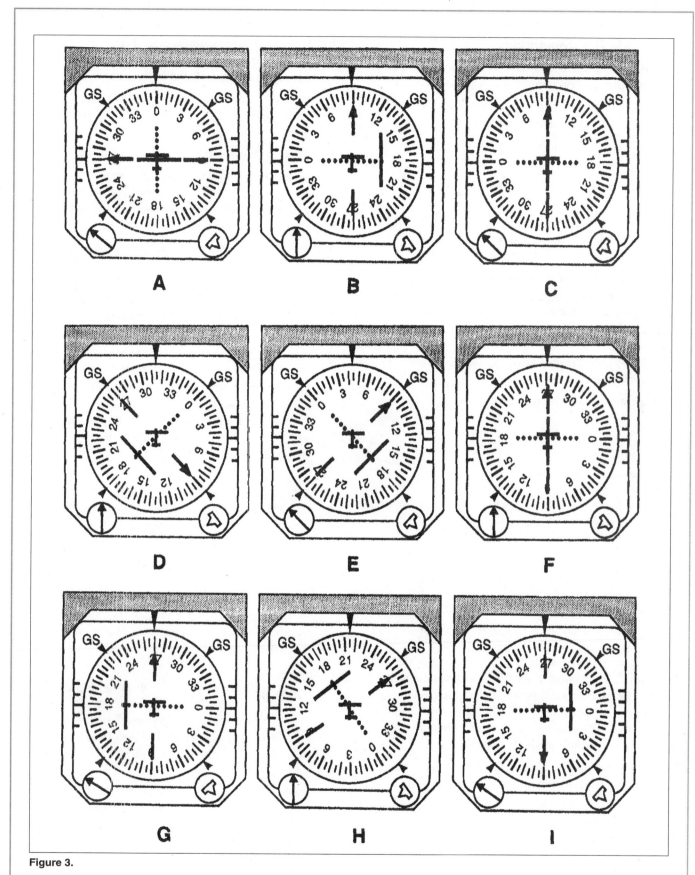

A

B

C

D

E

F

G

H

I

Figure 3.

Unusable ILS Components

1. If two components of an ILS are unusable, the appropriate minimum to use is:

    (a) the highest minimum required by any single component that is unusable.

    (b) the same minimum for the fully operational ILS.

    (c) the normal minimum plus 100 feet.

    ➤ (a)

2. What may be substituted for the ILS outer marker, if unusable? (six possibilities!)

    ➤ a compass locator, precision radar (PAR), surveillance radar (ASR), DME, VOR or a nondirectional fix authorized on the instrument approach chart.

3. What may be substituted for the ILS middle marker, if unusable?

    ➤ a compass locator, or precision radar (PAR)

4. Without the glideslope, the ILS becomes (completely unusable/a localizer approach)

    ➤ a localizer approach

5. If the glideslope of an ILS becomes unusable, the minimum is (raised/lowered/unchanged).

    ➤ raised

6. The minimums for the Durango-La Plata County, Colorado ILS/DME RWY 2 are:
    S-ILS-2 6839-½ 200 (200-½)
    S-LOC 2 6980-½ 341 (300-½)
    The ILS decision altitude is _____ feet MSL, which is approximately _____ feet above the touchdown point. If the glideslope warning flag appears after passing the final approach fix inbound, the minimum is _____ feet MSL, which is the (ILS/localizer) minimum, known as (decision height/minimum descent altitude).

    ➤ 6839 feet MSL, 200 feet HAT, 6980 feet MSL, localizer minimum, minimum descent altitude

7. If the glideslope warning flag appears after you have become visual on an ILS approach, are you permitted to continue the approach to a landing?

    ➤ yes (but recheck your minimums without a glideslope)

Flying the Approach

1. While being radar vectored, if crossing the ILS final approach course becomes imminent and an approach clearance has not been issued, what action should you take?

    ➤ maintain the assigned heading and query ATC

2. You think you will be not be able to lose sufficient height in time to commence an ILS correctly. Two options to enable you to lose the excess height are to request _____ or _____.

    ➤ a holding pattern or radar vectors

3. Ideally, drift corrections to maintain the localizer should be so accurately established before reaching the outer marker, that completion of the approach inside the outer marker should require heading changes no greater than ±_____°.

    ➤ ±2°

4. The rate of descent required to stay on an ILS glideslope depends on (true airspeed/indicated airspeed/groundspeed).

    ➤ groundspeed

5. If you reduce the indicated airspeed as you descend down an ILS glidepath in steady wind conditions, you would expect to (increase/decrease/not alter) the rate of descent to stay on slope.

    ➤ decrease (because of the lower groundspeed)

6. You are on slope, glideslope needle and localizer needle both centered, but 10 knots too fast. Your initial correction should be to adjust (power/pitch attitude).

    ➤ power

7. If you fly into a steadily decreasing headwind, then your ground speed will (increase/decrease/stay the same), and to stay on the ILS glideslope the rate of descent should be (increased/decreased/unchanged).

➤ increase, increased

8. When passing through an abrupt windshear which involves a shift from a tailwind to a headwind, your airspeed will tend to (increase/decrease/stay the same). To maintain a constant airspeed, power will initially have to be (increased/decreased) for a brief period.

➤ increase, decreased

9. When passing through an abrupt windshear which involves a shift from a headwind to a tailwind, your airspeed will tend to (increase/decrease/stay the same). To maintain a constant airspeed, power will initially have to be (increased/decreased) for a brief period.

➤ decrease, increased

10. While flying a 3° glideslope, a headwind shears to a tailwind. Airspeed will tend to (increase/decrease). Pitch attitude will tend to (increase/decrease). There will be a tendency to go (above/below) slope.

➤ airspeed and pitch attitude will decrease, tendency to go below slope

11. While flying a 3° glideslope, a tailwind shears to a headwind. Airspeed will tend to (increase/decrease). Pitch attitude will tend to (increase/decrease). There will be a tendency to go (above/below) slope.

➤ airspeed and pitch attitude will increase, tendency to go above slope

12. Describe what power management would normally be required to maintain a constant indicated airspeed and ILS glideslope when passing through an abrupt windshear which involves a shift from a tailwind to a headwind. Compared to an approach in calm conditions, the power setting:
   – before the shear is encountered will be (higher than/lower than/the same as) normal.
   – when the shear is encountered will be (higher than/lower than/the same as) normal.
   – after the shear is encountered will be (higher than/lower than/the same as) normal.

➤ lower than, lower than (a further decrease), higher than

13. Windshear can occur (only near ground level/at any level).

➤ at any level

14. If you do not become visual, the latest point at which you should commence the missed approach is at the _____ on the glideslope.

➤ decision height

Lighting, and Precision Instrument Runway Markings

1. The usual glideslope angle for an on-slope VASI indication is _____°.

➤ 3°

2. The on-slope indications of a 2-bar VASI are top bar (white/red) and bottom bar (white/red).

➤ top bar red, bottom bar white

3. The too-high indications of a 2-bar VASI are top bar (white/red) and bottom bar (white/red).

➤ top bar white, bottom bar white

4. The too-low indications of a 2-bar VASI are top bar (white/red) and bottom bar (white/red).

➤ top bar red, bottom bar red

5. The on-slope indications for the pilot of a small aircraft on a 3-bar VASI are top bar (white/red), middle bar (red/white) and bottom bar (white/red).

➤ top bar red, middle bar red, bottom bar white

6. The slightly too-high indications for the pilot of a small aircraft on a 3-bar VASI are top bar (white/red), middle bar (red/white) and bottom bar (white/red).

➤ top bar red, middle bar white, bottom bar white

7. The grossly too-high indications for the pilot of a small aircraft on a 3-bar VASI are top bar (white/red), middle bar (red/white) and bottom bar (white/red).

➤ top bar white, middle bar white, bottom bar white

8. The too-low indications for the pilot of a small aircraft on a 3-bar VASI are top bar (white/red), middle bar (red/white) and bottom bar (white/red).

➤ top bar red, middle bar red, bottom bar red

9. The pilot of a long-bodied airplane should treat the (top/bottom) two bars of a 3-bar VASI as a 2-bar VASI and neglect the (top/bottom) bar.

➤ top, bottom

10. The on-slope indications for the pilot of a long-bodied aircraft on a 3-bar VASI are top bar (white/red), middle bar (red/white) and bottom bar (white/red).

➤ top bar red, middle bar white, bottom bar white

11. If you are at a safe altitude with respect to obstacle clearance, for instance at the MDA, and all bars of a 3-bar VASI appear red, you should (make a missed approach/fly level until you intercept the slope, then descend).

➤ fly level until you intercept the slope, then descend

12. You have flown an ILS, become visual, and are using the VASI when the glideslope fails. You (may continue/must make a missed approach).

➤ may continue

13. A VASI provides safe guidance over obstacles in the approach path within plus or minus ____° of the extended runway centerline out to a distance of ____ nm.

➤ ±10°, 4 nm

14. The tri-color VASI shows ____ when the aircraft is above slope.

➤ amber

15. The tri-color VASI shows ____ when the aircraft is on slope.

➤ green

16. The tri-color VASI shows ____ when the aircraft is below slope.

➤ red

17. PAPI lights are white-white-red-red: you are (well above/above/on/below/well below) slope. The usual slope is ____°.

➤ on, 3°

18. PAPI lights are white-red-red-red: you are (well above/above/on/below/well below) slope. Your slope is likely to be ____°.

➤ below, 2.8°

19. PAPI lights are red-red-red-red: you are (well above/above/on/below/well below) slope. Your slope is likely to be ____°.

➤ well below, below 2.5°

20. PAPI lights are white-white-white-red: you are (well above/above/on/below/well below) slope. Your slope is likely to be ____°.

➤ above, 3.2°

21. PAPI lights are white-white-white-white: you are (well above/above/on/ below/well below) slope. Your slope is likely to be _____°.

➤ well above, above 3.5°

22. Synchronized flashing white lights specifically installed at an airport to enable you to identify the runway end on approach in reduced visibility are known as _____ identifier lights, abbreviated to _____.

➤ runway end identifier lights, REIL

23. On a precision approach runway, the distance from the approach threshold to the touchdown zone marker is _____ feet.

➤ 500 feet

24. On a precision approach runway, the distance from the approach threshold to the fixed distance marker is _____ feet.

➤ 1000 feet

25. On a precision approach runway, the distance from the beginning of the touchdown zone marker to the beginning of the fixed distance marker is _____ feet.

➤ 500 feet

26. A displaced threshold on an instrument runway is indicated by _____ leading to the threshold mark.

➤ arrows

27. A displaced threshold (is/is not) available for taxiing.

➤ is

28. A displaced threshold (is/is not) available for takeoff.

➤ is

29. A displaced threshold (is/is not) available for landing.

➤ is not

30. A displaced threshold at the runway stopping end (is/is not) available for landing rollout.

➤ is

31. At night you taxi out onto the end of a runway with the green displaced threshold lights visible ahead. You (may/must not) commence takeoff before you reach these lights.

➤ may

32. RVR represents (horizontal range down the runway/slant range down approach).

➤ horizontal range down the runway

33. Runway visibility $\frac{1}{2}$ sm is approx RVR _____.

➤ 2400 feet RVR

Simultaneous Approaches

1. When simultaneous approaches are in progress, you should listen out on (tower/approach) frequency for radar advisories.

➤ tower

2. Simultaneous approaches can only be made when there is at least _____ feet between the centerlines of the parallel runways.

➤ 4300 feet

The Sidestep Maneuver

1. You are cleared for the ILS Runway 7-left approach, sidestep to Runway 7-right. When should you commence the sidestep maneuver?

➤ as soon as you are visual and have the runway environment in sight

2. The sidestep maneuver may only be performed when the landing parallel runway is displaced (at least/not more than) _____ feet from the runway on which the precision approach aid is aligned.

➤ not more than 1200 feet

LDA, SDF and ILS Approaches

1. The width of an LDA course and a normal localizer course is approximately _____°.

➤ 5°

2. A normal localizer course (is/is not) aligned with the runway.

➤ is

3. An LDA course (is/is not) aligned with the runway.

➤ is not

4. The LDA (does/does not) provide glideslope guidance.

➤ does not

5. The SDF is (less/more) precise than the LDA.

➤ less

6. The width of an SDF course is either _____° or _____°.

➤ 6° or 12°

7. The SDF course (is/may not be) aligned with the runway.

➤ may not be

8. The SDF (does/does not) provide glideslope guidance.

➤ does not

9. A localizer front course with an associated glideslope is called an _____ system, or _____.

➤ instrument landing system, ILS

10. A localizer back course (may/will not) have an associated glideslope.

➤ will not

MLS Approaches

1. An MLS system has a _____-letter coded identifier beginning with the letter _____.

➤ 4-letter coded identifier, M

2. The MLS approach azimuth guidance angle coverage extends to at least _____ feet HAA.

➤ 20,000 feet HAA

3. MLS lateral approach angle is at least _____° either side of the extended runway centerline.

➤ at least 40°

4. MLS front and back guidance extends to at least _____ nm from the landing runway.

➤ at least 20 nm in front and 7 nm back

Area navigation (RNAV) allows you to fly point to point on a direct course without having to overfly ground-based radio aids. Instead of flying from VORTAC to VORTAC along Victor airways on what might be a circuitous route, you can fly direct from your departure airport to the destination airport, or from waypoint to waypoint, using RNAV. A **waypoint** is a predetermined geographical position usually specified by latitude and longitude, or by radial and distance from a VORTAC, and used to define an RNAV route or instrument approach.

Some RNAV systems can define a waypoint internally by the pilot inserting latitude and longitude into the computer, and then deriving data from navigation systems such as LORAN, inertial navigation systems (INS), VLF/Omega systems, and Doppler radar; other RNAV systems define waypoints relative to a VORTAC, using radial and distance (or latitude and longitude) to create "phantom" VORTACs, known as pseudo-VORTACs.

RNAV using Pseudo-VORTACs

Many general aviation aircraft have a course line computer system which, when used in conjunction with the VHF-NAV radio selected to a VORTAC, can electronically *relocate* that VORTAC, so that a pseudo-VORTAC is created at any desired waypoint. It does this by electronically adding a vector (radial and distance) to the position of the actual VORTAC.

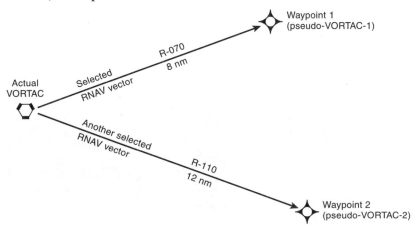

Figure 15-1. Electronically creating a "phantom" VORTAC

You can locate pseudo-VORTACs wherever you like, provided they are within signal reception range of the parent VORTAC, and thereby create a series of waypoints along your desired route.

The normal VHF-NAV receiver is selected to the parent VORTAC, and the computer is programmed to electronically add the vector (radial and distance) to received VORTAC signals. How this is done depends on the actual equipment in the cockpit—refer to equipment information in your Pilots Operating Handbook.

The **course deviation indicator (CDI)** in the cockpit receives its input via the computer, and indicates deviation from course between the waypoints—not an angular deviation as for normal VOR flying, but a lateral deviation in nautical miles, or fractions thereof. A 1 dot deviation of the CDI might be 1 nm off course during the en route phase; in the approach mode, a 1 dot deviation might be 0.25 nm off course.

The course between waypoints is maintained by keeping the CDI centered. Because it indicates *lateral* deviation in nautical miles, known as **crosstrack deviation**, rather than *angular* deviation, there is no "funneling" effect using the RNAV CDI. (Normal VOR tracking is 2° deviation per dot; normal localizer tracking is 0.5° per dot.) Distance to the waypoint is shown on the normal DME indicator.

The waypoints can normally be preset on the RNAV equipment, and then instantaneously recalled as you need them. As the flight progresses, you will proceed through the waypoints in order, keeping within signal range of each parent VORTAC by flying at a suitable altitude and distance from it. If the usable signal range is exceeded, the CDI OFF flag will show.

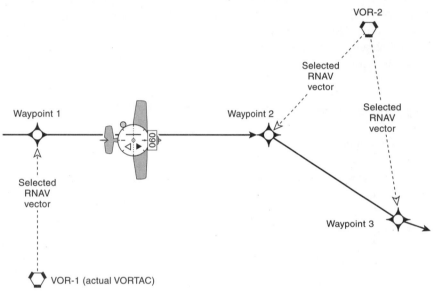

Figure 15-2. Tracking between waypoints

Typical RNAV systems can provide you with:

• crosstrack deviation from the selected course in nautical miles with TO/FROM information;

• distance to the waypoint in nautical miles;

• groundspeed in knots;

• time-to-waypoint in minutes.

Figure 15-3. A typical RNAV display

RNAV DPs and Approaches

An approved RNAV receiver is required for you to fly an RNAV approach, which is a nonprecision approach, and is flown like a VOR/DME approach, down to a minimum descent altitude (MDA).

Each RNAV approach must have at least two waypoints, but there are generally more. These waypoints should be preset, and then recalled as you need them. The RNAV waypoints are defined on the charts by both:

• latitude and longitude (expressed in order of keypad insertion); and

• radial and distance from the parent VORTAC.

The missed approach point (MAP) on an RNAV approach is indicated when
the TO flag changes to FROM, at which point you must commence the missed
approach procedure if you do not have the runway environment in view.

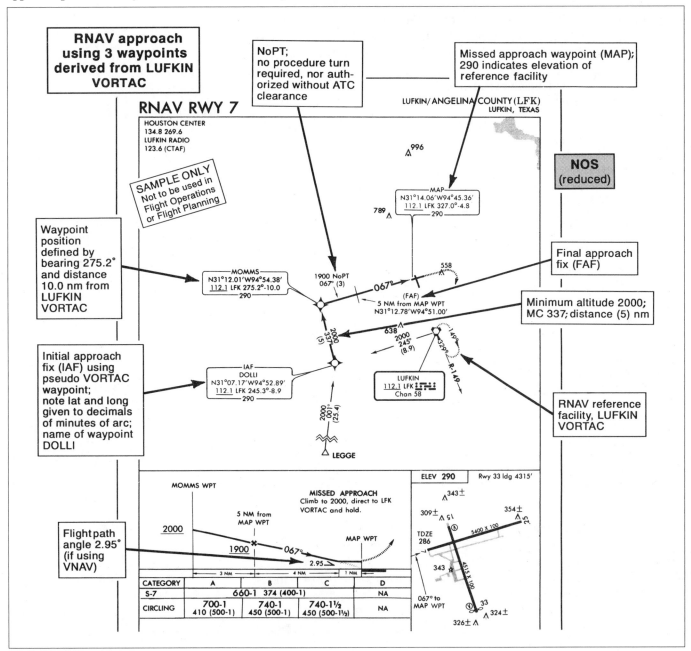

Figure 15-4. Lufkin/Angelina County (Texas) RNAV Rwy 7 approach

Note: Some advanced RNAV systems provide a vertical navigation (VNAV)
capability—in other words, three-dimensional area navigation. It may be
used en route, or it may be used in the approach phase to provide a particular flight path angle (FPA) to the runway, shown on the chart under the
final approach path. Most general aviation RNAV systems do not have
VNAV capability with their usual LNAV (lateral or horizontal navigation)
capability.

RNAV using LORAN

LORAN is a long-range navigation system originally designed for maritime use. In earlier days, it required rather complicated charts, a large table to spread them out on, and a trained navigator to interpret the LORAN signals and plot the position on the chart—obviously not a perfect system for small aircraft. However, the development of the microprocessor has changed that. What were complicated calculations are now performed automatically at high speed and with great accuracy, with position and other information presented to the pilot in the cockpit in digital form.

The cost of the equipment is within the range of the small aircraft owner, and so LORAN was a popular means of light aircraft navigation in the United States, particularly during the 1980s and early 1990s.

The LORAN-C system is a *hyperbolic* system. It measures the difference in time of arrival of radio pulses from a chain of transmitters which are separated by hundreds of miles. One station is the master station, and the others are secondary stations whose signals are synchronized with those from the master station.

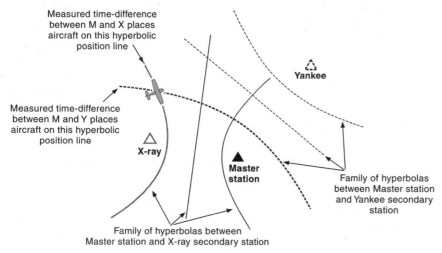

Figure 15-5. LORAN-C computes position using hyperbolas

The time-difference between the arrival of the various pulses from different directions allows the microprocessor to compute the position of the aircraft. All points having the same time-difference between pulses from two stations lie on a curve known as a hyperbola. With signals from a number of stations, more than one hyperbolic position line is known, and the intersection of two or more of these hyperbolas defines the position of the aircraft.

There are six LORAN chains providing good signal coverage over the United States. Normal accuracy is to 0.25 nm.

The capability of microprocessor technology is utilized in LORAN receivers to provide you with many pieces of information—in fact, so much that you must discriminate and only access what you need.

There are differences between LORAN sets from various manufacturers, but a typical LORAN set can provide you with:

- position (as latitude/longitude or radial/distance);
- track and groundspeed;
- wind speed and direction (using MH and TAS data);
- crosstrack error (lateral deviation from course in nautical miles);
- estimated time en route;

- memory storage of all airports, airspace and radio navigation aids in the United States, plus anything else that you care to add;
- Victor airways specifications with MEAs and MOCAs;
- course and distance to any selected point (no matter how far)—useful when considering diverting to an alternate airport; and
- an alert signal to warn you of an impending penetration of Class B or Class C airspace.

LORAN has been approved by the FAA as an en route navigation aid as well as for a number of nonprecision instrument approach procedures. Refer to the Aircraft Flight Manual supplement of your aircraft to determine the approval status of its LORAN equipment. LORAN equipment is typically certified as: basic VFR only, IFR (en route and terminal), or IFR (en route, terminal and approach).

Figure 15-6. A typical LORAN set

Global Positioning Systems (GPS)

Precise point-to-point navigation is now possible using satellite navigation systems that can compute aircraft position and height accurately by comparing signals from a global network of navigation satellites. The first global positioning systems (GPS) were designed for the U.S. Department of Defense, but in the early 1990s the government made GPS available for civil use.

Basically, three elements make up GPS:

1. a space element, consisting of a constellation of satellites orbiting the earth every 12 hours in six orbital planes, from an altitude of 11,000 nm (21,300 km);
2. a satellite control ground network responsible for orbital accuracy and control; and
3. a navigation receiver in the aircraft (many are small enough to be hand-held) capable of receiving and identifying several satellites at a time.

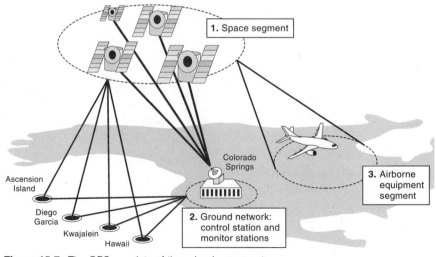

Figure 15-7. The GPS consists of three basic segments

Each satellite transmits its own computer code packet on frequency 1575.42 MHz (for civilian use), 1000 times a second. The satellite constellation typically guarantees that at least four satellites are in view and usable for positioning at any one time, from any position on earth. GPS equipment pinpoints an aircraft's horizontal position in lat-long coordinates, similar to other long-range navigation systems, such as VLF/Omega, and then, in the case of most aviation units, turns the information into a graphical moving map display of the aircraft's position in relation to surrounding airspace on an LCD or CRT screen. Most GPS receivers can also display a CDI presentation, along with groundspeed, time and distance to the next waypoint and the current altitude of the aircraft.

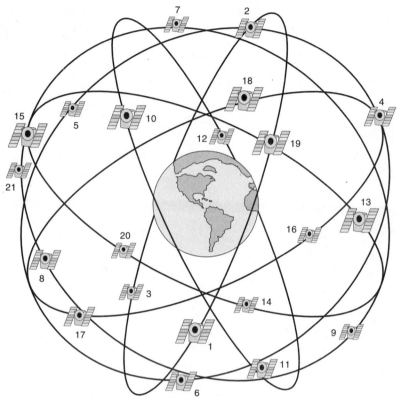

Figure 15-8. The relative orbital position of GPS satellites

Figure 15-9. Signals from satellites are received to establish an aircraft's position

GPS units have been approved for both en route and approach navigation, but, as with LORAN, not all units are approved for IFR use. IFR units must have their databases updated on a regular basis to remain IFR certified.

Nonprecision GPS approaches are available at most U.S. airports today. Precision GPS approaches, using a ground station to augment the satellite signals, were being researched in the late 1990s.

Some manufacturers have produced **navigation management systems**, which combine GPS, multi-chain LORAN and onboard fuel/air data sensors for light aircraft. Typical GPS panels are shown in Figure 15-10.

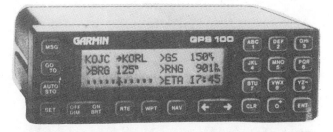

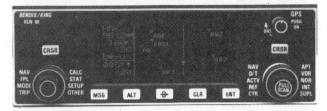

Figure 15-10. GPS and nav management receivers

✍ Review 15

1. A pseudo-VORTAC is a (real/phantom) VORTAC.
   ➤ phantom

2. A pseudo-VORTAC can be created (anywhere/anywhere within signal coverage).
   ➤ anywhere within signal coverage

3. A pseudo-VORTAC is created by electronically adding a _____ to the position of the real VORTAC.
   ➤ vector

4. The CDI, when being used as part of an RNAV system, displays (angular deviation/crosstrack error).
   ➤ crosstrack error

5. The fixes along an off-airways route are known as _____.
   ➤ waypoints

6. A predetermined geographical position used for an RNAV route or an RNAV instrument approach is called a _____.
   ➤ waypoint

7. LORAN-C uses time-difference measurement from widely separated LORAN stations to fix position using (parabolic/hyperbolic/straight/circular) position lines.
   ➤ hyperbolic

8. How can you determine if your LORAN-C or GPS equipped airplane is approved for IFR operations?
   ➤ by reference to the Aircraft Flight Manual supplement

Refer to Figure 1 for Questions 9–22.

9. On which radio navigation aid is this approach based, and how many waypoints must you insert?
   ➤ ETX VORTAC, 3 waypoints (ZARDO, MYRON, and MAP)

10. Approaching from the southeast, the more appropriate IAF is _____.
    ➤ ZARDO

11. To reverse direction at ZARDO for the inbound final approach course you should _____.
    ➤ make a holding pattern entry

12. The final approach course is MC _____, and the distance from ZARDO to the runway threshold is _____ nm.
    ➤ MC 067, 7 nm

13. Passing ZARDO, to what altitude can you descend?
    ➤ 1900 feet MSL

14. The minimums for a straight-in landing are MDA _____ feet MSL, which is _____ feet (HAT/HAA), visibility _____ (sm/nm).
    ➤ MDA 1400 feet MSL, 1006 feet HAT, vis 11/4 sm

15. The minimums for a circling approach to Rwy 32 are MDA _____ feet MSL, which is _____ feet (HAT/HAA), visibility _____ (sm/nm).
    ➤ MDA 1400 feet MSL, 1001 feet HAA, vis 11/4 sm

16. At what point are you able to descend to the MDA?
    ➤ after passing MYRON waypoint

17. The CDI indicates deviation in (degrees/fractions of a nautical mile).
    ➤ fractions of a nautical mile

18. The MAP is on the ETX _____ radial at _____ DME.
    ➤ R-104.7, 8.7 DME

19. Passing the MAP is indicated by _____.
    ➤ the TO flag changing to FROM

20. Following a missed approach, you should hold at the _____.

➤ ETX VORTAC

21. If you have VNAV, the FPA is _____°.

➤ 3.05°

22. What is the touchdown zone elevation (TDZE) for Rwy 7?

➤ 394 feet MSL

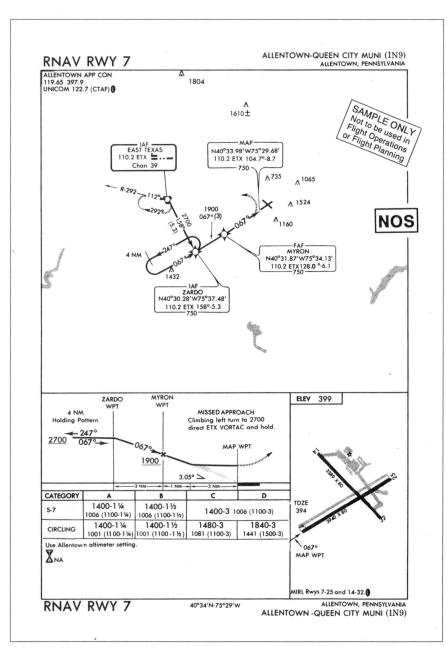

Figure 1. Allentown RNAV Rwy 7

VHF Direction Finding (DF) **16**

General Principle

Some airports are equipped with special radio antennas that can sense the direction of normal VHF-COM signals received from an airplane. These signals may be voice communications from the pilot, or simply transmissions made by pressing the transmit button on the microphone (carrier wave signals only).

Directional information is presented to the air traffic controller as a radial line on a cathode ray tube similar to a radar screen or, in the case of the most modern VDF equipment, as an accurate digital readout of bearing. The controller can then advise the pilot of his bearing relative to the airport, or provide him with a series of headings to steer toward the airport, known as DF steers.

Figure 16-1. VHF direction finding antennas at Santa Barbara airport

If simultaneous bearings are available from two or more VDF stations, then ATC can determine the actual position of the airplane, known as a DF fix. This procedure is known as very high frequency direction finding, and is often abbreviated to VHF D/F, VDF or simply DF.

An advantage of VDF is that no special airborne equipment is required other than a normal VHF communications radio, although it does require a special installation at the airport. Two typical designs for airport VDF antennas are the H-type antenna (a double-H dipole antenna in technical terms), or the Doppler-type VDF antenna.

VDF ground equipment from years ago was known as a "manual homer". It used an ADF-type null-seeking antenna that the operator had to rotate manually to determine the direction of the airplane. It also required long transmissions from the pilot while the operator sought the null position.

Modern equipment is fully automatic, with the ground operator having the direction of the airplane displayed to him automatically following only a short VHF-COM transmission from the pilot.

Using VDF

The VHF direction finder can help a pilot without him even being aware of its operation. It is used by ATC in locating and directing lost aircraft, and in helping to identify aircraft already on radar.

Bearing to a station is the most usual bearing requested by pilots. It is the heading to steer direct to the VDF station, provided no crosswind exists. In a crosswind, however, a wind correction angle must be used if a reasonably straight track is to be achieved, rather than homing. ATC can allow for this with their DF steers as they monitor the flightpath of the airplane. VDF is used like a simple radar.

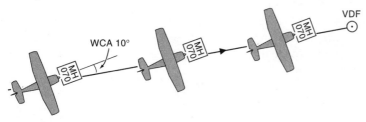

Figure 16-2. Tracking efficiently to a VDF ground station

In a distress or urgency situation, ATC may even be able to provide a DF instrument approach. Such a situation could involve a non-instrument pilot caught above a cloud layer and requiring descent to an airport. The DF specialist would provide him with DF steers, and tell him when to commence descent. The aim is to achieve maximum flight stability with small turns and wings-level descents.

The DF instrument approach in IFR conditions is considered an emergency procedure, but there is no reason why you should not request a practice one in VFR conditions at a suitably equipped airport (see your A/FD). The DF instrument approaches are not published in charts available to pilots.

✐ Review 16

VHF Direction Finding (DF)

1. The letters VDF stand for _____.
➤ VHF direction finding

2. VDF (is/is not) radar.
➤ is not

3. The airborne radio used for VDF is the (ADF/ VHF-NAV/VHF-COM).
➤ VHF-COM

4. A heading provided by ATC using VDF is known as a _____.
➤ DF steer

5. A VDF instrument approach in IFR conditions (is/is not) considered an emergency procedure.
➤ is

IFR Meteorology Section Three

17 **Icing** 371

18 **Visibility** 379

19 **Clouds** 387

20 **Thunderstorms** 401

21 **High-Level Meteorology** 415

22 **Wind, Air Masses and Fronts** 419

23 **Weather Reports and Forecasts** 431

Icing 17

Ice accretion on an airplane structure or within the engine induction system can significantly reduce flight safety by causing:

- **adverse aerodynamic effects**—ice buildup on the airframe structure can modify the airflow pattern around airfoils (wings and propeller blades), leading to a serious loss of lift and an increase in drag; ice/snow or frost has a thickness and/or roughness similar to medium or coarse sandpaper, and on the leading edge and upper surface of a wing it can reduce lift by as much as 50%, and increase drag also by as much as 50%;

- **a loss of engine power, or complete stoppage**, if ice blocks the engine air intake or carburetor ice forms;

- **a weight increase and a change in the CG position of the airplane,** as well as unbalancing of the various control surfaces and the propeller, perhaps causing severe vibration and/or control difficulties;

- **blockage of the pitot tube and/or static vent**, producing errors in the cockpit pressure instruments (airspeed indicator, altimeter, vertical speed indicator);

- **degradation in radio communications and radio navigation** (if ice forms on the antennas); and

- **loss of visibility** (if ice forms on the windshield).

The possibility of icing conditions can be determined from weather forecasts and prognostic charts, but the most accurate information on icing conditions, both current and forecast, can be obtained from PIREPs (pilot reports), SIGMETs (weather advisories that warn of conditions that could be dangerous to all aircraft) and AIRMETs (that warn of hazards primarily for small aircraft).

Structural Icing

For ice to form on the aircraft structure, two conditions must be satisfied:

- there must be visible moisture; and
- the temperature must be at or below freezing (0°C).

Aerodynamic cooling can lower the temperature of the airplane structure below that of the surrounding air by a few degrees, however, making it possible for ice to form on the structure even though the ambient air temperature is still a few degrees above freezing—so be on the watch for structural icing when the air temperature is below about +5°C and you are flying in visible moisture.

Temperature usually decreases in the atmosphere as you climb. The altitude where the temperature has fallen to 0°C is known as the **freezing level**, and it is possible to estimate this level, at least approximately.

The rate at which temperature falls with altitude (known as the **lapse rate**) depends on a number of variables, but the standard (average) lapse rate is a temperature decrease of 2°C for every 1000 feet of altitude gained. For instance, if the air temperature is +8°C at 5000 feet MSL, then you would need to climb approximately 4000 feet for the temperature to fall to 0°C, and so the freezing level in this case is at 9000 feet MSL.

Icing can be extremely hazardous to aircraft.

PIREPs, SIGMETs and AIRMETs provide the most accurate icing information.

There must be visible moisture and near or below freezing temperatures before ice can form.

In general terms, the worst continuous icing conditions are usually found near the freezing level in heavy stratified clouds or in rain, with icing possible up to 5000 feet higher, but rarely above this where the droplets in the clouds are already frozen. In cumuliform clouds with strong updrafts, however, large water droplets may be carried to high altitudes making structural icing a possibility up to high altitudes.

Clear Ice

Clear ice is the most dangerous form of structural icing. It is most likely to form when you are flying through *freezing rain*, which consists of raindrops that spread out and freeze on contact with the cold airplane.

It is possible for liquid water drops to exist in the atmosphere at temperatures well below the normal freezing point of water (0°C), possibly at –20°C or even lower. These are known as *supercooled* drops, and can occur when rain falls from air warmer than 0°C into a subzero layer of air beneath. Supercooled drops are in an unstable state, and will freeze on contact with a subzero surface—the skin of an airplane, or the propeller blades, for example.

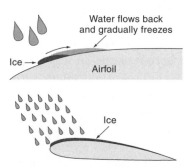

Figure 17-1. Clear ice formed from large, supercooled water drops

Each drop will freeze gradually because of the latent heat released in the freezing process, which allows part of the water drop to spread backward before it freezes. The slower the freezing process, the greater the spread-back of the water before it freezes. The spread-back is greatest at temperatures just below freezing. The result is a sheet of solid, clear, glazed ice with very little air enclosed.

The surface of clear ice is smooth, usually with undulations and lumps. It is quite tenacious but, if it does break off, it could be in large chunks capable of doing damage.

Clear ice can alter the aerodynamic shape of airfoils quite dramatically and reduce or destroy their effectiveness. Along with the increased weight, this creates a hazard to safety.

A good indication to a pilot that freezing rain may exist at higher altitudes is the presence of ice pellets, formed by rain falling from warmer air and freezing on the way down through colder air. Wet snow, however, indicates subzero temperatures at some higher altitude, and warmer air at your level. The snow that formed in the subzero air above is now melting to form wet snow as it passes through your level.

Rime Ice

Rime ice occurs when tiny, supercooled liquid water droplets freeze on contact with a surface of subzero temperature. Because the drops are small, the amount of water remaining after the initial freezing is insufficient to coalesce into a continuous sheet before freezing. The result is a mixture of tiny ice particles and trapped air, giving a rough, opaque, crystalline deposit that is fairly brittle.

Rime ice is the most common form of icing.

Rime ice often forms on leading edges and can affect the aerodynamic qualities of an airfoil or the airflow into the engine intake. It does cause a significant increase in weight.

Mixed (or Cloudy) Ice

Rain falling from clouds may consist of drops of many sizes. A mixture of clear ice (from large drops) and rime ice (from small drops) may result. This is known as *mixed ice,* (referred to in some countries as *cloudy ice*).

Frost

Frost forms when moist air comes in contact with a subzero-temperature surface. The water vapor, rather than condensing to form "liquid" water, changes directly to ice in the form of frost. This is a white crystalline coating that can usually be brushed off.

Frost remaining on the wings is especially dangerous during takeoff. It may disturb the airflow sufficiently to prevent the airplane from becoming airborne at its normal takeoff speed, or prevent it from becoming airborne at all.

Frost can form in clear air when the airplane is parked in subzero temperatures or when the airplane flies from subzero temperatures into warmer moist air—for example, on descent, or when climbing through a temperature inversion (where temperature increases with altitude).

Although frost is not as dangerous as clear ice, it can obscure vision through a cockpit window and can possibly affect the lifting characteristics of the wings, which can be extremely serious. Although frost does not alter the basic aerodynamic shape of the wing (like clear ice does), frost can disrupt the smooth airflow over the wing, causing early separation of the airflow from the upper surface of the wing and a consequent loss of lift.

Frost on the wings during takeoff may disturb the airflow sufficiently to prevent the airplane from becoming airborne at its normal takeoff speed, or prevent it from becoming airborne at all.

Structural Icing and Cloud Type

Cumulus-type clouds nearly always consist predominantly of liquid water droplets at temperatures down to about –20°C, below which either liquid-drops or ice-crystals may predominate. Newly formed parts of the clouds will tend to contain more liquid drops than in mature parts. The risk of airframe icing is severe in these clouds in the range 0°C to –20°C, and moderate to severe in the range –20° to –40°C, with only a small chance of structural icing below –40°C.

Since there is a lot of vertical motion in convective clouds, the composition of the clouds may vary considerably at the one level, and the risk of icing may exist throughout a wide altitude band in (and under) the clouds. Updrafts will tend to carry the water droplets higher and increase their size. If significant structural icing does occur, it may be necessary to descend into warmer air.

Stratiform clouds usually consist entirely or predominantly of liquid water drops down to about –15°C, with a risk of structural icing. If significant icing is a possibility, it may be advisable to fly at a lower level where the temperature is above 0°C, or at a higher level where the temperature is colder than –15°C. In certain conditions, such as stratiform clouds associated with an active front or with orographic uplift, the risk of icing is increased at temperatures lower than usual; continuous upward motion of air generally means a greater retention of liquid water in the clouds.

Raindrops and drizzle from any type of clouds will freeze if they meet an airplane whose surface is below 0°C, with a severe risk of clear ice forming the bigger the water droplets are. You need to be cautious when flying in rain at freezing temperatures. This could occur for instance when flying in the cool sector underlying the warmer air of a warm front from which rain is falling.

Structural icing is most likely to accumulate rapidly on an airplane in conditions of *freezing rain*, for instance when flying in below-freezing air underneath the surface of a warm front from which rain is falling.

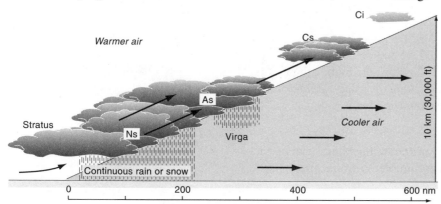

Figure 17-2. Danger area beneath a warm front

High-level clouds, such as cirrus, with their bases above 20,000 feet, are usually composed of ice crystals which will not freeze onto the airplane, and so the risk of structural icing is only slight in these clouds.

Structural icing is most likely to accumulate rapidly on an airplane in conditions of freezing rain, for instance when flying in below-freezing air underneath the surface of a warm front from which rain is falling.

Induction Icing

Carburetor Icing

Ice can form in the carburetor and induction system of an engine in moist air with outside air temperatures as high as +25°C (or even higher). It will disturb or prevent the flow of air and fuel into the engine, causing it to lose power, run roughly and perhaps even stop.

Cooling occurs when the induction air expands as it passes through the venturi in the carburetor (adiabatic cooling), and occurs also as the fuel vaporizes (absorbing the latent heat of vaporization). This can easily reduce what was initially quite warm air to a temperature well below zero and, if the air is moist, ice will form.

Throttle icing is more likely to occur at lower power settings when the partially closed butterfly creates a greater venturi cooling effect, compared with high power settings when the butterfly is more open and the venturi effect is less.

Carburetor ice can even form on a warm day in moist air.

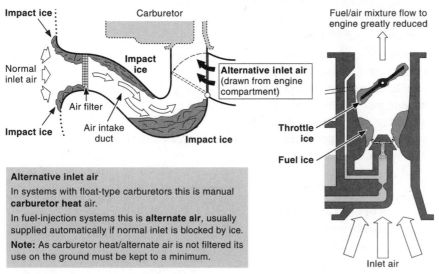

Figure 17-3. Carburetor ice

Most airplanes whose engines have carburetors are fitted with a **carburetor heat** control that can direct hot air from around the engine into the carburetor, instead of the ambient air. Being hot, the air should be able to melt the ice and prevent further ice from forming. The correct method of using carburetor heat for your airplane is found in the Pilot's Operating Handbook.

Engine Intake Icing

Structural icing near the engine air intake at subzero temperatures can restrict the airflow into the induction system and cause problems. Some aircraft have an alternate air system in case this occurs.

Instrument Icing

Icing of the pitot-static system can affect the readings of the pressure-operated flight instruments (the airspeed indicator, the altimeter, and the VSI). If the airplane has a pitot heater, then use it when appropriate.

Hints on Flying in Icing Conditions

Use all available information, such as forecasts and PIREPs, to plan your flight so that you avoid areas of icing, unless your airplane is equipped with de-icing or anti-icing equipment. Flight into known icing conditions is not authorized if the aircraft is not certified for flight into known icing.

Check that all the aircraft's airfoils are clean prior to takeoff. Frost, and indeed any contamination, should be removed from the wings and other lifting surfaces prior to flight if they are to produce lift efficiently.

If taxiing or taking off in below-freezing temperatures, avoid splashing water or slush onto the airplane, since it could freeze onto the structure. Always check full-and-free movement of the controls prior to commencing the takeoff roll.

Use de-icing and anti-icing equipment as recommended in icing conditions. If they are not adequate, then change course or altitude to fly out of icing conditions as quickly as possible. Consider making a 180° turn. Carry a little extra airspeed to give an added margin over what could be an increased stalling speed, and avoid abrupt maneuvers. Be alert for incorrect readings from the pressure instruments (airspeed indicator, altimeter, vertical speed indicator) if pitot heat is not available in your airplane.

Avoid cumuliform clouds if possible, since clear ice may occur at any altitude above the freezing level. If icing-up in stratiform clouds, either descend to warmer air above freezing, or climb to colder air well below freezing, say – 10°C or less. If descending, think carefully of the terrain below, and how far you will have to descend to fly into warmer air.

If icing-up in freezing rain, either climbing or descending may take you into warmer air. Act quickly and decisively before the build-up of clear ice is so great that it causes a significant deterioration in the airplane's performance.

Warning!

Ice of any type on the airframe or propeller, or in the carburetor and induction system, deserves the pilot's immediate attention and removal. Wings which are contaminated by ice prior to takeoff will lengthen the takeoff run because of the higher speed needed to fly—a dangerous situation!

An ice-laden airplane may even be incapable of flight. Ice or frost on the leading edge and upper forward area of the wings (where the majority of the lift is generated) is especially dangerous.

Most training airplanes are not fitted with airframe de-icers (removal) or anti-icers (preventive), so pilots of these airplanes should avoid flying in icing conditions (that is, in rain or moist air at any time the airframe is likely to be at subzero temperatures). If a pitot heater is fitted, use it to avoid ice forming over the pitot tube and depriving you of airspeed information.

Ice of any type on the airframe or propeller, or in the carburetor and induction system, deserves the pilot's immediate attention and removal.

An ice-laden airplane may be unable to fly.

Review 17

Structural Icing

1. What two conditions must be met for structural icing to occur on an airplane?

➤ visible moisture, temperature at or below freezing

2. Large supercooled droplets striking a subzero airplane are likely to form (clear ice/rime ice/frost).

➤ clear ice

3. Small supercooled droplets striking a subzero airplane are likely to form (clear ice/rime ice/frost).

➤ rime ice

4. If the air temperature is +6°C at 1500 feet MSL, and a standard temperature lapse rate exists, the freezing level will be approximately _____ feet MSL.

➤ 4500 feet MSL

5. If the air temperature is a+12°C at 1500 feet MSL, and a standard temperature lapse rate exits, the freezing level will be approximately _____ feet MSL.

➤ 7500 feet MSL

6. The formation of clear ice on the airplane structure is most likely if you are flying through (hail/snow/freezing rain).

➤ freezing rain

7. Freezing rain consists of (supercooled water drops/ice pellets/warm water drops).

➤ supercooled water drops

8. Freezing rain can result when rain falls into a layer of air that is (above/below) 0°C.

➤ below

9. Rain drops falling from warm air into subzero air may remain in liquid form as supercooled water drops, forming what is known as (hail/freezing rain/snow), or may freeze to form (fog/frost/ice pellets).

➤ freezing rain, ice pellets

10. If the supercooled water drops in freezing rain strike a subzero aircraft structure, they will spread out on impact, join together and freeze to form (frost/clear ice/rime ice), which (is/is not) dangerous.

➤ clear ice, is

11. The possibility of freezing rain at higher altitudes is indicated by (heavy rain/ice pellets/snow/light rain).

➤ ice pellets

12. Ice pellets falling at ground level are evidence of (freezing rain at a higher level/passage of a clod front/thunderstorms in the area)/

➤ freezing rain at a higher level

13. If you fly through rain which freezes on impact, then you know that temperatures at some higher altitude are (above/below) the freezing temperature of 0°C.

➤ above

14. If you fly through wet snow, then you know that temperatures at some higher altitude are (above/below) the freezing temperature of 0°C, and the temperature at your altitude is (above/below) 0°C.

➤ below, above

15. Clear ice (can/will not) after the basic aerodynamic shape of the wing

➤ can

16. Frost (can/will not) cause a loss of lift from the wing.

➤ can

17. Frost can cause a loss of lift by (changing the aerodynamic shape of the wing/causing early airflow separation from the wing).

➤ causing early airflow separation from the wing

18. You (should/need not) remove frost, ice or any other contaminant from the wings prior to flight.

➤ should

19. The risk of clear ice forming on the airplanes structure is greater when flying in (cumuliform/cirrus) clouds.

➤ cumuliform

20. The family of clouds least likely to contribute to structural icing on an airplane is (low-/middle-/high-) level clouds.

➤ high-level

21. Structural icing is most likely to have the highest rate of accumulation in (heavy, wet snow/freezing rain/cumulonimbus clouds/cloud, humid conditions).

➤ freezing rain

22. What three weather sources reflect the most accurate information on icing conditions, both current and forecast?

➤ PIREPs, SIGMETs, and AIRMETs

Induction Icing

1. For carburetor icing to occur, the outside air temperature (must/need not) be below freezing.

➤ need not

2. Ice can form in the carburetor when the ambient air temperature is (below freezing only/above or below freezing).

➤ above or below freezing

3. The air entering the carburetor and induction system (cools/warms) as it expands through the venturi.

➤ cools

4. The control in the cockpit used to protect you against carburetor icing is called the _____ control.

➤ carburetor heat

5. Carburetor ice (may/will not) form when you are flying in moist air at +10°C.

➤ may

Instrument Icing

1. If ice forms over the pitot tube, the instrument(s) likely to give faulty indications is/are the _____.

➤ airspeed indicator only

2. If ice forms over the static vents, the instrument(s) likely to give faulty indications is/are the _____.

➤ airspeed indicator, altimeter, vertical speed indicator

Visibility 18

Visibility is the greatest distance you can see and identify objects—it is a measure of how transparent the atmosphere is to the human eye.

The actual visibility is very important to pilots, and strict visibility requirements are specified for visual flight operation.

Slant visibility may be quite different from *horizontal* visibility. A runway clearly visible through stratus, fog or smog from directly overhead the airport might be impossible to see when you are trying to join final approach.

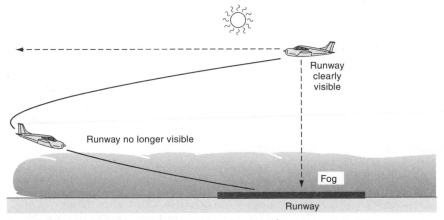

Figure 18-1. Slant visibility may be severely reduced by fog, smog or stratus

On a perfectly clear day visibility can exceed 100 nm, however this is rarely the case since there are always some particles suspended in the air preventing all of the light from a distant object reaching your eyes.

Rising air (unstable air) may carry these particles up and blow them away, leading to good visibility; stable air that is not rising, however, will keep the particles in the lower levels, and this may result in poor visibility.

Particles that restrict visibility include:

- **minute particles** so small that even very light winds can support them;
  - **dust or smoke** causing haze;
  - liquid water or ice producing mist, fog or clouds;
- **larger particles of sand, dust or sea spray** which require stronger winds and turbulence for the air to hold them in suspension; and
- **precipitation** (rain, snow, hail), the worst visibility being associated with very heavy rain or with large numbers of small particles, such as thick drizzle or heavy, fine snow.

Unstable air that is rising may cause cumuliform clouds to form, with poor visibility in the showers falling from them, but good visibility otherwise, since the rising unstable air will carry the obscuring particles away. As well as causing good visibility, the rising unstable air may cause bumpy flying conditions.

Visibility can be reduced by particles suspended in the air.

Rain or snow reduces the distance that you can see, as well as possibly obscuring the horizon and making it more difficult for you to keep the wings level or hold a steady bank angle in a turn. Poor visibility over a large area may occur in mist, fog, smog, stratus, drizzle or rain. As well as restricting visibility through the atmosphere, heavy rain may collect on the windshield and further restrict your vision, especially if the airplane is flying fast, and might also cause optical distortions. If freezing occurs on the windshield, either as ice or frost, vision may be further impaired.

Strong winds can raise dust or sand from the surface and, in some parts of the world, visibility may be reduced to just a few feet in dust and sandstorms.

Sea spray often evaporates after being blown into the atmosphere, leaving small salt particles suspended in the air that can act as condensation nuclei. The salt particles attract water and can cause condensation at relative humidities as low as 70%, restricting visibility much sooner than would otherwise be the case. Haze produced by sea salt often has a whitish appearance, and may often be seen along ocean coastlines.

The position of the sun can also have a significant effect on visibility. Flying down-sun (with the sun behind you) where you can see the sunlit side of objects, the visibility may be much greater than when flying into the sun. As well as reducing visibility, flying into the sun may also cause glare. If landing into the sun is necessary because of strong surface winds or other reasons, consideration should be given to altering your time of arrival at a destination.

Remember that the onset of darkness is earlier on the ground than at altitude and, even though visibility at higher altitudes might be good, flying low in the traffic pattern and approaching to land on a darkening field may cause problems.

Inversions and Reduced Visibility

An inversion occurs when the air temperature increases with altitude (rather than decreases, which is the usual situation).

An inversion occurs when the air temperature increases with altitude.

A temperature inversion can act as a blanket, stopping vertical convection currents—air that starts to rise meets warmer air and so will stop rising, i.e. temperature inversions are associated with a stable layer of air. Particles suspended in the lower layers will be trapped there causing a rather dirty layer of smoke, dust, or pollution, particularly in industrial areas. These small particles may act as condensation particles or nuclei, and encourage the formation of fog if the relative humidity is high, the combination of smoke and fog being known as smog. There is usually an abundance of condensation nuclei in industrial areas as a result of the combustion process (factory smoke, car exhausts, etc.), hence the poor visibility often found over these areas.

Similar poor visibility effects below inversions can be seen in rural areas if there is a lot of pollen, dust or other matter in the air.

Inversions can occur by cooling of the air in contact with the earth's surface overnight, or by subsidence associated with a high pressure system as descending air warms. The most common type of ground-based inversion is that produced by terrestrial radiation on a clear, relatively still night, often leading to poor visibility in the lower levels the following morning from fog, smoke or smog.

Flying conditions beneath a low-level inversion layer are typically smooth (because of the air being stable and not rising), with poor visibility, haze, fog, smog or low clouds. Because there is little or no mixing of the air above and below an inversion, the effect of any upper winds may not be carried down beneath the inversion. This may cause a quite sharp windshear as an airplane climbs or descends through the inversion.

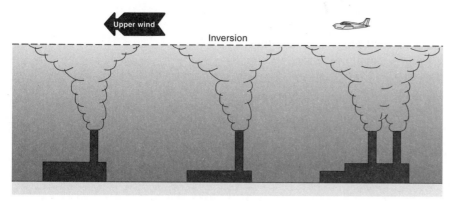

Figure 18-2. Reduced visibility and smooth flying conditions beneath the inversion, and possible windshear passing through it

High-level inversions are common in the stratosphere, but these are so high as to only affect high-flying jets.

Condensation

Visibility can be dramatically reduced when invisible water vapor in the air condenses out as visible water droplets and forms clouds or fog.

The amount of water vapor which a parcel of air can hold depends on its temperature—warm air is able to carry more water vapor than cold air. Warm air passing over a water surface, such as an ocean or a lake, is capable of absorbing much more water vapor than cooler air.

If the moist air is then cooled, say by being forced aloft and expanding or by passing over or lying over a cooling surface, it eventually reaches a point where it can no longer carry all of its invisible water vapor and is said to be *saturated.* The temperature at which saturation occurs is called the **dewpoint temperature** (or simply *dewpoint*) of that parcel of air. Any further cooling will most likely lead to the excess water vapor condensing out as visible water droplets and forming fog or clouds, a process encouraged by the presence of dust or other condensation nuclei in the air. If the air is extremely clean, with very few condensation nuclei, the actual condensation process may be delayed until the temperature falls some degrees below the dewpoint.

Air carrying a lot of water vapor, for instance warm air after passing over an ocean or large lake, will have a high dewpoint temperature compared with the relatively dry air over an arid desert. Moist air may only have to cool to a dewpoint of +25°C before becoming saturated, whereas less moist air may have to cool to +5°C before reaching saturation point. Extremely dry air may have to cool to a dewpoint temperature of –5°C before becoming saturated.

Clouds or fog form when the invisible water vapor condenses out in the air as visible water droplets. The closeness of the actual air temperature to the dewpoint of the air, often contained in surface aviation weather reports, is a good indication to the pilot as to how close the air is to saturation and the possible formation of clouds or fog.

If the water vapor condenses out on contact with a surface such as the ground or an airplane that is below the dewpoint of the surrounding air, then it will form **dew** (or **frost**, if the temperature of the collecting surface is below freezing).

The reverse process to condensation may occur in the air if its temperature rises above the dewpoint, causing the water droplets to evaporate into water vapor and, consequently, the fog or clouds to disperse.

Fog is simply a cloud layer reaching ground level.

Clouds or fog form when the invisible water vapor condenses out in the air as visible water droplets.

Fog

Fog is of major concern to pilots because it severely restricts vision near the ground. The condensation process that causes fog is usually associated with cooling of the air either by:

- an underlying cold ground or water surface (causing radiation or advection fog);
- the interaction of two air masses (causing frontal fog);
- the adiabatic cooling of a moist air mass moving up a slope (causing upslope fog); or
- very cold air overlying a warm water surface (causing steam fog).

The closer the *temperature/dewpoint* spread, and the faster the temperature is falling, the sooner fog will form. For instance, an airport with an actual air temperature of +6°C early on a calm, clear night, and a dewpoint temperature of +4°C (a temperature/dewpoint spread of 2°C) is likely to experience fog when the temperature falls 2°C or more from its current +6°C.

Radiation Fog

Radiation fog forms when air is cooled to below its dewpoint temperature by losing heat energy as a result of radiation. Conditions suitable for the formation of radiation fog are:

- a cloudless night, allowing the land to lose heat by radiation to the atmosphere and thereby cool, also causing the air in contact with the ground to lose heat (possibly leading to a temperature inversion);
- moist air and a small temperature/dewpoint spread (i.e. a high relative humidity) that only requires a little cooling for the air to reach its dewpoint temperature, causing the water vapor to condense onto small condensation nuclei in the air and form visible water; and
- light winds (5–7 knots) to promote mixing of the air at low level, thereby thickening the fog layer.

These conditions are commonly found with an anticyclone (or high-pressure system).

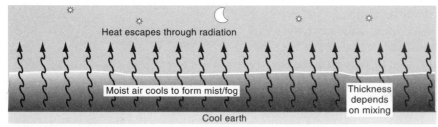

Figure 18-3. Radiation fog

Air is a poor conductor of heat, so that if the wind is absolutely calm, only the very thin layer of air 1–2″ thick actually in contact with the surface will lose heat to it. This will cause dew or frost to form on the surface itself, instead of fog forming in the air above it. Dew will form at temperatures above freezing, and frost will form at below freezing temperatures. This may inhibit the formation of radiation fog by removing moisture from the air. After dawn, however, the dew may evaporate and fog may form.

If the wind is stronger than about 7 knots, the extra turbulence may cause too much mixing and, instead of radiation fog right down to the ground, a layer of *stratus* clouds may form above the surface.

| No wind: dew/frost | Light wind: mist/fog | Strong wind: stratus |

Figure 18-4. Wind strength will affect the formation of dew/frost, mist/fog or stratus clouds

The temperature of the sea remains fairly constant throughout the year, unlike that of the land which warms and cools quite quickly on a diurnal (daily) basis. Radiation fog is therefore much more likely to form over land, which cools more quickly at night, than over the sea.

As the earth's surface begins to warm up again some time after sunrise, the air in contact with it will also warm, causing the fog to gradually dissipate. It is common for this to occur by early or mid-morning. Possibly the fog may rise to form a low layer of stratus before the sky fully clears.

If the fog that has formed overnight is thick, however, it may act as a blanket, shutting out the sun and impeding the heating of the earth's surface after the sun has risen. As a consequence, the air in which the fog exists will not be warmed from below and the radiation fog may last throughout the day. An increasing wind speed could create sufficient turbulence to drag warmer and drier air down into the fog layer, causing it to dissipate.

Note: Haze caused by particles of dust, pollen, etc., in the air of course cannot be dissipated by the air warming—haze needs to be blown away by a wind.

The dispersal of radiation fog depends on heating of the air.

Advection Fog

A warm, moist air mass flowing as a wind across a significantly colder surface will be cooled from below. If its temperature is reduced to the dewpoint temperature, then fog will form. Since the term *advection* means the horizontal flow of air, fog formed in this manner is known as advection fog, and can occur quite suddenly, day or night, if the right conditions exist, and can be more persistent than radiation fog.

For instance, a warm, moist maritime air flow over a cold land surface can lead to advection fog forming over the land. In winter, moist air from the Gulf of Mexico moving north over cold ground often causes advection fog extending well into the south-central and eastern United States.

Advection fog depends on a wind to move the relatively warm and moist air mass over a cooler surface. Unlike radiation fog, the formation of advection fog is not affected by overhead cloud layers, and can form with or without clouds obscuring the sky. Light to moderate winds will encourage mixing in the lower levels to give a thicker layer of fog, but winds stronger than about 15 knots may cause *stratus* clouds rather than fog. Advection fog can persist in much stronger winds than radiation fog.

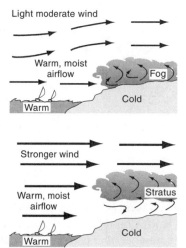

Figure 18-5. Fog or stratus caused by advection

Sea fog is advection fog, and it may be caused by:

- tropical maritime air moving toward the pole over a colder ocean or meeting a colder air mass; or by

- an air flow off a warm land surface moving over a cooler sea, affecting airports in coastal areas. Advection fog is common in coastal regions of California during summer.

Upslope Fog

Moist air moving up a slope will cool adiabatically and, if it cools to below its dewpoint temperature, fog will form. This is known as upslope fog. It may form whether there is cloud above or not. If the wind stops, the upslope fog will dissipate. Upslope fog is common on the eastern slopes of the Rockies and the Appalachian mountains.

Both upslope fog and advection fog depend on wind to exist (but not radiation fog).

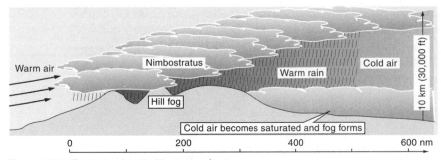

Figure 18-6. Upslope fog

Frontal Fog

Frontal fog forms from the interaction of two air masses in one of two ways:

- as clouds that extend down to the surface during the passage of the front (forming mainly over hills and consequently called **hill fog**); or
- as air becomes saturated by the evaporation from rain that has fallen, known as **precipitation-induced fog**.

These conditions may develop in the cold air ahead of a warm front (or an occluded front), the prefrontal fog possibly being widespread.

Rain or drizzle falling from relatively warm air into cooler air may saturate it, forming precipitation-induced fog which may be thick and long-lasting over quite wide areas. Precipitation-induced fog is most likely to be associated with a warm front, but it can also be associated with a stationary front or a slow-moving cold front.

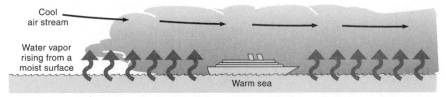

Figure 18-7. Fog associated with a warm front

Steam Fog

Steam fog can form when cool air blows over a warm, moist surface (a warm sea or wet land), cooling the water vapor rising from the moist surface to below its dewpoint temperature and thereby causing fog. Steam fog over polar oceans is sometimes called *Arctic sea smoke*. It forms in air more than 10°C colder than water, and can be thick and widespread, causing serious visibility problems for ships.

Figure 18-8. Low-level turbulence and the risk of severe icing can be present in steam fog

✍ Review 18

1. Poor visibility is more likely to result with (stable/unstable) air.

   ➤ stable

2. For an inversion to exist, temperature must (increase/decrease) with altitude.

   ➤ increase

3. Air and the particles it contains (will/will not) tend to rise through an inversion.

   ➤ will not

4. The presence of an inversion (increases/decreases) the risk of poor visibility.

   ➤ increases

5. The air beneath an inversion is (held down/forced aloft) by the inversion, forming a (stable/unstable) layer.

   ➤ held down, stable

6. Flying conditions beneath a low-level inversion are likely to be (good/poor) visibility with (smooth/bumpy) flying conditions.

   ➤ poor, smooth

7. There is (little/much) mixing of the air above and below an inversion with (some/no) risk of windshear to an airplane climbing or descending through the inversion.

   ➤ little, some

8. The amount of water vapor that a parcel of air can hold largely depends on (air temperature/relative humidity/stability of the air).

   ➤ air temperature

9. Warm air can hold (more/less/the same amount of) water vapor compared to cold air.

   ➤ more

10. Water vapor is (visible/invisible).

    ➤ invisible

11. Water droplets formed when water vapor condenses out of cooling air are (visible/invisible).

    ➤ visible

12. As a parcel of air is cooled, it is capable of holding (less/more) water vapor.

    ➤ less

13. The temperature to which a parcel of air must be cooled for it to become saturated is called its _____.

    ➤ dewpoint

14. Water vapor will condense out of air when it is (above/at or below) its dewpoint temperature—a process that is (encouraged/discouraged) by the presence of condensation nuclei in the air.

    ➤ at or below, encouraged

15. Clouds, fog, dew or frost form when (water vapor is present in the air/water vapor condenses/air temperature falls to the dewpoint).

    ➤ water vapor condenses (Note: The lack of condensation nuclei in clean air sometimes delays the condensation process until air temperature is below the dewpoint.)

16. Fog is formed when the air is cooled to its _____ temperature or below.

    ➤ dewpoint

17. The possibility of fog in industrial areas is increased because of the prevalence of _____ nuclei as a result of the combustion process.

    ➤ condensation nuclei

18. A mixture of smoke and fog is known as _____.

    ➤ smog

19. Radiation fog is more likely to form on a (cloudy/clear) night.

    ➤ clear

20. Radiation fog is more likely to occur when the temperature/dewpoint spread is (small/big).

➤ small

21. Radiation fog is more likely to form when the wind is (strong/light).

➤ light

22. Radiation fog is more likely to form by (night/day).

➤ night

23. At night, the land cools (faster/slower) than the sea.

➤ faster

24. Radiation fog is more likely to form over (land/sea).

➤ land

25. A common type of surface-based inversion that can lead to ground fog is caused by ground (heating/radiation) on (clear/cloudy), (warm/cool) (days/nights) with (light/strong) winds.

➤ radiation, clear, cool, nights, light

26. For dew to form, the temperature of the collecting surface must be (above/below) the dewpoint of the surrounding air, and the dewpoint must be (above/below) freezing.

➤ below, above

27. For frost to form, the temperature of the collecting surface must be (above/below) the dewpoint of the surrounding air, and the dewpoint must be (above/below) freezing.

➤ below, below

28. In order for advection fog to form, there (must/need not) be a wind.

➤ must

29. Advection fog is formed as (dry/moist) air is carried over a (warmer/cooler) surface.

➤ moist, cooler

30. Advection fog caused by a warm, moist airflow over a cold land surface is most likely in (inland/coastal) areas in (summer/winter).

➤ coastal, winter

31. Moist air flowing over a cold surface is likely to form (cumulonimbus clouds/fog/rain showers).

➤ fog

32. Advection fog may form on the lee side of a large lake, the side to which the wind is blowing, if the lake is (warmer/colder) than the air.

➤ colder

33. Advection fog may be lifted to form low stratus clouds by winds stronger than about (3/5/15) knots.

➤ 15

34. Moist, stable air being moved over gradually rising ground by a wind may lead to the formation of _____ fog.

➤ upslope

35. What types of fog depend on a wind in order to exist—radiation fog, advection fog, upslope fog?

➤ advection fog, upslope fog

36. Fog (may/cannot) be dissipated by heating of the air.

➤ may

37. Haze layers (may/cannot) be dissipated by heating of the air.

➤ cannot

38. Haze can be dissipated by (heating/a wind blowing it away).

➤ a wind blowing it away

Clouds 19

A cloud is a visible aggregate of minute particles of water and/or ice in the free air. The effect of clouds on aviation, particularly on flight, makes them an important topic in training to become an instrument-rated pilot.

Low stratus clouds formed in stable atmospheric conditions can sit low over the ground, possibly even on the ground as fog, and cause you to divert to an alternate destination. Towering cumulus clouds can form in unstable conditions due to moist air rising, and these can develop into one of the greatest hazards to an airplane, cumulonimbus clouds and thunderstorms.

The Naming of Clouds

Clouds may take on numerous different forms, many of which continually change. They are classified into four families according to height and named individually according to their nature. It is important to have an understanding of cloud classification because the meteorological forecasts and reports use this system to give you a picture of the weather.

Clouds are classified in four families according to height: high-level, mid-level, low-level and those with extensive vertical development.

Clouds belong to one of four families depending on height. They are:

1. **high-level clouds** with a base above approximately 20,000 feet, and composed mainly of ice crystals in the below freezing upper atmosphere (cirrus, cirrocumulus, cirrostratus);

2. **middle-level clouds** with a base above approximately 6500 feet (altocumulus, altostratus, nimbostratus);

3. **low-level clouds** with a base below approximately 6500 feet (stratocumulus, stratus, fair weather cumulus, nimbostratus); and

4. **clouds with extensive vertical development** (towering cumulus, cumulonimbus).

Clouds are named according to the following types:

- **cirriform** (or fibrous)—consisting mainly of ice crystals;
- **cumuliform** (or heaped)—formed by unstable air rising and cooling;

- **stratiform** (or layered)—formed by the cooling of a stable layer;
- **nimbus** (or rain-bearing);
- **fractus** (fragmented);
- **castellanus** (common base with separate vertical development, often in lines);
- **lenticularis** (lens-shaped, often formed in strong winds over mountainous areas).

For example, nimbostratus means stratified clouds from which rain is falling. Altocumulus is middle-level heaped clouds. Cumulus fractus is fragmentary cumulus clouds. Cirrostratus is high-level stratified clouds consisting of ice crystals. Standing lenticular altocumulus clouds are lens-shaped middle-level clouds standing in the one position, usually over a mountain range in strong winds.

Nimbostratus is a hybrid cloud in terms of classification since its base can be low level or middle level, and it can have great vertical depth. Sometimes nimbostratus is 10,000 feet or even 15,000 feet thick, making it very dark when seen from underneath and capable of causing heavy rain for many hours.

Flying in clouds means poor visibility and the risk of icing—not a great risk in the high-level cirriform clouds consisting of ice crystals, but very great in clouds of extensive vertical development which may contain large supercooled water drops that will freeze on contact with a cold airplane.

Some clouds are fine for flying through, while others are not. Know the difference.

Moisture in the Atmosphere

Clouds are formed when water vapor in the atmosphere condenses into water droplets or, in below freezing temperatures, into ice crystals. Water vapor is taken up into the atmosphere mainly by evaporation from the oceans and other bodies where water is present, or by sublimation directly from solid ice when the air overlies a frozen surface.

The Three States of Water

Water in its vapor state is not visible, but when the water vapor condenses to form water droplets we see it as cloud, fog, mist, rain or dew. Frozen water is also visible as high-level clouds, snow, hail, ice or frost. Water exists in three states—gas (vapor), liquid (water) and solid (ice).

Under certain conditions water can change from one state to another, absorbing heat energy if it moves to a higher energy state (from ice to water to vapor) and giving off heat energy if it moves to a lower energy state (vapor to water to ice). This heat energy is known as *latent heat* and is a vital part of any change of state. The absorption or emission of latent heat is important in meteorological processes such as cloud formation, and evaporation of rain (virga).

The three states of water, the names of the various transfer processes and the absorption or giving off of a latent heat are shown in Figure 19-1.

Water comes in three states: vapor (gas), liquid and solid. It can be found in all three forms in clouds.

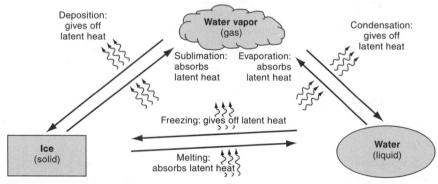

Figure 19-1. The three states of water

Relative Humidity

The amount of water vapor present in the air depends on the amount of evaporation, which will be greater over wet surfaces such as oceans and flooded ground than over a desert or continent.

The actual amount of water vapor in the air, known as **humidity**, is not as important as whether the air can support that water vapor or not. When a parcel of air is supporting as much water vapor as it can, it is said to be *saturated* and have a **relative humidity** of 100%.

Air supporting less than its full capacity of water vapor is said to be *unsaturated*, and will have a relative humidity of less than 100%.

In cloud and fog, the relative humidity is 100% and the air is saturated; over a desert, relative humidity might be 20%.

Cloud Formation

Clouds are formed when air is cooled to its dewpoint temperature, and the excess water vapor condenses as liquid water or ice crystals, depending on temperature. The cooling of a parcel of air can occur by various means, such as:

• rising air cooling adiabatically as it expands; or

• air flowing over, or lying over, a cooling surface.

Dewpoint Temperature

How much water vapor a particular parcel of air can support depends on the air temperature—warm air is able to support more water vapor than cold air. If the temperature of the air falls, it is capable of holding less water vapor, and so will move closer to being saturated, its relative humidity will rise. Relative humidity increases greatly with a decrease in temperature.

Warm air is able to support more water vapor than cold air.

The temperature at which the relative humidity reaches 100%, and the excess water vapor starts to condense as water droplets, is known as the **dewpoint temperature**. The condensation process may be delayed if there are insufficient condensation nuclei in the air, or conversely, certain types of condensation nuclei may induce condensation shortly before 100% relative humidity is reached. Typical condensation nuclei are small particles of hygroscopic (water-soluble) dust, salt, or other small particles. Clouds form only when the water vapor actually condenses.

A parcel of air that has a temperature higher than its dewpoint is unsaturated and its relative humidity is less than 100%, since it is capable of holding more moisture at its current temperature. The closer the actual temperature of the parcel of air is to its dewpoint, the closer it is to being saturated. As the spread between actual air temperature and the dewpoint temperature decreases as the air temperature falls, the relative humidity increases.

At its dewpoint, the air will be fully saturated. If it becomes cooler than its dewpoint, then the excess water vapor will condense as visible water droplets (or, in below freezing temperatures below the frost point, deposit as ice crystals). The actual value of the dewpoint temperature for a particular parcel of air varies, depending on the amount of water vapor it contains. If the air is moist (for instance over a tropical ocean), the dewpoint temperature may be quite high, say +25°C; if the air is dry, the dewpoint temperature may be quite low.

If the air temperature falls to a dewpoint temperature which is above freezing, the water vapor will condense as liquid water droplets and become visible as clouds, fog, or dew; if the dewpoint temperature is below freezing, the excess water vapor may change to ice crystals (like in high-level cirriform clouds, or frost on the ground on a below freezing night).

If the air in which clouds form is unable to support the water droplets (if they become too large and heavy), then the drops will fall as precipitation (rain, hail or snow).

Adiabatic Processes

The temperature of a gas depends on the number and energy of its molecules striking the measuring surface of a thermometer. In adiabatic processes, temperature can change as a result of pressure changes, even though heat energy is neither added to nor taken from the system. Expanding a gas and decreasing its pressure causes a lowering of temperature, because fewer molecules will collide with the measuring surface.

Conversely, compressing a gas and increasing its pressure will raise its temperature because more molecules will collide with the measuring surface. Placing your finger over the outlet of a bicycle pump illustrates that compressing air increases its temperature. Also, air that has been compressed and stored at room temperature will cool when it is released to the atmosphere and allowed to expand.

A common adiabatic process that involves the expansion of a gas and its cooling is when a parcel of air rises in the atmosphere. This can be initiated by the heating of the parcel of air over warm ground, causing it to expand and become less dense than the surrounding air, hence it will rise. A parcel of air can also be forced aloft as it blows over a mountain range, or as it is lifted over a front.

Unsaturated air will cool adiabatically at about 3°C/1000 feet as it rises and expands. This is known as the **dry adiabatic lapse rate (DALR)**. Air that is 12°C at ground level will cool adiabatically to 9°C if it is forced up to 1000 feet AGL, and to 6°C at 2000 feet AGL, provided it does not reach saturation point.

Cooler air can support less water vapor, so, as the parcel of air rises and cools, its relative humidity will increase. At the altitude where its temperature is reduced to the dewpoint temperature (relative humidity reaches 100%), water will start to condense and form cloud.

Above this altitude, the now-saturated air will continue to cool as it rises but, because latent heat will be given off as the water vapor condenses into the lower energy liquid state, the cooling will not be as great. The rate at which saturated air cools as it rises is known as the **saturated adiabatic lapse rate (SALR)** and may be assumed to have a value of approximately half the DALR, 1.5°C/1000 feet. Air that is, say, 5°C inside a cloud will, if it is forced 1000 feet higher, cool adiabatically to 3.5°C.

Note: At higher levels in the cloud where there is less water vapor to condense into water (since most of this has already occurred), there will be less latent heat given off and so SALR will increase.

Which Cloud Type Forms?

The structure or type of cloud that forms depends mainly on the stability of the air before lifting occurs.

Moist air that is unstable will continue rising, forming cumulus-type cloud with significant vertical development and turbulence, whereas moist air that is stable has no tendency to continue rising and so will form stratus-type clouds with little vertical development and little or no turbulence. Some stratus-type clouds, such as nimbostratus, can however form in a thick layer.

Dry air that is forced to rise, but does not cool to its dewpoint temperature, will not form clouds.

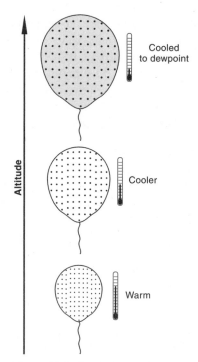

Figure 19-2. As air rises and expands, it cools adiabatically

The type of cloud which forms depends on stability of the air.

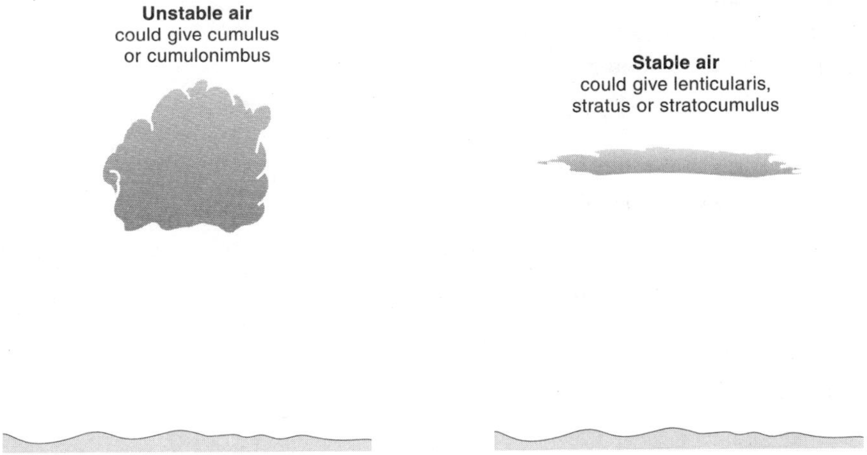

Unstable air
could give cumulus
or cumulonimbus

Stable air
could give lenticularis,
stratus or stratocumulus

Figure 19-3. Cumuliform clouds in unstable conditions; stratiform clouds form in stable conditions

Unstable air. As long as a parcel of air given vertical movement is warmer than its surroundings, it will continue to rise. This is known as an unstable parcel of air. Characteristics of unstable air are:

- turbulence in the rising air;
- the formation of cumuliform clouds (heaped clouds);
- showery rain from these clouds, if there is precipitation; and
- good visibility between the showers (caused by the rising air carrying any obscuring particles away).

Stable air. If the rising parcel of air is cooler than the ambient air around it, then it will stop rising because its density will be greater than the surroundings. An atmosphere in which air tends to remain at the one level, or to sink, is called a stable atmosphere.

Characteristics of stable air are:

- the formation of stratiform clouds (layer-type) with little vertical development and steady, if any, precipitation;
- poor visibility if there are any obscuring particles; and
- possibly smooth flying conditions with little or no turbulence.

The rate of temperature change as altitude is gained in the surrounding atmosphere (in the air that is not rising) is called the **environmental lapse rate (ELR)**, the ambient lapse rate or the actual lapse rate. Its relationship to DALR and SALR is the main factor in determining the levels of the bases and tops of the clouds that form. A great decrease in ambient air temperature with altitude (a high ELR) encourages warm air to keep rising (an unstable situation) and form clouds of great vertical development. A lesser ELR may indicate a stable situation. The stability in the atmosphere depends on the ambient lapse rate.

The **standard atmosphere**, which is simply a theoretical measuring stick against which the actual atmosphere at any time or place can be compared, assumes an ambient lapse rate of 2°C/1000 feet. The actual ELR in a real atmosphere, however, may differ greatly from this—it may be 1°C per 1000 feet gain in altitude, or it may be 2.5°C per 1000 feet gain in altitude. In a temperature inversion, the temperature will not decrease with altitude, but will increase. The actual environmental lapse rate varies from time to time and place to place.

The actual environmental lapse rate varies from time to time and place to place.

Clouds Formed by Convection Caused by Heating

Cold air moving over or lying over a warm surface will be warmed from below, and so become less stable. It will tend to rise, causing turbulence and good visibility. If the air is moist and unstable, cumuliform clouds will develop as the air ascends and cools adiabatically to its dewpoint temperature.

The ascending unsaturated air will cool at the dry adiabatic lapse rate of 3°C/1000 feet. The closer the air temperature is to the dewpoint, the lesser height it has to rise before condensing to form clouds. The dewpoint decreases at about 0.5°C/1000 feet, which means that the *air temperature/dewpoint* spread will decrease at approximately 2.5°C/1000 feet in rising unstable air.

For working in degrees Fahrenheit, DALR for unsaturated air is 5.4°F and dewpoint lapse rate is approximately 1°F, so they converge at approximately **4.4°F/1000 feet** (which is the same as 2.5°C/1000 feet).

$$Cloud\ base\ in\ thousands\ of\ feet\ = \frac{air\ temperature - dewpoint}{4.4°F\ (or\ 2.5°C)}$$

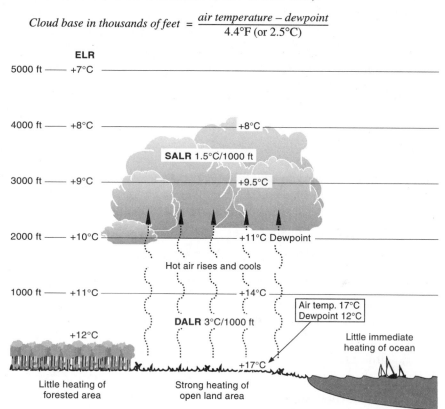

Figure 19-4. The temperature processes involved in the formation of a cumulus cloud

Example 1. If the temperature at a given level is 17°C and the dewpoint is 12°C, (a temperature/dewpoint spread of 5°C), then as the air rises this spread will decrease by approximately 2.5°C/1000 feet. The temperature and dewpoint will have the same value at an altitude approximately 2000 feet higher (5 ÷ 2.5 = 2).

The cloud base will form at a level 2000 feet higher and the air, if it is still unstable, will continue to rise and form a heaped cumuliform cloud. Because it is now saturated, latent heat will be given off as more and more water vapor condenses into liquid water droplets. This reduces the rate at which the rising saturated air cools to the saturated adiabatic lapse rate of approximately 1.5°C/1000 feet.

Example 2. What is the appropriate base MSL of clouds if the temperature at 3000 feet MSL is 68°F and the dewpoint is 46°F?

$$\text{Cloud base in thousands of feet} = \frac{68 - 46}{4.4} = \frac{22}{4.4} = 5$$

$$\text{therefore cloud base MSL} = 3000 \text{ ft MSL} + 5000 \text{ ft}$$
$$= 8000 \text{ ft MSL}$$

Clouds Formed by Orographic Uplift

Air flowing over mountains rises and is cooled adiabatically. If it cools to below its dewpoint temperature, then the water vapor will condense and clouds will form. Descending on the other side of the mountains, however, the airflow will warm adiabatically and, once its temperature exceeds the dewpoint for that parcel of air, the water vapor will no longer condense. The liquid water drops will now start to vaporize, and the clouds will cease to exist below this level.

The altitude at which the cloud base forms depends on the moisture content of the parcel of air and its dewpoint temperature. The cloud base may be below the mountain tops or well above them depending on the situation. Once having started to form, the cloud may sit low over the mountain as stratiform clouds (if the air is stable), or (if the air is unstable) the clouds will be cumuliform and may rise to high levels.

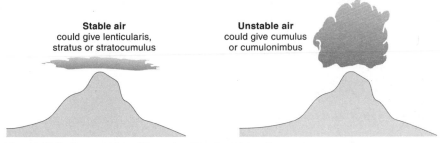

Stable air
could give lenticularis,
stratus or stratocumulus

Unstable air
could give cumulus
or cumulonimbus

Figure 19-5. Orographic uplift can lead to cloud formation

An almond-shaped or lens-shaped cloud that forms as a cap over the top of a mountain is known as a **lenticular cloud**. It will remain more or less stationary while the air flows through it, possibly at speeds of 50 knots or more.

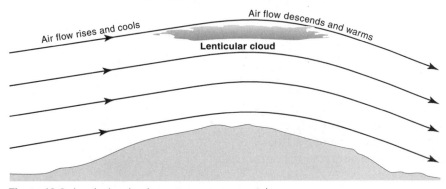

Air flow rises and cools

Air flow descends and warms

Lenticular cloud

Figure 19-6. Lenticular cloud as a cap over a mountain

Sometimes, when an airstream flows over a mountain range and there is a stable layer of air above, **standing waves** occur. This is a wavy pattern as the airflow settles back into a more steady flow and, if the air is moist, lenticular clouds may form in the crest of the lee waves, and a **rotor** or **roll cloud** may form at a low altitude. The presence of standing lenticular altocumulus clouds is a good indicator that strong **mountain wave turbulence** exists.

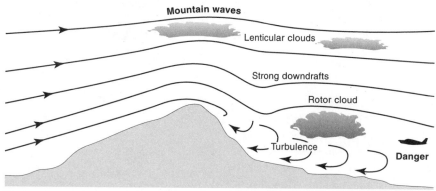

Figure 19-7. Mountain waves

The Foehn Wind Effect (or Chinook Wind Effect)

If the air rising up a mountain range is moist enough to have a high dewpoint temperature and is cooled down to it before reaching the top of the mountain, then cloud will form on the windward side. If any precipitation occurs, moisture will be removed from the airflow and, as it descends on the lee side of the mountain, it will therefore be drier. The dewpoint temperature will be less and so the cloud base will be higher on the lee side of the mountain.

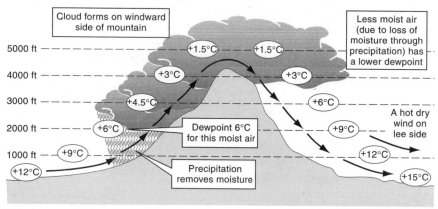

Figure 19-8. The foehn wind effect

As the dry air beneath the cloud descends, it will warm at the dry adiabatic lapse rate of 3°C/1000 feet, which is at a greater rate than the rising air cooled inside the cloud (saturated adiabatic lapse rate: 1.5°C/1000 feet). The result is a warmer and drier wind on the lee side of the mountains. This noticeable effect is seen in many parts of the world, for example the foehn (pronounced "*fern*") wind in Switzerland and southern Germany, from which this effect gets its name, the *Chinook* wind which blows down the eastern slope of the Rocky Mountains, and the Santa Ana wind which blows from the east or northeast in southern California.

Clouds Formed by Turbulence and Mixing

As air flows over the surface of the earth, frictional effects cause variations in local wind strength and direction. Eddies are set up which cause the lower levels of air to mix—the stronger the wind and the rougher the earth's surface, the larger the eddies and the stronger the mixing. The air in the rising currents will cool and, if the turbulence extends to a sufficient height, it may cool to the dewpoint temperature, water vapor will condense to form liquid water droplets and clouds will form.

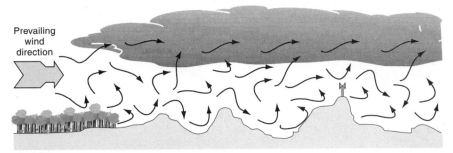

Figure 19-9. Formation of turbulence clouds

The descending air currents in the turbulent cloud layer will warm and, if the air's dewpoint temperature is exceeded, the liquid water droplets that make up the clouds will return to the water vapor state. The air will dry out and clouds will not exist below this altitude. With turbulent mixing, stratiform clouds may form over quite a large area, possibly with an undulating base. They may be continuous stratus or broken stratocumulus.

Clouds Formed by the Widespread Ascent of an Air Mass

When two large masses of air of differing temperatures meet, the warmer and less dense air will flow over (or be undercut by) the cooler air. As the warmer air mass is forced aloft it will cool and, if the dewpoint temperature is reached, clouds will form. The boundary layer between two air masses is called a **front**.

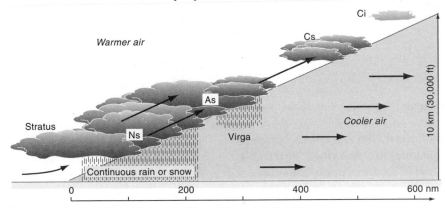

Figure 19-10. Cloud formation caused by widespread ascent

Widespread lifting can also result from *latitudinal pinching* of an air mass as it moves to higher latitudes and has to crowd into a smaller area.

Precipitation From Clouds

Precipitation refers to falling water that finally reaches the ground, including:

- **rain** consisting of liquid water drops;
- **drizzle** consisting of fine water droplets;
- **snow** consisting of branched and star-shaped ice crystals;
- **hail** consisting of small balls of ice;
- **freezing rain or drizzle**—liquid drops or droplets which freeze on contact with a cold surface (such as the ground or an aircraft in flight); and
- **dew, frost or ice**.

Intermittent or continuous precipitation (which often starts and finishes gradually, perhaps over a long period) is usually associated with *stratiform* clouds, including fine drizzle or snow from stratus and stratocumulus, heavy continuous rain or snow from nimbostratus, and steady rain from altostratus.

Figure 19-11. Showers fall from cumuliform clouds

Rain or snow showers are associated with *cumuliform* clouds, and very heavy rain may fall from cumulonimbus storm clouds. The strong updrafts in cumulonimbus clouds carry the water droplets up to cooler levels where the condensation process continues and the drops grow in size and weight before they fall.

It is possible to use precipitation as a means of identifying the cloud type— rain or snow showers generally falling from cumuliform clouds, and non-showery precipitation such as steady rain, light snow or drizzle from stratiform clouds, mainly altostratus and nimbostratus.

Figure 19-12. Non-showery (steady) precipitation from stratiform clouds

For precipitation reported to be of light or greater intensity, the cloud will usually have to be at least 4000 feet thick.

Rain (and snow) that falls from the base of clouds but evaporates before reaching the ground (hence is not really precipitation) is called **virga**. This can occur in areas of low humidity, often over deserts. One extremely important consequence of virga is that the evaporation of the rain absorbs latent heat from the air, creating a very cool and invisible parcel of air that may sink, or even plummet, quite rapidly toward the ground. This can sometimes result in a **microburst**, a lethal form of downflow that has brought many aircraft to grief.

Figure 19-13. Virga

Sometimes the only indications of a microburst are high-level virga and a ring of dust blown up on the ground. A sequence of color pictures showing a microburst appears in the *Private & Commerical* volume of this series. Microbursts are described in Chapter 20 of this book, *Thunderstorms*.

Virga is associated with microbursts.

Lifted Index

The lifted index of a parcel of air is a measure of its stability. The lifted index is calculated by:

(a) theoretically lifting the parcel of air from the surface to the 500 millibar pressure level, and calculating its temperature based on it cooling adiabatically by expansion; then

(b) subtracting this calculated value from the actual temperature of the air already at the 500 millibar pressure level.

$$\text{Lifted index} \quad = \quad \begin{array}{c} \textit{actual temperature} \\ \textit{at 500 mb level} \end{array} \quad - \quad \begin{array}{c} \textit{theoretical temperature} \\ \textit{at 500 mb level if surface} \\ \textit{air is raised} \end{array}$$

If the "lifted" parcel of air has a temperature less than that existing in the actual air at the 500 mb pressure level, then the parcel would have no tendency to keep rising, and the lifted index would have a positive value. A positive lifted index indicates stable air.

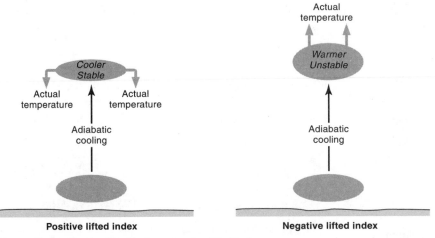

Figure 19-14. Positive lifted index; negative lifted index

If the "lifted" air is warmer than the environmental air, then it will tend to keep on rising, and the lifted index would have a negative value. A negative lifted index indicates unstable air.

1. Name the four families of clouds.
   ➤ High-, middle-, low-level clouds, and those with extensive vertical development

2. Clouds, fog or dew form when water vapor (is present/condenses).
   ➤ condenses

3. Clouds with a base above approximately 20,000 feet are known as _____ clouds.
   ➤ high-level

4. Clouds with a base below approximately 6500 feet are known as _____ clouds.
   ➤ low-level

5. The suffix *nimbus* and the prefix *nimbo*, used in naming clouds, means that the clouds are _____-bearing.
   ➤ rain-bearing

6. Clouds broken into fragments are often identified by the suffix (nimbus/cirrus/fractus).
   ➤ fractus

7. Clouds formed in strong winds over mountains are known as _____ clouds.
   ➤ lenticular (lenticularis)

8. The temperature to which air must be cooled to become saturated is called the _____ temperature.
   ➤ dewpoint

9. As a parcel of air is cooled, its relative humidity (rises/falls/remains unchanged).
   ➤ rises

10. As a parcel of air is cooled to its dewpoint temperature, its relative humidity will rise to _____%
    ➤ 100%

11. The amount of water vapor which air can hold largely depends on its (temperature/relative humidity/dewpoint).
    ➤ temperature

12. If air in contact with the ground cools to its dewpoint temperature, which is above freezing, the excess water vapor will condense out and form (frost/dew/ice).
    ➤ dew

13. If air in contact with the ground cools to its dewpoint temperature, which is below freezing, the excess water vapor will condense out and form (frost/dew/ice).
    ➤ frost

14. For frost to form, the dewpoint (must/need not) be below freezing, and the collecting surface (must/need not) be below freezing.
    ➤ must, must

15. The process of excess water condensing out of the air to form cloud or fog may be delayed if there are insufficient _____ nuclei in the air.
    ➤ condensation nuclei

16. Turbulence, good visibility, cumuliform clouds and showery precipitation indicate (stable/unstable) air.
    ➤ unstable

17. The presence of cumuliform clouds indicates (stable/unstable) air.
    ➤ unstable

18. The presence of stratiform clouds indicates (stable/unstable) air.
    ➤ stable

19. Steady precipitation and little or no turbulence is a characteristic of (cumuliform/stratiform) clouds that are formed in (stable/unstable) air.
    ➤ stratiform, stable

20. Poor visibility, stratiform clouds and steady precipitation are more likely when the ambient lapse rate is (high/low), which indicates (stable/unstable) air.

➤ low, stable

21. Stability can be determined from the value of the (ambient/dry adiabatic/saturated adiabatic) lapse rate.

➤ ambient lapse rate

22. The structure or type of clouds, such as stratiform or cumuliform, is determined by:

(a) the method by which the air is lifted.

(b) the relative humidity of the air;

(c) the prevalence of condensation nuclei;

(d) the stability of the air before lifting occurs.

➤ (d)

23. Unsaturated air being forced aloft will cool at a rate of _____°C per 1000 feet.

➤ 3°C per 1000 feet

24. Saturated air being forced aloft will cool at a rate of _____°C per 1000 feet.

➤ 1.5°C per 1000 feet

25. The ambient lapse rate in the theoretical standard atmosphere is assumed to be _____°C per 1000 feet. It (can/will not) vary significantly from this value in an actual atmosphere.

➤ 2°C/1000 feet, can

26. If an unstable air mass is forced to ascend a mountain slope, the cloud type most likely to develop is (cumuliform/stratiform) with (little/extensive) vertical development.

➤ cumuliform, extensive

27. If a stable air mass is forced to ascend a mountain slope, the cloud type most likely to develop is (cumuliform/stratiform) with (little/extensive) vertical development.

➤ stratiform, little

28. An unstable cold air mass moving over a warm surface may give rise to (cumuliform/stratiform) clouds, (turbulent/smooth) flying conditions, and (good/poor) visibility.

➤ cumuliform, turbulent, good

29. An indicator of very strong turbulence is the presence of (stratus/standing lenticular altocumulus/high-level) clouds in mountain areas.

➤ standing lenticular altocumulus

30. The lowest cloud in a stationary group of clouds associated with a mountain wave could be a (standing lenticular/low stratus/rotor) cloud.

➤ rotor

31. The clouds with the greatest turbulence are (cumulus/cumulonimbus/nimbostratus/stratus) clouds.

➤ cumulonimbus

32. High-level clouds are composed mainly of (water vapor/water droplets/ice crystals).

➤ ice crystals

33. Flying conditions at and below the level of fair weather cumulus clouds are often (smooth/turbulent).

➤ turbulent

34. Flying conditions above fair cumulus clouds, compared with below them, are often (smoother/rougher).

➤ smoother

35. The presence of standing lenticular altocumulus over a mountain range is a good indication of (smooth flying conditions/strong turbulence).

➤ strong turbulence

36. Drizzle or steady rain is more likely from (stratiform/cumuliform) clouds.

➤ stratiform

37. Showers are more likely from (stratiform/cumuliform) clouds.

➤ cumuliform

38. The growth rate of raindrops is enhanced by (updrafts/no vertical movement), which is most likely in (cumulonimbus/cirrus) clouds.

➤ updrafts, cumulonimbus

39. There is (little/great) risk of structural icing when flying in clouds of extensive vertical development since they may contain (ice crystals/large supercooled water drops).

➤ great, large supercooled water drops

40. There is (little/great) risk of structural icing when flying in high-level cirriform clouds, since they consist mainly of (large supercooled water drops/ice crystals).

➤ little, ice crystals

41. For precipitation of light or greater intensity to occur, the clouds generally have to be at least (1000/2000/4000/10,000) feet thick.

➤ 4000 feet

42. Rain which evaporates before it reaches the ground is called _____.

➤ virga

43. Evaporating rain will cause the temperature to (increase/decrease).

➤ decrease

44. There (may/will not) be very strong downdrafts beneath virga.

➤ may

45. A very dangerous and localized downflow of air that may be quite narrow in extent is known as a _____.

➤ microburst

Thunderstorms

A thunderstorm is one or more *cumulonimbus* clouds accompanied by sudden electrical discharges known as lightning, which cause a sharp rumbling sound known as thunder. Thunderstorms generate spectacular weather which may be accompanied by lightning, thunder, heavy rain showers, and sometimes hail, squalls and tornadoes.

Thunderstorms are only associated with cumulonimbus clouds, and there may be several thunderstorm cells within the one cloud mass. Thunderstorms constitute a severe hazard to the aviator and must be avoided.

Thunderstorms must be avoided!

Lightning and Thunder

Lightning is simply a discharge of static electricity that has built up in the cloud. The air along the path that the lightning follows experiences intense heating, causing it to expand violently. It is this expansion of air that produces the familiar clap of thunder. By definition, all thunderstorms have lightning—since it is the lightning which causes the thunder.

Thunderstorm Formation

Three conditions are necessary for a thunderstorm to develop, and they are:

1. **deep instability in the atmosphere**, so that once the air starts to rise it will continue to rise (for example, a steep unstable lapse rate with warm air in the lower levels of the atmosphere and cold air in the upper levels);

2. **a high moisture content**, so that clouds can readily form; and

3. **a trigger action** (catalyst or lifting force) to start the air rising, possibly caused by:

   – a front forcing the air aloft;

   – a mountain or other terrain forcing the air aloft, (orographic ascent);

   – strong heating of the air in contact with the earth's surface causing convective ascent;

   – heating of the lower layers of a cold polar air mass as it moves by advection to warmer latitudes, causing convective ascent and known as a cold stream thunderstorm;

   – advection of cold air in an upper layer, over warm air beneath, which will then tend to rise;

   – less dense moist air moving up and over drier and denser continental air; or

   – cooling of the tops of large clouds at night by radiation which will cause the lower warmer air to rise (for instance, thunderstorms in tropical areas at night or in the early mornings).

The Life Cycle of a Thunderstorm

1. The Cumulus Stage

As moist air rises, it is cooled until its dewpoint temperature is reached. Then the water vapor starts to condense out as liquid droplets, forming clouds. Latent heat is given off in the condensation process, and so the rising air cools at a lesser rate, with the release of large amounts of latent heat energy driving along the formation of the storm cloud. At this early cumulus stage in the formation of a thunderstorm, there are strong, warm **updrafts** over a diameter of one or two miles, with no significant downdrafts.

Air is drawn horizontally into the cell at all levels and causes the updraft to become stronger with altitude. The temperature inside the cloud is higher than the outside environment (because of the release of latent heat during the condensation), and the cloud continues to build to greater and greater altitudes. This growth often occurs at such a rate that an airplane cannot out-climb the growing cloud.

The strong, warm updrafts carry the water droplets higher and higher, to levels often much higher than the freezing level, where they may freeze or continue to exist as liquid water droplets in a supercooled state. Water condensation occurs, and the liquid droplets coalesce to form larger and larger drops.

The cumulus stage as a thunderstorm forms typically lasts 10 to 20 minutes and is characterized by continuous updrafts. If the cumulus cloud develops into a towering cumulus 25,000 feet high in only 10 minutes, then the average updraft strength exceeds 2000 fpm.

2. The Mature Stage

The water drops eventually become too large and too heavy to be supported by the updrafts, even though the updrafts may be in excess of 6000 fpm, and so start to fall. As the drops fall in great numbers inside the cloud, they drag air along with them causing strong **downdrafts**. Often the first lightning flashes and the first rain from the cloud base will occur at this stage.

Rain commencing to fall from the base of a cumulonimbus cloud to the surface is an indication that the thunderstorm has entered the mature stage, and it is in this stage that the thunderstorm reaches its greatest intensity.

The descending air warms adiabatically, but the very cold drops of water slow down the rate at which this occurs, resulting in very **cool downdrafts** in contrast to the **warm updrafts**. Heavy rain or hail may fall from the base of the cloud at this stage, generally being heaviest for the first five minutes. The strong wind currents associated with the thunderstorm may throw the **hailstones** well out from the core of the storm, possibly several miles where they may fall in clear air.

The top of a storm cloud in this mature stage may reach as far up as the tropopause, which is perhaps 30,000 feet MSL in temperate latitudes and 50,000 feet MSL in the tropics. The storm cloud may now have the typical shape of a cumulonimbus, with the top spreading out in an *anvil* shape in the direction of the upper winds. Extremely large cumulonimbus with strong vertical development can sometimes push through the tropopause and into the stratosphere. Over the Midwestern plains, some thunderstorms reach well above 50,000 feet MSL.

The violent updrafts and downdrafts (which are very close to each other in a mature thunderstorm) cause extremely strong **windshear** and **turbulence**, which can result in structural failure of the airframe. The rapidly changing direction from which the airflow strikes the wings could also cause a stall, so intentionally flying into a mature cumulonimbus cloud is a foolhardy thing to do.

Thunderstorms have a distinct lifecycle consisting of three stages: cumulus, mature and dissipating.

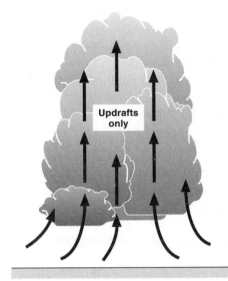

Figure 20-1. The cumulus stage in the development of a thunderstorm

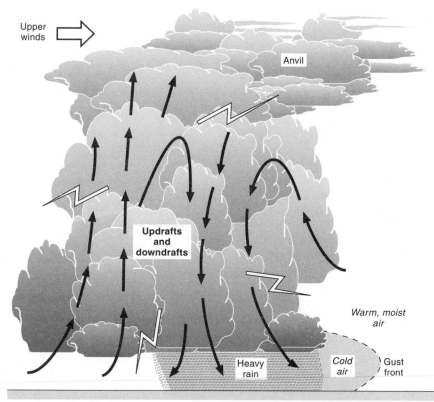

Figure 20-2. The mature stage

As the cold downdrafts flow out of the base of the cloud at a great rate, they change direction and begin to flow horizontally as the ground is approached. Strong windshear and turbulence will occur—and this has caused the demise of many aircraft, large and small. The outflowing cold air will undercut the inflowing warmer air and, like a mini cold front, a gusty wind and a sudden drop in temperature may precede the actual storm.

Squalls may occur at the surface—a squall being defined as a sudden increase in wind speed of at least 15 knots, with the peak being at least 20 knots and lasting more than one minute.

A **gust** is less dramatic than a squall and is defined as a brief increase in wind speed of at least 10 knots.

A **roll cloud** may also develop at the base of the main cloud where the cold downdrafts and warm updrafts pass, indicating possible extreme turbulence.

The mature stage of a thunderstorm typically lasts between 20 and 40 minutes, and is characterized by updrafts and downdrafts, and by precipitation. There is so much water falling through the cloud toward the end of the mature stage that it starts to wash out the updrafts.

3. The Dissipating Stage

The cold downdrafts gradually cause the warm updrafts to weaken, thereby reducing the supply of warm, moist air to the upper levels of the cloud. The cool downdrafts continue (since they are colder than the ambient air surrounding the cloud) and spread out over the whole cloud, which starts to collapse from above. The dissipating stage of a thunderstorm is characterized by **downdrafts**.

Eventually the temperature inside the cloud warms to reach that of the environment, and what was once a towering cumulonimbus cloud may collapse into stratiform cloud.

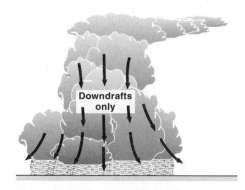

Figure 20-3. The dissipating stage

Severe Thunderstorms

Sometimes severe thunderstorms develop, containing more than one storm cell, and with a prolonged mature stage of updrafts and downdrafts, with extremely strong windshears resulting. The cells within the one large storm may be at different stages in their life cycle. Strong winds aloft may cause the updrafts to slope. The rain and resulting downdrafts will be well-separated from the sloping updrafts, and so will not affect the updrafts and the moisture they are carrying up to the upper levels of the clouds. This can lead to the development of large cumulonimbus clouds and **supercell** thunderstorms.

The strong downdrafts, on approaching the ground, tend to spread out in all directions, with the forward edge in front of the cloud forming a gust front. As the gust front advances, air is forced aloft and new storm cells can form.

Embedded Thunderstorms

Sometimes cumulonimbus clouds are embedded in a general cloud layer and, unlike many isolated and scattered thunderstorms, may not be detected by pilots flying visually below the clouds or by pilots flying without weather radar.

Figure 20-4. Embedded thunderstorms

The presence of embedded thunderstorms might be indicated to a pilot flying visually beneath the cloud base by heavy rain showers. In general, however, you should not fly into or under a cloud mass containing embedded thunderstorms unless you have airborne weather radar or lightning detection equipment such as a Stormscope or Strikefinder (lightning has been associated with the severe turbulence found in thunderstorms).

Icing

The most critical icing levels for airplanes inside a cumulonimbus cloud is from the freezing level (0°C) up to an altitude where the temperature is –15°C, the range where it is most likely to encounter supercooled water drops (freezing rain). If possible, avoid this temperature band inside clouds.

Hailstones

Large hailstones often form inside cumulonimbus clouds as water adheres to already formed hailstones and then freezes, leading to even larger hailstones. In certain conditions hailstones can grow to the size of an orange. Heavy hail can damage the skin of an airplane and damage its windshield.

Almost all cumulonimbus clouds contain hail, with most of it melting before reaching the ground where it falls as rain. Strong air currents can sometimes throw hailstones out of the storm for a distance of several miles. On cold days, with freezing level at or near ground level, hail will fall from the cloud and reach the ground before melting.

Lightning Strikes

Lightning strikes can cause damage to electrical equipment in the airplane and to the airplane skin and antennas. It can also temporarily blind the pilot, especially if flying at night in a darkened cockpit with his eyes adjusted to the darkness. A good precaution against this is to turn up the cockpit lights when in the vicinity of thunderstorms.

Lightning strikes seem to be most likely when flying in or near to cumulonimbus clouds at altitudes near the freezing level (±5°C, within about ±2500 feet of the freezing level).

Turbulence

So that pilots and FSS can communicate efficiently regarding turbulence, certain classifications are used and should be generally understood.

- **Light turbulence** causes slight, erratic changes in attitude and/or altitude. Pilots may feel a slight pull from the seatbelt.
- **Moderate turbulence** causes some changes in attitude and/or altitude, and possibly in airspeed, but the aircraft stays in positive control at all times. Pilots will feel more pronounced pulls from the seatbelt.
- **Severe turbulence** causes large changes in attitude and/or altitude, probably with large changes in airspeed, and the aircraft may occasionally be momentarily out of control. Pilots will experience severe pulling from the seatbelt.
- **Extreme turbulence** causes violent changes in attitude and/or altitude and airspeed, with possible structural damage.

The duration of the turbulence can be described by:

- **occasional**—less than $\frac{1}{3}$ of the time;
- **intermittent**—$\frac{1}{3}$ to $\frac{2}{3}$ of the time;
- **continuous**—more than $\frac{2}{3}$ of the time.

Turbulence in the vicinity of a thunderstorm that causes large changes in attitude, altitude and airspeed, with the aircraft occasionally out of control for a moment, and causing you to experience severe pulling from the seatbelt for about three quarters of the time, would be described as *continuous severe turbulence*.

Downbursts and Microbursts

Strong downdrafts that spread out near the ground are known as **downbursts**. A very strong downburst not exceeding 2 nm in diameter is called a **microburst**.

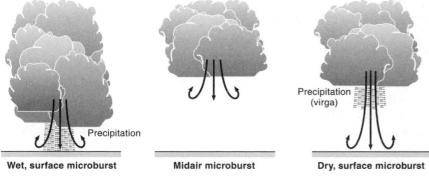

| Wet, surface microburst | Midair microburst | Dry, surface microburst |

Figure 20-5. Some types of microbursts

Airplanes may not have the performance capability or the structural strength to combat the extremely strong downdrafts, turbulence and windshear in downbursts and microbursts, and can be destroyed. You should avoid such weather phenomena at all costs.

Downbursts and microbursts are mainly associated with cumulonimbus clouds, but they may also occur with smaller clouds, such as cumulus, or with clouds from which virga is falling. As rain falls from high clouds and evaporates (virga), it absorbs latent heat and creates a very cold parcel of air beneath the cloud which may plummet toward the ground as a downburst or a microburst. This can sometimes be detected visually by a ring of dust being blown up where the microburst hits the ground and spreads out.

Microbursts and downbursts may appear very suddenly and may or may not last very long. A typical life cycle lasts about 15 minutes from when the very strong shaft of downdrafts first strikes the ground. The wind spreads out horizontally in all directions, with the horizontal winds usually increasing in strength for the first 5 minutes and peak wind strength lasting 2–4 minutes.

In extreme cases, microbursts have been known to blow hundreds of trees down in a radial pattern, and to blow trains off rails.

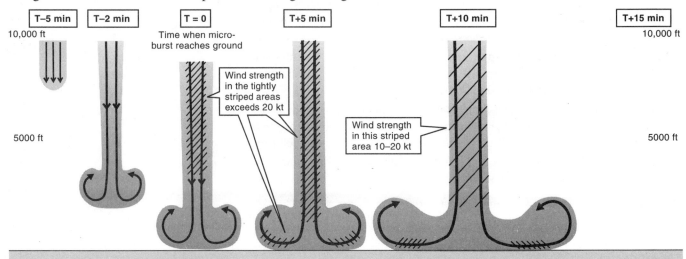

Figure 20-6. Typical life-cycle of a microburst

Even though one airplane might make an approach satisfactorily underneath a large cloud, a following aircraft may not. There are a number of accidents to illustrate this. Always be on the watch for large clouds with a bulging under-surface, for virga, or for any other indication of downbursts or microbursts.

Effects of a Microburst on Aircraft Performance
An aircraft entering the area of a microburst within 1000–3000 feet AGL will first encounter an increasing headwind. The aircraft will initially maintain its inertial speed over the ground (its groundspeed) and the increased headwind will cause it to have a higher airspeed, therefore increased performance. It will tend to fly above the original flightpath. Then the aircraft will enter the down-burst shaft and will be carried earthward in the strong downward air current—a loss of performance.

As the aircraft flies out of the downburst shaft (hopefully), the situation is not greatly improved. It will fly into an area of increasing tailwind. As the aircraft will tend to maintain its inertial groundspeed initially, the increasing tailwind will cause the airspeed to decay—a reduced airspeed, resulting in reduced performance.

Even with the addition of full power and suitable adjustments to pitch attitude by the pilot, the airplane may struggle to maintain a safe airspeed and flightpath. Traversing some small, strong microbursts safely may be beyond the performance capabilities of any aircraft.

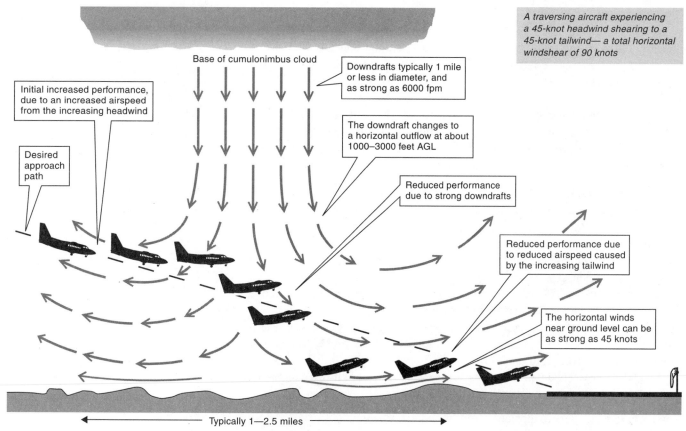

Figure 20-7. The dangers of a microburst on approach to land

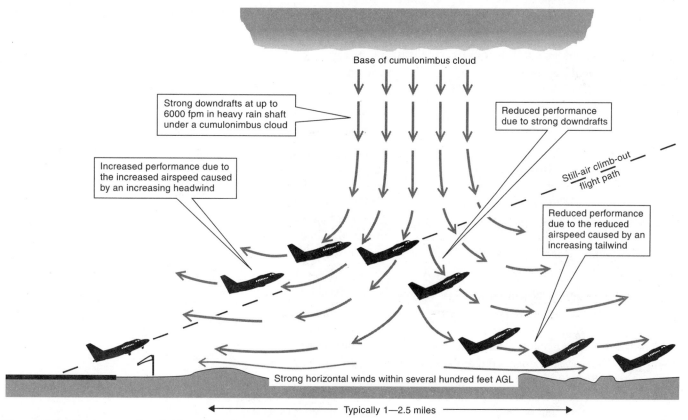

Figure 20-8. The dangers of a microburst following takeoff

Tornadoes and Water Spouts

A strongly growing large cumuliform cloud may "suck" air into it as an updraft. These strong updrafts may commence from just beneath the base of the cloud, or they may commence well below the cloud base from near the ground, from where they may raise objects or, if over a water surface, cause a water spout.

Tornadoes and water spouts are rotating funnels of air of very small diameter. The central pressure will be much lower than in the surrounding air, creating a vortex of wind with speeds possibly exceeding 150 knots. Tornadoes and water spouts are a great hazard to aviation. Avoid them at all costs!

Thunderstorms are Hazardous to Aviation

The dangers to aviation from a thunderstorm do not exist just inside or just under the storm cloud, but for up to 10 or 20 nm or more.

Most jet transport aircraft and advanced airplanes are equipped with weather radar to enable the pilots to identify the position of storm cells and to divert around them by an appropriate distance. The visual pilot without weather radar has to use his eyes and common sense. This may be difficult if the storms are embedded and rising out of a general cloud base or out of layers of clouds that obscure the storm clouds. Frequent lightning from within a cumulonimbus cloud, the presence of rain clouds, and the presence of a roll cloud indicate a severe thunderstorm.

SIGMETs are issued whenever possible to warn pilots of known or forecast thunderstorms and other meteorological hazards.

Figure 20-9. A tornado

Some obvious dangers to airplanes from thunderstorms include:

- severe windshear (which may cause large flightpath deviations and handling problems, loss of airspeed, and possibly structural damage);
- severe turbulence (causing loss of control and possible structural damage);
- severe icing (possibly the dangerous clear ice that forms from large super-cooled water drops striking a below-freezing surface);
- damage from hail (to the airframe and to the cockpit windows);
- reduced visibility;
- damage from lightning strikes, including electrical damage; and
- interference to radio communications and radio navigation instruments.

The most severe flying conditions, such as heavy hail and destructive winds, may be produced in a **squall line**, which is a nonfrontal band of very active thunderstorms, possibly in a long line that requires a large detour to fly around. This line of thunderstorms (sometimes more than one line) can form in the relatively warm air ahead of a cold front, and can be quite fast-moving. A squall line may contain a number of severe steady-state thunderstorms, destructive winds, heavy hail, tornadoes, and can present a most intense hazard to aircraft.

Squall lines can produce the most severe flying conditions. These lines of thunderstorms are a serious hazard to aircraft.

Flying Near Active Thunderstorms

Do not land or take off if there is an active thunderstorm approaching the airport. Sudden wind changes, severe turbulence and windshear are possible.

Avoid thunderstorms in flight by at least 10 nm and, in severe situations, by 20 nm. If you are passing downwind of them, you should perhaps increase this distance even further. Use your weather radar, Stormscope or Strikefinder, if available, otherwise detour visually making use of heavy rain showers, towering clouds, lightning, and roll clouds as indicators of where mature storm cells are likely to be.

Remember that embedded thunderstorms may be obscured from sight by the general cloud layers, so avoid areas where embedded cumulonimbus clouds are forecast, unless you are equipped with a serviceable weather avoidance equipment. Also avoid areas with 6/10 or more of thunderstorm coverage. Any thunderstorm with tops 35,000 feet or higher should be regarded as extremely hazardous.

Fasten seatbelts and shoulder harnesses, and secure any loose objects in the cockpit. Turn up the cockpit lights at night to lessen the danger of temporary blindness from nearby lightning. Do not fly under thunderstorms, because you may experience severe turbulence, strong downdrafts, microbursts, heavy hail, and windshear. High-flying aircraft should divert upwind of the tops of thunderstorms if possible, avoiding flying downwind of or under the anvil, where there may be strong turbulence. Clearing the tops by 1000 feet or more, if the airplane has the altitude performance capability, should avoid turbulence. A good rule-of-thumb is 1000 feet of altitude above the tops for each 10 knots of wind speed at the cloud tops.

If you cannot avoid flying through or near a thunderstorm:

- Plan a course that will take minimum time through the hazardous area.
- Establish a power setting for the recommended turbulence penetration speed (which may be near the maneuvering speed, V_A); the wing will stall before becoming overloaded, so flying at V_A reduces the risk of structural damage.
- Turn on pitot heaters (to avoid loss of airspeed indication), carburetor heat or jet-engine anti-ice (to avoid power loss) and other anti-icing equipment (to avoid airframe icing).
- Maintain your heading by keeping the wings level with ailerons, and do not make sudden changes in pitch attitude with the elevators—just hold the pitch attitude steady and allow the altitude to fluctuate in updrafts and downdrafts ("ride the waves"). Sudden changes in pitch attitude may overstress the airplane structure. It may be advisable to disconnect the autopilot, or at least its altitude-hold and speed-hold functions, to avoid the autopilot making sudden changes in pitch attitude (causing additional structural stress) and sudden changes in power (increasing the risk of a power loss).
- Avoid turns if possible, as this increases g-loading—continue heading straight ahead and avoid turning back once you have penetrated the storm, as a turn will increase stress on the airframe and also increase the stall speed. Maintaining the heading will most likely get you through the storm in the minimum time.
- Allow the airspeed to fluctuate in the turbulence, and avoid rapid power changes.

The most critical icing band within a cloud is from the freezing level (0°C) up to an altitude where the temperature is about –15°C, which is the temperature band where supercooled water drops may exist. Avoid this temperature band in large clouds if possible.

Monitor the flight and engine instruments, avoiding looking out of the cockpit too much to reduce the risk of temporary blindness from lightning. Use the weather radar effectively, occasionally tilting the antenna up or down to allow detection of thunderstorm activity at altitudes other than the one being flown.

Note: You may sometimes experience **St. Elmo's fire,** a spectacular static electricity discharge across the windshield, or from sharp edges or points on the airplane's structure, especially at night. St. Elmo's fire is not dangerous.

Weather Radar

Airborne weather radar installed in sophisticated aircraft is a type of primary radar that can detect water drops. It cannot detect air currents, turbulence, windshear, hail, or the fact that instrument-flying conditions exist, but it can warn you of the possibility of these phenomena, since they are associated with cumulonimbus clouds, which do contain large water drops—a case of guilt by association.

Large water drops reflect the radar beam transmitted from the airplane, and this reflected signal is shown on the radarscope in the cockpit as a radar echo. The radar display can be either monochrome or color, depending on the equipment installed. Color weather radar displays are extremely effective in portraying the weather, with a number of strong colors representing the intensity of the returns—usually graded from *green* for light rain, through *yellow* and *red*, to *magenta* for severe rain showers. Monochrome displays rely on "gray-scales" to display gradations of echo intensity.

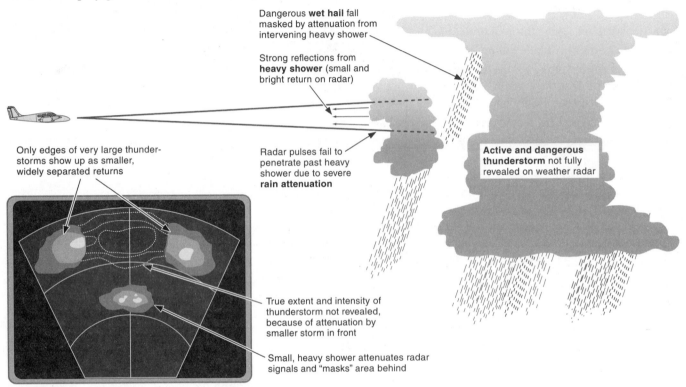

Figure 20-10. Storm cells appearing as echoes on a weather radarscope

Not all storm cells containing large drops of water will be detected initially, since nearer cells may mask the presence of more distant cells. An extremely strong storm may also show up as a "hole" in the radar picture.

Any storm cells strong enough to cause a radar echo should be avoided by at least 20 miles. To achieve this separation between two storm cells, they must be at least 40 miles apart. If not you should consider flying to one side of the pair of cells.

While strong windshear, turbulence and/or a microburst cannot be detected directly by most weather radar, you should suspect their presence if there is a weather radar return from an overlying cumulonimbus cloud.

Radar is sophisticated equipment, and works only as well as the operator is trained. Pilots who use airborne weather radar are encouraged to take time out to learn their particular system.

Stormscopes

Some aircraft have *Stormscope* or *Strikefinder* displays, which show the location of lightning. This equipment shows clusters of lightning strikes on a CRT screen as clusters of dots or plus signs (+). Since the lightning is always associated with thunderstorms in the mature (most dangerous) stage, avoiding the lightning allows pilots to avoid the thunderstorms. This equipment does not suffer from "masking" or "shadows," as does weather radar, and is somewhat easier to use. *Stormscopes* and *Strikefinders* are more likely to be found in light aircraft than weather radar because of their relatively simple installations, light weight and generally lower cost.

✍ Review 20

Thunderstorms

1. All thunderstorms have (lightning/rain/hail).
   ➤ lightning

2. The requirements for the formation of a thunderstorm are (moist/dry) air, a (stable/unstable) ambient lapse rate, and a (lifting/sinking) action in the atmosphere.
   ➤ moist, unstable, lifting

3. An *unstable* lapse rate means that the lapse rate is (high/low) and that rising air will tend to keep rising.
   ➤ high

4. Name the three stages of a typical thunderstorm.
   ➤ cumulus stage, mature stage, dissipating stage

5. The cumulus stage of a thunderstorm is characterized by (updrafts/downdrafts/updrafts and downdrafts).
   ➤ updrafts

6. The growth rate of raindrops is enhanced by (updrafts/downdrafts).
   ➤ updrafts

7. The mature stage of a thunderstorm is characterized by (updrafts/downdrafts/updrafts and downdrafts).
   ➤ updrafts and downdrafts

8. The dissipating stage of a thunderstorm is characterized by (updrafts/downdrafts/updrafts and downdrafts).
   ➤ downdrafts

9. Rain falling from the base of a storm cloud is an indication that (updrafts/downdrafts) have developed, and that the _____ stage in its life cycle has commenced.
   ➤ downdrafts, mature

10. Thunderstorms that grow out of a massive cloud layer that possibly obscures them are known as _____ thunderstorms.
    ➤ embedded thunderstorms

11. The most severe flying conditions, including heavy hail and destructive winds, are often found in _____ lines, which should be avoided.
    ➤ squall lines

12. Hazardous windshear and turbulence (may/will not) be encountered outside of a thunderstorm cloud.
    ➤ may

13. Hazardous windshear and turbulence may occur (beneath/within/on all sides of/beneath, within and on all sides of) a thunderstorm cloud.
    ➤ beneath, within and on all sides of

14. If squalls are reported at your destination airport, you should expect:
    (a) a brief increase in wind speed of at least 10 knots.
    (b) heavy rain but no wind.
    (c) sudden increases in wind speed.
    ➤ (c)

15. If gusts are reported at your destination airport, you should expect:

    (a) a brief increase in wind speed of at least 10 knots.

    (b) heavy rain but no wind.

    (c) sudden increases in wind speed.

➤ (a)

---

16. Airborne weather radar, when correctly used, can detect (large water drops/large water drops and small water droplets/turbulence and windshear/fog).

➤ large water drops

---

17. Cumulonimbus clouds, which cause thunderstorms and have associated turbulence and windshear, (do/do not) contain large water drops.

➤ do

---

18. Airborne weather radar can be used to detect the large water drops in some cumulonimbus clouds, giving a pilot warning of possible turbulence, windshear, hail, icing and instrument weather conditions. Can weather radar also warn a pilot of other possible instrument weather conditions such as fog or stratiform clouds?

➤ no

---

19. As a general rule, you should avoid severe thunderstorms by at least _____ nm.

➤ 20 nm

---

20. For you to fly between two severe thunderstorms, they should be separated by at least _____ nm, so that you can maintain a separation from each one of at least _____ nm.

➤ 40 nm, 20 nm

---

21. Airborne weather radar (can/cannot) be used to avoid all instrument weather conditions.

➤ cannot

---

22. The downdraft in a microburst encounter may be as strong as (8000/7000/6000/5000/4000) feet per minute.

➤ 6000 fpm

---

23. The downdraft from a microburst will spread out within a few hundred feet of the ground, causing horizontal winds as strong as (45/10/5) knots.

➤ 45 knots

---

24. A typical microburst may last (2 hours/15 minutes/1 minute) from the time the burst strikes the ground until dissipation.

➤ 15 minutes

---

25. Any change of windspeed and/or wind direction between two points is known as (windshear/turbulence/wind variation).

➤ windshear

---

26. An aircraft that encounters a headwind of 45 knots as it enters a microburst is likely to encounter a downdraft followed by a _____ knot (headwind/tailwind) as it exits the microburst.

➤ 45 knot tailwind

---

27. An aircraft that encounters a headwind of 45 knots near the surface as it enters a microburst can expect a total windshear of _____ knots across the microburst.

➤ 90 knots

---

28. An aircraft entering a microburst and encountering an increasing headwind will, without a change in pitch attitude or power, experience an (increase/decrease) in performance. It is likely to (gain/lose) airspeed and (gain/lose) altitude.

➤ increase, gain, gain

---

29. Having entered a microburst, an aircraft flies from headwind conditions into a strong downdraft and then into a decreasing tailwind. It will experience an (increase/decrease) in performance and, unless the pilot takes action, is likely to (lose/gain) airspeed and (lose/gain) altitude.

➤ decrease, lose, lose

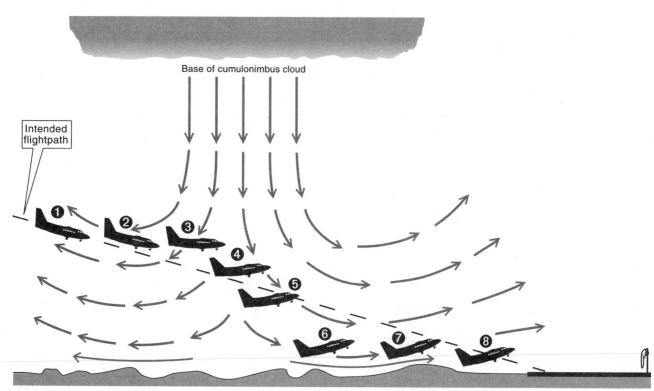

Figure 1. Microburst on approach; use for questions 30–32.

Refer to Figure 1 for Questions 30–32.

30. The airplane at position 2 will experience an (increase/decrease) in performance due to (increasing headwind/increasing tailwind/decreasing tailwind/a strong downdraft).

➤ increase, increasing headwind

31. The airplane at positions 4 and 5 will experience an (increase/decrease) in performance due to (increasing headwind/increasing tailwind/decreasing tailwind/a strong downdraft).

➤ decrease, a strong downdraft

32. The airplane at position 6 will experience an (increase/decrease) in performance due to (increasing headwind/increasing tailwind/decreasing tailwind/a strong downdraft).

➤ decrease, increasing tailwind

33. If you unintentionally penetrate a thunderstorm, you should set the power for the recommended _____ penetration airspeed, (alter/maintain) heading, and hold (attitude/altitude) with the elevator.

➤ turbulence penetration airspeed, maintain heading, hold attitude

34. If you enter an area of severe turbulence, you (should/should not) attempt to hold the wings level with the ailerons and hold a constant (pitch attitude/altitude) even if the (altitude/pitch attitude) varies.

➤ should, pitch attitude, altitude

35. In severe turbulence, reducing the airspeed to the design maneuvering airspeed (will/will not) protect the wings from a potential overload.

➤ will

36. If you fly into severe turbulence, you should attempt to maintain a constant (airspeed/level-flight attitude/altitude).

➤ level-flight attitude

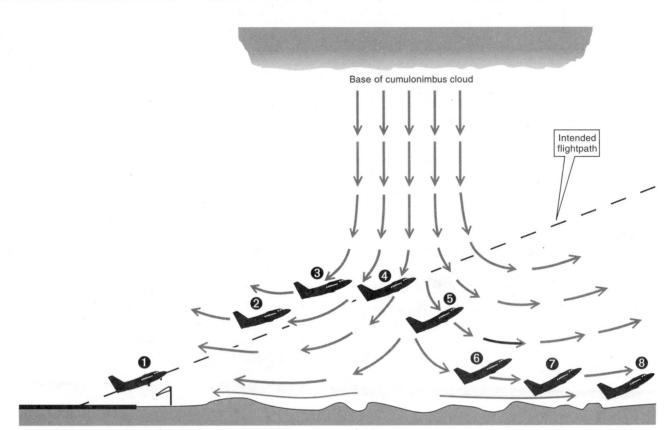

Figure 2. Microburst after takeoff; for Questions 37–39.

Refer to Figure 2 for Questions 37–39.

37. The airplane at position 2 will experience an (increase/decrease) in performance due to (increasing headwind/increasing tailwind/ decreasing tailwind/a strong downdraft).

➤ increase, increasing headwind

38. The airplane at position 5 will experience an (increase/decrease) in performance due to (increasing headwind/increasing tailwind/ decreasing tailwind/a strong downdraft).

➤ decrease, a strong downdraft

39. The airplane at positions 7 and 8 will experience an (increase/decrease) in performance due to (increasing headwind/increasing tailwind/ decreasing tailwind/a strong downdraft).

➤ decrease, increasing tailwind

High-Level Meteorology 21

High-level meteorology applies near to and above the **tropopause**, which is the border between the troposphere and the stratosphere. It varies in altitude from about 20,000 feet over the poles to 55,000 to 65,000 feet over the equator. In mid-latitudes, it is approximately 37,000 feet, and this is its assumed level in the standard atmosphere.

The tropopause is characterized by a sudden change in the temperature lapse rate, with temperature above the tropopause no longer decreasing with altitude. Temperatures and winds vary significantly near the tropopause, and knowledge of these can help you achieve an efficient and comfortable flight.

The tropopause is characterized by a sudden change in the temperature lapse rate, and is generally found in mid-latitudes at approximately 37,000 feet.

Jetstreams

The tropopause is not a continuous "sheet" from the equator to the poles, but descends in a number of steps from overhead the equator to overhead the poles. These steps are like breaks in the tropopause with intensified temperature gradients. Often the winds reach maximum values in narrow *jetstream* tubes along these breaks in the tropopause, with narrow bands of windshear and severe turbulence.

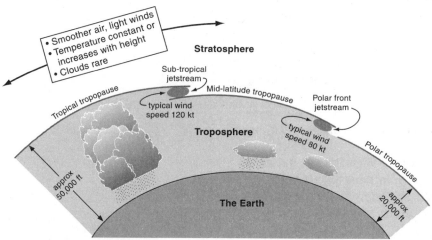

Figure 21-1. The tropopause

In the winter months in the Northern Hemisphere the whole system moves further south (along with the sun), and the jetstreams increase in strength. The position of the jetstream over North America varies, but it is (in general terms) further south and stronger in winter, and moves further north in summer and is somewhat weaker.

The position of the jetstream and its associated clear air turbulence can sometimes be visually identified by long streaks of high-level cirrus clouds.

A jetstream is typically 5000 feet thick and is associated with a deep low-pressure trough situated in the upper atmosphere near the tropopause. It may run in a curved path for thousands of miles around the earth at high altitude basically from west to east, but its path may meander quite a bit.

Clear air turbulence and long streaks of high-level cirrus clouds may show the presence of a jetstream.

By definition, the wind strength in a jetstream is 50 knots or greater, with the strongest winds existing in the "core" of the jetstream tube. It is possible sometimes for a second and third jetstream to form.

High-flying jets often take advantage of the strong winds in the core of the jetstream when they are flying from west to east, perhaps giving them a tailwind of 100 knots or more, but avoid the jetstream when flying in the other direction.

The wind strength in a jetstream is 50 knots or greater, with the strongest winds existing in the "core" of the jetstream tube.

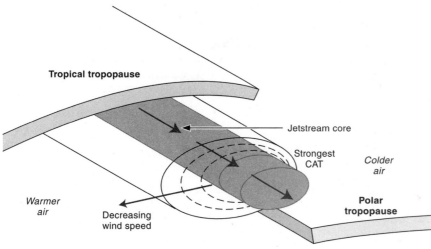

Figure 21-2. A jetstream

CAT near Jetstreams

Flying conditions can be smooth in a jetstream, but turbulence can be expected on its edges where it meets with slower moving air—so **clear air turbulence (CAT)** is always a possibility near a jetstream.

CAT is likely to be greatest on the edges of the jetstream core, especially on the cold polar side of the jetstream where there may be strong windshear, strong curvature in the airflow, and cold air moving in by advection associated with sharply curving strong upper-level troughs. A strong windshear can be expected on the low-pressure side of a jetstream core if speed at the core is greater than 110 knots.

A curving jetstream associated with a deep upper-level trough will create the greatest turbulence, especially during the winter months when the jetstream wind speeds are greater.

If encountering CAT associated with a jetstream at high altitude, it is good airmanship to report it, and also to determine from other pilot's reports if smooth flight is being achieved at other levels. You might fly out of the CAT by climbing or descending several thousand feet, or by moving some miles laterally from the jetstream.

How a Jetstream Forms

Wind velocity changes with altitude, and this is caused by uneven temperatures in the horizontal.

A warm air mass alongside a cold air mass (as is the case at the polar front) will be less dense and have relatively expanded pressure levels. Even though the pressures may be the same at ground level in the two air masses (with no pressure gradient), the pressure at altitude in the warm air mass will be greater than that at the same level in the cold air mass. A pressure gradient force will exist and a wind will be initiated. In general, the higher the altitude in the troposphere, the steeper the pressure gradient and the stronger the wind.

Once the wind starts to flow, the Coriolis force turns it to the right in the Northern Hemisphere. In the situation in Figure 21-3, the wind will flow out of the page (from west to east as a westerly wind), and will be stronger at higher altitudes in the troposphere. If you look at weather charts and winds-aloft forecasts, you will often see westerlies that increase with altitude.

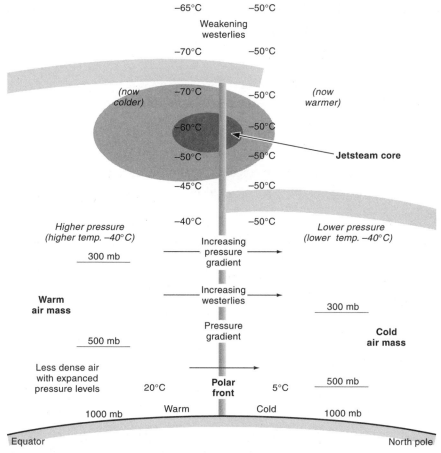

Figure 21-3. The polar front bringing cold air down from polar regions

At the tropopause, temperature stops decreasing. Since the polar tropopause is lower than the mid-latitude tropopause, temperature above it will stop decreasing with altitude, whereas temperature will continue decreasing in the "warm" air mass until its tropopause is reached, by which time it may be significantly colder than the "cold" air mass at the same level.

As well as the temperature gradient reversing with altitude, the pressure gradient will also start to reverse, and so the westerlies will start to weaken with increasing altitude above the tropopause, and may even become easterlies at great altitudes.

The westerly winds reach their maximum intensity in the break between the two tropopause sheets, often blowing in a narrow jetstream tube at speeds well in excess of 100 knots.

Clouds at High Levels

High-altitude cirriform clouds which form in the cold air at high levels usually consist of ice crystals, and so generally do not create a significant icing hazard, although you may experience continuous turbulence. Streaks of cirrus clouds may be associated with a jetstream. It is possible, also, for strong thunderstorms to punch their way up to high levels, even above the tropopause, and these can create the usual cumulonimbus problems for high-flying pilots.

Haze layers sometimes exist at high levels near the tropopause, consisting of cirrus clouds with a low density of ice crystals. They may not be visible from the ground but, when flying in them, your visibility might be greatly restricted and the ride may not be smooth. Sometimes both visibility and smoothness of ride can be improved by climbing above the haze, or by descending beneath it.

Water vapor from the exhausts of high-flying jets sometimes condenses in the cold air at high altitudes to form exhaust condensation trails, known as **contrails**.

✍ Review 21 — High-Level Meteorology

1. A jetstream is defined as a wind of _____ knots or greater.

   ➤ 50 knots

2. The tropopause is characterized by an abrupt change in _____ rate.

   ➤ temperature lapse rate

3. The average height of the tropopause in mid-latitudes is _____ feet.

   ➤ 37,000 feet

4. The jetstream is generally (stronger/weaker) and further (north/south) in the summer compared with in the winter.

   ➤ weaker and further north

Wind, Air Masses and Fronts 22

The Nature of the Atmosphere

The earth is surrounded by a mixture of gases which are held to it by gravity. The mixture of gases is called air, and the space it occupies is called the atmosphere. The atmosphere is important to pilots because it is the medium in which we fly.

Air density and air pressure decrease with altitude. Temperature also decreases with altitude, until a certain level in the atmosphere known as the **tropopause**, above which the temperature does not vary much. Another way of saying this is that at the tropopause the temperature lapse rate changes abruptly.

The space between the earth's surface and the tropopause is called the **troposphere**, and it is in this part of the atmosphere that most of the water vapor is contained, and where most of the vertical movement of air and the creation of "weather" (clouds) occurs. Unstable air, if forced aloft, will tend to keep rising and possibly cause cumuliform clouds. Stable air, if forced aloft, will tend to stop rising and possibly form stratiform clouds. The term wind refers to the flow of air over the earth's surface. This flow is almost completely horizontal, with only about $\frac{1}{1000}$ of the total flow being vertical.

The tropopause is approximately 65,000 feet above the equator, and descends in steps to approximately 20,000 feet over the poles. Jetstream tubes of winds 50 knots or greater can form along the breaks. The average altitude of the tropopause in mid-latitudes is about 37,000 feet.

The part of the atmosphere directly above the tropopause is called the **stratosphere**, and high-flying jets often cruise up there. It experiences little change in temperature or vertical movement of air, contains little moisture, and so there is an absence of clouds.

Air density and air pressure decrease with altitude up to the tropopause, where the lapse rate changes abruptly.

Wind direction is the direction from which the wind is blowing.
Wind strength is expressed in knots.

The Cause of Weather

The primary cause of weather is uneven heating of different areas of the earth by the sun. The warmer air is less dense and tends to rise, causing pressure changes, and so circulation of the air begins.

The primary cause of weather is uneven heating of different areas of the earth by the sun.

Winds

On weather charts, places of equal pressure are joined with lines called **isobars**. Air will tend to flow into the lower pressure areas (resulting from the warm air rising) from the higher pressure areas. The greater the **pressure gradient**, the closer the isobars are together, the greater the pressure gradient force causing winds to start blowing across the isobars. See Figure 22-1.

The wind that initially moves across the isobars is caused to turn right (in the Northern Hemisphere) by the **Coriolis force**. The Coriolis force acts on a moving parcel of air. It is not a real force, but an apparent force resulting from the passage of the air over the rotating earth.

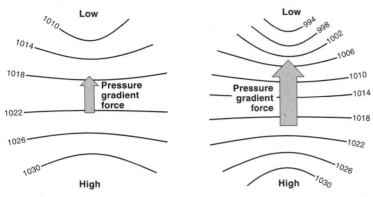

Figure 22-1. The pressure gradient force will start a parcel of air moving

Refer to Figure 22-2. Imagine a parcel of air that is stationary over point A on the equator. It is in fact moving with point A as the earth rotates on its axis from west to east. Now, suppose that a pressure gradient exists with a high pressure at A and a low pressure at point B, directly north of A. The parcel of air at A starts moving toward B, but still with its motion toward the east due to the earth's rotation.

The further north one goes away from the equator, the less is this easterly motion of the earth, and so the earth will lag behind the easterly motion of the parcel of air. Point B will only have moved to B′, but the parcel of air will have moved to A″. In other words, to an observer standing on the earth's surface the parcel of air will appear to turn to the right. This effect is caused by the Coriolis force.

If the parcel of air was being accelerated in a southerly direction from a high pressure area in the Northern Hemisphere toward a low near the equator, the earth's rotation toward the east would "get away from it" and so the air flow would appear to turn right also—A having moved to A′, but the airflow having only reached B′ to the west.

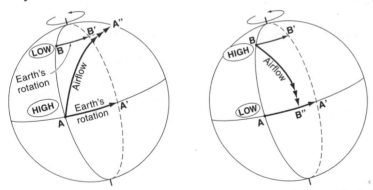

Figure 22-2. The Coriolis force acts towards the right in the Northern Hemisphere

The faster the airflow, the greater the wind speed, the greater the Coriolis effect—if there is no air flow, then there is no Coriolis effect. The Coriolis effect is also greater in regions away from the equator and toward the poles, where changes in latitude cause more significant changes in the speed at which each point is moving toward the east.

In the Northern Hemisphere, the Coriolis force deflects the winds to the right, until the Coriolis force balances the pressure gradient force, resulting in the **geostrophic wind** or the **gradient wind** that flows parallel to the curved isobars, clockwise around a high and counterclockwise around a low. (In the Southern Hemisphere, the situation is reversed and winds are deflected to the left.)

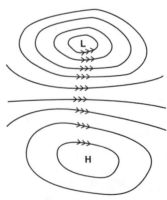

Figure 22-3. Winds flow clockwise around a high and counterclockwise around a low in the Northern Hemisphere

In the *friction layer* between about 2000 feet AGL and the surface, friction slows the winds down—a lower wind speed means less Coriolis effect, and so winds, due to the friction effect reducing the wind speed, will tend to flow at an angle across the isobars toward the lower pressure.

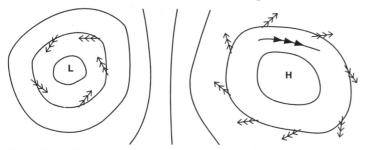

Figure 22-4. Friction causes the surface winds to weaken in strength and flow across the isobars

Windshear

Windshear is the variation of wind speed and/or direction from place to place. It affects the flightpath and airspeed of an airplane and can be a hazard to aviation.

Windshear is generally present to some extent as an airplane approaches the ground for a landing, because of the different speed and direction of the surface wind compared to the wind at altitude. Low-level windshear can be quite marked at night or in the early morning when there is little mixing of the lower layers, for instance when a temperature inversion exists.

Windshear can also be expected when a sea breeze or a land breeze is blowing, or when in the vicinity of a thunderstorm. Cumulonimbus clouds have enormous updrafts and downdrafts associated with them, and the effects can be felt up to 10 or 20 nm away from the actual cloud. Windshear and turbulence associated with a thunderstorm can destroy an airplane.

Windshear is the variation of wind speed and/or direction from place to place, and is often present around cold or warm fronts.

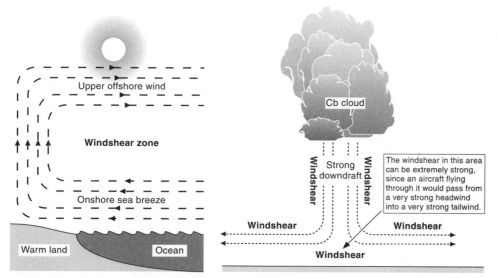
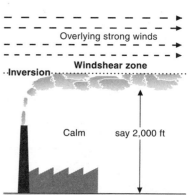

Figure 22-5. Windshear is a change of wind speed and/or direction between various places

Windshear often is present in the wind changes that occur around fronts, usually prior the passage of a warm front, and during or just after the passage of a cold front. It is also likely to be present in the air surrounding a fast moving jetstream.

Air Masses and Frontal Weather

Air Masses

An air mass is a large parcel of air with fairly consistent properties (such as temperature and moisture content) throughout. It is usual to classify an air mass according to:

• its origin;

• its path over the earth's surface; and

• whether the air is diverging or converging.

An air mass is a large parcel of air with fairly consistent properties.

The Origin of an Air Mass

Maritime air flowing over an ocean will absorb moisture and tend to become saturated in its lower levels; continental air flowing over a land mass will remain reasonably dry since little water is available for evaporation.

Air Mass Movement

The track of an air mass across the earth's surface. Polar air flowing toward the lower latitudes will be warmed from below and so become unstable. Conversely, tropical air flowing to higher latitudes will be cooled from below and so become more stable.

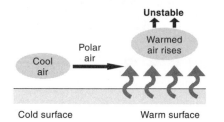

Figure 22-6. Polar air warms and becomes unstable

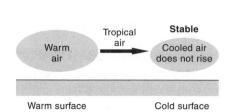

Figure 22-7. Tropical air cools and becomes stable

Divergence or Convergence

An air mass influenced by the **divergence** of air flowing out of a high pressure system at the earth's surface will slowly sink (known as subsidence) and become warmer, drier and more stable. An air mass influenced by **convergence** as air flows into a low pressure system at the surface will be forced to rise slowly, becoming cooler, moister and less stable.

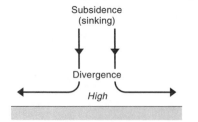

Figure 22-8. Subsiding air, resulting from divergence, is stable

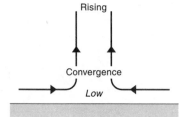

Figure 22-9. Rising air, resulting from convergence, is unstable

Frontal Weather

Air masses have different characteristics, depending on their origin and the type of surface over which they have been passing. Because of these differences there is usually a distinct division between adjacent air masses. These divisions are known as **fronts**, and there are two basic types—*cold fronts* and *warm fronts*. Frontal activity describes the interaction between the air masses, as one mass replaces the other. There is always a wind change when a front passes.

A front defines the border between two different air masses. The wind changes when a front crosses over, known as frontal passage.

The Warm Front

If two air masses meet so that the warmer air replaces the cooler air at the surface, a warm front is said to exist. The boundary at the earth's surface between the two air masses is represented on a weather chart as a line with semi-circles pointed in the direction of movement.

The slope formed in a warm front as the warm air slides up over the cold air is fairly shallow and so the clouds that form in the (usually quite stable) rising warm air is likely to be stratiform. In a warm front the frontal air at altitude is actually well ahead of the line as depicted on the weather chart. The cirrus could be some 600 nm ahead of the surface front, and rain could be falling up to approximately 200 nm ahead of it. The slope of the warm front is typically 1 in 150, much flatter than a cold front, and has been exaggerated in the diagram.

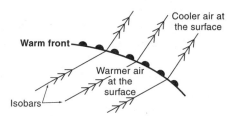

Figure 22-10. Depiction of a warm front on a weather chart

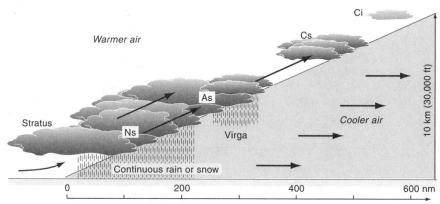

Figure 22-11. Cross-section of a warm front

The Warm Front from the Ground

As a warm front gradually passes, an observer on the ground may first see high cirrus clouds, which will slowly be followed by a lowering base of cirrostratus, altostratus and nimbostratus.

Rain may be falling from the altostratus and possibly evaporating before it reaches the ground, virga, and from the nimbostratus. The rain from the nimbostratus may be continuous until the warm front passes and may, due to its evaporation, cause fog. Also, the visibility may be quite poor.

The atmospheric pressure usually falls continuously as the warm front approaches and, as it passes, either stop falling or falls at a lower rate. The air temperature rises as the warm air moves in over the surface. The warm air holds more moisture than the cold air, and the dewpoint temperature in the warmer air is higher.

In the Northern Hemisphere, the wind direction will veer (a clockwise change of direction) as the warm front passes (counterclockwise change of direction in the Southern Hemisphere). Behind the warm front, and after it passes, there is likely to be stratus. Visibility may still be poor. Weather associated with a warm front may extend over several hundred miles.

The general characteristics of a warm front are:
- lowering stratiform clouds;
- increasing rain, with the possibility of poor visibility and fog;
- possible low-level windshear before the warm front passes;
- a falling atmospheric pressure that slows down or stops;
- a wind that veers (clockwise change of direction); and
- a temperature that rises.

The Warm Front from the Air

What a pilot sees, and in which order he or she sees it, will depend on the direction of flight. The pilot may see a gradually lowering cloud base if in the cold sector underneath the warm air and flying toward the warm front, with steady rain falling.

If the airplane is at subzero temperatures, the rain may freeze and form ice on the wings, thereby decreasing their aerodynamic qualities. The clouds may be as low as ground level (hill fog) and sometimes the lower layers of stratiform clouds can conceal cumulonimbus and thunderstorm activity. Visibility may be quite poor.

There will be a wind change either side of the front and a change of heading may be required to maintain course.

The Cold Front

If a cooler air mass undercuts a mass of warm air and displaces it at the surface, a cold front is said to occur. The slope between the two air masses in a cold front is generally quite steep (typically 1 in 50) and the frontal weather may occupy a band of only 30 to 50 nautical miles.

The boundary between the two air masses at the surface is shown on weather charts as a line with barbs pointing in the direction of travel of the front. The cold front moves quite rapidly, with the cooler frontal air at altitude lagging behind that at the surface.

The air that is forced to rise with the passage of a cold front is unstable and so the clouds that form are cumuliform in nature, cumulus and cumulonimbus. Severe weather hazardous to aviation, such as thunderstorm activity, squall lines, severe turbulence and windshear, may accompany the passage of a cold front.

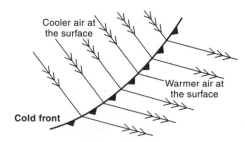

Figure 22-12. Depiction of a cold front on a weather chart

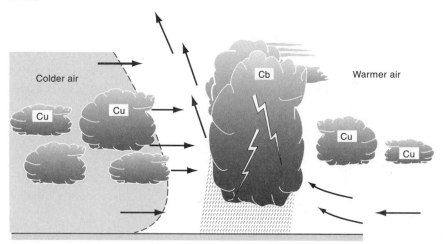

Figure 22-13. Cross-section of a cold front

The Cold Front from the Ground

The atmospheric pressure will fall as a cold front approaches and the change in weather with its passage may be quite pronounced. There may be cumulus and possibly cumulonimbus clouds with heavy rain showers, thunderstorm activity and squalls, with a sudden drop in temperature and change in wind direction as the front passes (the direction shifting clockwise in the Northern Hemisphere, and counterclockwise in the Southern Hemisphere).

The cooler air mass contains less moisture than the warm air, and so the dewpoint temperature after the cold front has passed is lower. Once the cold front has passed, the pressure may rise rapidly.

The general characteristics of a cold front are:
- cumuliform clouds—cumulus, cumulonimbus;
- a sudden drop in temperature, and a lower dewpoint temperature;
- possible low-level windshear as or just after the front passes;
- a veering of the wind direction; and
- a falling pressure that rises once the front is past.

The Cold Front from the Air

Flying through a cold front may require diversions to avoid weather. There may be thunderstorm activity, violent winds (both horizontal and vertical) from cumulonimbus clouds, squall lines, windshear, heavy showers of rain or hail, and severe turbulence. Icing could be a problem. Visibility away from the showers and the clouds may be quite good, but it is still a good idea for a pilot to consider avoiding the strong weather activity that accompanies many cold fronts. A squall line may form ahead of the front.

The Occluded Front

Because cold fronts usually travel much faster than warm fronts, it often happens that a cold front overtakes a warm front, creating an *occlusion* (or occluded front). This may happen in the final stages of a frontal depression (which is discussed shortly). Three air masses are involved and their vertical passage, one to the other, will depend on their relative temperatures. The occluded front is depicted by a line with alternating barbs and semicircles pointing in the direction of motion of the front.

The clouds that are associated with an occluded front will depend on what clouds are associated with the individual cold and warm fronts. It is not unusual to have cumuliform clouds from the cold front as well as stratiform clouds from the warm front. Sometimes the stratiform clouds can conceal thunderstorm activity. Severe weather can occur in the early stages of an occlusion as unstable air is forced upward, but this period is often short.

Flight through an occluded front may involve encountering intense weather, as both a cold front and a warm front are involved, with a warm air mass being squeezed up between them. The wind direction will be different on either side of the front.

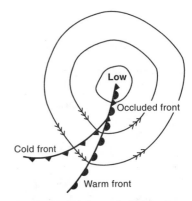

Figure 22-14. An occluded front on a weather map

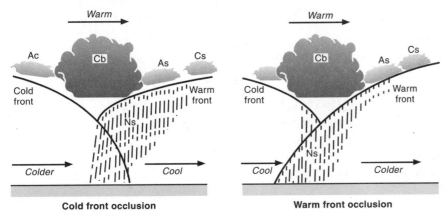

Figure 22-15. Cross-sections of occluded fronts

Depressions—Areas of Low Pressure

A **depression** or **low** is a region of low pressure at the surface, the pressure gradually rising as you move away from its center. A low is depicted on a weather chart by a series of concentric isobars joining places of equal sea level pressure, with the lowest pressure in the center.

In the Northern Hemisphere, winds circulate counterclockwise around a low. Flying toward a low, an airplane will experience right drift.

Depressions generally are more intense than highs, being spread over a smaller area and with a stronger pressure gradient (change of pressure with distance). The more intense the depression, the "deeper" it is said to be. Lows move faster across the face of the earth than highs and do not last as long.

Because the pressure at the surface in the center of a depression is lower than in the surrounding areas, there will be an inflow of air, known as convergence. The air above the depression will rise and flow outward.

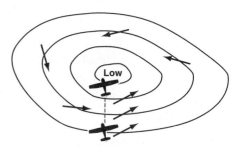

Figure 22-16. A depression or low pressure system

The three-dimensional pattern of airflow near a depression is:

- convergence (inflow) in the lower layers;
- rising air above; and
- divergence (outflow) in the upper layers.

The depression at the surface may in fact be caused by the divergence aloft removing air faster than it can be replaced by convergence at the surface.

Weather Associated with a Depression

In a depression, the rising air will be cooling and so clouds will tend to form. Instability in the rising air may lead to quite large vertical development of cumuliform clouds accompanied by rain showers. Visibility may be good (except in the showers), since the vertical motion will tend to carry away all the particles suspended in the air.

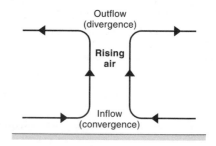

Figure 22-17. The three-dimensional flow of air near a low

Troughs of Low Pressure

A V-shaped extension of isobars from a region of low pressure is called a trough. Air will flow into it (convergence will occur) and rise. If the air is unstable, weather similar to that in a depression or a cold front will occur, cumuliform clouds, possibly with cumulonimbus and thunderstorm activity.

The trough may in fact be associated with a front. Less prominent troughs, possibly more U-shaped than V-shaped, will generally have less severe weather.

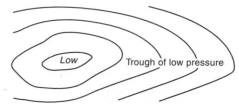

Figure 22-18. A trough

The Wave or Frontal Depression

The boundary between two air masses moving (relative to one another) side by side is often distorted by the warmer air bulging into the cold air mass, with the bulge moving along like a wave. This is known as a **frontal wave**. The leading edge of the bulge of warm air is a warm front and its rear edge is a cold front.

The pressure near the tip of the wave falls sharply and so a depression forms, along with a warm front, a cold front, and possibly an occlusion. It is usual for the cold front to move faster across the surface than the warm front, but even then, the cold front moves only relatively slowly. Frontal waves can also form on a stationary front.

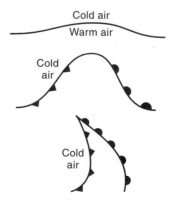

Figure 22-19. The frontal depression

The Hurricane or Tropical Revolving Storm

Tropical revolving storms are intense cyclonic depressions and can be both violent and destructive. They occur over warm tropical oceans at about 10–20° latitude during certain periods of the year. In the U.S. they occur off the Pacific southwest coast, in the Gulf of Mexico, the Atlantic Ocean and in the Caribbean Sea.

Occasionally, weak troughs in these tropical areas develop into intense depressions. Air converges in the lower levels, flows into the depression and then rises—the warm, moist air forming large cumulus and cumulonimbus clouds. The deep depression may be only quite small (200–300 nm in diameter) compared to the typical depression in temperate latitudes, but its central pressure can be extremely low.

Winds in hurricanes can exceed 100 knots, with heavy showers and thunderstorm activity becoming increasingly frequent as the center of the storm approaches. Despite the strong winds, hurricanes move quite slowly and usually only dissipate after encountering a land mass, which gradually weakens the depression through surface friction. They are then usually classified as tropical storms.

The eye of a hurricane is often only some 10 nm in diameter, with light winds and broken clouds. It is occupied by warm subsiding air, which is one reason for the extremely low pressure. Once the eye has passed, a strong wind from the opposite direction will occur. In the Northern Hemisphere, pronounced right drift caused by a strong wind from the left will mean that the eye of the hurricane is ahead (and vice versa in the Southern Hemisphere).

In addition to the term hurricane, the tropical revolving storm is also known by other names in different parts of the world—*tropical cyclone* in Australia and the South Pacific, and *typhoon* in the South China Sea.

Tropical revolving storms are best avoided by all aircraft.

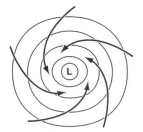

Figure 22-20. A tropical revolving storm or hurricane

Anticyclones—Areas of High Pressure

An **anticyclone** or **high** is an area of high pressure at the surface surrounded by roughly concentric isobars. Highs are generally greater in extent than lows, but with a weaker pressure gradient and slower moving, although they are more persistent and last longer.

In the Northern Hemisphere, the wind circulates clockwise around the center of a high. Flying toward a high an aircraft will experience left drift.

The three-dimensional flow of air associated with an anticyclone is:

- an outflow of air from the high pressure area in the lower layers (divergence);
- the slow subsidence of air over a wide area from above; and
- an inflow of air in the upper layers (convergence).

The high pressure area at the surface originates when the convergence in the upper layers adds air faster than the divergence in the lower layers removes it.

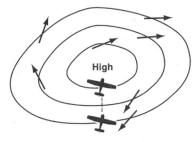

Figure 22-21. The anticyclone or "high"

Weather Associated with a "High"

The subsiding air in a high pressure system will be warming as it descends and so any clouds will tend to disperse as the dewpoint temperature is exceeded and the relative humidity decreases. Subsiding air is stable.

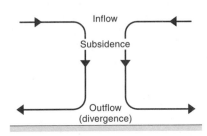

Figure 22-22. The three-dimensional flow of air near a "high"

It is possible that the subsiding air may warm sufficiently to create an inversion, with the upper air warming to a temperature higher than that of the lower air, and possibly causing stratiform clouds to form (stratocumulus, stratus) and/or trapping smoke, haze and dust beneath it. This can happen in winter in some parts of the country, leading to rather gloomy days with poor flight visibility. In summer, heating by the sun may disperse the clouds, leading to a fine but hazy day.

If the sky remains clear at night, greater cooling of the earth's surface by radiation heat-loss may lead to the formation of fog. If the high pressure is situated entirely over land, the weather may be dry and cloudless, but with any air flowing in from the sea, extensive stratiform clouds in the lower levels can occur.

A Ridge of High Pressure

Isobars which extend out from a high in a U-shape indicate a *ridge* of high pressure (like a ridge extending from a mountain). Weather conditions associated with a ridge are, in general, similar to the weather found with anticyclones.

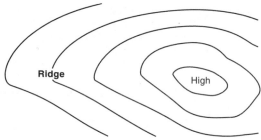

Figure 22-23. A ridge

A Col

The area of almost constant pressure (and therefore indicated by a few widely spaced isobars) that exists between two highs and two lows is called a *col*. It is like a "saddle" on a mountain ridge.

Light winds are often associated with cols, with fog a possibility in winter and high temperatures in summer possibly leading to showers or thunderstorms.

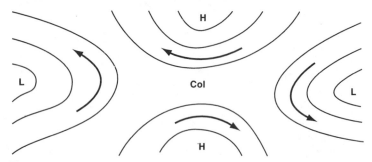

Figure 22-24. A col

1. The tropopause is defined by an abrupt change in _____ lapse rate.

    ➤ temperature

2. The stratosphere is the atmospheric layer (above/below) the tropopause, has a (high/low) moisture content, (little/great) vertical movement, and (small/large) changes in temperature with an increase in altitude.

    ➤ above, low, little, small

3. Stable air, if forced aloft, (will/will not) tend to keep rising.

    ➤ will not

4. Unstable air, if forced aloft, (will/will not) tend to keep rising.

    ➤ will

5. The primary cause of all changes in weather is variations in _____ of the earth's surface.

    ➤ solar heating

6. The force that acts at a right angle to the wind and deflects it to the right in the Northern Hemisphere until it is flowing parallel to the isobars is known as the _____ force.

    ➤ Coriolis force

7. The surface winds are usually (stronger/weaker) than the winds at 2000 feet AGL because of _____.

    ➤ weaker, friction

8. While the winds at 2000 feet AGL and above tend to flow parallel to the isobars, the surface winds tend to cross the isobars at an angle toward the (higher/lower) pressure, because they are (faster/slower) and therefore (more/less) affected by the Coriolis force.

    ➤ lower, slower, less

9. The surface wind tends to flow across the isobars toward the lower pressure because of (the Coriolis force/the reduced Coriolis force caused by friction).

    ➤ the reduced Coriolis force caused by friction

10. Windshear can be associated with any change in wind (speed/direction/speed or direction) at any level in the atmosphere.

    ➤ speed or direction

11. Windshear can be associated with a low-level temperature _____, a _____, or a _____ zone.

    ➤ inversion, jetstream, frontal zone

12. If a strong temperature inversion exists, there (may/will not) be a strong windshear as you pass through the inversion layer.

    ➤ may

13. There is a likelihood of (weak/strong) windshear within and near a thunderstorm.

    ➤ strong

14. With a warm front, the most critical period for low-level windshear above an airport is (before/after) the warm front has passed.

    ➤ before

15. With a cold front, the most critical period for low-level windshear above an airport is as or just (after/before) the cold front passes.

    ➤ as or just after

16. An extensive body of air with fairly uniform temperature and moisture content horizontally is known as an _____.

    ➤ air mass

17. Whenever a front passes, a (wind/pressure/temperature) change will always occur.

    ➤ wind change

18. Squall lines often develop ahead of a (cold/warm) front

➤ cold

19. Frontal waves normally form on (fast/slow) moving cold fronts or stationary fronts.

➤ slow

20. Squall lines most often develop (ahead of/behind) a cold front.

➤ ahead of

Weather Reports and Forecasts

23

Weather conditions vary from place to place and from time to time. It is good airmanship (common sense) that you make yourself aware of the weather that you are likely to encounter en route. You can do this by making your own observations to a limited extent but, for flights away from the local airport, you should obtain weather reports and forecasts.

Weather that has actually been observed is contained in weather *reports*. Weather that is expected to occur at some time in the future is contained in weather *forecasts* or shown graphically on *prognostic charts*.

Reports and forecasts are available before flight from Flight Service Stations (FSS) and other offices by telephone, in person and (sometimes) by facsimile. They are also available via a personal computer on the direct user access terminal (DUAT) system. When you are airborne, reports or forecasts are available from the nearest FSS, or from Flight Watch on the designated en route flight advisory service (EFAS) frequency of 122.0 MHz at the lower altitudes, transcribed weather broadcasts (TWEB), hazardous in-flight weather advisory service (HIWAS), the automatic terminal information service (ATIS) and automated observing systems (AWOS and ASOS).

Obtaining a Weather Briefing

Obtaining Weather from Flight Service Stations

In the United States, the primary method of obtaining the most current aviation weather information is by calling a Flight Service Station. In most parts of the country, you can receive a briefing by dialing 1-800 WX BRIEF, or you can look up the telephone number of an FSS under U.S. Government, Department of Transportation, Federal Aviation Administration, in a telephone book. The FAA's Airport/ Facility Directory (A/FD) gives telephone numbers for weather briefings for all public-use airports. Pilots may also call National Weather Service offices for briefings.

Sometimes it is possible to visit a Flight Service Station office or a National Weather Service office for a briefing, but with the consolidation of smaller Flight Service Stations into larger automated stations, walk-in briefings are becoming uncommon. When possible, a walk-in briefing is best because it allows you to examine charts and data yourself, and not depend only on what the briefer says.

When you call for a briefing, you can usually listen to recordings giving local conditions and forecasts and then talk with a briefer to obtain whatever additional information you need.

Obtaining Weather by Computer and Fax

More and more pilots are obtaining weather information using personal computers and facsimile equipment, either at home or at a fixed-base operator at an airport. These methods have become the most common ways of obtaining preflight weather information.

Any certificated pilot in the United States may obtain a basic weather briefing on a personal computer under the FAA's direct user access terminal

(DUAT) system. These free briefings are in code, which you must learn to understand (some DUAT systems offer a "plain language" mode, but you still must learn the code). Pilots with a computer and modem can also access weather services through on-line connections and the Internet.

Pilot Responsibility

The growing use of recorded briefings and computer briefings means that you must assume more responsibility than in the past for obtaining needed weather data. It also means you are less likely than in the past to be able to talk face-to-face or by telephone with a meteorologist or briefer who can help you understand the reports and forecasts.

You must learn how to read and understand coded forecasts and the various kinds of weather charts of reports and forecasts. One key to American weather reports and forecasts is *Aviation Weather Services*, a document published by the Federal Aviation Administration and National Weather Service as FAA Advisory Circular AC 00-45E. The U.S. METAR code is described in the *Federal Meteorological Handbook (FMH) No. 1 "Surface Observations and Reports,"* while the U.S. TAF code procedures used by the National Weather Service are described in the *Weather Service Operations Manual,* Chapter D-31. These are available from the Federal Government Printing Office and from many fixed-base operators and pilot-supply shops.

The "Big Picture" from TV and Newspapers

Before obtaining a specific briefing for a flight, you can get a good idea of general weather trends—the big picture—from newspaper weather forecasts and television weather programs. The Weather Channel, which is available on cable television systems across the country, broadcasts nothing but weather reports and forecasts, including segments specifically for pilots, 24 hours a day. Local television stations give detailed reports and forecasts for their viewing areas on evening news shows. These usually include moving satellite pictures, live local radar images and maps that give you a good idea of the national picture for the coming day. Many of these local weather shows are presented by knowledgeable weathercasters using sophisticated graphics, and watching them is a good way to further your weather education.

Specific Aviation Briefings

No matter how good the information you receive from a newspaper or television weather program, both common sense and the regulations require that you obtain a specific briefing for a flight to a destination away from your takeoff point. Use DUAT, the internet and/or a FSS.

When you telephone or visit a FSS, first tell the briefer you want a flight weather briefing and give him the following information: you are a pilot, whether the flight will be VFR or IFR, the aircraft's N number, the aircraft type, your departure point, your proposed route, your destination, the altitude you plan to fly at, the estimated time of departure, and your estimated time en route. This information will enable the briefer to give you the information you need as a pilot.

The standard briefing should follow the items specified in the FAA's *Flight Service Handbook*. If the briefer follows the standard format, you will receive all the needed information, but there is always a slight chance that the briefer might not give you a complete briefing. Also, if you are using a personal computer to gather weather information, you need some way to ensure that you receive all the needed data. For these reasons, you should have a form like the one shown below. If you fill in all of the blanks and complete the Pilot's

Weather "Go or No-Go" Checklist, you will be assured of getting a complete briefing every time.

Pilots Weather "Go or No-Go" Checklist		
Synopsis and area WX	Destination WX forecast	Temperature/dewpoint spread
Adverse WX, including SIGMETs/ AIRMETs	Winds & temperatures aloft forecast	Better WX area forecast
Current en route WX	PIREPs, including top levels	Alternate airport WX forecast
Forecast en route WX	Freezing levels	NOTAMs

Figure 23-1. The weather "Go or No-Go" checklist

A good weather briefing should include at least the following:

- **Adverse conditions**—information about any conditions that could be a hazard to your flight, such as thunderstorms, low ceilings, poor visibility, icing.
- **Weather synopsis**—a brief statement explaining the causes of the weather. This should include the locations and movements of highs, lows, and fronts.
- **Severe weather warnings**—includes AIRMETs, SIGMETs and Convective SIGMETs, and ATC weather advisories.
- **Freezing levels**—to aid in predicting any possibility of icing conditions en route.
- **Current weather**—if you are leaving within two hours, reports of the current weather along your route should be included.
- **An en route forecast**—the briefer should summarize the expected en route conditions in a logical order; this is departure, climb-out, en route and arrival.
- **Destination terminal forecast**—this will be the forecast for one hour before your expected arrival time until an hour later.
- **Winds aloft**—a summary of the forecast winds aloft at and near your planned cruise level. The briefer can also supply the expected temperatures.
- **Notices to airmen (NOTAMs)**—current NOTAMs for your route will be provided, but you have to ask for information about military training routes and NOTAMs that have been published. Only Flight Service Stations, not National Weather Service offices, can supply NOTAMs.

Note:

1. Other types of briefing: In addition to standard briefings, an FSS can offer two other kinds of briefings. When your planned departure is six or more hours away you should ask for an *outlook briefing*. It will include general information about expected weather trends that should help your planning. You need to ask for a more complete briefing later on, when it is closer to your takeoff time. When you need to update a previous briefing or to supplement mass-disseminated data or recorded data received by telephone or radio, you should ask for an *abbreviated briefing*. Tell the briefer the type of previous information you received and when you received it.

2. Updating your weather information in flight: Once you are in the air you can update weather information by contacting *Flight Watch* on 122.0 MHz. This is a Flight Service Station (FSS) frequency, which is the same all over the USA, exclusively for the exchange of weather information. The information should flow two ways. In addition to receiving updated information, you should give Flight Watch pilot weather reports, known as PIREPs. Since weather observation stations are often far apart, PIREPs are an important source of information on what is going on between stations. They give other pilots information which meteorologists usually cannot obtain from satellite photos and other sources, such as how turbulent the air is. You can also tune in to certain NDBs and VORs which broadcast transcribed weather broadcasts (TWEB), continuous tape-recorded messages containing weather and NOTAM information, and hazardous in-flight weather messages (HIWAS).

✍ Now complete **Review 23, Weather Briefings,** on page 462.

Weather Reports

You should start your briefing by finding out what the current weather is along your planned route and what it has been doing the last few hours. When you have a good idea of the current conditions, you are ready to look at forecasts of what the weather is expected to be doing at the time of your flight.

Weather Depiction Charts

If you are obtaining a walk-in briefing or if you have a personal computer with graphics capability, the weather depiction chart is a good place to begin. The chart gives a broad-brush snapshot of the actual weather, showing fronts and areas of clouds and precipitation. It is a good chart for determining general weather conditions (IFR or VFR) on which to base your flight planning.

Weather depiction charts are prepared from surface aviation (METAR) reports. They give a broad overview of flying conditions at the validity time of the chart, allowing you to determine general weather conditions quite readily, and so provide a good starting point when flight planning. More specific information, however, does need to be obtained from forecasts, prognoses, and the latest pilot, radar and surface weather reports to augment the general information shown on weather depiction charts.

Weather depiction charts show:
- areas of IFR, marginal VFR (MVFR), and VFR conditions, as determined by cloud base and visibility;
- the position of fronts;
- sky cover, cloud height or ceiling, weather (including types of precipitation or obstructions to vision) and reduced visibilities as observed at various stations.

At each station:
- sky cover is shown in the station circle (with "M" indicating missing data);
- cloud height or ceiling above ground level (AGL) is shown under the station circle in hundreds of feet (when the total sky cover is few or scattered, the height shown on the weather depiction chart is the base of the lowest layer);
- weather and obstructions to vision symbols are shown left of the station circle;
- visibility (if 6 miles or less) is shown to the left of the symbols for weather and obstructions to vision.

On weather depiction charts:
IFR conditions are shown by a shaded area—with ceilings less than 1000 feet AGL and/or visibility less than 3 miles.
MVFR (marginal VFR) areas are shown by contoured areas without shading—with cloud ceilings 1000–3000 feet AGL and/or visibility 3–5 miles.
VFR areas are shown by no contours at all—there the ceiling is above 3000 feet AGL and visibility greater than 5 miles.

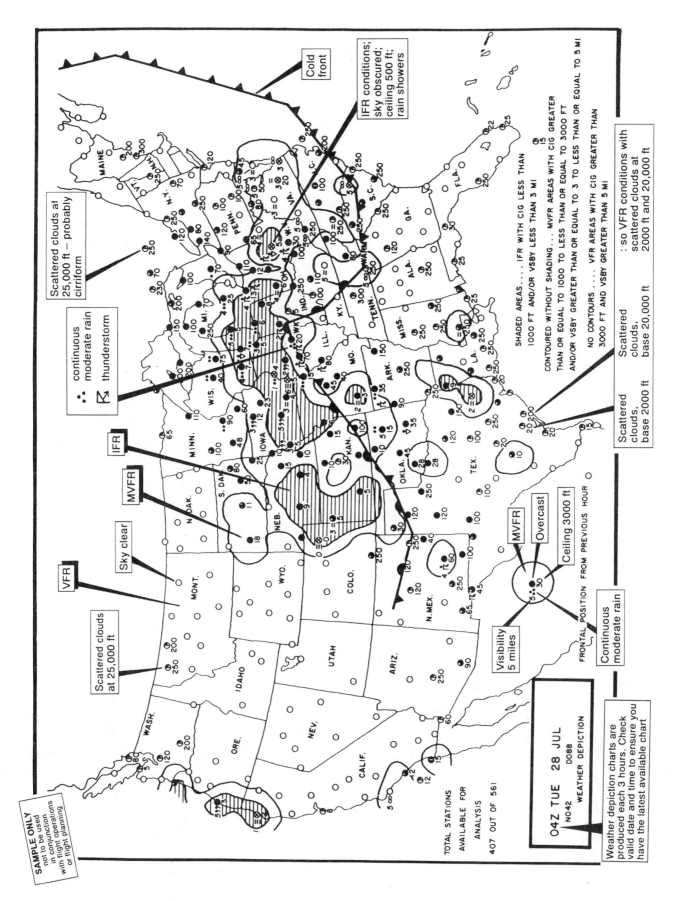

Figure 23-2. A typical weather depiction chart

For example, rain is indicated by small black dots to the left of the station circle—a single dot representing intermittent rain, two dots side-by-side representing continuous rain, and three dots arranged in a triangle representing continuous moderate rain. Fog is indicated by two or three horizontal lines, arranged one above the other—three lines: visibility is less than $1/4$ mile; two lines it is $1/4$ mile or greater (and a visibility value would usually be added to the left of the fog symbol).

Symbol	Total sky cover
O	Sky clear
◐	Less than $1/10$ (Few)
◑	$1/10$ to $5/10$ inclusive (Scattered)
◕	$6/10$ to $9/10$ inclusive (Broken)
◉	$10/10$ with breaks (BINOVC)
●	$10/10$ (Overcast)
⊗	Sky obscured or partially obscured

Figure 23-3. (above) Sky cover

Plotted	Interpreted
◐₈	Few clouds, base 800 feet, visibility more than 6
▽ ◕₁₂	Broken sky cover, ceiling 1,200 feet, rain shower
5∞ ◉	Thin overcast with breaks, visibility 5 in haze
▲ ◑₃₀	Scattered at 3,000 feet, clouds topping ridges
2 ≡ O	Sky clear, visibility 2, ground fog or fog
½ ⊢ ⊗	Sky partially obscured, visibility ½, blowing snow
¼ ✻ ⊗₅	Sky obscured, ceiling 500, visibility ¼, snow
1 ⚡ ●₁₂	Overcast, ceiling 1,200 feet, thunderstorm, rain, visibility 1

Figure 23-4. (right) Typical station plots. (Note: Some common weather symbols are shown in Figure 23-11 and Figure 23-12.)

✍ Now complete **Review 23, Weather Depiction Charts,** on page 462.

Surface Analysis Charts

The surface analysis chart, also known as the surface weather chart, provides an overview of the *observed* situation at the surface (ground level), and allows you to:

- locate the position of pressure systems and fronts at ground level; and
- overview surface winds, temperatures, dewpoints, visibility problems and total sky cover at chart time.

Note: The surface analysis chart does not show cloud heights or tops (even though it shows total sky cover in the small station model circle), nor does it show the expected movement of weather pressure systems (even though it shows their position at chart time).

The National Weather Service (NWS) prepares these charts from observations taken at many weather stations, and the validity time of the chart in *coordinated universal time* (UTC, or Zulu) corresponds to the time of observation. When using surface analysis charts, you should remember that weather moves and conditions change, so what is portrayed on the chart at its validity time may have changed.

The actual chart may appear to be a bit jumbled, but the main features are shown below. The information for each station is set out in standard format, known as a *station model*. Detailed decoding information is available at Flight Service Stations and in FAA weather publications such as AC 00-45E.

The closer the isobars are, the stronger the pressure gradient. If the pressure gradient is weak, sometimes dashed isobars are inserted at 2 hPa (hectopascals) intervals (instead of the usual 4 hPa).

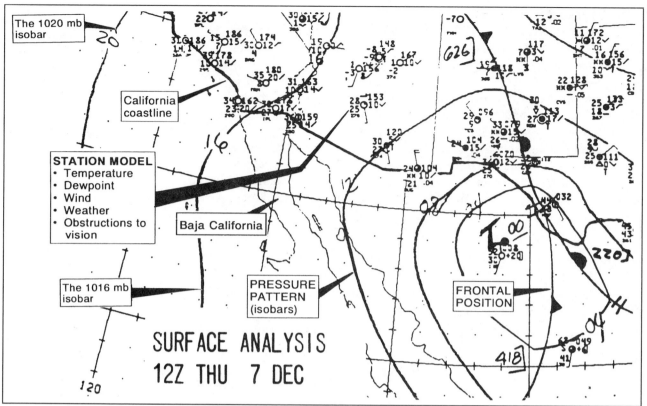

Figure 23-5. Extract from a typical surface analysis chart

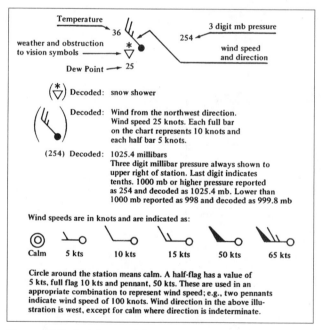

Figure 23-6. A station model

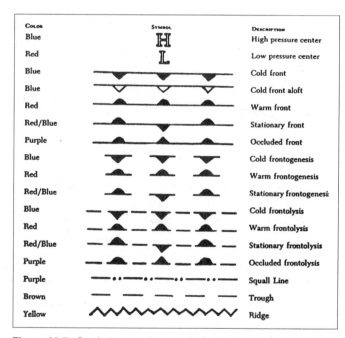

Figure 23-7. Symbols on surface analysis charts

✍ Now complete **Review 23, Surface Analysis Charts,** on page 464.

Radar Summary Charts

A radar summary chart shows areas of heavy precipitation detected by various radar stations around the country, and predicts their direction of movement. You should use the radar summary chart at the preflight planning stage, in conjunction with other charts, reports and forecasts. For instance, used in conjunction with a weather depiction chart, it can help provide a three-dimensional picture of clouds and precipitation. *Severe weather watch* areas (thunderstorms and tornadoes) are enclosed by boxes.

Heavy precipitation is often associated with thunderstorms and accompanied by the usual thunderstorm hazards, so is best avoided. Lines and cells of potentially dangerous thunderstorms, which are not shown on other charts, are shown on radar summary charts. Fog and clouds containing only small droplets are not shown.

Radar echoes may be:

- **individual cells**—with individual movement indicated by an arrow with speed;
- **an area of cells**—shown as a contoured area that is hachured, with movement of the area indicated by a shaft to show direction, and barbs to show speed;
- **a line of cells,** such as in a *squall line*—shown as a line with the direction of movement indicated.

The intensity of the radar echoes is shown by contours, one within the other if necessary:

- **first contour**—weak to moderate (radar levels 1 and 2);
- **second contour**—strong to very strong (levels 3 and 4); and
- **third contour**—intense and extreme (levels 5 and 6).

Be aware that the radar summary chart can show where thunderstorms were, and where they were headed at the chart's valid time, but not where they are right now.

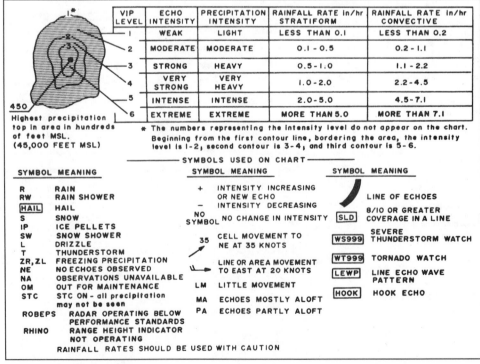

Figure 23-8. Key to radar summary charts

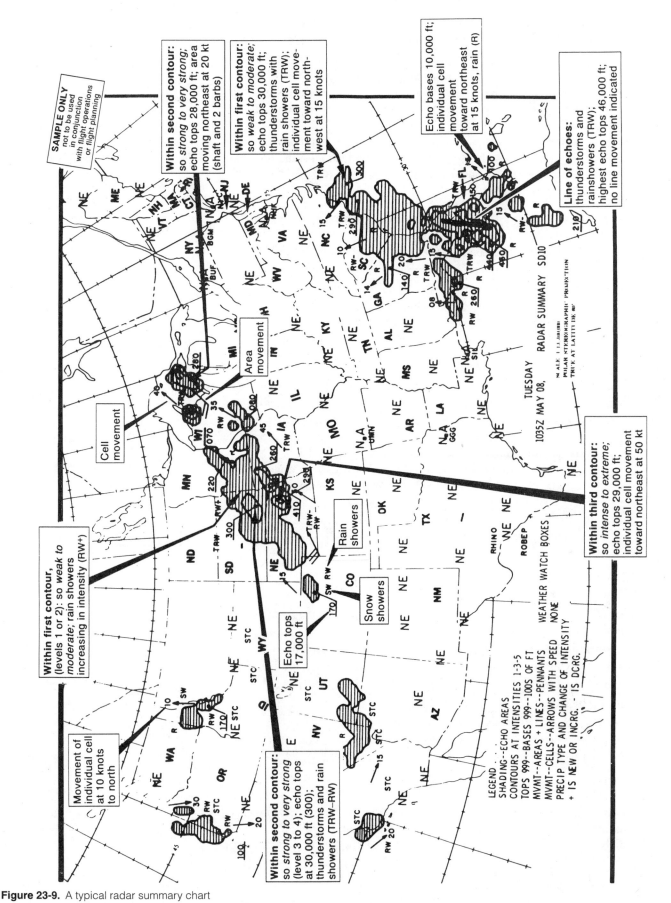

Figure 23-9. A typical radar summary chart

The height of the tops and bases of the precipitation echoes is shown in hundreds of feet above and below a horizontal line (no number below the line indicates no reported echo base). The trend of liquid precipitation is indicated by "+" for increasing, and "–" for decreasing. For instance, "RW–" means decreasing rain showers, "TRW+" means increasing thunderstorms and rain showers. Be aware that radar can detect only precipitation—it cannot detect clouds, fog or icing conditions.

> Radar can detect only precipitation—it cannot detect clouds, fog or icing conditions.

Severe weather watch areas are outlined on the radar summary chart by heavy dashed lines, usually in the shape of a rectangle, labeled something like "WS821", which is severe thunderstorm watch number 821, or "WT184", which is tornado watch number 184.

> Do not confuse a Canadian radar report with a severe weather watch box. The Canadian radar reports are enclosed by a solid line, while the severe weather watch box is enclosed with a dashed line.

✍ Now complete **Review 23, Radar Summary Charts,** on page 464.

Aviation Routine Weather Reports (METAR/SPECI)

Your best source of information about the current weather or past weather at a particular airport is the hourly aviation routine weather reports, known as METAR reports. The SPECI acronym roughly translates as "Aviation Selected Special Weather Report." At weather stations all over the world, observers note the weather about five or ten minutes before the end of each hour and transmit their observations. The coded reports follow a format that makes them relatively easy to translate once you understand the system.

There are a few differences, worldwide, in how the reports are coded. In the U.S., winds are reported in knots, cloud layer heights and runway visual range in feet, visibility in statute miles and altimeter settings in inches of mercury. In other parts of the world, metric measurements and hectopascals are used. Temperatures throughout the world are reported in degrees Celsius.

While the METAR code uses some non-English words for some present weather phenomena, the U.S. standard for METAR was developed in a cooperative effort. Some of the coding groups (such as GR for hail or FU for smoke) are based on French words, but many English abbreviations have been adopted. For example, the international abbreviations for *fog* and *rain* are FG and RA, respectively.

A METAR observation will contain some or all of the following elements in the following order:

1. **Type of report**—METAR or SPECI is included in all reports, and is separated from the element following it by a space.
2. **The station identifier**—denotes where the report was taken from. Station identifiers are always given in four-letter ICAO code (KLAX, for example).
3. **The date and time** of the report—the day of the month is shown first, followed by Zulu time of the report.
4. **Modifier**—if used, tells if report is automated (AUTO).
5. **Wind**—is reported as the full three-digit true direction, to the nearest 10°. (Note that ATC towers and ATIS report wind as magnetic.)
6. **Visibility**—reported in statute miles. Runway visual range (RVR) is reported in feet.
7. **Weather and obstructions to visibility**—reported in the format: intensity/ proximity/descriptor/precipitation/obstruction to visibility/other.
8. **Sky conditions**—reported by their amount, height above ground level and type. Cloud coverage is categorized in eighths, or octas. SKC, sky clear, is just what it says. FEW is 0–2 octas coverage, SCT is 304 octas coverage,

BKN is 5–7 octas coverage and OVC is 8 octas, or total coverage. Indefinite ceilings may be listed as VV (giving vertical visibility in feet).

9. **Temperature and dewpoint**—reported in degrees Celsius. This is sometimes found in the Remarks section of a METAR.

10. **Altimeter setting** in inches of mercury—consists of **A** followed by four digits. Just add a decimal point in the middle to decode.

11. **Remarks**—if included, follow the altimeter setting. Some stations will note the sea level pressure (SLP) in hectopascals to the nearest tenth here. Temperature and dewpoint, coded as 9 characters, may also be listed, as well as other temperatures. Remarks are best decoded with the aid of a decoder card (see illustration).

Note: Any information that is missing in a METAR/SPECI report will simply be left out of the report. For this reason, take care when decoding the reports.

Decode the following METAR report, using the decoder illustrated.

METAR KFMY 141647Z VRB05KT 15SM SKC 30/16 A3003

This breaks down into:

1	2	3	4	5	6	7	8	9
KFMY	141647Z	VRB05KT	15SM	SKC	30/16	A3003		

1. KFMY is Fort Myers, Florida.
2. The report was taken the 14th day of the month, at 16:47 Zulu.
3. The wind direction is variable at 5 knots.
4. The visibility is 15 miles.
5. The sky is clear.
6. The temperature is 30°C and the dewpoint is 16°C.
7. The altimeter setting is 30.03 in. Hg.

That was a nice day in Fort Myers, Florida. Next, decode a more complicated report:

METAR KMCO 141653Z 23006KT 10SM FEW040 27/14 A3004 RMK A02 SLP170 T02720144

This breaks down into:

1	2	3	4	5	6	7	8	9
KMCO	141653Z	23006KT	10SM	FEW040	27/14	A3004	RMK A02 SLP170 T02720144	

1. The report is from Orlando International Airport, Florida.
2. The day is the 14th, the time is 16:53Z.
3. The wind is from 230 degrees, at 6 knots.
4. The visibility is 10 statute miles.
5. There are a few clouds (0–2 octas coverage) at 4000 feet.
6. The temperature is 27°C and the dewpoint 14°C, not close enough for you to have to worry about fog at the present time.
7. The altimeter is 30.04 in. Hg.
8. The remarks tell us that an automated observation that can determine precipitation (AO2) was used. We also see that the sea level pressure is

1017.5 hPa and the temperature/dewpoint spread is a + 27.2°C and 14.4°C, respectively.

Another typical METAR/SPECI weather report is:

SPECI KTPA 141056Z 35003KT 6SM BR SCT250 21/18 A2998 RMK AO2 SLP152 TO2060183

This decodes to:

"Special weather observation for Tampa International Airport at the 14th day of the month, 10:56Z. The wind is 350 at 3 knots. There is 6 miles visibility with mist. There are scattered clouds (3–4 octas coverage) at 25,000 feet. The temperature is 21°C and the dewpoint is 18°C. The weather was taken by an automated observer capable of noting precipitation. The sea level pressure is 1015.2, and the precise temperature/dewpoint spread is +20.6°C/+18.3°C."

✍ Now complete **Review 23, METAR/SPECI Weather Reports,** on page 465.

Pilot Weather Reports (PIREPs)

Pilot reports can be your best source—sometimes the only source—of information about what is going on between weather stations. Since the reports are voluntary, PIREPs may not be available to you on every flight, but you should still ask for them.

Pilot reports (PIREPs), identified by UA or by UUA if urgent, are often appended to surface aviation weather reports. The form of a PIREP is:

UA followed by the mandatory items /OV (over location); /TM (time); /FL (altitude or flight level); /TP (aircraft type); and then by the optional items /SK (sky cover); /WX (flight visibility and weather); /TA (temperature in degrees Celsius); /WV (wind velocity °M/kt); /TB (turbulence); /IC (icing); /RM (remarks).

A typical PIREP, decoded below, is:

UA/OV 12 NW MDB/TM 1540/FL 120/TP BE55/SK 026 BKN 034/044 BKN-OVC/TA –11/IC MDT RIME 060-080/RM R TURBC INCRS WWD MH 270 TAS 185

"PIREP, 12 nm northwest of MDB, at time 1540 UTC, altitude 12,000 feet MSL, type Beech Baron, sky cover is first cloud layer base 2600 feet MSL broken with tops at 3400 feet MSL and second cloud layer base 4400 feet MSL broken occasionally overcast with no reported tops, temperature minus 11 degrees Celsius, icing moderate rime between 6000 and 8000 feet MSL, remarks are turbulence increasing westward, magnetic heading 270, true airspeed 185 knots."

You can generally interpret the abbreviations without too much trouble. For example: FL080/SK INTMTLY BL means an airplane at 8000 feet MSL is flying intermittently between layers; /TB MDT means turbulence moderate; / TP B727 means type Boeing 727; /SK OVC 075/085 OVC 150 means sky cover is an overcast layer with tops 7500 feet MSL and no reported base, with a second overcast layer base 8500 feet MSL and tops 15,000 feet MSL.

If the METAR at the place where the UA PIREP contained those last cloud details above also contained OVC009, then it is possible to calculate the thickness of the lower cloud layer. If the station elevation is say 2300 feet MSL, then the cloud base is 3200 feet MSL (elevation 2300 feet MSL + ceiling 900 feet AGL). Since the pilot reported the tops of the lower layer at 7500 feet MSL, the thickness of this layer is 4300 feet (7500 – 3200).

Examples of typical PIREPs follow.

ONT UA/OV PDZ/TM 2109/FL 085/TP PA28/SK SCT–BKN 090/TA 05

"The report is from Ontario, California at 2109Z. The aircraft was over the Paradise (PDZ) VOR at 8500 feet. It was a Piper Cherokee (or Warrior, the FAA uses the PA-28 designation for both). The pilot reported scattered to broken clouds with tops at 9000 feet. The temperature at 8500 feet was +5 degrees Celsius."

SFO UUA/OV SFO 020030/TM 2100/FL 100/TP C130/IC MDT–SVR/RM HAIL

"The aircraft was on the 020 radial from the San Francisco VOR, 30 miles out. The report was made at 2100 UTC. The airplane was at 10,000 feet. It was a C130 Lockheed Hercules. Under IC for icing, the pilot reported moderate to severe icing. Under remarks (RM), he noted there was hail. While no comment is made on the weather, we can conclude that thunderstorms or violent towering cumulus clouds are around to generate the hail and, even though the pilot has not made a specific turbulence report, it probably exists—any cloud that can produce hailstones will be turbulent. The icing was probably caused by supercooled water in cloud updrafts hitting the airplane."

AHN UA/OV AHN/TM 2038/FL DURGD/TP CE152/SK 055 SCT–BKN 080/TB MDT BLO 040

"The report is from Athens, Georgia, and the aircraft was over the Athens VOR at 2038 UTC. The DURGD under FL means the pilot reported during descent. ('During climb' is written DURGC.) Aircraft type Cessna 152. The pilot encountered a scattered to broken layer of clouds with the bases at 5500 feet and the tops at 8000 feet. Note that all heights in PIREPs are referenced to mean sea level (MSL), since the pilot will be making estimates of height with reference to his altimeter. He also reported moderate turbulence below 4000 feet."

When reporting turbulence, use standard criteria so that other pilots derive correct information from your PIREP.
- Duration:
    - **occasional** is less than one-third of the time;
    - **intermittent** is one-third to two-thirds of the time;
    - **continuous** is more than two-thirds of the time.
- Intensity:
    - **light turbulence** causes slight, erratic changes in altitude and/or attitude, with the occupants feeling slight strain on their seatbelts. Rhythmic bumpiness, without appreciable changes in altitude and/or attitude, should be reported as "light chop" rather than light turbulence.
    - **moderate turbulence** causes changes in altitude and/or attitude, and usually causes variations in indicated airspeed, but the aircraft remains in positive control at all times: the occupants will feel definite strains on their seatbelts and unsecured objects in the aircraft may be dislodged. Rapid bumps or jolts, without appreciable changes in altitude and/or attitude, should be reported as "moderate chop" rather than moderate turbulence.
    - **severe turbulence** causes large, abrupt changes in attitude and/or altitude and usually large changes in indicated airspeed, and the aircraft

may be momentarily out of control; the occupants will be forced violently against their seatbelts and unsecured objects in the aircraft will be tossed about.

– **extreme turbulence** will toss the aircraft about violently and the aircraft may be practically impossible to control—structural damage may result.

✍ Now complete **Review 23, PIREPs,** on page 466.

Weather Forecasts

If you visit a FSS or Weather Service Office and check over the charts and reports described above, and also look at satellite photos, you should have a good idea of what the weather was doing at the time the information was gathered. Knowing what the weather is doing now, and what it has been doing in the last few hours, makes it easier to understand the forecasts of what it should be doing later on during your flight.

You need to develop a three-dimensional picture of current weather, and then judge how this picture will change with time.

To take a single example: you are planning a two-hour trip to another airport; the weather is forecast to be good at the destination when you expect to arrive, and the weather is now good at your departure point. The forecast, however, predicts that thunderstorm activity will cease at your destination about an hour before your estimated time of arrival.

Obviously, you need to know more. What is the weather likely to be along your planned route? Will the thunderstorms be moving across your planned route? If the thunderstorms are moving away from both the destination and your route, are there any indications that they are in fact moving away as predicted by the forecast? What will you do if you arrive at your destination and find that the forecast is inaccurate and the storms have not ended?

Having studied the recently observed weather, it is now time to study the forecasts of what the weather is predicted to do in the hours ahead.

Low-Level Significant Weather Prognostic Charts

Prognostic charts are *forecasts*, rather than observations, and are the only charts that can give you a good overall view of the weather that is expected to occur. The low-level significant weather prog is a four-panel chart that shows the general conditions that are forecast to occur from the surface to 24,000 feet MSL (the 400 millibar (hPa) pressure level) at the valid time (VT) of the chart, the two left hand panels for 12 hours from the issuance time, and the two right hand panels for 24 hours from the issuance time. Prognostic charts are usually issued four times daily. See example in Figure 23-10.

The upper panels show the *significant weather prognosis* (the forecast from the surface up to 24,000 feet):

- **forecast IFR**—enclosed by smooth lines;
- **forecast MVFR**—enclosed by scalloped lines;
- **forecast VFR areas**—not outlined;
- **forecast moderate or stronger turbulence**—enclosed by long-dashed lines, with the upper and lower limits of the forecast turbulence given in hundreds of feet above and below a line, and the intensity of the turbulence represented by a symbol;
- **forecast freezing level**—short dashed lines at 4000 feet levels (dots when freezing level is at the surface).

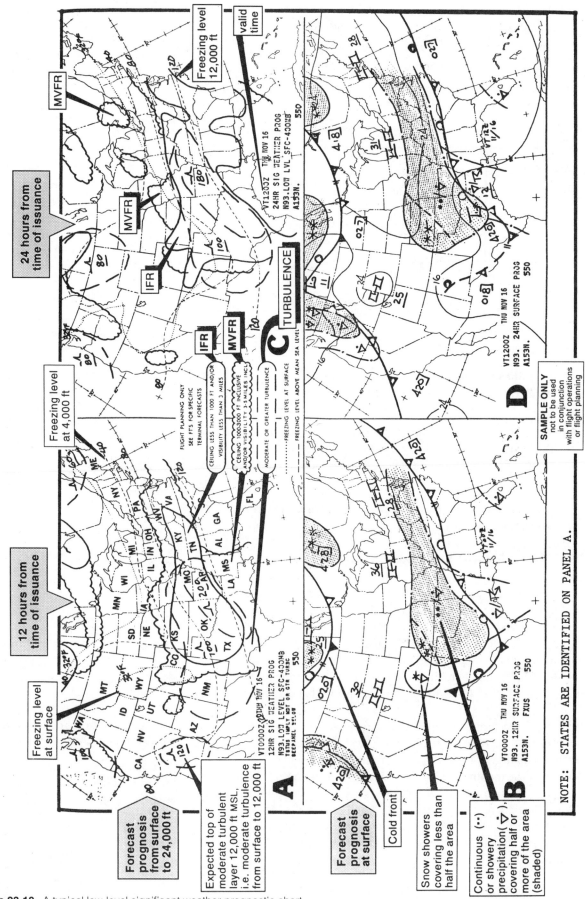

Figure 23-10. A typical low-level significant weather prognostic chart

The lower panels show the *surface prognosis* (the forecast at the surface):
- **forecast position and movement of pressure systems** (highs, lows, fronts);
- **forecast areas of precipitation and/or thunderstorms**.

Note: The method of outlining the IFR and MVFR areas differs from that on the weather depiction charts.

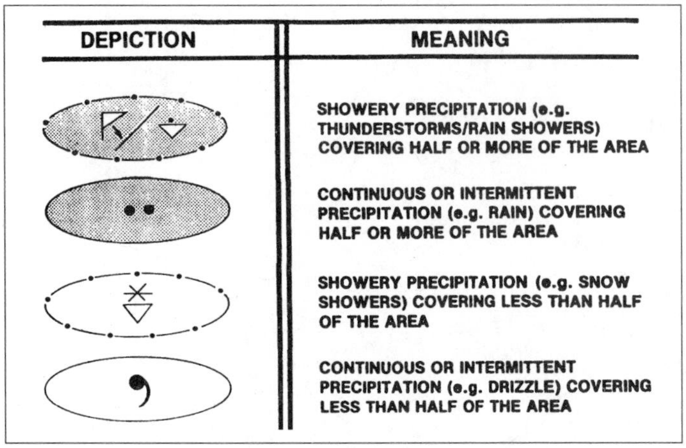

Figure 23-11. Some significant weather prognostic symbols

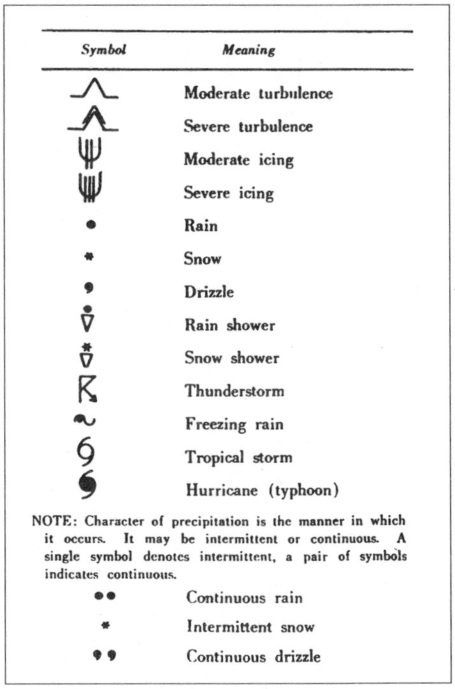

The low-level significant weather prognostic chart as shown in Figure 23-10, can be used to determine which areas to avoid, those with non-VFR weather, turbulence, and the possibility of icing above the freezing level.

Note: There is also a *high-level* significant weather chart covering the airspace from 24,000 feet (400 mb) to 63,000 feet (70 mb). Small scalloped lines are used to show areas of cumulonimbus clouds. See Figure 23-21 on page 457.

✎ Now complete **Review 23, Low-level Significant Weather Prognostic Charts,** on page 467.

Terminal Aerodrome Forecasts (TAF)

As the name indicates, terminal aerodrome forecasts (TAF) predict the weather at particular airports. They are issued four times a day and are valid for a 24-hour period. If the weather changes significantly between scheduled forecasts, amendments are issued.

The forecast is for cloud heights and amounts, visibility, weather and wind that would affect flying within five miles of the airport's center. If the forecast uses the term VCNTY, an abbreviation for *vicinity*, it is referring to weather expected in the area from 5 to 25 miles from the airport that could affect flying there.

The format of the terminal aerodrome forecast is essentially that of the METAR, but a few examples will illustrate the differences. There will be a date-time group, such as 141730Z, which means that the forecast was issued on the 14th day of the month at 1730Z. Forecasts are given in UTC (Zulu time), but you can translate them into local times if it makes it easier for you. Eastern daylight time (EDT) is found by subtracting 4 hours from the UTC time.

Next come the valid times, 141818, meaning, the 14th day, from 1800Z to 1800Z. From there on out, the forecast reads much like a METAR, except with multiple levels.

Figure 23-12. Some standard weather symbols

Terminal aerodrome forecasts (TAF) are the ones most used by pilots.

A code, much like that used for METAR weather reports, is used for the forecasts.

For example:

```
TAF KRSW 141730Z 141818 27008KT P6SM SCT0040 SCT200
BECMG 2122 34007KT
BECMG 0203 VRB04KT SCT150 SCT200
TEMPO 1014 BKN150
FM1400 33007KT P6SM SCT035 SCT150
TEMPO 1418 BKN150
```

"This terminal forecast is for Southwest Florida International Airport on the 14th day of the month, issued at 13:30 local time and valid from 14:00 local time until 14:00 local time on the 15th. The wind is forecast to be from 270 degrees at 8 knots, with a visibility of more than 6 miles, with a scattered layer of clouds (3–4 octas coverage) at 4000 feet, and another scattered layer of clouds at 20,000 feet. This becomes, between 17:00 and 18:00 local time, a wind from 020 degrees, variable at 4 knots, with scattered clouds at 15,000 and 20,000 feet. Temporary changes are expected between 06:00 and 10:00 local time, when clouds are expected to be broken at 15,000 feet. From 10:00 local time, winds are forecast from 330 degrees at 7 knots, with scattered clouds at 3500 feet."

International Differences

Pilots who fly outside of the U.S. will notice that all METAR and TAF reports are not quite the same.

- International altimeter settings are given in hectopascals and noted as Q1013.

- Wind may be reported in knots, meters per second (mps) or kilometers per hour (kph). Low-level windshear that is not associated with convective activity does not get reported outside of the U.S., Canada or Mexico.

- Visibility is reported in thousands of meters, with reference to the lowest visibility in a geographic sector and a trend (for instance, 3000SWD, which means visibility of 3000 meters to the southwest, reducing).

- Finally, in international METAR/TAF the code CAVOK means that there are no clouds below 1500 meters (5000 feet) or the lowest ATC sector altitude and the visibility is 10 kilometers or better.

✍ Now complete **Review 23, TAFs,** on page 470.

Area Forecasts, TWEB Forecasts and the Convective Outlook

While TAFs provide detailed predictions for airports, they do not tell you what to expect between airports. When obtaining a weather briefing, it is a good idea to look at the forecasts for airports along and near your route for an indication of what to expect. Two other kinds of forecasts are available to help you see the en route weather picture—area forecasts and TWEBs.

Area Forecasts (FA)

Area Forecasts—coded "FA"—are issued three times a day (every eight hours) for six different areas of the 48 contiguous States and separately for Alaska and Hawaii. They are valid for 12 hours plus a 6-hour *outlook* period. The outlook gives a generalized forecast.

Area forecasts are supplied in 4 sections. The first two contain:

- **communication and product header section**—shows where the FA was issued from, the date and time of its issue, the product name, valid times and the States the FA covers.

- **a precautionary statement section**—lets the reader know immediately if and where any IFR conditions, mountain obscurations or thunderstorm hazards exist. It also warns the reader that heights, for the most part, are given in AGL.

Then, two weather sections contain:

- **a synopsis**—a brief summary of the location and movement of weather fronts, pressure systems and circulation patterns for the 18-hour period; plus

- **a statement of VFR clouds and weather**—a 12-hour forecast, in broad terms, of clouds and weather significant to VFR flights, giving a summary of the sky condition, cloud heights, visibility, weather and/or obstructions to visibility, and surface winds of 30 knots or more. It concludes with a categorical outlook valid for 6 hours.

TWEB Forecasts

Transcribed Weather Broadcast (TWEB) Route Forecasts provide information similar to an area forecast, except that they are in a route format covering weather 25 miles either side of particular routes. TWEB can be monitored by calling selected locations (TEL-TWEB numbers are in the A/FD) and, in flight, by tuning to suitable navigational facilities (shown on Sectionals and IFR charts).

Pilots often have more trouble deciphering area forecasts than other reports and forecasts because they use more contractions than plain English words and also because they describe the location of areas of turbulence and icing by referring to VORs—often VORs that are outside the area covered in the forecast. Practice, with a list of the most common contractions, is the only way to learn to read area forecasts. When checking the turbulence and icing parts of the forecast, look for VORs along or within 100 miles or so on either side of your planned route. If you find such a VOR listed, then you can look closer to see if your flight is likely to be affected.

A detailed explanation of a typical area forecast is shown in Figure 23-13 and Figure 23-14.

The Convective Outlook (AC)

The convective outlook (AC) forecasts the possibility for general, as well as severe, thunderstorm activity during the following 24 hours.

```
SFOC FA 101145
SYNOPSIS AND VFR CLDS/WX
SYNOPSIS VALID UNTIL 110600...CLDS/WX VALID UNTIL 110000
OTLK VALID 110000-110600   WA OR CA AND CSTL WTRS
```
> **AREA FORECAST (FA) VALIDITY & COVERAGE**

The data originated from the San Francisco weather center, and it is an Area Forecast (FA) for the 10th of the month, effective from 1145Z (UTC). It contains a synopsis, and clouds and weather appropriate to VFR operations. The synopsis is valid until 0600Z on the 11th; the significant clouds and weather group is valid until 0000Z on the 11th.

Outlooks (in the forecasts) are valid from 0000Z, and cover a six-hour period (to 0600Z). The forecast and attached Airmets cover Washington State, Oregon, California and coastal waters.

Note: We mainly show the information for a part of Oregon in this example.

```
SEE AIRMET SIERRA FOR IFR CONDS AND MTN OBSCN.
TSTMS IMPLY SVR OR GTR TURBC SVR ICG LLWS AND IFR CONDS.
NON MSL HGTS NOTED BY AGL OR CIG
```
> **REFERENCE TO IMPORTANT WEATHER**

Refer to Airmet Sierra (later in the briefing data) for details of IFR (Instrument Flight Rules) weather conditions and any mountain obscuration. Where thunderstorms are mentioned, this implies severe or greater turbulence, severe icing, low-level windshear and IFR conditions.

Non-mean sea level heights are appended with the terms *AGL* (above ground level) or *CIG* (ceiling).

```
SYNOPSIS...WEAK HIGH LVL TROF OVER THE SFO FA AREA. TROF XPCD
TO DRFT EWD THRU 06Z. RDG ALF BLDG ACRS THE ERN PAC.
```
> **THE SYNOPSIS**

Synopsis of the weather situation:

There is a weak high-level trough over the San Francisco area-forecast area. The trough is expected to drift eastward through 0600Z.

A ridge (of high pressure) aloft is building across the eastern Pacific Ocean area.

```
OR CASCDS WWD
CSTL SXNS...10-20 BKN 40 BKN 100. VSBYS 3-5L-F. 18Z-20Z BCMG 15
SCT-BKN 35 BKN 80 BKN. WDLY SCT RW-. OTLK...VFR.
WILLAMETTE VLY-NRN CASCDS...15 SCT-BKN 40 BKN 100. OCNL VSBYS 3-
5L-F. 19Z-21Z BCMG 30-50 BKN 80 BKN. WDLY SCT RW-. OTLK...VFR.
```
> **SIGNIFICANT CLOUDS AND WEATHER**

Significant clouds and weather for Oregon, Cascades westward (includes the slopes of the Cascades):

Coastal sections—broken clouds (5–7 oktas—that is, 5 to 7 eighths of the sky covered), base 1,000 to 2,000 feet MSL; broken clouds, base 4,000 feet MSL up to 10,000 feet MSL. Visibility 3 to 5 miles in light drizzle *(the hyphen after the L means that the drizzle is light)* and fog.

Between 1800Z and 2000Z, clouds becoming scattered (1–4 oktas) to broken, base 1,500 feet MSL; broken clouds, base 3,500 feet MSL; and again at base 8,000 feet MSL. Widely scattered light rain showers. The outlook for this region is for the weather conditions to become suitable for VFR operations.

For the Willamette valley to the northern *Cascades*—scattered to broken clouds, base 1,500 feet MSL; broken clouds, base 4,000 feet MSL up to 10,000 feet MSL. Occasionally, the visibility will be between 3 to 5 miles in light drizzle and fog.

Then, between 1900Z and 2100Z, the clouds will lift to become broken, base between 3,000 and 5,000 feet MSL; and also broken, base 8,000 feet MSL. Widely scattered light rain showers are forecast. The outlook for this region is also for VFR conditions.

Figure 23-13. A typical area forecast for the Dallas/Fort Worth area

```
AIRMET TANGO FOR TURBC VALID UNTIL 102000...WA OR
OCNL LGT ISOLD MDT TURBC BLO 150 W OF CASCDS ASSOCD WITH LGT-
MDT WLY WNDS. CONDS CONTG THRU 20Z..ENDG 02Z
```

> **TURBULENCE (T)**

Turbulence Airmet (Tango): for Washington and Oregon, valid until 2000Z—occasional light and isolated moderate turbulence below 15,000 feet MSL West of the Cascades associated with light to moderate westerly winds; continuing thru 2000Z, ending around 0200Z.

> **IFR WEATHER AND MOUNTAIN OBSCURATION (S)**

```
AIRMET SIERRA FOR IFR AND MTN OBSCN VALID UNTIL 102000
AIRMET IFR...OR
FROM 40SSW ONP TO 30NNE MFR TO 30S MFR TO 80WSW MFR TO 40SSW ONP
OCNL CIG BLO 10 VSBY BLO 3 FOG. CONDS ENDG 17Z-19Z.
AIRMET MTN OBSCN...WA OR CA ID MT
FROM YQL TO 50N TWF TO REO TO 20SW UKI TO 20NW FOT TO 20N TOU TO YQL
MTNS OCNL OBSCD IN CDS/PCPN F. CONDS SPRDG EWD AND CONTG BYD 20Z THRU 02Z
```

IFR Weather and Mountain Obscuration Airmet (Sierra): valid until 2000Z on the 10th.

IFR weather for Oregon—within a line joining points 40 nautical miles south-southwest of ONP VOR to 30 nm north-northeast of MFR VOR to 80 nm west-southwest of MFR VOR to 40 nm south-southwest of ONP VOR. Occasionally ceilings below 1,000 feet AGL and visibility below 3 miles in fog. These conditions to end between 1700Z and 1900Z.

Mountain obscuration data for Washington, Oregon, California, Idaho and Montana—within the specified area, mountains occasionally obscured in clouds, precipitation and fog. Conditions spreading eastward and continuing beyond 2000Z through 0200Z.

> **ICING AND FREEZING LEVELS (Z)**

```
AIRMET ZULU FOR ICG AND FRZLVL VALID UNTIL 102000
AIRMET ICG...WA OR CA ID MT
FROM YQL TO LKT TO REO TO FOT TO 20N TOU TO YQL
LGT OCNL MDT MXD ICGICIP FRZLVL TO 160. CONDS SPRDG EWD AND CONTG
BYD 20Z THRU 02Z. FRZLVL 40-60 NW SLPG TO 70-90 SE.
FRZLVL...WA-OR..040-060 NW OF A GEG-MFR LN. 070-090 SE OF THE LN.
```

Icing and Freezing Level Airmet (Zulu): valid until 2000Z on the 10th.

Icing for Washington, Oregon, California, Idaho and Montana—within the specified area, light and occasionally moderate mixed icing in clouds and in precipitation from the freezing level up to 16,000 feet MSL. Conditions spreading eastward and continuing beyond 2000Z.

The freezing level in this region is 4,000–6,000 feet MSL in the northwest, sloping up to 7,000–9,000 feet MSL in the southeast.

Freezing level data for Washington and Oregon—the freezing level (zero degrees Celsius) is 4,000–6,000 feet MSL northwest of a line joining GEG and MFR VORs. The freezing level is 7,000–9,000 feet MSL southeast of the line.

Figure 23-14. Explanation of area forecast for the Dallas/Fort Worth area

✐ Now complete **Review 23, Area Forecasts, TWEB Forecasts and the Convective Outlook,** on page 470.

Winds and Temperatures Aloft Forecasts (FD)

Winds and temperatures aloft forecasts contain forecast upper winds in degrees true and knots, and forecast upper temperatures in degrees Celsius.

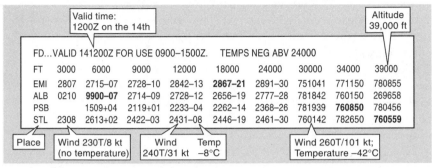

Figure 23-15. Winds and temperatures aloft forecast

"2867–21 at 18,000 feet MSL decodes as a wind from 280 degrees true (by adding a 0 after the first two digits) at 67 knots and temperature –21 degrees Celsius (+/– precedes temperature up to 24,000 feet, above this all temperatures will be below zero and so no signs need be given); at 30,000 feet 256830 decodes as a wind from 250 degrees magnetic at 68 knots and temperature –30 degrees Celsius; at 3000 feet MSL 2908 decodes as a wind from 290 degrees true at 8 knots with no forecast temperature (usually temperature is not forecast for the 3000 feet MSL level or for a level within 2500 feet AGL of the station elevation—also winds aloft are not forecast for levels within 1500 feet AGL of the station elevation); 9900 decodes as winds light and variable (less than 5 knots); and for winds aloft in the 100–199 knots range, to overcome the problem that only two digits are available for wind speed the forecaster adds 50 to the direction and subtracts 100 from the speed, which you need to reverse when decoding; at 34,000 feet 764255 decodes as a wind from 260 degrees magnetic (76 – 50 = 26) at 142 knots (100 + 42 = 142) and temperature –55 degrees Celsius; at 39,000 feet 780458 decodes as a wind from 280 degrees magnetic at 104 knots and –58 degrees Celsius."

You can *interpolate* to estimate the winds and temperatures at intermediate levels. For example, if the winds and temperatures aloft forecast shows:

24000 ft	30000
2367–26	781938

You can estimate the conditions at FL270 by interpolating:

FL240 is wind 230° at 67 knots and temperature –26°C
FL300 is wind 280° at 119 knots and temperature –38°C
Differences: 50°,   52 knots, and   12°C

Interpolating for FL270 (halfway between) gives differences of 25 in direction, 26 knots in speed, and 6°C in temperature. So the estimated values are wind from 255 degrees true (230 + 25) at 93 knots (67 + 26) and temperature –32°C (–26 – 6).

Temperatures may be asked for in the written test in °C, or as a deviation from the ISA standard (which is +15°C at MSL, decreasing at 2°C per 1000 feet, and remaining constant at –57°C above approximately 36,000 feet). At 24,000 feet, ISA = 15 – (2 × 24) = 15 – 48 = –33°C; a temperature here of, say, –35°C (2°C cooler) is ISA–2. A temperature of –26°C, which is 7°C warmer, is ISA+7.

✍ Now complete **Review 23, Winds and Temperatures Aloft Forecast,** on page 471.

Convective Outlook Charts (AC)

The convective outlook chart is issued each morning and provides a preliminary 48-hour outlook for thunderstorm activity, tornadoes and watch areas. It is presented in two panels, the first for the time period of 24 hours, and the second for the next day. It is used for advanced planning only.

An area of forecast general thunderstorm activity is represented by a line with an arrowhead—when you face in the direction of the arrowhead, thunderstorm activity is expected to the right of that line.

Forecast severe thunderstorms are shown by a single-hatched area, which may be labeled SLGT (slight risk), MDT (moderate risk) or SVR (high risk). Any tornado watches in effect at chart time are shown by crosshatched areas.

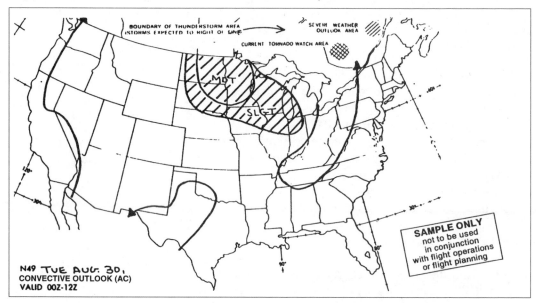

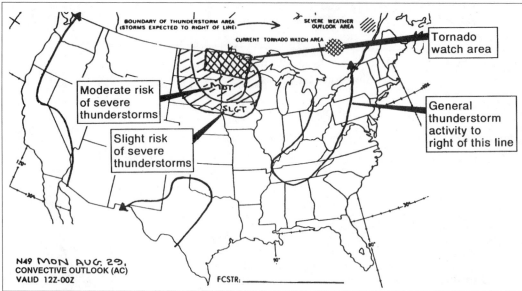

Figure 23-16. Example of a convective outlook chart

✍ Now complete **Review 23, Convective Outlook Charts,** on page 471.

Constant Pressure Analysis Charts

A constant pressure analysis chart shows meteorological data at a particular *pressure level* in the atmosphere, rather than at a particular altitude. They are useful for determining winds and temperatures aloft. The upper air measurements are usually taken by radiosonde instruments carried aloft by balloon, with the information then radioed back to the ground station.

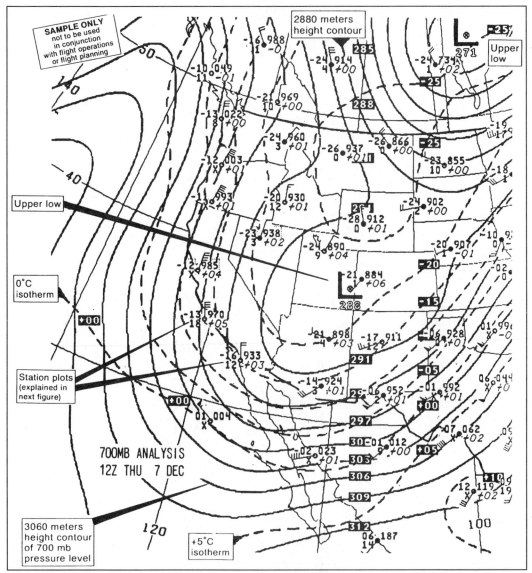

Figure 23-17. Part of a 700 mb constant pressure analysis chart (pressure alt. 10,000 ft)

In contrast to constant pressure charts, surface charts, with which you are already familiar, are based on a constant altitude, with pressure variations being plotted. They show *isobars*, which are lines joining points of equal pressure, and allow you to estimate wind direction and strength near that level in the atmosphere, based on the pattern of high and low pressure systems and the closeness of the isobars. The wind in the northern hemisphere, once you are above the friction layer (more than about 2000 feet AGL), flows clockwise around a high pressure system and counterclockwise around a low pressure system. The closer the isobars, the stronger the wind.

At upper levels in the atmosphere, however, the lower air density causes the relationship between the isobars and the wind to alter, and constant pressure charts become more useful than constant altitude charts. They are just a different means of plotting the same data to better describe the same meteorological situation. The pressure systems in the upper levels may differ from those shown on surface charts, and often they have more bearing on the actual flying weather.

The various constant pressure charts relate to approximate altitudes MSL:

- 850 mb/hPa and 5000 feet—this chart is good for forecasting poor weather which often occurs in the lower levels, such as heavy clouds, thunderstorms, rain, snow, overcast, fronts, etc.;
- 700 mb/hPa and 10,000 feet;
- 500 mb/hPa and 18,000 feet;
- 300 mb/hPa and 30,000 feet;
- 200 mb/hPa and 39,000 feet.

If you plan on cruising at 10,000 feet MSL, you should look at the 700 mb/hPa chart especially. The 700 mb/hPa pressure level, which is equivalent to about 10,000 feet pressure altitude in the standard atmosphere, will vary in its height MSL in any real atmosphere. By plotting contour lines showing the altitudes MSL at which the specified pressure level is found, 700 mb in this case, an upper air picture of pressure distribution is formed, in exactly the same way that variations in height are shown by contours on an ordinary survey map.

Plotted at each reporting station, at the level of the specified pressure, are:

- **height of that pressure surface** (in meters);
- **changes in this height over the past 12 hours**;
- **temperature**;
- **temperature/dewpoint spread** (useful in determining the possibility of cloud or fog formation); and
- **wind direction and speed**.

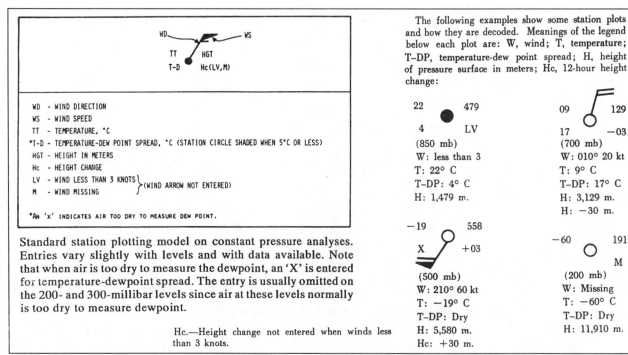

Figure 23-18. Station model

Height contours join places where the pressure level is at equal heights MSL, and these height pattern contours depict highs, lows, troughs and ridges in the upper atmosphere in a similar way to isobars on the surface charts. A *high height center* on a 700 mb/hPa constant pressure chart is analogous to a *high pressure center* at about 10,000 feet. Winds will parallel the contours, flowing clockwise around a *high* height center in the northern hemisphere and counterclockwise around a *low*. Fronts, if they reach as high as the specified pressure level, are depicted in the normal manner.

Isotherms are dashed lines joining places of equal temperatures, and these allow you to determine if you are flying toward warmer or cooler air. Temperatures near to and below freezing and a temperature/dewpoint spread of 5°C or less indicate a risk of structural icing.

Isotachs are short dashed lines joining places of equal wind strength. Strong wind areas are indicated by hachuring. Areas with winds of 70–110 knots will be hachured, and these areas may include a clear area of stronger winds of 110–150 knots, and perhaps contain another hachured area of even stronger winds.

If the constant pressure surface is high, then it has warm air beneath it. A consequence of this is that a parcel of warm air will not tend to rise through the already warm air, and so the weather in the vicinity of a *warm upper high* is likely to be typical of a high pressure system, good, although with a possibility of restricted visibility. Conversely, if the constant pressure surface is low, then it has cool air beneath it. A parcel of warm air that starts to rise from the surface will tend to keep rising through the cooler air, an unstable situation, and so a *cold upper low* is an indicator of possible unstable conditions and poor flying weather.

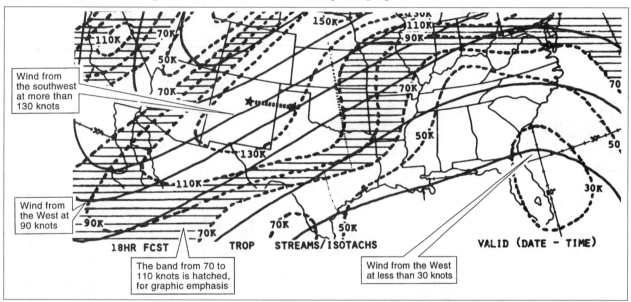

Figure 23-19. Extract from a chart showing isotachs (tropopause wind prog chart)

✍ Now complete **Review 23, Constant Pressure Analysis Charts,** on page 472.

Tropopause Data Charts

The tropopause data chart has various panels which show:

- the observed winds, pressures and temperatures at the tropopause;
- a prognosis (forecast) for high-level significant weather, and maximum winds;
- a prognosis for tropopause height/vertical windshear; and
- observed winds aloft for 34,000 feet (250 mb).

Note: *Aviation Weather Services* (FAA Advisory Circular 00-45E) no longer covers the tropopause data charts; they are included here for aid in understanding high-level significant weather charts, and for comparison to the other available charts.

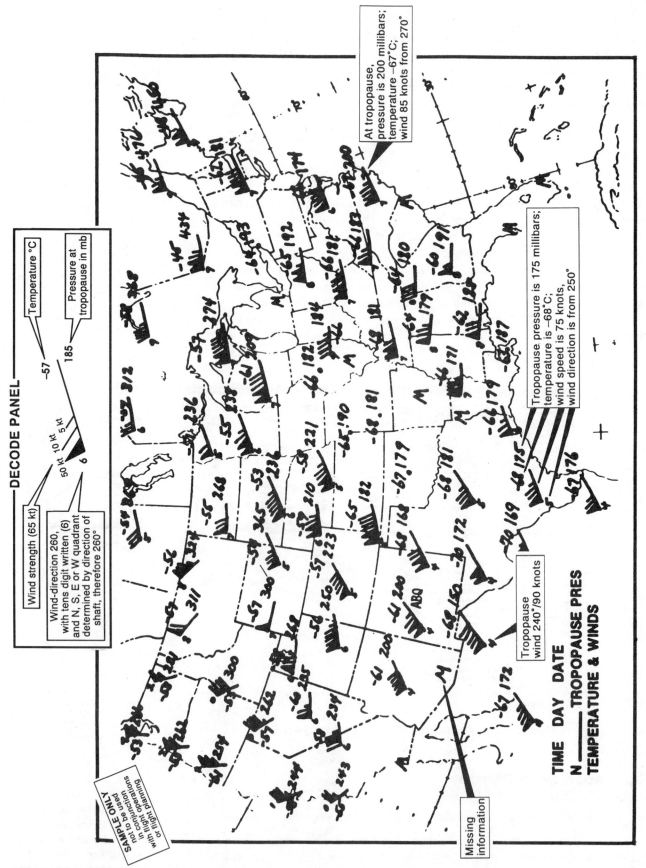

Figure 23-20. Extract of observed tropopause pressure, temperature and winds panel

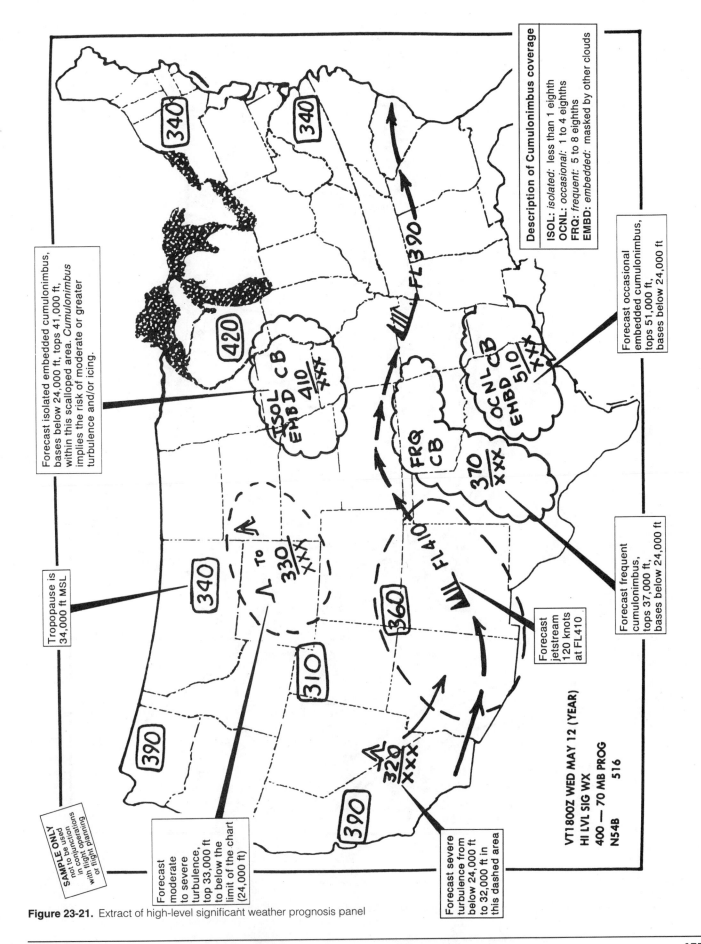

Figure 23-21. Extract of high-level significant weather prognosis panel

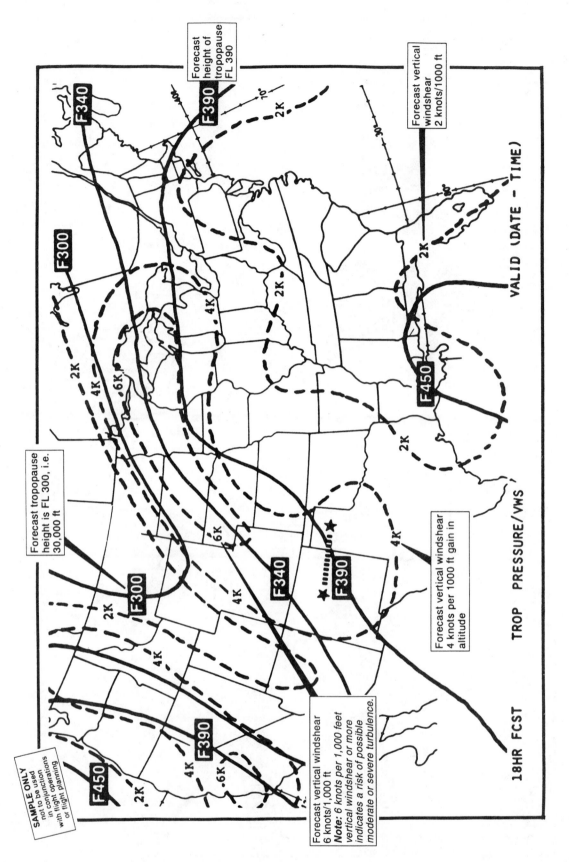

Forecast height of tropopause FL 390

Forecast vertical windshear 2 knots/1000 ft

VALID (DATE – TIME)

Forecast tropopause height is FL 300, i.e. 30,000 ft

Forecast vertical windshear 4 knots per 1000 ft gain in altitude

TROP PRESSURE/VWS

SAMPLE ONLY not to be used in conjunction with flight planning or flight operations

Forecast vertical windshear 6 knots/1,000 ft
Note: 6 knots per 1,000 feet vertical windshear or more indicates a risk of possible moderate or severe turbulence.

18HR FCST

Figure 23-22. Extract of tropopause height/vertical windshear prognosis panel

✍ Now complete **Review 23, Tropopause Data Charts,** on page 472.

Other Weather Information

RADAT

Sometimes freezing level data, obtained from upper air (rawinsonde) observation stations and codified by the term RADAT, is provided in surface aviation weather reports. It includes:

- relative humidity at the freezing level in percent; and
- the height (in hundreds of feet above mean sea level) at which the upper air sounding passed through the 0°C isotherm (freezing level).

RADAT 86 0 55 decodes as relative humidity 86% at freezing level, and freezing level (0°C) was passed at 5500 feet MSL.

Composite Moisture Stability Chart

The composite moisture stability chart has one panel which is an analysis of observed freezing level data from upper air observations.

Radar Weather Reports (SD)

Sometimes radar weather reports are available indicating the position and intensity of thunderstorm cells detected by a radar station. For example:

DFW 1735 LN 7TRW++/+ 75/30 160/50 170/110 12W C2520 MT470 AT 140/45

This decodes as: Dallas-Ft. Worth at 1735Z, a line of very heavy thunderstorms, increasing in intensity and covering 7/10 of the sky, in the area defined by 075 bearing from DFW radar site at a distance of 30 nm, 160 bearing 50 nm, 170 bearing 110 nm, 12 nm wide band, cells moving from 250° at 20 knots, maximum tops (MT) of 47,000 feet located on 140 bearing at 45 nm.

✍ Now complete **Review 23, Other Weather Information,** on page 473.

Staying Informed in the Air

After receiving a briefing and taking off, you should remain aware that weather forecasts are just that—forecasts. They are scientific estimates of what the weather will be like at various times in the future. Forecasts can and do go wrong. Stay alert to what you see as you fly. There is no real excuse for being caught by unforecast weather changes.

If the weather shows any signs of turning out to be worse than you and your airplane are prepared to deal with, then you must devise an alternative plan of action. You may have to land short of your destination or divert to an alternate airport and wait out the weather.

The **en route flight advisory service (EFAS)** is the best source of weather information en route. Call Flight Watch on 122.0 MHz (between 0600–2200 local time) with your aircraft identification and the name of the nearest VOR. This puts you in contact with someone at a Flight Service Station with immediate access to the latest weather information, including "live" weather radar. Flight Watch is an information exchange frequency for pilots and weather briefers. You can normally expect to receive actual weather and thunderstorm activity along your proposed route from Flight Watch, but not complete weather briefings. Actual destination weather and the terminal forecast will be provided on request. To assist the EFAS specialists and other pilots, you are encouraged to report good as well as bad weather, and to confirm expected conditions as well as unexpected conditions. Flight Service Stations that provide EFAS are listed in the A/FD and indicated on en route charts.

Also, the National Weather Service and Federal Aviation Administration issue and broadcast various kinds of weather alerts on navigation and air traffic control radio. These are designed to warn pilots of weather that may not have been forecast when they received their briefings. These alerts include:

SIGMETs warn of conditions that could be dangerous to all aircraft.

Convective SIGMETs are observations and/or forecasts that warn of conditions associated with thunderstorms, such as tornadoes or large hail, that could be dangerous to all aircraft.

AIRMETs warn of hazards primarily to small aircraft. Flight Service Stations broadcast SIGMETs and AIRMETs on receipt, and at periodic intervals thereafter (15 minutes past the hour and 45 minutes past the hour for the first hour after issuance).

Transcribed Weather Broadcasts (TWEB) are continuous broadcasts on certain NDBs and VORs of tape-recorded weather and NOTAM information, generally oriented to within 25 miles either side of a particular route. FSS will transcribe any important new data onto the tape periodically, making TWEB a very useful source of current data. Stations carrying TWEB are specified on aeronautical charts and in the A/FD. Some TWEBs are also accessible by telephone (with the telephone numbers listed in the A/FD). TWEBs are made available for preflight and in-flight planning, but are not substitutes for specialist-provided preflight briefings.

Hazardous In-Flight Weather Advisory Service (HIWAS) provides a continuous broadcast of in-flight weather advisories including summarized SIGMETs, AIRMETs and PIREPs. A HIWAS alert will be broadcast on all except emergency frequencies and the HIWAS message itself will be transmitted over certain VORs.

Airport Weather Broadcasts

The Automatic Terminal Information Service (ATIS) is a continuous broadcast of recorded noncontrol information at certain airports containing weather information, runway in use and other pertinent remarks. ATIS broadcasts are updated on the receipt of any official weather, regardless of content change and reported value. The ATIS may be broadcast on a discrete VHF frequency (requiring you to listen using a VHF-COM radio). ATIS frequencies are published on instrument charts and in the AF/D, which also includes their hours of operation. For example, Yakima Air Terminal ATIS operates between 1400–0600Z. Time conversion is GMT–8 (–7 DT), making the hours 0600–2200 local standard time. The symbol indicates that the same local times apply when daylight saving time (DT) is in effect, still 0600–2200 local time.

Weather at many airports is reported by automated weather observing equipment:

AWOS (automated weather observing system) transmits data over a COM or navaid frequency at the airport (see A/FD).

- AWOS-A reports altimeter setting;
- AWOS-1 reports altimeter setting, wind data and usually temperature, dewpoint and density altitude;
- AWOS-2 reports the same as AWOS-1 plus visibility;
- AWOS-3 reports the same as AWOS-1 plus visibility and cloud/ceiling data.

ASOS (automated surface observing system) reports the same as AWOS-3 plus precipitation (type and intensity) and freezing rain occurrence (a future enhancement). ASOS is a more sophisticated and newer system than AWOS and as well as being transmitted on radio frequencies, the observations are fed into the weather observation system METAR reports, which are appended with A02A (facility attended) and A02 (facility unattended) in the remarks. A METAR report that comes from a completely automated site may also be notated in the remarks section with the word AUTO.

Note: Automated observing equipment has fixed sampling paths, and unlike a human observer who can take into account variations that are evident, the automated equipment may observe readings of, say, cloud base and visibility which are significantly different (better or worse) than an arriving pilot may encounter at the end of an instrument approach to the airfield.

✍ Now complete **Review 23, Staying Informed in the Air,** on page 473.

Weather Briefings

1. Weather reports and forecasts are usually obtained from a F_____ S_____ S_____, but may also be obtained from a N_____ W_____ S_____ office.

➤ Flight Service Station (FSS), National Weather Service office

2. The number to call for a telephone weather briefing in most of the US is _____ .

➤ 1-800-WX-BRIEF

3. Weather information may be obtained by personal computer and fax. (true/false)?

➤ true

4. One government book with information about weather reports and forecasts is _____.

➤ Aviation Weather Services (FAA Advisory Circular AC 00-45E)

5. A pilot may obtain all of the weather information needed for a flight from television programs, such as those seen on the Weather Channel. (true/false)?

➤ false

6. Usually you need to receive a (standard/abbreviated/outlook) briefing before a flight.

➤ standard

7. A brief statement explaining the causes of the weather is called a _____, and for the next day's expected weather, you should ask for an _____ briefing.

➤ synopsis, outlook

8. In flight, you may receive weather updates by calling _____ on frequency _____.

➤ Flight Watch, 122.0 MHz

9. Information you should give a weather briefer includes:

    (a) _____

    (b) _____

    (c) _____

    (d) _____

    (e) _____

    (f) _____

    (g) _____

    (h) _____

    (i) _____

    (j) _____

➤ (a) the fact that you are a pilot; (b) VFR or IFR; (c) N-number of aircraft; (d) aircraft type; (e) departure point; (f) the route; (g) destinations; (h) en route altitude; (i) time of departure; (j) time en route

10. To obtain a complete weather briefing for a planned flight, you should request a s_____ briefing.

➤ standard

11. If your planned departure time is 6 or more hours away, you should request an o_____ briefing.

➤ outlook

12. If you already have obtained mass-disseminated weather data, you should supplement this with an a_____ briefing from an FSS.

➤ abbreviated

Weather Depiction Charts

1. A weather depiction chart shows (actual weather as reported/forecast weather).

➤ actual weather as reported

2. A weather depiction chart shows weather as reported by (weather reporting stations/aircraft en route).

➤ weather reporting stations

3. A weather depiction chart is of most value in determining (general weather/specific cloud/icing) conditions.

➤ general weather

4. The general weather shown on a weather depiction chart includes which of the following: actual sky cover as reported; forecast sky cover; actual restricted visibility; forecast restricted visibility; actual temperature; forecast temperature; actual weather, including type of precipitation at weather reporting stations; actual en route weather; forecast en route weather?

➤ actual sky cover as reported; actual restricted visibility; actual weather, including type of precipitation at weather reporting stations

5. On a weather depiction chart, a shaded area represents (IFR/MVFR/VFR) conditions.

➤ IFR

6. IFR conditions mean ceiling less than (1000 feet/1500 feet/3000 feet) and/or visibility less than (1 mile/3 miles/5 miles).

➤ 1000 feet, 3 miles

7. On a weather depiction chart, an area without contours represents (IFR/MVFR/VFR) conditions.

➤ VFR

8. VFR conditions mean ceiling greater than (1000 feet/1500 feet/3000 feet) and/or visibility greater than (1 mile/3 miles/5 miles).

➤ 3000 feet, 5 miles

9. On a weather depiction chart, a contoured area without shading represents (IFR/MVFR/VFR) conditions.

➤ MVFR

10. MVFR conditions means that the ceiling is at or between _____ feet AGL and _____ feet AGL, an/or the visibility is at or between _____ miles and _____ miles.

➤ 1000–3000 feet AGL, 3–5 miles

11. On a weather depiction chart, a station symbol of an empty circle means (sky clear/sky obscured).

➤ sky clear

12. On a weather depiction chart, a station symbol of a black circle means (sky clear/sky overcast).

➤ sky overcast

13. On a weather depiction chart, a station symbol of a circle including a cross means _____.

➤ sky obscured or partially obscured

14. The station circle on a weather depiction chart is fully black, with the number "7" beneath it. This indicates that the (reported/forecast) sky cover is (scattered/broken/overcast) with a ceiling of (7/70/700/7000) feet above (ground/sea) level.

➤ reported, overcast, 700 feet above ground level

15. The letter "M" in the station circle on a weather depiction chart indicates _____.

➤ missing data

16. The station circle on a weather depiction chart is three-quarters shaded with the number "5" beneath it. This indicates that the sky coverage is (clear/few/scattered/broken/overcast), which means a sky coverage of from _____ tenths to _____ tenths, with a base of _____ feet (AGL/MSL)

➤ broken, 6/10 to 9/10, 500 feet AGL

17. The letter "X" in the station circle on a weather depiction chart indicates _____.

➤ sky obscured or partially obscured

18. The station circle on a weather depiction chart has the symbol "≡" to the left of it. This indicates _____.

➤ thick fog (visibility less than $\frac{1}{4}$ mile)

19. The station circle on a weather depiction chart has the symbol "2=" to the left of it. This indicates _____.

➤ light fog with visibility 2 miles

20. Two dots to the left of the station circle on a weather depiction chart indicates (intermittent rain/continuous rain/fog/snow).

➤ continuous rain

Refer to Figure 23-2 on page 435 for Questions 21–25.

21. The ceiling in southeast New Mexico in the contoured area without shading is _____ feet and the sky (is/is not) overcast. There (are/are not) thunderstorms, and the visibility is _____ miles. Conditions are (IFR/MVFR/VFR).

➤ 6000 feet, is, are, 4, MVFR

22. The front extending from New Mexico to Indiana is a (stationary/warm/cold/occluded) front.

➤ stationary

23. The IFR weather in eastern Texas is due to (fog/rain/dust).

➤ fog

24. The IFR conditions along the coast of Oregon and California is caused by low ceilings of _____ feet with f_____ and d_____.

➤ 300 feet, fog and drizzle

25. The weather for a flight from Arkansas to southeast Alabama will have broken to scattered clouds at _____ feet.

➤ 25,000 feet

26. Areas where reports indicate a ceiling of greater than _____ feet AGL and visibility greater than _____ miles are not enclosed by a contour line on a weather depiction chart.

➤ 3000 feet AGL, 5 miles

Surface Analysis Charts

1. A surface analysis chart is valid (a) at some time in the future; (b) at the time the observations were taken.

➤ (b)

2. A surface analysis chart (shows/does not show) the position of pressure systems and fronts at ground level.

➤ shows

3. A surface analysis chart (shows/does not show) the expected direction of movement of fronts and pressure systems.

➤ does not show.

4. A surface analysis chart (shows/does not show) total sky cover.

➤ shows

5. A surface analysis chart (shows/does not show) cloud tops and heights.

➤ does not show

6. A surface analysis chart (shows/does not show) temperature and dewpoint at various stations.

➤ shows

7. A surface analysis chart (shows/does not show) obstructions to vision.

➤ shows

Radar Summary Charts

1. A fair-weather cumulus cloud (will/will not) be detected by radar.

➤ will not

2. Heavy precipitation from a cumulonimbus cloud (will/will not) be detected by radar.

➤ will

3. Icing conditions (will/will not) be detected by radar.

➤ will not

4. Radar echoes can determine the tops and bases of (clouds/heavy precipitation).

➤ heavy precipitation

5. Radar echoes, such as lines or cells of hazardous thunderstorms, are shown on (radar summary charts/weather depiction charts/both).

➤ radar summary charts

6. On a radar summary chart, the movement of a cell at 20 knots to the east is depicted by a (single arrow/shaft and barbs).

➤ single arrow

7. On a radar summary chart, the movement of an area of radar echoes at 10 knots to the northeast is depicted by a (single arrow/shaft and barbs).

➤ shaft and barbs

8. The shaft shows the (direction/speed) and the barbs show the (direction/speed).

➤ direction, speed

9. A three-dimensional picture of clouds and precipitation can be formed prior to flight by considering the _____ summary chart and the _____ depiction chart.

➤ radar summary chart, weather depiction chart

10. The area within the first contour on a radar summary chart indicates conditions that are (weak to moderate/strong to very strong).

➤ weak to moderate

11. The area within the second contour on a radar summary chart indicates conditions that are (weak to moderate/strong to very strong/intense to extreme).

➤ strong to very strong

12. The area within the third contour on a radar summary chart indicates conditions that are (weak to moderate/strong to very strong/intense to extreme).

➤ intense to extreme

13. What does a rectangle labeled "WT762" on a radar summary chart indicate?

➤ tornado watch number 762

14. What does a rectangle labeled "WS657" on a radar summary chart indicate?

➤ severe weather watch number 657

METAR/SPECI Weather Reports

1. METAR reports are (scheduled hourly observation/unscheduled special observation indicating a significant change in one or more elements of the weather/scheduled observation indicating a significant change in weather).

➤ scheduled hourly observation

2. The code SPECI at the beginning of a report indicates a (scheduled hourly observation/unscheduled special observation indicating a significant change in one or more elements of the weather/scheduled observation indicating a significant change in weather).

➤ unscheduled special observation indicating a significant change in one or more elements of the weather

3. Times in METAR reports are (local/UTC) time.

➤ UTC (coordinated universal time)

4. Decode this surface aviation weather report for Bartow, Florida.

    SPECI KBOW 141130Z 00000KT 3SM HZ SKC 19/16 A3004

➤ Special report for Bartow, 14th day of the month at 11:30Z. Wind is calm, with 3 statute miles visibility and haze. The sky is clear and the altimeter setting is 30.04 in. Hg.

5. Decode the remarks "A02" in a METAR weather report.

➤ Automated weather observation system capable of detecting precipitation used.

6. A ceiling is defined as the (highest/lowest) layer of clouds or obscuring phenomena aloft that is reported as (BKN/OVC/BKN or OVC).

➤ lowest, broken or overcast

7. If the station originating the following weather report has a field elevation of 1600 feet MSL, what is the thickness of the one continuous cloud layer?

00000KT VV000 FG OVC040

➤ 2400 feet thick (ceiling is indefinite, indicated by "VV000", so the sky cover extends from the surface at 1600 feet MSL to the top of the overcast layer at 4000 feet MSL)

8. A METAR for a particular airport that specifies BKN014 is amended by a later SPECI that specifies BKN030. This means that the _____.

➤ ceiling improved by 1600 feet (3000 – 1400)

9. If an element is not encoded in a METAR report does not occur or cannot be observed then it is (listed as not observed/omitted completely).

➤ omitted completely

PIREPs

1. PIREPs are symbolized by the two letters _____, or if urgent by the three letters _____, and (are/are not) often appended to surface aviation weather reports, which are symbolized by the two letters _____.

➤ UA, UUA, are, SA

2. Specify the four mandatory items to be reported by a pilot making a PIREP which are necessary for the PIREP to have any significance. What letters symbolize these four items in the PIREP?

➤ over location (/OV), time (/TM), flight level or altitude (/FL), aircraft type (/TP)

3. What are the optional items that a pilot may report in a PIREP, which are symbolized by the letters /SK, /WX, /TA, /WV, /TB, /IC and /RM?

➤ sky cover, flight visibility and weather, temperature in degrees Celsius, wind velocity, turbulence, icing, and remarks

4. Which of the following weather could you observe in flight and report in a PIREP— jetstream winds, level of the tropopause, structural icing?

➤ structural icing

5. Interpret the following extract from a PIREP:

SK INTMTLY BL

➤ intermittently between layers

6. The level of cloud bases and tops in PIREPs, which are based on pilot reports, are related to (MSL/AGL).

➤ MSL

7. Interpret the PIREP:

UA/OV 20S ATL 1620 FL050/TP BE 18/IC MDT RIME ICE

➤ 20 nm south of Atlanta at 1620Z, a pilot flying at 5000 feet MSL in a Beech 18 reported moderate rime ice.

8. What significant cloud coverage is reported by a pilot in this UA? What is the thickness of the lower layer of clouds if the station elevation is 1000 feet MSL, and the current METAR reports the ceiling as OVC008?

UA/OV 14 NW POR 1345/SK OVC 030/050 OVC 080

➤ The pilot report mentions the top of the lower overcast layer at 3000 feet MSL (OVC 030), and then a second overcast layer with base 5000 feet MSL and tops 8000 feet MSL (050 OVC 080). Base of the lower overcast layer is 800 feet AGL (OVC008), which is 1800 feet MSL, giving a thickness of 1200 feet (3000 – 1800).

9. Interpret the following PIREP:

UA/OV MRB /TM 1835 /FL 060/TP PA28/SK INTMTLY BL/TB MDT/RM R TURBC INCRS WWD

➤ PIREP/overhead MRB/time 1835 UTC/altitude 6000 feet MSL/aircraft type PA28/sky cover— intermittently between layers/turbulence: moderate/remarks: rain and turbulence increasing westward

10. How would you report turbulence that momentarily causes slight, erratic changes in altitude and/or attitude, one-third to two-thirds of the time?

➤ "intermittent light turbulence"

11. Slight, rapid and somewhat rhythmic bumpiness without appreciable changes in attitude and/or altitude, less than one-third of the time would be reported as _____.

➤ "occasional light chop"

12. How would you report turbulence that causes changes in altitude and/or attitude more than two-thirds of the time, but the aircraft remains in positive control at all times?

➤ "continuous moderate turbulence"

Low-level Significant Weather Prognostic Charts

1. A forecast of future weather is often called a (report/prog).

➤ prog

2. The chart that gives you an overall view of the weather forecast for particular times in the future is called the _____.

➤ low-level significant weather prog chart

3. The low-level significant weather prog chart (does/does not) allow you to avoid areas of non-VFR weather and to avoid altitudes where turbulence or the risk of icing exists.

➤ does

4. How do you know what time the forecast shown in a particular panel of a low-level significant weather prog chart is for?

➤ VT—valid time—in the lower left corner of the chart

Refer to Figure 1 on page 468 for Questions 5–8.

5. Interpret the weather symbol depicted in the southern California area on the 12-hr significant weather prognostic chart.

➤ moderate turbulence from the surface to 18,000 feet

6. The band of weather associated with the cold front in the western states is expected to move in a direction toward the _____ at a speed of _____ knots.

➤ east, 30 knots

7. What weather is forecast for the Gulf Coast area just ahead of the cold front during the first 12 hours?

➤ Marginal VFR (outlined by scalloped lines) with some areas of IFR (outlined by smooth lines) as shown in upper chart, and some associated thunderstorms and showers shown in lower chart.

8. What is the approximate freezing level over Oklahoma City?

➤ 10,000 feet MSL (by interpolation between 8000 and 12,000)

Refer to Figure 2 on page 469 for Questions 9–11.

9. In the forecast for 1800 UTC for Dec. 25, the weather over the state of Michigan is expected to be (VFR, MVFR, IFR).

➤ IFR

10. In the prog chart forecast for 1800 UTC, Dec. 25, the weather over the state of North Dakota is expected to be (VFR, MVFR, IFR).

➤ MVFR

11. What is the freezing level forecast to be over the southernmost part of California on the prog chart for 1800 UTC Dec. 25?

➤ 12,000 feet or higher

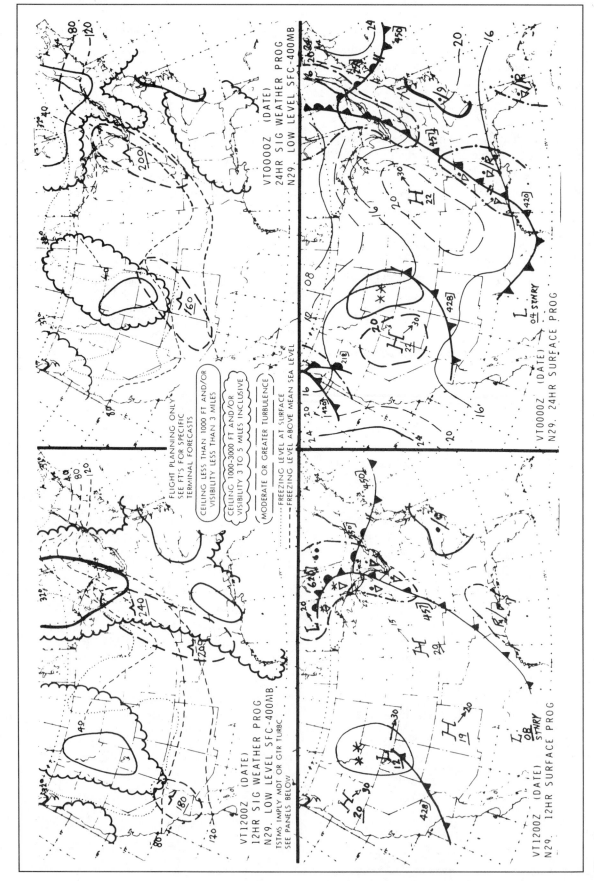

Figure 1.

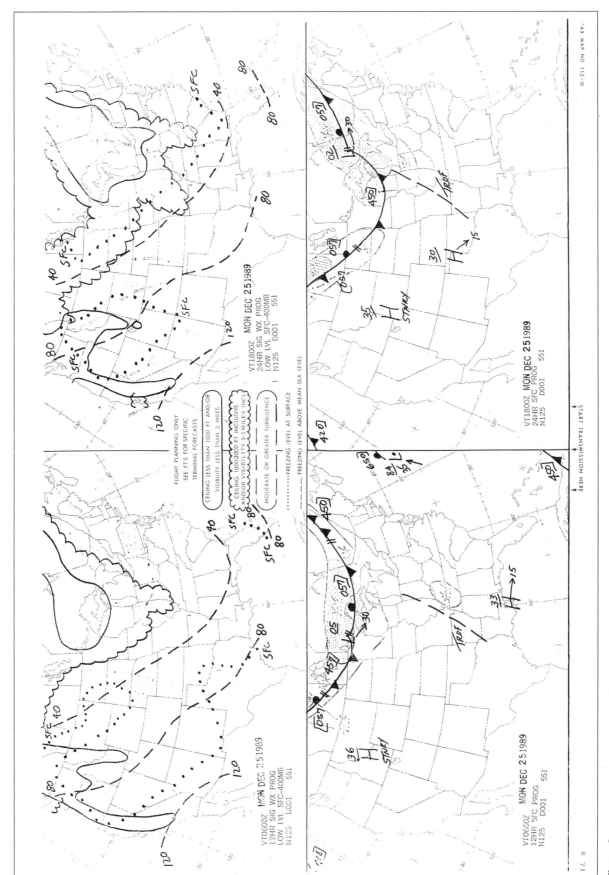

FLIGHT PLANNING ONLY
SEE FTS FOP SPECIFIC
TERMINAL FORECASTS

CEILING LESS THAN 1000 FT AND/OR
VISIBILITY LESS THAN 3 MILES

CEILING 1000-3000 FT INCLUSIVE
AND/OR VISIBILITY 3-5 MILES INCL

MODERATE OR GREATER TURBULENCE

········· FREEZING LEVEL AT SURFACE

— — — FREEZING LEVEL ABOVE MEAN SEA LEVEL

VT1800Z MON DEC 25 1989
24HR SIG WX PROG
LOW LVL SFC-400MB
N125   D001   551

VT0600Z MON DEC 25 1989
12HR SIG WX PROG
LOW LVL SFC-400MB
N125   D001   551

VT1800Z MON DEC 25 1989
24HR SFC PROG
N125   D001   551

MON DEC 25 1989
12HR SFC PROG
N125   D001   551

START TRANSMISSION HERE

Figure 2.

12. The symbol of two dots side-by-side •• on a low-level significant weather prognostic chart indicates _____.

➤ continuous rain

13. The symbol of two dots side-by-side •• inside a shaded oval on a low-level significant weather prognostic chart indicates continuous rain covering (more/less) than half the area.

➤ more

14. The symbol of a dot above an inverted triangle ∇̇ on a low-level significant weather prognostic chart indicates _____.

➤ rain shower

TAFs

1. The primary source of information regarding the weather expected to exist at your destination at your estimated time of arrival is the (terminal/area) (forecast/report), which is abbreviated as (METAR/AF/TAF).

➤ terminal forecast, abbreviated as TAF

2. The term "TAF" refers to a _____, which covers an area out to _____ nautical miles. If the term "VCNTY" is used, an area from _____ nm out to _____ nm is considered.

➤ terminal forecast, 5 nm, 5 nm out to 25 nm

3. A visibility entry of "P6SM" in a TAF implies that the surface visibility is _____.

➤ more than 6 statute miles

4. A wind entry of "VRB" in a TAF implies that the wind is expected to be _____ and less than _____ knots.

➤ variable in direction, 6 knots

5. The term "TEMPO" in a TAF means that the following conditions are expected to _____.

➤ be temporary, during the time mentioned in the forecast

6. The term "VV000" in a terminal forecast means _____.

➤ vertical visibility zero, used to describe an indefinite ceiling

7. The term "PROB40" in a terminal forecast (TAF) means that conditions are forecast to occur _____.

➤ with a probability of 40%

8. The term *squalls* means a sudden increase in wind speed of at least _____ knots to a sustained speed of _____ knots or more for a period of at least _____ minute.

➤ 15 knots, 20 knots, 1 minute

Area Forecasts, TWEB Forecasts and the Convective Outlook

1. Information regarding frontal movement, turbulence and icing conditions for a specific area are found in an (TAF/FA/PIREP/TWEB), the letters of which stand for _____

➤ FA, area forecast

2. Forecast weather conditions for a given area the size of several states are contained in an _____ forecast, abbreviated _____.

➤ area forecast, FA

3. The section of the area forecast (FA) entitled *A Statement of VFR Clouds and Weather* contains a _____ hour forecast that identifies and locates weather significant to VFR flights.

➤ 12 hour

4. The section of an FA, which is an _____ forecast, entitled *Synopsis* contains a summary of location and movement of fronts (in a given area/along a specified route).

➤ area forecast, in a given area

5. TWEB stands for _____, and provides information like in an FA, except that it is (in a given area/along a specified route).

➤ transcribed weather broadcast, along a specified route

6. Which weather forecast describes the prospects for an area coverage of severe or general thunderstorm activity during the following 24 hours, and what is its abbreviation?

➤ convective outlook, AC

Winds and Temperatures Aloft Forecast

1. Wind direction on a winds and temperatures aloft forecast are in degrees (true/magnetic), wind strength is in (knots/mph), temperature is in degrees (Celsius/Fahrenheit/as a deviation from standard).

➤ true, knots, °Celsius

2. On a winds and temperatures aloft forecast, "9900+03" at 6000 feet MSL decodes as _____.

➤ wind light and variable, temperature +3°C

3. On a winds and temps aloft forecast, 2745–20 at 18,000 feet MSL decodes as _____.

➤ a wind from 270 degrees true at 45 knots and temperature –20°C

4. On a winds and temps aloft forecast, "1608" at 3000 feet MSL decodes as _____.

➤ a wind from 160 degrees true at 8 knots and no reported temperature

5. On a winds and temperatures aloft forecast, temperature is omitted for the _____ feet MSL level and when the level is within _____ feet of station elevation.

➤ 3000 feet MSL, 2500 feet of station elevation

6. On a winds and temperatures aloft forecast, the wind group is omitted for one of the usual forecast levels when it is within _____ feet of station elevation.

➤ 1500 feet of station elevation

7. On a winds and temperatures aloft forecast, "841558" at 39,000 feet decodes as _____.

➤ a wind from 340 degrees true at 115 knots and temperature –58°C

8. How would you encode a wind from 290 degrees true at 60 knots and a temperature of minus 40 degrees Celsius at FL300 in a winds and temperatures aloft forecast?

➤ 296040

9. How would you encode a wind from 170 degrees true at 140 knots and a temperature of minus 45 degrees Celsius at FL300 in a winds and temperatures aloft forecast?

➤ 674045

10. How would you encode a wind from 340 degrees true at 8 knots and a temperature of minus 9 degrees Celsius at 9000 feet MSL in a winds and temperatures aloft forecast?

➤ 3408–09

11. Planning for a flight at FL270, the winds and temperatures aloft forecast predicts:

24000	30000
2891–30	751041

What approximate wind direction, speed and temperature (in °C and also as a deviation from standard) can you expect?

➤ wind from 265 degrees true at 100 knots, and temperature –36°C or ISA+3 (since at FL270, ISA = 15 – (2 × 27) = 15 – 54 = –39°, and –36° is 3° warmer or ISA+3)

12. Planning for a flight at FL270, the winds and temperatures aloft forecast predicts:

24000	30000
2368–26	781939

What approximate wind direction, speed and temperature (in °C and also as a deviation from standard) can you expect?

➤ wind from 255 degrees true at 93 knots and temperature –33°C (or ISA+6)

Convective Outlook Charts

1. The convective outlook chart is a preliminary (12/24/48)-hour outlook chart and shows (actual/forecast) areas of thunderstorm activity, tornadoes and watch areas.

➤ 48-hour, forecast

2. A single-hatched area on a convective outlook chart means that there is a forecast risk of _____.

➤ severe thunderstorms

3. The letters "MDT" on a convective outlook chart mean that there is a _____ risk of severe thunderstorm activity in that area.

➤ moderate

4. The letters "SLGT" on a convective outlook chart mean that there is a _____ risk of severe thunderstorm activity in that area.

➤ slight

5. A crosshatched area on a convective outlook chart means that there is a forecast risk of _____.

➤ tornadoes

6. A line with an arrowhead plotted on a convective outlook chart represents an area of forecast general thunderstorm activity to the (left/right) of the line when you face in the direction of the arrow.

➤ right

Constant Pressure Analysis Charts

1. Constant pressure charts show meteorological data collected at a particular (height/pressure level) in the atmosphere.

➤ pressure level

2. Constant pressure charts are useful for quickly determining the (winds/turbulence) and (cloud heights/temperatures) aloft.

➤ winds and temperatures

3. For a flight at 5000 feet MSL, the most relevant constant pressure chart is that for (850/700/500/300/200) mb/hPa.

➤ 850 mb/hPa

4. For a flight at 18,000 feet MSL, the most relevant constant pressure chart is that for (850/700/500/300/200) mb/hPa.

➤ 500 mb/hPa

5. An upper high has relatively (warm/cool) air beneath it, and indicates a (stable/unstable) atmosphere with probably (good/poor) flying conditions, with the risk of (poor/good) visibility.

➤ warm air, stable atmosphere, good flying conditions, possibly poor visibility

6. An upper low has relatively (warm/cool) air beneath it, and indicates a (stable/unstable) atmosphere with possibly (good/poor) flying conditions.

➤ cool air, unstable atmosphere, poor flying conditions

7. Clouds are more likely to form if there is a (wide/small) temperature/dewpoint spread.

➤ small

8. Be on the watch for structural icing if there is a (wide/small) temperature/dewpoint spread, and the temperature is below about _____°C.

➤ small, +5°C

9. State five pieces of information shown on constant pressure charts.

➤ height of pressure surface, changes in this height over last 12 hours, temperature, temperature/dewpoint spread, wind direction and speed

Tropopause Data Charts

1. The U.S. high-level significant weather prognostic chart forecasts significant weather in the airspace from _____ feet MSL, which is the _____ pressure level, up to _____ feet MSL, which is the _____ mb pressure level.

➤ 24,000 feet MSL, 400 mb/hPa, 63,000 feet MSL, 70 mb/hPa

2. What weather is implied on a "HI LVL SIG WX PROG" chart in an area enclosed by small scalloped lines?

➤ cumulonimbus clouds, and the associated icing and moderate or greater turbulence

3. Decode the following symbol:

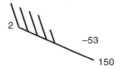

➤ tropopause pressure 176 mb/hPa, temp –66°C, wind 240/75

4. Decode the following symbol:

➤ tropopause pressure 150 mb/hPa, temp –53°C, wind 320/45

5. On a tropopause height/vertical windshear prognosis panel, a dashed line labeled "4K" indicates _____.

➤ a vertical windshear of 4 knots per 1000 feet

6. On the same chart as in previous question, a line labeled "F300" indicates _____.

➤ the tropopause along this line is at flight level 300

7. On a high-level significant weather prog chart, "310" enclosed in a box indicates _____.

➤ the tropopause in this area is at flight level 310

Other Weather Information

1. One panel of the c_____ m_____ s_____ chart is an analysis of observed freezing level data from upper air observations.

➤ composite moisture stability chart

2. What does "MT 460 AT 140/55" mean in a RAREP (radar weather report)?

➤ maximum tops of thunderstorm cells is 46,000 feet, located on a bearing of 140°M from the station at 55 nm

3. What does "RADAT 67055" mean in the remarks section of an hourly aviation weather report?

➤ relative humidity was 67%, and the freezing level (0°C) was at 5500 feet MSL

Staying Informed in the Air

1. SIGMETs are warnings of weather that is potentially hazardous to (all/light) aircraft.

➤ all

2. The quickest means of obtaining a relevant SIGMET in flight is to _____.

➤ contact the nearest FSS

3. AIRMETs contain information most relevant to pilots of (airline/light) aircraft.

➤ light

4. FSS will broadcast current AIRMETs on receipt, and then at H+_____ and H+_____, during the _____ hour(s) after issuance.

➤ H+15, H+45, during the first hour after issuance.

5. A widespread sandstorm lowering visibility to less than 3 miles would be reported in (an AIRMET/a SIGMET).

➤ SIGMET

6. A sustained surface wind of 30 knots or more would be reported in (an AIRMET/a SIGMET).

➤ an AIRMET

7. The best source of weather information en route is by calling F_____ W_____ on _____ MHz.

➤ Flight Watch on 122.0

The IFR System Section Four

24 **Regulations Important to the Instrument Pilot**   477
25 **Preparation for Flight** 505
26 **Instrument Departures** 531
27 **En Route** 543
28 **Holding Patterns, Procedure Turns & DME Arcs** 553
29 **Instrument Approaches** 575
30 **Visual Maneuvering** 603

Regulations Important to the Instrument Pilot

24

The regulations described in this chapter are the basic rules you need to know to fly IFR in the U.S. Because the FAA is continually changing these regulations, it is imperative that you invest in a current copy of the Code of Federal Regulations, Section 14 (14 CFR) and keep that copy up to date at all times. 14 CFR, and its companion manual, the Aeronautical Information Manual (AIM) are available from a variety of publishers, as well as from the FAA Internet site and on CD-ROM.

Study from a current set of rules.

Terminology

Before beginning any chapter on rules and regulations, it is always helpful to clarify certain terms.

An **authorized instructor** is an instructor who has a valid ground instructor certificate or current flight instructor certificate with appropriate ratings issued by the Administrator; an instructor authorized under Part 121 (SFAR 58), Part 135, or Part 142 to give instruction under those parts; or any other person authorized by the Administrator to give instruction.

An **airplane flight simulator** is a device that is a full-sized airplane cockpit replica of a specific type of airplane, or make, model and series of airplane; and includes the hardware and software necessary to represent the airplane in ground operations and in flight; and uses a force cueing system that provides cues at least equivalent to those provided by a 3° freedom of motion system; and uses a visual system with at least a 45° horizontal and 30° vertical visual field simultaneously for each pilot; and has been evaluated, qualified and approved by the Administrator.

An airplane flight simulator uses a force cueing system.

A **flight training device** is a full-sized replica of instruments, equipment, panels and controls of an airplane or rotorcraft, in an open flight deck area or in an enclosed cockpit, including the hardware and software for systems installed, necessary to simulate the aircraft in ground and flight operations. It does not have to have a motion system or a visual system, but it does have to be evaluated, qualified and approved by the Administrator.

A flight training device does not have to have a motion system or a visual system, but it does have to be evaluated, qualified and approved by the Administrator.

PCATDs are desktop computers that simulate an airplane type or make, model, and series. They are beneficial, when used under an authorized instructor's guidance, for proficiency in procedural tasks such as area departures and arrivals, navigational aid tracking, holding pattern entries, instrument and missed approach procedures. AC 61-126 suggests a schedule of training time on qualified PCATDs, to reduce the total flight hours that would otherwise have to be completed in an aircraft to meet instrument rating requirements.

PCATD: Personal Computer-based Aviation Training Device.
PCATDs are highly beneficial when used under an authorized instructor's guidance for learning procedural tasks such as area departures and arrivals, navigational aid tracking, holding pattern entries, instrument and missed approach procedures.

Responsibility and Authority of the Pilot-in Command (14 CFR Part 91)

The pilot-in-command of an aircraft is directly responsible for, and is the final authority as to, the operation of that aircraft. In an in-flight emergency requiring immediate action, the pilot-in-command may deviate from the regulations to the extent required to meet the emergency. A written report of the deviation may be requested at a later date by the Administrator of the FAA.

As you complete each regulation, go through its review questions.

What is IFR? (14 CFR Part 91)

IFR is simply any "non-VFR" situation.

Part 91: Basic VFR weather minimums

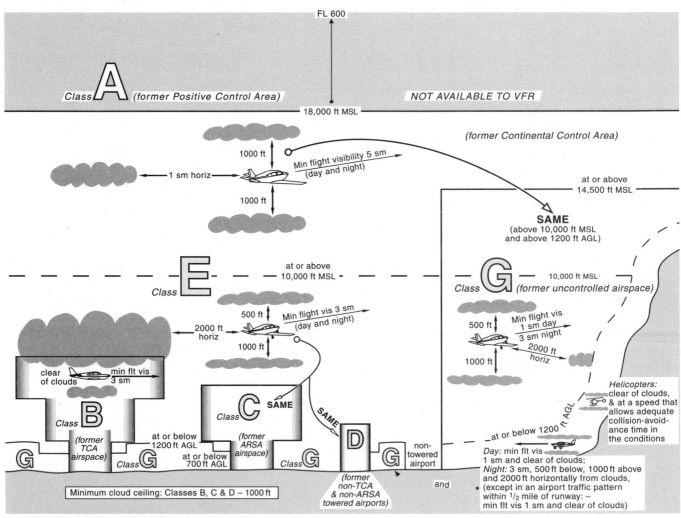

Figure 24-1. U.S. VFR minimums

	Class A airspace	Class B airspace	Class C airspace	Class D airspace	Class E airspace (general controlled airspace)	Class G airspace (uncontrolled airspace)
VFR minimum visibility	Not applicable (IFR only)	3 statute miles	3 statute miles	3 statute miles	*3 statute miles	**1 statute mile
VFR minimum distance from clouds	Not applicable (IFR only)	Clear of clouds	500 feet below; 1000 feet above; and 2000 feet horizontal	500 feet below; 1000 feet above; and 2000 feet horizontal	*500 feet below; 1000 feet above and 2000 feet horizontal	**500 feet below, 1000 ft above and 2000 ft horizontal

*Different visibility minimums and distance from cloud requirements exist for operations above 10,000 ft MSL in Class E airspace.

**Different visibility minimums and distance from cloud requirements exist for night operations, operations above 10,000 ft MSL, and operations below 1200 ft AGL in Class G airspace.

Part 91: Special VFR Weather Minimums

Except for airports where special VFR is prohibited (these are listed in section 3 of 14 CFR Part 91 Appendix D), a pilot operating within the lateral boundaries of the surface areas of Class B, C, D, or E airspace designated for an airport may be issued an ATC clearance to operate under **special VFR**. This reduces the normal requirements to:

- flight visibility 1 sm; and
- clear of clouds.

To take off or land at any airport where special VFR is permitted, the ground visibility at the airport must be at least 1 sm. If ground visibility is not reported, then the flight visibility during takeoff or landing must be at least 1 sm.

A non-instrument-rated pilot may be issued a special VFR clearance by day but, to operate under special VFR at night, you must be instrument-rated, instrument-current and in an IFR-equipped airplane.

When the visibility is less than 3 statute miles but not less than 1 statute mile during night hours, an airplane may be operated VFR clear of clouds if operated in an airport traffic pattern within one-half mile of the runway.

Am I Qualified to Fly IFR Today? (14 CFR Part 61)

Part 61: Requirements for Certificates, Ratings, and Authorizations

To operate as pilot-in-command under instrument flight rules (IFR), or in weather conditions less than the minimums prescribed for VFR flight, you are required to hold an **instrument rating**. Since an IFR clearance is required to operate in Class A airspace, you must hold an instrument rating to do this.

Upon request from the FAA Administrator, an authorized representative of the National Transportation Safety Board (NTSB), or any federal, state or local law enforcement officer, you must present your pilot certificate for inspection.

Part 61: Required Equipment for Practical Tests

You must supply an aircraft appropriate and qualified for the test you are about to take. You must have on board the equipment necessary to complete the test of your skills. You also must provide a view limiting device approved by both the flight test examiner and the Administrator.

Part 61: Pilot Logbooks

The aeronautical training and experience to meet the requirements for a certificate or rating, or the recent flight experience requirements, must be shown by a reliable record. The logging of other flight time is not required.

A pilot may log as **instrument flight time** only that time during which he operates the aircraft solely by reference to instruments, under actual or simulated instrument flight conditions. Each entry must include:

- Total time of flight or flight lesson.
- (Except for simulated flight), the place, or points of departure and arrival.
- Type and identification of aircraft, flight simulator, or flight training device.
- Type of pilot experience or training.
- Pilot in command or solo.
- Second in command.
- Flight instruction received from an authorized flight instructor.
- Instrument flight instruction from an authorized flight instructor.
- Pilot ground trainer instruction.

- Participating crew (for lighter than air aircraft).
- Other pilot time.
- Instruction in a flight simulator or in a flight training device.
- Conditions of flight.
- Day or night.
- Actual instrument time.
- Simulated instrument conditions in actual flight, in a flight simulator or a flight training device.
- The place and type of each instrument approach completed; and
- The name of the safety pilot for each simulated instrument flight conducted.
- An instrument flight instructor may log as instrument time that time during which he acts as instrument flight instructor in actual instrument weather conditions.
- All time logged as instruction must be certified by the authorized instructor from which it was received.

Part 61: Qualification and Approval of Flight Simulators and Flight Training Devices

If you intend to log simulator or flight training device time for the purposes of a rating or currency, the training device or simulator must be qualified and approved by the Administrator.

Part 61: Recent Flight Experience; Pilot-In-Command

General Experience. To act as pilot-in-command of an aircraft carrying passengers, you must have made 3 takeoffs and 3 landings as the sole manipulator of the flight controls in an aircraft in the preceding 90 days in an aircraft of the same category and class or, if a type-rating is required, of the same type. You can fly the aircraft for the purpose of achieving this currency even after your currency has expired, as long as you do not carry persons or property other than as necessary for the compliance with this rule. The takeoffs and landings may be performed in an approved flight simulator at a Part 142 training facility.

Night Experience. If you intend to carry passengers at night, you must have made at least 3 takeoffs and 3 landings to a full-stop at night as the sole manipulator of the flight controls in an aircraft in the preceding 90 days in the category and class of aircraft to be used. The takeoffs and landings may be performed in an approved flight simulator at a Part 142 training facility.

Night is defined as the period beginning 1 hour after sunset and ending 1 hour before sunrise (as published in the American Air Almanac).

Instrument Experience. To act as pilot-in-command under IFR, or in weather conditions less than the minimums prescribed for VFR, you must have, within the previous 6 calendar months, logged at least 6 instrument approaches under actual or simulated IFR conditions, as well as holding patterns and tracking and intercepting through the use of navigation systems. The approaches may have been in either an aircraft or a simulator. For the purposes of glider instrument currency, additionally, 3 hours of IFR flight needs to be logged every 6 months for passenger carrying purposes (1 $\frac{1}{2}$ hours if no passengers are carried).

To act as pilot-in-command under IFR, or in IMC, you must have, within the previous 6 calendar months, logged at least 6 instrument approaches under actual or simulated IFR conditions, as well as holding patterns and tracking and intercepting skills through the use of navigation systems.

If you run out of IFR-currency, you have a period of 6 calendar months thereafter to achieve the above requirements to regain your IFR privileges. For instance, suppose you logged 6 approaches and one holding pattern on January 1, and then navigation and tracking on July 7; you are instrument-current until July 31. At any time in the next 6 calendar months following July 7 (until the end of January), you may regain instrument currency by adding to the navigation on July 7 with holding and 6 approaches, which will keep you instrument-current until January 31. You must always look at the last 6 calendar months to ensure your instrument currency.

If the above conditions cannot be met, an alternative way to remain current for IFR is to pass an **instrument proficiency check** in the category of aircraft involved. This will be conducted by an FAA inspector, an FAA-designated examiner, or a certificated instrument flight instructor. An instrument proficiency check qualifies you as current for IFR flight for the next 6 months. You can, of course, submit yourself to an instrument proficiency check at any time.

Part 61: Flight instruction; Simulated Instrument Flight and Certain Flight Tests

To operate in simulated instrument flight (under the hood), you must have a **safety pilot** occupying the other control seat. The safety pilot must possess at least a private pilot certificate with category and class ratings appropriate to the aircraft being flown. The safety pilot must have adequate vision forward and to either side of the aircraft, or his vision must be complemented by another competent observer in the aircraft. Additionally, the aircraft must be equipped with functioning dual controls. However, the safety pilot is permitted to make a determination that a single, throw-over control is adequate, provided certain conditions are met.

Part 61: Airplane Rating; Aeronautical Experience

If you hold a Commercial Pilot Certificate, you may carry passengers for hire. If you hold a Commercial Pilot Certificate, but not an instrument rating, then you may not carry passengers for hire in airplanes:

- on cross-country flights of more than 50 nm; or
- at night.

Is the Airplane suitable for IFR?

Part 91: Civil Aircraft Airworthiness

You shall not operate an aircraft that is not in an airworthy condition. As pilot-in-command, you are responsible for determining this. You should discontinue a flight when unairworthy mechanical, structural or electrical conditions occur.

Inspections. You may not operate an airplane unless within the preceding 12 calendar months it has had either:

1. an annual inspection; or
2. an inspection for the issuance of an airworthiness certificate.

As a general rule, you may not operate an aircraft carrying persons for hire, or give flight instruction for hire, unless within the preceding 100 hours the aircraft has received either:

1. an annual inspection; or
2. an inspection for the issuance of an airworthiness certificate; or
3. a 100-hour inspection.

The annual inspection is required, and is the normal inspection that is done during the life of the airplane following the initial airworthiness inspection. With FAA approval, a series of progressive checks through the year may replace the annual/100-hour inspections. People who own their own airplanes and operate them privately, and not for hire, typically do not have 100-hour inspections done.

Part 91: Certifications Required

The aircraft should carry within it:

1. the current airworthiness certificate; and

2. an effective registration certificate.

Part 91: Civil Aircraft Flight Manual, Marking, and Placard Requirements

You must operate within the limitations specified in the approved Flight Manual, on markings and placards, or as otherwise prescribed. Within the aircraft, there should be an approved Flight Manual or Pilot's Operating Handbook (and this will include weight-and-balance information).

Note: The required documents can be remembered using the word AROW:

A airworthiness certificate;

R registration certificate;

O operating limitations (Flight Manual, POH, placards, etc.);

W weight-and-balance information (in the Flight Manual, POH, or separate).

An FCC radio station license is also required if the airplane is flown outside of the U.S., according to ICAO rules.

Part 91: Instrument and Equipment Requirements

Powered civil aircraft with a standard category United States airworthiness certificate must satisfy the following instrument and equipment requirements:

VFR by Day

1. Airspeed indicator.

2. Altimeter.

3. Magnetic direction indicator (magnetic compass).

4. Tachometer for each engine.

5. Oil pressure gauge for each engine using pressure system.

6. Temperature gauge for each liquid-cooled engine.

7. Oil temperature gauge for each air-cooled engine.

8. Manifold pressure gauge for each altitude engine.

9. Fuel gauge indicating the quantity of fuel in each tank.

10. Landing gear position indicator (for retractables).

11. Approved flotation gear for each occupant, and at least one pyrotechnic signaling device (if aircraft is operated for hire over water beyond the power-off gliding distance from shore).

12. Approved safety belts for all occupants two years or older.

13. Approved shoulder harness for each front seat (for small civil airplanes manufactured after July 18, 1978).

VFR by Night

As above, plus:

14. Approved position lights.

15. An approved anti-collision light (aviation red or aviation white).

16. At least one electric landing light (if the airplane is operated for hire).

17. An adequate source of electrical energy for all installed electric and radio equipment.

18. One spare set of fuses, or three spare fuses of each kind required.

A pilot may operate at night without anti-collision lights if he determines that they must be turned off for safety reasons. If the anti-collision lights fail, the pilot may continue the flight to an airport where repairs can be made.

IFR

As above (for day or night flight as appropriate), plus:

19. A two-way radio communications system and navigation equipment appropriate to the ground facilities to be used (including DME for all flights at and above 24,000 feet MSL within the 50 states and the District of Columbia for which VOR is required—these altitudes are, of course, within Class A airspace, and IFR operations are therefore required at all times).

20. A gyroscopic rate-of-turn indicator (turn coordinator or turn-and-slip indicator).

21. A slip-skid indicator (coordination ball).

22. A sensitive altimeter, adjustable for barometric pressure.

23. A clock displaying hours, minutes, and seconds with a sweep second pointer or digital presentation.

24. Gyroscopic bank and pitch indicator (attitude indicator or artificial horizon).

25. Gyroscopic direction indicator (heading indicator).

Part 91: Operations in Class B Airspace

To operate in Class B airspace, you require the following communications and navigation equipment:

- An operable VOR receiver (for IFR operations, but not required for VFR operations).

- An operable two-way radio capable of communications with ATC.

- A Mode C (altitude-reporting) 4096 transponder. A new Mode S transponder is, of course, also acceptable.

Having satisfied the equipment requirements, you also require prior authorization from ATC to operate in Class B airspace (an ATC clearance).

Part 91: ATC Transponder and Altitude Reporting Equipment and Use

A Mode C (or better) transponder is required to be carried by all aircraft operating:

- in Class A, Class B and Class C airspace, and, within the lateral boundaries of Class B and C airspace areas designated for an airport, up to 10,000 feet MSL;

- within 30 nm of an airport listed in section 1 of Appendix D of the new 14 CFR Part 91 (this list contains most major U.S. airports, for example Atlanta, Denver, Los Angeles, Miami, Minneapolis, both New York airports, St. Louis and both Washington airports), from the surface up to 10,000 feet MSL;

- in all airspace of the 48 contiguous states and the District of Columbia at and above 10,000 feet MSL (except at and below 2500 feet AGL); and

- from the surface to 10,000 feet MSL within a 10 nm radius of any airport in 14 CFR 91 Appendix D, section 2 (currently only one airport listed—Billings, MT), except the airspace below 1200 feet outside the lateral boundaries of the surface area of the airspace designated for that airport.

If your transponder fails in flight, and you are, or will be, operating in airspace where it is required equipment, you should notify ATC immediately. ATC may authorize deviation from the requirement to have an operating transponder to allow you to continue to the airport of your ultimate destination, including any intermediate stops, or to proceed to a place where suitable repairs can be made, or both. For a continuing waiver you should make a request to ATC at least one hour before the proposed flight.

Part 91: ATC Transponder Tests and Inspections

To be used, the transponder must have been tested and inspected satisfactorily within the preceding 24 calendar months.

Part 91: Altimeter System and Altitude Reporting Equipment Tests and Inspections

To operate under IFR each static pressure system, each altimeter instrument, and each automatic pressure altitude reporting system must have been tested and inspected satisfactorily within the preceding 24 calendar months. You may not operate under IFR at an altitude above the maximum at which the systems were tested.

Part 91: VOR Equipment Check for IFR Operations

To use the VOR under IFR, the aircraft's VOR receiving equipment must either:

(a) be maintained, checked and inspected under an approved procedure; or

(b) have been operationally checked within the preceding 30 days, and found to be within the permissible limits. The accuracy for the VOR equipment was covered in Chapter 13 of this manual, and is specified in this regulation.

Each person making an operational check of the VOR shall enter in the aircraft log, or other permanent record:

1. date;

2. place;

3. bearing error; and

4. signature.

Part 91: Supplemental Oxygen

Crew Oxygen Requirements. Crew members are not required to use oxygen up to a cabin pressure altitude of 12,500 feet MSL (although you may).

At cabin pressure altitudes above 12,500 feet up to and including 14,000 feet, the required minimum flight crew may fly without supplemental oxygen for up to 30 minutes only. However, supplemental oxygen must be provided and used for at least the time in excess of 30 minutes at these cabin pressure altitudes.

At cabin pressure altitudes above 14,000 feet, the required minimum flight crew must be provided with and use supplemental oxygen during the entire time at those cabin altitudes.

Passenger Oxygen Requirements. At cabin pressure altitudes above 15,000 feet, each occupant (flight crew and passengers) must be provided with supplemental oxygen, although it is not required that the passengers actually use it.

Note: Commercial pilots operating under 14 CFR Part 135 and Part 121 have different oxygen requirements. Consult a current set of regulations for details.

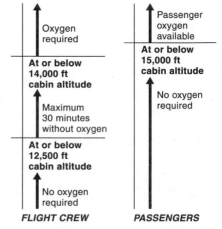

Figure 24-2. Supplemental oxygen requirements

Part 91: Emergency Locator Transmitters

Your aircraft should be equipped with an ELT. If it is battery powered, the batteries should be recharged or replaced after use for more than 1 cumulative hour, or if 50% of their useful life has expired.

Part 91: Operation under IFR in Controlled Airspace; Malfunction Reports

Any loss of navigation or air/ground communications capability must be reported immediately to ATC. This report should include:

1. aircraft identification;

2. equipment affected;

3. any impairment of IFR capability; and

4. the nature and extent of ATC assistance desired.

Part 91: Maintenance Required

Each owner or operator of an aircraft shall have the aircraft regularly inspected as prescribed, and have any discrepancies repaired as prescribed. Maintenance personnel shall make appropriate entries in the aircraft maintenance records indicating that the aircraft has been approved for return to service. Any inoperative instrument, or item of equipment permitted to be inoperative by 14 CFR 91, shall be repaired, replaced, removed, or inspected at the next required inspection. Inoperative instruments or equipment shall be placarded.

Part 91: Inoperative Instruments and Equipment

You may not take off in an aircraft with an inoperative instrument or inoperative equipment unless 14 CFR 91 permits it and unless the equipment is properly placarded as inoperative. In general, flight is not permitted if the inoperative instrument or equipment is part of the VFR-day required instruments and equipment or, for an IFR flight, part of the IFR-required instruments and or equipment. Under certain stringent conditions, the FAA may issue a special flight permit.

NTSB 830
Rules pertaining to the notification and reporting of aircraft accidents or incidents and overdue aircraft, and preservation of aircraft wreckage, mail, cargo, and records

The NTSB is the United States National Transportation Safety Board, which is charged with investigating aircraft accidents and incidents. The procedures a pilot should use to report such matters are specified in document NTSB 830.

An **accident** involves the death or serious injury of a person, or substantial damage to an aircraft, between the time any person boards the aircraft with the intention of flight and the time they disembark.

An **incident** is an occurrence other than an accident, associated with the operation of an aircraft, which affects or could affect the safety of operations.

IFR Operations (14 CFR Part 91)

Part 91: Preflight Action

A pilot-in-command shall, before beginning a flight, familiarize himself with all available information concerning that flight. This information must include:

- runway lengths, and takeoff and landing distance information, at airports of intended use, and the performance capabilities of the aircraft (such as takeoff and landing distances required); and

- for a flight under IFR or not in the vicinity of an airport:
  - weather reports and forecasts;
  - fuel requirements;
  - alternatives available if the planned flight cannot be completed;
  - any known traffic delays advised by ATC.

Part 91: Fuel Requirements for Flight in IFR Conditions

The fuel required to operate in IFR conditions must be sufficient to:

1. complete the flight to the airport of first intended landing;

2. fly from that airport to the alternate airport (see below); and

3. fly after that for 45 minutes at normal cruising speed.

Remember the 1-2-3 rule for determining the need for an alternate.

Item 2 does not apply if the first airport of intended landing has a standard instrument approach procedure, and for at least 1 hour before and 1 hour after the estimated time of arrival there, the weather reports and/or forecasts indicate:

- the ceiling will be at least 2000 feet above the airport elevation; and
- visibility will be at least 3 statute miles.

This can be remembered as 1-2-3: ETA ±1 hour, 2000 feet, 3 miles. Additional fuel should also be carried for any known traffic delays.

Part 91: Flight plan; Information Required

These regulations list the usual information that you must include on a flight plan, but here we consider the information especially relevant to an IFR flight plan.

In the case of an IFR flight plan, you shall include an **alternate airport** unless, at the first airport of intended landing:

1. There is a prescribed standard instrument approach; and
2. For at least one hour before and one hour after the estimated time of arrival, the weather reports or forecasts or any combination of them indicate:

   (a) the ceiling will be at least 2000 feet above the airport elevation; and

   (b) visibility will be at least 3 statute miles. (This is the 1-2-3 requirement to avoid naming an alternate.)

To be suitable as an alternate, the current weather forecasts must indicate that, at the estimated time of arrival at the alternate airport, the ceiling and visibility will be at or above the following alternate airport weather minimums:

1. If an instrument approach procedure has been published for the proposed alternate airport:

   (a) the alternate airport minimums specified in the instrument approach procedure for that alternate airport; or

   (b) if no alternate airport minimums are so specified, the following minimums:

      (i) precision approach procedure (ILS): ceiling 600 feet, visibility 2 statute miles;

      (ii) nonprecision approach procedure: ceiling 800 feet, visibility 2 statute miles.

2. If no instrument approach procedure has been published for the proposed alternate airport, the ceiling and visibility minimums are those allowing descent from the minimum en route altitude (MEA), approach and landing, all under basic VFR.

Note: *Alternate minimums* listed above are those required to be met for you to select the airport as a suitable alternate airport. These alternate minimums are significantly better conditions than the *landing minimums*, so you should be able to approach and land at the alternate even if conditions deteriorate a little below the alternate minimums while you are en route. Having selected it as alternate, and then diverted to it, you may make an approach and landing at the alternate airport provided the landing minimums for the approach to be used are met.

When looking for an alternate airport, remember: if no alternate minimums are specified and the airport supports a precision approach, you need a 600 ft ceiling and 2 miles visibility. If there's only a nonprecision approach you need an 800 ft. ceiling and 2 miles visibility. If there's no approach, you need the airport to be VFR from your cruising altitude on down.

Part 91: ATC Clearance and Flight Plan Required

To operate in controlled airspace under IFR, you must (1) file an IFR flight plan; and (2) receive an appropriate ATC clearance.

Part 91: Operations in Class A Airspace

To fly within Class A airspace:

1. You must be instrument rated.

2. The airplane must be equipped for IFR operations.

3. You must operate under IFR at a specific flight level assigned by ATC (you need to submit an IFR flight plan and receive an ATC clearance).

4. The airplane must be equipped with applicable equipment specified in 14 CFR 91 and capable of direct pilot/controller communication on the frequency specified by ATC; (capable of frequencies such as 135.725 MHz).

Part 91: Compliance with ATC Clearances and Instructions

No pilot-in-command may deviate from an ATC clearance unless an amended clearance is obtained, an emergency exists, or the deviation is in response to a traffic alert and collision avoidance system (TCAS) resolution advisory. If you must deviate, notify ATC of that deviation as soon as possible. If you are given priority by ATC in an emergency, you should submit a detailed report of that emergency within 48 hours to the manager of that ATC facility, if requested by ATC.

Part 91: Altimeter Settings

You shall maintain cruising altitude or flight level, as the case may be, by reference to an altimeter with its pressure window set to:

- below 18,000 feet MSL: the current reported altimeter setting of a station along the route and within 100 nm of the aircraft (at altitudes); or

- at or above 18,000 feet MSL: 29.92 in.Hg (at flight levels).

Part 91: VFR Cruising Altitude or Flight Level

VFR cruising altitudes or flight levels, when more than 3000 feet AGL, are:

- on a magnetic course of magnetic north to MC 179: **odds + 500 feet**; 3500 feet MSL, 15,500 feet MSL, FL195, FL235; and

- on a magnetic course of MC 180 to MC 359: **evens + 500 feet**; 4500 feet MSL, 16,500 feet MSL, FL185, FL285.

Although this regulation covers VFR levels even above FL290, it is a mandatory requirement in the USA to operate IFR in Class A airspace, which is from 18,000 feet MSL up to FL600. This regulation also applies to an IFR flight operating on a VFR-on-top clearance above a cloud layer.

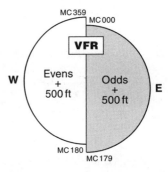

Figure 24-3. VFR cruise levels "WEEO + 500" (West evens, East odds, plus 500 feet)

Part 91: IFR Cruising Altitude or Flight Level

An IFR flight should plan to cruise at:

- on a magnetic course of north to MC 179: **odds**; 5000 feet MSL, 15,000 feet MSL, FL190, FL230; and

- on a magnetic course of MC 180 to MC 359: **evens**; 4000 feet MSL, 16,000 feet MSL, FL180, FL280.

In controlled airspace, however, maintain the altitude or flight level assigned by ATC. If ATC assigns you a VFR-on-top clearance, you should maintain a VFR altitude or flight level.

This regulation applies up to FL290.

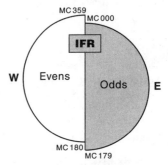

Figure 24-4. IFR cruise levels "WEEO" (West evens, East odds)

Part 91: Minimum Altitudes for IFR Operations

You may not operate under IFR below a prescribed minimum altitude. If both an MEA (minimum en route altitude) and a MOCA (minimum obstruction clearance altitude) are prescribed for a particular route or route segment, you may operate below the MEA down to, but not below, the MOCA within 22 nm (25 sm) of the VOR concerned, based on your reasonable estimate of that distance.

The MEA assures obstruction clearance and radio navigation aid reception; MOCA is lower and only assures obstruction clearance, plus radio navigation aid reception within 22 nm (25 sm) of the aid.

If no applicable minimum altitude is prescribed, then you must maintain a clearance height above the highest obstacle, within a horizontal distance of 4 nautical miles of the course to be flown, of:

• 2000 feet in designated mountainous areas (shown in 14 CFR Part 95: IFR Altitudes subpart B); otherwise

• 1000 feet.

You should climb to a higher minimum IFR altitude immediately after passing the point beyond which that minimum altitude applies, except that, when ground obstructions intervene, the point beyond which the higher minimum altitude applies shall be crossed at the applicable MCA (minimum crossing altitude).

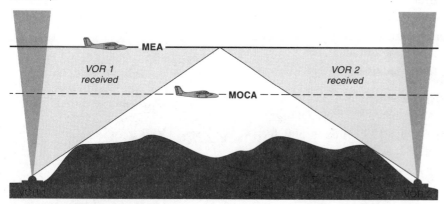

Figure 24-5. MEA and MOCA

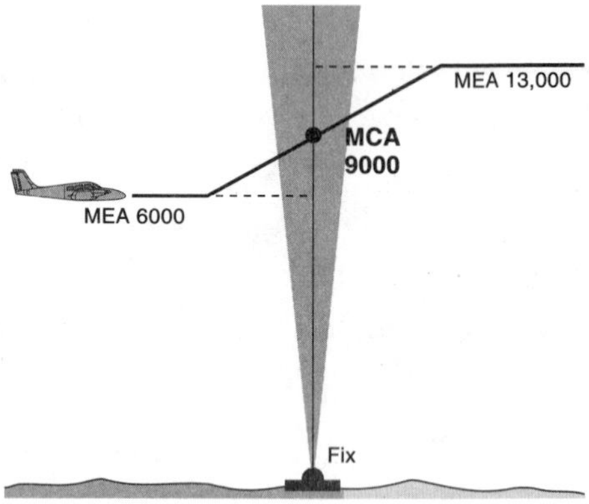

Figure 24-6. MCA

Part 91: Course to be Flown (IFR)

Unless otherwise authorized by ATC, in controlled airspace, under IFR you should:

• fly along the centerline of an airway (±4 nm from airway centerline when within 51 nm of the VOR); or

• on any other route, directly between fixes.

You may, however, maneuver the aircraft to pass well clear of other traffic.

Part 91: Takeoff and Landing under IFR; General

Instrument approaches. When an instrument approach to a civil airport is necessary, you shall use a published standard instrument approach procedure (SIAP) unless otherwise authorized.

Authorized DH or MDA. The authorized **decision height (DH)** or **minimum descent altitude (MDA)** is the higher of:

• the DH or MDA prescribed for the pilot-in-command; and

• the DH or MDA for which the aircraft is equipped.

Operation below DH or MDA. You may not operate the aircraft below the authorized DH or MDA unless:

- the aircraft is continuously in a position from which a safe landing may be made using normal maneuvers;
- the flight visibility is not less than the prescribed visibility in the standard IAP;
- one of the following visual references for the intended runway is distinctly visible and identifiable to the pilot (except for Category II or III approaches):
    1. the approach light system;
    2. the threshold, threshold markings or threshold lights, or the runway end identifier lights (REIL);
    3. the visual approach slope indicator (VASI);
    4. the touchdown zone, touchdown markings or touchdown zone lights;
    5. the runway, runway markings or runway lights; or
- the aircraft has reached the specified visual descent point (VDP) for certain nonprecision IAPs.

Landing. You may not land when the flight visibility is less than the visibility prescribed in the standard IAP being used.

Missed Approaches. You shall immediately execute a missed approach if, at the DH or below on a precision approach or below the MDA on a nonprecision approach, the above visibility requirements are not met, or if you lose sight of the airport environment (except in normal banked turns when maneuvering).

Takeoff Minimums. Takeoff weather minimums for each runway are published with the instrument approach charts and departure procedures, otherwise standard minimums apply. For one- and two-engine airplanes involved in 14 CFR Part 135 (Air Taxi or Commercial) operations, the standard takeoff minimum is visibility 1 statute mile.

These IFR takeoff minimums do not apply in a legal sense to Part 91 operations (that is, private flights, flight instruction and airwork), however they are a very good guide for you to follow.

Comparable Values of Runway Visual Range (RVR) and Visibility. RVR 2400 feet = $\frac{1}{2}$ statute mile; RVR 5000 feet = 1 statute mile.

Use of Radar during Instrument Approaches. ATC may issue radar vectors as course guidance through the segments of an approach procedure to the final approach fix (FAF). When you have received an approach clearance, you shall hold the last altitude assigned until established on a segment of a published route or the IAP, after which the published altitudes apply within each succeeding route or approach segment (unless a different altitude is assigned by ATC).

Limitations on Procedure Turns. In the case of a radar vector to a final approach course or fix, a timed-approach from a holding fix, or an approach for which the procedure specifies "NoPT", you may not make a procedure turn unless cleared to do so by ATC.

Part 91: Flight Crew Members at Station

Each required crew member shall be at his station with his seatbelt fastened during takeoff and landing and while en route, unless his absence is necessary in the performance of other operational duties or to satisfy physiological needs. If a shoulder harness is available, it shall be used during takeoff and landing.

Part 91: Use of Seatbelts and Safety Harnesses

You must brief each person on board how to fasten and unfasten their safety belt, and shoulder harness if installed, and ensure that they are used during takeoff and landing. This does not apply to children less than 2 years old and held by an adult, or to sport parachutists (who still must wear a safety belt even if they use the floor of the aircraft for a seat).

Part 91: Aircraft Speed

- Maximum 250 KIAS below 10,000 feet MSL, unless otherwise authorized by ATC in Class A or Class B airspace; (Class A is mainly above 18,000 feet MSL, so usually not affected).

- Maximum 200 KIAS at or below 2500 feet AGL within 4 nm of the primary airport of a Class C or Class D airspace area, unless otherwise authorized or required by ATC.

- Maximum 200 KIAS in the airspace underlying a Class B airspace area designated for an airport, or in a VFR corridor designated through such a Class B airspace area.

Part 91: Portable Electronic Devices

You may not allow the operation of any portable electronic device, other than those listed below, while operating under IFR:

- portable voice recorders;
- hearing aids;
- heart pacemakers;
- electric shavers; or
- any other portable electronic device that the operator of the aircraft has determined will not cause interference with the navigation or communication system of the aircraft. This determination may be made by the commercial operator, or by the pilot-in-command of a private IFR flight.

Part 91: IFR Radio Communications

You shall maintain a continuous radio watch on the appropriate frequency when flying IFR, and report by radio as soon as possible:

- time and altitude at each designated reporting point, except when under radar control;
- any unforecast weather conditions encountered; and
- any other information relating to the safety of the flight.

Part 91: IFR Operations; Two-Way Radio Communications Failure

If, when operating under IFR, two-way radio communications fail, you are required to take the following action:

- In VFR conditions: remain in VFR and land as soon as practicable.
- In IFR conditions:
1. Route:
    (a) Follow the route in the last ATC clearance received.

    (b) If being radar vectored—by the direct route from the point of radio failure to the fix, route or airway specified in the vector clearance.

    (c) In the absence of an assigned route, by the route that ATC has advised you to expect in a further clearance, otherwise the route filed in the flight plan.

2. Altitude:

At the highest of the following altitudes or flight levels for the route segment being flown:

(a) The altitude or flight level in the last ATC clearance received.

(b) The minimum altitude for IFR operations.

(c) The altitude or flight level that ATC has advised you to expect in a further clearance.

3. Leave Clearance Limit:

(a) When the clearance limit is a fix from which the approach begins, commence descent or descent and approach as close as possible to the *expect further clearance* (EFC) time if one has been received or, if one has not been received, as close as possible to the estimated time of arrival (ETA) as calculated from the filed or amended (with ATC) estimated time en route.

(b) If the clearance limit is not a fix from which an approach begins, leave the clearance limit at the EFC time if one has been received or, if none has been received, upon arrival over the clearance limit, and proceed to a fix from which an approach begins, and commence descent or descent and approach as close as possible to the ETA as calculated from the filed or amended (with ATC) estimated time en route (ETE).

Note: In cases of radio communications failure, make use of your transponder to alert radar controllers by squawking code 7600. If you divert to an alternate airport, and you have not filed route or altitude, you should fly the published airways and minimum en route altitude (MEA).

14 CFR Part 142

If the flight school at which you're training uses flight simulators and flight training devices extensively for both pilot training and for checkrides, the odds are you are training at a school governed by 14 CFR Part 142 rules, which went into effect in August 1996. Schools that operate under these rules can use simulators and flight training devices extensively in their syllabi, and can certify pilots for private, instrument and commercial ratings in less flight time than schools operating under 14 CFR Part 61 or 14 CFR Part 141. The rules are geared toward hi-tech pilot training programs using standardized training. Most Part 142 facilities train airline and corporate turbojet and turboprop pilots.

✍ Review 24   Regulations Important to the Instrument Pilot

Responsibility and Authority of the Pilot-In-Command

1. Who is directly responsible for the operation of an aircraft?

➤ the pilot-in-command

_____

2. Who is responsible to ensure that you are adequately qualified to commence an IFR flight and that the aircraft is serviceable for flight?

➤ you are, as pilot-in-command

_____

3. Who is responsible that all items of equipment required for IFR flight have been tested and inspected, and found to be satisfactory, within the prescribed periods?

➤ you are, as pilot-in-command

_____

4. If an IFR flight plan is required to be filed, whose responsibility is that?

➤ yours, as pilot-in-command

_____

5. If you experience an in-flight emergency, you (may/must not) deviate from 14 CFR to the extent required to meet the emergency.

➤ may

Basic VFR Weather Minimums

1. You may not operate under basic VFR at an airport that is within Class E airspace beneath the ceiling when the ceiling is less than _____ feet AGL?

➤ 1000 feet

2. VFR minimums for flight by day in Class G airspace that starts at the surface are: flight visibility _____; distances from clouds: _____.

➤ 1 sm; clear of clouds

3. VFR minimums for flight in Class G airspace below 10,000 feet, but higher than 1200 feet AGL (regardless of MSL altitude) by day are: flight visibility of _____; and distances from clouds: _____ below; _____ above; _____ horizontal.

➤ 1 sm; 500 feet below, 1000 feet above and 2000 feet horizontal

4. VFR minimums for flight in Class E airspace below 10,000 feet or less than 1200 feet AGL (regardless of MSL altitude) are: flight visibility _____; distances from clouds: _____.

➤ 3 sm; 500 feet below, 1000 feet above and 2000 feet horizontally from clouds

5. VFR minimums for flight in Class E airspace at or above 10,000 feet MSL, and more than 1200 feet AGL are: flight visibility _____; distances from clouds: _____.

➤ 5 sm; 1000 feet below, 1000 feet above and 1 sm horizontal

6. VFR minimums for flight in Class B airspace are: flight visibility _____; distances from clouds _____.

➤ 3 sm; clear of clouds

7. VFR minimums for flight in Class C airspace are: flight visibility _____; distances from clouds _____.

➤ 3 sm; 500 feet below, 1000 feet above and 2000 feet horizontal

8. VFR minimums for flight in Class D airspace are: flight visibility _____; distances from clouds _____.

➤ 3 sm; 500 feet below, 1000 feet above and 2000 feet horizontal

9. VFR minimums for flight in Class G airspace at or above 10,000 feet MSL, and more than 1200 feet AGL are: flight visibility _____; distances from clouds: _____.

➤ 5 sm; 1000 feet below, 1000 feet above and 1 sm horizontal

10. VFR minimums for a VFR-on-top flight in Class G airspace at 13,500 feet MSL (above 1200 feet AGL) during daylight hours are: flight visibility _____; distances from clouds: _____.

➤ 5 sm; 1000 feet below, 1000 feet above and 1 sm horizontal

11. VFR minimums for a VFR-on-top flight in Class E airspace at 13,500 feet MSL (above 1200 feet AGL) during daylight hours are: flight visibility _____; distances from clouds: _____.

➤ 5 sm; 1000 feet below, 1000 feet above and 1 sm horizontal

12. VFR minimums for a VFR-on-top flight in Class G airspace at 8500 feet MSL (above 1200 feet AGL) during daylight hours are: flight visibility _____; distances from clouds: _____.

➤ 1 sm; 500 feet below, 1000 feet above and 2000 feet horizontal

13. VFR minimums for a VFR-on-top flight in Class E airspace at 8500 feet MSL during daylight hours are: flight visibility _____; distances from clouds: _____.

➤ 3 sm; 500 feet below, 1000 feet above and 2000 feet horizontal

14. VFR minimums for a VFR-on-top flight at 10,500 feet MSL (above 1200 feet AGL) during daylight hours are (a) in Class E airspace; (b) in Class G airspace: flight visibility _____; distances from clouds: _____.

➤ both (a) and (b): 5 sm; 1000 feet below, 1000 feet above and 1 sm horizontal

15. VFR minimums for flight in Class G airspace 1200 feet or less AGL by night are: flight visibility _____; distances from clouds: _____.

➤ 3 sm; 500 feet below, 1000 feet above and 2000 feet horizontal

16. VFR minimums for flight in Class G airspace more than 1200 feet AGL but less than 10,000 feet MSL by night are: flight visibility _____; distances from clouds: _____.

➤ 3 sm; 500 feet below, 1000 feet above and 2000 feet horizontal

Special VFR Weather Minimums

1. In what airspace may a special VFR clearance be issued by ATC?

➤ within the lateral boundaries of the surface areas of Class B, C or D airspace, except at airports listed in section 3 of Appendix D of 14 CFR Part 91

2. Visibility and distance from clouds requirements of a special VFR clearance are _____.

➤ visibility 1 sm and clear of clouds

3. May a non-instrument-rated pilot fly special VFR at night?

➤ no

Requirements for Certificates, Ratings, and Authorizations

1. Do you require an instrument rating to be pilot-in-command of an IFR flight?

➤ yes

2. Do you require an instrument rating to be pilot-in-command of an IFR flight in VFR conditions?

➤ yes

3. Do you require an instrument rating to be pilot-in-command of a flight in weather conditions less than the minimums prescribed for VFR flight?

➤ yes

4. Do you require an instrument rating to operate in Class A airspace?

➤ yes

Pilot Logbooks

1. Must you be flying in actual IFR conditions to log the time as instrument time?

➤ no, it can be in simulated instrument conditions

2. Can the total flight time of a flight on an IFR flight plan be logged as instrument flight time?

➤ no, only the time in actual or simulated instrument conditions may be logged

3. Which part of the total flight time under an IFR flight plan can be logged as instrument flight time?

➤ the time during which you operated the airplane solely by reference to instruments under actual or simulated instrument conditions

4. If you enter some flight time as being simulated instrument conditions, what additional qualifying information must also be entered?

➤ place; type of instrument approach or procedure completed; and the name of the safety pilot

5. Can an instrument flight instructor log as instrument time the total flight time for an instrument training flight?

➤ no

6. Can an instrument flight instructor log as instrument time the flight time during an instrument training flight that the student is under the hood in simulated instrument conditions?

➤ no

7. Can an instrument flight instructor log as instrument time the flight time during an instrument training flight that the student is actually in instrument weather conditions?

➤ yes

Recent Flight Experience; Pilot-In-Command

1. The minimum instrument time required within the last 6 months for you to be current for IFR is _____.

➤ there is no minimum time requirement (except for glider pilots)

2. How much flight in actual IFR conditions is required to remain instrument current?

➤ none, all flights can be in simulated IFR conditions

3. How many instrument approaches must have been flown in the previous 6 months for you to be current for IFR operations? How many of these instrument approaches must have been in an aircraft?

➤ 6 instrument approaches, none—they can all be in a simulator

4. To remain current for IFR operations , you must have accomplished during the last _____ months at least _____ instrument approaches, and _____.

➤ 6 months, 6 instrument approaches, holding patterns and IFR en route navigation skills.

5. If these conditions cannot be met, you may complete an _____ check in the category of aircraft to be flown.

➤ instrument proficiency check

6. After your recent IFR experience lapses, how much time do you have before you must pass an instrument proficiency check to act as pilot-in-command under IFR?

➤ 6 months

7. After successfully completing an instrument proficiency check you remain current for IFR flight for a period of _____, even if no further IFR flights are made.

➤ 6 months

8. Do you require any recent IFR experience to submit yourself to an instrument proficiency check with an FAA inspector, a designated examiner or a certificated instrument flight instructor?

➤ no (but it is recommended)

9. Your recent IFR experience expires on June 1 of this year. What is the latest date that you can meet the IFR recent experience requirement without having to take an instrument proficiency check?

➤ Nov. 30 this year (6 months after the expiration of your IFR recency requirements)

10. Your present instrument experience within the last 6 months is: simulator: 3 hours and 1 instrument approach; airplane: 3 hours and 1 instrument approach. What additional IFR experience do you require to meet the recent IFR requirements to act as pilot-in-command under IFR?

➤ 4 approaches, holding patterns and navigation skills

Flight Instruction; Simulated Instrument Flight and Certain Flight Tests

1. For you to practice simulated IFR flight under the hood in VFR conditions, what minimum requirements must be met?

➤ you require a safety pilot sitting in the other control seat

2. Define the qualifications that your safety pilot must possess.

➤ at least a private pilot certificate with category and class ratings appropriate to the aircraft being flown

Airplane Rating; Aeronautical Experience

1. As a commercial pilot, do you require an instrument rating to carry passengers for hire at night?
   > yes

2. As a commercial pilot, do you require an instrument rating to carry passengers for hire on a cross-country flight of 45 nm by day?
   > no

3. As a commercial pilot, do you require an instrument rating to carry passengers for hire on a cross-country flight of 45 nm by night?
   > yes

4. As a commercial pilot, do you require an instrument rating to carry passengers for hire on a cross-country flight of 73 nm by day?
   > yes

Civil Aircraft Airworthiness

1. Who is responsible for determining if an aircraft is in a condition safe for flight?
   > pilot-in-command

2. If an unairworthy mechanical, structural or electrical condition occurs in flight, you should:
   (a) continue the flight normally to the destination.
   (b) discontinue the flight.
   > (b)

Inspections

1. One of three inspections must have been carried out within the last 100 hours to permit normal operations for hire. What are they?
   > the annual inspection, the airworthiness inspection, or the 100-hour inspection

Certifications Required

1. Must the airworthiness certificate be carried within the aircraft?
   > yes

2. Must the registration certificate be carried within the aircraft?
   > yes

Civil Aircraft Flight Manual, Marking, and Placard Requirements

1. Name the documents required to be carried in an aircraft.
   > AROW (airworthiness certificate, registration certificate, operating limitations, weight and balance)

Instrument and Equipment Requirements

1. If the clock does not have a digital presentation, a sweep second hand (is/is not) a requirement for IFR flight?
   > is

2. A gyroscopic direction indicator (is/is not) required for operations under IFR.
   > is

3. A dual VOR system (is/is not) required for operations under IFR.
   > is not

4. Is DME required for flight at and above 24,000 feet MSL?
   > yes, if VOR is required (which is almost always the case)

5. For IFR flight, you (do/do not) require navigation equipment appropriate to the ground facilities to be used.
   > do

Operations in Class B Airspace

1. Do you require an operable VOR to fly IFR in a Class B airspace area?
   > yes

2. Do you require an operable ADF to fly IFR in a Class B airspace area?
   > no

3. Do you require two-way radio communications to fly in a Class B airspace area?

➤ yes

4. Do you require an altitude-reporting transponder to fly in a Class B airspace area?

➤ yes

5. An altitude-reporting capability on a transponder is known as Mode _____.

➤ Mode C

6. Is an ATC clearance required to fly in a Class B airspace area?

➤ yes

ATC Transponder and Altitude Reporting Equipment and Use

1. An operable coded transponder equipped with Mode C capability is required in all airspace above _____ feet MSL, except if that airspace is within _____ feet of the ground.

➤ 10,000 feet MSL, 2500 feet AGL

2. Is an operable coded transponder equipped with Mode C capability required in Class A or B airspace?

➤ yes, for both

3. Is an operable coded transponder equipped with Mode C capability required in a Class C or D airspace?

➤ Class C—yes; Class D—no

4. Is an operable coded transponder equipped with Mode C capability required within 30 nm of the primary airport of a Class B airspace area?

➤ yes

5. Your transponder fails when you are flying in a Class B airspace area. ATC (may/will not) allow you to continue without your transponder functioning.

➤ may

6. If your transponder is inoperative and you wish to fly into Class B airspace, you should request a waiver from the transponder requirement at least _____ hour before the proposed flight.

➤ 1 hour

ATC Transponder Tests and Inspections

1. The ATC transponder, to be used, must have been tested and inspected satisfactorily within the preceding _____.

➤ 24 calendar months

Altimeter System and Altitude Reporting Equipment Tests and Inspections

1. An aircraft altimeter system test and inspection must be accomplished within _____.

➤ 24 calendar months

2. Your aircraft had the static pressure system and altimeter tested and inspected on September 13 of this year, and was found to comply with FAA standards. These systems must be reinspected and approved for use in controlled airspace under IFR by which date and how many years hence?

➤ September 30, 2 years hence

3. The altitude-reporting system of the transponder must be checked within _____.

➤ 24 calendar months

VOR Equipment Check for IFR Operations

1. To operate under IFR, an operational check of the aircraft VOR equipment must have been accomplished within the preceding _____.

➤ 30 days

2. When making an airborne check of a dual VOR system, the maximum tolerance between the two indicators when set to identical radials of a VOR is _____.

➤ plus or minus 4 degrees

3. What four items should be entered in the aircraft log, or other permanent record, by each person who carries out the VOR operational check?

➤ date, place, bearing error, and signature

4. The maximum tolerance allowed for an operational VOR equipment check when using a VOT is _____.

➤ plus or minus 4 degrees

Supplemental Oxygen

1. As pilot of an unpressurized airplane, are you required to use supplemental oxygen cruising at 12,000 feet?

➤ no

2. As pilot of an unpressurized airplane, are you required to use supplemental oxygen cruising at 12,500 feet?

➤ no

3. As pilot of an unpressurized airplane, are you required to use supplemental oxygen cruising at 13,000 feet?

➤ yes, for any period in excess of 30 minutes above 12,500 feet

4. What is the maximum cabin pressure altitude at which you can fly for longer than 30 minutes without using supplemental oxygen?

➤ 12,500 feet

5. As pilot of an unpressurized airplane operating above 12,500 feet MSL, but not more than 14,000 feet MSL, for a period of 1 hour 40 minutes, for what period are you required to use supplemental oxygen?

➤ 1 hour 10 min

6. As pilot of an unpressurized airplane operating above 15,000 feet MSL for a period of 1 hour 40 minutes, for what period are you required to use supplemental oxygen?

➤ 1 hour 40 min

7. Crew must use oxygen for the whole time above _____ feet MSL cabin pressure altitude.

➤ 14,000 feet

8. Passengers must (be provided with/use) oxygen for flight above _____ feet MSL cabin pressure altitude.

➤ be provided with, 15,000 feet

9. You are flying a pressurized airplane at FL310 (31,000 feet). The cabin is pressurized to 8500 feet. Must you wear your oxygen mask?

➤ no, cabin pressure altitude is 12,500 feet or lower

10. Cruising at FL 310, your airplane experiences a depressurization. You put your oxygen mask on and commence a rapid descent to a lower altitude. If you level off at 16,000 feet MSL, may you remove your oxygen mask to improve voice communications?

➤ no

11. If you level off at 15,000 feet MSL, may you remove your oxygen mask to improve voice communications?

➤ no

12. If you level off at 14,000 feet MSL, may you remove your oxygen mask to improve voice communications?

➤ yes, but only for a period of 30 minutes or less

13. If you level off at 12,500 feet MSL, may you remove your oxygen mask to improve voice communications?

➤ yes

14. If you level off at 16,000 feet MSL, may the passengers remove their oxygen masks?

➤ yes, above 15,000 feet cabin altitude passenger oxygen must be provided, but does not have to be used

Emergency Locator Transmitters

1. The batteries of an ELT must be replaced or recharged after _____ hours of cumulative use, or if _____% of their usable life has expired.

➤ 1 hour, 50%

Operation under IFR in controlled airspace; malfunction reports

1. Are you required to report the malfunction of your VOR receiver to ATC if you are operating on an IFR flight plan?

➤ yes

Maintenance Required

1. Maintenance personnel (shall/need not) make an entry in the aircraft maintenance records to indicate that an aircraft is approved for return to service following the replacement of a faulty attitude indicator.

➤ shall

2. A known inoperative ADF (should/need not) be placarded.

➤ should

Inoperative Instruments and Equipment

1. When taxiing for takeoff prior to an IFR flight, you notice that the turn coordinator is not functioning. Is a takeoff permitted?

➤ no

2. In your preflight inspection prior to an IFR flight, you notice that the VSI has been placarded as inoperative by the maintenance personnel. Is a takeoff permitted?

➤ yes

3. In your preflight inspection prior to an IFR flight, you notice that the only VOR in the aircraft has been placarded as inoperative by the maintenance personnel. Is a takeoff permitted without further reference to the FAA?

➤ no

NTSB 830

1. The publication which covers the procedures required for aircraft accident and incident reporting responsibilities for pilots is the _____.

➤ NTSB 830

Preflight Action

1. May you depart on a cross-country flight in VFR conditions to an airport whose runway lengths cannot be determined?

➤ no

2. May you depart on a cross-country flight in IFR conditions to an airport whose runway lengths cannot be determined?

➤ no

3. May you depart on a flight if unaware of the performance capabilities of the aircraft?

➤ no

4. What are some of the important performance capabilities of your airplane that you should be familiar with before you depart on a flight?

➤ the takeoff distance required, and the landing distance required

5. For an IFR flight, you are (required/encouraged) to familiarize yourself with weather reports and forecasts.

➤ required

6. For an IFR flight, you are (required/encouraged) to familiarize yourself with fuel requirements.

➤ required

7. For an IFR flight, you are (required/encouraged) to familiarize yourself with alternatives available if the planned flight cannot be completed.

➤ required

8. For an IFR flight, you are (required/encouraged) to familiarize yourself with any known traffic delays advised by ATC.

➤ required

9. List six items you must familiarize yourself with prior to an IFR flight.

➤ runway lengths, aircraft performance, weather reports and forecasts, fuel requirements, alternatives, known traffic delays

Fuel Requirements for Flight in IFR Conditions

1. What minimum conditions must exist at the destination airport to avoid listing an alternate airport on an IFR flight plan when a standard instrument approach is available?

➤ within ETA±1 hour, forecast ceiling 2000 feet, forecast visibility 3 miles

2. Is an alternate required for a destination airport served with an instrument approach procedure, and which has a ceiling forecast to be 1500 feet, and a forecast visibility of 3 miles? Justify your answer.

➤ yes; ceiling must be at least 2000 feet above airport elevation

3. If conditions requiring an alternate are forecast to improve above alternate conditions 45 minutes prior to your ETA, you (must/need not) carry an alternate.

➤ must

4. If excellent weather conditions at your destination are forecast to deteriorate below alternate minimums 55 minutes after your ETA, you (must/need not) carry an alternate.

➤ must

5. Is an alternate required for a destination airport served by an instrument approach, and with a ceiling forecast to be 2500 feet, and a forecast visibility of 3 miles? Justify your answer.

➤ no; ceiling exceeds 2000 feet height above airport elevation (HAA), visibility exceeds 3 miles

6. Is an alternate required for a destination airport not served by an instrument approach, and with a ceiling forecast to be 2500 feet, and a forecast visibility of 3 miles? Justify your answer.

➤ yes; the IFR destination must be served by an IAP

7. Is an alternate required for a destination airport with a ceiling forecast to be 2000 feet, and a forecast visibility of 3 miles? Justify your answer.

➤ no; ceiling must be at least 2000 feet, and visibility must be at least 3 miles—this airport just makes it!

8. The destination airport has a ceiling forecast to be 1500 feet, and a forecast visibility in excess of 3 miles. Is an alternate required? What minimum fuel must you carry?

➤ yes; fuel to destination, fuel to alternate, plus 45 minutes at normal cruising speed

9. The destination airport has a ceiling forecast to be 3000 feet, and a forecast visibility in excess of 3 miles. Is an alternate required? What minimum fuel must you carry?

➤ no; fuel to destination, plus 45 minutes at normal cruising speed

10. If there are known traffic delays of 30 minutes, should you carry 30 minutes additional fuel?

➤ yes

11. If the weather at your destination airport is currently good, but the ceiling is forecast to drop to 1500 feet approximately 50 minutes after your estimated time of arrival, is an alternate required?

➤ yes

12. If the weather at your destination airport is currently good, but the ceiling is forecast to drop to 1500 feet approximately 1 hour after your estimated time of arrival, is an alternate required?

➤ yes

13. If the weather at your destination airport is currently good, but the ceiling is forecast to drop to 1500 feet approximately 90 minutes after your estimated time of arrival, is an alternate required?

➤ no

14. If the weather at your destination airport is currently ceiling 1500 feet, visibility 2 miles, but is forecast to improve to ceiling 2500 feet, visibility 4 miles approximately 75 minutes after your estimated time of arrival, is an alternate required?

➤ yes, the improvement is more than 1 hour after your ETA

15. If the weather at your destination airport is currently ceiling 1500 feet, visibility 2 miles, but is forecast to improve to ceiling 2500 feet, visibility 4 miles approximately 45 minutes before your estimated time of arrival, is an alternate required?

➤ yes, the improvement is required at least 1 hour before your ETA

Flight Plan; Information Required

1. The alternate minimums that must be forecast at the proposed alternate airport if it has only a nonprecision approach procedure are ceiling _____ feet (HAA/MSL) and visibility _____ (sm/nm).

➤ 800 feet HAA (height above airport elevation), 2 sm

2. The alternate minimums that must be forecast at the proposed alternate airport if it has a precision approach procedure are ceiling _____ feet (HAA/MSL) and visibility _____ (sm/nm).

➤ 600 feet HAA, 2 sm

3. The alternate minimums that must be forecast at the proposed alternate airport if it has only a VOR approach procedure are ceiling _____ feet (HAA/MSL) and visibility _____ (sm/nm).

➤ 800 feet HAA, 2 sm

4. The alternate minimums that must be forecast at the proposed alternate airport if it has published VOR and ILS approach procedures are ceiling _____ feet (HAA/MSL) and visibility _____ (sm/nm).

➤ 600 feet HAA, 2 sm

5. The alternate minimums apply to the (ETA/ETA ±1 hour) at the alternate airport.

➤ ETA

6. An airport without an authorized instrument approach procedure may be included on an IFR flight plan as an alternate, if the current weather forecast indicates that the ceiling and visibility at the ETA _____.

➤ will allow descent from the MEA followed by an approach and landing, all under basic VFR

7. You have diverted to the alternate airport. When making an approach to land there, you are restricted to the (alternate/landing) minimums.

➤ landing minimums for the approach to be used

ATC Clearance and Flight Plan Required

1. To operate in controlled airspace (Class A–E) under IFR you must file a _____ and receive an _____.

➤ flight plan, ATC clearance

2. Do you need to file an IFR plan to operate in instrument conditions (IMC) in controlled airspace?

➤ yes

3. Do you need to file an IFR plan to operate in IMC in Class G airspace?

➤ no

4. Do you need to have an instrument rating to operate as pilot-in-command in IMC in Class G airspace?

➤ yes

5. When departing in IMC conditions from an airport located in Class G airspace, must you file a flight plan and receive an ATC clearance before takeoff?

➤ no

6. When departing in IMC conditions from an airport located in Class G airspace, must you file a flight plan and receive an ATC clearance before entering IFR conditions?

➤ no

7. When departing in IMC conditions from an airport located in Class G airspace, must you file a flight plan and receive an ATC clearance before arriving at the en route portion of the flight?

➤ no

8. When departing in IMC conditions from an airport located in Class G airspace, must you file a flight plan and receive an ATC clearance before entering controlled airspace?

➤ yes

9. When departing in IMC conditions from an airport located in Class G airspace, you must file a flight plan and receive an ATC clearance before:

   (a) takeoff
   (b) entering IFR conditions
   (c) entering controlled airspace
   (d) arriving at the en route portion of the flight

➤ (c)

Operations in Class A Airspace

1. Do you need to file an IFR plan if you intend to operate in Class A airspace?

➤ yes

2. The Class A airspace area begins at _____ feet MSL.

➤ 18,000 feet MSL

3. Having filed an IFR plan, do you also require an ATC clearance to operate in Class A airspace?

➤ yes

4. Will the ATC clearance to operate in Class A airspace contain an assigned flight level?

➤ yes

5. No person may operate an aircraft in controlled airspace under IFR unless he has filed a flight plan and received a clearance:

   (a) by telephone prior to takeoff.
   (b) prior to joining an airway.
   (c) prior to entering controlled airspace.

➤ (c)

Compliance with ATC Clearances and Instructions

1. While on an IFR flight, you have an emergency that causes you to deviate from your ATC clearance. What action must be taken?

➤ notify ATC of the deviation as soon as possible

2. If you experience a distress condition, such as mechanical problems, you (should/should not) declare an emergency and obtain an amended clearance, time permitting.

➤ should

3. When may ATC request a detailed report of an emergency, even though a rule has not been violated?

➤ when ATC has given you priority

Altimeter Settings

1. Below 18,000 feet MSL, the pressure window of the altimeter should be set to _____, and this should be for a station along the route and within _____ nm of the aircraft.

➤ current reported altimeter setting, 100 nm

2. The pressure window of the altimeter should be set to 29.92 in.Hg for cruising (at/at and above/above) _____ feet MSL.

➤ at and above 18,000 feet MSL

VFR and IFR Cruising Level

1. What is the next higher appropriate cruising altitude or flight level to 5000 feet MSL for a VFR flight along an airway whose magnetic course is MC 090?

➤ 5500 feet MSL

2. What is the next higher appropriate cruising altitude or flight level to 5000 feet MSL for an IFR flight along an airway whose magnetic course is MC 090?

➤ 7000 feet MSL

3. What is the next higher appropriate cruising altitude or flight level to 5000 feet MSL for an IFR flight along an airway whose magnetic course is MC 180?

➤ 6000 feet MSL

4. What is the next higher appropriate cruising altitude or flight level to 5000 feet MSL for a VFR flight along an airway whose magnetic course is MC 180?

➤ 6500 feet MSL

5. What is the next higher appropriate cruising altitude or flight level to 18,000 feet MSL for an IFR flight along an airway whose magnetic course is MC 330?

➤ FL200

6. What is the next higher appropriate cruising altitude or flight level to 5000 feet MSL for an IFR flight with a VFR-on-top clearance above a cloud layer with tops at 7000 feet along an airway whose magnetic course is MC 135?

➤ 9500 feet MSL (don't forget VFR vertical separation from clouds)

Minimum Altitudes for IFR Operations

1. MEA is the M_____ E_____ A_____.

➤ minimum en route altitude

2. The MEA (assures/does not assure) obstruction clearance.

➤ assures

3. The MEA (assures/does not assure) radio navigation aid reception.

➤ assures

4. MOCA is the _____.

➤ minimum obstruction clearance altitude

5. The MOCA (assures/does not assure) obstruction clearance.

➤ assures

6. The MOCA (assures/does not assure) radio navigation aid reception.

➤ does not assure

7. The MOCA is (higher/lower) than the MEA.

➤ lower

8. MCA is the _____.

➤ minimum crossing altitude

9. On a particular route segment the MEA is 7000 feet, and on the next route segment, after passing an intersection, it is 9500 feet. When is the latest you may start your climb if you are initially cruising at 7000 feet and the airplane can achieve a climb of 500 fpm? No MCA is noted at the intersection.

➤ at the intersection

10. On a particular route segment the MEA is 6000 feet, and on the next route segment, after passing an intersection, it is 12,000 feet. When is the latest you may start your climb if you are initially cruising at 7000 feet and the airplane can achieve a climb of 500 fpm? An MCA of 8500 feet is noted at the intersection for this route.

➤ 3 minutes before your ETA at the intersection

11. If no applicable minimum altitude is prescribed for your route, which is in a designated mountainous area, you should plan to maintain a clearance of at least _____ feet above the highest obstacle within a horizontal distance of _____ nm of the course to be flown.

➤ 2000 feet, 4 nm

12. If no applicable minimum altitude is prescribed for your route, which is not in a designated mountainous area, you should plan to maintain a clearance height of at least _____ feet above the highest obstacle within a horizontal distance of _____ nautical miles of the course to be flown.

➤ 1000 feet, 4 nm

Course to be Flown (IFR)

1. Should you plan to fly directly between fixes on an IFR flight?

➤ yes

Takeoff and Landing under IFR; General

1. May you continue with an approach to land if an excessive rate of descent to the runway is required?

➤ no

2. May you continue with an approach to land if a steep turn is required to align the aircraft with the runway?

➤ no

3. May you continue to maneuver below the MDA for a landing if you lose sight of the airport environment behind a cloud bank?

➤ no

4. The landing minimum is specified as a (visibility/ cloud ceiling/both).

➤ visibility

5. If you decide to discontinue an approach at or below the DH of a precision approach, or below the MDA of a nonprecision approach, what procedure should you follow?

➤ the missed approach procedure

6. Standard takeoff minimums for one- or two-engine airplane carrying people for 14 CFR Part 135 operations are _____, and for flights operated under Part 91 are _____.

➤ visibility 1 sm, none

7. The equivalent visibility in statute miles for RVR 2400 feet is _____ sm.

➤ $\frac{1}{2}$ sm

8. The equivalent visibility in statute miles for RVR 5000 feet is _____ sm.

➤ 1 sm

Flight Crew Members at Station

1. Should you wear a shoulder harness, if available, during takeoff and landing?

➤ yes

2. Must you wear a shoulder harness, if available, en route?

➤ no

3. Should you wear your seatbelt en route?

➤ yes

4. In a multi-crew airplane, is it permitted for one pilot to leave his station en route?

➤ yes

Use of Seatbelts and Safety Harnesses

1. Is a 1 yr-old child permitted to be held by an adult passenger during takeoff and landing?

➤ yes

Aircraft Speed

1. The maximum speed below 10,000 feet MSL, in any airspace class, is _____ KIAS. In Class B airspace, ATC (has/does not have) the authority to override this requirement.

➤ 250 KIAS, has

2. The maximum speed at or below 2500 feet AGL within 4 nm of the primary airport of a Class C or D airspace area is _____ KIAS.

➤ 200 KIAS

3. The maximum speed in the airspace underlying Class B airspace that is designated for an airport is _____ KIAS.

➤ 200 KIAS

4. The maximum speed in a VFR corridor through Class B airspace is _____ KIAS.

➤ 200 KIAS

Portable Electronic Devices

1. May a portable voice recorder be used when operating under IFR?

➤ yes

2. Are you, as pilot-in-command of a private IFR flight, permitted to determine if any other portable electronic device may be used in flight?

➤ yes

IFR Radio Communications

1. Are you required to make a radio call at a compulsory position reporting point designated on your chart when you are under radar control?

➤ no

2. Are you required to make a radio call at a compulsory position reporting point designated on your chart when you are not under radar control?

➤ yes

3. You are (required/encouraged) to report by radio any unforecast weather encountered, such as a thunderstorm.

➤ required

IFR Operations; Two-way Radio Communications Failure

1. What action should you take if you experience two-way radio communications failure in VFR conditions?

➤ squawk 7600; continue the flight under VFR and land as soon as possible

2. You enter a holding pattern at a fix, but which is not the approach fix, and receive an EFC time of 1620Z. At 1610Z you experience a complete two-way communications failure. You should depart the (holding/approach) fix at the EFC time of 1620Z, and complete the approach.

➤ holding fix

3. If you are in IFR weather conditions and experience a two-way radio communications failure, what action can you take with the transponder to alert ATC, and what altitude and route should you follow?

➤ squawk 7600; continue flight on the last assigned route and fly the last assigned altitude or the MEA, whichever is higher

Preparation for Flight **25**

Careful planning for a flight on instruments is important. Besides satisfying normal IFR requirements, an instrument pilot flying in clouds or at night must be conscious of high terrain or obstacles that cannot be seen, and ensure that a safe height above them is maintained.

You must be aware of the danger of icing (both airframe and carburetor icing) and take appropriate precautions; you must have an alternate airport in mind in case a diversion becomes necessary; and you must have sufficient fuel to get there, and still have a safety margin remaining in the tanks on arrival.

The best time to organize these things is prior to flight.

Good flight planning is essential.

Flight planning procedures learned early in your basic training will have prepared you thoroughly. As a reminder of some of the vital points, a number of the review questions will test your knowledge in these areas. Do not be afraid to review previously learned knowledge! Always remember that, as pilot-in-command, you are responsible for the safety of the flight.

Preflight Considerations for an IFR Flight

Preflight considerations, which are all logical, include:

- Am I properly qualified (instrument-rated, instrument-current and type-qualified)?
- Am I medically fit today?
- Is the airplane suitably equipped (serviceable radios, anti-icing equipment, lighting, etc.)?
- What is the weather? Are changes expected?
- Is the departure airport suitable for my operation?
- Is the destination airport suitable for my operation?
- Is an alternate airport required (or more than one)?
- What routes are suitable in terms of terrain, weather and available en route radio navigation aids?

- Are there any relevant NOTAMs?
- Preparation of charts (DPs, en route charts, instrument approach charts, VFR sectionals, etc.).
- Compilation of a flight log with courses, distances, times, MEAs and cruising altitudes calculated.
- Compilation of a fuel log, with adequate fuel reserves.
- Filing an IFR flight plan.
- Preparation of the airplane.
- Organizing the cockpit for flight—selecting the charts, ensuring a flashlight is kept handy for night flying, etc.
- Briefing of passengers.

Beware that charts are updated constantly. You must ensure that your charts are current before beginning an IFR flight.

En Route Charts

It is essential that you can read IFR charts quickly and accurately, and this takes practice. Study your own charts, and become familiar with the legend. Each chart carries an enormous amount of vital information concerning radio navigation aids, airways, safe altitudes, airports, airspace, and communications. You have the choice of *National Ocean Service* (NOS) or *Jeppesen* charts—we consider both types here. The instrument rating FAA Knowledge examination is based on NOS low-altitude en route charts.

Airports

Airports are shown on the en route charts, accompanied by some basic information, such as elevation. NOS en route charts have Air-to-Ground Voice Communication panels that include tower hours of operation. More complete information on each airport and its facilities, such as control tower hours of operation, traffic pattern altitude (TPA), elevation, runway data, communications, radio navigation aids, instrument approach procedures (IAPs), and servicing facilities may be found in the **Airport/Facility Directory (A/FD)** booklet.

```
MT OLIVE MUNI   (W40)   3 NE    UTC–5(–4DT)    N35°13.33' W78°02.27'                    CHARLOTTE
    168    B    S4   FUEL 100LL                                                          L-20G, 27C
RWY 05-23: H3697X75 (ASPH)    S-20    MIRL                                                    IAP
    RWY 05: VASI(V2L)—GA 3.0°TCH 23'. Ground.        RWY 23: VASI(V2L)—GA 3.25° TCH 20'. Crops.
AIRPORT REMARKS: Attended 1300-2300Z‡. Parachute Jumping. Low level military activity near arpt.—5' drainage
    ditch 100' left of centerline of Rwy 05. Rwy 05 and 23 VASI out of svc indefinitely.
COMMUNICATIONS: CTAF/UNICOM 122.8
    RALEIGH FSS (RDU) TF 1-800-WX-BRIEF. NOTAM FILE RDU.
Ⓡ SEYMOUR JOHNSON APP/DEP CON 123.7
RADIO AIDS TO NAVIGATION: NOTAM FILE ISO.
    KINSTON (L) VORTAC 109.6    ISO    Chan 33    N35°22.26' W77°33.50'    254° 25.2 NM to fld. 70/05W.
```

Figure 25-1. A sample airport entry in the A/FD

Navigation Aids

VORs and VORTACs are prominently displayed on the en route charts, as they form the basis of the airways. Civil pilots use the VOR for course guidance, and the DME function of the TACAN for distance information. Many VORs transmit HIWAS messages (hazardous in-flight weather advisory service) or TWEB (transcribed weather broadcast—a broadcast of weather and aeronautical information). NDBs are also depicted if they provide an en route function or transmit HIWAS or TWEB broadcasts.

Localizer front courses and/or back courses are only shown on NOS en route charts if, as well as providing approach guidance to an airport, they also serve an additional ATC function such as defining an intersection, and are therefore part of the en route structure. The same applies to LDAs, SDFs and MLSs.

Routes

Airways, also known as **federal airways**, are controlled airspace established in the form of a corridor, the centerline of which is defined by radio navigation aids, usually VORTACs.

Below 18,000 feet MSL, the airways are known as VOR, or **Victor airways**, and are labeled with a "V" and their designated number, "V223". They exist down to 1200 feet AGL (higher in some instances), and are depicted on the low altitude en route charts. Various information is shown along the airways, such as the magnetic course, distance, MEA and MOCA. All distances are in nautical miles, and all directions are in degrees magnetic. Breaks in airways are shown at intersections (published fixes) by a triangle, and at mileage break points not coincident with an intersection by a small cross. DME distance to the relevant VORTAC is shown at intersections, if appropriate.

A segment of an airway common to more than one route carries the numbers of each of these routes, "V107-301", but you only need to indicate the number of the route you are using on your flight plan, "V301". Alternate airways are identified by their location with respect to the associated main airway, "V12W" is to the west of "V12".

From 18,000 feet MSL up to and including FL 600, the airspace is Class A. Flight in Class A airspace is IFR only, and the airways from 18,000 feet MSL up to and including FL 450, are known as **jet routes**. These are labeled with a "J" and their designated number, "J 84" eastbound from San Francisco. The low altitude en route charts are not designed for flights above 18,000 feet MSL.

Minimum En Route IFR Altitude (MEA)

The MEA appears as a number, such as 9500, along the airway, and is the lowest published altitude between radio fixes that assures:

- **acceptable navigation signal coverage** (but not necessarily 2-way communications coverage); and

- **meets obstacle clearance requirements between those fixes** (1000 feet normally, 2000 feet in designated mountainous areas) within ±4 nm of the route to be flown.

It is usual to maintain an IFR altitude at or above the MEA that is in accordance with the hemispherical rule (WEEO: West-evens; East-odds), according to your magnetic course. Occasionally, an MEA may be approved with a *gap* in navigation signal coverage, and this will be depicted on NOS charts with the words "MEA GAP", and on *Jeppesen* charts by a broken bar. Some routes have **directional MEAs**, the MEA depending on which direction you are traveling—the MEA flying toward high ground being higher than when flying in the opposite direction away from high ground.

A bar crossing an airway at an intersection indicates that there is a change of MEA. You do not have to commence a climb to a higher MEA until reaching the intersection where the MEA change occurs, unless a minimum crossing altitude (MCA) is specified.

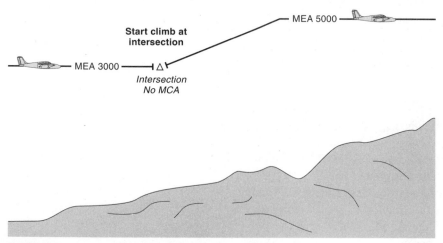

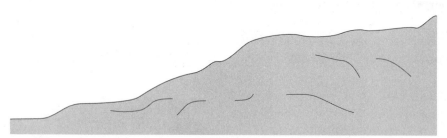

Figure 25-2. Approaching a higher MEA, with no MCA specified

Minimum Crossing Altitude (MCA)

The MCA is the lowest altitude at certain fixes at which an aircraft may cross when proceeding in the direction of a higher MEA. The MCA is usually specified for obstacle clearance requirements, but it may also be specified to assure adequate reception of navigation signals so that you can identify the intersection. MCA is indicated by a "flagged X" on NOS charts, and as an airway number and altitude alongside the intersection on *Jeppesen* charts ("V-25 11000S" means MCA 11,000 feet MSL flying south on V-25).

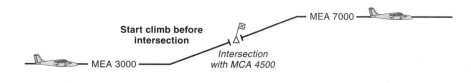

Figure 25-3. Approaching a higher MEA, with an MCA specified for the following course

Minimum Obstruction Clearance Altitude (MOCA)

The MOCA is the lowest published altitude in effect between radio fixes on VOR airways, off-airway routes, or route segments which meets obstacle clearance requirements for the entire route segment, and which ensures acceptable navigation signal coverage only within 22 nautical miles (25 statute miles) of a VOR. The MOCA, if shown, is differentiated from the MEA by an asterisk on NOS charts (*2500), and a "T" on *Jeppesen* charts (2500T). If the MOCA is the same as the MEA, it is not shown.

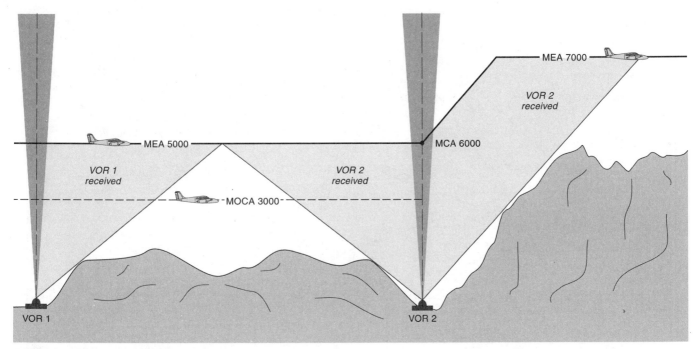

Figure 25-4. MEA, MOCA and MCA

Minimum Reception Altitude (MRA)

The MRA is the lowest altitude at which an intersection can be determined. At altitudes lower than the MRA, navigation signal coverage is not assured, and you may not be able to identify the intersection. An MRA is indicated by a "flagged R" on NOS charts, and by "MRA" on *Jeppesen* charts (MRA 9000).

Changeover Points (COPs)

A changeover point (COP) is the position en route between two adjacent navigation facilities where changeover in navigation guidance should occur, from the ground station behind to the ground station ahead. If the COP is not at the midway point, then it will be shown on aeronautical charts with the appropriate DME distances. COPs are designed to prevent the loss of navigation guidance, to prevent frequency interference from other ground facilities, and to prevent use of different facilities by different aircraft that are operating in the same airspace. You should use COPs to the fullest extent.

Maximum Authorized Altitude (MAA)

The MAA is the highest usable altitude for an airspace structure or route segment at which adequate reception of navigation signals is assured. At altitudes above the MAA, there may be navigation signal interference from another station on the same frequency. It is rare to see an MAA on a chart.

Sample excerpts of NOS and *Jeppesen* low-altitude En Route IFR Charts appear on the four next pages.

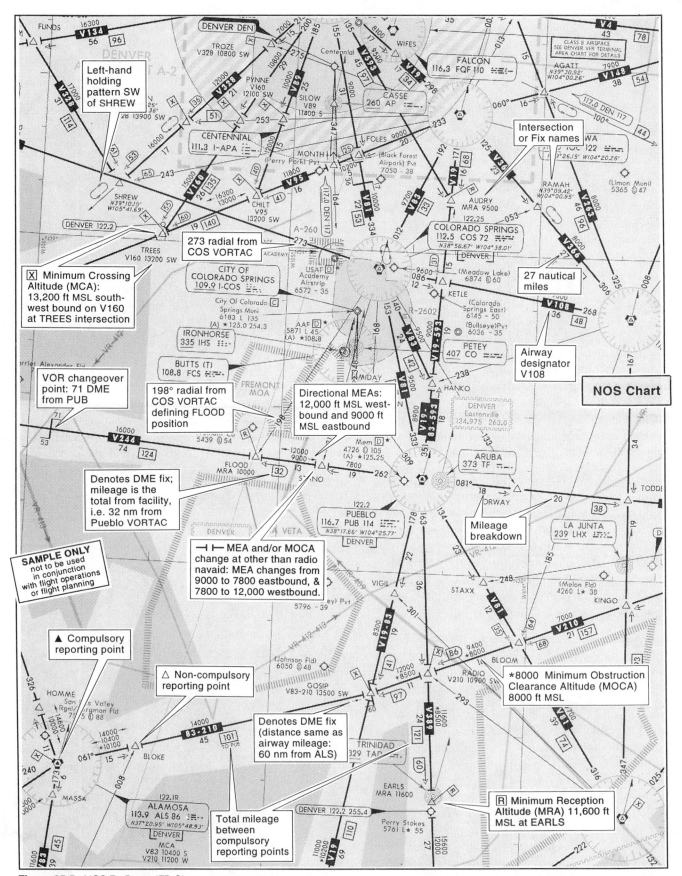

Figure 25-5. NOS En Route IFR Chart—route structure

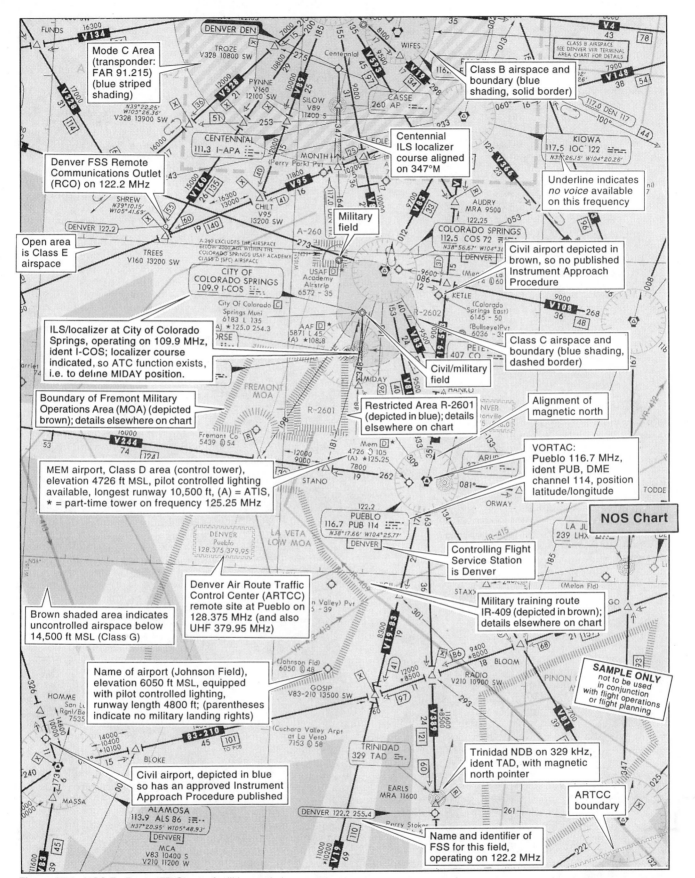

Figure 25-6. NOS En Route IFR Chart—facilities and airspace structure

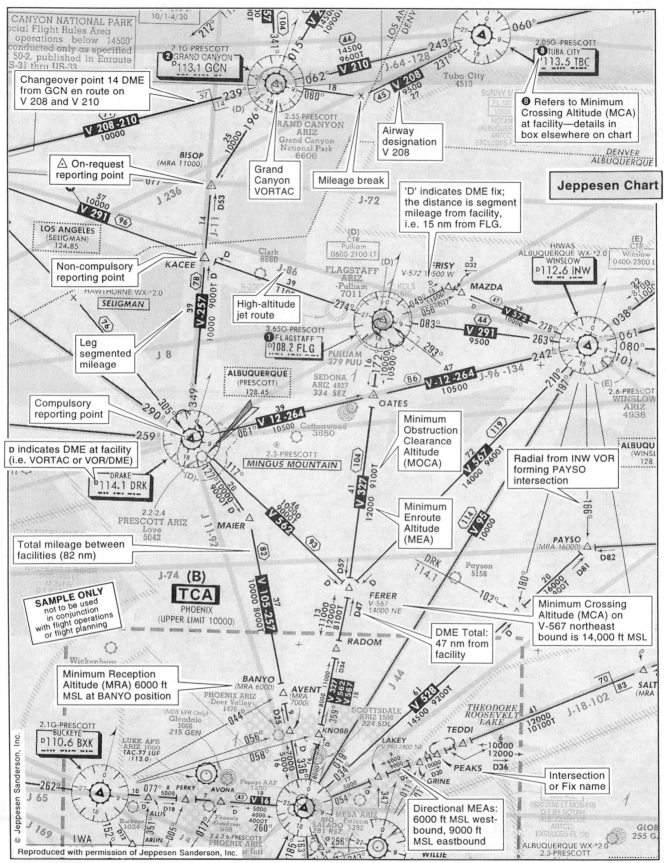

Figure 25-7. *Jeppesen* En Route IFR Chart—route structure

The following labels appear on the chart:

- Changeover point 14 DME from GCN en route on V 208 and V 210
- ⚠ On-request reporting point
- Non-compulsory reporting point
- Leg segmented mileage
- Compulsory reporting point
- D indicates DME at facility (i.e. VORTAC or VOR/DME)
- Total mileage between facilities (82 nm)
- Minimum Reception Altitude (MRA) 6000 ft MSL at BANYO position
- Grand Canyon VORTAC
- Mileage break
- High-altitude jet route
- Airway designation V 208
- 'D' indicates DME fix; the distance is segment mileage from facility, i.e. 15 nm from FLG.
- ❽ Refers to Minimum Crossing Altitude (MCA) at facility—details in box elsewhere on chart
- **Jeppesen Chart**
- Minimum Obstruction Clearance Altitude (MOCA)
- Minimum Enroute Altitude (MEA)
- Radial from INW VOR forming PAYSO intersection
- Minimum Crossing Altitude (MCA) on V-567 northeast bound is 14,000 ft MSL
- DME Total: 47 nm from facility
- Intersection or Fix name
- Directional MEAs: 6000 ft MSL westbound, 9000 ft MSL eastbound

SAMPLE ONLY not to be used in conjunction with flight operations or flight planning

© Jeppesen Sanderson, Inc.

Reproduced with permission of Jeppesen Sanderson, Inc.

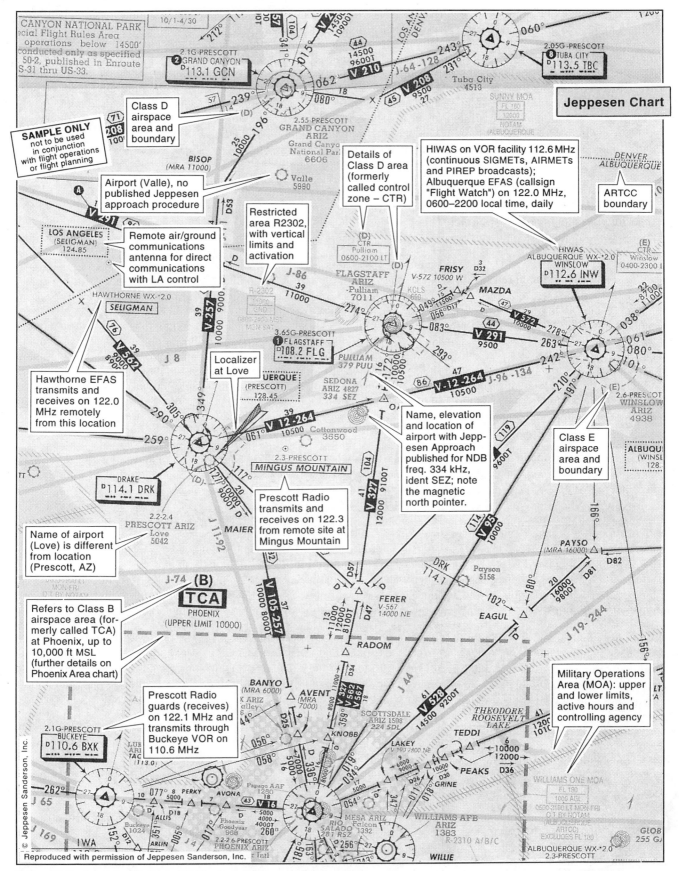

Figure 25-8. *Jeppesen* En Route IFR Chart—facilities and airspace structure

Airspace

U.S. airspace is organized into six classes (A, B, C, D, E and G), in line with International Civil Aviation Organization (ICAO) standards. This classification system is designed to simplify the airspace and align it with the rest of the world aviation community. Classes A through Class E are allocated to controlled airspace—Class A being the most restrictive and Class E for general controlled airspace. Uncontrolled airspace is allocated Class G. (Class F, although available in the ICAO system, has not been allocated in the U.S.)

The airspace classification system links various parameters to each airspace class, including:

- entry requirements (radio contact for all aircraft in Class C airspace; ATC clearance for IFR flights in controlled airspace);
- minimum pilot qualifications;
- two-way communication and transponder equipment requirements;
- VFR weather minimums (where VFR is available—Classes B–E and G); and
- aircraft separation, conflict resolution and traffic advisory services.

Subdivision of Airspace

The structure of U.S. airspace is as follows:

Class A is generally that airspace extending from 18,000 feet MSL up to FL600: specified as IFR only.

Class B airspace extends from a surface area and attached stepped tiers, up to a designated altitude. This airspace is established at all major U.S. airports and requires a Mode C transponder and an ATC clearance for all flights, and an operable VOR for IFR flights.

Class C airspace extends from a surface area of 5 nm radius, usually with one stepped tier of 10 nm radius at 1200 feet AGL, up to a designated altitude (usually 4000 feet HAA, expressed as MSL). This airspace is established at designated airports where ATC provides radar vectoring and sequencing on a full-time basis for all IFR and VFR traffic.

Class D is airspace surrounding any other tower-operated airport, extending from a surface area up to 2500 feet AGL (expressed as an MSL altitude). Areas are normally cylindrical in shape, plus any extensions up to 2 nm that are necessary to include any instrument approach and departure paths. Extensions stretching more than 2 nm from the Class D "core" area become all Class E airspace.

Class E is allocated to general controlled airspace. This includes airports without control towers, transition areas (upward from 700 feet AGL at airports with published instrument approaches, and upward from 1200 feet AGL when associated with airway route structures or segments) designed to contain IFR operations within controlled airspace when transiting between the terminal and en route environments; federal airways; plus all unallocated airspace over the U.S. from 14,500 feet MSL up to the Class A area commencing at 18,000 feet MSL.

Class G is allocated to all remaining airspace, which is uncontrolled.

Note: Special-use airspace is not allocated a class.

Maximum Aircraft Speeds

- Maximum 250 KIAS below 10,000 feet MSL (unless ATC authorizes otherwise in Class A or B airspace).
- Maximum 200 KIAS within 4 nm of the primary airport of a Class C or D airspace area (unless ATC authorizes or requires otherwise).

- Maximum 200 KIAS in the airspace underlying a Class B area designated for an airport, or in a VFR corridor through Class B airspace.

Note: Some airports offer radar advisory services known as Terminal Radar Service Areas (TRSAs). The primary airport of a TRSA is Class D airspace, with the remaining portion usually overlying Class E (transition) airspace.

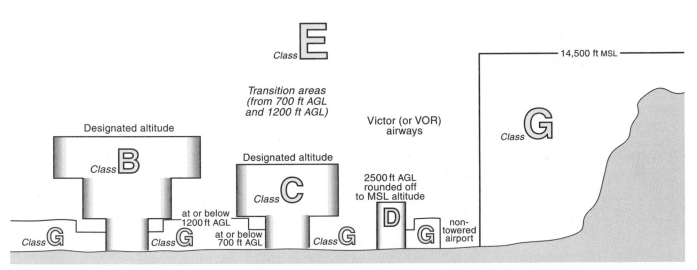

Figure 25-9. Summary of U.S. airspace classifications

AIRSPACE FEATURES	Class A airspace	Class B airspace	Class C airspace	Class D airspace	Class E airspace	Class G airspace
Flight operations permitted	IFR	IFR and VFR	IFR and VFR	IFR and VFR	IFR and VFR	IFR and VFR
Entry prerequisites	ATC clearance	ATC clearance	IFR clearance/VFR radio contact	IFR clearance/VFR radio contact	Clearance/radio contact for IFR	None
Minimum pilot qualifications	Instrument rating	Private Pilot Cert./*endorsed student	Student Certificate	Student Certificate	Student Certificate	Student Certificate
Two-way radio comms	Yes	Yes	Yes	Yes	IFR	No
VFR minimum visibility	*not applicable*	3 statute miles	3 statute miles	3 statute miles	**3 statute miles	***1 statute mile
Aircraft separation	All	All	IFR, SVFR and runway operations	IFR, SVFR and runway operations	IFR, SVFR	None
Conflict resolution (collision avoidance)	*not applicable*	*not applicable*	Between IFR and VFR flights	No	No	No
Traffic advisories	*not applicable*	*not applicable*	Yes	Workload permitting	Workload permitting	Workload permitting
Safety advisories	Yes	Yes	Yes	Yes	Yes	Yes

*Operations at some Class B airports require a minimum of a Private Pilot Certificate—see 14 CFR 91.
**Visibility and cloud clearance requirements increase above 10,000 feet MSL.
***Visibility and cloud clearance requirements decrease below 1200 feet AGL; increase above 10,000 feet MSL, and at night —see 14 CFR 91 or AIM 3.

Figure 25-10. Summary of the U.S. airspace classification system

Airspace Depiction on Low-Altitude En Route Charts

NOS low-altitude en route charts show all airspace up to, but not including, 18,000 feet MSL.

- Class B areas—light-blue shading with a solid-blue border line;
- Class C areas—similar light-blue shading, but with a dashed-blue border line;
- Class C and Class D airports (the appropriate letter placed inside a box);
- Class E airspace is shown as open white space;
- Class G airspace (uncontrolled airspace, below 14,500 feet MSL) is shown as brown shaded areas;
- Mode C areas (encoding altimeter mandatory)—striped blue tint lines; and
- Special-use airspace—blue or brown hatched lines (prohibited areas, restricted areas, military operations areas [MOAs]). Military training routes, alert areas, and controlled firing areas are also delineated (use a chart legend for details).

Jeppesen Low-Altitude en route Charts show airspace classifications with the appropriate letter in parentheses: (B), (C), & (D).

Chart legends are your best source for discovering what kind of airspace you are about to fly through.

Flight Plan and ATC Clearance

IFR flights must submit a full flight plan and receive an air traffic clearance for all operations within controlled airspace—Classes A through E. The flight plan should be submitted at least 30 minutes prior to the estimated time of departure (ETD). The procedure is covered in more detail later in the chapter.

Communications

FSS VHF communications frequencies are shown on en route charts near navaid boxes, 122.45 on NOS, and 2.45 on *Jeppesen* (the initial 12 of the 122.45 not being shown because it is always 12). The standard FSS frequency is 122.2 MHz. You normally transmit and receive on the one COM frequency.

There are some frequencies, however, that you can contact FSS on, but they cannot reply. These frequencies are labeled R on NOS (for FSS receive only), and G on *Jeppesen* (for FSS guarded), 122.1R (NOS), 2.1G (*Jeppesen*). FSS will reply to you on the associated VOR frequency, 110.0 MHz. Therefore, when using this method of radio communication, you would select VHF-COM to 122.1 for you to transmit on, and select the VHF-NAV to 110.0 with the audio ON to hear the response from FSS.

The **emergency frequency 121.5 MHz** is available at almost all FSSs, and is not shown on the charts. This is one frequency that you should remember. It is used internationally.

Remote communications outlets (RCOs) are unmanned communications facilities, remotely controlled by ATC personnel, used to extend communication to pilots operating well away from direct radio coverage. RCOs allow communications at some remote satellite airports (for the issuance of clearances, closing flight plans, etc.) and, as a secondary function, are used for advisory purposes when the aircraft is below coverage of the primary air/ground frequency. They are labeled RCO on NOS charts, with the controlling FSS beneath, and associated with the airport data on *Jeppesen* charts, with the controlling FSS above.

Note: Some limited remote communications facilities are not equipped with the emergency frequency 121.5 MHz.

The boundary of an **ARTCC (Center)** area of responsibility is shown by a ragged line (NOS) or dotted line (*Jeppesen*) across the en route chart, with the appropriate Center name either side of the line. The Center frequencies are shown in boxes (ragged or dotted) in various places in the appropriate areas.

The **common traffic advisory frequency (CTAF)**, used for traffic advisory purposes at an airport without an operating control tower, is found in the Airport/Facility Directory, and on SID and IAP charts. The CTAF frequency may be a UNICOM, MULTICOM, FSS or tower frequency. UNICOM is a non-government frequency.

Flight Planning

The most current en route and destination flight information should be obtained from the FSS when planning an IFR flight. You should obtain a thorough weather briefing. Select the most suitable route to your destination, using the en route charts, and check for nonstandard takeoff minimums, special IFR departures and DPs at the departure airport, STARs and instrument approach procedures at the destination and alternate airports. Check the A/FD for further information on the airports. Confirm that takeoff and landing distances are adequate.

Check NOTAMs. There are three categories of NOTAM:

- **NOTAM (D)**—given distant dissemination beyond the area of responsibility of the FSS;
- **NOTAM (L)**—given local dissemination;
  (Both D and L NOTAMs contain information such as runway closures, nonavailability of certain radio navaids, etc.)
- **FDC NOTAMs**—given wide dissemination and advising of flight data changes, such as might affect instrument approach procedures prior to them being republished, or changes in aeronautical charts, or temporary flight restrictions due to natural disasters or large-scale public events.
  NOTAMs are given either:
  - Class 1 distribution via telecommunications if the information is time critical, and you will receive these along with your weather briefing, or
  - Class 2 distribution by means other than telecommunications, and not provided with your weather briefing unless specifically requested.

Preferred IFR Routes
Preferred IFR routes have been established between busier airports to facilitate traffic flow. IFR clearances are generally issued on the basis of these routes, unless severe weather or some other reason dictates otherwise.

Preferred IFR routes are listed in the NOS Airport/Facility Directory (A/FD), and in the *Jeppesen* airway manual. For instance, the preferred IFR route from Houston-Hobby airport to New Orleans is: "V198 TBD V552". This means: out of Houston on V198 to TBD VORTAC and then along V552 to New Orleans. Shorthand is sometimes used: "TBD093101" means track out on the TBD 093 radial to 101 DME.

Routing between particular airports and fixes on preferred IFR routes is often via SIDs and STARs, or radar vectors.

Tower En Route Control (TEC) Routes
TEC routes link approach control areas between certain city pairs, allowing the flight to be completed using *tower* communications (approach/departure) only. TEC is designed for short low-level flights in a busy traffic environment. You may request it by writing TEC in the remarks section of your flight plan. Tower en route clearances are available in many places without filing a flight plan, simply by calling *clearance delivery* and requesting a tower en route clearance.

TEC is designed for short low-level flights in a busy traffic environment.

Shortest Route via Airways

To facilitate Air Traffic Control, you should file via airways or jet routes established for your planned altitudes or flight levels, and describe the route on your flight plan using the published type-number designators, such as "V262" for airway Victor 262, or "J5" for jet route 5.

If you plan to use more than one airway or jet route, clearly indicate the point of transition, which will usually be a VORTAC or waypoint. For instance, the route: "V27 MQO V113" indicates that you will fly along airway Victor 27 until the point MQO (Morro Bay VORTAC) where you will turn to Victor 113.

After takeoff from some airports, you can join the airway via a standard instrument departure (SID), and then leave an airway for an approach into the destination airport via a standard terminal arrival (STAR). For instance, the route: "SBA HABUT 2 GVO V27 MQO V113 PRB" indicates: from SBA (Santa Barbara) airport via the HABUT 2 SID to the point GVO (Gaviota) where airway Victor 27 will be joined and followed to MQO (Morro Bay) VORTAC, from where Victor 113 will be followed to PRB (Paso Robles).

Direct route segments not along airways can be defined by fixes. For instance, "GVO FLW" indicates from Gaviota direct to Fellows.

Direct Routes

For off-airways navigation, for instance using area nav (RNAV) or GPS equipment, calculation of a **safety altitude** is important, since terrain and other obstacles may not be seen in IFR conditions, and there are no published MEAs or MOCAs for off-airways routes.

Plan a cruising altitude that provides at least 1000 feet vertical clearance above the highest obstacle within 5 sm either side of each route segment (2000 feet in designated mountainous areas).

VFR sectional charts are most valuable to an IFR pilot who wants to know where the obstructions are.

VOR service volumes are an important consideration for planning an off-airways route (see Chapter 13). Also check the A/FD for unusable VOR radials.

VFR sectional charts are most valuable to an IFR pilot who wants to know where the obstructions are.

Selection of Altitude

Consider the en route winds and weather, and select an altitude that is:

1. an IFR altitude (WEEO);
2. at or above the MEA; and
3. with favorable winds, and preferably not in icing conditions.

Alternate Airports

Apply the ETA ±1 – 2 – 3 rule to your destination airport to see if it requires an alternate. For the period 1 hour either side of your destination ETA, the ceiling and visibility must be at least 2000 feet/3 sm for there to be no need for an alternate. To be suitable as an alternate, the alternate airport forecast must be:

- at least the alternate minimums as published for that airport (in the front of the applicable NOS IAP booklet, and on *Jeppesen* IAP charts); otherwise
- ceiling 600 feet, visibility 2 sm, if it has a precision approach;
- ceiling 800 feet, visibility 2 sm, if it has a nonprecision approach.

When you actually arrive at the alternate after diverting, whether you may land or not depends on the landing minimums, not the alternate minimums.

Some airports may have high alternate minimums, and some airports are not authorized (NA) for use as an alternate.

Fuel Requirements

Fuel requirements should be calculated carefully, with consideration being given to arrival at an alternate airport with adequate reserves still remaining. Being tight on fuel increases pilot stress if a diversion becomes necessary.

The minimum fuel requirements for an IFR flight are for:

- departure to destination; plus
- destination to alternate (if required); plus
- 45 minutes fuel reserve calculated at normal cruise rate.

In the absence of more specific figures, you should allow approximately 15 mins for each takeoff and departure, missed approach, and approach and landing. Any extra fuel in excess of the above requirements is available for holding.

The Flight Plan

To operate in controlled airspace (Classes A–E) under IFR, you are required to:

- file an IFR flight plan (usually done in person or by telephone to FSS or ATC on the ground at least 30 minutes prior to the flight); and
- obtain an air traffic clearance (usually requested by radio immediately prior to entering the controlled airspace).

The 30 minutes is required to allow time for ATC to process your flight data and (hopefully) avoid delays to your flight. The preferred methods of filing a flight plan are: in person or by telephone—by radio is permitted, but discouraged because of the time it takes. Closing a flight plan by radio is usual, since it takes just a few seconds.

Closing an IFR flight plan is automatically done by ATC at tower-controlled airports after landing. At an airport without an active control tower, you must close the flight plan with FSS or ATC by radio or telephone. Do this within 30 minutes of the latest advised ETA, otherwise search and rescue (SAR) procedures will begin.

- An IFR flight plan is required in both IMC and VMC in Class A airspace, and in IMC conditions in Classes B, C, D & E (controlled) airspace (and also in VMC, if you desire flight following or for practice);
- An IFR flight plan is not required in Class G (uncontrolled) airspace.

To assist you in completing the flight plan and performing the flight, you should compile a navigation log, calculating time intervals and fuel requirements. A typical navigation log is shown in Figure 25-11 (page 520), and a typical flight plan form is shown in Figure 25-13 (page 522).

Important navigation log items to be inserted on the flight plan include:

- the planned route;
- the initial cruise altitude or flight level (later altitudes or flight levels can be requested in flight);
- the estimated time en route (ETE), in hours and minutes, from departure to touchdown at the first point of intended landing;
- the total usable fuel on board at takeoff, converted to endurance in hours and minutes.

If you wish to fly part of the route according to IFR procedures and part according to VFR procedures, you can file a composite flight plan, signified by you checking both IFR and VFR in the Item 1 box on the flight plan form. You should also indicate the clearance limit fix in the flight-planned route box, to show where you plan to transition from IFR to VFR.

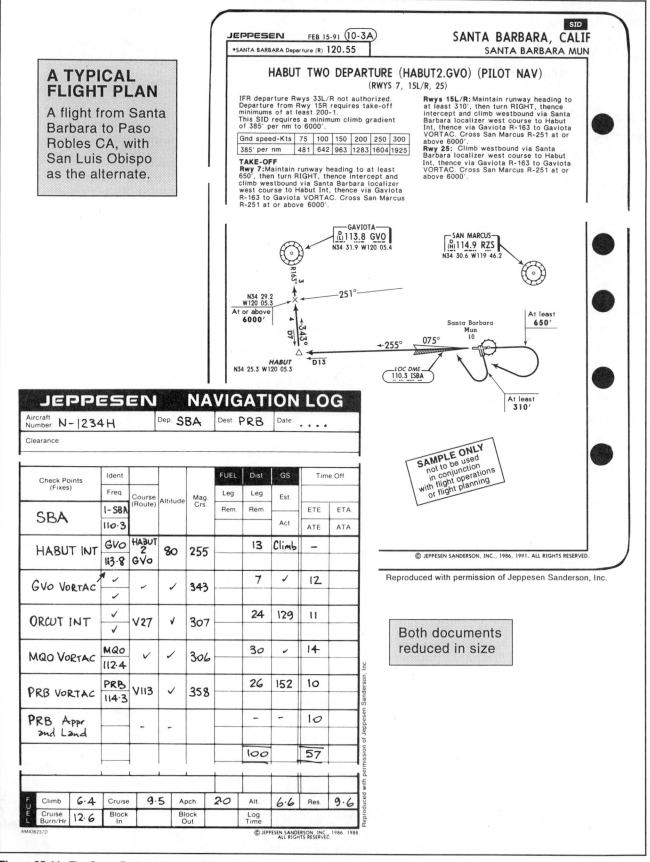

A TYPICAL FLIGHT PLAN

A flight from Santa Barbara to Paso Robles CA, with San Luis Obispo as the alternate.

Both documents reduced in size

Figure 25-11. The Santa Barbara Habut 2 SID (or, DP) (*Jeppesen* plate), and a typical flight plan

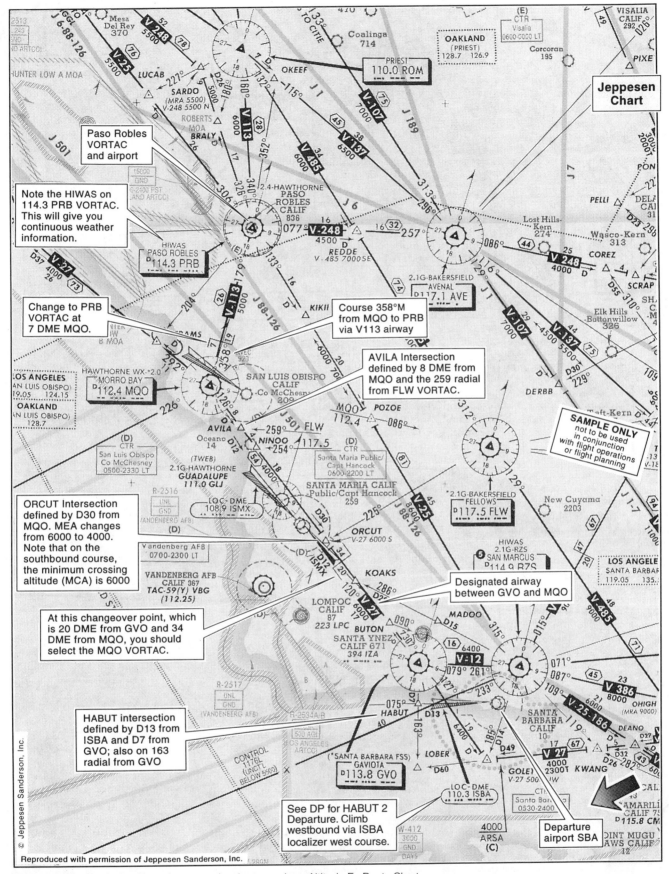

Figure 25-12. The flight planned route on the *Jeppesen* Low-Altitude En Route Chart

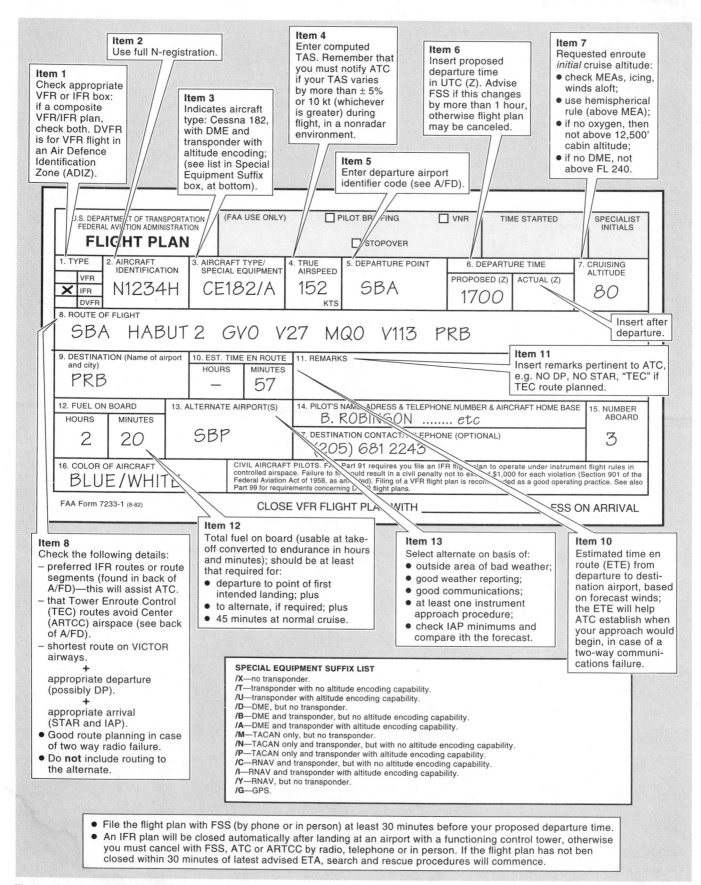

Item 1
Check appropriate VFR or IFR box: if a composite VFR/IFR plan, check both. DVFR is for VFR flight in an Air Defence Identification Zone (ADIZ).

Item 2
Use full N-registration.

Item 3
Indicates aircraft type: Cessna 182, with DME and transponder with altitude encoding; (see list in Special Equipment Suffix box, at bottom).

Item 4
Enter computed TAS. Remember that you must notify ATC if your TAS varies by more than ± 5% or 10 kt (whichever is greater) during flight, in a nonradar environment.

Item 5
Enter departure airport identifier code (see A/FD).

Item 6
Insert proposed departure time in UTC (Z). Advise FSS if this changes by more than 1 hour, otherwise flight plan may be canceled.

Item 7
Requested enroute *initial* cruise altitude:
- check MEAs, icing, winds aloft;
- use hemispherical rule (above MEA);
- if no oxygen, then not above 12,500' cabin altitude;
- if no DME, not above FL 240.

U.S. DEPARTMENT OF TRANSPORTATION
FEDERAL AVIATION ADMINISTRATION
FLIGHT PLAN
(FAA USE ONLY) ☐ PILOT BRIEFING ☐ VNR TIME STARTED SPECIALIST INITIALS
☐ STOPOVER

1. TYPE	2. AIRCRAFT IDENTIFICATION	3. AIRCRAFT TYPE/ SPECIAL EQUIPMENT	4. TRUE AIRSPEED	5. DEPARTURE POINT	6. DEPARTURE TIME		7. CRUISING ALTITUDE
☐ VFR ☒ IFR ☐ DVFR	N1234H	CE182/A	152 KTS	SBA	PROPOSED (Z) 1700	ACTUAL (Z)	80

8. ROUTE OF FLIGHT
SBA HABUT 2 GVO V27 MQO V113 PRB

Insert after departure.

Item 11
Insert remarks pertinent to ATC, e.g. NO DP, NO STAR, "TEC" if TEC route planned.

9. DESTINATION (Name of airport and city)	10. EST. TIME EN ROUTE		11. REMARKS
PRB	HOURS –	MINUTES 57	

12. FUEL ON BOARD		13. ALTERNATE AIRPORT(S)	14. PILOT'S NAME, ADDRESS & TELEPHONE NUMBER & AIRCRAFT HOME BASE	15. NUMBER ABOARD
HOURS 2	MINUTES 20	SBP	B. ROBINSON .... etc	3

17. DESTINATION CONTACT/TELEPHONE (OPTIONAL)
(205) 681 2243

16. COLOR OF AIRCRAFT
BLUE/WHITE

CIVIL AIRCRAFT PILOTS. FAA Part 91 requires you file an IFR flight plan to operate under instrument flight rules in controlled airspace. Failure to file could result in a civil penalty not to exceed $1,000 for each violation (Section 901 of the Federal Aviation Act of 1958, as amended). Filing of a VFR flight plan is recommended as a good operating practice. See also Part 99 for requirements concerning DVFR flight plans.

FAA Form 7233-1 (8-82)   CLOSE VFR FLIGHT PLAN WITH _____ FSS ON ARRIVAL

Item 8
Check the following details:
- preferred IFR routes or route segments (found in back of A/FD)—this will assist ATC.
- that Tower Enroute Control (TEC) routes avoid Center (ARTCC) airspace (see back of A/FD).
- shortest route on VICTOR airways.
  +
appropriate departure (possibly DP).
  +
appropriate arrival (STAR and IAP).
- Good route planning in case of two way radio failure.
- Do **not** include routing to the alternate.

Item 12
Total fuel on board (usable at take-off converted to endurance in hours and minutes); should be at least that required for:
- departure to point of first intended landing; plus
- to alternate, if required; plus
- 45 minutes at normal cruise.

Item 13
Select alternate on basis of:
- outside area of bad weather;
- good weather reporting;
- good communications;
- at least one instrument approach procedure;
- check IAP minimums and compare with the forecast.

Item 10
Estimated time en route (ETE) from departure to destination airport, based on forecast winds; the ETE will help ATC establish when your approach would begin, in case of a two-way communications failure.

SPECIAL EQUIPMENT SUFFIX LIST
/X—no transponder.
/T—transponder with no altitude encoding capability.
/U—transponder with altitude encoding capability.
/D—DME, but no transponder.
/B—DME and transponder, but no altitude encoding capability.
/A—DME and transponder with altitude encoding capability.
/M—TACAN only, but no transponder.
/N—TACAN only and transponder, but with no altitude encoding capability.
/P—TACAN only and transponder with altitude encoding capability.
/C—RNAV and transponder, but with no altitude encoding capability.
/I—RNAV and transponder with altitude encoding capability.
/Y—RNAV, but no transponder.
/G—GPS.

- File the flight plan with FSS (by phone or in person) at least 30 minutes before your proposed departure time.
- An IFR plan will be closed automatically after landing at an airport with a functioning control tower, otherwise you must cancel with FSS, ATC or ARTCC by radio, telephone or in person. If the flight plan has not ben closed within 30 minutes of latest advised ETA, search and rescue procedures will commence.

Figure 25-13. A typical IFR flight plan

✍ Review 25

Preparation for Flight

En Route Charts (a)

1. MEA is the abbreviation for _____.

    ➤ minimum en route altitude

    ___

2. Does the MEA between two fixes meet obstacle clearance requirements between the two fixes?

    ➤ yes

    ___

3. Does the MEA between two fixes guarantee adequate navigation signal coverage between the two fixes?

    ➤ yes

    ___

4. Does the MEA between two fixes guarantee two-way radio communications when flying between the two fixes?

    ➤ no

    ___

5. Does the MEA between two fixes guarantee radar coverage between the two fixes?

    ➤ no

    ___

6. Does the MEA between two fixes guarantee DME reception between the two fixes?

    ➤ no

    ___

7. Does the MEA between two fixes guarantee reception of more than one navigation signal at all points between the two fixes?

    ➤ no

    ___

8. MOCA is the abbreviation for _____.

    ➤ minimum obstruction clearance altitude

    ___

9. Does the MOCA between two fixes meet obstacle clearance requirements between the two fixes?

    ➤ yes

    ___

10. Does the MOCA between two fixes guarantee adequate navigation signal coverage between the two fixes?

    ➤ no

    ___

11. An acceptable navigation signal coverage at the MOCA is assured only to a distance of _____ nm, or _____ sm, from the VOR.

    ➤ 22 nm or 25 sm

    ___

12. MOCA is (lower/higher) than MEA.

    ➤ lower

    ___

13. Reception of signals from an off-airway radio facility when flying at the MEA may be inadequate to identify a fix or intersection. The minimum altitude at which the reception will be adequate is called the _____, and abbreviated as _____.

    ➤ minimum reception altitude, MRA

    ___

14. You are cruising at the MEA of 7000 feet MSL and have 30 nm to reach a radio fix beyond which the MEA is 8500 feet MSL. If no MCA is specified, the lowest altitude at which you may cross the fix is _____. The airplane is capable of a 500 fpm climb which should be initiated, at the latest,:

    (a) 3 minutes before reaching the fix.

    (b) immediately after passing the fix.

    ➤ 7000 feet MSL, (b)

    ___

15. In the case of operations within a designated mountainous area, where no other minimum altitude is specified, no person may operate an aircraft under IFR below _____ feet above the highest obstacle.

    ➤ 2000 feet

    ___

16. In the case of operations within a designated mountainous area, no person may operate an aircraft under IFR below 2000 feet above the highest obstacle within a horizontal distance of _____ from the course flown.

    ➤ 4 nm

    ___

17. The MEA (assures/does not assure) acceptable navigation signal coverage, and (meets/does not meet) obstruction clearance requirements.

➤ assures, meets

18. If no COP is shown on an en route chart for an airway between two VORTACs, then you would change VOR frequencies at _____.

➤ the midway point

19. If the COP is not at the midway point between two VORs, then it is shown on the en route charts with the _____ to each VOR.

➤ distance

20. A waypoint is a predetermined geographical position defined by (radio navigation aids/latitude and longitude/either).

➤ either

21. Victor airways (are/are not) depicted on en route low-altitude charts.

➤ are

22. Class A airspace begins at _____ feet MSL, and (is/is not) depicted on en route low-altitude charts.

➤ 18,000 feet MSL, is not

23. Maximum speed below 10,000 feet MSL is _____, and within 4 nm of the primary airport of a Class C airspace area is _____.

➤ 250 KIAS, 200 KIAS

24. Special-use airspace, an MOA, (is/is not) depicted on en route low-altitude charts.

➤ is

25. Extensions to Class D airspace to accommodate an instrument approach, and which extend more than 2 nm from the Class D core area, are entirely Class _____ airspace.

➤ Class E

26. Transition area extensions associated with an airport with an instrument approach procedure at an airport that is in a Class D airspace area, commence at _____ feet (AGL/MSL) and extend upward.

➤ 700 feet AGL

27. Transition areas associated with the airways route structure commence at _____ feet (AGL/MSL) and extend up to the overlying airspace.

➤ 1200 feet AGL

28. Airspace beneath a transition area and down to the surface is (controlled/uncontrolled) airspace.

➤ uncontrolled (Class G)

29. The areas established to separate certain military activities from IFR traffic are known as _____ and abbreviated to _____.

➤ military operations areas, MOAs

30. Unshaded white areas on NOS low-altitude en route charts are Class _____ airspace

➤ Class E

31. ATC (is/is not) responsible for the control of air traffic in Class G airspace.

➤ is not

32. A mode-C equipped transponder is required for all flights above _____ feet MSL, as well as all flights in Class _____ airspace.

➤ 10,000 feet MSL, Class B and Class C

33. DME is required to plan for flight at and above _____.

➤ FL 240

34. Class C airspace usually has (one/two/three) stepped tier(s) and extends upward to (a designated altitude/18,000 feet/2500 feet).

➤ one, designated altitude

35. Class D airspace at an airport is indicated by _____, and extends upward usually to _____.

➤ A boxed "D" beside the airport name, 2500 feet AGL—expressed as an MSL altitude

36. Minimum equipment required for flight within Class B airspace is _____.

➤ two-way communications, a Mode C transponder, and an operable VOR for IFR flights

37. You are inbound and close your IFR flight plan 10 miles from your destination, which is a Class D towered airport; you should be in contact with the control tower _____.

➤ prior to entering the Class D airspace

38. If the control tower is not operating, but there is an FSS at the airport, you will receive (a control/an advisory) service

➤ an advisory

39. Hours of operation of a control tower can be found in the applicable _____ booklet and on the NOS IFR en route chart _____; the times are expressed in (UTC/local time).

➤ A/FD booklet, in the A/G Voice Communication legend; UTC (also expressed as Z),

40. The time difference between local time and UTC at a particular airport (can/cannot) be found in the A/FD.

➤ can

En Route Charts (b)

Refer to Figure 1 on page 526 for the following questions.

1. The VOR changeover point when flying east on V306 from Daisetta to Lake Charles is _____ nm east of Daisetta.

➤ 30 nm

2. Are LDA aproaches indicated on en route charts?

➤ yes, if they serve an ATC function such as defining an intersection

3. VHF communications frequencies normally available at all FSSs, and not shown above the Air/Ground communication boxes on NOS en route charts, are _____ and _____.

➤ 121.5 and 122.2

4. What is the appropriate FSS to communicate with in the Lake Charles area?

➤ De Ridder FSS

5. On which frequencies can you receive De Ridder FSS during the day in the Lake Charles area?

➤ 121.5, 122.2 and 122.3

6. What is the appropriate FSS to communicate with over the Daisetta VOR?

➤ Montgomery County

7. Can you talk to, and receive messages from, Montgomery County FSS on 122.1 in the Daisetta area?

➤ talk to—yes, receive from—no

8. How can you receive messages from Montgomery County FSS in reply to a call you have made on 122.1 in the Daisetta area?

➤ on the VOR frequency 116.9 with voice selected

9. What frequencies can you receive Montgomery County FSS on during the day in the Daisetta area?

➤ 121.5, 122.2 and VOR 116.9

10. What does the striped area around the Houston Class B airspace indicate?

➤ Mode C transponder required

11. At Jefferson County airport, why is the back course of the localizer depicted, but not the front course.

➤ because the back course serves an ATC function (defining the PORTZ intersection), whereas the front course serves no such function

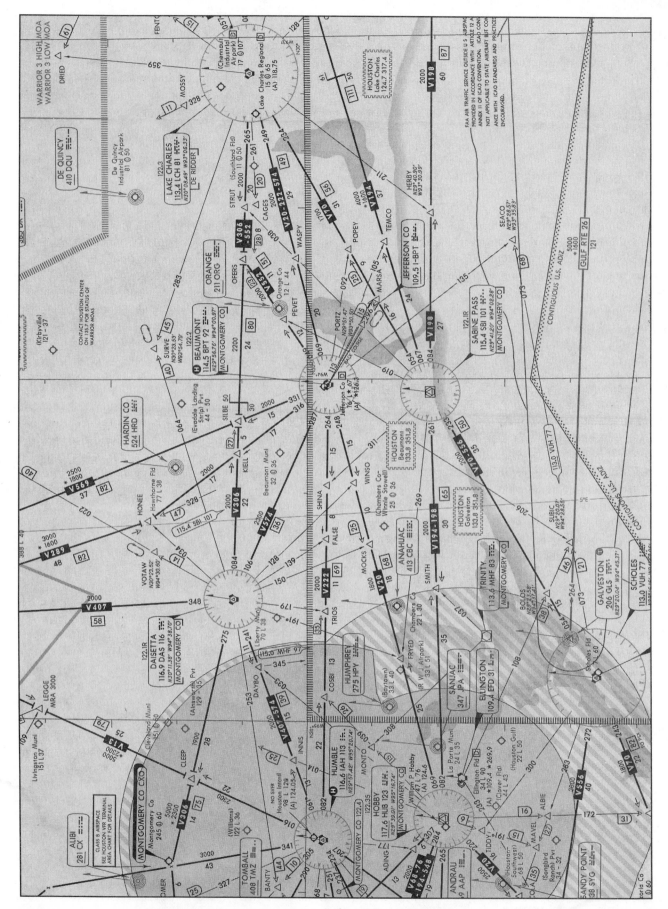

Figure 1. L-17 NOS low-altitude en route chart; excerpt of Galveston, Texas area (reduced in size)

12. What airspace exists at Jefferson County airport?

➤ Class D (boxed-D symbol)

---

13. When flying southwest from Jefferson County along V20 to Hobby, the VOR changeover point is at _____.

➤ the halfway point (otherwise it would be designated on the chart)

---

14. When flying from Jefferson County along V20 to Hobby, the VOR changeover point is _____ nm from _____.

➤ 34 nm from BPT VORTAC

---

15. What are the MEAs when flying northwest from Jefferson County to Daisetta along V574, and north from Jefferson County to SILBE intersection along V569?

➤ 2300 feet MSL, 2000 feet MSL

---

16. What is the MEA flying north from SILBE intersection along V569? Is adequate obstruction clearance assured at this altitude? Is adequate navigation signal coverage assured at this altitude?

➤ 2500 feet MSL, yes, yes

---

17. What is the meaning of the symbol: "*1800" flying north from SILBE intersection along V569? Is adequate obstruction clearance assured at this altitude? Is adequate navigation signal coverage assured at this altitude?

➤ 1800 feet MSL is the MOCA, yes, no

---

18. What are the ARTCC VHF frequencies in the Jefferson County and the Lake Charles areas?

➤ 133.8 MHz, 124.7 MHz

---

19. On what frequency is an en route flight advisory service, EFAS, available in the Jefferson County to Lake Charles area?

➤ standard frequency 122.0 MHz at low altitude (up to 18,000 feet MSL)

---

20. H_____ I_____ W_____ A_____ S_____ is available in the area near Jefferson County airport on frequency _____, which you would select on your (ADF/VHF-NAV/VHF-COM).

➤ Hazardous In-Flight Weather Advisory Service, 114.5 MHz, VHF-NAV)

---

21. Areas shaded light brown on NOS low altitude en route charts Class _____ airspace below _____ feet MSL. This is (controlled/uncontrolled) airspace.

➤ Class G, 14,500 feet MSL, uncontrolled

---

22. What available lighting is indicated on the chart at Lake Charles Regional airport?

➤ pilot controlled lighting

---

23. What is the responsible ARTCC unit and frequency in the Lake Charles area?

➤ Houston Center, 124.7 MHz

Flight Planning

Continue reference to Figure 1 on page 526 for the following questions.

1. The most current en route and destination flight information for planning an IFR flight should be obtained from (ATIS/FSS/Class 2 NOTAMs).

➤ FSS

---

2. Changes in flight data, such as changes on IFR approach and en route charts, will be notified in (L/D/FDC) NOTAMs obtained from _____.

➤ FDC, FSS

---

3. The latest status of a runway can be determined from the A/FD, as amended by (L/D/FDC) NOTAMs.

➤ L and D NOTAMs

You are to plan an IFR flight from Lake Charles Regional to Montgomery County airport via V306, with cruise TAS 180. An extract of the meteorological FD is:

FT	3000	6000	9000	12000
LCH	2115	2325+08	2335+02	2340–04

4. What is the elevation of Lake Charles Regional airport?

➤ 15 feet MSL

---

5. Using an average groundspeed of 140 knots, and a rate of climb of 650 fpm, the distance to reach cruise altitude 8000 feet will be _____.

➤ 28 nm (8000 feet at 650 fpm = 12 min at GS 140 = 28 nm)

---

6. The initial route out of LCH is V306–552. V552 goes from LCH to _____ VORTAC via _____ intersection.

➤ Beaumont VORTAC via OFERS Intersection

---

7. At OFERS intersection the MEA on V306 changes from _____ MSL to _____ MSL.

➤ 2000 feet, 2200 feet

---

8. The calibrated airspeed (CAS) which must be used to maintain the filed TAS at the flight plan altitude of 8000 feet is _____ KCAS.

➤ 158 KCAS (use temperature +04 by interpolation from forecast)

---

9. The estimated time interval from OFERS to DAS using the wind entry nearest your planned altitude 8000 feet is _____ minutes. Magnetic variation at LCH is shown as 7E in the A/FD.

➤ 20 minutes (MC 265, 9000 feet wind 230/35 true, 223/35 Magnetic. Groundspeed 153 knots, MH 257, distance 52 nm = estimated time 20 minutes)

---

10. The distance from OFERS intersection to the VOR changeover point is _____ nm.

➤ 22 nm (LCH to COP 50 nm, LCH to SILBE 52 nm, OFERS to COP = 24–2 = 22 nm)

---

11. The course and distance out of DAS to the turning point beside Montgomery County airport is MC _____ and _____ nm.

➤ MC 275, 42 nm

---

12. The highest MEA DAS to the turning point is _____ feet.

➤ 5000 feet

---

13. The MOCA from DAS to Cleep is _____ feet, and from Cleep to the turning point is _____ feet.

➤ 1900 feet, 2300 feet

---

14. To determine whether or not the destination requires an alternate, apply the ETA ±1,2,3 rule, which means that, in the destination forecast, the ceiling must be at least _____ feet, and the visibility at least _____ sm, for the period _____ hour either side of your ETA.

➤ 2000 feet, 3 sm, 1 hour either side of ETA

---

15. To be suitable as an alternate airport, the forecast must be at least its published alternate minimums, otherwise ceiling _____ feet and _____ sm visiblity if serviced by an ILS; and ceiling _____ feet and _____ sm visiblity if serviced only by a VOR IAP.

➤ 600 feet ceiling, 2 sm; 800 feet ceiling, 2 sm

---

16. Fuel requirements for an IFR flight are _____.

➤ fuel for departure to destination, plus to alternate if required, plus 45 minutes at normal cruise rate

---

17. What is the highest altitude a westbound flight can normally plan on a Victor airway?

➤ 16,000 feet (WEEO rule; Victor airways go up to, but do not include, 18,000 feet MSL)

18. The wind and temperatures aloft forecast predicts a wind of 340° at 30 knots at 9000 feet altitude in the area of your planned flight. If the average magnetic variation is 20° east and your planned TAS at 9000 feet is 170 knots, then determine the flight plan heading and groundspeed for the following magnetic courses.
(a) MC 080 (b) MC 110 (c) MC 140 (d) MC 170 (e) MC 020 (f) MC 040

➤ (a) MH 071, GS 183 (b) MH 105, GS 195 (c) MH 140, GS 200 (d) MH 175, GS 195 (e) MH 011, GS 153 (f) MH 030, GS 163; (wind is 320 degrees magnetic at 30 knots)

19. To achieve a filed TAS of 180 knots, you would need to fly at CAS _____ knots if the OAT is +8°C at 8000 feet.

➤ 156 KCAS

20. To achieve a filed TAS of 158 knots, you would need to fly at CAS _____ knots if the OAT is 0°C at 8000 feet.

➤ 140 KCAS

Flight Plan Form

Refer to sample Flight Plan form on page 522, or your own copy.

1. For an IFR flight, you should check the _____ box in Block 1 on the flight plan form. For a composite flight plan, you should check the _____ and _____ boxes.

➤ IFR, IFR and VFR

2. If your aircraft is fitted with RNAV and a Mode C transponder, you should insert the letter _____ in Block 3 of the flight plan form.

➤ /I (see panel below flight plan form in Figure 25-13 on page 522)

3. If your aircraft is fitted with DME, but no transponder, you should insert the letter _____ in Block 3 of the flight plan form.

➤ /D

4. What code should be entered in Block 3 of the flight plan form if your airplane is equipped with DME and a Mode C transponder?

➤ /A

5. In Block 6, insert the proposed departure time (UTC/local); to avoid cancelation of the flight plan, you should advise ATC of any delay beyond _____ minutes.

➤ UTC (Z), 60 minutes

6. In Block 7, enter the (initial/intermediate/final) requested cruising altitude or FL.

➤ initial

7. How would you enter the following route into Block 8: "Bakersfield (AVE) along airway Victor 248 to Paso Robles (PRB), then along airway Victor 113 to Morro Bay (MQO), the along Victor 27 to the ORCUT intersection, and then direct to Fellows (FLW)"?

➤ AVE V248 PRB V113 MQO V27 ORCUT FLW

8. When filing a composite flight plan where the first portion of the flight is IFR, Block 8 should indicate: fixes where you transition from one airway to another—(yes/no); fixes defining direct route segments—(yes/no); the IFR clearance limit fix—(yes/no).

➤ yes, yes, yes

9. Insert in Block 10 the estimated time from departure to (top of climb/touchdown at airport of first intended landing/initial approach fix at destination).

➤ touchdown at airport of first intended landing

10. If you do not have your DP and STAR charts, you should enter _____ in the remarks section of the flight plan form.

➤ No DP, No STAR

11. Insert in Block 12 the fuel endurance in (gallons/hours and minutes) based on the (total usable fuel on-board/minimum fuel required)

➤ hours and minutes, total usable fuel on-board

12. An IFR flight plan is required, and an ATC clearance is required, for IFR operations in Class (A/B/C/D/E/G) airspace. (More than one answer is correct.)

➤ A, B, C, D and E

13. If IMC exist, an IFR flight plan and clearance (is/is not) required to operate in Class G airspace, which is (controlled/uncontrolled); to enter Class E airspace from Class G airspace in IMC, an IFR flight plan (is/is not) required.

➤ is not, uncontrolled, is

14. To avoid delays, an IFR flight plan should be submitted at least _____ prior to the proposed time of departure.

➤ 30 minutes

15. An IFR flight plan (will/will not) be automatically closed by ATC when you land at an airport with an operating control tower, and (will/will not) be automatically closed by ATC if you land at an airport without an operating control tower.

➤ will, will not

16. Search and rescue procedures will begin if a flight plan has not been closed by _____ after the latest advised ETA.

➤ 30 minutes

17. An IFR flight plan can be closed in flight if VFR conditions exist when flying in Class (A/B/C/D/E) controlled airspace. (More than one answer is correct.)

➤ B, C, D and E

18. When is an IFR flight plan and clearance required to fly in VFR conditions?

➤ in Class A airspace

Instrument Departures

26

A pilot should not take off unless he is certain that conditions at the departure airport are suitable, and that conditions at the destination or alternate airport will allow a landing to be made. Operating in adverse weather can be safe only within certain limits. It is strongly recommended, therefore, that a careful decision to operate or not is made before every IFR flight, taking into account all the available relevant information.

Use all relevant information when making a sound Go/No-Go decision.

Weather at the Departure Airport

The **automatic terminal information service (ATIS)** provides a description of the current weather and non-control information at that airport. ATIS broadcasts are updated on receipt of any official weather, regardless of content change and reported values. If the weather is above ceiling/sky condition of 5000 feet and the visibility 5 sm or more, it is possible that these items may not be included in the ATIS. You should listen to the ATIS prior to taxiing, and notify ATC on initial contact that you have received it.

The ATIS broadcast will be updated on receipt of any official weather regardless of content change or reported values.

Some airports have **automated weather observing systems** (ASOS or AWOS). Refer to the AIM and A/FD for details.

ATC often operate the **airport rotating beacon** in daylight hours to indicate a ground visibility of less than 3 sm and a ceiling less than 1000 feet HAA.

Beware of standing water or slush on the runway, which may cause the tires to *hydroplane* by separating them from the runway surface. Surface friction is greatly reduced, causing directional control problems and greatly reduced braking capability. This is important, especially if you attempt to abandon the takeoff, or if you return for a landing.

Takeoff Minimums

Published takeoff minimums (either standard minimums or specific minimums applicable to a particular runway or airport) apply to commercial operations only, and are intended to protect the traveling public. If you are pilot-in-command of an FAR Part 91 operation (private, flight instructional or airwork operation), then you are not legally bound to comply with these published minimums, however they do provide good guidance as to whether you should take off or not.

Standard takeoff minimums are stated as *visibility only*, since normal climb-out performance after takeoff will keep the airplane above any obstructions in a normal obstacle-clear takeoff area. Standard takeoff minimums are:

If conditions are considered to be too poor for highly trained professional pilots in commercial aircraft, then probably they are too poor for you.

- 1 statute mile visibility for airplanes with 1 or 2 engines;
- $\frac{1}{2}$ statute mile visibility for airplanes with 3 or more engines.

If the standard takeoff minimums apply to a particular runway, and are met, then, provided a climb gradient of 200 ft/nm or better can be achieved, you may make a normal IFR takeoff. You should climb straight ahead to at least 400 feet before turning to intercept the outbound course.

A climb gradient of 200 ft/nm will keep the airplane above any obstructions during the climb to the applicable **minimum en route altitude (MEA)**. A gradient of 200 ft/nm is 1 in 30, or 2°. If you are confident that your airplane will achieve a rate of climb that will satisfy this gradient, then you may takeoff in low visibility, immediately enter clouds, and still be confident of clearing all obstacles.

- At groundspeed 60 kt, 200 ft/nm is achieved with a rate of climb of 200 fpm.
- At groundspeed 90 kt, 200 ft/nm is achieved with a rate of climb of 300 fpm.
- At groundspeed 120 kt, 200 ft/nm is achieved with a rate of climb of 400 fpm.

An **obstacle identification surface (OIS)** is projected from a point no higher than 35 feet above the departure end of the runway at a gradient of 1 in 40, which is 1.5° or 152 ft/nm. If no obstacles penetrate this OIS, then standard takeoff minimums apply (visibility 1 sm for 1- or 2-engined airplanes), a normal takeoff and climb can be made, and no special IFR procedures need to be published. If the airplane achieves a climb gradient of 200 ft/nm, then clearance above obstacles on the climb to the MEA will increase by at least 48 feet for each nm traveled (200 – 152).

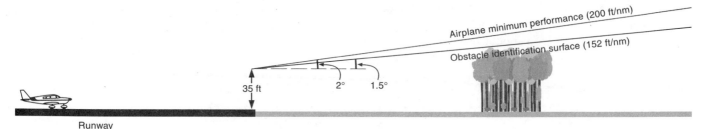

Figure 26-1. Obstacle clearance in the takeoff area

If, however, there are significant obstacles that do penetrate this obstacle identification surface, then obstacle avoidance procedures are specified, which may be either:

- **a higher climb gradient** in excess of the standard 200 ft/nm, so that the airplane will clear the obstacles on a normal straight flightpath, and the standard minimums still apply (visibility 1 sm for airplanes with 1 or 2 engines, and with no reference to a ceiling minimum); or
- takeoff minimums expanded to include a **cloud ceiling** as well as a visibility minimum, allowing a pilot to see and avoid the obstacle; or
- **a prescribed IFR departure procedure**, describing the flightpath to be followed (turns, heading, altitudes) to avoid the obstructions; or
- a combination of the above.

If special takeoff minimums and/or special IFR departure procedures apply to an airport, then this is indicated on the instrument charts:

- NOS instrument charts have a symbolic "T" in an inverted black triangle, directing you to the front of the NOS booklet for details of *IFR Takeoff Minimums and Departure Procedures*; and
- *Jeppesen* instrument charts display *Takeoff and IFR Departure Procedures* on the front or rear face of the airport chart.

On some runways, an IFR takeoff may not be authorized because of obstacle clearance problems.

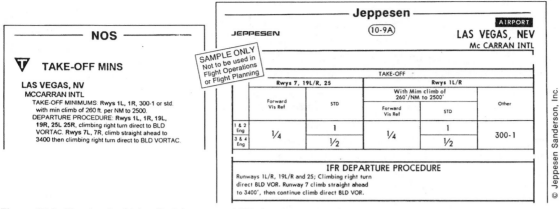

NOS

▽ **TAKE-OFF MINS**

LAS VEGAS, NV
MCCARRAN INTL
TAKE-OFF MINIMUMS: Rwys 1L, 1R, 300-1 or std.
with min climb of 260 ft. per NM to 2500.
DEPARTURE PROCEDURE: Rwys 1L, 1R, 19L,
19R, 25L 25R, climbing right turn direct to BLD
VORTAC. Rwys 7L, 7R, climb straight ahead to
3400 then climbing right turn direct to BLD VORTAC.

Jeppesen

JEPPESEN   (10-9A)   **AIRPORT**   **LAS VEGAS, NEV**
Mc CARRAN INTL

	TAKE-OFF				
	Rwys 7, 19L/R, 25		**Rwys 1L/R**		
			With Mim climb of 260'/NM to 2500'		
	Forward Vis Ref	STD	Forward Vis Ref	STD	Other
1 & 2 Eng	1/4	1	1/4	1	300-1
3 & 4 Eng		1/2		1/2	

IFR DEPARTURE PROCEDURE
Runways 1L/R, 19L/R and 25; Climbing right turn
direct BLD VOR. Runway 7 climb straight ahead
to 3400', then continue climb direct BLD VOR.

© Jeppesen Sanderson, Inc.

Figure 26-2. Nonstandard takeoff minimums and IFR departure procedure

Note: Sometimes horizontal visibility along a runway is expressed in terms of **runway visual range (RVR)** in feet, measured by a transmissometer placed near the runway. If the minimums on the chart are prescribed as an RVR, but the transmissometer(s) is(are) inoperative, then you may convert the RVR minimum in feet to an equivalent visibility in statute miles, and apply that (1 sm = 5000 feet; $\frac{1}{2}$ sm = 2400 feet).

For Las Vegas Runway 1L or 1R, the standard takeoff minimums (visibility 1 sm for airplanes with 1 or 2 engines) only apply if you can achieve a climb gradient of 260 ft/nm or better to an altitude of 2500 feet MSL. At a ground-speed of 90 knots, this would require a rate of climb of 390 fpm. If you cannot climb at this higher rate, then the takeoff minimums are increased to ceiling 300 feet/visibility 1 sm; the 300 feet ceiling requirement enabling the pilot climbing at only 200 ft/nm to visually avoid any obstacles below this level. Additionally, an IFR departure procedure applies to this runway, requiring a climbing right turn direct to the Boulder City VORTAC. This procedure *must* be flown, irrespective of whatever minimums apply to the takeoff.

Prior to every IFR takeoff, you should carefully consider obstacle clearance and climb capability. In particular, beware of taking off in a tailwind—this means a higher groundspeed for the same airspeed, and consequently a flatter climb path over the ground. To achieve the same climb gradient as in still air, a higher rate of climb will therefore be required, and the airplane may not be capable of achieving this. In addition, a 5-knot tailwind on the ground may well increase to a 10-knot, or even 20- or 30-knot tailwind soon after takeoff, further penalizing the climb performance, this is known as an undershoot (or performance-decreasing) windshear. You should also plan your takeoff to avoid possible wake turbulence from a preceding heavy aircraft.

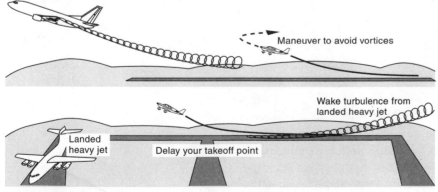

Figure 26-3. Avoid wake turbulence on your takeoff

Setting Course

Most departures on an instrument flight involve maneuvering after takeoff to intercept the departure course to or from a particular radio navigation aid. It is good airmanship to have in mind the direction of turns necessary, and the approximate time required to intercept the course. If it is a complicated procedure, take time to review it before entering the runway.

The tower controller will normally inform you of the departure control frequency and, if appropriate, the transponder code, prior to takeoff. The transponder should not be operated until ready to start the takeoff roll, and you should not change to departures control until requested. Ensure that the current local altimeter setting is set in the pressure window for takeoff and departure so that the altimeter indicates vertical distance above mean sea level, and ensure that your heading indicator is aligned with the magnetic compass.

Standard takeoff and departure procedure is to climb straight ahead to at least 400 feet HAA before making any turns, and then to climb to the en route MEA at best rate of climb. Change from the tower frequency to departure control when requested. Any IFR departure procedure, standard instrument procedure or other clearance specified by ATC, and accepted by you, should be followed. ATC should be notified if your rate of climb to cruising altitude is less than 500 fpm. For the last 1000 feet of the climb to the cleared cruising altitude, the rate of climb should be reduced to between 500 and 1500 fpm.

Figure 26-4 shows an airplane taking off and intercepting the MC 270 course outbound from an NDB positioned near the airport.

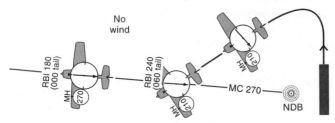

Figure 26-4. Intercepting the departure course using an NDB

Figure 26-5 shows an airplane intercepting the MC 030-TO course to a VOR (the 210 radial), and then tracking outbound on the 090 radial.

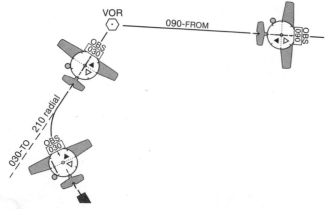

Figure 26-5. Intercepting departure course using a VOR

Note: Many instrument departures are made in visual conditions, and you should take advantage of this to scan the sky for other aircraft to reduce the risk of a collision. Climb on the centerline of the airway and systematically focus on different segments of the sky for short intervals, occasionally making gentle banks left and right to clear the area under the nose.

Instrument Departure Procedures (DPs)

At many busy controlled airports, specific Instrument Departure Procedures (DPs) are published for the use of instrument-rated pilots.

A DP is a published IFR departure procedure providing a standard route from the terminal to the appropriate en route structure. In some cases a DP may have an associated **transition**, which is a published procedure connecting the end of the DP to one of several en route structures.

DPs considerably simplify the issuance of departure clearances, allowing ATC to simply specify the DP by name without having to describe any further tracking details, since these are provided in diagrammatic and textual form on the pilot's DP charts. The clearance may include the basic DP name and number, plus a transition to the desired route. The departure control frequency, normally passed to a pilot with his IFR departure clearance, may be omitted by ATC since it is published on the DP page.

To accept a DP, you must have at least a textual description of it available in the cockpit. An example of a DP, the MEAD-7 DP for Las Vegas, is shown in Figure 26-6, on page 536. ATC may issue DPs without a specific pilot request. If you do not wish to accept a DP, then you should advise ATC, preferably by inserting "No DP" in the remarks section of the filed flight plan, otherwise verbally. (The same applies to STARs—Standard Terminal Arrival Routes.) This does not preclude ATC from reading to you the textual form of a DP as your clearance.

Instrument departure procedures (DPs) are designed to:
- separate departing traffic from arriving traffic;
- provide efficient interception of outbound course;
- avoid noise-sensitive areas near the airport;
- simplify the issuance of departure clearances; and
- reduce radio talk.

There are two basic forms of DPs:
- **pilot navigation DPs**, where the pilot is primarily responsible for navigation along the published DP route (as in the Las Vegas case in Figure 26-6); and
- **vector DPs**, where ATC will provide radar vectors to a filed/assigned route or to a fix depicted on the DP.

Typical DPs issued by ATC as part of an IFR departure clearance are:

"..., Mead-7 departure, ...;"

"..., Mead-7 departure, Drake transition, ...;"

"..., Mead-7 departure, Drake transition, cross Boulder City VORTAC at or below six thousand, ..."

ATC Clearances

To operate in controlled airspace under IFR, you are required to file an IFR flight plan and obtain a clearance.

An ATC clearance is an authorization by ATC for you to proceed under specified conditions within controlled airspace.

Clearances are normally issued for the altitude and route as filed (AF) by the pilot, however this is not always the case, depending upon traffic flow, congestion, etc. You should always write down any clearance issued to you by ATC (using clearance shorthand), and then read it back without error as a double-check.

> A DP is a published IFR departure procedure providing a standard route from the terminal to the appropriate en route structure. To accept a DP, you must have at least have it written down in the cockpit.

> Always write down an ATC clearance, and read it back.

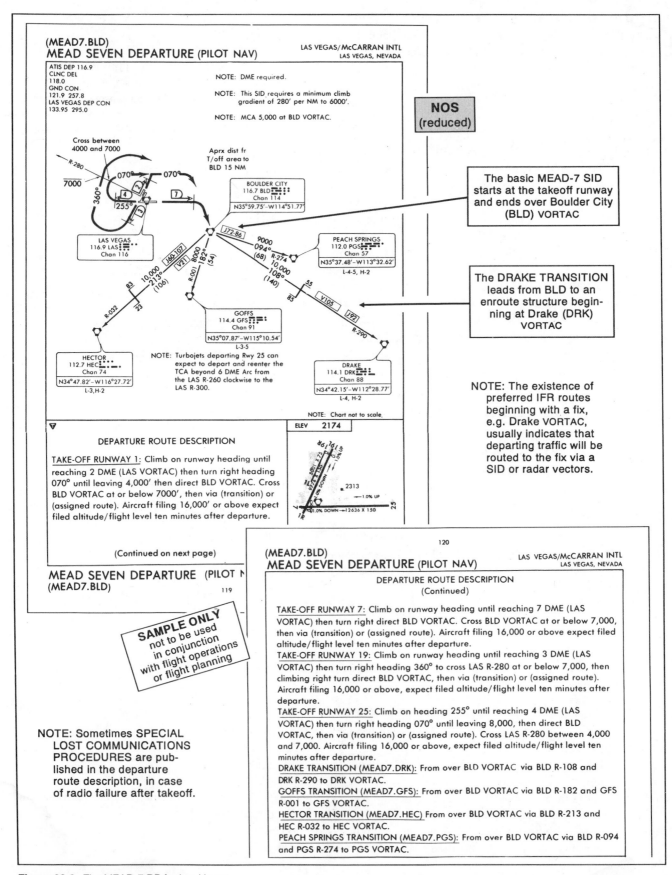

Figure 26-6. The MEAD-7 DP for Las Vegas

You, as pilot-in-command, are ultimately responsible for the safety of your aircraft (14 CFR Part 91), so do not accept a clearance that would cause you to deviate from any rule or regulation or that would place the aircraft in jeopardy. Instead, request an amended clearance.

Do not accept a clearance that causes you to break a rule or break your aircraft. Request an amended clearance instead.

Pre-Taxi Clearance Procedures

If operating on an IFR flight plan, you should communicate with the control tower on the appropriate ground control or clearance delivery frequency, prior to starting engines, to receive engine-start time, taxi and/or clearance information. At certain airports, you may obtain your IFR clearance before taxiing by calling Clearance Delivery or Ground Control not more than 10 minutes prior to the proposed taxi time, otherwise request it prior to takeoff.

Sometimes the clearance is available immediately, and sometimes there is a delay. An ATC response of "Baron 1543 Foxtrot—clearance on request" or "Baron 1543 Foxtrot—standby", means that your clearance is not yet available. When it is ready, they will advise you "Baron 1543 Foxtrot—clearance", which you may then receive at a convenient time.

The clearance will contain:
- your identification;
- the clearance limit (often the destination airport, otherwise an en route fix);
- the departure procedure or DP to be followed;
- altitude(s);
- any holding instructions;
- any other special information;
- radio frequency and transponder code information.

The route issued in the clearance, if it is the same as you filed in your IFR flight plan, may be abbreviated to "as filed," and you can write this down as AF. This is known as an **abbreviated clearance**, and it will always contain at least:
- the name of the destination airport or a fix;
- DP and transition, if appropriate; and
- altitude.

The clearance may contain a delay, such as "hold for release—expected delay 10 minutes", which you can write as "H-10". Develop a clearance shorthand to speed up the process of copying clearances. You must be fast and accurate.

A **clearance void (CV) time** stated in the clearance when departing from an airport not served by a control tower means that you must depart by the CV time for the clearance to remain valid. If you decide not to depart before the CV time, you should advise ATC of your intentions as soon as possible, but no later than 30 minutes, to avoid unnecessary ATC action following a false assumption that you have departed.

An altitude assignment "maintain 6000" instructs you to fly *at* that altitude. An altitude assignment "cruise 6000" means that you can fly at any altitude from the minimum IFR altitude up to and including the altitude specified in the clearance, and you may alter your level within this layer of airspace without advising ATC. Most IFR clearances in the busy United States airspace are to "maintain" the specified altitude, rather than cruise within a layer.

Strict adherence to clearances by the pilot-in-command is essential to safety, so you must know the exact conditions of your clearance throughout the flight, even though it might be amended by ATC from time to time. IFR departure clearances should be copied, and then read back, as mutual pilot/controller verification of accuracy.

The items in an ATC clearance are issued in a predictable order, and you should develop a shorthand pattern of writing them down, as shown below:

Cleared to..........................

Via...

Climb to & maintain............ Expect................. minutes after departure

Instructions on departure....................................

Departure Frequency................... Squawk........

This can be abbreviated to:

C.....................

Via..

C & M............ E................. >dpt.

On dpt ....

Dpt freq................... Sqk ....

With practice this reminder pattern can be dispensed with altogether.

The following IFR departure clearances were written down exactly as spoken by actual controllers, except for certain abbreviations in brackets that will help you practice your clearance shorthand. The term "cleared to" is used by ATC; the term "ATC clears …" is used by a Flight Service Station (FSS) relaying an ATC clearance to you.

Example 1. Teterboro NJ (TEB) to Allentown PA (ABE).
King Air 280SC
cleared to Allentown airport
via Teterboro-2 departure
expect radar vectors to Lanna intersection
Victor-30 East Texas (ETX VORTAC)
direct
expect 6000 10 minutes after departure
departure frequency will be 127.6
squawk 4317

> C-ABE
> TEB-2 RV LANNA V30 ETX DIR
> 6000/10
> 127·6   4317

Note: The Teterboro-2 departure off runway 19 (which you will read from your DP booklet) is:

Maintain runway heading until leaving 800 feet, then turn right heading 280, maintain 1500 feet until crossing the Patterson NDB 195 bearing (PNJ NDB), then climb and maintain 3000 feet, then expect radar vectors to Lanna intersection.

Example 2. Teterboro NJ (TEB) to Fulton County GA (FTY).
Gulfstream N1040
cleared to Fulton County Airport (FTY)
via Teterboro-2 departure (TEB-2)
expect radar vectors to Lanna intercept
then J-48 to Fort Mill (FML VORTAC)
direct Awson-7 arrival
expect FL 430 10 minutes into departure
departure frequency will be 127.6
squawk 4354

> C-FTY
> TEB-2 RV LANNA J48 FML
> DIR AWS-7
> F430/10
> 127·6   4354

Example 3. Santa Barbara CA (SBA) to Paso Robles CA (PRB).
Baron 4123G
cleared to Paso Robles airport (PRB)
via Gaviota (GVO VORTAC)
Victor-27 to Morro Bay (MQO VORTAC)
direct
climb and maintain 6000
hold for release
departure frequency 119.05
squawk 4576

```
C-PRB
GVO  V27 MQO DIR
6000  (H)
119·05   4576
```

Example 4. Santa Barbara CA (SBA) to San Diego CA (SAN).
November 3456D
cleared to San Diego Lindbergh Field (SAN)
via radar vectors to Ventura (VTU VORTAC)
Victor-299 to Los Angeles (LAX VORTAC)
Victor-23 Oceanside (OCN VORTAC)
direct Mission Bay (MZB VORTAC)
San Diego Lindbergh Field
climb and maintain 6000
expect 12,000 5 minutes after departure
you are released—clearance void if not off by 0045 Zulu
departure frequency 119.05
squawk 4273

```
C-SAN
RV TU  V299 LAX
          V230CN DIR MZB SAN
6000  12,000/5
CV 0045Z
119·05   4273
```

Example 5. Rock Springs WY (RKS) to Denver International (DEN).
ATC clears Rocky Mountain Flight 2247
from Rock Springs airport to Denver airport
via Victor-4 Laramie (LAR VORTAC) then as filed
climb and maintain 17,000
contact Salt Lake Center on 119.25 after departure
squawk 6035

```
C-DEN
V4 LAR AF
17,000
119·25  6035
```

Example 6. Rock Springs WY (RKS) to Liberal KA (LBL).
ATC clears Cessna 9478G
to Liberal airport from Rock Springs airport
via Victor-4 Laramie then as filed
climb VFR through 9000 up to and maintain 17,000
contact Salt Lake Center on 119.25 after departure
squawk 6074

```
C-LBL
V4 LAR AF
9000 VFR  17,000
119·25   6074
```

Example 7. El Paso TX (ELP) to Dallas Love Field TX (DAL).
November 3812S
cleared to Dallas (DAL)
via radar vectors to join Victor-16 to Wink (INK VORTAC)
Victor-15 to Dallas
maintain 11,000
on departure fly runway heading
departure frequency 119.7
squawk 4205

```
C-DAL
RV V16 INK V15 DAL
11,000
RWY HDG
119·7  4205
```

Example 8. Spokane WA (GEG) to Seattle WA (SEA).

Northwest 1289
cleared to Seattle
direct Ephrata (EPH VORTAC)
Jay-70 Seattle
climb to and maintain 12,000
expect FL 230 5 minutes after departure
hold for release—expect 15 minutes departures delay
departure frequency 124.3
squawk 4650

```
C-SEA
DIR EPH J70 SEA
12,000 F230/5   (H-15)
124.3   4650
```

Example 9. Spokane WA (GEG) to Yakima WA (YKM).

Cessna 541S
cleared to Yakima airport via Spokane-4 departure
Victor-2 Seattle
Victor-23 Battleground (BTG VORTAC)
Victor-448
climb to and maintain 12,000
departure frequency 124.3
squawk 4705

```
C-YKM
GEG-4 V2 SEA V23 BTG V448
12,000
124.3   4705
```

✍ Review 26

Instrument Departures

Takeoff Minimums

1. Standard takeoff minimums are stated as (visibility/cloud ceiling/both).

   ➤ visibility only

2. Standard takeoff minimums for airplanes with 1 or 2 engines are _____; this is equivalent to an RVR of _____ feet.

   ➤ visibility 1 sm, RVR 5000 feet

3. The A_____ T_____ I_____ S_____ is updated (every 30 min/upon receipt of any official weather).

   ➤ automatic terminal information service, upon receipt of any official weather

4. The absence of sky condition and visibility on an ATIS broadcast implies a ceiling of more than _____ feet (MSL/AGL) and visibility _____.

   ➤ 5000 feet AGL, unrestricted

5. Standard takeoff minimums require a climb gradient of _____ ft/nm or better.

   ➤ 200 ft/nm

6. If standard takeoff minimums apply, and you estimate your groundspeed will be 60 knots, the required rate of climb is _____ knots.

   ➤ 200 fpm

7. If standard takeoff minimums apply, and you estimate your groundspeed will be 90 knots, the required rate of climb is _____ knots.

   ➤ 300 fpm

8. To achieve the same climb gradient taking off with a tailwind, compared with no-wind or a headwind, will require a (higher/lower/similar) rate of climb.

   ➤ higher rate of climb

9. What does a T in an inverted black triangle mean on NOS charts?

   ➤ takeoff minimums not standard and/or special IFR departure procedures are published

10. If standard takeoff minimums apply, the airplane must climb at _____ ft/nm or better to remain well above the obstacle-clear surface which climbs at _____ ft/nm.

   ➤ 200 ft/nm, 152 ft/nm

11. A T in an inverted black triangle on NOS charts alerts you to:

    (a) check the front of the NOS booklet.

    (b) check the minimums section of the NOS chart.

    (c) check the NOS en route chart.

➤ (a)

12. If a nonstandard takeoff minimum climb gradient of 240 ft/nm applies, what rate of climb must you achieve if your groundspeed is 120 knots?

➤ 480 fpm

13. Nonstandard takeoff minimums may contain a _____ requirement as well as a visibility requirement, so that the pilot may see and avoid obstructions.

➤ cloud ceiling

14. During an IFR departure in visual conditions you (should/need not) scan the sky for other aircraft.

➤ should

15. During an IFR departure in visual conditions, you should climb (on the centerline/to one side) of the airway, and you (should/need not) make gentle banks occasionally to improve your visual scanning.

➤ on the centerline, should

16. After takeoff, you should change from tower control frequency to departure control (immediately/on request).

➤ on request

17. You should climb to the assigned altitude at (optimum rate of climb/500–1500 fpm), except for the last _____ feet when you should reduce to between _____ and _____ fpm.

➤ optimum rate of climb, 1000 feet, 500–1500 fpm

DPs

1. If you do not have DP charts available, then you should insert _____ in the remarks section of your flight plan.

➤ NO DP

2. To accept a DP you must have with you in the cockpit at least:

    (a) a textual description.

    (b) a diagram.

    (c) a textual description and a diagram.

    (d) neither (a) nor (b).

➤ (a)

3. The two basic forms of standard instrument departure are _____ DPs and _____ DPs.

➤ pilot nav DPs, vector DPs

4. May ATC issue you with a DP without you making a specific request?

➤ yes

5. Preferred IFR routings beginning with a fix indicate that departing aircraft will normally be routed to the fixing aid via a _____ or by _____.

➤ DP, radar vectors

Refer to Figure 26-6 on page 536 (MEAD-7 DP for Las Vegas) for Questions 6–15.

6. Can you accept the MEAD-7 DP if your DME is inoperative?

➤ no (see chart)

7. The basic MEAD-7 DP, with runway 25 being used for takeoffs, starts at _____ and ends at _____.

➤ runway 25, BLD VORTAC

8. The DRAKE transition leads from _____ to _____.

➤ BLD to DRAKE

9. What minimum climb gradient is required for the MEAD-7 DP, and what rate of climb would you need to achieve this at groundspeed 120 knots?

➢ 280 ft/nm to 6000 feet MSL, 560 fpm

10. The minimum crossing altitude at the Boulder City VORTAC is _____?

➢ MCA 5000 feet

11. The maximum altitude at which you may cross the Boulder City VORTAC when using a Rwy 1 DP is _____?

➢ 7000 feet (see route description)

12. What is the Las Vegas VHF departure frequency?

➢ 133.95 (shown on the DP chart)

13. If you were to track southwest from Las Vegas, which transition would you use, and which low-level en route chart would you need?

➢ Hector transition, L-3 (shown beneath Hector frequency box)

14. What is the distance from BLD to HEC?

➢ 106 nm

15. At what DME from BLD would you transfer to HEC VOR?

➢ COP 83 DME from BLD

16. A particular DP requires a minimum climb rate of 210 feet per nautical mile. With an airspeed of 120 knots and a 20-knot tailwind, this requires a minimum rate of climb of _____ feet per minute.

➢ 490 fpm (2.3 nm per minute × 210 feet per nm)

17. In some cases, Special Lost Communications Procedures (are/are not) published on a DP departure route description.

➢ are

ATC Clearances

1. The words "cleared as filed" indicate an (abbreviated/full) clearance.

➢ abbreviated

2. The destination airport or a fix (is/is not) stated in an abbreviated clearance.

➢ is

3. The cleared en route altitude (is/is not) stated in an abbreviated clearance.

➢ is

4. In a radar environment at an airport with standard instrument departures available, the cleared DP/transition (is/is not) stated in an abbreviated clearance.

➢ is

5. Which items are given in an abbreviated clearance?

➢ destination or fix, DP/transition if appropriate, altitude

6. If your clearance to depart an airport not served by a control tower contains a void time, and you do not make it off before this void time, you should advise ATC of your intentions as soon as possible, but no later than _____ minutes.

➢ 30 minutes

7. If your clearance is to "maintain 7000", must you fly at 7000, or may you cruise below it?

➢ 7000 feet only

8. If your clearance is to "cruise 7000", must you fly at 7000, or may you cruise below it?

➢ 7000 feet or below (but above minimum IFR altitude)

9. With a clearance to "cruise at 6000", must you advise ATC if you wish to descend to 5000 feet?

➢ no

10. With a clearance to "maintain 6000", must you advise ATC if you wish to descend to 5000 feet?

➢ yes

Now return to the ATC clearances given in full in this chapter, and practice writing them in your own shorthand. Assume that they are being read by a controller at normal speaking rate.

En Route 27

The en route phase of flight follows your departure from one airport, and lasts until your arrival at another. There are a number of tasks for the instrument pilot to perform en route, such as maintaining course, making the required radio reports, preparing for the descent, arrival and approach at the destination airport, and making the appropriate calculations in case a diversion to an alternate airport is necessary. Fuel is always an important consideration.

Radar Service

Normally you will change to departure frequency when instructed to by the tower after takeoff. Initial radar identification of your aircraft by a controller will be advised by the phrase "radar contact." Transponder Mode C (or S) should always be selected, unless otherwise requested, to provide ATC with altitude reporting. The controller will follow your flight on radar, until "radar contact lost" or "radar service terminated" is advised, or until you have been cleared for a visual approach with a preceding aircraft in sight, or until after you have landed. If the controller instructs you to "resume own navigation," then you are responsible for your own navigation even though *radar flight-following* will continue.

En Route Clearances

Pilots of airborne aircraft, upon receiving a clearance or instruction from ATC, should read back the numbers (altitudes, altitude restrictions, radar vectors), and any data needing verification. Altitudes in charted procedures (DPs, STARs, IAPs) need not be read back unless they are specifically stated by the controller. It is your responsibility, as pilot-in-command, to accept the clearance, or to refuse it. Any changes of altitude should be made without delay, unless the clearance includes "at pilot discretion." You should change altitude at the optimum rate of climb or descent consistent with normal operation of the airplane, until the last 1000 feet which should be at 500–1500 fpm. Advise ATC if you cannot achieve a 500 fpm climb/descent rate.

Operating on a composite VFR/IFR flight plan:

- If you are changing from VFR to IFR, you should close the VFR portion of your flight plan with FSS and request an ATC clearance, but remain in VMC until operating in accordance with the IFR clearance.

- If you are changing from IFR to VFR, you should close the IFR portion of the flight plan with ATC when overhead the IFR clearance-limit fix, and then contact the nearest FSS to activate the VFR portion of the flight plan.

- If you do not wish to change from IFR to VFR, but to continue IFR, advise ATC at least 5 minutes prior to reaching the IFR clearance-limit fix and request a further IFR clearance. Do not proceed IFR past the IFR clearance-limit fix until you have obtained the onward ATC clearance—hold in a published holding pattern at the fix, otherwise in a standard holding pattern on the radial or course to the fix.

Position Reports

ATC needs to know where aircraft are in the IFR environment, and this is achieved by:

- ATC radar, where possible, supported by limited reports from aircraft; or
- full position reports from aircraft in a nonradar environment.

A **full position report** contains:

- aircraft identification;
- position;
- time;
- altitude (specifying VFR-on-top if appropriate);
- type of flight plan (not necessary if in contact with Center or Approach);
- ETA and name of next reporting point;
- name only of the following reporting point; and
- pertinent remarks.

Example 1.

> Sacramento, Cessna 238 Sierra
> Sacramento at two eight
> Niner thousand
> Manteca four seven
> Following-point Panoche
> Moderate turbulence.

Compulsory reporting points are shown on en route charts by solid triangles; on request reporting points are shown by open triangles, requiring reports only when requested by ATC. When flying on a direct route, reports shall also be made over each fix defining the route.

In a radar environment, after having been informed of being in radar contact by ATC, you may discontinue position reports. The words "radar contact" signify that you have been identified on the radar controller's display, and that radar flight-following will be provided until radar service is terminated or radar contact lost. You should use transponder Mode C (altitude reporting capability) at all times, unless ATC requests you not to. If ATC advise "radar contact lost" or "radar service terminated," you should resume normal position reporting.

Even in a radar environment, you should maintain a flight log, so that, in the event of loss of radar contact, you are able to continue with full position reporting.

In a radar environment, after having been informed of being in radar contact by ATC, you may discontinue position reports.

Additional Compulsory Radio Reports

You should initiate the following radio reports without any specific request from ATC:

(a) at all times

- when vacating a previously assigned altitude for a newly assigned altitude;
- when an altitude change will be made while operating VFR-on-top;
- when unable to climb or descend at a rate of at least 500 fpm;
- after initiating a missed approach;
- if you change the TAS at cruising altitude by 5% or 10 knots (whichever is greater) from that filed in the flight plan;
- the time and altitude upon reaching a holding fix or clearance limit;

- when leaving any assigned holding fix or point;
- any loss of navigation or communications capability in controlled airspace;
- any information relating to the safety of flight; and
- any unforecast weather, or any hazardous conditions encountered (forecast or not).

(b) when not in radar contact

- when leaving the final approach fix (FAF) inbound on a nonprecision approach (VOR/NDB/LOC/LDA/SDF);
- when leaving the outer marker (OM), or fix used in lieu of the outer marker, inbound on a precision approach (ILS/MLS/PAR);
- when an estimate previously submitted is in error by in excess of 3 minutes, and a revised estimate is required.

Flying the Airways

You should fly along the centerline of airways, except to pass well clear of other traffic in VFR conditions, keeping in mind that the protected airspace of an airway is at least ±4 nm, making a corridor 8 nm wide. Maintain calculated IFR safe altitudes when flying IFR routes and procedures, since this is your only protection from obstacles and terrain that you may not see.

> An airway corridor is 8 nm wide. Strive to fly in this protected airspace.

If climbing, cruising or descending outside of clouds, you should keep a good lookout, and make gentle banks periodically to assist you in detecting other traffic. When weather conditions permit, you are responsible to see-and-avoid, even if you are under radar control. The radar controller may advise you of nearby traffic using the clock-code based on the direction your radar blip is moving across his display, based on your ground track and not your heading.

En Route Information

As you proceed toward your destination, you should stay aware of the current weather. The En Route Flight Advisory Service (EFAS) is probably the best source of information as you fly along; it was described in detail in Chapter 23. EFAS operates on frequency 122.0 MHz usually between the hours of 0600–2200 local time. To obtain the EFAS, call Flight Watch on 122.0 MHz with your aircraft identification and the name of the nearest VOR. FSSs that provide EFAS are listed in the A/FD and indicated on en route charts.

En Route information is also broadcast over selected VORs and NDBs, predominantly through the Hazardous In-flight Weather Advisory Service (HIWAS).This service provides a continuous broadcast of severe weather forecast alerts (AWW), SIGMETs, convective SIGMETs, center weather advisories, AIRMETs and urgent pilot reports (PIREPs).

At locations where HIWAS is not implemented, ARTCCs and terminal facilities will broadcast HIWAS information on all but emergency frequencies.

The availability of en route information broadcasts is shown on NOS charts by:

- a white "H" in a black circle in the top left-hand corner of the navaid data box for HIWAS broadcasts; and
- a white "T" in a black circle for transcribed weather en route broadcasts (TWEB).

On *Jeppesen* en route charts, the weather service, HIWAS or TWEB, is listed immediately above the navaid identifier box.

Note: Underlining of the frequency in the navaid data box on NOS en route charts indicates that no voice is transmitted on that frequency.

High-Altitude Flying and Oxygen

You must use oxygen for all of the time that you are above a cabin altitude of 14,000 feet, and for the time in excess of 30 minutes above 12,500 feet up to and including 14,000 feet. The onset of **hypoxia**, a lack of oxygen, is gradual and insidious. You may not even be aware of it—you might feel euphoric and think that you are the world's greatest pilot, when in reality your performance is dreadful.

Note: Hypoxia is different from **hyperventilation** which is a result of too much air being breathed into the lungs. If you suspect hyperventilation, breathe at a slower rate than normal. If you suspect hypoxia, use oxygen.

You may not recognize the symptoms of hypoxia before your reactions are affected, so use oxygen at high cabin altitudes!

VFR-on-Top

If you are operating on an IFR clearance, and suitable conditions exist, you may "request VFR-on-top" in lieu of an assigned IFR altitude. A clearance to operate VFR-on-top will not be initiated by ATC; it must be initiated by the pilot. It allows you to climb through cloud layers, if necessary, to reach the VFR conditions on top of clouds, or to stay in VFR conditions below clouds.

An "on top" clearance requires VFR conditions at altitude.

You must fly at a VFR altitude based on magnetic course (*WEEO plus 5: West evens+5; East odds+5*); comply with VFR visibility and distance-from-cloud criteria; and comply with IFR requirements such as MEAs, position reporting and adherence to ATC clearances. With a VFR-on-top clearance, you are still on an IFR flight plan, but ATC is no longer responsible for your separation from other IFR aircraft. You must see and avoid other traffic. A VFR-on-top clearance is not available in Class A airspace.

Note: Under certain circumstances, it is possible to get a short-range IFR clearance to VFR conditions over the top. This is most frequently used at coastal airports to climb up through a cloud layer, then cancel IFR and proceed VFR once on top of the layer. This is often a **tower en route clearance (TEC)**, and may not require even the filing of a flight plan.

DME Failure

If VOR equipment is required, then DME is also required for you to file FL 240 or above. If the DME fails at or above FL 240, then you should notify ATC immediately, and continue operations at and above FL 240 until the next airport of intended landing at which repairs or replacement can be made.

En Route Diversions

As you proceed toward your destination, you should stay aware of the suitability of en route airports in case you have to make an unexpected diversion. You may be able to obtain the current weather at these airports from:

• automatic terminal information service (ATIS);

• transcribed weather broadcasts (TWEB);

• airport automated weather observation systems (ASOS or AWOS).

Failing that, the en route flight advisory service (EFAS) on 122.0 MHz can provide airport weather information on request.

Diversion to an Alternate Airport

If the weather is bad at your destination airport, you may decide to hold in the vicinity in the hope that it will improve, making an approach and landing possible. You should carefully consider the amount of fuel that you have available for holding, after allowing for:

- flight from the holding point to the destination airport, with an approach followed by a possible missed approach and climb-out;
- diversion to the alternate airport with an approach and landing; plus
- 45 minutes reserve.

Note: At the flight planning stage you will have considered the alternate minimums at your proposed alternate airport. Once you arrive there, however, you may fly the approach to the usual landing minimums, which are lower. Alternate minimums are for planning purposes only.

"Minimum Fuel"

If your fuel state is such that you cannot accept any undue delay at your destination, you should advise ATC: "minimum fuel." This is not declaration of a fuel emergency, but an advisory message to ATC that you may have to declare an emergency and receive priority if there is any undue delay.

Canceling an IFR Flight Plan

If operating an on IFR flight plan to an airport with a functioning control tower, the flight plan is automatically closed upon landing. You do not need to request the cancellation. If operating on an IFR flight plan to an airport with no functioning control tower, however, you must initiate the cancellation.

If conditions at the destination airport are IFR, you should wait until after landing before closing your IFR plan, which you can do by radio or telephone to any FSS or ATC facility (but do not forget, as this will increase the workload on FSS/ATC, who will try to trace you).

You may cancel an IFR flight plan in flight only if you are operating in VFR conditions outside Class A airspace, by advising the controller "cancel my IFR flight plan." You should then take action to change to the appropriate air/ground frequency, VFR transponder code, and VFR altitude. ATC separation and information services will be discontinued, including radar services where applicable. Request VFR radar advisory service, if desired.

Review 27

Radar Service

1. You should normally have Mode C (selected/deselected).

➤ selected

---

2. Your IFR clearance consists of a DP to follow radar vectors and intercept a Victor airway. As you approach the airway on an intercept heading, you are advised "resume own navigation". Radar flight-following (is/is not) terminated. You should turn to intercept the airway (when advised/on your own initiative).

➤ is not, on your own initiative

En Route Clearances

1. Should you read back any altitude ATC assigns you when airborne?

➤ yes

---

2. Should you read back any heading ATC assigns you when airborne?

➤ yes

---

3. Should you read back any speed restriction ATC assigns you when airborne?

➤ yes

---

4. The term used by ATC to indicate that your aircraft has been radar identified and that radar flight-following will be provided is _____.

➤ "radar contact"

---

5. If ATC issues an instruction or a clearance, some aspect of which is not clear to you, should you request verification?

➤ yes

En Route

6. If you are instructed to climb from your current altitude 6000 feet MSL to 13,000 feet MSL, you should climb:

(a) at 500 fpm throughout.

(b) at the optimum rate of climb throughout.

(c) at the optimum rate of climb, reducing to 1000 fpm for the last 500 feet.

(d) at the optimum rate of climb, reducing to 500–1500 fpm for the last 1000 feet.

➤ (d)

---

7. If you are instructed to descend from your current altitude 16,000 feet MSL to 13,000 feet MSL, you should descend:

(a) at 500 fpm throughout.

(b) at the optimum rate throughout.

(c) at the optimum rate, reducing to 500–1500 fpm for the last 1000 feet.

(d) at the optimum rate, reducing to 1000 fpm for the last 500 feet.

➤ (c)

---

8. You are operating on a composite flight plan. What radio calls would you make to change from VFR to IFR?

➤ prior to transitioning from VFR to IFR, close the VFR portion of your plan with FSS and request an IFR clearance

Radio Reports

1. Is full position reporting normally required in a radar environment?

➤ no

---

2. Is full position reporting normally required in a nonradar environment?

➤ yes

---

3. Compulsory reporting points in a nonradar environment are shown on en route charts by (open/solid) triangles.

➤ solid triangles

4. If your estimate at the next fix, not advised to ATC because you are in a radar environment, is in error by more than 3 minutes, must you advise ATC?

➤ no

5. If your estimate at the next fix, in a nonradar environment, is in error by more than 3 minutes, must you advise ATC?

➤ yes

6. Are you required to report if unable to climb or descend at 500 fpm or better?

➤ yes

7. Are you required to report when vacating a previously assigned altitude for a newly assigned altitude?

➤ yes

8. Are you required to report if you alter the cruising TAS to 120 knots, if you filed 115 knots?

➤ no

9. Are you required to report if you alter the cruising TAS to 130 knots, if you filed 115 knots?

➤ yes

10. What are you required to report upon reaching an assigned holding fix?

➤ time and altitude

11. Are you required to report leaving an assigned holding fix?

➤ yes

12. Are you required to report over fixes you have selected, and filed, to define a direct route?

➤ yes

13. When should Mode C be selected for an IFR flight?

➤ at all times, unless otherwise requested by ATC

14. Are you required to report the failure of your only VHF-NAV?

➤ yes

15. Are you required to report the failure of your no. 1 VHF-NAV, which has ILS capability, if your no. 2 VHF-NAV, without ILS capability, remains serviceable?

➤ yes

16. You fly into unexpected moderate turbulence and reduce speed from cruise speed 145 KIAS to maneuvering speed VA 110 KIAS while attempting to maintain a level flight attitude. What, if anything, should you report to ATC?

➤ speed reduction (5% of TAS or 10 knots), moderate turbulence

17. You cross ETX VORTAC at 0432 Zulu, and pass a full position report with an estimate of 0458 Zulu at the next compulsory reporting point at 60 DME ETX. You pass 20 DME ETX at 0442 Zulu. What action, if any, should you take in a nonradar environment?

➤ advise ATC of revised estimate 0502Z, since it differs by more than 3 minutes from previously advised estimate (GS 120 for next 40 nm = 20 min)

18. Are you required to report at the FAF inbound on a nonprecision approach in a nonradar environment?

➤ yes

19. Are you required to report at the FAF inbound on a nonprecision approach in a radar environment?

➤ no

20. Are you required to report at the outer marker inbound on a precision approach in a nonradar environment?

➤ yes

21. Are you required to report at the outer marker inbound on a precision approach in a radar environment?

➤ no

22. Are you required to report after commencing a missed approach?

➤ yes

Flying the Airways

1. The protected airspace either side of an airway is at least _____ nm.

➤ 4 nm

2. Operating on an IFR flight plan, but not in clouds, you (are/are not) responsible to see and avoid other traffic.

➤ are

3. The radar controller advises "traffic 2 o'clock." You are holding 20° correction for a crosswind from the right. You should look for the traffic approximately (straight ahead/20° right/40° right).

➤ 40° right

4. Availability of HIWAS en route weather broadcasts at a navaid facility is indicated on NOS en route charts by _____, and on *Jeppesen* en route charts by _____.

➤ NOS—a white "H" in a black circle in the top LH corner of the navaid data box; *Jeppesen*—the service will be shown immediately above the navaid data box

5. Underlining of the navaid frequency in the data box on an NOS en route chart indicates _____.

➤ no voice is transmitted on the frequency

6. For access to a weather specialist at a Flight Service Station you should call _____ on frequency _____, giving _____.

➤ (FSS name) Flight Watch on 122.0, aircraft identification and name of nearest VOR

7. Flight Service Stations that provide the en route flight advisory service (are/are not) listed in the appropriate Airport/Facility Directory booklet.

➤ are (rear cover)

High Altitude Flying and Oxygen

1. A lack of oxygen is known as _____.

➤ hypoxia

2. To combat hypoxia, you should _____.

➤ use oxygen

3. Too much air being breathed into the lungs is known as _____, and the remedy is to _____.

➤ hyperventilation, slow your breathing rate

4. You are cruising at 15,000 feet MSL in an unpressurized airplane. What are the oxygen requirements for crew and passengers?

➤ required minimum crew must be using supplemental oxygen; passengers do not require oxygen—only above 15,000 feet (14 CFR 91, see Chapter 24)

5. Symptoms of hypoxia are (easy/difficult) to recognize before your reactions are affected.

➤ difficult

VFR-on-Top

1. ATC (may/may not) authorise VFR-on-top operations to an IFR flight without a specific request from the pilot to operate in VFR conditions.

➤ may not

2. Does a clearance to operate IFR to VFR-on-top allow you to climb through cloud layers to reach the VFR conditions on top?

➤ yes

3. What words should an instrumented-rated pilot use to request an ATC clearance to climb through a cloud layer, or an area of reduced visibility, and then to continue the flight VFR, but still remain on an IFR plan?

➤ "IFR to VFR-on-top"

4. May you operate on a VFR-on-top clearance below a cloud layer?

➤ yes, provided VFR criteria are met

5. Must a VFR-on-top cruising altitude comply with VFR weather minimums?

➤ yes

6. Must a VFR-on-top cruising altitude comply with the appropriate VFR altitude?

➤ yes

7. Must a VFR-on-top cruising altitude also meet the minimum IFR altitude?

➤ yes

8. The VFR-on-top cruising altitude is based on:

(a) true course.

(b) magnetic course.

(c) magnetic heading.

➤ (b)

9. When flying VFR-on-top, you use (VFR/IFR) cruising altitudes.

➤ VFR

10. An appropriate VFR-on-top cruising altitude on magnetic course MC 170 is (6000/6500/7000/7500) feet MSL.

➤ 7500 feet MSL

11. An appropriate VFR-on-top cruising altitude on magnetic course MC 190 is (6000/6500/7000/7500) feet MSL.

➤ 6500 feet MSL

12. An appropriate VFR-on-top cruising altitude on MC 180 is (6000/6500/7000/7500) feet MSL.

➤ 6500 feet MSL

13. When operating VFR-on-top, (VFR/IFR/both VFR and IFR) rules apply.

➤ both VFR and IFR

14. VFR-on-top operations (are/are not) prohibited in Class A airspace.

➤ are prohibited

15. Class A airspace lies above _____ feet MSL.

➤ 18,000 feet MSL

16. You are cruising IFR on course MC 340 at a correct altitude of (16,000/16,500/ 17,000/ 17,500) feet MSL. After you request "to VFR-on-top", ATC assign you a VFR-on-top clearance at the next higher suitable altitude, which is _____ feet MSL.

➤ 16,000 feet MSL, 16,500 feet MSL

17. Can you cruise VFR-on-top on course MC 097 at FL195?

➤ no, VFR-on-top is not permitted in Class A airspace above 18,000 feet MSL

18. VFR-on-top operations (are/are not) permitted in Class D airspace.

➤ are

19. VFR-on-top operations (are/are not) permitted in Class B airspace.

➤ are

20. VFR-on-top operations (are/are not) permitted in controlled airspace.

➤ are permitted, except in Class A airspace (above 18,000 feet MSL)

21. Radio reports from an airplane on an ATC VFR-on-top clearance should be the same reports that are required for any (IFR/VFR) flight.

➤ IFR

22. VFR-on-top flights must be (above/below) the MEA, and below the _____ that begins at _____ feet MSL.

➤ above MEA, below Class A airspace, 18,000 feet MSL

DME Failure

1. If your DME fails while maintaining FL 240 or above, you (must/need not) advise ATC.

➤ must

2. If your DME fails while maintaining FL 240 or above, you (must/need not) descend to a lower altitude.

➤ need not

3. If your DME fails, you should notify ATC and you:

   (a) must land immediately.

   (b) may continue to the nearest airport where repairs can be made.

   (c) may continue to the next airport of intended landing where repairs can be made.

➤ (c)

En Route Diversions

1. EFAS stands for _____ and usually operates on frequency _____ between the hours of _____ and _____.

➤ en route flight advisory service, 122.0, 0600–2200 local time

2. The weather at your destination is below minimums, but improving. You decide to hold at a VOR 20 nm away. How would you calculate how much fuel is available for holding?

➤ see our text

3. If you are unable to accept any undue delay at the destination because of your fuel state, you should advise ATC "_____" . This (is/is not) declaration of an emergency.

➤ "minimum fuel", is not

Radio Communications Failure

1. While operating on an IFR clearance you experience 2-way radio communications failure. You are in VFR conditions. You should squawk _____. Your plan of action should be to _____.

➤ 7600; continue under VFR and land as soon as practicable

2. You are operating on an IFR flight plan in IFR conditions when you experience 2-way radio communications failure shortly after takeoff. You should squawk _____, and you (should/should not) follow the route as cleared. If you have been assigned 3000 feet and advised to expect 9000 feet, with a route segment MEA of 4000 feet, you should climb to and maintain _____ feet.

➤ 7600, should, 9000 feet

Canceling an IFR Flight Plan

1. You (must/need not) initiate the closure of your IFR flight plan after landing at an airport with no functioning control tower.

➤ must

2. Your IFR flight plan (is/is not) automatically closed after landing at an airport with a functioning control tower.

➤ is

3. You may close an IFR flight plan prior to completing the flight only in (IFR/VFR) conditions (within/outside) Class A airspace.

➤ VFR conditions outside Class A airspace

Holding Patterns, Procedure Turns & DME Arcs

There are various maneuvers that an instrument pilot must be able to perform efficiently, including:

- **holding patterns**—for delaying action in a racetrack pattern;
- **procedure turns**—for course reversal in instrument approaches; and
- **DME arcs**—for transiting from en route to final approach course.

Unless suitable fixes, radar vectoring by ATC, or a DME arc permit a direct entry into an instrument approach procedure, a positioning turn of some kind may be necessary. **Course reversals** can be made using procedure turns, teardrop turns, or by following the appropriate sector entry for a published racetrack pattern.

Holding Patterns

A **holding pattern** is a predetermined maneuver designed to keep an aircraft within a specified airspace while awaiting further clearance from ATC. Holding is a delaying action, and onward flight ceases until the airplane is cleared to proceed.

> A holding pattern is a delaying action on the part of ATC. Being asked to hold is essentially being asked to wait.

The delaying action could be required for a number of reasons, such as waiting for further en route clearance, waiting until other aircraft have commenced an ILS approach and an approach slot has become available, or waiting until a storm has moved away from the destination airport.

A holding pattern is generally a *racetrack* shape with five basic elements:

1. **the holding fix**;
2. **the holding radial or bearing**;
3. **the position of the holding pattern relative to the fix**, expressed as one of the eight cardinal points of the compass (northeast, south, etc.);
4. **the direction of turns** (usually right-hand); and
5. **the timing** (or, in the case of mileage legs, distance).

Also, the holding altitude is important, and the time at which you can expect a further clearance.

The **minimum holding altitude (MHA)** is the lowest holding altitude prescribed for a holding pattern which:

- assures navigation signal coverage;
- assures communications; and
- meets obstacle clearance requirements.

A typical holding pattern, as illustrated in Figure 28-1, uses a VOR ground station as the holding fix, the 250 radial southwest of the VOR as the holding radial (inbound leg is 070-TO the holding fix), with standard right-hand turns.

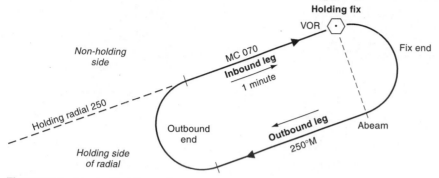

Figure 28-1. A typical holding pattern

Holding Fixes

The location of an IFR holding fix is usually specified by reference to one or more radio navaids or some other navigation device. The most common holding fixes are:

- **overhead a radio navigation aid**, such as a VOR, NDB, or the outer marker on a localizer; or
- **an intersection of two VOR radials** (a VOR/VOR fix), or a DME fix along a particular VOR radial (a VOR/DME fix).

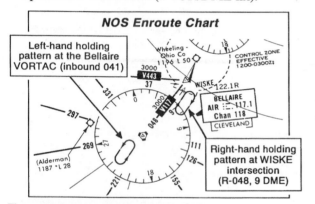

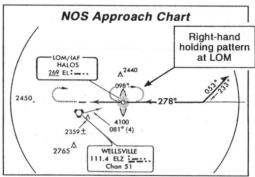

Figure 28-2. Examples of holding fixes

The Standard Holding Pattern

The standard holding pattern, as shown in Figure 28-1, has:

- **right-hand turns**; and
- **a one-minute inbound leg**.

If left-hand turns are required, then "left turns" will be specified in the ATC clearance or on the chart. If no mention is made of the direction of turns, then they are right-hand. The "1 minute" applies to holding at or below 14,000 feet MSL. Above 14,000 feet MSL, the time is extended to $1\frac{1}{2}$ minutes. It may also be extended by ATC. Some holding patterns, rather than being based on *time*, are based on *DME distance outbound*.

Published Holding Patterns

Many holding patterns are published on the en route charts and instrument approach charts as illustrated in Figure 28-2, and an ATC clearance to hold in that pattern would be given as: "cleared to (fix), hold (direction) as published." For example: "cleared to Bellaire VORTAC, hold southwest as published."

Not all holding patterns are illustrated on charts, but those that are will be in sufficient detail for you to enter and maintain correctly. They may have other chart details superimposed on them, but with experience, the holding details are easily read. Holding patterns should be flown within any time limitations or published leg length.

Non-Published Holding Patterns

If the holding pattern is not charted, ATC will issue you with holding instructions at least 5 minutes prior to reaching the fix, if possible. ATC instructions to hold will include the following information:

Never accept a holding clearance without an EFC!

- **the holding fix;**
- **the direction of holding** from the fix in terms of the eight cardinal compass points (southeast, west, northwest, etc.);
- **the radial,** course, bearing, airway or route on which the aircraft is to hold;
- **leg length** (in minutes if different to standard timing, or as a DME distance outbound);
- **direction of turn** if left-hand turns are required (otherwise right turns);
- **expect further clearance (EFC)** time, and any pertinent additional delay information.

Some typical ATC clearances to hold are:

"Cleared to the Huguenot VORTAC, hold east on the zero nine zero radial, expect further clearance at 1134."

"Cleared to the Revloc VORTAC, hold southwest on the two one zero radial, left turns, expect further clearance at 2215, anticipate additional two zero minute en route delay."

"Hold south of RUBER on the zero one niner radial of the Huguenot VORTAC, expect further clearance at 1905."

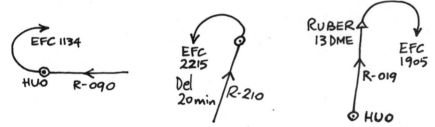

Figure 28-3. Sketching impromptu holding patterns

These improvised holding patterns sometimes cause problems for inexperienced instrument pilots but, if you develop good techniques to handle them, they will cause you no concern at all. When given a clearance to hold in a nonpublished holding pattern, you should write down the details, or sketch a diagram.

1. Start at the fix.
2. Draw the specified direction from the fix, then show an arrow on it toward the fix (the direction of the inbound leg).
3. Show the direction of turn at the fix (left turn if specified, otherwise right).
4. Note any other details (EFC, DME distance, etc.).

Speeds in Holding Patterns

The maximum speed for a propeller-driven aircraft in holding patterns at all altitudes is 175 KIAS, to ensure that it stays within protected airspace.

If you are cruising at a speed greater than 175 knots, and have not received a clearance beyond a certain limit, you are required to start a speed reduction when 3 minutes or less from the clearance limit so that you will cross the fix, initially, at or below the maximum holding speed of 175 knots. ATC will give you holding instructions at least five minutes before the fix if possible, so you should have two minutes or more to get organized before having to slow down. If ATC does not issue holding instructions or a further clearance before you reach a clearance limit, then you should hold. Enter the published holding pattern at the fix, or if there is no published holding pattern, enter a standard right-turn one-minute holding pattern.

When you advance to flying jets, the maximum holding speeds are different: from the minimum holding altitude (MHA) through 6,000 feet, 200 KIAS; above 6,000 through 14,000 feet, 230 KIAS (or 210 KIAS where published); and above 14,000 feet, 265 KIAS.

Timing in Holding Patterns

A complete one-minute holding pattern will, if flown perfectly in no-wind conditions, take four minutes. The inbound leg should be one minute at or below 14,000 feet MSL (one-and-one-half minutes above 14,000 feet MSL). The 180° standard-rate turns at either end should each take one minute, and the outbound leg, in no-wind conditions, will also take one minute—making a total of four minutes.

> It takes 4 minutes to complete one circuit of a basic holding pattern.

Normal timing of the outbound leg commences from abeam the fix outbound. If the abeam position cannot be determined, then start timing when the wings are level after rolling out of the turn, at the outbound wings-level position. In a two-minute holding pattern, the straight legs are increased to two minutes, the complete pattern then taking six minutes in no-wind conditions, and occupying more airspace.

Occasionally, the delay required during holding is less than four minutes, in which case the timing of the outbound leg can be adjusted for the airplane to arrive overhead the fix at the desired time. For instance, if you arrive at the fix inbound at 1443 UTC and have an EFC 1446, then you have only three minutes to absorb. The 180° turns at either end of the holding pattern will each take one minute, leaving only one minute to be lost in the outbound and inbound legs. In no-wind conditions, a thirty second outbound leg should give you a thirty second inbound leg, with the airplane arriving overhead the fix inbound at 1446. In windy conditions, some timing adjustment outbound will be required.

> Adjust your holding pattern legs to arrive over the fix at your EFC.

Tracking in Holding Patterns

The main tracking leg of a holding pattern is the inbound leg toward the holding fix. Normal tracking procedures are followed using the tracking aid, which may be a VOR, NDB or localizer, by applying a wind correction angle so that the desired inbound course is maintained.

Monitor the tracking periodically on the VOR cockpit indicator, or the ADF if the hold is based on an NDB. The tracking aid will act as your navigation performance instrument. Most of your attention should be on the attitude flying instruments (monitoring altitude, airspeed and heading), with an occasional scan of the navigation instruments (VOR, DME, ADF). Any adjustments to heading called for by deviations on the navigation instruments should be made with reference to the attitude indicator and the heading indicator.

The outbound turns after crossing the fix, and the inbound turn at the end of outbound leg, should be standard-rate turns, and should never exceed 30° bank angle (25° if a flight director system is used).

During the turn outbound, and on the outbound leg, there is no direct tracking aid, so you have to estimate a suitable heading. Both the turns and the outbound leg of the holding pattern are modified according to the estimated wind effect, so that the standard-rate turn to rejoin the inbound leg will bring the airplane out right on course. You should check the tracking instrument during this inbound turn to determine if you will overshoot or undershoot the inbound course, in which case you can take early corrective action.

Corrections for Wind in Holding Patterns

The aim when flying a normal holding pattern is to fly a neat pattern, and intercept an inbound leg that takes 1 minute exactly to the fix.

Aim for a neat pattern with a 1 minute inbound leg.

The initial outbound leg should be flown for 1 minute, so that the wind effect can be established on the subsequent inbound leg. The initial pattern is, more or less, a trial run so you can make timing and tracking adjustments to later patterns. It may take several patterns before you get the tracking and timing perfect.

In no-wind conditions, the ground track of the holding pattern will be a straightforward racetrack pattern, with the outbound timing commencing as the airplane passes abeam the fix, and with the outbound leg (where there is no tracking aid) simply being the reciprocal of the inbound leg and flown for one minute.

Headwinds and Tailwinds

If there is a strong tailwind outbound, however, then 1 minute outbound will carry the airplane much further than in no-wind conditions, and it will be carried even further downwind during the turn inbound. With an airspeed of 90 knots, for instance, the groundspeed will be 110 knots outbound with a 20-knot tailwind and only 70 knots inbound. The 20-knot wind acting for the 3 minutes from overhead the fix to rejoining the inbound leg will have carried the airplane an extra 1 nm downwind compared with the no-wind situation. It will be a long haul at the slower groundspeed back to the fix (well in excess of one minute), unless some correction to the outbound timing is made.

A reasonable correction is to reduce the timing of the next "1-minute" outbound leg by 2 seconds per knot of the estimated tailwind. For instance, with a 20 knot tailwind outbound, reduce the timing by 40 seconds to only 20 seconds outbound before commencing the standard-rate turn inbound. Conversely, in a strong headwind outbound, add 2 seconds per knot. The timing is commenced when abeam the fix, or when the wings are level.

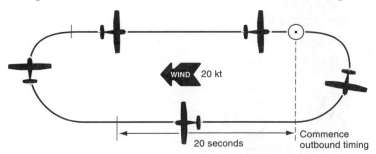

Figure 28-4. Adjust outbound timing to allow for head/tail wind

The effect of your outbound timing correction will become evident on the next inbound leg. Further timing corrections to the following outbound legs may be required to achieve the perfect one-minute inbound leg.

Another method of adjusting the timing of the outbound leg is to double the inbound time deviation from the desired one minute, and apply it appropriately to the next outbound leg. For instance, if the inbound leg takes only 45 seconds, 15 seconds short of the desired one minute, double this to 30 seconds and add it on to the next outbound leg. This will extend the outbound leg, and lengthen the inbound leg (hopefully to 1 minute exactly). Conversely, if the inbound leg took 1 minute 10 seconds, then shorten the next outbound leg by $2 \times 10 = 20$ seconds.

The correction to timing can also be found by setting the following formula on your navigation computer, when outbound again after the first pattern:

$$\frac{\text{Initial outbound time}}{\text{Initial inbound time}} = \frac{\text{Adjusted outbound time (to be found)}}{\text{Required inbound time (say 60 sec, know)}}$$

Crosswinds

In strong crosswind conditions, the airplane will tend to be carried downwind both on the straight legs and during the turns. The inbound course to the fix is the easiest part of the pattern to fly, since the inbound course has a direct tracking aid, and a suitable wind correction angle on the inbound leg can easily be found by applying normal tracking corrections to maintain the inbound course.

For both the turns and the outbound leg, however, measures to counter the wind effect can only be estimated, since they have no direct tracking aid. One turn will be downwind, the outbound leg will have a crosswind, and the other turn will be into a headwind. Common sense and a little experience, however, will enable you to handle this effectively, and to fly an outbound leg that will enable you to intercept the inbound leg with a neat standard-rate turn.

In the holding pattern illustrated below, a strong tailwind on the standard-rate turn outbound will increase its **ground radius**, the path followed over the ground. If the airplane then flies the published outbound heading without any adjustment for wind, it will be carried even further downwind. The standard-rate turn inbound, with its much smaller ground radius into the wind, will then place the airplane well short of the required inbound course, and the attempt to regain it will require a long haul back into the wind. The result is an unsatisfactory holding pattern. With some thought, however, this can be remedied.

On the outbound leg, simply applying a comparable drift allowance to that used on the inbound leg will cause the airplane to parallel the inbound leg; however it will not overcome the problem of the different ground radiuses of the turns. To allow for this, it is recommended that when a particular wind correction angle (WCA) is used on the inbound leg, you should apply a triple wind correction angle into the wind on the outbound leg, to a maximum of 30°.

Note: This is one of many techniques. Your instructor will advise his or her preferred method—many prefer only a double WCA, or even less if the outbound leg exceeds 60 seconds.

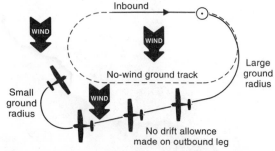

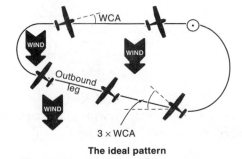

The ideal pattern

Figure 28-5. Apply 3 × WCA on the outbound leg

For instance, if an 8° WCA to the left is used inbound, then a 24° right WCA should be applied outbound. This means that the outbound heading will be modified from 270° to 294°. The standard-rate turn at the outbound end of the holding pattern should then bring the airplane back onto the required inbound course, or at least close to it.

The triple drift allowance can be thought of as:

- one drift allowance to allow for the wind effect during the outbound turn; plus
- a second drift allowance to allow for the drift on the outbound leg; plus
- a third drift allowance to allow for wind effect during the turn to the inbound leg.

If the triple drift allowance (to a maximum of 30°) results in an outbound heading within 30° of the wind direction, then there will be little drift on the outbound leg itself, in which case the correction can be reduced to a double drift allowance, $2 \times$ WCA, to allow for the wind effect only in the turns.

The success of the outbound leg drift allowance will be discovered when turning to rejoin the inbound leg. It is unlikely that it will have been perfect. If too great a correction was made, then the airplane will fly through the inbound course. Continue the turn, not exceeding standard-rate or a 30° bank angle, and make a shallow intercept of the inbound leg from the non-holding side. If the outbound wind correction was too small, then the turn inbound will have to be stopped early until the inbound course is regained.

Aim to regain the inbound course without delay, and then make suitable adjustments to tracking and timing for the next run around the pattern. It may take several complete holding patterns to get the timing and the tracking really tied down. There is protected airspace around holding patterns to allow for minor deviations, but you should always aim to be as accurate as possible.

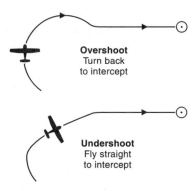

Figure 28-6. Rejoining the inbound leg

Summary of the Wind Corrections for a Holding Pattern

1. Apply a triple wind correction angle outbound, to a maximum of 30°. If the resulting outbound heading is within 30° of the wind direction, reduce it to a double WCA.

2. Reduce the outbound timing by 2 seconds per 1 knot of tailwind (and increase it by 2 seconds per knot for a headwind component), or (Method 2) double the time-deviation inbound, and apply to the next outbound leg.

Entering a Holding Pattern

There may be some maneuvering required to join a holding pattern, since an airplane can approach the holding fix from any direction. Surprisingly, entering the holding pattern is often more difficult than maintaining the pattern.

Three types of **sector entry** have been devised, based on the direction of the inbound holding course and an imaginary line angled at 70° to it, from the fix and cutting the outbound leg at about one-third of its length. How the airplane joins the pattern depends on the heading of the airplane as it initially approaches the holding fix.

There are 3 standard holding entries: parallel, teardrop and direct. You may, however, enter the hold any way you please, as long as you stay within the protected area.

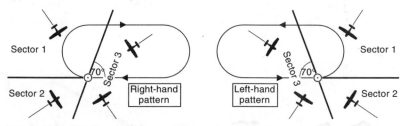

Figure 28-7. The three sectors

A Sector 1 Entry is a Parallel Entry

- Fly to the fix and turn to an outbound heading to parallel the inbound course. Do not backtrack on it—just fly parallel to it on the non-holding side for a period of 1 minute.
- Turn in the direction of the holding side through more than 180° to either intercept the inbound leg or return to the fix (you will actually cut across the inbound leg, and re-intercept it from the holding side).
- On reaching the fix, turn to follow the holding pattern.

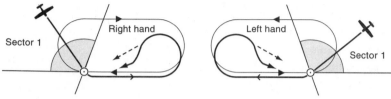

Figure 28-8. The Sector 1 parallel entry

A Sector 2 Entry is a Teardrop Entry

- Fly to the fix and turn to a heading for a 30° teardrop, to make good a track within the pattern (on the holding side) at 30° to the reciprocal of the inbound leg for a period of one minute.
- Turn in the direction of the holding pattern to intercept the inbound leg.
- Track to the fix, and proceed with normal holding patterns.

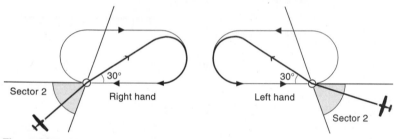

Figure 28-9. The Sector 2 teardrop entry

A Sector 3 Entry is a Direct Entry

- Fly to the fix and turn to follow the holding pattern
- If a full 180° turn (or greater) is required to take up the outbound heading, then commence turning immediately you reach overhead the fix. If, however, the turn to the outbound leg is less than 180°, then hold heading for an appropriate time past the fix before commencing the standard-rate turn. For instance, if the turn is less than 180° by 45° (which at standard-rate of 3° per second would take 15 seconds), maintain the original heading for 15 seconds before turning.

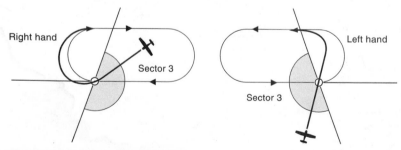

Figure 28-10. The Sector 3 direct entry

Entering a holding pattern correctly and efficiently, and at the right speed (175 KIAS or less for propeller-driven aircraft), is a sign of a good instrument pilot. Holding patterns often precede an instrument approach, so a good holding pattern, including the entry, is a good start to the approach.

You should report at the holding fix and your altitude as you fly over it initially. You should also report leaving the holding fix as you depart the holding pattern having received a further clearance.

How to Determine the Sector Entry

There are two simple methods of determining which sector entry to use when joining a holding pattern—one method using a chart, the other visualizing the entry on the heading indicator.

Method (a). On a chart. This method involves sketching the allocated holding pattern on your chart, placing the 70° line over the fix and the one-third point of the outbound leg, and then determining your sector entry. This is the traditional method shown in the previous figures.

Method (b). Using the heading indicator (HI). It is easy to visualize the entry using the heading indicator as you approach the holding fix. First, imagine the holding fix to be at the center of the HI. For the standard **right-hand holding pattern**, place your right thumb on the HI and imagine a line sloping up to the right at the 70° position relative to your heading. The teardrop sector is immediately above your thumb; (Thumb = Teardrop). If the inbound course of the holding pattern lies:

1. Ahead to the left—a Sector 1 parallel entry.

2. Ahead to the right—a Sector 2 teardrop entry.

3. Behind—a Sector 3 direct entry.

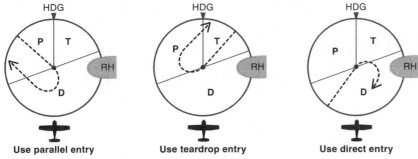

Use parallel entry   **Use teardrop entry**   **Use direct entry**

Figure 28-11. Visualizing the sector entry on the HI—standard right-hand pattern

Note: The easiest way to determine in which sector the inbound course lies is to note where the outbound course from the holding fix is. For instance, if the inbound course of the holding pattern is MC 060, then look for its reciprocal 240 on the HI.

For the nonstandard **left-hand holding pattern**, the situation ahead is simply reversed. Place your left thumb on the HI and imagine a line sloping up to the left at the 70° position relative to your heading. The teardrop sector is immediately above your thumb; (Thumb = Teardrop). If the inbound course of the holding pattern lies:

1. Ahead to the right—a Sector 1 parallel entry.

2. Ahead to the left—a Sector 2 teardrop entry.

3. Behind—a Sector 3 direct entry.

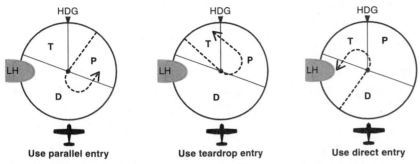

Use parallel entry **Use teardrop entry** **Use direct entry**

Figure 28-12. Visualizing the sector entry on the HI—nonstandard left-hand pattern

Holding at an NDB

Many holding patterns use an NDB or locator as the holding fix. In Figure 28-13, typical ADF indications are shown as the pilot initially tracks to the NDB, and then joins the holding pattern.

Passage over the NDB is indicated by the ADF needle swinging from ahead to behind.

Timing on the outbound leg should begin abeam the fix. If you cannot determine the abeam position, then commence timing at the wings-level position at completion of the outbound turn.

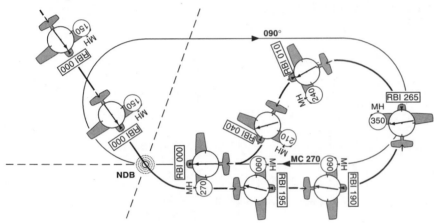

Figure 28-13. Making a Sector 1 entry using the ADF

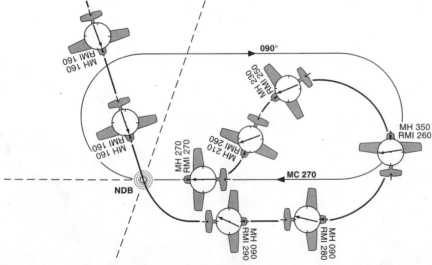

Figure 28-14. Making the same Sector 1 entry using an RMI

Holding at a VOR

Many holding patterns use a VOR ground station as the fix. In Figure 28-15, typical VOR cockpit indications are shown as the pilot initially tracks to the VOR ground station, and then joins the racetrack holding pattern.

Passing overhead the fix will be indicated by the first complete reversal of the TO-FROM flag.

While not essential, you may track out on the teardrop entry with the appropriate radial selected in the OBS. What is essential, however, is that you must select the inbound course in the OBS throughout the holding pattern.

Timing of the outbound leg should commence at the abeam fix position, indicated by the TO-FROM flag changing from FROM to TO, provided the inbound course is selected in the OBS.

Remember that when flying outbound in the pattern you will be flying a heading, and not tracking on a radial. When outbound, the VOR indicator will show reverse commands (since it has the inbound course selected in the OBS), with the CDI on the opposite side of the instrument to the inbound course.

When turning inbound, however, you will be heading in the same direction as the course selected in the OBS, and so the VOR indicator will be a command display. The usual VOR cockpit indicator is not heading-sensitive, hence the reverse commands outbound; if you are lucky enough to have an HSI, then the slaved compass card will make it a command instrument throughout the whole pattern.

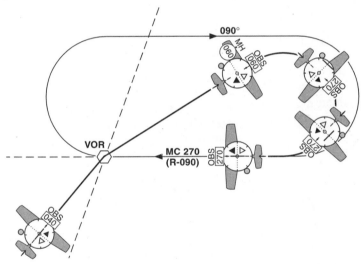

Figure 28-15. Making a Sector 2 entry using the VOR

Holding at a VOR/VOR Fix

Holding at a fix defined by two VOR radials, as many intersections are, is made easier if you have two VOR sets in the cockpit.

- **Use VOR-1** to track on the desired course, which may be an airway; and
- **Select VOR-2** to the crossing radial that pinpoints the fix. When its CDI centers, you are at the fix.

If you select the crossing radial (*from* the VOR, rather than the bearing to the station) on VOR-2, the CDI will be on the *same side* as the ground station as you approach the radial, will center, and then move to the other side as you pass the radial.

It may be difficult to determine the abeam position outbound in this pattern, since you are abeam an intersection rather than a ground station, in which case you can start the outbound timing from wings-level on the outbound heading.

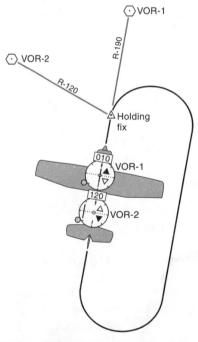

Figure 28-16. Holding at an intersection using two VORs

Ensure that you copy the holding instructions accurately: "Cleared to Avery intersection, hold southwest on Victor-One-Two-Three" is a different clearance from "Cleared to Avery intersection, hold northeast on Victor-One-Two-Three."

After crossing the fix initially, select the OBS to the inbound course of the holding pattern. If you are holding toward the VOR, the TO flag will show throughout the pattern. If you are holding away from the VOR, the FROM flag will show throughout the pattern.

With only one VOR cockpit display, holding at a fix defined by radials from two different VOR ground facilities becomes a little more difficult, with switching between VORs necessary.

When established on the course to the fix using the *tracking* VOR, and approaching the fix, select the frequency of the second VOR and set the *intersecting* radial in the OBS.

When the CDI centers, you are at the fix, and can start the standard-rate turn to the outbound leg.

There is no need to reselect the tracking VOR and the inbound course until you are about to turn inbound. Then, having established the airplane on the inbound course, and being certain of tracking overhead (or close to the fix) by the tracking CDI remaining centered, reselect the second VOR and its radial to determine the fix.

Repeating the procedure amounts to only two re-selections every pattern.

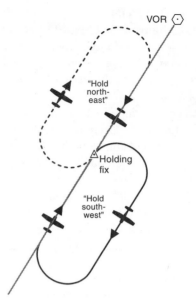

Figure 28-17. Holding toward, and away from, a VOR at an intersection

Holding at a VOR/DME Fix

A holding fix can also be specified using a DME distance along a particular VOR radial. Many intersections are determined in this manner.

In a **DME hold**, the controller will specify the length of the outbound leg that you should fly, rather than specifying an inbound time. If the fix distance is 15 DME, and the specified leg length is 5 nm, then you would turn outbound at the 15 DME holding fix, and commence your turn inbound at:

• 20 DME if the inbound holding course is *toward* the VOR; or

• 10 DME if the inbound holding course is *away* from the VOR).

Use the 7-Ts at each turn to ensure that all appropriate tasks are completed. *Time–turn–twist–tracking–throttle–talk–think.* **While you should consider all of the Ts, some of them need not be actioned in a holding pattern, such as** *twist***, because the OBS will remain the same right around the pattern.**

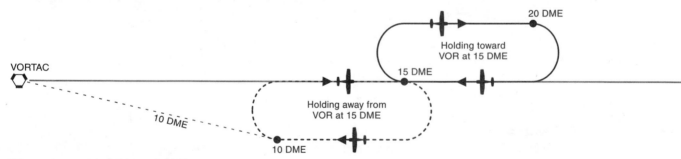

Figure 28-18. Holding at a VOR/DME fix

Holding at an ILS Outer Marker

This method of holding is often shown on ILS approach charts.

The inbound course to the holding fix is the localizer (supported by the locator NDB if needed), with the fix being defined by passage over the outer marker or locator. (See Figure 28-19.)

Because the localizer CDI is four times as sensitive as the VOR CDI, the locator NDB can prove useful when intercepting the inbound course, since close in to the airport the CDI may move from the full-scale position with a rush, whereas the ADF needle will move progressively and continually show position.

Timed Approaches from a Holding Fix

At busy airports, ATC may use timed approaches by assigning each pilot in an approach sequence a time to depart the holding fix inbound. For nonprecision approaches (VOR, NDB), the holding fix may be the final approach fix (FAF).

For precision approaches (ILS), the holding fix may be the outer marker, or a fix used in lieu of the outer marker. Nonradar procedures or radar vectors may be used by ATC.

When given a time to leave the holding fix, you should adjust the timing of the last outbound leg to leave the fix inbound as closely as possible to the designated time. Normally the preceding aircraft will be two minutes ahead of you, and the one to follow you will be given a time two minutes behind you.

The normal separation is 2 minutes or 5 miles, which will be extended to 3 minutes or 6 miles for a small aircraft behind a heavy aircraft. If a number of aircraft are holding in a stack, they will be descended progressively by ATC as the lower levels in the pattern are vacated.

Adjust the timing of the last outbound leg to leave the fix inbound at the designated time

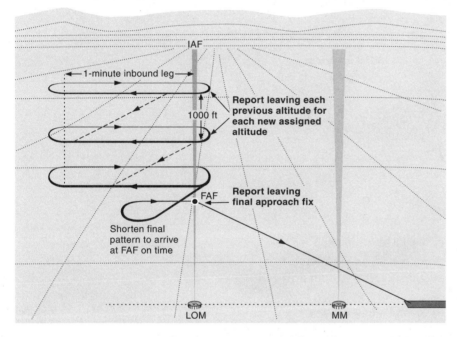

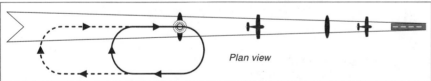

Figure 28-19. Separation on approach and landing using timed approaches

Timed approaches will only be conducted under the following conditions:

1. A control tower is in operation.
2. Direct ATC/pilot communications are maintained.
3. If more than one missed approach procedure is available, none require a course reversal.
4. If only one missed approach procedure is available, course reversal is not required, and the reported ceiling and visibility are equal to or better than the highest prescribed circling minimums for the approach.
5. When cleared for the approach, the pilot shall *not* make a procedure turn.

Procedure Turns

A procedure turn is a common maneuver used for course reversal, and is often used to position an airplane on the intermediate approach segment or final approach course of an instrument approach to land.

The maximum speed in a procedure turn is not greater than 250 KIAS, and the maneuver should normally be completed within 10 nm of the procedure turn fix (or as published on the individual chart). This is commonly known as the **procedure turn limit.** The procedure turn fix can be identified on the profile view of the approach as the point where the instrument approach procedure begins.

The 45°/180° Procedure Turn

The 45° procedure turn is the course reversal procedure most commonly shown on instrument approach charts. It is the maneuver used to reverse the direction of an airplane flying outbound, and to establish it inbound on the intermediate or final approach course.

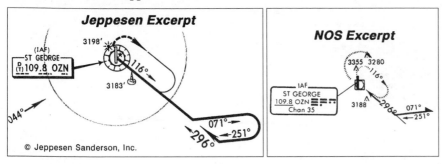

Figure 28-20. The 45° procedure turn

The 45° procedure turn consists of:

- an outbound track from the fix (normally for one or two minutes);
- a turn of 45° away from the outbound track (usually held for one minute from the start of the turn, plus or minus wind correction in terms of both drift and time);
- a 180° turn in the opposite direction, to intercept the inbound track.

Left or right in a description of the procedure turn refers to the direction of the initial turn.

The 80°/260° Procedure Turn

The 80° procedure turn may be used in lieu of the 45° procedure turn although, for various reasons, it is a less common method in the U.S. It consists of:

- an outbound course away from the fix;
- a turn of 80° away from the outbound course in the prescribed direction;
- followed almost immediately by a 260° turn in the opposite direction to intercept the inbound course.

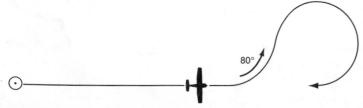

Figure 28-21. The 80° procedure turn

If the initial turn is into a strong headwind, then the 80° heading can be held for a brief time (an extra 1 second per knot of headwind), before the 260° turn is commenced.

If the initial turn puts a strong tailwind behind the airplane, then stop turning before 80° is reached, and gently roll immediately into the reversal turn.

The Base Turn, or Teardrop Turn

The base turn, used to reverse direction by more than 180°, is a teardrop pattern which consists of:

- a specified outbound course and timing or distance;
- followed by a turn to intercept the inbound course.

A teardrop procedure, or penetration turn, is sometimes used to permit an aircraft to reverse direction and lose considerable altitude within reasonably limited airspace. It may consist of departure from an initial approach fix on an outbound course, followed by a turn toward and intercepting the inbound course prior to the intermediate fix or point (see Figure 28-22).

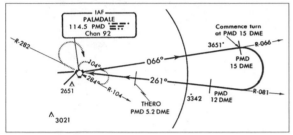

Figure 28-22. A base turn (NOS chart)

A standard-rate turn in slower aircraft may result in too small a radius of turn, and a short straight leg might be required in the middle of the turn, before continuing the turn to intercept the inbound course.

Positioning in a Racetrack Pattern

Many instrument approaches commence at the holding fix, and simply by carrying out a sector entry into the holding pattern, the airplane is in position to commence the approach.

When a holding pattern replaces the procedure turn, the standard entry and the holding pattern must be followed, except when radar vectoring is provided or when NoPt is shown on the approach course.

If there is any delay in approval to commence the approach, however, or if you need to lose excess altitude, the airplane can remain in the holding pattern (with ATC approval).

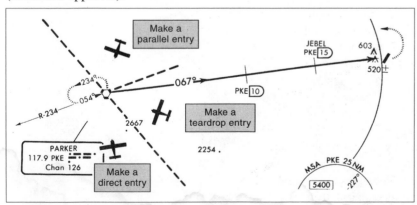

Figure 28-23. Positioning in a holding pattern (NOS chart)

DME Arcs

A DME arc is a curved maneuver flown at a specific distance from the DME ground facility. It is usually flown as a series of short straight legs, rather than as a steady curve. The DME arc is often used to transition from the en route phase of a flight to the intermediate approach segment or final approach course of an instrument approach to land. DME arcs are also used in some Departure Procedures (DPs).

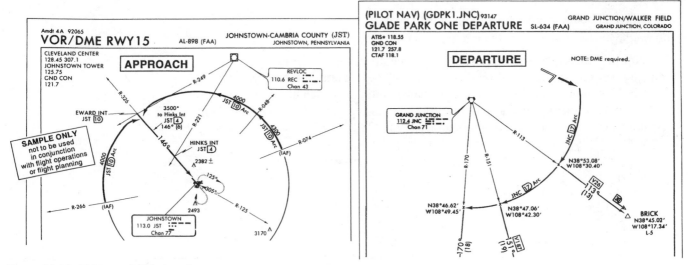

Figure 28-24. DME arcs (NOS charts)

Intercepting a DME Arc

If you are tracking directly to a VOR/DME ground facility, then you will have to turn 90° to intercept the DME arc. Commencing the 90° turn with just under 1 nm to run to the arc should give you an accurate intercept, to join the 10 DME arc, start turning at about 10.5 DME. The heading to use can be easily read off the VOR indicator or the HSI 90° wingtip position prior to commencing the turn.

Maintaining a DME Arc Using an RMI or ADF

The easiest way to maintain a DME arc is to use an RMI (or an ADF if appropriate), by keeping the needle approximately on the wingtip, and flying a series of short straight legs, keeping the DME distance within the required limits. The protected airspace of a DME arc is the same as an airway, extending 4 nm either side of the arc, but you should aim to stay within 1 nm of the specified arc.

If the airplane flies a straight path tangential to the arc, it will fly away from it, the DME distance will increase, and the needle will fall behind the wingtip. As the needle falls to 10° behind the wingtip, turn 20° in the direction of the arc, which will place the needle 10° ahead of the wingtip.

Then fly a constant heading until the needle falls behind the wingtip again, and repeat the procedure. The DME distance will decrease slightly as you fly abeam the ground station, and then increase again. Make your turns so that the DME arc accuracy is met. If anything, a DME arc is easier to maintain if you are a little on the inside of it, since a straight path will tend to increase the distance and bring you back onto the arc, whereas if you are on the outside of it and do not make a correcting turn, you will fly further away from the arc.

Having conquered the DME arc with 20° heading changes, you might like to try holding it more accurately with only 10° heading changes, from 5° ahead of the wingtip reference to 5° behind it. A good way to practice DME arcs is to fly part of a 12 DME arc around a VORTAC in one direction, turn and fly an 11 DME arc in the other direction, followed by progressively smaller arcs in alternating directions.

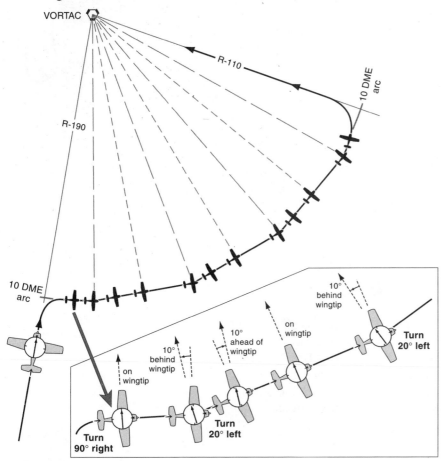

Figure 28-25. Flying a DME arc

Allowing for Wind in a DME Arc

If there is any crosswind, then a wind correction angle into the wind will be required, and the abeam reference will need to be either a little ahead of the wingtip (if the wind is from within the arc), or a little behind the wingtip if the wind is from outside the arc. The wind effect will change as your heading changes. Monitor DME distance and keep it within limits with appropriate turns. See Figure 28-26.

Maintaining a DME arc Using the VOR Indicator

To use a normal VOR cockpit display to maintain a DME arc, the easier method is to select the radial 10° ahead of the current position, just giving full-scale CDI deflection on the same side as the VOR ground facility.

As you approach the selected radial, the CDI will center, and then move to full-scale deflection on the side away from the arc. Make a 20° correction turn in the direction of the arc, and select a new radial 20° further on, causing the CDI to move to full-scale on the inside of the arc.

Monitor the DME distance and keep it within limits with appropriate turns. For each deviation of $^1/_2$ nm outside the arc, a correction of 10–20° toward the arc should be sufficient.

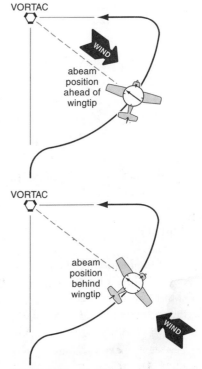

Figure 28-26. Allowing for a crosswind in a DME arc

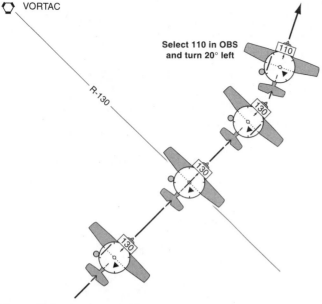

○ VORTAC

Select 110 in OBS
and turn 20° left

R-130

110

130

130

130

Figure 28-27. Maintaining a DME arc using VOR indicator

Intercepting the Approach Radial from a DME Arc

As you move around the arc, you will eventually approach the inbound radial. On a 10 DME arc, commencing the intercept turn 5° before reaching the required radial is generally sufficient (at half-scale deflection if using a VOR) for you to roll out right on the inbound course. Closer in than 10 DME, or if traveling at high speed, you should increase the lead angle. Some charts specify a lead-in radial to the inbound course as guidance. You may like to vary this depending on your airspeed and the wind-effect. Tracking inbound, you should set the inbound course with the OBS so that the VOR indicator is a command instrument.

☞ Review 28

Holding Patterns, Procedure Turns & DME Arcs

1. The shape of a typical holding pattern is a:
   (a) circle. (b) racetrack. (c) rectangle. (d) ellipse.

   ➤ (b)

2. A complete 1-minute holding pattern will take _____ minutes if flown perfectly in no-wind conditions.

   ➤ 4 minutes

3. In strong head/tailwind conditions on the outbound leg of a holding pattern, the timing should be adjusted by _____ second per knot of the estimated head/ tailwind component.

   ➤ 2 seconds per knot

4. With an estimated 15-knot tailwind component on the outbound leg of a holding pattern, it is reasonable to adjust the timing by _____.

   ➤ reducing the 60 seconds by half, and flying outbound for 30 seconds

5. While tracking guidance is usually available to you on the inbound leg to the holding fix, on the outbound leg there generally is none. In strong crosswind conditions, it is suggested that a correction of _____ be applied on the outbound leg.

   ➤ triple the wind correction angle

6. If a 5° WCA to the left is required to track correctly on the inbound leg of a holding pattern, then a suitable correction on the outbound leg is _____.

➤ 15° right

7. Sketch three diagrams of a holding pattern showing the three sector entries.

➤ refer to our text

8. A Sector 1 entry is also known as a _____ entry.

➤ parallel entry

9. A Sector 2 entry is also known as a _____ entry.

➤ teardrop entry

10. A Sector 3 entry is also known as a _____ entry.

➤ direct entry

11. Sketch the pattern of a 45°/180° procedure turn used to reverse direction.

➤ refer to our text

12. Refer to Figure 1. You arrive at the 15 DME fix steering MH 350 with an ATC clearance to: "Hold west of the one five DME fix on the zero eight six radial of the XYZ VORTAC, five mile legs, left turns". The correct procedure is to join holding pattern (A/B) using a (parallel/direct/teardrop) entry, with an initial turn after passing the fix (left/right) to MH _____.

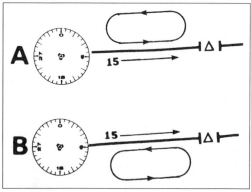

Figure 1.

➤ pattern A (because the holding fix is always at the end of the inbound leg), direct entry, MH 266

13. Refer to Figure 2. You arrive at the 15 DME fix steering MH 250 with an ATC clearance to: "Hold west of the one five DME fix on the two six eight radial of the DEF VORTAC, five mile legs, left turns".
The correct procedure is to join holding pattern (A/B) using a (parallel/direct/teardrop) entry, with an initial turn after passing the fix (left/right) to MH _____.

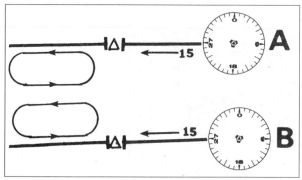

Figure 2.

➤ B (because the holding fix is always at the end of the inbound leg), parallel entry, MH 268

14. The timing for the first leg outbound in a nonstandard holding pattern should commence when (starting the turn outbound from overhead the fix/abeam the fix).

➤ abeam the fix

15. If the position abeam the holding fix cannot be determined, you should commence timing when _____ after turning outbound.

➤ the wings are level

16. To ensure proper airspace protection, the recommended maximum speed in a holding pattern is _____ KIAS for propeller-driven aircraft.

➤ 175 KIAS

17. The recommended maximum speed in a holding pattern above 14,000 feet MSL is _____ KIAS for propeller-driven aircraft (and if you are flying a jet _____ KIAS).

➤ 175 KIAS (265 KIAS)

18. The recommended maximum speed for a jet in a holding pattern below 14,000 feet MSL is _____ KIAS. The lowest holding altitude that provides adequate protection is known as the (MHA/MSA/MEA), which stands for _____.

➤ 230 KIAS (210 where published), MHA, minimum holding altitude

---

Refer to Figure 3 for Questions 19–23.

Figure 3.

19. A pilot receives this ATC clearance: "cleared to the Point Reyes VORTAC, hold west on the two seven zero radial." The pattern will be (left/right) turns. The inbound leg of the holding pattern is MC_____. (to/away from) the fix. What is the recommended procedure to enter the holding pattern? The first turn after crossing the VOR should be (left/right) to approximately MH _____.

➤ right, 090-TO, direct, right to MH 270

---

20. A pilot receives this ATC clearance: "cleared to the Point Reyes VORTAC, hold north on the three six zero radial, left turns." The pattern will be (left/right) turns. The inbound leg of the holding pattern is MC _____ (to/away from) the fix. What is the recommended procedure to enter the holding pattern? The first turn after crossing the VOR should be (left/right) to approximately MH _____.

➤ left, 180-TO, direct, left to MH 360

---

21. When established in a holding pattern at an NDB, the timing outbound should begin _____.

➤ abeam the fix

---

22. When established in a holding pattern at a VOR, the timing outbound should begin _____.

➤ abeam the fix

---

23. A pilot receives this ATC clearance: "cleared to the Point Reyes VORTAC, hold south on the one eight zero radial." The pattern will be (left/right) turns. The inbound leg of the holding pattern is MC _____ (to/away from) the fix. What is the recommended procedure to enter the holding pattern? The first turn after crossing the VOR should be (left/right) to approximately MH _____.

➤ right, 360-TO, teardrop, right to MH 180 (the outbound heading)

Refer to Figure 4 for Questions 24–27.

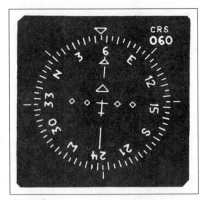

Figure 4.

24. A pilot receives this ATC clearance: "hold east of the Dingo VOR on the zero niner zero radial, left turns." The pattern will be (left/right) turns. The inbound leg of the holding pattern is MC _____ (to/away from) the fix. What is the recommended procedure to enter the holding pattern? The first turn after crossing the VOR should be (left/right) to approximately MH _____.

➤ left, 270-TO, parallel, right to MH 090

---

25. A pilot receives this ATC clearance: "hold south of the Dingo VOR on the one eight zero radial." The pattern will be (left/right) turns. The inbound leg of the holding pattern is MC _____ (to/away from) the fix. What is the recommended procedure to enter the holding pattern? The first turn after crossing the VOR should be (left/right) to approximately MH _____.

➤ right, 360-TO, direct, right to MH 180

---

26. A pilot receives this ATC clearance: "hold north of the Dingo VOR on the three six zero radial, left turns." The pattern will be (left/right) turns. The inbound leg of the holding pattern is MC _____ (to/away from) the fix. What is the recommended procedure to enter the holding pattern? The first turn after crossing the VOR should be (left/right) to approximately MH _____.

➤ left, 180-TO, teardrop, left to MH 030

27. A pilot receives this ATC clearance: "cleared to the Dingo VOR, hold west on the two seven zero radial." The pattern will be (left/right) turns. The inbound leg of the holding pattern is MC _____ (to/away from) the fix. What is the recommended procedure to enter the holding pattern? The first turn after crossing the VOR should be (left/right) to approximately MH _____.

➤ right, 090-TO, direct, right to MH 270

Refer to Figure 5 for Questions 28–30.

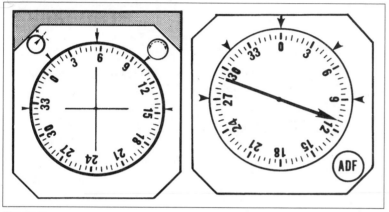

Figure 5.

28. You receive this ATC clearance: "cleared to the Gaffa NDB, hold southwest on the two three zero degree bearing." At station passage, you note the indications as shown in the figure. The pattern will be (left/right) turns. The inbound leg of the holding pattern is MC _____ (to/away from) the fix. What is the recommended procedure to enter the holding pattern? The first turn after crossing the NDB should be (left/right) to approximately MH _____.

➤ right, 050-TO, direct, right to MH 230

29. You receive this ATC clearance: "cleared to the Gaffa NDB, hold northeast on the zero four zero degree bearing, left turns." At station passage, you note the indications as shown in the figure. The pattern will be (left/right) turns. The inbound leg of the holding pattern is MC _____ (to/away from) the fix. What is the recommended procedure to enter the holding pattern? The first turn after crossing the NDB should be (left/right) to approximately MH _____.

➤ left, 220-TO, teardrop, right to MH 070

30. You receive this ATC clearance: "cleared to the Gaffa NDB, hold southeast on the one four zero degree bearing, left turns." At station passage, you note the indications as shown in Figure 5. The pattern will be (left/right) turns. The inbound leg of the holding pattern is MC _____ (to/away from) the fix. What is the recommended procedure to enter the holding pattern? The first turn after crossing the VOR should be (left/right) to approximately MH _____.

➤ left, 320-TO, parallel, right to MH 140

31. Adjustments in timing of each holding pattern are made on the (outbound/inbound) leg.

➤ outbound

32. Where a holding pattern is specified in lieu of a procedure turn, the holding maneuver must be executed within the _____ minute time limitation or the published leg length. The maneuver is considered completed when established inbound.

➤ 1 min or published leg length

33. For a timed approach from a holding fix, a control tower (must/need not) be in operation.

➤ must

34. For a timed approach from a holding fix, there (must/need not) be direct communication between the pilot and ATC.

➤ must

35. For a timed approach from a holding fix, if there is more than one missed approach procedure, then there (may/must not) be any course reversal required.

➤ must not

36. When making a timed approach from a holding fix at the outer marker, the pilot should leave the (final approach fix/holding fix/initial approach fix) inbound at the assigned time. The holding pattern (may/must not) be adjusted to achieve this.

➤ final approach fix, may

37. For a timed approach from a holding fix, the pilot (need not/must) be in communications with the tower.

➤ need not—he must be in contact with ATC, which may be center or approach control, before switching to the tower

38. For a timed approach from a holding fix with only one missed approach procedure available, the reported ceiling and visibility minimums must be (lower/equal to or greater) than the prescribed (straight-in/circling) minimums for the instrument approach procedure.

➤ equal to or greater, circling

39. If you are far too high to commence an approach for which you have been cleared, excess altitude (may/may not) be lost in the holding pattern.

➤ may

40. A procedure turn is a common maneuver used for course _____.

➤ reversal

41. A procedure turn should normally be completed within _____ nm of the procedure turn fix, or as otherwise published on the instrument approach chart.

➤ 10 nm

42. To maintain a right-hand DME arc with no cross-wind component, the bearing pointer should be (on/ahead of/behind) the right wingtip.

➤ on

43. To maintain a right-hand DME arc with a right crosswind component, the bearing pointer should be (on/ahead of/behind) the right wingtip.

➤ ahead of

44. To maintain a right-hand DME arc with a left crosswind component, the bearing pointer should be (on/ahead of/behind) the right wingtip.

➤ behind

45. For each $1/2$ nm you have drifted outside a DME arc, a suitable heading change is approximately _____ to _____ degrees (toward/away from) the arc.

➤ 10–20°, toward

46. Course reversal or positioning to commence an instrument approach can (sometimes/never) be achieved by entering an appropriate holding pattern.

➤ sometimes

47. You are required to hold at an intersection, with an EFC time of 1245. At 1238 you experience a 2-way radio communications failure. What action should you take with your transponder? At what time should you depart the holding fix? In IFR conditions you should (return to departure airport/continue on cleared route).

➤ squawk 7600; 1245; continue on cleared route

Instrument Approaches 29

Arrivals

Arrival planning should begin early in the cruise, so that your descent and arrival in the terminal area is at the correct speed and altitude, with you in a relaxed, but alert, condition. Appropriate charts should be close at hand.

Before beginning a descent, you must consider conditions at the planned destination airport to determine if an approach is desirable. Thunderstorms over the airport, reported windshear, contaminated runways or a crosswind well above the maximum for your airplane might encourage you to divert from cruise altitude to the alternate. Standing water or slush on a runway will cause poor or nonexistent braking, and possibly *hydroplaning*, where the tire does not contact the runway, but glides along the water/slush surface. Do not land in hydroplaning conditions.

To calculate a descent point, you may work backward from the approach and landing. Start by obtaining the airport information—ATIS (automatic terminal information service) or an automated weather observing system (AWOS or ASOS) at the airport. To begin an ILS at 3000 feet some 10 nm the other side of the airport adds distance to your route, and so your descent may be delayed compared with descent for a straight-in approach from an en route segment.

You should commence descent promptly following a descent clearance unless it is qualified by "at pilot discretion." The normal descent procedure is to maintain the optimum descent rate, reducing it to 500–1500 fpm for the last 1000 feet. If you are flying an unpressurized airplane, then 500 fpm throughout the whole descent is a reasonable rate that should not harm any eardrums. As an example of descent planning, losing 6000 feet at 500 fpm takes 12 minutes which, if your groundspeed is 120 knots (2 nm per minute), will require 24 nm.

ATC requirements may, of course, lead to a descent different from that planned. ATC may require speed adjustments, which you should maintain as closely as possible, but certainly within ±10 knots, and also altitude and tracking adjustments. You may have to track using pilot navigation with radio navaids onto the final approach course, or you may receive radar vectors if the airport is in a radar environment. You may also have to hold, and perhaps become one aircraft in a series of timed approaches from a holding fix. Allow yourself some flexibility to cope with reasonable unexpected variations.

If making a VFR practice instrument approach and ATC assigns a heading or altitude that will take you into clouds, then avoid the clouds, remain VFR and advise ATC that the assigned altitude or heading will not permit VFR.

Standard Terminal Arrival Routes (STARs)

STARs are published in textual and diagrammatic form to simplify clearance delivery to IFR arrivals at some airports. A STAR is a published IFR arrival procedure that provides transition from the en route structure to a fix or waypoint in the terminal area leading into the instrument approach. ATC may issue a STAR without a specific pilot request; if you do not want a STAR, advise ATC, preferably by writing "No STAR" in the remarks section of your flight plan.

Plan your arrival long before you reach your destination.

VFR practice approaches are just that, VFR. Do not accept headings or altitudes that will take you into IMC. Request amended instructions from ATC.

To accept a STAR, you must have at least a textual description in the cockpit. If not, ATC may still issue you with an arrival clearance identical to the STAR, but they will have to read it out in full.

STARs are found alphabetically in a group at the front of the applicable NOS *Terminal Procedures* booklet, and are included with the other instrument charts for that particular airport in the *Jeppesen* airway manual.

Shown here is the DINGO standard terminal arrival route at Tucson, Arizona, with the Gila Bend transition. It is written as "GBN.DINGO 4". The actual arrival begins overhead DINGO, with the Gila Bend transition providing the routing from the en route phase of the flight to DINGO. Flown properly, and with good pilot/controller cooperation, this STAR will lead you to the TUS Rwy 11 ILS at the ideal commencement altitude.

STARs are *not* approach clearances, so you must not descend below the last assigned altitude until you receive an approach clearance and are on a published segment for that approach.

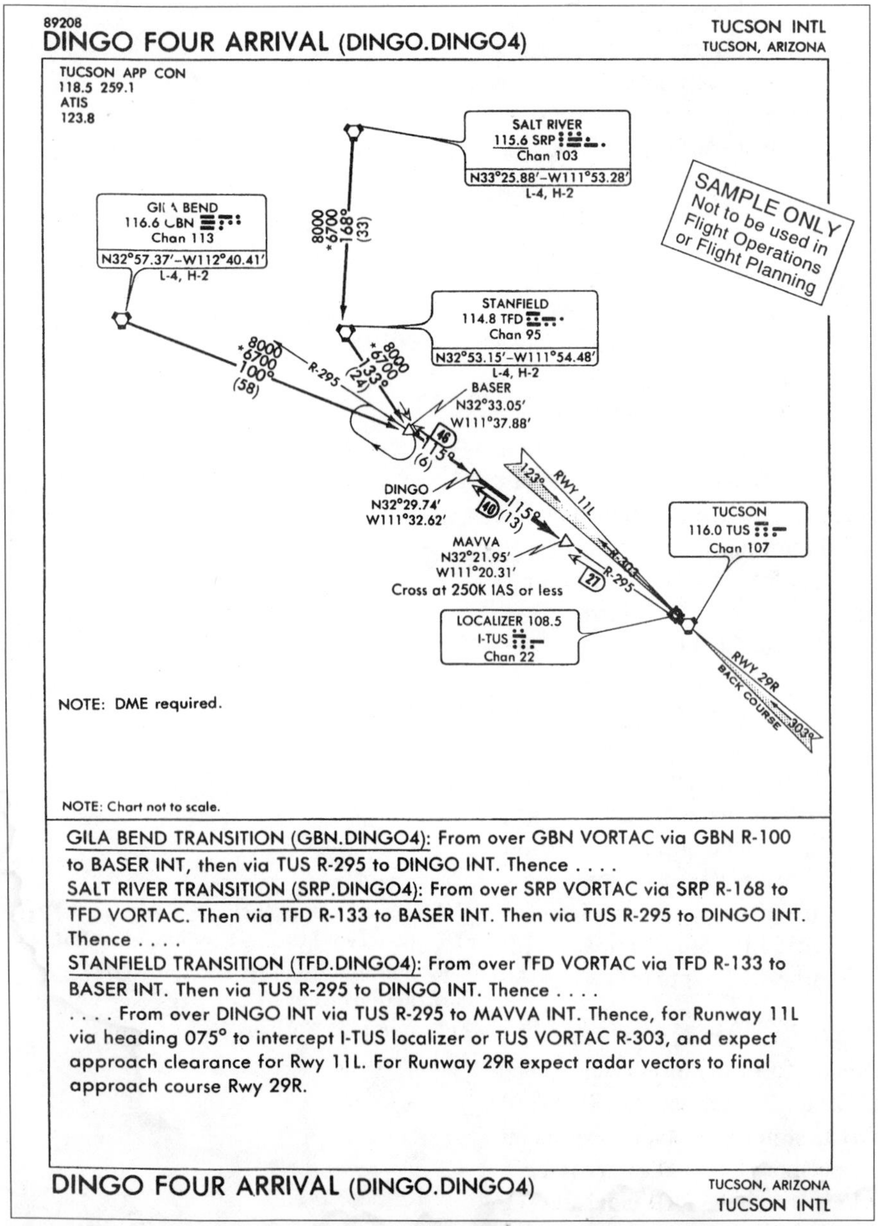

To accept a STAR, you must have at least a textual description in the cockpit.

Figure 29-1. NOS chart for DINGO STAR at Tucson, Arizona, with the Gila Bend transition

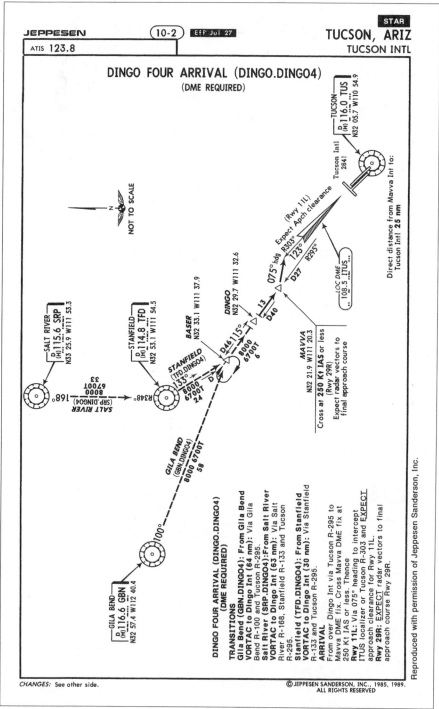

Figure 29-2. *Jeppesen* chart for DINGO STAR at Tucson, Arizona (reduced)

Vertical Navigation

Correct vertical navigation is vital during instrument flight when terrain, obstacles and other airplanes may not be seen. Vertical navigation is based mainly on the indications of the altimeter, therefore the correct altimeter setting is most important. It is so important that each new subscale setting advised by ATC, and its location, should be read back by the pilot as confirmation. The datum for vertical navigation is mean sea level, and the correct altimeter setting in the pressure window causes the correct altitude MSL to be indicated.

Read back all altimeter settings for confirmation.

The Instrument Approach

Having arrived in instrument conditions at the initial approach fix (IAF), the airplane is then in a position to commence the instrument approach. Delaying action, if necessary, can be taken by entering a holding pattern if cleared by ATC.

When an instrument approach is designed by an airplane performance specialist, the first consideration is the final approach course to the runway for a straight-in procedure, or to the airport for a circle-to-land procedure. The procedure is then designed backward from this desirable final approach course through a number of segments, with the aim of providing a suitable flightpath between the en route phase of the flight and final approach. Generally, the fewer the turns and the less complicated the approach, the better it is for the pilot and for ATC.

The Segments of an Instrument Approach

The complete instrument approach procedure (IAP) may be divided into up to five separate segments that blend into each other. They are:

1. arrival segment, or feeder route;
2. initial approach segment;
3. intermediate approach segment;
4. final approach segment; and
5. missed approach segment.

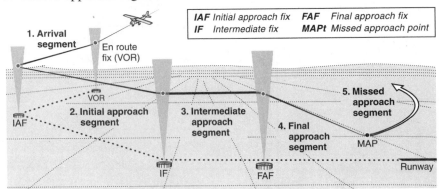

Figure 29-3. A simple and well-designed instrument approach

1. The Arrival Segment

The feeder route, also known as the arrival segment, is the route followed from the en route phase of the flight to the initial approach fix (IAF). It usually starts at an en route fix and ends at the initial approach fix (IAF), often the first navigation facility associated with the procedure. The IAP chart will show the feeder route, if any, with its minimum altitude, course to be flown, and distance to the IAF.

There may be a number of feeder routes into the one instrument approach procedure to cater for airplanes arriving from different directions, or there may be none. Many procedures do not require a feeder route—for instance, if the en route tracking ends at an initial approach fix (IAF).

2. The Initial Approach Segment

In the initial approach segment, the airplane is maneuvered to enter the intermediate segment which aligns it, at least approximately, with the final approach course. The initial approach segment commences at the initial approach fix (IAF), and may consist of a particular course, radial, DME arc, procedure turn, holding pattern, radar vector, or any combination of these.

---

3. The Intermediate Approach Segment

The intermediate approach segment blends the initial approach segment and the final approach segment. It is the segment in which aircraft configuration, speed and positioning adjustments should be completed prior to entering the final approach segment, by which time all cockpit prelanding checks should normally be completed, with the airplane established in a suitable condition for landing. Your instructor will explain the procedures you are to use for your particular airplane.

The intermediate approach segment ends at the final approach fix (FAF), and may begin either:

- at a designated intermediate approach fix (such as an NDB or a locator outer marker—LOM); or
- on completion of a dead-reckoning course, a procedure turn, or a reversal turn in a racetrack pattern.

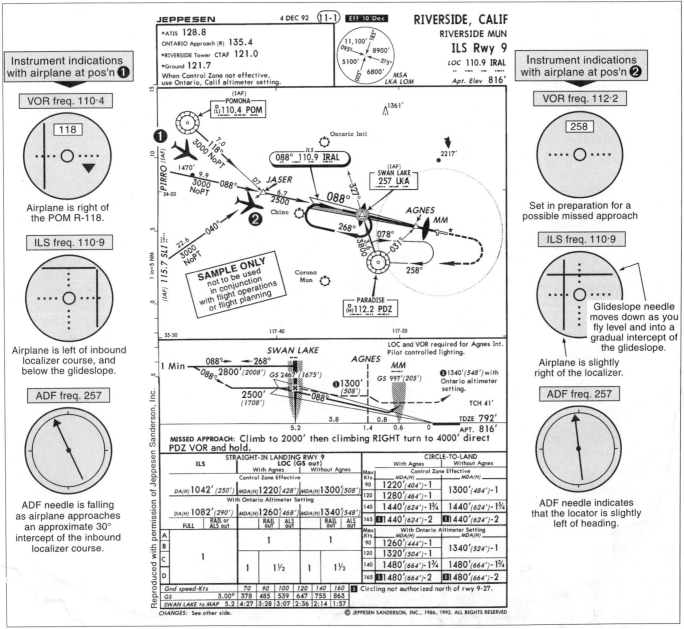

Figure 29-4. Riverside CA, ILS Rwy 9 (*Jeppesen,* reduced)

4. The Final Approach Segment

The final approach segment of a nonprecision approach (such as an NDB approach) begins at the final approach fix (FAF), and is the segment in which the alignment and descent for landing are accomplished. It ends at the missed approach point (MAP).

In some instrument approaches, the final approach fix is the same as the initial approach fix (the IAF may be the locator outer marker LOM when flying outbound, and the FAF is the same locator outer marker when flying inbound).

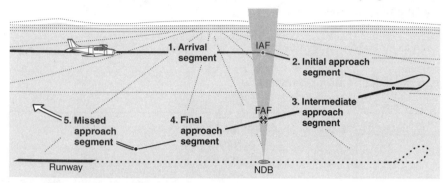

Figure 29-5. The five segments of a typical NDB approach

Final approach may be made to a runway for a straight-in landing, or it may be made for a circling approach (visual maneuvering for at least a partial traffic pattern) to a runway with which the final approach of the instrument approach procedure is not aligned, provided of course that the pilot becomes visual at a suitable time. The final approach fix on nonprecision approaches should be crossed at or above the specified altitude before final descent is commenced. The FAF is marked on IAP charts with a Maltese cross or a lightning bolt symbol. If ATC directs a lower-than-published glideslope intercept altitude, then the FAF is the resultant actual point of glideslope intercept. Where no final approach fix is shown, final descent should not be commenced until the airplane is established within ±5° of the final approach course.

Step-down fixes, if published on the chart profile diagram, are limiting altitudes, and should be crossed at or above their minimum crossing altitudes.

The final approach segment for a precision approach commences at the final approach point (FAP), where the intermediate segment of the procedure intersects the glidepath for the precision part of the ILS. The ILS approach is designed so that the airplane will intercept the glideslope from below, generally by flying level until the slope is intercepted, to avoid the possibility of following one of the false glideslopes that may exist at steep angles such as 12°.

Avoid false glideslopes! Intercept the glideslope on an ILS from below.

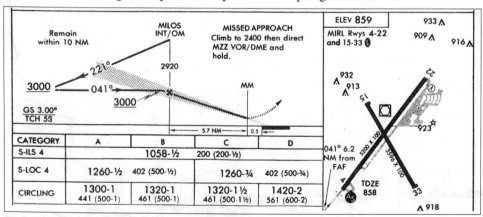

Figure 29-6. The final approach segment of an ILS

Final descent slope guidance on an ILS is provided by the electronic glideslope. Descent on the glidepath should not be initiated by the pilot unless the airplane is on course (within half-scale deflection of the localizer). A fix or facility, usually the outer marker (OM) (but it could be a compass locator, a DME distance, or a radar fix), is provided to allow the pilot to verify the glidepath/altitude relationship at one point on the precision approach.

Timing should commence at the FAF to assist in determining arrival at the missed approach point for some nonprecision approaches.

It is most important that a pilot does not descend below his minimum permitted altitude for a particular approach unless he has become visual, and can continue his approach to land visually with the runway environment and nearby ground features in view. The items that constitute runway environment such as the approach lights, are listed in Part 91 in Chapter 24.

5. The Missed Approach Segment

If the pilot has not become visual by a particular point or minimum altitude on final descent, then a missed approach must be made.

If the pilot has not become visual by a particular point or minimum altitude on final descent, then a missed approach must be made.

For a **precision approach**, such as the ILS, the **missed approach point** is defined by the intersection of the glidepath with the pilot's **decision height (DH)**, and therefore is not shown diagramatically on the charts. Unless visual, the pilot should begin the missed approach *immediately* the DH is reached.

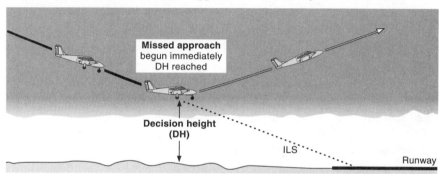

Figure 29-7. If not visual, commence the missed approach at DH on a precision approach

For a **nonprecision approach**, the **missed approach point** is defined by either a **fix**, **facility** or by **timing**, and is shown on both the plan and profile diagrams as a dotted line. It is also described in text. If a turn is specified in the missed approach procedure, then it should not be commenced until the airplane has passed the MAP and is established in the climb.

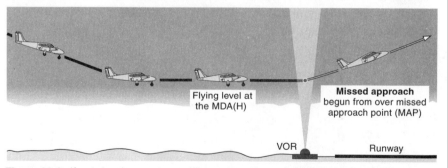

Figure 29-8. If not visual on a nonprecision approach, track in to the MAP at MDA

If, for some reason, you want to execute an early missed approach, before reaching the MAP, you may commence climbing at any time, but you should continue tracking to the MAP and then follow the prescribed missed approach course (unless otherwise directed by ATC).

The pilot may not descend below his calculated **minimum descent altitude (MDA)** on a nonprecision approach unless he becomes visual, however (unlike on a precision approach), he may track in as far as the MAP at or above this level in the hope of becoming visual, before having to commence a missed approach. It is possible that he may become visual in a position from which it is not possible to complete a straight-in landing safely, in which case some maneuvering to position the airplane will be necessary, known as a *circle-to-land* maneuver.

The missed approach segment is considered to be completed at an altitude sufficient to allow either:

- initiation of another instrument approach;
- return to a designated holding pattern; or
- resumption of en route flight to a diversion airport.

Instrument Approach Charts

Instrument approach procedure (IAP) charts provide a graphic presentation to the pilot of:

- **holding procedures** (if required prior to commencing the instrument approach);
- **the instrument approach procedure**; and
- **the missed approach procedure**.

Instrument approach charts are designed to be readable in the cockpit, although some difficulty may be experienced in turbulence and/or poor light. The actual instrument approach is shown in both plan and profile on the chart.

IAP charts are available for all airports where instrument approach procedures have been established and approved by the FAA. Charts acceptable to the FAA are those published by NOS (the National Ocean Service) and *Jeppesen*.

You must study carefully the actual instrument approach charts that you will be using, since presentation of the same instrument approach by the various publishers is not identical. The symbols and abbreviations used will also differ. We have used both NOS and *Jeppesen* charts as examples.

Only current instrument approach charts must be used! They are regularly revised and amendments made available. Changes to the actual procedure, the appearance of significant new obstacles, such as buildings or masts in the approach or missed approach areas, changes to radio frequencies or the addition of new radio navaids relevant to that approach will require a current chart. Urgent amendments of a timely nature may be advised to pilots by NOTAM. Check currency of chart, and check the NOTAMs for any amendments.

Update your approach charts at the designated intervals.

The Elements of an Instrument Approach Chart

The information provided on an instrument approach chart includes:

- identification of the particular approach;
- a *plan* view of the approach and the missed approach;
- a *profile* view of the approach and the missed approach;
- holding procedures associated with the approach;
- full details of radio facilities associated with the instrument approach, missed approach and holding;
- necessary airport and topographical information (coastlines, lakes and rivers, relief, built-up areas, etc.) pertinent to the safe execution of the approach; and
- a landing chart, showing the runway layout.

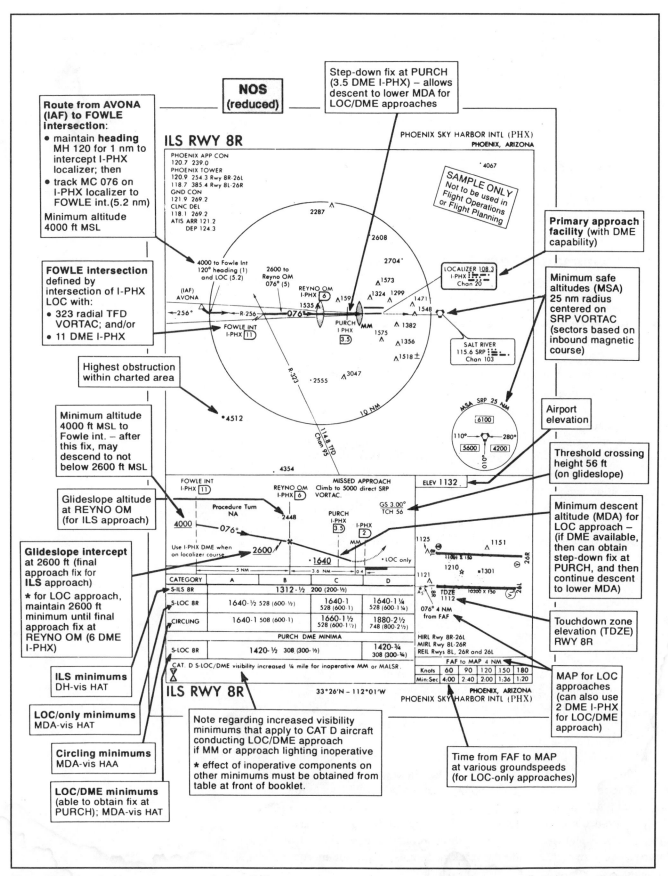

Figure 29-9. A typical instrument approach chart (ILS)

The following are the labels and callouts on the chart:

Route from AVONA (IAF) to FOWLE intersection:
- maintain **heading MH 120** for 1 nm to intercept I-PHX localizer; then
- track **MC 076** on I-PHX localizer to FOWLE int.(5.2 nm)

Minimum altitude 4000 ft MSL

FOWLE intersection defined by intersection of I-PHX LOC with:
- 323 radial TFD VORTAC; and/or
- 11 DME I-PHX

Highest obstruction within charted area

Minimum altitude 4000 ft MSL to Fowle int. – after this fix, may descend to not below 2600 ft MSL

Glideslope altitude at REYNO OM (for ILS approach)

Glideslope intercept at 2600 ft (final approach fix for **ILS** approach)

* for LOC approach, maintain 2600 ft minimum until final approach fix at REYNO OM (6 DME I-PHX)

ILS minimums DH-vis HAT

LOC/only minimums MDA-vis HAT

Circling minimums MDA-vis HAA

LOC/DME minimums (able to obtain fix at PURCH); MDA-vis HAT

NOS (reduced)

Step-down fix at PURCH (3.5 DME I-PHX) – allows descent to lower MDA for LOC/DME approaches

SAMPLE ONLY Not to be used in Flight Operations or Flight Planning

Primary approach facility (with DME capability)

Minimum safe altitudes (MSA) 25 nm radius centered on SRP VORTAC (sectors based on inbound magnetic course)

Airport elevation

Threshold crossing height 56 ft (on glideslope)

Minimum descent altitude (MDA) for LOC approach – (if DME available, then can obtain step-down fix at PURCH, and then continue descent to lower MDA)

Touchdown zone elevation (TDZE) RWY 8R

MAP for LOC approaches (can also use 2 DME I-PHX for LOC/DME approach)

Time from FAF to MAP at various groundspeeds (for LOC-only approaches)

Note regarding increased visibility minimums that apply to CAT D aircraft conducting LOC/DME approach if MM or approach lighting inoperative

* effect of inoperative components on other minimums must be obtained from table at front of booklet.

ILS RWY 8R

PHOENIX SKY HARBOR INTL (PHX)
PHOENIX, ARIZONA

PHOENIX APP CON
120.7 239.0
PHOENIX TOWER
120.9 254.3 Rwy 8R-26L
118.7 385.4 Rwy 8L-26R
GND CON
121.9 269.2
CLNC DEL
118.1 269.2
ATIS ARR 121.2
DEP 124.3

LOCALIZER 108.3
I-PHX Chan 20

SALT RIVER
115.6 SRP Chan 103

MSA SRP 25 NM
110° — 280°
6100
5600 / 4200

MISSED APPROACH
Climb to 5000 direct SRP VORTAC.

ELEV 1132

GS 3.00°
TCH 56

CATEGORY	A	B	C	D
S-ILS 8R	1312-½ 200 (200-½)			
S-LOC 8R	1640-½ 528 (600-½)		1640-1 528 (600-1)	1640-1¼ 528 (600-1¼)
CIRCLING	1640-1 508 (600-1)		1660-1½ 528 (600-1½)	1880-2½ 748 (800-2½)
	PURCH DME MINIMA			
S-LOC 8R	1420-½ 308 (300-½)			1420-¾ 308 (300-¾)

CAT. D S-LOC/DME visibility increased ¼ mile for inoperative MM or MALSR.

ILS RWY 8R   33°26'N – 112°01'W
PHOENIX SKY HARBOR INTL (PHX)

HIRL Rwy 8R-26L
MIRL Rwy 8L-26R
REIL Rwys 8L, 26R and 26L

TDZE 1112
076° 4 NM from FAF

FAF to MAP 4 NM					
Knots	60	90	120	150	180
Min:Sec	4:00	2:40	2:00	1:36	1:20

Chapter 29 **Instrument Approaches**   **583**

Identification of an Instrument Approach Chart

An instrument approach chart is normally identified at the top by:

- the name of the airport;
- an abbreviation of the type of radio facility (further identified by the runway served in the case of a runway approach as against an airport approach); and
- additional information to distinguish between separate charts for the same airport.

"ILS DME Rwy 9" indicates that the approach requires both an ILS and a DME, whereas "ILS Rwy 27" indicates that DME is not required. If a letter follows the aid, such as VOR-A or VOR-B, it indicates that circling minimums only are published, either because the IAP is not aligned with the runway, or the descent gradient from the FAF to the touchdown zone straight-in is too steep.

Radio Communications Frequencies

The relevant VHF communications frequencies, usually in the order in which a pilot will use them, are also listed near the top of the chart.

Plan View of the Instrument Approach

The plan view is a *conformal* projection that displays correct angular relationships. The scale is such that the approach charts are of a convenient small size for use in the cockpit, yet large enough to show the intermediate approach area as well as the final approach and missed approach areas. A scale of 5 nm to the inch is typical. A graduated scale line is shown down the left hand side of the *Jeppesen* charts.

A reference circle of 10 nm radius centered on a fix or facility on NOS charts (5 nm centered on the airport on *Jeppesen* charts) emphasizes to the pilot any obstructions or features close to the airport. Horizontal distances along the approach are measured in *nautical miles* to facilitate use of the DME which reads in nm, however remember that runway distances and runway visual range (RVR) are specified in *feet*, and visibility in *statute miles*.

The airport is clearly shown on the plan view, including the runway pattern and any other distinctive patterns perhaps formed by taxiways or aprons. Even though obstacle clearance is provided for in the design of the instrument approach, significant topographical and other data, although not part of the actual instrument approach, may be shown on the chart to assist the pilot when and if he becomes visual. It is handy, for instance, for a pilot to know the runway layout and the position of any nearby obstacles that he can expect to see when and if he becomes visual on final approach.

The plan position of each of the radio aids required for the procedure is shown, with frequencies, ident, and defined courses in *degrees magnetic*.

The **main procedure course** is shown as a heavily printed full line with its magnetic direction and a directional arrow. Any procedure turn required to reverse direction is also clearly shown.

The **missed approach** is shown as a dashed line with its magnetic direction and a directional arrow. The latest point at which the pilot may commence a missed approach according to the procedures is referred to as the missed approach point (MAP).

The **holding pattern**, which, strictly speaking, is not part of most approaches, is shown with magnetic direction and a directional arrow. Some approaches, however, use the racetrack pattern as part of an alternative intermediate segment, replacing a procedure turn.

Profile View

The profile view of the instrument approach is published directly beneath the plan view. The **main procedure course** is a solid line with a directional arrow and magnetic course. In the profile view, the angles shown are generally not correct, but exaggerated for display purposes.

Approach slopes are really quite gentle (a typical ILS glideslope, for instance, is only 3° to the horizontal, a gradient of 1 in 20). The profile view of any reversal or procedure turn is shown as a horizontal line, which may have associated altitude, distance or time requirements stated nearby.

Relevant radio facilities (LOM, MM) are also shown in profile. The missed approach procedure is shown as a dotted line with a directional arrow, and with a written description nearby.

Vertical distances are shown in *feet MSL*. **Airport elevation** is the vertical distance (in feet MSL) of the highest point on the landing area of the airport, and is published on all instrument approach procedure (IAP) charts:

- on NOS charts as *Elev* near the airport diagram;
- on *Jeppesen* charts as *Apt. Elev* (airport elevation) at top-right, and as *Apt.* near the runway on the profile diagram.

Airport elevation is the reference level for cloud ceiling. For instance, a cloud ceiling of 800 feet at an airport, elevation 5200 feet, would be encountered at altitude 6000 feet MSL. Height above the airport elevation is written as HAA, and is used when specifying circling minimums and alternate minimums for an airport.

Touchdown zone elevation (TDZE) is the highest elevation in the first 3000 feet of the runway, and is shown near the runway on the IAP chart when straight-in landing minimums are authorized. Height above touchdown zone is abbreviated to HAT, and is used when straight-in minimums are published.

Threshold crossing height (TCH) is the theoretical height above the runway threshold at which the aircraft's glideslope antenna would be if the aircraft is flown right on the ILS/MLS glideslope. Note that TCH is not wheel height above the threshold—the wheels might be considerably lower.

The Minimum Safe Altitude Circle (MSA)

The MSA circle, which may be broken into sectors, indicates minimum safe altitudes that provide 1000 feet obstruction clearance within 25 nm of the radio facility on which the MSA circle is based. These altitudes, while they guarantee obstruction clearance, do not guarantee reception of navigation or communication radio signals, and so are considered as *emergency* minimum altitudes for an IFR flight.

Approach Minimums

Approach minimums are a critical part of each instrument approach. The appropriate minimums to use depend on the qualifications and experience of the pilot, the performance category of the aircraft, the equipment carried in the aircraft, and the approach itself.

The **performance category** of the aircraft is based on its maneuverability, which depends to a large extent on its airspeed. An airplane flying slowly is able to maneuver in less airspace than a fast airplane.

The categories are based on $1.3 \times V_{S0}$, where V_{S0} is the stall speed in the landing configuration at maximum landing weight. $1.3 V_{S0}$ is a measure of maneuvering speed, and is the speed that would be used on approach (at least approximately, depending on actual weight and conditions).

$1.3 \, V_{S0}$	Performance Category
90 kt and below	A
91 kt to 120 kt	B
121 kt to 140 kt	C
141 kt to 165 kt	D
166 kt and above	E

Most general aviation airplanes fall into Categories A or B; *Boeing 757s* are in Category C, and *Boeing 767s* are in Category D.

You must know your airplane category before you can determine the approach minimums. If your airplane has V_{S0} = 50 knots, then $1.3V_{S0}$ = 1.3×50 = 65 knots, which places it in Category A. Another airplane, with V_{S0} = 70 knots $(1.3V_{S0} = 1.3 \times 70 = 91)$ would be in Category B. The approach minimums consist of an altitude by which you must be visual, and a required visibility.

Once you are visual, the landing minimum is determined by visibility alone, which may be **runway visual range (RVR)** in feet or visibility in statute miles. RVR is measured by a *transmissometer* installed beside the runway—if this is inoperative, and the prescribed minimum is expressed in RVR, you may convert the RVR in feet to a comparable ground visibility in statute miles (using tables published in the IAP booklets, or by using RVR 2400 feet = $\frac{1}{2}$ sm, RVR 5000 feet = 1 sm).

Minimums are raised if:
- you approach at a higher speed than for your normal category—then you must use the minimums for the higher category; or
- components are inoperative (MM not available). See the front of the NOS IAP booklet, and on the *Jeppesen* IAP charts, to see what penalties apply.

The minimums (in order of meeting them on the approach) can be thought of as:
- circle-to-land minimums, for other than straight-in landings;
- straight-in nonprecision minimums (localizer only if the ILS glideslope is not available);
- straight-in precision minimums (ILS);
- landing minimums (RVR or visibility only).

Note: The **alternate minimums**, which are used for flight planning purposes to determine if you may file that airport as an alternate, are higher minimums than the approach minimums and are not found on the approach charts, but at the front of the NOS IAP booklet. They are on the *Jeppesen* airport charts.

Some nonprecision approaches have a **visual descent point (VDP)** from which normal descent from the minimum descent altitude (MDA) may be commenced, provided the runway environment is clearly visible.

For certain instrument approaches, there may be a **sidestep maneuver**, where you fly an ILS approach to one runway (say ILS Rwy 25R), but are cleared to land on another parallel runway (25L) that is within 1200 feet laterally. The **sidestep minimum** may be higher than the minimum for a straight-in approach to the initial runway, but lower than the circle-to-land minimums. You should perform the sidestep maneuver as soon as you have the landing runway environment in view.

Timing to the Missed Approach Point

For a *nonprecision* approach where the approach aid is well away from the airport and acts as the final approach fix (FAF), a small table at the bottom of the chart shows the time from the final approach fix to the missed approach point (MAP). On ILS charts, this information is useful in situations where the electronic glideslope is not available, and a nonprecision localizer approach has to be made.

Always start timing at the FAF, even on an ILS approach. If the glideslope fails after the FAF, you can still proceed with a nonprecision localizer approach and recognize the MAP.

Some Typical Instrument Approach Charts

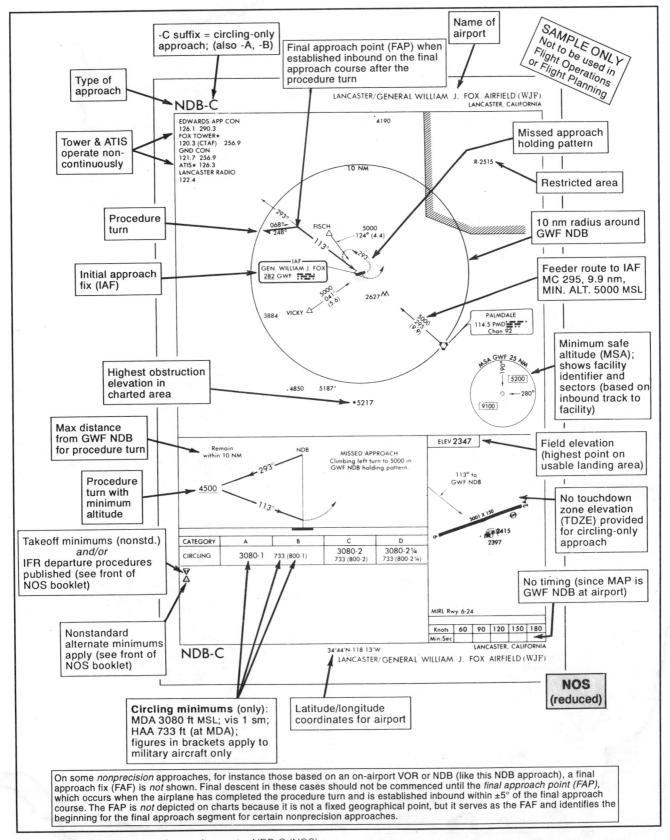

Type of approach → NDB-C

-C suffix = circling-only approach; (also -A, -B)

Final approach point (FAP) when established inbound on the final approach course after the procedure turn

Name of airport

SAMPLE ONLY
Not to be used in
Flight Operations
or Flight Planning

LANCASTER/GENERAL WILLIAM J. FOX AIRFIELD (WJF)
LANCASTER, CALIFORNIA

Tower & ATIS operate non-continuously

EDWARDS APP CON
126.1 290.3
FOX TOWER*
120.3 (CTAF) 256.9
GND CON
121.7 256.9
ATIS* 126.3
LANCASTER RADIO
122.4

4190

Missed approach holding pattern

R-2515

Restricted area

10 NM

Procedure turn

293°
068°
248°

FISCH   5000
124° (4.4)

113°   293°

10 nm radius around GWF NDB

Initial approach fix (IAF)

IAF
GEN. WILLIAM J. FOX
282 GWF

5000
041°
(5.6)

2627

VICKY

3884

Feeder route to IAF MC 295, 9.9 nm, MIN. ALT. 5000 MSL

5000
295
(9.9)

PALMDALE
114.5 PMD
Chan 92

Highest obstruction elevation in charted area

.4850   5187°

•5217

MSA GWF 25 NM
5200
9100   280°

Minimum safe altitude (MSA); shows facility identifier and sectors (based on inbound track to facility)

Max distance from GWF NDB for procedure turn

Remain within 10 NM   NDB

ELEV 2347

Field elevation (highest point on usable landing area)

MISSED APPROACH
Climbing left turn to 5000 in
GWF NDB holding pattern.

293°

113° to
GWF NDB

Procedure turn with minimum altitude

4500

113°

5001 X 150

24
2415
2397

No touchdown zone elevation (TDZE) provided for circling-only approach

Takeoff minimums (nonstd.) *and/or* IFR departure procedures published (see front of NOS booklet)

CATEGORY	A	B	C	D
CIRCLING	3080-1	733 (800-1)	3080-2 733 (800-2)	3080-2¼ 733 (800-2¼)

No timing (since MAP is GWF NDB at airport)

MIRL Rwy 6-24

Knots	60	90	120	150	180
Min:Sec					

LANCASTER, CALIFORNIA

Nonstandard alternate minimums apply (see front of NOS booklet)

NDB-C

34°44'N-118 13'W
LANCASTER/GENERAL WILLIAM J. FOX AIRFIELD (WJF)

NOS
(reduced)

Circling minimums (only): MDA 3080 ft MSL; vis 1 sm; HAA 733 ft (at MDA); figures in brackets apply to military aircraft only

Latitude/longitude coordinates for airport

On some *nonprecision* approaches, for instance those based on an on-airport VOR or NDB (like this NDB approach), a final approach fix (FAF) is *not* shown. Final descent in these cases should not be commenced until the *final approach point (FAP)*, which occurs when the airplane has completed the procedure turn and is established inbound within ±5° of the final approach course. The FAP is *not* depicted on charts because it is not a fixed geographical point, but it serves as the FAF and identifies the beginning for the final approach segment for certain nonprecision approaches.

Figure 29-10. Tracking aid at airport—Lancaster NDB-C (NOS)

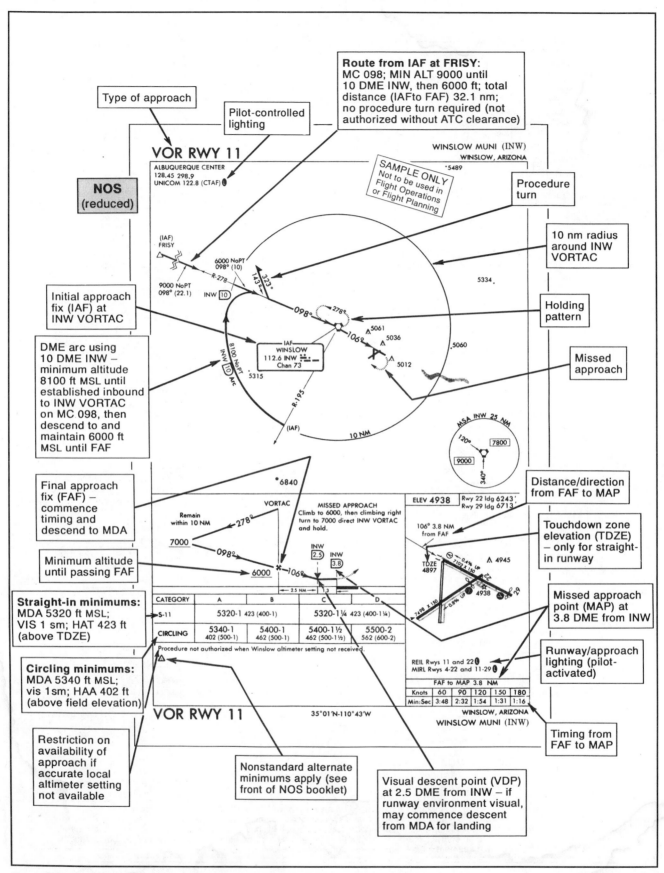

Figure 29-11. An off-airport tracking aid—Winslow VOR Rwy 11 (NOS)

The annotations and content within the figure:

Type of approach

Pilot-controlled lighting

Route from IAF at FRISY:
MC 098; MIN ALT 9000 until
10 DME INW, then 6000 ft; total
distance (IAF to FAF) 32.1 nm;
no procedure turn required (not
authorized without ATC clearance)

VOR RWY 11

ALBUQUERQUE CENTER
128.45 298.9
UNICOM 122.8 (CTAF)

WINSLOW MUNI (INW)
WINSLOW, ARIZONA

NOS (reduced)

SAMPLE ONLY
Not to be used in
Flight Operations
or Flight Planning

Procedure turn

10 nm radius around INW VORTAC

(IAF) FRISY

6000 NoPT 098° (10)

9000 NoPT 098° (22.1)

INW 10

5334.

Initial approach fix (IAF) at INW VORTAC

Holding pattern

DME arc using 10 DME INW — minimum altitude 8100 ft MSL until established inbound to INW VORTAC on MC 098, then descend to and maintain 6000 ft MSL until FAF

IAF
WINSLOW
112.6 INW
Chan 73

5315

8100 NoPT INW 10 Arc

R-278

143°

323°

098°

278°

106°

5061
5036
5012
.5060

Missed approach

(IAF)

R-195

10 NM

MSA INW 25 NM
120° 7800
9000
340°

Final approach fix (FAF) — commence timing and descend to MDA

•6840

Remain within 10 NM

VORTAC

278°

7000

098°

6000

106°

MISSED APPROACH
Climb to 6000, then climbing right
turn to 7000 direct INW VORTAC
and hold.

ELEV 4938

Rwy 22 ldg 6243
Rwy 29 ldg 6713

106° 3.8 NM from FAF

Distance/direction from FAF to MAP

Touchdown zone elevation (TDZE) — only for straight-in runway

Minimum altitude until passing FAF

INW 2.5
INW 3.8

2.5 NM   1.3

TDZE 4897

0.4% UP
7102 X 150

4945

7498 X 150

0.8% UP

4938

22
29

Missed approach point (MAP) at 3.8 DME from INW

CATEGORY	A	B	C	D
S-11	5320-1 423 (400-1)		5320-1¼ 423 (400-1¼)	
CIRCLING	5340-1 402 (500-1)	5400-1 462 (500-1)	5400-1½ 462 (500-1½)	5500-2 562 (600-2)

Procedure not authorized when Winslow altimeter setting not received.

Straight-in minimums:
MDA 5320 ft MSL;
VIS 1 sm; HAT 423 ft
(above TDZE)

Circling minimums:
MDA 5340 ft MSL;
vis 1 sm; HAA 402 ft
(above field elevation)

Runway/approach lighting (pilot-activated)

REIL Rwys 11 and 22
MIRL Rwys 4-22 and 11-29

FAF to MAP 3.8 NM

Knots	60	90	120	150	180
Min:Sec	3:48	2:32	1:54	1:31	1:16

VOR RWY 11

35°01'N-110°43'W

WINSLOW, ARIZONA
WINSLOW MUNI (INW)

Timing from FAF to MAP

Restriction on availability of approach if accurate local altimeter setting not available

Nonstandard alternate minimums apply (see front of NOS booklet)

Visual descent point (VDP) at 2.5 DME from INW — if runway environment visual, may commence descent from MDA for landing

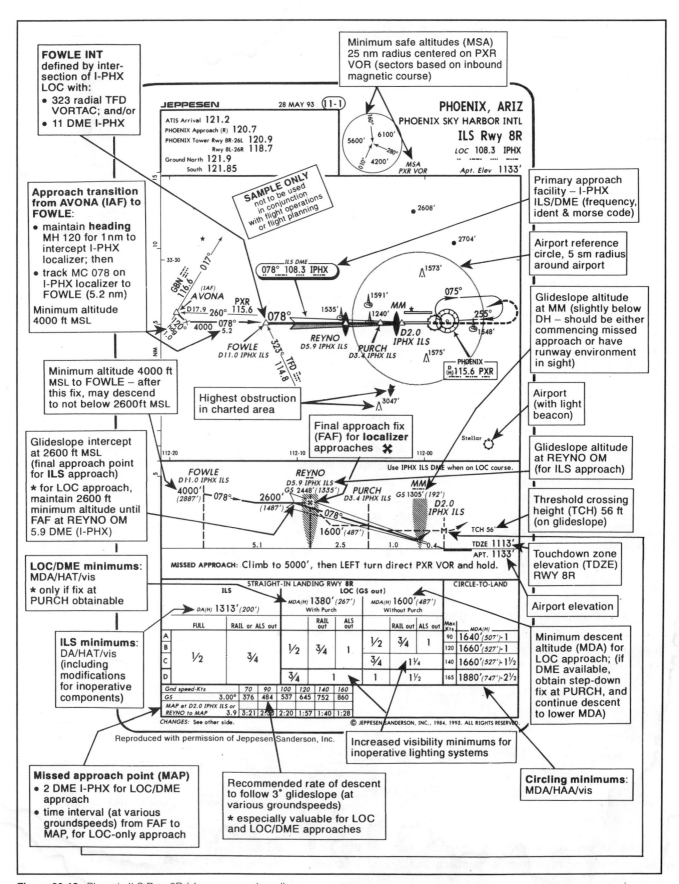

FOWLE INT
defined by inter-
section of I-PHX
LOC with:
- 323 radial TFD
  VORTAC; and/or
- 11 DME I-PHX

**Approach transition
from AVONA (IAF) to
FOWLE:**
- maintain **heading**
  MH 120 for 1 nm to
  intercept I-PHX
  localizer; then
- track MC 078 on
  I-PHX localizer to
  FOWLE (5.2 nm)

Minimum altitude
4000 ft MSL

Minimum altitude 4000 ft
MSL to FOWLE – after
this fix, may descend
to not below 2600ft MSL

Glideslope intercept
at 2600 ft MSL
(final approach point
for **ILS** approach)
★ for LOC approach,
maintain 2600 ft
minimum altitude until
FAF at REYNO OM
5.9 DME (I-PHX)

LOC/DME minimums:
MDA/HAT/vis
★ only if fix at
PURCH obtainable

ILS minimums:
DA/HAT/vis
(including
modifications
for inoperative
components)

Missed approach point (MAP)
- 2 DME I-PHX for LOC/DME
  approach
- time interval (at various
  groundspeeds) from FAF to
  MAP, for LOC-only approach

Recommended rate of descent
to follow 3° glideslope (at
various groundspeeds)
★ especially valuable for LOC
and LOC/DME approaches

Increased visibility minimums for
inoperative lighting systems

Circling minimums:
MDA/HAA/vis

Minimum descent
altitude (MDA) for
LOC approach; (if
DME available,
obtain step-down
fix at PURCH, and
continue descent
to lower MDA)

Airport elevation

Touchdown zone
elevation (TDZE)
RWY 8R

Threshold crossing
height (TCH) 56 ft
(on glideslope)

Glideslope altitude
at REYNO OM
(for ILS approach)

Airport
(with light
beacon)

Glideslope altitude
at MM (slightly below
DH – should be either
commencing missed
approach or have
runway environment
in sight)

Airport reference
circle, 5 sm radius
around airport

Primary approach
facility – I-PHX
ILS/DME (frequency,
ident & morse code)

Minimum safe altitudes (MSA)
25 nm radius centered on PXR
VOR (sectors based on inbound
magnetic course)

Highest obstruction
in charted area

Final approach fix
(FAF) for **localizer**
approaches ✖

Figure 29-12. Phoenix ILS Rwy 8R (*Jeppesen*, reduced)

General Comments On Instrument Approaches

It is most important that the cockpit be well organized prior to starting an instrument approach, since the workload during the approach will be high. The instrument approach procedures to be used, including the missed approach, should be reviewed en route, preferably well before the airport is approached and even prior to commencing descent from cruise altitude.

You must also consider:
- runway surface conditions (dry, wet, standing water, slush, ice);
- crosswind;
- airplane performance (landing distance required).

Students should think of these points before commencing the approach.

Given a choice of instrument approaches to an airport or to a particular runway, a pilot will generally opt for a precision approach, such as an ILS, over a nonprecision approach. As well as making it easier to fly an accurate final descent, the glideslope guidance of a precision approach will permit a lower minimum altitude, possibly making the difference between becoming visual or having to make a missed approach.

Given the choice, a precision approach is preferred over a nonprecision approach. The best approach, however, may be the one that allows a straight-in approach into the wind.

The charts required should be arranged in order, consideration of minimums completed, and intended action in the case of a missed approach determined (diversion, return for a second approach, etc.). Fuel on board is an important consideration, especially if a diversion to an alternate becomes necessary.

The radio navigation aids required for the approach should be set up as early as convenient, although some delays may be necessary. For instance, the VHF-NAV may need to remain selected to a VOR for en route tracking prior to the commencement of an ILS approach. Make use of every available means of navigation to assist you in forming a picture of exactly where the airplane is. Do not leave the VHF-NAV, ADF or DME idle if they can be tuned to useful aids, even if those aids are not part of the published procedure.

Ensure that the altimeter setting is correct for precise vertical navigation. If a high speed has been used on the cruise and descent, it may be appropriate to slow the airplane to a more suitable maneuvering speed before reaching the initial approach fix, and to complete any necessary cockpit checks at that time.

If the instrument approach uses the same facility for the initial approach fix (IAF) and the final approach fix (FAF), the pilot will track outbound from the IAF, reverse course by making a procedure turn inbound, and then track to the final approach fix. Some instrument approaches are designed so that a base turn (rather than a procedure turn) is used to align the airplane on the final approach course (see Figure 29-13). Others use a holding pattern.

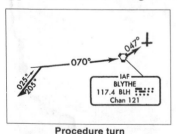

Procedure turn

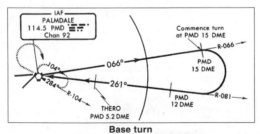

Base turn

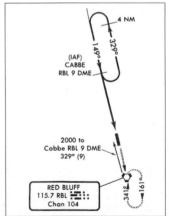

Holding pattern and reversal turn

Figure 29-13. Aligning the airplane on final approach course

Under **radar control**, a pilot may be radar vectored directly to the final approach course of any instrument approach, and cleared to descend to suitable altitudes by ATC, so that a smooth intercept of final approach may be made. If *feeder routes* are published for the particular approach, then the pilot will possibly be routed by ATC via one of these routes. Sometimes it is possible to track via a DME arc from the en route phase to intercept the final approach course. In all of these cases, reversal turns may be avoided.

The **minimum altitude** at which the pilot may fly in any particular segment using pilot nav will be shown on the chart, although ATC may assign a higher level. Do not leave the last assigned level unless you have been cleared for the approach, and do not intercept final approach off a radar vector unless you have been cleared for the approach (you may give the controller a reminder that you are about to cross the final approach course). The radar controller will be using a **minimum vectoring altitude (MVA)** to provide you with adequate obstruction clearance (1000 feet normally, 2000 feet in mountainous areas), and at least 300 feet above the floor of controlled airspace to give you the protection of controlled airspace.

During the **intermediate approach segment**, the airplane is being maneuvered to be positioned on final approach at a suitable altitude and airspeed. The actual configuration of the airplane (the position of flaps and landing gear) and the speed at which it should be flown at various stages in the approach will vary between airplane types, and clear instructions in this regard will be given to you by your instructor, and in the Pilot's Operating Handbook. If you think that you will be far too high to commence the approach, you can request a holding pattern or radar vectors in order to lose the excess altitude. If you are doing a visual practice instrument approach and look like you will be flying into actual instrument conditions, remain VFR and advise ATC.

Ready your airspeed, altitude, and mental attitude for the approach during the intermediate segment.

During **final approach**, normal attitude flying techniques should be used, with constant reference to the flight instruments and regular reference to the navigation instruments. During an ILS, the glideslope should be maintained with small adjustments of pitch attitude on the attitude indicator using the elevator, and airspeed should be maintained on the ASI with power adjustments using the throttle. For a nonprecision approach, a suitable steady rate of descent should be set up. For example, to lose 1500 feet of altitude in 5 nm (300 feet per nm) at a groundspeed of 90 knots (1.5 nm per min), a suitable rate of descent is $1.5 \times 300 = 450$ feet per minute.

When on final approach, the pilot should have clearly fixed in his mind his *minimum*, and the *missed approach procedure*. If not visual with the runway environment in sight at the calculated minimum altitude:

- **DH** for a **precision approach**—a missed approach should be commenced immediately; or
- **MDA** for a **nonprecision approach**—the airplane may continue tracking at MDA to the missed approach point (MAP) in the hope of becoming visual, but a missed approach must be commenced at or before the MAP if visual flight does not become possible. Early missed approach climbs are permitted, but tracking for the missed approach must be as published, unless otherwise authorized by ATC.

What is "Visual Reference" at the DH or MDA?

Visual reference is the minimum visual reference that a pilot should have in view before continuing the approach below the DH or MDA. The visual segment should contain sufficient physical features (approach lights, runway lights, runway markings, and features in the general runway environment) to ensure that the position of the aircraft relative to the desired flightpath can be positively ascertained. This then enables the pilot to make an informed judgment at DH or MDA, and thereafter to maintain stable flight toward the runway. After becoming visual, the **landing minimum** is visibility alone (or RVR).

Approach lights, runway lights, runway markings, and features in the general runway environment are all visual references the pilot looks for before descending below DH or MDA.

Visual   **Not visual**

Figure 29-14. Visual, or not visual

A precision approach such as an ILS will be aligned with the extended runway centerline and the electronic glideslope will provide an ideal slope to the touchdown zone. Therefore, if you have flown a stable ILS approach in clouds with localizer and glideslope needles centered, you should be in a good position, when and if you become visual, to continue the stable approach without any dramatic alterations of heading or rate of descent (unless necessitated by windshear or turbulence).

The localizer allows you to track accurately along the extended runway centerline—so remember that, if a significant crosswind exists, you can expect to see the runway not directly straight ahead through the windshield, but slightly left or right depending on the wind direction. Do not make any large changes of heading immediately you become visual—wait briefly to see if you already have the correct wind correction angle—likely to be the case if you have tracked accurately down the localizer. Of course, you may have to make some minor adjustments to heading to keep your flightpath aligned with the extended runway centerline.

Nonprecision approaches using a VOR or an NDB, may or may not be aligned with the runway centerline—you can determine this from the approach charts—so you should prepare yourself and know where to look for the runway when and if you become visual. If not aligned with the centerline and/or if not on a suitable approach slope, when you become visual you should maneuver into a position so that you can fly a straight and stable last few hundred feet to the touchdown zone on the runway.

Even when you are out of the clouds and visual, you should always be prepared to make a **missed approach**:

- if you feel your approach is too unstable or too far out of alignment with the runway centerline; or
- if you are unable to maintain a safe rate of descent to the touchdown zone or to control the airspeed sufficiently well; or
- if the runway is obstructed.

Make use of any VASI to assist you in achieving the correct approach slope. If at the MDA on a nonprecision approach the VASI lights are all red (showing you well below slope) then fly level at the MDA until you are on slope, then proceed with the landing.

Keep in mind the runway, its length and surface conditions (wet, slushy, etc.) and the possibility of wake turbulence or low-level windshear. There is a lot to think about on approach but, with practice and experience, it becomes a lot easier. Always keep in mind: a good landing requires a good approach.

Visual Illusions on Approach

Be prepared for visual illusions. A narrower-than-usual or upsloping runway will give the impression that you are high on slope, leading some pilots to make a lower-than-normal approach. Haze creates the illusion that the runway is further away, and can lead some pilots into making a lower-than-normal approach.

Most runways are of standard width and on flat ground. On every approach, you should try to achieve the same flightpath angle to the horizontal, and your eyes will become accustomed to this, allowing you to make consistently good approaches along an acceptable glideslope merely by keeping your view of the runway through the windshield in standard perspective.

Runway slope. If you are approaching a sloping runway, however, the perspective will be different. A runway that slopes upward will look longer and you will feel that you are high on slope, when in fact you are right on slope. The tendency will be for you to fly lower and make a shallower approach. If you know that the runway does have an upslope, you can avoid this tendency.

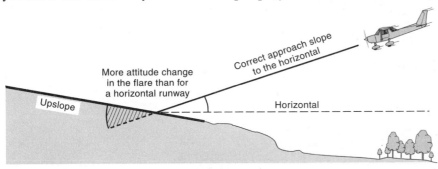

Figure 29-15. An upward sloping runway creates a "too-high" illusion

A runway that slopes downward will look shorter and you will feel that you are low on slope, when in fact you are on slope. The tendency will be for you to go higher and make a steeper approach. If you know that the runway does have a downslope, you can avoid this tendency. If you know the slope of the runway, you can allow for it in your visual estimation of whether you are high or low on slope.

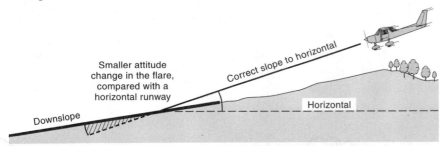

Figure 29-16. A downward sloping runway creates a "too-low" illusion

Runway size and shape. A runway that is larger than usual will appear to be closer than it really is. Conversely, a runway that is smaller than usual will appear to be further away than it really is.

A wide runway, because of the angle at which you view it peripherally in the final stages of the approach and landing, will cause an illusion of being too low, and you may flare and hold-off too high as a result, leading to "dropping in" for a heavy landing. Conversely, a narrow runway will cause an illusion of being too high, and you may delay the flare and make contact with the runway earlier (and harder) than expected.

If you know that the runway is wider or narrower than what you are familiar with, then you can allow for this in your visual judgment of flare height and hold-off.

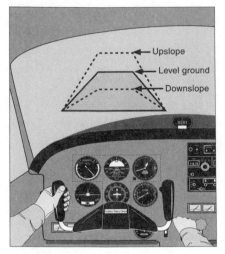

Figure 29-17. How runways of different slopes should appear at the same point on final

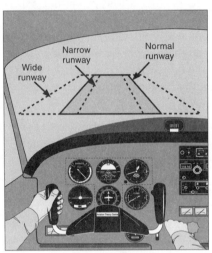

Figure 29-18. How runways of different widths should appear at the same point on final

Poor visibility. In hazy conditions, you may be closer to the runway than you appear to be, an illusion that may lead to an unnecessarily hard landing if you are not aware of the effect of haze on your vision.

Heavy rain on the windshield—a frequent occurrence when flying IFR—can create a visual illusion that you are higher than you actually are, causing some pilots to fly a lower-than-normal approach. Using a VASI (visual approach slope indicator system), or referring to the electronic glideslope needle if usable, can help a pilot maintain a suitable approach slope.

Flying into fog or clouds on approach can create an illusion of pitching up, causing some pilots (who do not recognize this as an illusion by failing to check their instruments or the VASI) to pitch the nose down and steepen the flightpath unnecessarily, sometimes quite abruptly!

If the runway is situated in featureless terrain, or is surrounded by water, snow, or darkened areas, then an illusion can be created that the airplane is higher than it actually is, causing a tendency to fly a lower-than-normal approach.

The Night Approach

A powered approach is preferable at night, rather than a glide approach, providing a normal well-controlled approach at normal speeds. In modern training aircraft, the powered approach is generally used by day also. Power gives the pilot more control, a lower rate of descent and, therefore, a less steep approach slope. The approach to the aiming point should be stable, using any available aids, such as the runway lighting and a VASI if available.

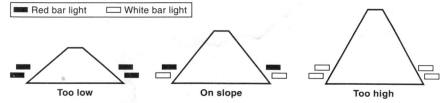

Figure 29-19. Perspectives on approach using a VASI

Using the runway edge lighting only, correct tracking and slope is achieved when the runway perspective is the same as in daylight. For correct tracking, the runway should appear symmetrical in the windshield. Guidance on achieving the correct approach slope is obtained from the apparent spacing between the runway edge lights.

If you are low on slope, the runway lights will appear to be closer together. If you are above slope, then the runway lights will appear to be further apart. Attention should also be paid to the airspeed indicator throughout the approach, to ensure that the correct airspeed is being maintained.

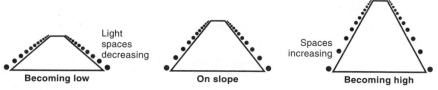

Figure 29-20. Perspectives on approach using runway edge lighting

A VASI will provide correct slope guidance day or night, but the perspective provided by runway edge lighting may be slightly misleading if you do not allow for any runway slope.

At night, you must be careful not to mistake a well-lit road for the runway, which may have less intense lighting than nearby roads. Lights of townships built on the side of a hill may provide a false horizon, so refer regularly to your flight instruments to avoid unwanted banking. Bright runway and approach lights, especially when surrounded by dark areas with little or no lighting, may create the illusion that you are closer to the runway than you really are, causing a tendency to fly a higher-than-normal approach.

You can take action to avoid being misled by these visual illusions by:

- Anticipating the possibility of visual illusions at unfamiliar airports, especially at night or in adverse weather conditions.

- Making a visual inspection of an unfamiliar airport before landing, if you feel it is needed and conditions permit.

- Use a VASI or electronic glideslope (ILS) for slope guidance on final approach, if they are available.

- Even when visual on an approach, regularly refer to your airspeed indicator and your altimeter, vertical speed indicator and glideslope needle if you think it is useful.

- Pay special attention to the flightpath and airspeed if you run the risk of being distracted by an abnormality, emergency or other non-normal activity.

- Maintain optimum proficiency in your approach, landing and missed approach procedures.

✍ Review 29

Arrivals

1. A clearance to descend to 4000 feet at pilot's discretion means you (must commence descent immediately/may delay the commencement of your descent).

➤ may delay the commencement of your descent

2. You are doing a VFR practice instrument approach and your clearance appears likely to take you into clouds. You should (continue as cleared/remain VFR and advise ATC).

➤ remain VFR and advise ATC

3. Approaching the airport, ATC requests you to reduce speed to 160. What speed range should you remain within?

➤ 160±10 knots, but exactly 160 is better

4. The radar controller advises "traffic at 2 o'clock, 5 miles, southbound." Wind is calm. You should look approximately _____° (left/right).

➤ 60° right

5. The radar controller advises "traffic at 2 o'clock, 5 miles, southbound." You are holding a 20° correction for a crosswind from the right. You should look approximately _____° (left/right).

➤ 40° right

6. The term "radar contact" signifies that your aircraft has been identified on the radar display. Radar flight-following (will/will not) be provided, and you (are/are not) required to give position reports.

➤ will, are not

7. A S _____ T _____ A _____ R _____ is established to (separate IFR and VFR traffic/reduce traffic congestion/simplify clearance delivery procedures).

➤ Standard Terminal Arrival Route, simplify clearance delivery procedures

Instrument Approaches

8. To accept a STAR you need at least a (textual/graphic/textual and graphic) description of it in the cockpit.

➤ textual

9. ATC (may/will not) issue a STAR without a specific request from the pilot.

➤ may

10. If you do not want a STAR, you should write _____ in the remarks section of your flight plan.

➤ No STAR

Refer to the *Jeppesen* DINGO-4 STAR chart on page 577 for Questions 11–15

11. You are cleared for the DINGO-4 arrival via the SALT RIVER transition. The actual arrival begins at (SRP/TFD/BASER/DINGO).

➤ DINGO

12. The SALT RIVER transition begins at _____.

➤ SRP VORTAC

13. The STANFIELD transition begins at _____.

➤ TFD VORTAC

14. Can you accept this clearance if you do not have an operational DME?

➤ no (see top of chart)

15. How can you obtain the current weather conditions at Tucson International?

➤ ATIS frequency 123.8

16. Does a STAR give you approval to commence the actual approach?

➤ no, you need an approach clearance

Instrument Approach Charts

1. An initial approach fix is represented on an instrument approach chart by the letters _____.

➤ IAF

2. A procedure turn (is/is not) part of the initial approach segment.

➤ is

3. Aircraft approach categories are based on _____ times the stall speed in the (landing/clean) configuration at maximum gross landing weight.

➤ 1.3, landing

4. A T in an inverted black triangle in the minimums section on an NOS instrument approach chart means takeoff minimums (are/are not) standard and/or departure procedures (are/are not) published. You (should/need not) consult the alternate takeoff procedures.

➤ are not, are, should

5. The letter A in black triangle in the minimums section of an NOS instrument approach chart indicates that _____.

➤ special alternate minimums apply (refer to Chapter 25)

6. The letters MSA on an instrument approach chart mean _____.

➤ Minimum Safe Altitude

7. The published MSA provides _____ feet obstacle clearance within a _____ mile radius of the navigation facility.

➤ 1000 feet, 25 mile

8. The MSA (assures/does not assure) acceptable navigation signal coverage within a 25 mile radius of the navigation facility.

➤ does not assure

9. When being radar vectored for an ILS approach, at what point may you start a descent from your last assigned altitude if cleared for the approach?

➤ when established on a segment of a published route or instrument approach procedure

10. Your current radar vector is about to take you through the localizer. You have been cleared for the approach. You should _____.

➤ intercept the localizer

11. Your current radar vector is about to take you through the localizer. You have not been cleared for the approach. You should _____.

➤ maintain heading and query ATC

12. If cleared for an approach over a waypoint labeled NoPT, you should commence final approach (after/without) making a procedure turn.

➤ without

13. Circle-to-land minimums are based on aircraft (speed/weight).

➤ speed

14. If your aircraft has a published V_{S0} of 52 knots, it will be Category (A/B/C/D).

➤ A (since $1.3 \times V_{S0}$ 52 = 67 knots)

15. If your aircraft has a published V_{S0} of 77 knots, it will be Category (A/B/C/D).

➤ B (since $1.3 \times V_{S0}$ 77 = 100 knots)

16. When may a pilot make a straight-in landing if using an instrument approach procedure having only circling minimums?

➤ a straight-in landing may be made if the pilot has the runway in sight in sufficient time to make a normal approach for landing, and has been cleared to land

17. The pilot of a Category B aircraft decides to circle-to-land at a speed 5 knots faster than the maximum speed for that category. He should use the Category (A/B/C/D) approach minimums.

➤ Category C

18. When the approach procedure involves a procedure turn, the maximum speed should not be greater than _____ knots.

➤ 250 knots

19. If a DME is inoperative, its code tone (will/will not) be transmitted.

➤ will not

20. Is a DME that has locked-on, but has no identifiable coded tone, usable for navigation?

➤ no

21. If you are holding at an intersection, and cannot determine the abeam position, timing on the outbound leg should commence _____.

➤ at wings-level after completion of the turn outbound

RVR

1. Minimums for an ILS approach, with all components operative, normally establish a visibility requirement of _____ feet or _____ sm.

➤ RVR 2400 feet, vis $\frac{1}{2}$ sm

2. RVR represents the following distance a pilot can see:

   (a) in-flight slant range at the minimum.

   (b) in-flight slant range crossing the threshold on glideslope.

   (c) horizontal distance down the runway from the approach end of the runway.

➤ (c)

3. The RVR is not available for a particular instrument approach. The published RVR minimum (may/may not) be converted from feet to miles and used as ground visibility minimum for the landing.

➤ may

4. If the RVR equipment is inoperative for an instrument approach that specifies a minimum RVR 2400, the visibility requirement should be a ground visibility of _____.

➤ $\frac{1}{2}$ statute mile

5. In haze, you appear to be (closer to/further from) the runway than what you really are.

➤ further from

Sidestep Maneuver

1. When cleared to execute a published sidestep maneuver for a specific approach and landing on the parallel runway, you should commence this maneuver (at the minimum/as soon as the runway environment is in sight/prior to becoming visual).

➤ as soon as the runway environment is in sight

Missed Approaches

1. You commence an early missed approach prior to reaching the published MAP, which is a left turn from the MAP. After applying power and commencing a missed-approach climb, you should:

   (a) turn left immediately.

   (b) track to the MAP before commencing the turn.

   (c) declare an emergency

➤ (b)

2. You become visual on an instrument approach before reaching the MAP, and commence a circle-to-land maneuver. During this maneuver, you lose visual reference. What should your actions be?

➤ commence a missed approach, make a climbing turn toward the landing runway and continue the turn until on the missed approach course

Equipment Requirements

1. The minimum aircraft radio-navigation equipment needed to perform an ILS approach is (ILS/VOR/DME/ADF/approved RNAV receiver).

➤ ILS

2. The minimum aircraft radio-navigation equipment needed to perform an ILS/DME approach is (ILS/VOR/DME/ADF/approved RNAV receiver).

➤ ILS, DME

3. The minimum aircraft radio-navigation equipment needed to perform a VOR approach is (ILS/VOR/DME/ADF/approved RNAV receiver).

➤ VOR

4. The minimum aircraft radio-navigation equipment needed to perform a NDB approach is (ILS/VOR/DME/ADF/approved RNAV receiver).

➤ ADF

5. The minimum aircraft radionavigation equipment needed to perform an RNAV approach is (ILS/VOR/DME/ADF/approved RNAV receiver).

➤ approved RNAV receiver

Visual Illusions on Approach

1. When flying in haze, you may experience the illusion of objects being (closer/further away) than what they actually are.

➤ further away

2. To reduce the danger of spatial disorientation occurring when flying in poor visual conditions, you should rely on (your bodily sensations/the flight instruments).

➤ the flight instruments

3. In hazy conditions, another object may be (closer/further away) than it appears to be.

➤ closer

4. A runway that is larger than usual will appear to be (further away/closer) than it really is.

➤ closer

5. A runway that is smaller than usual will appear to be (further away/closer) than it really is.

➤ further away

6. A narrow runway will give the pilot on the correct approach slope an impression of being (high/low) on slope.

➤ high

7. A wide runway will give the pilot on the correct approach slope an impression of being (high/low) on slope.

➤ low

8. When on approach to land on an upsloping runway without slope guidance, the tendency is to approach on a flightpath that is too (steep/shallow).

➤ shallow

9. When on approach to land on a downsloping runway without slope guidance, the tendency is to approach on a flightpath that is too (steep/shallow).

➤ steep

Riverside ILS Rwy 9 Chart

Refer to Figure 1 on page 601, and use Category A aircraft.

1. Approaching from the southwest, the M _____ S _____ A _____ is _____ feet within _____ nm of _____.

➤ minimum safe altitude, 5100 feet, 25 nm of LKA locator

2. The ATIS at Riverside can be received on frequency _____, which requires a (VHF-COM/VHF-NAV) radio set to be used.

➤ 128.8 MHz, VHF-COM

3. Ontario approach control frequency is _____

➤ 135.4

4. Riverside control tower frequency is _____, and it (is/is not) manned continuously.

➤ 121.0, is not

5. Ground control frequency is _____

➤ 121.7

6. Approaching from the southwest and planning to use SEAL BEACH as the I _____ A _____ F _____, appropriate navaid selections would be: VOR frequency and ident _____, ILS frequency and ident _____, and ADF frequency and ident _____.

➤ initial approach fix, VOR 115.7 SLI, ILS 110.9 I-RAL, ADF 257 LKA

7. Approaching the localizer from the SEAL BEACH IAF, the minimum altitude is _____ feet.

➤ 3000 feet

8. Are DME indications available when the VHF-NAV is selected to SLI VORTAC?

➤ yes

9. Are DME indications available when the VHF-NAV is selected to the I-RAL localizer?

➤ no

10. Once you have intercepted the localizer you may descend to _____ feet prior to SWAN LAKE.

➤ 2500 feet

11. The FAF is at _____.

➤ SWAN LAKE (LKA)

12. What is the distance from SEAL BEACH to SWAN LAKE?

➤ 29.3 nm

13. Approaching SWAN LAKE after following the feeder route from the SLI IAF, and cleared for the approach, are you required to enter the holding pattern at LKA?

➤ no

14. The glideslope angle is _____° and the threshold crossing height (TCH) of the glidepath is _____ feet.

➤ 3°, 41 feet

15. The touchdown zone elevation on Rwy 9 is _____ feet MSL.

➤ TDZE 792 feet MSL

16. The decision height for a straight-in landing is _____ feet MSL, which is _____ feet HAT. Assume V_{S0} = 60 knots, which gives $1.3V_{S0}$ = _____ knots, which places the aircraft in Category _____.

➤ 1042 feet MSL, 250 feet HAT, 78 knots, Category A

17. The visibility required to continue with the landing is _____.

➤ one statute mile

18. If the glideslope fails, and you have to make a localizer-only approach, the minimum becomes (DH/MDA) _____ feet MSL which is _____ HAT. You can recognize the MAP by _____.

➤ MDA 1300 feet MSL, 508 feet HAT, timing from the FAF

19. To identify the AGNES intercept while you are flying a localizer (no glideslope) approach, you (will/will not) need a second VHF-NAV. If you are able to identify the AGNES intercept, you may cross AGNES at or above _____ feet MSL, and then descend to an MDA of _____ feet MSL. Visibility required to land is _____.

➤ will, 1300 feet MSL, 1220 feet MSL, one statute mile

20. You can fix your position at AGNES intercept with the VHF-NAV 1 on the localizer and VHF-NAV 2 on _____.

➤ PDZ VOR radial 031

21. After you have become visual with the runway in sight, the localizer fails. You (may continue/must make a missed approach).

➤ may continue

22. The localizer fails before you have become visual; you (may continue/must make a missed approach).

➤ must make a missed approach

23. Following a missed approach, the method of entering the holding pattern at PDZ is a (parallel/teardrop/direct) entry.

➤ direct

24. Approaching Riverside from the southeast, you may reverse direction to join the localizer inbound by (making a procedure turn/making an appropriate holding pattern entry).

➤ making an appropriate holding pattern entry

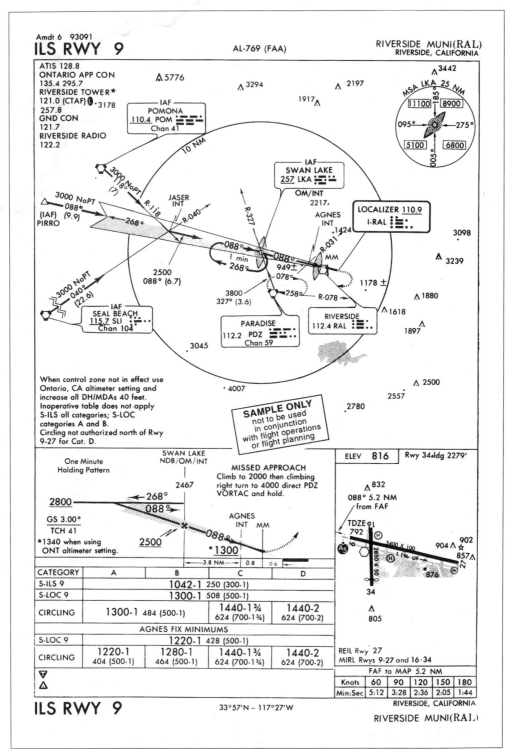

Figure 1. Riverside ILS Rwy 9 (NOS, reduced)

25. You are holding at the LOM for an ILS approach, and ATC has advised you to expect clearance for the approach at time 0915. At 0907 you experience two-way radio communications failure. What action, if any, should you take with your transponder? At what time would you begin your approach?

➤ squawk 7600; commence approach at 0915 (see Part 91, Chapter 24)

26. You are approaching JASER intercept from SLI at 3000 feet MSL and slightly right of course. Sketch how your navigation instruments might appear on the instrument faces below.

VOR freq. ....

ILS freq. ....

ADF freq. ....

➤ answer:

VOR freq. 115·7
040

ILS freq. 110·9

ADF freq. 257

27. Is a DME required for this approach?

➤ no

28. How many initial approach fixes are there for this approach?

➤ four (SLI VORTAC, POM VORTAC, PIRRO intercept and LKA NDB)

29. When Riverside Tower is not operating, the runway/approach lighting is (operating continuously/pilot-activated).

➤ pilot-activated

30. What radio equipment and frequency would you use to activate the lighting?

➤ VHF-COM, 121.0 MHz

31. What type of approach lighting is available on Rwy 9 at Riverside (hint: use a current NOS Approach Chart Legend if you don't know the answer)?

➤ Medium Intensity Approach Lighting System, with RAIL/SFL

32. Due to excessive crosswind on Rwy 9, you have been cleared for an ILS Rwy 9 approach for a landing on Rwy 34. What minimums are applicable for this procedure?

➤ circling minimums (MDA 1300 feet MSL, visibility 1 sm)

33. What landing distance is available on Rwy 34?

➤ 2279 feet (displaced threshold)

34. Is Riverside Municipal airport equipped with its own radar?

➤ no (no ASR/PAR mentioned in communications area of chart)

The preceding questions relate to the NOS chart. You may repeat the questions using the equivalent *Jeppesen* chart in Figure 29-4, page 579.

Visual Maneuvering **30**

As you near your destination airport in IFR conditions, there are three types of approach possible:

- **a standard instrument approach** as published by NOS and *Jeppesen*, followed by a circle-to-land maneuver if not a straight-in approach procedure;
- **a contact approach** if visibility is at least 1 sm (special VFR conditions); or
- **a visual approach** (if VFR weather conditions exist).

Contact and visual approaches allow a pilot to avoid flying what may be a time-consuming instrument approach if VFR or special VFR conditions exist. They expedite the flow of air traffic and reduce pilot/controller workload by shortening the flightpath to the landing.

To assist maneuvering pilots to locate the airport in conditions of visibility less than 3 miles and/or ceiling below 1000 feet, the airport rotating beacon may be operated.

Circling to Land

If the final approach direction of an instrument approach procedure does not align the airplane within ±30° of the landing runway, then it is technically no longer a *straight-in* procedure, and significant visual maneuvering (probably involving at least part of a traffic pattern) will be required to align the airplane with the landing runway.

Visual maneuvering is also known as **circling**, or **circle-to-land**. These terms are used to describe the *visual* phase of flight after completing an instrument approach, with the aim of maneuvering an aircraft into position for a landing on a runway to which a straight-in approach is not possible.

Circling to land is most commonly used when it is necessary to make an instrument approach to one runway, but you wish to land on another runway. After becoming visual, you must then maneuver the airplane for a landing on the favored runway—for instance, using a Runway 27 ILS to become visual, followed by a circling approach and landing on the into-wind Runway 9, which is not served by an instrument approach.

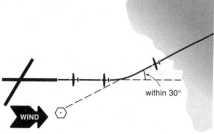

Figure 30-1. A straight-in approach

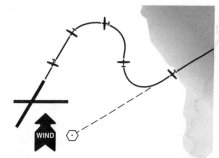

Figure 30-2. A circling approach

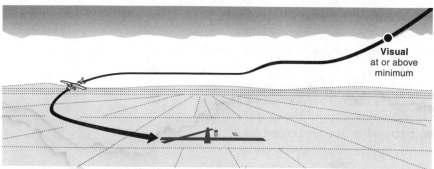

Figure 30-3. Typical maneuvering (circling) after becoming visual following an instrument approach

The flightpath that the pilot chooses to fly will vary depending on the situation—for instance, he might choose to circle in a direction that avoids high terrain, low clouds or a heavy shower.

A circling approach is a more difficult maneuver than a straight-in approach, because it often involves close-in maneuvering under low cloud bases and in rain or poor visibility. It will require precise attitude flying, with close attention to maintaining altitude, while flying a suitable flightpath to position the airplane for a landing, keeping the runway environment in view, and maintaining a good lookout for obstructions and other aircraft.

The Visual Circling Maneuver

If you become visual at or above the **circling MDA** for the instrument approach, then you should maintain circling MDA, or higher, while you maneuver within the circling area, until you are in a position to commence descent to intercept a normal final approach. A circling approach is a visual flight maneuver, and you must remain visual throughout, otherwise a missed approach is to be carried out.

Each circling situation is different because of variables such as:

- the final approach direction of the instrument approach;
- the runway layout;
- wind direction and wind speed, and the selected runway for landing;
- local terrain; and
- meteorological conditions (especially cloud bases and visibility).

For instance, wind direction and speed usually determine the runway that should be used for landing. Cloud bases usually determine what pattern altitude is flown. If there is a fog bank on one side of the airport, then a circling approach on the other side of the airport in good visibility is preferable, irrespective of whether a left or right pattern is involved.

If conditions permit, however, it is advisable to follow the normal traffic pattern, which at most airports is left-handed to provide the captain in the left seat with a good view of the runway, and to fly at the normal pattern altitude. If the clouds are lower, however, then a circling approach is legal at altitudes down to the circling minimum.

The term *circling* does not imply that the visual maneuvering should follow a circular pattern, but rather that the traffic pattern should be adjusted to suit the conditions. As a general rule, however, circling should be as close to a normal traffic pattern as conditions allow. This helps other aircraft in the pattern, as well as ATC, and keeps things as standard as possible for the pilot. If, for instance, you become visual at 2000 feet HAA on the instrument approach, well above the permitted minimum, then you should continue descent to normal pattern altitude and fly a normal pattern, rather than descend to a lower circling MDA. While training, however, your instructor may ask you to fly a pattern assuming particular cloud bases even though actual conditions do not require it.

Good attitude control is essential in the circling maneuver, with bank angle limited to 20° or standard-rate (maximum 30°), altitude maintained at or above circling MDA, and airspeed as desired. The airplane must also be configured for landing (with the landing gear and flaps extended as required), and all checks completed, before the landing is made. A well-flown circling approach is the sign of a competent pilot.

When circling to land, follow the normal traffic pattern at or above MDA, if conditions permit. Otherwise, use common sense and stay VFR if you can.

Descent Below Circling MDA

Descent below the circling MDA should not be made until:

- visual reference with the airport environment is established and maintained;
- the landing threshold is in sight; and
- the required obstacle clearance can be maintained on approach and the airplane is in a position to carry out a landing.

The most appropriate time to commence the descent from the circling MDA for a landing is when the normal landing descent profile is intercepted. The lower the circling MDA, the closer this will be to the airport. If, for instance, the airplane is circling at 400 feet HAA, the landing descent would not be commenced until on final. For higher circling MDAs, say 1200 feet HAA, the descent for a landing may be commenced earlier to avoid unnecessarily high descent rates on final.

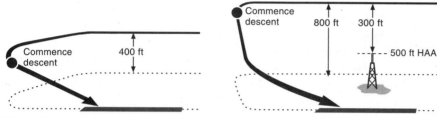

Figure 30-4. Achieve a normal landing profile

Some instrument approaches do not have a straight-in minimum published, but only a circling minimum. If, however, you have the runway in sight when you are at or above the circling MDA, and you still have sufficient room to make a normal approach for landing straight in (and provided the runway is suitable in the wind conditions), you are permitted to land straight in without circling.

Pilot Initiative and Judgment is Required

It is impossible to design a single procedure that will cater for all circling situations—this is an area for pilot judgment and decision. Because the circling maneuver may have to be carried out in poor conditions, the pilot must be able to make firm decisions fairly quickly. This ability will come with experience and with good planning. The basic assumption in circling approaches is that, after initial visual contact, the runway environment (the runway, the runway threshold or approach lighting aids, or other markings identifiable with the runway) should be kept in sight while maneuvering in the traffic pattern at or above the circling MDA.

The actual height to be flown while maneuvering in the circling area will be governed by obstacle clearance and cloud ceiling. It is unusual for cloud bases to be absolutely flat; normally they are rather irregular or ill-defined, and fluctuate in height. For this reason, it is recommended that a vertical clearance of at least 200 feet is maintained between the airplane (flying at circling MDA or higher) and the actual cloud bases. This separation is impossible to measure accurately of course, so it requires realistic estimation by the pilot who must:

- remain visual; and
- not descend below the circling MDA until in a position for a safe descent for landing.

If, for example, the circling MDA published for a particular airport is 550 feet HAA, then the pilot, seeing a forecast or reported cloud ceiling of 800 feet HAA, knows that he will probably be operating in marginal conditions. You must not circle at a lower height than the circling MDA, no matter what the

If you fly into clouds while circling at the MDA, you must make a missed approach.

clouds do—if you fly into clouds while circling at the MDA, you must make a missed approach.

The other consideration in circle-to-land maneuvers (besides cloud bases) is the minimum visibility required, typically 1 sm, $1\frac{1}{4}$ sm, or $1\frac{1}{2}$ sm for circling maneuvers. The precise visibility is impossible for you to measure in flight, but you can estimate it, keeping in mind that it is your responsibility as pilot-in-command to judge whether sufficient visibility exists for safe visual maneuvering.

Keep the runway in sight at all times, except when it disappears beneath a wing in normal maneuvering, or if you are flying directly over the top of the runway to position yourself. If at any time during a circling approach you feel uncomfortable for any reason (such as lowering cloud bases, decreasing visibility, heavy rain or hail, turbulence, or windshear), or if you lose visual contact, then don't hesitate to execute a missed approach.

The Visual Maneuvering (Circling) Area

The **visual maneuvering area** (or circling area) is the area around an airport in which obstacle clearance has been considered by the FAA for aircraft having to maneuver visually before landing. To avoid penalizing slower and more maneuverable aircraft (that require less maneuvering area than faster airplanes), different aircraft categories based on maximum speed for circling have been devised. Circling speed is based on $1.3V_{S0}$ – 1.3 times the stalling speed at maximum weight in the landing configuration.

Category A airplanes maneuvering at 90 knots or less have a circling area defined by 1.3 nm radii from the runway thresholds. Category B airplanes maneuvering at between 91 and 120 knots have a circling area defined by 1.5 nm radii from the runway thresholds—a slightly larger area which might contain higher obstacles and therefore require a higher circling MDA.

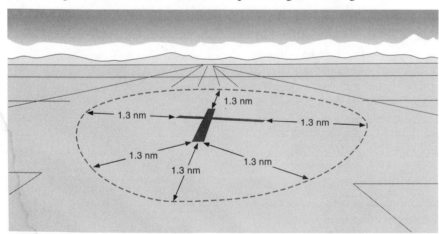

Figure 30-5. The visual maneuvering area for Category A airplanes (less than 90 knots)

If you decide to circle your Category A airplane at a speed higher than 90 knots (say 100 knots because of turbulence), then this effectively moves you into category B, with a larger circling area and possibly a higher MDA.

Note: NOS approach charts use Category A, B, C, and D to specify circling minimums. *Jeppesen* charts now specify actual maximum speeds against the corresponding circling MDA and visibility (90 KIAS, 120 KIAS, etc.). Use the circling MDA applicable to your actual circling speed if using *Jeppesen* charts.

Obstacle Clearance in the Visual Maneuvering (Circling) Area

Once the FAA has established its circling area, obstacles within this area are surveyed, and a safety margin of 300 feet added to ensure safe clearance from these obstacles at the circling MDA.

- If, for instance, the highest obstacle in the circling area is a tower 1290 feet MSL, then the circling MDA is (1290 + 300 =) 1590 feet MSL.

- If there are no specific obstacles, then 100 feet is allowed for the growth of trees and the 300 feet safety margin added to this to give a lowest circling MDA of 400 feet HAA.

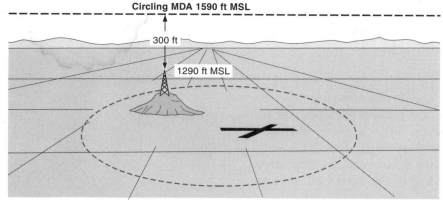

Figure 30-6. Calculation by FAA of circling MDA

Sectorized Visual Maneuvering (Circling) Areas

The lower the circling MDA, the more accessible the airport is in poor weather, since it will allow a pilot to operate beneath lower cloud bases. In an attempt to achieve lower circling MDAs, the FAA can exclude from the circling area a sector that contains a particularly high and restrictive obstacle, provided it lies outside the final approach and missed approach areas.

If the FAA does exercise this option, and thereby lowers the circling MDA, then the pilot is prohibited from circling at this lowered altitude within the excluded sector that contains the obstacle(s).

For instance, an obstacle 800 feet HAA in the normal circling area requires a circling MDA of (800 + 300) 1100 feet HAA, which operationally is very restrictive. By removing a sector that contains this obstacle from the permissible circling area, the FAA may be able to lower the circling MDA to say 400 feet HAA. A statement that circling in the excluded area is not authorized will be included on the instrument approach chart, such as "circle-to-land NA [not authorized] south of Rwy 8-26."

The Missed Approach Procedure When Circling

If you lose visual reference when circling to land after an instrument approach, then the missed approach procedure for that particular instrument approach should be followed.

The airplane may be in a slightly awkward position to follow the published missed approach procedure, depending on its position in the pattern, but it is expected that you will make an initial climbing turn toward the landing runway to track overhead the airport, from where you will continue climbing on the published missed approach course to the required altitude. This should keep the airplane clear of obstacles, first in the circling area and then in the missed approach area.

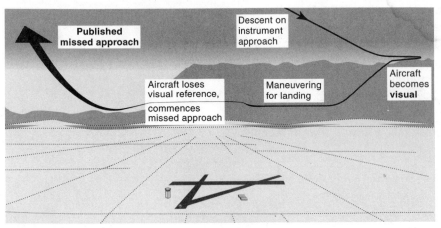

Figure 30-7. Making a missed approach when circling

Since the circling maneuver may be accomplished in more than one direction, and since the airplane could be anywhere in the traffic pattern when visual reference is lost, the pilot will have to devise and follow a suitable flightpath to establish the airplane on the prescribed missed approach course. This would depend on the airplane's position in the circling maneuver at the time visual reference is lost and the climb-out commenced, relative to the missed approach course itself.

When you decide to execute a missed approach, you must fly the airplane according to the procedure laid down in the airplane's flight manual—transitioning smoothly to a climb-out in a positive manner with prompt and precise attitude and power changes. A typical missed approach procedure may be:

- adopt the missed approach attitude and simultaneously apply go-around power;
- assume the missed approach configuration (gear up when a positive climb is achieved, flaps as required).

As soon as comfortably established in the climb (there need be no rush!), turn toward the runway and the missed approach course. Attitude flying will require most of the pilot's attention, so at least from the time he commences the circle-to-land maneuver he should have in mind:

Remember the order of importance: aviate (fly the airplane!); navigate (head it toward where you have to go); and, finally, communicate (advise ATC).

- an initial heading to turn to if he loses visual contact;
- the missed approach course; and
- the missed approach altitude.

When convenient, and once comfortably established in the climb-out, the pilot should advise ATC that he has commenced a missed approach.

Approaches With Circling Minimums Only

Some instrument approach procedures have only circle-to-land minimums published (no straight-in minimums). This is because the:

- runway is more than 30° out of alignment with the final approach path; and/or
- descent gradient from the FAF to the runway is excessive (greater than 400 ft/nm maximum), requiring a high rate of descent for a straight-in landing.

An example is the VOR/DME-A to South Lake Tahoe, CA. The "-A" (or "-B", or "-C") indicates *circling minimums only*. Circling MDA is 2536 feet HAA. While the procedure is designed for circle-to-land, you may land straight-in if you see the runway early enough, and a normal stable approach and landing can be made. Extreme caution should be used in executing this type of approach. Good judgment might dictate that a circling approach is the safest procedure.

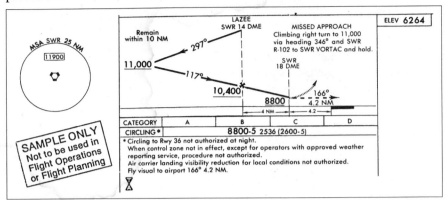

Figure 30-8. South Lake Tahoe (CA) VOR/DME-A

Airports that Do Not Have a Published IAP

If arriving at an airport which does not have a published instrument approach procedure, the pilot should, where possible, become visual well away from the airport to allow time for orientation and planning of the visual pattern. The options available to achieve this are:

1. Establish the aircraft in VFR minimums or better (for example, by requesting a clearance to descend to MEA/MOCA), then cancel IFR and proceed VFR to the airport; or

2. Descend through clouds using a published instrument approach procedure at a nearby airport, and transit visually to the destination airport in accordance with VFR.

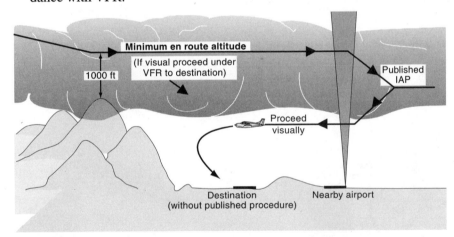

Figure 30-9. Arriving at an airport that does not have a published instrument approach

Contact Approach

A contact approach may be used by an IFR pilot, with authorization from ATC, in lieu of a standard instrument approach procedure to that airport.

The pilot must request a contact approach—it may *not* be initiated by ATC—and the *special VFR* conditions that must exist are:

- clear of clouds;
- at least 1 statute mile visibility; and
- a reasonable expectation that these conditions, or better, will continue to the airport.

ATC will issue a clearance for a contact approach on request if satisfied that:

- reported ground visibility at the airport is at least 1 sm;
- adequate separation from other IFR and special VFR traffic will exist; and
- weather conditions make this contact approach practical.

If not satisfied, ATC will deny your request for a contact approach, in which case you will proceed, as cleared, for a standard instrument approach. The pilot on a contact approach is responsible for obstruction clearance and separation from VFR traffic.

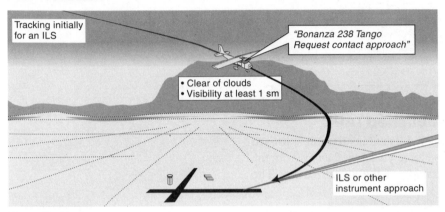

Figure 30-10. A contact approach

Visual Approach

ATC may issue a visual approach clearance, with or without pilot request, provided that VFR conditions exist. Prior to requesting, or accepting, a visual approach clearance, you must either:

- have the airport in sight; or
- have the preceding aircraft identified and in sight (in which case you should follow it, taking responsibility for separation and avoidance of wake turbulence).

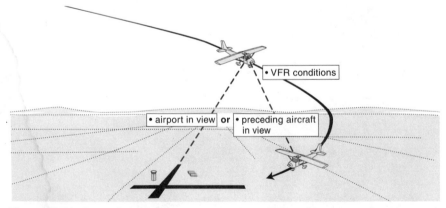

Figure 30-11. A visual approach

If you have the airport in sight, but not the preceding aircraft, ATC may still issue a clearance for a visual approach, but will retain responsibility for separation. Radar service, if provided, is automatically terminated when you are instructed to contact the tower.

A visual approach clearance is an IFR authorization, and does not alter your IFR flight plan cancellation responsibility. For instance, you must still cancel your IFR flight plan if you land at an uncontrolled airport.

At airports without an operating control tower, ATC will only authorize a visual approach if you advise them that a descent and landing can be completed in VFR conditions.

Visual Illusions

This topic was covered in some detail toward the end of the previous chapter. This serves as a reminder that visual illusions are possible to experience having transferred from instrument flight to visual flight—which hopefully will have occurred at or above the circling MDA (minimum descent altitude). When maneuvering visually for a landing after an instrument approach, you should be well prepared to experience visual illusions but not be affected by them.

- **At night**, or in dark conditions, you should avoid the use of bright white light in the cockpit so that night-adaptation of your eyes is not impaired.

- **Hazy conditions** create an illusion of greater distance—pilots who are not aware of this illusion tend to fly too low on approach and touch the ground sooner than they expect.

- **Narrow runways** also create the illusion of being high—leading unsuspecting pilots into making too-low approaches and early touchdowns.

- **Upsloping runways** also create the illusion of being high—leading unsuspecting pilots into making too-low approaches and early touchdowns.

- **Downsloping runways** will appear short and you will feel you are low on slope, creating a tendency to make a steeper than normal approach.

Wake Turbulence on Approach

Wake turbulence is caused by wingtip vortices from preceding aircraft, especially large and heavy airplanes that are flying slowly in a relatively clean configuration, at a high angle of attack. Heavy weights, high angles of attack and relatively clean configurations are typical after takeoff.

If such aircraft are ahead of you (taking off or landing), try to picture where their wake turbulence will be. The vortices will gradually drift down and be carried downwind. A light crosswind may carry the upwind vortex from a preceding aircraft on approach into your flightpath, and a light tailwind may move its vortices into your touchdown zone—so be careful when making an approach in a light quartering tailwind.

Be careful of wingtip vortices when making an approach in a light quartering tailwind.

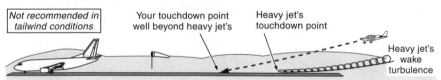

Figure 30-12. Avoidance of wake turbulence on your approach

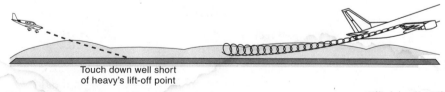

Figure 30-13. Landing behind a "heavy" that has just taken off

In general, if you are approaching to land behind a large jet airplane, try and stay above its flightpath if possible and land beyond its touchdown point.

Hydroplaning

Hydroplaning occurs when a small layer of water exists between the airplane tire and the runway surface. This can happen near takeoff and touchdown speeds when there is water or slush on the runway, especially if the runway is smooth. There will be almost no friction between the tire and the runway, in fact the tire may not even spin up, and so directional control may be difficult and braking may be totally ineffective.

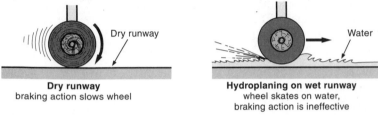

Dry runway
braking action slows wheel

Hydroplaning on wet runway
wheel skates on water,
braking action is ineffective

Figure 30-14. Low-friction surfaces significantly affect runway performance

If you suspect hydroplaning is a possibility because of standing water on the runway during heavy rain, you should consider delaying your takeoff or landing, or diverting to another airport.

✍ Review 30

1. A straight-in procedure aligns the airplane within ± _____ ° of the landing runway; an instrument approach procedure that is not straight-in will be followed by a _____-to-land maneuver, once the pilot is visual at or above the (circling/straight-in) MDA.

➤ ±30°, circle-to-land, circling MDA

2. You should circle-to-land at the:
   (a) decision height.
   (b) circling MDA.
   (c) straight-in MDA.
   (d) alternate minimum.

➤ (b)

3. You should commence descent from the circling MDA:
   (a) only when aligned with the landing runway.
   (b) to intercept a reasonable final approach path not requiring abnormal maneuvers.
   (c) at any time in the pattern.

➤ (b)

Visual Maneuvering

4. May you make a straight-in landing if you are flying an instrument approach that has only circling minimums published?

➤ yes, if you have the runway (which must be suitable, of course) in sight and sufficient room to make a normal approach

5. Obstruction clearance in the circling area is _____ feet .

➤ 300 feet

6. If the highest obstacle in the circling area is 450 feet HAA, you would expect the circling MDA to be _____ feet HAA.

➤ 750 feet HAA

7. If the circling MDA is 950 feet HAA, you would expect the highest obstacle in the circling area to be _____ feet HAA.

➤ 650 feet HAA

8. The circling area for an airplane that maneuvers at 90 knots or less is defined by _____ nm radii from the runway end.

➤ 1.3 nm

9. The circling area for an airplane that maneuvers at 120 knots or less is defined by _____ nm radii from the runway end.

➤ 1.5 nm

10. If V_{S0} for your airplane is 80 knots, then your circling MDA is that for airplanes maneuvering at less than (90/120/140/165) knots, which is Category (A/B/C/D).

➤ 120 knots, Category B ($1.3V_{S0}$ = 104 knots)

11. If V_{S0} for your airplane is 65 knots, then your circling MDA is that for airplanes maneuvering at less than (90/120/140/165) knots, which is Category (A/B/C/D).

➤ 90 knots, Category A ($1.3V_{S0}$ = 85 knots)

12. If you lose visual reference circling-to-land, then you should commence a missed approach:

    (a) straight ahead.

    (b) with an initial climbing turn toward the runway, then out on the missed approach course published for the IAP used.

➤ (b)

13. You (are/are not) required to notify ATC that you have commenced a missed approach.

➤ are

14. If conditions are suitable, what sorts of approach may you make, with ATC approval, to avoid having to fly a standard instrument approach procedure?

➤ a contact approach or a visual approach

15. Does the issuance of a clearance to make a visual approach cancel your IFR flight plan?

➤ no

16. What two conditions are necessary before ATC can authorize a visual approach?

➤ you must have the airport in sight or a preceding aircraft to follow, and be able to proceed to the airport in VFR conditions

17. ATC (may/may not) issue a visual approach without pilot request.

➤ may

18. ATC (may/may not) issue a contact approach without pilot request.

➤ may not

19. The weather minimums for a visual approach are (higher than/lower than/the same as) those for a contact approach.

➤ higher than

20. What weather minimums must exist for a visual approach?

➤ VFR conditions

21. What weather minimums must exist for a contact approach?

➤ 1 mile visibility and clear of clouds

22. Must a pilot request a contact approach?

➤ yes

23. If the reported visibility is less than 1 mile and you request a contact approach, would you expect ATC to issue one?

➤ no

24. Can ATC assign a visual approach without pilot request?

➤ yes

25. On visual approaches, radar service is automatically terminated when:

    (a) ATC so advises.

    (b) the pilot is instructed to contact the tower.

    (c) after landing.

➤ (b)

26. To avoid impairing your night-adaptation you should (use/avoid) bright white light in the cockpit.

➤ avoid

27. An upsloping runway may cause an illusion of being (high/low), leading unsuspecting pilots into making (too-high/too-low) approaches.

➤ high, too-low

28. A narrower-than-usual runway may create an illusion of being (high/low), leading unsuspecting pilots into making a (too-high/too-low) approach.

➤ high, too-low

29. Haze creates an illusion of distance from the runway being (greater/less) than what it really is, leading unsuspecting pilots into flying a (too-high/too-low) approach.

➤ greater, too-low

30. The wind condition which prolongs wake turbulence of a preceding aircraft on the runway for the longest period of time is a (strong headwind/strong tailwind/strong crosswind/light crosswind/light quartering tailwind).

➤ light quartering tailwind

31. Wake turbulence is caused by (jet engines/wingtip vortices) and is greatest behind (light/heavy) aircraft flying at (high/low) angles of attack.

➤ wingtip vortices, heavy, high

32. A light crosswind may carry the (upwind/downwind) wingtip vortex of a preceding airplane over the runway.

➤ upwind

33. If possible, try to land (at/before/beyond) the touchdown point of a preceding heavy jet airliner.

➤ beyond

34. If a strong headwind on approach suddenly shears to a calm wind, as can happen if you fly through a temperature inversion on approach, you would expect (no change in/a sudden loss of/a sudden gain of) airspeed.

➤ a sudden loss of

35. Hydroplaning may occur at (high/low) speeds on a (dry/wet and slushy) runway.

➤ high, wet and slushy

36. During hydroplaning, the tire is (in contact with/separated from) the runway surface.

➤ separated from

37. Hydroplaning (improves/decreases dramatically) a pilot's ability to achieve directional control and good braking on the runway.

➤ decreases dramatically

38. If an airport rotating beacon is operating during daylight hours in Class B, C or D airspace, this indicates that the ground visibility is less than _____ miles and/or the ceiling is less than _____ feet.

➤ 3 miles, 1000 feet

39. What action could a tower controller take during daylight hours to assist maneuvering pilots to locate the airport in poor conditions with visibility less than 3 miles and/or ceiling less than 1000 feet?

➤ activate the airport rotating beacon

AC severe weather outlook chart

ACLT actual calculated landing time

ADF automatic direction finder (usually tuned to a nondirectional beacon, NDB)

ADIZ Air Defense Identification Zone

ADR advisory route

A/FD airport/facility directory

AGL above ground level

AH artificial horizon

AI attitude indicator

AIM Aeronautical Information Manual

AIRMET airman's meteorological information, urgent items that might affect some aircraft

Airspace Classification System system in which Classes A through E and G are allocated to the various components of controlled and uncontrolled airspace, conforming closely to ICAO format

ALS approach lighting system

ALT altitude

alternate alternative destination airport, designated for use if a landing is not possible at planned destination

altitude vertical distance above mean sea level

ALTN alternate airport

AMA area minimum altitude (Jeppesen charts)

A/P autopilot

APP approach

approach control ATC service for aircraft approaching (or departing, or in vicinity of) a controlled airport

approach plate a published navigation document describing an instrument approach, usually including a horizontal map, a vertical profile, courses, heights, and weather minimums

APT airport

area navigation (R-Nav or RNAV) navigation system that does not confine the navigation of aircraft to routes passing overhead ground-based radio navaids

ARSR air route surveillance radar

ARTCC air route traffic control center

ASR airport surveillance radar

ASD accelerate–stop distance

ASI airspeed indicator

ASOS automated surface observing system, which provides weather information at airports

ATA actual time of arrival

ATC air traffic control

ATCRBS air traffic control radar beacon system

ATD actual time of departure

ATIS automatic terminal information service

attitude relation of the three airplane axes to an external reference system

AT-VASI abbreviated T-VASI—a set of lights to one side of the runway to provide slope guidance on approach

AWOS automated weather observing system, in varying capabilities: AWOS-A, AWOS-1, AWOS-2 and AWOS-3

AWW severe weather forecast alerts

azimuth horizontal bearing or direction

base cloud base (height above ground level of the underside surface of cloud)

basic-T standard-T layout of primary flight instruments on cockpit instrument panel

BFO beat frequency oscillator (additional equipment in ADF installation needed to enable identification of certain NDBs, especially some in Europe)

C Celsius temperature scale (formerly centigrade)

CAS calibrated airspeed—indicated airspeed corrected for any position error of the pitot tube

CAT clear air turbulence

CAT I, II or III ILS approach categories, each having a specific combination of decision height and visibility (or runway visual range); for bad weather landings following an ILS approach

category performance category of aircraft, used to determine approach minimums

CDI course deviation indicator—component of cockpit VHF-NAV display instrument

ceiling vertical distance above the surface level of the base of the lowest layer of cloud; greatest altitude that an airplane can reach

14 CFR Code of Federal Regulations; regulations pertaining to the construction, maintenance and operation of aircraft in the U.S.

Class see airspace classification system

"cleared" authorized to carry out a particular maneuver in flight operations (such as "cleared for takeoff," "cleared for the approach," "cleared to land")

clear air turbulence (CAT) significant turbulence encountered outside clouds, often at altitude near the jetstream, or near mountains

clearance authorization by air traffic control (ATC) for an aircraft to proceed under specified conditions

clearance limit fix or waypoint to which a flight may be cleared, there to receive a further clearance towards the destination

command bars principal reference index on flight director cockpit instrument

compass locator see locator

contact approach variation to the standard instrument approach procedure available in certain conditions, with authorization from ATC

converging approaches simultaneous ILS approach procedures to converging runways at the same airport

COP changeover point

course direction of intended flight, usually expressed in degrees magnetic

CRT cathode ray tube

CW continuous wave radio transmissions

CWA center weather advisory

DA density altitude

DA(H) Decision Altitude (Height); international (ICAO) system of specifying minimum for a precision approach, such as an ILS. It is a combination of DA (Decision Altitude, based on MSL) and DH (decision height, based on runway touchdown zone, HAT). Jeppesen approach plates now utilize this international system, and pilots should be alert to the NOS use of the term Decision Height, 'DH', which is based on MSL.

DALR dry adiabatic lapse rate

departure point navigational checkpoint (such as a VOR, NDB or visual fix) used as the point from which to set course

dewpoint temperature at which air becomes 100% saturated and begins to condense into clouds

DH lowest point at which a missed approach must be commenced if the required conditions to continue approach to land have not been established following a precision approach, such as an ILS. This presentation is used by NOS. Two values are specified—the first is MSL altitude; the second is height above runway touchdown zone (HAT). Refer also to ICAO term: DA(H).

DME distance measuring equipment

DP departure procedure

DR dead reckoning (from term deduced reckoning)

DUAT direct user access terminal for weather data

EAT expected approach time

EET estimated elapsed time

EFAS enroute flight advisory service (callsign .... Flight Watch) operating on 122.0 MHz

ELEV elevation, vertical distance of airport, or place, measured from mean sea level

ELR environmental lapse rate of ambient air

ETA estimated time of arrival

ETE estimated time en route

ETD estimated time of departure

ETI estimated time interval

F Fahrenheit temperature scale

FA area forecast

FAA Federal Aviation Administration

FAF final approach fix

false glideslope false indication of being on ILS glideslope

fan marker radio position-fixing beacon radiating in a vertical, fan-shaped pattern (see marker beacon)

FD winds and temperatures aloft forecast

final approach IFR inbound flight from the final approach fix

fix a determined aircraft position

FL flight level

flag warning flag, usually red, to warn pilot of electrical or signal failure to an instrument

Flight Watch callsign for radio contact with EFAS FSS

FPA flightpath angle

FSS Flight Service Station

g acceleration due to gravity

GCA ground controlled approach (radar) (see PAR approach)

glidepath, GP path formed by intersection of localizer and glideslope planes of an ILS, the ideal flightpath for the ILS approach

glideslope inclined radio beam of ILS, providing vertical guidance

GPS global positioning system

GS glideslope; groundspeed

HAA height above airport; height of the MDA above the airport elevation

HAT height above touchdown —the height of the DH above the highest runway elevation in the touchdown zone

heading angle between horizontal reference datum, usually magnetic north, and the longitudinal axis of aircraft, usually expressed as a three-figure group

HF high frequency radio transmissions

HI heading indicator (formerly directional gyro, direction indicator)

HIWAS hazardous in-flight weather advisory service

hPa hectopascal (unit of pressure used internationally)

HSI horizontal situation indicator

IAF initial approach fix

IAP instrument approach procedure

IFR instrument flight rules

ILS instrument landing system

IMC instrument meteorological conditions

instrument approach prescribed procedure for maneuvering, based on specified radio navaid(s), to enable descent on instruments to a safe minimum altitude in the vicinity of an airport

IR instrument rating

ISA international standard atmosphere

isobar line joining points of equal atmospheric pressure

isotach line joining points of a equal wind speed

isotherm line joining points of equal temperature

Jeppesen U.S. company producing domestic and international aeronautical charts and approach plates

KCAS knots calibrated airspeed

KIAS knots indicated speed

KTAS knots true airspeed

LDA localizer type directional aid

LF low frequency radio transmissions

LIFR low IFR, used on some meteorological charts

LLWAS low-level windshear alert system

LNAV lateral (or horizontal) navigation

localizer component of ILS providing track guidance along extended runway centerline

locator low-powered NDB, usually associated with ILS

LOM locator outer marker

LORAN a long-range navigation system

MAA maximum authorized altitude

magnetic variation difference, in degrees, between magnetic north and true north at a place

MALS medium intensity approach light system

MAP missed approach point

marker beacon component of ILS, providing horizontal position fixing

mb millibar (unit of pressure used in some countries, mostly now replaced by equivalent unit hectopascal)

MC magnetic course

MCA minimum crossing altitude

MDA minimum descent altitude (MSL), for nonprecision instrument approach (VOR, NDB)

MDA(H) international (ICAO) method of specifying nonprecision approach minimum, used by Jeppesen; term is a combination of minimum descent altitude (MSL) and height above airport (HAA)

MEA minimum enroute altitude

METAR/SPECI surface weather observations issued hourly, or, in the case of a SPECI, whenever significant changes to weather at a location have occurred

MF medium frequency radio transmissions

MH magnetic heading

MHA maximum holding altitude

MLS microwave landing system

MM middle marker, beacon on ILS

MOA military operations area

MOCA minimum obstruction clearance altitude

MORA minimum off route altitude (Jeppesen charts)

MRA minimum reception altitude

MSA minimum safe altitude (circle)

MSL mean sea level; above mean sea level

MTA military training area

MVA minimum vectoring altitude

MVFR marginal VFR

NDB nondirectional beacon

NOS National Ocean Survey—U.S. Government producer of instrument charts and approach plates for domestic operations

NOTAM notice to airmen

NTSB National Transportation Safety Board

OBI omni bearing indicator

OBS omni bearing selector

OFT outer fix time

OM outer marker (beacon on ILS)

omni abbreviated term often used for VOR, from omni-directional

PAPI precision approach path indicator

PAR precision approach radar

PAR approach a precision instrument approach guided by ATC precision radar

PIREP pilot weather report

PPI plan position indicator

pressure altitude vertical distance, expressed in feet, referenced to standard pressure 29.92 in. Hg (1013.2 hPa); a flight level is a pressure altitude.

PVASI pulsating visual approach slope indicator

RADAT freezing level data in SA

RAIL runway alignment indicator lights

RB relative bearing

RBI relative bearing indicator (fixed-azimuth cockpit ADF display)

RCLS runway centerline lighting system

RCO remote communications outlet

REIL runway end identifier lights

RMI radio magnetic indicator (rotating-azimuth cockpit ADF display)

RNAV area navigation equipment

RVR runway visual range

squawk activate a transponder on a specified code

SALR saturated adiabatic lapse rate

SALS short approach lighting system

SDF simplified directional facility, similar to a localizer

SFL sequenced flashing lights (approach light system)

SIAP standard instrument approach procedure

SIGMET significant meteorological information that might affect all categories of aircraft

SSR ATC secondary surveillance radar system

SSV standard service volume of VOR or NDB

STAR standard terminal arrival route

surface area term referring to the lateral dimensions at the surface of Class B, C, D or E airspace areas

TACAN tactical air navigation—UHF military radio navigation aid giving both bearing and distance information to suitably equipped aircraft

TAF terminal aerodrome forecast

TCH threshold crossing height

TDZE touchdown zone elevation

TDZL touchdown zone lighting

TEC tower en route control (routes)

tropopause division between troposphere and stratosphere

TTS time to station

TRSA terminal radar service area

TWEB transcribed weather broadcast

UTC coordinated universal time or zulu time (formerly GMT)

variation see magnetic variation

VASI visual approach slope indicator

VDF VHF direction finding procedure

VDP visual descent point

VFR visual flight rules

VHF very high frequency radio transmissions

visual maneuvering (circling) area area around an airport in which obstacle clearance has been considered by FAA

VLF/Omega very low frequency long-range navigation equipment using network of global transmitters to fix aircraft position

VMC visual meteorological conditions

V-NAV vertical navigation, usually referring to capability of cockpit navigation equipment to schedule climb/descent profiles

VOR VHF omni-directional radio range

VORTAC combination of VOR and TACAN offering VOR azimuth information and TACAN DME distance information to suitably equipped aircraft

VSI vertical speed indicator

WA AIRMET

WS SIGMET

Z short for Zulu. ATC reference to UTC time standard (UTC was formerly known as GMT.)

Index

A

ADF *see* automatic direction finder
adiabatic
    dry lapse rate 390
    processes 390
    saturated lapse rate 390
advection fog 383
air masses 422
AIRMETs 460
airspace classification 478, 514–516
airspeed
    in steep turns 126
    in turns 124
    management 24, 76, 80, 82, 86–92, 96,
        115, 151
    monitoring 20, 22–26, 75, 79
airspeed indicator 31, 36–40
    calibration 37
    color coding 37
    errors 40
    in climb 23, 96, 98
    in descent 103
    in straight-and-level 24, 73, 75, 79
    instrument flying use 20, 22, 25
    limit speed markings 38
    partial panel use 143, 146, 153
    pitot heat use 59
    pitot-static system and 58
    pitot tube blockage, effect 59, 144
    preflight checks 61
    static line blockage, effect 59, 144
    TAS indicators 39
AI *see* attitude indicator
alternate
    airports 486, 518
    minimums 586
altimeter 31, 46–52
    accuracy 47
    altimetry procedures 48, 74, 104, 487
    altitude-encoding 49, 192
    calibration 46, 50
    density error 50
    digital 49
    in climb 23, 96, 100
    in descent 103, 104
    in straight-and-level 23, 73, 79
    instrument flying use 20, 22, 25, 26, 27
    interpretation 48
    in turns 114, 115
    Kollsman window 47

operation 46
partial panel use 143, 146, 153
pitot-static system and 58
position error 52
preflight checks 50, 61
presentation 48
pressure error correction 52
pressure window 47
static line blockage, effect 59, 144
tests and inspections 484
altimeter setting
    altimetry procedures and 48
    altitude indications and 48, 51
    for instrument approach 253, 302, 577
altitude
    altimeter setting and 47, 48
    density altitude 51
    management 23, 78–82, 87, 89, 90
    monitoring 20, 22–27, 74, 76, 78–82
    pressure changes and 46, 47
    true altitude 51
anticyclones 427
anti-icers on aircraft 375
approach
    minimums 585–586
    timing to MAP 586
    visual illusions on 611
    wake turbulence on 611
Arctic sea smoke 384
area forecasts 447
    international differences 447
ASI *see* airspeed indicator
ATIS *see* automatic terminal information
    service
atmosphere 419
    moisture content 388
attitude indicator 31–35
    errors 33, 84
    failure 33, 84–85, 143, 146
    in climb 95
    in descent 102
    in straight-and-level 73, 76
    instrument flying use 19, 20, 22, 23, 27
    in turns 114, 125
    pitch and bank limits 34
    power source 60
    preflight checks 34, 62
    resetting in flight 84
automated surface observing system 461
automated weather observing system 431,
    460, 531, 575

automatic direction finder 213–229
    airborne equipment 220
    antennas 220–223
    control panel 223
    DME arcs and 568
    indicators 224, 228
    NDB approach 252–255, 270
    RBI 225
        course intercepts 235–240, 534
        orientation 214, 226, 231–234
        tracking 241–252
    RMI 259
        course intercepts 260–262
        orientation 259
        tracking 262–270
    rotatable-card ADF 227, 259
automatic terminal information service 431,
    460, 531, 575

B

balance
    management 26, 56, 102, 115, 143
    monitoring 20, 26, 54, 55, 115, 143
    partial panel display 147
bank angle
    attitude indicator display 32
    partial panel display 147–149
    required accuracy 115, 125
    turn coordinator display 54
    turn indicator display 54
    turn rate and 111
base turns 567, 590

C

calibrated airspeed 40
carburetor icing 374
castellanus clouds 388
CAT *see* clear air turbulence
change-over point (COP) 278, 509
Chinook wind effect 394
circling approach 580, 603–609
    circling area 606
    circling MDA 604, 606
    circling minimums 606
    circling-only instrument approaches 584,
        608
    descent below circling MDA 591, 605
    missed approach 607
    non-IAP airports 609
    visual reference 591

cirrus clouds 387, 417
Class A airspace 487, 507
clear air turbulence 416
clearances 486, 535
    abbreviated clearances 537
    clearance shorthand 538
    compliance with 487
    departure clearances 537
    en route clearances 543
clear ice 372
climb
    constant-rate 100–101
    control instruments 95
    leveling off 97
    management 23, 95–102
    monitoring 20, 23, 26, 95–102
    partial panel display 147, 152–154
    required accuracy 96, 177, 178
    speeds 98
clock
    in climb 100
    in turns 116, 118
    partial panel use 157
    requirement for IFR flight 57
    setting 57
clouds 387–397
    formation 389
        air stability and 390
        convection 392
        orographic uplift 393
        turbulence and mixing 394
        widespread lifting 395
    high-level clouds 417
    low-level clouds 387
    naming of 387
    precipitation and 395
    rotor 393
    structural icing and 373
    types 387
cloudy ice 372
cold fronts 424, 425
cols 428
composite moisture stability chart 459
constant pressure analysis charts 453–455
contact approach 609
contrails 418
controlled airspace
    en route chart presentation 511, 513
convective SIGMETs 460
convergence 426
converging approaches 338
coordination ball 54–56
    in climb 96
    in straight-and-level 75, 77
    instrument flying use 20, 22, 26
    in turns 56, 114–115, 121, 125
    on descent 102, 103
    partial panel use 143, 147, 153
    preflight checks 61

Coriolis force 419–421
    jetstream formation and 416
cruise levels
    en route changes 543
    for IFR flight plan 518
    IFR 487, 507, 537
    VFR 487
    VFR-on-top 546
cumulonimbus clouds 401
    see also thunderstorms
cumulus clouds 387

D

decision altitude 337
decision height 488, 581, 591
de-icers on aircraft 375
departure procedures 535
    transition in 535
depressions 426
descent
    constant-rate 106
    control instruments 95, 102
    leveling off 104
    management 95, 102–106
    monitoring 20, 26, 102–106
    partial panel display 147, 154–156
    required accuracy 104, 105, 177, 178
descent point calculations 575
dew 381
dewpoint 393
    spread with temperature, and fog 382
    temperature 389
direction indicator *see* heading indicator
direct user access terminal 431
distance measuring equipment 207–211
    DME/ILS frequency pairing 211
    DME/VOR frequency pairing 210, 279
    DME arcs 211, 270, 335, 568–570
    DME failure 546
    groundspeed display 208
    ground stations 210
    LOC/DME approach 325
    position fixes 208, 210, 285
    range 210
diversions 546
    to alternate airports 547
DME *see* distance measuring equipment
downbursts 405–407
DP *see* departure procedures
dry adiabatic lapse rate 390
DUAT *see* direct user access terminal

E

EFAS *see* en route flight advisory
    service 431
electrical failure, effects 144
embedded thunderstorms 404, 409
engine intake icing 374

en route
    clearances 543
    diversions 546
    level changes 543
    position reports 544
    preferred IFR routes 517
    radar service 543
    reporting requirements 544–545
    track-keeping requirements 545
    VFR-on-top 546
en route charts 278, 506
    airports 506
    airspace structure 511, 513
    COP presentation 509
    MAA presentation 509
    MCA presentation 508
    MEA presentation 507
    MOCA presentation 508
    MRA presentation 508
    radio communications 511, 513, 516
    radio navigation aids 506, 511, 513
    route structure 507, 510, 512
en route flight advisory service 431, 459,
    545, 546
environmental lapse rate 391
equivalent airspeed 40
exhaust condensation trails 418

F

FA *see* area forecasts
FD *see* winds and temperatures aloft
    forecasts
final approach fix 254, 580
flight director 58
flight-following, radar service 544
flight instruments 31–62
    failure 143
    preflight checks 61
flight plan
    airway routes 518
    alternate airports 518
    altitude selection 518
    cancellation requirements 547
    fuel requirements 519
    off-airways routes 518
    preferred IFR routes 517
    tower en route control routes 517
    typical IFR flight plan 522
Flight Watch 434
fluxgate 228
fluxvalve 228
foehn wind effect 394
fog 384
    advection fog 383
    formation 382
    precipitation-induced 384
    radiation fog 382
    steam fog 384
    upslope fog 384
fractus clouds 388

fronts 395, 422
  frontal fog 384
  frontal wave 426
  frontal weather 422
frost 372
  formation process 381
fuel
  minimum fuel 547
  requirements for IFR flights 485, 519

G

geostrophic wind 420
glideslope 317–323
  false glideslope 319
  flying technique 319, 322–323, 336
  frequency 320
  indicator 320–323
  principles 319
  technique 319
  threshold crossing height 318
global positioning systems (GPS) 361
gradient wind 420
gust 403
gyroscope 60
  attitude indicator and 32
  heading indicator and 40
  power sources 60
  precession errors 33, 60
  turn coordinator and 53

H

hailstones 402, 404
hazardous in-flight weather advisory
    service 460, 545
heading
  management 27, 77, 87, 89
  monitoring 20, 22, 25, 26, 75, 77
  partial panel display 143, 149, 150, 153
heading indicator 31, 40–43
  alignment with compass 40, 43, 117
  errors 42
  failure 43, 143
  in climb 96, 98
  in straight-and-level 74, 77
  instrument flying use 20, 22, 25, 26
  interpretation 41
  in turns 115, 117
  on descent 103
  pitch and bank limits 43
  power source 60
  preflight checks 43, 62
hectopascal 46
high-level weather 415
HI see heading indicator
HIWAS see hazardous in-flight weather
    advisory service
holding patterns 553–565
  components 553
  entry procedures 559–562
  ground radius 558

holding fixes 554
  in instrument approaches 567
  maximum speeds 555–556
  at NDB 562
  non-published 555
  at outer marker 564
  prior to instrument approach 335
  published 554
  standard patterns 554
  timing 556
  tracking 556
  at VOR 563
  at VOR/DME fix 564
  at VOR/VOR fix 563
  wind corrections 557–559
horizontal situation indicator 45, 299
  tracking using 300
  use on ILS approach 316
HSI see horizontal situation indicator
hurricanes 427
hydroplaning 531, 575, 612
hyperventilation 546
hypoxia 546

I

ice accretion, hazardous effects 371
icing
  carburetor 374
  clear 372
  cloudy or mixed 372
  engine intake 374
  frost 372
  induction type 374
  instrument 375
  rime ice 372
  structural type 371
IFR departure procedures 531–540
IFR operations
  aircraft speed 490
  alternate airports 486, 518
  clearance requirements 486
  compliance with ATC clearances 487
  compulsory radio reports 544
  cruise levels 487, 507, 518, 537
  DME failure 546
  flight planning 486, 517–522
  fuel requirements 485, 519
  IFR flight plan cancelation 547
  inoperative instruments and
    equipment 485
  instrument and equipment
    requirements 482–483
  malfunction reports 484
  minimum altitudes 488, 507–509, 518,
    585–586, 608
  off-airways routes 518
  portable electronic devices 490
  position reports 544
  preferred IFR routes 517
  preflight considerations 485, 505

radio communications 490
radio failure procedures 490–491
recent experience requirements 480
takeoff and landing 488, 531
tower en route control routes 517
VFR-on-top 546
ILS see instrument landing system
inclinometer 54
  see also coordination ball
indicated airspeed 36
  calibrated airspeed and 40
  dynamic pressure and 36
  performance and 38
  true airspeed and 38
induction icing 374
initial approach fix 578
instrument and equipment
    requirements 482–483
  Class B airspace 483
  IFR 483
  VFR 482
instrument approach
  altimeter setting 253, 302, 577
  approach minimums 585–586
  circling-only approaches 608
  descent profile 189, 317
  DF approach 368
  general considerations 590–591
  ILS/DME approach 325
  ILS approach 107–108, 309–339, 580
  inoperative components 332
  LDA approach 339
  LOC/DME approach 325
  LOC approach 322, 337
  NDB approach 252–255, 270
  RNAV approach 358
  SDF approach 340
  segments 578–582
  timed approaches 565, 575
  timing to MAP 586
  visual descent point (VDP) 586
  visual reference 591
  VOR approach 295, 300–302
instrument approach charts
  approach minimums 585
  circle-to-land only 584, 608
  general features 582–589
  ILS approach 333, 337, 589
  LDA approach 339
  NDB approach 252–255, 580, 587
  RNAV approach 358
  SDF approach 340
  VOR/DME-A approach 608
  VOR approach 300–302, 588
instrument icing 375
instrument landing system 309–347
  airborne equipment 310
  associated visual aids 310, 326
  components 107, 309–314, 317–322,
    324–326

instrument landing system (*continued*)
   ILS/DME approach 325
   ILS/DME frequency pairing 211
   ILS approach 107, 108, 309–339
   simultaneous converging
      approaches 338
Instrument Rating
   instrument flight time 479
   practical test standards 177
instrument scan
   basic-T scan 25
   circular scan 27
   establishing instrument failure 143
   inverted-V scan 28
   selective radial scan 23, 26
   techniques 20–28
   vertical scan 28
intercepting course
   using RBI 235–240, 534
   using RMI 260–262, 299
   using VOR 296–299, 534
inversions
   reduced visibility and 380
isobars 419
isotachs 455
isotherms 455

J

jetstreams 415
   clear air turbulence and 416
   formation 416

K

Kollsman window 47

L

landing minimum 591
lapse rate
   ambient 391
   dry adiabatic 390
   environmental 391
   saturated adiabatic 390
latent heat 390
lenticular clouds 388, 393
lifted index 397
lighting
   airport rotating beacon 531
   approach lighting 326
   control 331
   PAPI 329
   pilot-controlled 331
   PVASI 329
   runway lighting 326, 330
   taxiway lights 331
   tri-color VASI 329
   T-VASI 330
   VASI 326–330
lightning 401

localizer 310–317
   back course 312, 316
   blue-right course 316
   failure 314
   flying technique 314–317, 335
   frequency 311, 312
   indicator 310, 312–317
   LOC approach 322, 337
   range 311
   sensitivity 311, 313
localizer-type directional aid 339
LORAN 360
low-level significant weather prog chart 444

M

Mach indicator 40
Mach number 40
magnetic compass 56–57
   compass correction card 41, 56
   errors 41, 56, 119
   HI alignment 40, 43
   partial panel use 143, 147, 149, 153, 157
   preflight checks 57, 61
   turns with 119
   vertical compass 57
marker beacons 324–325
   back course marker 325
   fan markers 325
   frequency 324
   indicator 324
   inner marker 325
   middle marker 324
   outer marker 324
maximum authorized altitude 509
METAR 440
microbursts 396, 405–407
microwave landing system 341
millibar 46
minimum crossing altitude 508
minimum descent altitude 488, 582, 591
   circling MDA 604, 606
   operation below MDA 489, 591, 605
minimum en route altitude 277, 488, 507,
   532
   for off-airways route 518
   on en route charts 507
minimum fuel 547
minimum holding altitude 553
minimum obstruction clearance
    altitude 277, 488, 508
   on en route charts 508
minimum reception altitude 278, 509
   on en route charts 509
minimum safe altitude 252, 300, 585
minimum vectoring altitude 186, 591
missed approach 581, 591, 592
   examples 254, 337
   from circling approach 607
   partial panel 156

   requirements 489
   technique 105, 607
missed approach point 580
   determination 586
   timing to 586
mountain wave turbulence 393

N

National Weather Service 431, 436
navigation management systems 363
NDB *see* nondirectional beacon
night approach, visual illusions 594
nimbus clouds 388
no-gyro approaches 191
nondirectional beacon 213–219
   antenna types 217
   classification 218
   compass locator 216, 218
   holding patterns 562
   identification 219
   information sources 217
   limitations 218
   NDB approach 252–255, 270, 580, 587
   range 218
nonprecision approach 580
   missed approach point 581
NOTAMs 433, 517
NWS *see* National Weather Service

O

OAT gauge 58
obstacle clearance
   during circling approach 605, 607
   on takeoff 532
occluded fronts 425
orientation
   using RBI 231–234, 235
   using RMI 259, 299
   using VOR 280, 284–290
overshoot effect 344
oxygen
   crew oxygen requirements 484, 546
   high-altitude flight and 546
   passenger oxygen requirements 484

P

PAR approach 184, 187
   procedures 190
partial panel
   bank attitude on 147–149
   causes 143–145
   climbs on 152–154
   descents on 154–156
   missed approach 156
   pitch attitude on 146–147
   procedures 145
   stall recovery 141
   straight-and-level on 150–152
   turns on 157–160
   unusual attitudes 135, 137, 139

performance category 585
pilot weather reports 434, 442–444
PIREPs *see* pilot weather reports
pitch attitude
    attitude indicator display 32
    partial panel display 146–147, 153
pitot heat 375
pitot-static system 58
    pitot tube blockage 59, 144
    static line blockage 59, 144
position reports 544
power
    in steep turns 124
    management 24, 73, 81, 82, 86–92, 100,
        102
    monitoring 24, 73
    power changes, effect 86, 96, 102
power indicator 35
    engine pressure ratio (EPR) gauge 35
    in climb 95
    in descent 102
    in straight-and-level 73
    instrument flying use 21
    manifold pressure gauge 35, 58
    tachometer 35, 58
precision approach 580
    missed approach point 581
preferred IFR routes 517
preflight considerations for IFR flight 505
pressure
    altitude and 46–47
    standard atmosphere 46
procedure turns 566–567
    base turns 567, 590
    limitations 489, 566
    maximum speed 566
    teardrop turns 567
prognostic charts 431

R

radar 183–204
    Airport Surveillance Radar 183, 197
    Air Route Surveillance Radar 183, 197
    antenna 194
    approaches 184, 185–191
    contact, significance 544
    control, on instrument approach 590
    en route radar service 543
    Precision Approach Radar 184, 197
    primary radar 197–200
    principles 193–204
    range 195–197
    screens 198–200, 202
    secondary surveillance radar 184,
        201–203
    surveillance radar types 183, 197
    uses 183
radar altimeter 58
radar reports 459
radar summary charts 438

radar traffic information service 183
radar vectoring
    en route radar service 543
    instrument approaches 185–191, 489
    instrument departures 185
    procedures 185
RADAT 459
radiation fog 382
    dispersal 383
radio communications
    common traffic advisory frequency
        (CTAF) 517
    compulsory radio reports 544
    en route chart presentation 516
    IFR requirements 490
    radio failure procedures 491
    remote communications outlets
        (RCO) 516
radio magnetic indicator
    course intercepts 260–262, 299
    DME arcs and 270, 568
    needle function selection 229, 298
    orientation 259, 299
    principles 227–229, 259
    tracking 262–270
radio waves 193, 194
rain showers 396
RBI *see* relative bearing indicator
regulations 477–491
relative bearing, on ADF 215, 225
relative bearing indicator 225
    see also automatic direction finder
relative humidity 389
remote indicating compass 43–45
    free gyro mode 45
    slaving meter 43
ridges of high pressure 428
rime ice 372
RMI *see* radio magnetic indicator
RNAV 357–363
    approaches 358
    global positioning systems 361
    indications 358
    lateral navigation (LNAV) 359
    pseudo-VORTACs 357
    vertical navigation (VNAV) 359
    waypoints 357
roll cloud 393, 403
rotor cloud 393
runway markings 332
runway visibility 440
runway visual range 533, 586

S

Santa Ana wind 394
saturated adiabatic lapse rate 390
sea fog 383
Seven-Ts check 163
severe weather watch areas 440

sidestep maneuver 339, 586
    sidestep minimums 586
SIGMETs 408, 460
simplified directional facility 340
simulators for instrument training 163
simultaneous approaches 338
slant visibility 379
spatial disorientation 14
special VFR 479
speed of sound 40
squall 403
    line, with thunderstorm 408
St. Elmo's fire 409
stall recovery, on instruments 140
standard atmosphere 46, 391
standard instrument approach
        procedure 488
standard pressure 48
    altimetry procedures and 48
standard-rate turns 111–112, 118
standard terminal arrival routes 575
standing waves 393
STAR *see* standard terminal arrival routes
steam fog 384
stormscopes 411
straight-and-level
    configuration changes 90–92
    control instruments 73
    energy management 82
    management 73–92
    monitoring 25, 73–92
    partial panel indications 150–152
    performance instruments 73
    required accuracy 89, 177
stratosphere 415, 419
stratus clouds 387, 388
structural icing 371
    cloud type and 373
surface analysis charts 436, 437
    station model 436
surveillance approach 184, 187
    procedures 188–190
    typical approach chart 187

T

TACAN 279
TAF *see* terminal aerodrome forecasts
takeoff
    minimums 489, 531–533
    obstacle clearance 532
    on instruments 101, 534
taxiway lighting 331
TCAS 204
teardrop turns 567
terminal aerodrome forecasts 446
thunder 401
thunderstorms 401–411
    aviation hazard 408
    downbursts and microbursts 405
    embedded 404

thunderstorms (continued)
    formation 401
    hailstones from 402, 404
    hints when flying near 408
    life cycle 402
    lightning and thunder 401
    severe 404
    SIGMETs issued 408
    squall lines 408
    St. Elmo's fire and 409
    stormscopes and 411
    tornadoes and waterspouts 408
    weather radar and 410
timed approaches 565, 575
tower en route control routes 517
tracking
    in holding patterns 556
    using RBI 241–252
    using RMI 262–270
    using VOR 274, 278, 290–296
training maneuvers 163–176
    vertical-Ss 164
    warm-up procedures 164
transcribed weather broadcasts 431, 448,
    460
transition, DP 535
transmissometer 586
transponder 49, 184, 191–193, 201
    codes 192, 203
    encoding altimeter and 49
    IDENT function 192
    mode 3/A 202
    Mode C 202
    Mode S 204
    operation 191–193
    radio terminology 192
    requirements 203, 483
    squawk 192
    tests and inspections 483
tropical cyclones 427
tropical revolving storms 427
tropopause 415, 419
tropopause data charts 455, 458
troposphere 415, 419
troughs 426
turbulence
    extreme 405
    light 405
    moderate 405
    mountain wave 393
    reporting in PIREPs 443
    severe 405
    thunderstorms and 402
    wake turbulence 346
turn coordinator 31, 53–55
    calibration 118
    failure 144
    in straight-and-level 74, 77
    instrument flying use 20, 22, 26
    in turns 114, 118

partial panel use 143, 147, 153, 157
power source 60
preflight checks 55, 61
turn indicator 53–54
turns
    bank angle vs turn rate 111
    climbing turns 120–121, 158
    constant-bank angle 113
    control instruments 115
    coordination 56
    descending turns 122–123, 159
    forces in a turn 111, 124
    management 20, 111–129
    medium level turns 114–116
    monitoring 20, 26, 53, 114–129
    partial panel display 149, 157–160
    performance instruments 115
    rate 20, 75, 78, 111, 118
    required accuracy 115, 120, 125, 178
    roll-in and roll-out 113
    steep descending turns 128–129
    steep level turns 124, 125, 126, 127
    timed turns 116–119
    to particular headings 116
    using magnetic compass 119
TWEB forecasts 431, 448, 460
Type Performance Table 164

U

undershoot effect 344
unusual attitudes 133–141
    partial panel display 135, 137, 139
    recognition 133, 135
    recovery 84, 126, 136–141
    recovery, test standards 178
    stall recovery 140
upslope fog 384

V

vacuum system
    attitude indicator and 32, 33
    failure 143
VASI systems 326–330, 594
    PVASI 329
    tri-color VASI 329
    T-VASI 330
vertical speed indicator 31, 52–53
    in climb 96, 100
    in descent 103
    in straight-and-level 73, 79
    instrument approach use 189
    instrument flying use 20, 22, 26
    in turns 114, 115, 116
    partial panel use 143, 146, 147, 154
    pitot-static system and 58
    preflight checks 53, 61
    static line blockage, effect 59, 144
    turbulence, effect 26, 79
VFR-on-top 546

VFR weather minimums 478
    special VFR 479
VHF direction finding 367–368
    DF approach 368
    DF fix 367
    DF steers 367
Victor airways 279, 507
    type-number designators 518
virga 396
visibility 379–384
    condensation and 381
    factors affecting 379
    fog and 382
    inversions and 380
    slant visibility 379
visual approach 186, 610
visual descent point (VDP) 586
visual illusions on approach 593, 611
visual reference 591
VOR 273–302
    airborne equipment 273
    classification 276–277
    course intercepts 296–299, 534
    DME arcs and 569
    holding patterns 563–564
    indicators 273, 280–282, 289, 298–300
    information sources 277, 278
    orientation 280, 284–290
    position fixes 284–290
    radials 274
    range 276
    receiver checks 283, 484
    RMI 298–299
    tracking 274, 278, 290–296
    VOR/DME 279
    VOR approach 295, 300–302, 588
    VORTAC 279
VSI see vertical speed indicator 52

W

wake turbulence 346
    on approach 611
    on takeoff 533
warm fronts 423
water spouts 408
waypoints 357
weather
    cause of 419
    from Flight Service 431
    high-level 415–418
    information from Flight Watch 434
    information while in flight 459
    radar 408, 410
    synopsis, in weather briefings 433
weather briefings
    abbreviated briefing 433
    obtaining 431
    outlook briefing 433
    pilot responsibility 432
    standard briefing 432

weather depiction charts 434
    station circle 436
    station plot 436
weather forecasts 444
    area forecasts 447
    convective outlook 448
    low-level significant weather prog
        chart 444
    terminal aerodrome forecasts (TAF) 446
    transcribed weather broadcast 448
    TWEB forecasts 448
    winds and temperatures aloft
        forecasts 451
weather minimums
    alternate airports 486, 518
    circling 606
    landing 489, 591
    takeoff 489, 531, 532
weather reports 434
    aviation routine weather reports 440
    composite moisture stability charts 459
    constant pressure analysis charts 452
    METAR/SPECI 440
    radar reports 459
    radar summary charts 438
    station model 454
    surface analysis charts 436
    tropopause data charts 455
    weather depiction charts 434
wind direction 419
winds and temperatures aloft forecast 451
windshear 343–347, 421
    causes 346
    definition 421
    effects on aircraft 343, 345
    overshoot effect 344
    performance-decreasing 344
    performance-increasing 344
    pilot actions 346
    terminology 343
    thunderstorms and 402
    undershoot effect 344

NOTES

NOTES

NOTES

NOTES